THE ROUTLEDGE HANDBOOK OF SHAKESPEARE AND MEMORY

The Routledge Handbook of Shakespeare and Memory introduces this vibrant field of study to students and scholars, whilst defining and extending critical debates in the area. The book begins with a series of 'Critical introductions' offering an overview of memory in particular areas of Shakespeare such as theatre, print culture, visual arts, post-colonial adaptation and new media. These essays both introduce the topic but also explore specific areas such as the way in which Shakespeare's representation in the visual arts created a *national* and then a *global* poet.

The entries then develop into more specific studies of the genre of Shakespeare, with sections on Tragedy, History, Comedy and Poetry, which include insightful readings of specific key plays. The book ends with a state of the art review of the area, charting major contributions to the debate, and illuminating areas for further study. The international range of contributors explores the nature of memory in religious, political, emotional and economic terms which are not only relevant to Shakespearean times, but to the way we think and read now.

Andrew Hiscock is Professor of English at the University of Bangor, UK.

Lina Perkins Wilder is Associate Professor of English at Connecticut College, USA.

THE ROUTLEDGE HANDBOOK OF SHAKESPEARE AND MEMORY

*Edited by Andrew Hiscock
and Lina Perkins Wilder*

LONDON AND NEW YORK

First published 2018
by Routledge
2 Park Square, Milton Park, Abingdon, Oxon OX14 4RN

and by Routledge
711 Third Avenue, New York, NY 10017

Routledge is an imprint of the Taylor & Francis Group, an informa business

© 2018 selection and editorial matter, Andrew Hiscock and Lina Perkins Wilder; individual chapters, the contributors

The right of Andrew Hiscock and Lina Perkins Wilder to be identified as the authors of the editorial material, and of the authors for their individual chapters, has been asserted in accordance with sections 77 and 78 of the Copyright, Designs and Patents Act 1988.

All rights reserved. No part of this book may be reprinted or reproduced or utilized in any form or by any electronic, mechanical, or other means, now known or hereafter invented, including photocopying and recording, or in any information storage or retrieval system, without permission in writing from the publishers.

Trademark notice: Product or corporate names may be trademarks or registered trademarks, and are used only for identification and explanation without intent to infringe.

British Library Cataloguing-in-Publication Data
A catalogue record for this book is available from the British Library

Library of Congress Cataloging-in-Publication Data
A catalog record has been requested for this book

ISBN: 978-1-138-81676-3 (hbk)
ISBN: 978-1-315-74594-7 (ebk)

Typeset in Bembo
by Book Now Ltd, London

Printed in the United Kingdom
by Henry Ling Limited

For all the Hiscock family, most especially David Hiscock
and
For Calliope Wilder and Gideon Wilder

CONTENTS

List of illustrations xi
Notes on contributors xiii
Acknowledgements xvii

    Introduction 1
    Andrew Hiscock and Lina Perkins Wilder

PART I
Critical introductions 9

1 Shakespeare, memory, and the early modern theatre 11
  Zackariah Long

2 Shakespeare, memory, and print culture 23
  Amanda Watson

3 Shakespeare, memory and post-colonial adaptation 34
  Andrew J. Power

4 Shakespeare, memory and the visual arts 46
  Shearer West

5 Shakespeare, memory, film and performance 62
  Sarah Hatchuel and Nathalie Vienne-Guerrin

Contents

  6 Shakespeare, memory, and new media   73
      Rory Loughnane

  7 Shakespeare, memory and contemporary performance:
     Shakespeare in Shoreditch   91
      Sarah Dustagheer

PART II
Tragedy   **103**

  8 'The raven o'er the infectious house':
     contagious memory in *Romeo and Juliet* and *Othello*   105
      Evelyn Tribble

  9 'Lest we remember ... our Troy, our Rome': historical
     and individual memory in *Titus Andronicus* and *Troilus and Cressida*   116
      Jesús Tronch

10 Fooling with tragic memory in *Hamlet* and *King Lear*   135
      Kay Stanton

11 Fatal distraction: eclipses of memory in *Julius Caesar*
     and *Antony and Cleopatra*   149
      Jonathan Baldo

PART III
History   **163**

12 Handling memory in the Henriad: forgetting Falstaff   165
      William E. Engel

13 *Henry VI* to *Richard III*: forgetting, foreshadowing, remembering   180
      Nicholas Grene

14 Rumour's household: truth, memory, fiction, history
     in *2 Henry IV* and *All Is True*   191
      Ed Gieskes

15 Cultural memories of the legal repertoire in
     Richard III and *Richard II*: criticizing rites of succession   208
      Anita Gilman Sherman

PART IV
Comedy   **223**

16   Memory and subjective continuity in *As You Like It* and *All's Well That Ends Well*   225
      Erin Minear

17   Veiled memory traces in *Much Ado About Nothing*, *Pericles*, and *The Winter's Tale*   239
      Lina Perkins Wilder

18   Illyria's memorials: space, memory, and genre in Shakespeare's *Twelfth Night*   253
      Susan Harlan

19   'Have you forgot your love?': material memory and forgetfulness in *Love's Labour's Lost* and *Measure for Measure*   266
      Christine Sukic

PART V
Poetry   **279**

20   'Suppose thou dost defend me from what is past': Shakespeare's *Venus and Adonis* and *The Rape of Lucrece* and the appetite for ancient memory   281
      Andrew Hiscock

21   Monumental memory and little reminders: the fantasy of being remembered by posterity   297
      Grant Williams

PART VI
Review   **313**

22   The state of the art of memory and Shakespeare studies   315
      Rebeca Helfer

Bibliography   *329*
Index   *351*

ILLUSTRATIONS

Figures

4.1	Peter Scheemakers, monument to Shakespeare, 1740, Westminster Abbey	50
4.2	George Carter, *The Apotheosis of Garrick, c.* 1782	51
4.3	James Northcote, *The Meeting of Edward V and his brother Richard, Duke of York, contemplated by King Richard III,* 1799	54
4.4	William Hogarth, *David Garrick as Richard III,* 1745	55
4.5	John Singer Sargent, *Ellen Terry as Lady Macbeth,* 1889	57
4.6	Ellen Terry as Lady Macbeth, Window & Grove platinum print, 1888	59
6.1	References to the 'Art of Memory' in searchable *EEBO* texts 1473–1699	80
6.2	References to '*memento mori*' in searchable *EEBO* texts 1473–1699	86
7.1	Image courtesy of Zoe Bramley, author of *The Shakespeare Trail: A Journey into Shakespeare's England* (Amberley Publishing, 2015)	91
12.1	Francis Kirkman, *The Wits, or sport upon sport* (London, 1662), frontispiece	169

Tables

6.1	Shakespeare's potential reading in the Art of Memory	84
6.2	Shakespeare's potential reading about *memento mori*	87

CONTRIBUTORS

Jonathan Baldo is Professor of English at the Eastman School of Music, the University of Rochester, and has published numerous articles on Shakespeare and early modern culture. His most recent book, *Memory in Shakespeare's Histories: Stages of Forgetting in Early Modern England* (2012), reflects his ongoing interest in the partnership of remembering and forgetting in early modern constructions of the past. He is currently co-editing with Isabel Karremann a collection of essays entitled *Forms of Faith: Literary Form and Religious Conflict in Early Modern England* (2017).

Sarah Dustagheer is Lecturer in Early Modern Literature at the University of Kent. She researches playwriting, performance and theatre space in early modern London, as well as contemporary Shakespearean performance. Sarah is the co-author of *Shakespeare in London* (2014) and has published in *Moving Shakespeare Indoors* (2014), *Shakespeare Jahrbuch*, *Literature Compass*, *Cahiers Élisabéthains* and *The Shakespeare Encyclopaedia: The Complete Guide to the Man and His Works* (2009). Her first book, *Shakespeare's Playhouses: Repertory and Theatre Space at the Globe and the Blackfriars, 1599–1613* is forthcoming.

William E. Engel teaches English and Humanities at the University of the South, in Sewanee, TN, where he is the Nick B. Williams Professor of Literature. He is the author of five books on literary history and applied mnemonics, and co-editor of *The Memory Arts in Renaissance England: A Critical Anthology* (2016). He is on the editorial board of *Renaissance Quarterly* and is the Renaissance Society of America's Discipline Representative for 'Emblems'.

Edward Gieskes is Associate Professor of English at the University of South Carolina. He teaches courses on Shakespeare and early modern drama. He is the author of *Representing the Professions: Administration Law and Theatre in Early Modern England* (2006). He edited (with Kirk Melnikoff) the essay collection *Writing Robert Greene* (2008). He is completing a book on generic change in early modern literature.

Nicholas Grene is Emeritus Professor of English Literature at Trinity College Dublin. His books include *Shakespeare's Tragic Imagination* (1992), *The Politics of Irish Drama* (1999), *Shakespeare's Serial History Plays* (2002), *Yeats's Poetic Codes* (2008) and *Home on the Stage* (2014). The *Oxford Handbook of Modern Irish Theatre*, which he co-edited with Chris Morash, was published in 2016.

Contributors

Susan Harlan is Associate Professor of English Literature at Wake Forest University. Her book *Memories of War in Early Modern England: Armor and Militant Nostalgia in Marlowe, Sidney, and Shakespeare* was published in 2016. She has written articles on the subjects of masculine postwar character in Shakespeare's *Much Ado About Nothing*, found military objects in Shakespeare's *Pericles* and militant prologues and memory in Shakespeare's *Henry V* and *Troilus and Cressida*.

Sarah Hatchuel is Professor of English Literature and Film at the University of Le Havre (France), President of the Société Française Shakespeare and head of the 'Groupe de recherché Identités et Cultures'. She has written extensively on screen adaptations of Shakespeare's plays and on TV series. She is general editor of the *Shakespeare on Screen* collection (with Nathalie Vienne-Guerrin) and of the online journal *TV/Series* (with Ariane Hudelet).

Rebeca Helfer is an Associate Professor of English at the University of California-Irvine, where she specializes in early modern literature and memory. She is the author of *Spenser's Ruins and the Art of Recollection* (2012), which explores the importance of the art of memory in Edmund Spenser's poetics. Rebeca is currently working on *The Art of Memory in Early Modern Writing*, which argues that the early modern memory arts were a poetics in practice.

Andrew Hiscock is Professor of English Literature at Bangor University, Wales, and Marie Sklodowska-Curie Research Fellow at the Institut de Recherche sur la Renaissance, l'Âge Classique et les Lumières, Montpellier III. He is a Fellow of the English Association, editor (English Literature) of *MLR* and the *Yearbook of English Studies*, and series co-editor of *Arden Early Modern Drama Guides*. He has published widely on early modern English and French literature and his most recent monograph is *Reading Memory in Early Modern Literature* (2011).

Zackariah Long is Associate Professor of English at Ohio Wesleyan University. He has published essays on early modern memory, trauma, and theatre in journals such as *English Literary Renaissance* and *Journal of Literature and Trauma* as well in essay collections including *Staging Pain, 1580–1800* and *Forgetting in Early Modern English Literature and Culture*. He is currently working on parallel monographs on memory disorders on the English Renaissance stage and on early modern trauma theory and Shakespeare.

Rory Loughnane is Lecturer in Early Modern Drama and Literature at the University of Kent, Canterbury. He is an Associate Editor of *The New Oxford Shakespeare* (Oxford University Press, 2016–), for which he edited ten plays and co-authored a book-length study of 'The Canon and Chronology of Shakespeare's Works'. He has co-edited three essay collections about early modern drama, and is the co-editor of *The Memory Arts in Renaissance England: A Critical Anthology* (2016).

Erin Minear is Associate Professor of English at the College of William & Mary. She is the author of *Reverberating Song in Shakespeare and Milton: Language, Memory, and Musical Representation* (2011), and has written articles on topics including music and gender in *Troilus and Cressida*, memory and subjectivity in Shakespearean comedy and eavesdropping and interpretation in *Othello*. Her current project examines the intersection of dramatic and narrative modes in Shakespeare's plays.

Contributors

Andrew J. Power is Lecturer of Shakespeare and Early Modern Literature and English Program Director at Saint Louis University – Madrid Campus. He has also taught at Trinity College Dublin, University College Dublin, and the University of Cyprus. He is the co-editor of *Late Shakespeare, 1608–1613* and of a special issue of *The Yearbook of English Studies* 2014, on 'Caroline Literature'. His forthcoming monograph is entitled *Stages of Madness: Sin, Sickness and Seneca in Shakespearean Drama* (2017).

Anita Gilman Sherman is Associate Professor of Literature at American University in Washington and author of *Skepticism and Memory in Shakespeare and Donne* (2007). She has published essays on various Renaissance writers in journals and edited collections, as well as on Poland's reputation in early modern England, on the Revels office as a rehearsal space and on W. G. Sebald. Her current book project is titled 'Forms of Skepticism in Early Modern English Literature'.

Kay Stanton is Professor of English at California State University at Fullerton, specializing in Shakespeare studies. She has presented over 100 professional conference papers, in 12 foreign countries and 21 American states, and has published over 30 scholarly articles on Shakespeare, Milton and Arthur Miller. Her book *Shakespeare's 'Whores': Erotics, Politics, and Poetics* has recently been published, and she is currently at work on a book on Shakespeare and quantum physics.

Christine Sukic is Professor of Early Modern English Literature and Culture at the University of Reims Champagne-Ardenne, France. She is the author of *Le Héros inachevé: éthique et esthétique dans les tragédies de George Chapman (1559?–1634)* (2005) and has translated Chapman's *Bussy D'Ambois* into French for the Pléiade collection (2009). Her research interests focus on the heroic body and representations of the immaterial. She is the chief editor of the scholarly online journal *Études Épistémè*.

Evelyn Tribble is Professor and Donald Collie Chair of English at the University of Otago, Dunedin, New Zealand. She is the author of *Cognition in the Globe: Attention and Memory in Shakespeare's Theatre* (2011). Her most recent book is *Early Modern Actors and Shakespeare's Theatre: Thinking with the Body* (2017).

Jesús Tronch is Senior Lecturer at the Universitat de València, where he teaches English literature and creative translation. His main research interests are textual criticism (specifically on Shakespeare and early modern drama), and translation and reception studies (specifically the presence of Shakespeare in Spain), both converging on an open-access, hypertextual and multilingual database-collection of early modern European theatre (EMOTHE) developed by the ARTELOPE research project at the University of Valencia.

Nathalie Vienne-Guerrin is Professor in Shakespeare Studies at the université Paul-Valéry Montpellier 3 and director of the IRCL, Institute for Research on the Renaissance, the Neo-classical Age and the Enlightenment (CNRS). She has published on Shakespeare's evil tongues. She is co-general editor of the *Shakespeare on Screen* collection (with Sarah Hatchuel) and of the 'Shakespeare on Screen in Francophonia' database (with Patricia Dorval). She is co-editor in chief of the international journal *Cahiers Elisabéthains*.

Amanda Watson, a former CLIR Postdoctoral Fellow in Academic Libraries, is the Librarian for English and Comparative Literature at New York University. She recently published an article in the journal *Book History*, and is currently working on a book-length project provisionally titled *Original and Selected: Commonplace Books, Readers, and Poems in Nineteenth-Century America*.

Shearer West is Deputy Vice-Chancellor of the University of Sheffield and former Head of the Humanities Division at Oxford University. She has published nine books on eighteenth-, nineteenth- and twentieth-century European art, including *Portraiture* and *Italian Culture in Northern Europe in the Eighteenth Century*, and many peer-reviewed essays and articles. Most recently, she has published essays on Bluestocking portraits, the pastellist Rosalba Carriera and theatrical spectacle, with forthcoming work including studies of 'selfhood' in the Enlightenment and of portraits of immigrants in eighteenth-century England.

Lina Perkins Wilder is Associate Professor of English at Connecticut College. She is the author of *Shakespeare's Memory Theatre: Recollection, Properties, and Character* (2010). Her essays have been published in *Shakespeare Quarterly*, *Renaissance Drama* and *Modern Drama*. Her current book project is entitled *Recording Technologies in Renaissance Literature*.

Grant Williams is Associate Professor at Carleton University, Ottawa Canada. He has co-edited three collections of essays, *Forgetting in Early Modern English Literature and Culture* (2004), *Ars Reminiscendi* (2009) and *Taking Exception to the Law* (2015). He has also co-edited with Rory Loughnane and Bill Engel a critical anthology of texts on mnemonic culture, *The Memory Arts in Renaissance England* (2016).

ACKNOWLEDGEMENTS

We would like to thank Routledge for proposing this project and for the team's continued support and encouragement throughout the period of the collection's gestation. Our sincere gratitude is also extended to each and every one of the contributors to this volume. Their commitment, enthusiasm and good humour has meant that our editorial duties have been a pleasure throughout. Nonetheless, as the dedication to this collection indicates, *Shakespeare and Memory* would not have come into being without the patience, support and indulgence of our families. This collection is dedicated to them.

Andrew and Lina

INTRODUCTION

Andrew Hiscock and Lina Perkins Wilder

In Shakespeare's plays, acts of memory are articulated in a host of different contexts. Remembering can be intimately involved with bids for moral authority, power assertion or appropriation. Notable and repeated exertions of the faculty can denote intellectual prowess, a fine-grained sensibility negotiating change or elsewhere the mental life of those rendered inert by the burdens of the past. Equally importantly, in all Shakespearean writing, to recollect has the potential to bind and loose human communities, and in a play such as *A Midsummer Night's Dream* this potential comes to be seen as profoundly unsettling. After their night in the woods outside Athens, the young lovers are awoken by Theseus, who demands an account of the night's events. Like Bottom, the lovers find a clear narrative of their experiences in the woods to be elusive. 'I wot not by what power—', Demetrius tells Theseus, 'But by some power it is—my love to Hermia, / Melted as the snow, seems to me now / As the remembrance of an idle gaud / Which in my childhood I did dote upon' (IV.1.161–164). Theseus departs, and Demetrius adds:

> These things seem small and indistinguishable
> Like far-off mountains turned into clouds.
> *Hermia* Methinks I see these things with parted eye,
> When everything seems double.
> *Helena* So methinks,
> And I have found Demetrius like a jewel,
> Mine own and not mine own.
> *(IV.1.184–189)*

On one level, Helena's remark accurately describes the effect of Oberon's lingering enchantment: Demetrius is '[her] own' because he loves her; he is 'not [her] own' because his love is the result of enchantment, not his own choice or inclination. Understood differently, Helena is also, like Hermia and Demetrius, making a statement about memory. To Demetrius—as Erin Minear discusses in this volume—the past seems remote, transformed (by enchantment, but also simply by time) into something seen from a physical distance. Hermia's perception of the past is also indistinct, although she explains its indistinctness not as the effect of distance but as a result of her own perception. Like Demetrius's and Hermia's, Helena's perception of the past (or is it the past and the present together?) is 'double'.

1

As well as offering mastery of the passage of time and providing the requisite talents for public service and citizenship, memory was frequently conceptualized in the early modern period as something that could be seen. Thus, framed by university curricula investing deeply in rhetorical practice and mnemotechnology, the operations of the faculty were thought to traverse space—for those whose minds had undergone the appropriate training. Under this intellectual regime, memories themselves, no matter what their sensory origin, were shaped and stored in the brain as *imagines*; and trained memories might navigate through a frieze, a tableau, or a collection of ordered objects which were scanned visually in sequence so that the desired information was retrieved in the required pattern. For Demetrius and Hermia, however, memory's visual quality is compromised, and rather than being remembered, the past has 'melted', disappeared, transformed (like the affections of childhood or like distant objects that appear to be something other than what they are), or doubled. While the lovers' inability to remember allows the finale to take place and thus shapes the play's genre, their tentative recollection also suggests the limits of sensory perception (let alone ownership) as a metaphor for memory. However, the metaphor is so strong that Helena can imagine the difference between her memory of Demetrius (he did not love her) and her perception of Demetrius (he loves her) as two sides of the same coin, 'mine own and not mine own'.

One of the events that has come loose from the lovers' memories as a result of Oberon's enchantment and the confusion of the night's events is the disagreement between Hermia and Helena. The argument was itself a dispute over memory: thinking that Hermia has joined with Lysander and Demetrius to mock her with their pretended (really, enchanted) love, Helena exclaims 'O, is all quite forgot?' (III.2.202). Her memory of the childhood friendship she shared with Hermia is coloured by this sense of loss. Pained by what she thinks is Hermia's mockery of her, Helena recalls what her friendship with Hermia had been like: they 'grew together, / Like to a double cherry: seeming parted, / But yet an union in partition' (III.2.209–211). The intensity of Hermia's and Helena's friendship, as Helena describes it, is presented to the theatre audience only as memory. While the confidence between Hermia and Helena at the beginning of the play might lead us to infer a close friendship, the immediate betrayal of that friendship by Helena indicates that it is already less close than it was. Their lost friendship is a source of mutual understanding and a register of the shifting ground on which the lovers stand as they negotiate their new roles as married couples. In forgetting (if they do forget) the argument about their friendship, Helena and Hermia seem affected by a perhaps deeper *pathos*: as women successfully partnered with eligible men, they do not even have the capacity or the space to recall their own feelings of loss about a female friendship that was itself already lost. These earlier feelings of lack are, apparently, subsumed into the wonder of the marriages that shape the ending of this comedy.

However, while Helena and Hermia do not explicitly recall their argument and seem to have forgotten it, their language recalls the earlier exchange implicitly. In so doing, their words provide evidence—albeit sparse and equivocal evidence—of loyalties and still-existing disagreements that may trouble the play's solution to the problems brought out in the forest. Their implicit memory of the argument reminds us of the cost of the marriage plot and the complexity of feeling that goes into making a 'happy ending'. Picking up Helena's word 'double' in the later exchange, Hermia revises its meaning: not a joining together of two separate people but splitting a single event into two different perceptions. Still evoking this earlier doubling, she and Helena share a line, a sentence, and a common vocabulary ('methinks'). They are once again in agreement, erasing or effacing the quarrel of a few hours before. It is almost as if the events in the forest have not happened, or even that an entire chapter of their history together has 'melted as the snow': Demetrius loves Helena again; Helena and Hermia are friends; and the

Introduction

only change is that Lysander and Hermia's marriage has now received official approval. Helena and Hermia either have forgotten an important event, their quarrel, or remembered the more important fact of their friendship (although they do not speak to one another directly); similarly, either Demetrius is afflicted by amnesia, or an earlier and more powerful memory has reasserted itself. Befuddled by Oberon's enchantment, the young lovers experience memory as having and not having, examining what it past and is therefore not available for direct examination. In so doing, they remind us of the fictionality of the visual metaphor that (still) pervades memory studies. To remember is to examine something that was once available to the senses but is no longer available and can be understood only as a mental process or a physical trace or reminder. Remembering is a turn inward in the form of a turn outward, but a turn toward an object that escapes direct apprehension. The apprehension of memory is always 'double': the event is experienced, and then, after a gap of time, it is examined again.

This one brief passage reflects the breadth and variousness of memory as a topic. Scholarly work on memory and Shakespeare in the past 25 years has reminded us that memory is the striving for an ordering technique and for an underlying cohesion to the continuum of human experience. In the early modern period, as was indicated above, the faculty was fashioned as a practical and necessary skill, a discursive practice, a moral and religious imperative, an aspect of *prudentia*, but also as a gendered competency, an indication of a particular sensibility, as a human potential residing in the hindmost of the brain's three ventricles—and, latterly, as a cognitive process whose workings are unfolding under the gaze of modern neuroscience. Memory can give poignancy to lack, loss and change ('O is all quite forgot?'), and its failures and distortions can be transformative and, on occasion, a source of consolation. The faculty evades complete management, although for early modern Europe its control was seen as imperative.

Thus, understanding memory and Shakespeare is a complex task, and the considerable body of scholarship on the topic is reviewed in Rebeca Helfer's (Chapter 22) wide-ranging and thought-provoking discussion at the close of this volume. More generally, ranging across many of Shakespeare's plays and poems, including works that are often read in the context of memory studies and works that are seldom read for their insights into memory, this collection expands the study of early modern and modern memory in the context of Shakespeare's writing by exploring its many and varied functions in the different genres and forms in which he chose to write. A central question taken up implicitly, and sometimes explicitly, in this collection is the relationship between memory and genre. In tragedy, memory provides an awareness of loss. In history, memory in many ways represents an alternative to the genre itself, although the different valences of memory can be folded into the project of history-making. In comedy, memory draws attention to the discontinuities required by the transformative effects of comic structure; or it draws the plays toward other genres, creating generic ambiguities, frictions and synergies. As will become apparent, in the poetry, Shakespeare's writing enters all of these domains.

Depending upon reading strategies adopted, the chapters which follow may be read individually, in succession or clustered according to theme, genre or questions of textual production, for example. The flexibility of *Shakespeare and Memory* is that it responds to a host of different needs and designs on the part of its readership. In Part I, the reader encounters a succession of critical introductions, each in their own way reviewing key areas of memory studies in relation to Shakespeare's writing, offering a representative sample of the many subfields to which memory is relevant in modern critical discourse and looking forward to the discussions in later sections. As well as introducing the general topic, each of these critical introductions also expands and explores a particular area of interest within the topic. Zackariah Long's chapter (Chapter 1) on 'Shakespeare, memory, and the early modern theatre' gives an account of the overlap between theatre and memory-training in the historical record and in the scholarship of the past 50 years. Giulio Camillo's memory theatre, Long suggests, provides a powerful and unexplored model for theatrical practice, which Long details in a reading of Hamlet's 'distracted globe'. Long argues that the architecture of Camillo's theatre has direct equivalents in the Globe Theatre and that the different sources of Hamlet's distraction in this moment can be understood as aspects of memorial practice. In Chapter 2 on 'Shakespeare, memory, and print culture', Amanda Watson offers an overview of the study of print culture and places Shakespeare's work within that account, discussing two examples of Shakespeare in print which 'remember' the text: Shakespeare in anthologies and Shakespeare in American commonplace books. By examining these textual sources, Watson establishes the principle of fragmentation as part of the textual 'memory' of Shakespeare's plays. Subsequently, taking a central interest in playtexts such as *A Midsummer Night's Dream*, *Macbeth* and *The Two Noble Kinsmen* in Chapter 3, 'Shakespeare, memory and post-colonial adaptation', Andrew J. Power invites us to consider questions of canonicity, colonial legacy and political agency which continue to worry away at the ever-increasing formulations of *global* and *local* Shakespeares. Engaging tightly with current critical and political debate on the question of adaptation and transferral, Power's carefully wrought discussion urges us to scrutinize further the freighted operations of memory when negotiating the undertakings of performance and indeed of criticism itself.

Building upon a number of emphases in Power's discussion, in Chapter 4, 'Shakespeare, memory and the visual arts', Shearer West highlights how the visual arts strategically invested in the making of a *national*, and subsequently *global* poet. Some of the earliest examples of the production, circulation and consumption of Shakespearean images look back to the eighteenth century, but West emphasizes how generations of artists were drawn to create objects of commemoration linked directly with cultural institutions and political value systems. Thus, a succession of examples from the visual arts in the centuries that followed Shakespeare's death is seen to have participated in acts of collective remembering and, on occasions, modes of national identity-formation. In Chapter 5, 'Shakespeare, memory, film and performance', Sarah Hatchuel and Nathalie Vienne-Guerrin concentrate upon European and North American cinematic and televisual cultures, drawing attention to the particular timeliness of certain commitments to re-membering Shakespeare on screen for audiences in different locations and at different points in the twentieth century. Strikingly, Hatchuel and Vienne-Guerrin query the status and functions of film as a 'medium of permanence' and probe the ways in which screenings of Shakespeare maintain the potential for forgetting as well as selective remembrance. This discussion engages closely in dialogue with those that follow, Rory Loughnane's 'Shakespeare, memory and new media' (Chapter 6) and Sarah Dustagheer's 'Shakespeare, memory and contemporary performance' (Chapter 7). Loughnane's chapter focuses upon the ever-expanding powers of data retrieval made available in the digital age and how these might be seen variously to mirror, resist and thwart early modern formulations of active recollection in the *ars memorativae*. In direct comparison with Hatchuel and Vienne-Guerrin, Loughnane draws reader attention to the potential for loss and occlusion in seemingly transparent investments in searching, retrieving and scrutiny. Mindful of such concerns, Dustagheer's discussion brings this section to a close by concentrating upon contemporary theatre and how Shakespeare's playhouses and play-making continue to be reformulated for contemporary taste cultures both in and outside performance auditoria. Like West, Hatchuel and Vienne-Guerrin, Dustagheer probes the cultural anxieties surrounding questions of legacy, renewal and reinterpretation which continue to accompany the mediation of Shakespeare for contemporary audiences. In addition, she explores the thorny questions involved in the cultural and performative undertaking in producing Shakespeare—an undertaking which remains *in process* into the twenty-first century.

Part II of this collection turns to readings of Shakespeare's works, beginning with Shakespearean tragedy. In Chapter 8, '"The raven o'er the infectious house": contagious memory

Introduction

in *Romeo and Juliet* and *Othello*', Evelyn Tribble guides the reader on a stimulating journey examining how the mental gymnastics which acts of memory can trigger and how the desire itself to remember may serve to de-stabilize strategically our very understandings of fiction-making and of mental autonomy. This concern with the ways in which memory exposes the fragility of our mental life is also pursued by Jesús Tronch in Chapter 9, '"Lest we remember ... our Troy, our Rome": historical and individual memory in *Titus Andronicus* and *Troilus and Cressida*'. Tronch develops this interest by focusing on collective acts of nation-building and constructs of political heroism. Shakespeare's concern in both plays to demythologize and to chronicle ancient societies on the point of collapse is shown here to subvert any faith placed in the faculty to restore the possibility of human exchange for the future. In these brutalized stage environments given over wholly to the pleasure principles of verbal and physical violence, the potential to dis-member, rather than re-member, remains ever-present. In Chapter 10, 'Fooling with tragic memory in *Hamlet* and *King Lear*', Kay Stanton returns reader attention to the relationships between acts of memory and the construction of subjectivity. Engaging creatively with recent advances in neuropsychological research, Stanton reflects upon the ways in which memorial narrativization takes place in the psyche of those inhabiting Shakespeare's tragic worlds and how memory itself remains an embattled mental terrain where the brain variously recalls, develops, prunes, revises and erases the data it receives, thus creating an unending palimpsest for the Shakespearean subject to revisit. This section devoted to Shakespearean tragedy is brought to a close with Jonathan Baldo's 'Fatal distraction: eclipses of memory in *Julius Caesar* and *Antony and Cleopatra*' (Chapter 11). Here, Baldo refocuses attention on memorial training and its status in the early modern period as a requisite discipline for service to the *civitas*. Like Tronch, Baldo concentrates upon collective acts of commemoration, but in this latter discussion attention turns to material objects (calendars, images, statues and monuments) and to the ways in which both playtexts invest vigorously in acts of forgetting and 'distraction' as well as those of recollection in order to promote models of political commitment.

From the tragedies, we move to the histories. With their intense focus on the creation of cultural memories and the re-creation of events from the past with direct impact on the politics of the present, Shakespeare's history plays remain fertile ground for memory scholars. The chapters in Part III explore the mutually reinforcing dynamics of cultural memory, audience response and theatrical staging. William E. Engel contextualizes one of the most memorable figures in Shakespeare in Chapter 12, 'Handling memory in the Henriad: forgetting Falstaff'. Here, Engel argues that the numerous ways in which the Henriad brings us back to Falstaff can be understood as different aspects of memorial practice. Falstaff is emblematic of the way the histories re-write and over-write the past and inscribe themselves in their audiences' memories using methods that are at once theatrical and mnemotechnic. Nicholas Grene takes a somewhat different approach in Chapter 13, '*Henry VI* to *Richard III*: forgetting, foreshadowing, remembering'. Grene argues that the first tetralogy was written and performed in chronological order and that the disappearance and 'forgetting' in one play of characters central to the previous play reflects the relative unimportance of interiority to Shakespeare's early drama. However, what ties the plays together is broader: the narrative progression from unrest to bloody war. In Chapter 14, 'Rumour's household: truth, memory, fiction, history in *2 Henry IV* and *All Is True*', Ed Gieskes establishes the use of fiction to create memorable historical narratives. In their emphasis on 'chosen truth' and retelling, both plays suggest that history cannot be engrained in memory without a mixture of untruth or selective truth. Finally, Anita Gilman Sherman explores the creation of new and combative rituals in two plays not often read together in 'Cultural memories of the legal repertoire in *Richard III* and *Richard II*: criticizing rites of succession' (Chapter 15).

Part IV turns to the operations of memory in Shakespeare's comedies. With the exception of the generically mixed late plays, Shakespeare's comedies have received less attention from memory scholars than his other plays. Comedy, to some extent, depends on *not* remembering. The chapters in this part explore the complexity of remembering, forgetting and failing to remember in the comedies and the late plays. In Chapter 16, 'Memory and subjective continuity in *As You Like It* and *All's Well That Ends Well*', Erin Minear argues that memory in comedy is defined by discontinuity: when characters 'remember' they draw attention to the difference between their present and past selves. Nonetheless, since the comedic ending looks forward to some form of permanence, characters in comedy attempt to explain their transformations in a way that establishes a continuous form of selfhood, and memory becomes as much a fantasy as a form of record. The objects of memory are the focus of Chapter 17, Lina Perkins Wilder's 'Veiled memory traces in *Much Ado About Nothing*, *Pericles*, and *The Winter's Tale*', which argues that the veiled women in Shakespeare's comedies challenge gender hierarchy by challenging the hierarchy of male rememberer and female memory image. By remembering, characters as various as Hero, Thaisa, Marina and Hermione make memory dialectical rather than the property of a single individual and resist the play's attempts to subsume them into memory allegory. Susan Harlan traces the generic complexity attached to space and memory in Chapter 18, 'Illyria's memorials: space, memory, and genre in Shakespeare's *Twelfth Night*'. Nostalgically 'longing for home', the play's characters, like figures in romance, use memory of place to create narratives that define them while also exposing those narratives as fiction. The relationship between memory and the book is explored by Christine Sukic in Chapter 19, '"Have you forgot your love?": material memory and forgetfulness in *Love's Labour's Lost* and *Measure for Measure*'. Embedded in a culture that is both invested in the written word and recognizes its potential for instability, these comedies rely on a 'palimpsestic aesthetics' in which the records of the past are subject to oblivion as well as repurposing.

The two discussions in Part V, which follow this section on Shakespearean comedy, are devoted to his poetry. Andrew Hiscock's '"Suppose thou dost defend me from what is past": Shakespeare's *Venus and Adonis* and *The Rape of Lucrece* and the appetite for ancient memory' (Chapter 20) opens this section by considering the early modern context for the deployment of classical mythology in poetic narrative and how mythology itself is pressed into the service of memorial debate as Shakespeare's early poems unfold. Hiscock reflects upon how the modes of the epyllion, the complaint and rhetorical debate in these texts constantly urge the reader to consider the remorselessly competitive nature of the will to retrieve from the past and the multifarious ways in which we formulate environments for future remembering. In Chapter 21, 'Monumental memory and little reminders: the fantasy of being remembered by posterity', Grant Williams maintains this interest in futurity with particular reference to Shakespeare's *Sonnets*. In this discussion, like Baldo, Williams studies the implications of monumentalization for our understanding of early modern memory and how recent scholarship has sought to theorize the role which the faculty has to play in the formulation of subjectivity at the turn of the sixteenth century. Strikingly, like Stanton, Williams explores the possibility of considering Shakespearean writing as 'cognitive scripts' in which we encounter the ruins of the past as well as the materials of expectation, desire and ambition.

The collection comes to a close with Rebeca Helfer's vigorous interrogation of the field of early modern memory studies. As her discussion unfolds, Helfer charts some of the major contributions in recent decades to this field of analysis and, equally illuminatingly, offers key perspectives for future areas of critical study. Helfer's ambitious and wide-ranging chapter makes a fitting close to the collection as a whole, underlining the thriving nature of contemporary memory studies devoted to the early modern period and demonstrating both the scholarly range that scholars bring to Shakespeare's writing and the complexity of this broad and growing field. However we frame the topic of memory (and there are many frames, as both Helfer's chapter and the discussions throughout this volume make clear), it remains a powerful and flexible device for understanding such concepts as time, subjectivity, loss and others central to Shakespeare studies.

PART I
Critical introductions

1
SHAKESPEARE, MEMORY, AND THE EARLY MODERN THEATRE

Zackariah Long

In 1988, Bernard Richards published a brief piece in *Notes and Queries* entitled 'Hamlet and the Theatre of Memory.'[1] In it he observes with some surprise that in *The Art of Memory* (1966) and *Theatre of the World* (1969) Frances Yates does not remark upon a possible allusion to Renaissance memory theatre in Hamlet's second soliloquy: 'Remember thee? | Ay, thou poor ghost, whiles memory holds a seat | In this distracted globe.'[2] Noting that theatres were among the structures recommended by memory theorists as models for mnemonic systems, Richards speculates that the great unacknowledged referent of Hamlet's soliloquy may be the Renaissance theatre of memory. Yates's failure to remark on this possibility is particularly striking because in her books Yates advances the argument that Robert Fludd's illustration of a memory theatre in *History of the Two Worlds* (1619) was modelled on Shakespeare's Globe theatre. If it is possible that one of the most important memory theatres of the Renaissance was patterned on the Globe, then it seems equally possible that the Globe may have been imagined as a kind of memory theatre.

Since Yates's books and Bernard's provocative note, Shakespeare scholars, theatre historians, and students of memorial culture have expressed regular, if cautious, interest in the possibility of a connection between Renaissance memory theatres and Shakespeare's 'wooden O.'[3] However, there has been surprisingly little sustained critical attention to this relationship, perhaps because of the scepticism that originally greeted Yates's thesis.[4] At the same time, there has been a growing recognition of the manifold connections between the broader memorial culture that produced the memory theatres and early modern theatrical aesthetics, stagecraft, and performance. In textured and wide-ranging examinations of characters, stage properties, and performance conditions, histories, and practices, scholars have documented how the 'memory work' of Shakespeare's theatre is in constant dialogue with the theories and practices of a variety of mnemonic forms.[5] This expanded critical context suggests that the time may be ripe for a fresh look at the relationship between the Renaissance memory theatre and Shakespeare's Globe.

In this chapter, I would like to sketch a set of conceptual links between Shakespeare's Globe and the memory theatre, especially as manifested in that most famous memory theatre of the European Renaissance, Giulio Camillo's. The context for this argument will be a close reading of Hamlet's invocation of the 'distracted globe' in his second soliloquy. This soliloquy has long been recognized as an epicentre for the play's exploration of memory, and a speech that constellates and condenses a number of important early modern mnemonic terms and concepts.

I will have occasion to touch on a number of these concepts; however, my main objective is to offer a fresh reading of the lines themselves, which I believe crystallize the relationship between Shakespeare's theatre and the Renaissance theatre of memory. In identifying the Globe theatre as a seat of memory, and by punning on 'globe' as head, theatre, and world, Hamlet links the project of Shakespearean soliloquy to the project of visionaries like Camillo, who sought to use mnemonic technologies to recreate the order of the universe within the mind of man.[6] At the same time, by admitting that this theatre is 'distracted,' Hamlet measures the distance between this grand vision and Shakespeare's 'wooden O.' It is in the gap between these two theatres that we can find Hamlet.

Camillo's theatre

The cultural fantasy that animated Renaissance memory theatres has been aptly termed by Julie Stone Peters 'the fantasy of mnemonic totality': the attempt to distil the entirety of human knowledge into an epitomized form that can be taken in at a single glance.[7] This fantasy was supported by a particular view of human knowledge—'knowledge as the ordered representation of everything ... *spatialized* and *visual*, *objective* in the sense that it existed independently of its knowers'—and was made possible by an 'at least physical and perhaps psychological or ontological' separation of the knower from the known, observer from observed. Given these specular and epistemological needs, it is not surprising that the theatre was tapped as a conceptual and aesthetic model. By physically or imaginatively placing himself within a theatre (a 'place for seeing'), a memory artist could view the objects of his contemplation as a totality. Moreover, the figure of the theatre sorted nicely with the desire to 'map the world's order and to construct a universal theory of everything.'[8] Thanks to the ancient metaphor of the *theatrum mundi*, early moderns were already used to thinking of the theatre as a model for the world; it was only a short step to making this metaphor literal. And the physical and spatial characteristics of theatres themselves—both the semi-circular ancient amphitheatre, with its orderly division of seating bays into horizontal and vertical tiers, and the circular Elizabethan playhouse, with its symmetrical stage doors and upper and lower galleries—provided the regularity, stability, and orderliness necessary for a mnemonic system.[9] This is why several memory theorists, including those potentially linked to Shakespeare's Globe, Giulio Camillo, Robert Fludd, and John Willis, adopted the theatre as their mnemonic schema.

Given the spatial, temporal, and aesthetic proximity of Fludd's and Willis' memory theatres to the Globe, it is not surprising that their treatises have received the most critical attention in recent Shakespeare scholarship.[10] However, for the purposes of this analysis, I believe Camillo's memory theatre offers the most profound point of comparison. First, Camillo's theatre, unlike Fludd's or Willis's, adopts the point of view of Hamlet's soliloquy. When Hamlet invokes the 'distracted globe,' he is looking outward at the audience. In both Fludd's and Willis' theatres, in contrast, the mnemonist adopts the vantage point of an audience member viewing the stage. Second, the relationship between the theatre and the cosmos that informs Camillo's theatre is closest to that of the Globe. Like Shakespeare's theatre, Camillo's is a theatre of the world: it inscribes the proportions of the universe within its dimensions. Fludd's memory theatre is just the opposite: it is only one of a series of theatres *in* the world, literally positioned alongside other theatres within the circular circumference of the zodiac. (Willis, meanwhile, makes no claim to his theatres having microcosmic significance at all.) Of course, there is less likelihood of a direct relationship of influence between Camillo and Shakespeare's Globe as there is with Fludd or Willis; but, as I hope to show, this is not as important as Shakespeare's clearly demonstrable knowledge of the vision that informs it.

To understand Shakespeare's engagement with this vision, though, we need to examine Camillo's theatre more closely. We have already noted that Camillo's is a theatre of the world, so we should expect its symbolic topography to mirror the Neoplatonic universe on which it is modelled. First, it contains three worlds: supercelestial, celestial, and subcelestial. The supercelestial world is represented by the orchestra: this is the world of 'divine emanations,' and is where Camillo's mnemonist stands, looking outward at the amphitheatre's seating area. The seating area, in turn, is divided into the celestial world of 'first causes,' represented by the first row of seats, and the subcelestial world of the elements, which extends upward over the next six rows. As we shall see, this tripartite grouping is a major structural principle of the theatre, and a key to understanding its design. However, it is balanced by another structural principle centred on groupings of seven. We have already noted that the theatre's seating area is divided into seven tiers or grades, running from the orchestra to the back wall. Camillo endows these seven tiers with special significance: they represent phases in the creation of the universe, echoing the seven days of creation in Genesis. Camillo then divides these seven tiers into seven sections, running from left to right, that represent the seven planetary influences.[11] The result is a gently sloping grid of forty-nine loci, and in each locus Camillo places a gate emblazoned with memory images that epitomize qualities of the region associated with it.

As for the images positioned within this mnemonic grid, they too are structured by a complex symbolic system. Each phase of creation is given its own master image, which serves to connect it to its neighbours on the same tier. Then, under these master images are subsidiary images that focus upon the planetary series to which they are assigned. By standing in the centre of the orchestra and inspecting these images, Camillo's mnemonist could not only contemplate the universe's macrocosmic structure, but inspect that design on the microcosmic level. As an example, consider Tier Four of the Saturn Series. On this tier, which in Camillo's Neoplatonic history corresponds to the creation of man's soul, the master image is the three Gorgon Sisters, which symbolize the tripartite soul, and the subsidiary image is Hercules battling Antaeus, which symbolizes man's 'struggle with earth to rise to heights of contemplation.'[12] In scrutinizing these images the mnemonist becomes aware of their microcosmic significance—of how the tripartite soul recapitulates the tripartite structure of the universe—as well as how these three worlds inform the Hercules image, since the hero is imagined as occupying an intermediate region between earth (below) and heaven (above). The mnemonist then applies this macrocosmic perspective to the lesson of the image itself—that man cannot defeat his 'earthy' (Saturnine) character through aggressive action; instead, he must consecrate his flesh (Antaeus) to the heavens. By meditating on the other memory images on this gate, the mnemonist internalizes the fruits of such a victory: the 'memory of things above: learning, imagination, and contemplation' (another tripartite division); meanwhile, if he progresses (or, rather, regresses) along the Saturn series to Tier Five, he discovers what happens when one loses this battle, since on this level the master image is Pasiphae and the Bull, which symbolizes the fate of the soul when it 'falls into a state of desiring the body.'[13] By inspecting all of the memory images within the theatre's loci, and by toggling between these macrocosmic and microcosmic perspectives, Camillo's ideal mnemonist eventually comes to comprehend every dimension the world not only in its local manifestation, but in its cosmic significance—the whole in the part, the part in the whole.

Describing Camillo's mnemonist in this way makes him sound like an almost divine figure—and in fact this is the point. For in standing in the centre of supercelestial realm, looking down on the history of creation as it radiates outward from first to secondary causes and incorporeal to corporeal forms, the mnemonist stands in the position of God. Viglius Zuichemus, who was given a tour of the wooden theatre by Camillo, clearly grasped this concept:

He calls this theatre of his by many names, saying that it is a built or constructed mind and soul, and now that it is a windowed one. He pretends that all things that the human mind can conceive and which we cannot see with the corporeal eye, after being collected together by diligent meditation may be expressed by certain corporeal signs in such a way that the beholder may at once perceive with his eyes everything that is otherwise hidden in the depths of the human mind.[14]

'*So that the beholder may at once perceive ... everything*': Camillo's theatre is designed to make the universe simultaneously present to the mnemonist as it appears in the mind of God. By standing in the heavens and contemplating the order of creation, the mnemonist hopes that the distance between his mortal eyes and those of God will shrink to the point where he unites himself with the One. In doing so, he would fulfil not only the Renaissance 'fantasy of mnemonic totality,' but the destiny set out by Pico della Mirandola in his 'Oration on the Dignity of Man': 'you shall be able to be reborn out of the judgment of your own soul into the higher beings, which are divine.' 'A great miracle is man,' indeed.[15]

The 'distracted globe'

In tracking the efforts of Camillo's magus-mnemonist to unify the contents of his memory with the supercelestial harmony, we may seem to have travelled very far from the world of *Hamlet*—a world characterized by confusion, scepticism, and disenchantment. We may also seem to have travelled far from Shakespeare's theatre: after all, according to Hamlet, the Globe is 'distracted.' In due course we will consider this distraction; however, in order to judge it aright, I would like to begin by foregrounding those qualities that Hamlet's Globe has in common with Camillo's theatre—and we should expect to find similarities, for at the heart of Hamlet's disillusionment is an intense idealism:

> What a piece of work is a man—how noble in reason; how infinite in faculties, in form and moving; how express and admirable in action; how like an angel in apprehension; how like a god; the beauty of the world; the paragon of animals!
>
> (II.2.269–73)

This is Hamlet's version of Pico della Mirandola's 'miracle of man.' The problem is that Hamlet's ability to see this godly potential has been obscured by his melancholy: 'And yet to me what is this quintessence of dust? Man delights not me' (273–75). The experience of seeing *Hamlet* is thus akin to witnessing a pall being cast over a mind which, in other circumstances, may have gladly partaken of Camillo's idealism. We should therefore expect to see in Hamlet's 'distracted globe' both potential and disappointment, light and shadow—outlines of a Camillo-like memory theatre just visible through the haze of Hamlet's disillusion.

These outlines certainly become visible in Shakespeare's second soliloquy. 'Remember me,' the Ghost commands, and as those words echo into the night, Hamlet attempts to collects his thoughts, and also collect himself, as he grapples with the implications of this injunction. Interestingly, Hamlet's first impulse upon doing so is to locate himself in space. Moving downstage and addressing the audience surrounding him on three sides, Hamlet cries:

> O, all you host of heaven! O earth!—what else?—
> And shall I couple hell?
>
> (II.5.9293)

Through his apostrophic exclamations, Hamlet articulates the sense of a vertically organized universe, divided into separate spheres; and, as in Camillo's theatre, they are three in number: heaven, earth, and hell. Hamlet stands at the centre of this universe, much like Camillo's mnemonist, and so Hamlet's words take on a double reference. The 'host of heaven,' as editors point out, are not only the heavenly host, but those audience members sitting in the uppermost galleries. By extension, the residents of the 'earth' are those seated in the lower galleries on the same horizontal plane as Hamlet, which leaves the groundlings as the denizens of 'hell,' the term for the crawl space beneath the stage on the same level as the pit. Hamlet's invocation of the 'distracted globe' then unites these facets through an allusion to *theatrum mundi*.

Of course, if Hamlet addresses these thoughts to the audience, then it follows that these audience members are the repositories of those thoughts. Indeed, this point is made explicit in Hamlet's promise that he will remember his father's words 'while memory *holds a seat* | In this distracted globe.' On one level, of course, Hamlet is talking about his mind. But 'seat' can also mean the literal seats or benches upon which audience members sit. In this way, memory's abode—its 'locus,' another meaning of 'seat' (OED 19b)—is not only Hamlet's head but the audience that surrounds him. As Lina Wilder notes, this notion of auditors as memory loci recurs throughout *Hamlet*, with characters repeatedly asking each other to remember words that have been entrusted to them.[16] It is also reinforced by the speech act of the soliloquy, a vow that Hamlet swears to uphold several times over the course of the speech (II.5.96, 97–98, 104, 112). By calling on the audience to serve as witnesses to this vow ('O, all ye host of heaven!'), Hamlet implicitly casts them in the role of 'remembrancers,' those who will hold him to account for his promise. Finally, the sense of the audience as locus is reinforced by the fact that Hamlet is speaking in soliloquy at all, for as every student of original practices is eager to tell us, the Shakespearean soliloquy is not only a conversation the actor has with himself but with the audience. Like Camillo's mnemonist, Hamlet turns to the audience that surrounds him in an attempt to externalize his thoughts in a carefully organized mnemonic space.

How is this space organized, and how does it compare to Camillo's theatre? Camillo's theatre reflects the structure of the universe and, as we have seen, at least one aspect of its structure—its division into three vertical spheres—is echoed in Hamlet's soliloquy. But there are other echoes too. Although the galleries of the Globe are not divided into seven forty-nine loci corresponding to the phases of creation and the planetary gods, they do possess both a 'horizontal' and 'vertical' structuring system. Standing at the edge of the stage, the actor delivering Hamlet's soliloquy would see ten horizontal bays of seated galleries, organized into three vertical tiers—the lower, middle, and upper galleries—to create a grid of thirty compartments. Anyone who has had the chance to visit the New Globe in London will notice that these rows look like boxes neatly stacked one atop one another. Indeed, the individual cubicles created by the Globe's twenty sides bear a striking resemblance to the '*Theatre*' or '*Repository*' that John Willis recommends as an apt memory place in *Mnemonica*.[17] Although the number of these mnemonic loci are different, the animating design is the same.

Of course, this grid only represents the exoskeleton of the theatre, the system of loci within which memory images are placed. The true depositories of memory in both Camillo and *Hamlet* are the images themselves. In Camillo's theatre, these images are emblazoned on gates put there by the theatre's mnemonist. At first glance, there doesn't seem to be any obvious equivalent to these gates in Shakespeare. However, while audience members may not have been placed in particular galleries by the company's actors, the thoughts and images with which these audience members are entrusted clearly are. To search for the Shakespearean equivalent of Camillo's emblazoned gates, therefore, one must not look to the audience—at least initially—but rather to the words the actor delivers to his audience. For if the analogy between Camillo's and

Shakespeare's memory theatre holds, then Hamlet's soliloquy, through the arrangement of its parts (*divisio*), should not only map out a symbolic system for the classification and retention of its *res* ('heavens ... earth ... hell'), but the *res* that fill out this symbolic system should provide the Shakespearean equivalent of Camillo's memory images. The speech 'turned outward' onto the audience becomes the actor's mnemonic system, like a transparent overlay in a map book or medical textbook that can superimposed atop neighbouring pages.

Viewed from this perspective, Hamlet's soliloquy appears in a different light. Hamlet's ejaculations at the opening of the speech ('O, all you host of heaven! O earth!') don't simply express anger and wonder, but enumerate the major loci in his memory theatre. In terms of specular distance, the point of view assumed by this part of the soliloquy is quite remote, with Hamlet 'stepping back,' as it were, so he can take in the full sweep of the theatre's loci. It is appropriate, then, that this part of the soliloquy should culminate in Hamlet's vow to the heavens, since of all the parts of the soliloquy this is the one closest to a bird's eye view. However, in the second part of the soliloquy, this perspective changes. Leaving his macrocosmic perch, Hamlet describes concrete steps that he will take to ensure that he makes good on his promise—specifically, he will expunge all 'trivial and fond records' from his thoughts. This part of the soliloquy quite literally 'comes down to earth,' as Hamlet considers his place in the macrocosm, and by extension the place of memory in his mind. We can therefore imagine these lines being delivered to those audience members in the lower galleries, roughly on Hamlet's own level—in Camillo's theatre, this would be Tier Four, the grade of the Gorgon Sisters, who represent the three parts of the soul in man, including memory. Finally, in the third part of the soliloquy, Hamlet articulates what he intends to deposit in this locus: his father's injunction that will live 'all alone' within 'the book and volume of [his] brain, | Unmixed with baser matter' (I.5.99, 102–03). Note that in pitting himself against 'baser matter,' Hamlet implicitly casts himself in a role not unlike Camillo's Hercules, who strives against his earthy nature to 'rise to heights of contemplation'; and this desire to exercise control, in turn, explains why Hamlet is attracted to the architectural mnemotechnic. Memory theatre is Hamlet's way of stabilizing his memory, a strategy for anchoring it in something outside himself.

The tragedy is, this strategy doesn't work. It doesn't work in the play's plot, as Hamlet repeatedly delays in avenging his father's murder, and it doesn't work in the soliloquy either. Indeed, this failure is presaged in the very lines in which Hamlet announces his resolve: the globe, as Hamlet points out, is 'distracted.' What does this mean? On the most literal level, 'distracted' means 'drawn apart,' 'rendered asunder,' or 'divided,' from Latin root *trahere*, to draw or pull' (OED 1). The danger, then, is dis-integration—of parts not acting in harmonious relationship with one another—and much mnemonic scholarship of *Hamlet* might fairly be described as an attempt to catalogue the sources of this disintegration. However, they may be easily summed up in Hamlet's triplicate pun on 'globe': Hamlet's head (the globe of his mind); the theatre to which he would turn for external support (the Globe); and the macrocosm ('the great globe itself'). None of these loci proves capable of providing the support that Hamlet needs to stabilize his memory, and the effects of this incapacity ripple outward from the soliloquy, fracturing the mnemonic edifice which Hamlet would construct. Indeed, the soliloquy enacts, in miniature, the sources of Hamlet's memory problems writ large in the rest of the play.

The fact that Hamlet's head is distracted is signalled within the first few lines of the soliloquy. As we have seen, Hamlet's first impulse when attempting to collect himself after the Ghost's revelation is to address the audience, and the macrocosm of which they are representatives. This is the moment when Hamlet sketches the architecture of his memory theatre, dividing it into its major regions. What we have not yet acknowledged is that Hamlet's immediate reaction to this effort is physical collapse:

> O, fie! Hold, hold, my heart,
> And you, my sinews, grow not instant old
> But bear me stiffly up.
>
> (I.5.93–95)

From Hamlet's address to his heart and sinews it is clear that he is suffering from an irascible passion—likely anger, given his disgusted response ('O, fie!'). Hamlet grasps his heart because there is a surge of choler and spirits invading it, and the weakness in his sinews is a result of the emptying of his extremities by this sudden influx. One wouldn't think such a surge would be a problem for Hamlet, since the ultimate cause of his anger—Claudius—is also the object of his revenge. However, as natural philosophers observe, there is a point at which violent emotions disrupt, rather than reinforce, memory—a point at which they distract:

> [I]f the Spirit be disturbed by the violent Passions of Anger, Fear, Despair, &c. the exercise of Memory can never be so free, because it requires a sedate and quiet Temper of Mind as well as a Soundness in the Body. All the Alarms and Troubles of the Soul blot out the Ideas that are already entertained, and hinder others from coming in. They obstruct all the Passages; and the Crowd of thoughts that in such cases arise is a great hindrance to Memory.[18]

Hamlet's sudden incapacitation suggests that his anger, rather than serving as fuel for memory and vengeance, simply recoils on itself, becoming self-consuming and distracting. Certainly elsewhere in the play Hamlet associates such outbursts with such distraction. In his fourth soliloquy, for example, after being provoked by the player's tears for Hecuba, Hamlet flies into a rage and upbraids himself for 'unpacking his heart with words' (II.2.520) rather than taking action. This outburst interrupts the forward momentum of the soliloquy, just as, on a larger structural level, the soliloquies themselves interrupt the forward momentum of the revenge plot. This entire trajectory is foreshadowed in the second soliloquy.

The same process unfolds with reference to the second potential source of 'distraction' in Hamlet's triplicate pun, the theatre. As we have seen, Hamlet not only turns to his own memory to hold himself accountable for fulfilling the Ghost's command; he also turns to the audience, casting them as 'remembrancers' who would hold him to account. However, the question inevitably arises: Are Hamlet's auditors up to the task? Early modern accounts of playgoing are chock-full of references to the ill and erratic behaviour of the audience, especially commoners standing in the pit. Later in the play Claudius refers to such commoners as 'the distracted multitude' (II.3.4), an appellation with mnemonic resonance we are now in a position to appreciate. A moment ago we noted that Hamlet's disgusted reaction occurs immediately after he sketches the broad contours of his memory theatre; however, what was left uncommented upon is that one of these loci is not like the others. Unlike the 'heavens' and 'earth,' 'hell' is prefaced by an interrogative ('What else?'), and then when it is introduced, it is introduced *as* an interrogative ('And shall I couple hell?'). In short, Hamlet seems ambivalent about whether the habitants of hell are fit repositories of memory—and perhaps with good reason. After all, in addition to its reputation as a locus for 'the distracted multitude,' the pit is also qualitatively different from other loci. The galleries of the Globe theatre are divided into neatly stacked cubicles; they are therefore conducive to mnemonic deposition. The pit, on the other hand, is a single, large, undifferentiated mass of bodies. Its very structure—or lack of it—suggests distractedness, the collective equivalent of the 'crowd of thoughts' invading Hamlet's mind.

If this reading is correct, then it may explain Hamlet's 'inward turn' in the next part of the soliloquy to 'the book and volume of [his] brain,' and his concomitant impulse to expunge from his memory all 'baser matter.' Rather than relying on the 'base' residents of hell, Hamlet will rely on his own memory and the inhabitants of 'earth' as fitter receptacles for his thoughts. But if so, this impulse is remarkably short-lived. For no sooner does Hamlet articulate this wish than his rage once more explodes to the surface.

> O most pernicious woman!
> O villain, villain, smiling, damned villain!
> *(I.5.105–06)*

In a kind of lived demonstration of the 'Don't think of an elephant!' principle, no sooner does Hamlet vow to rise above 'baser matter' than his mind immediately recoils upon it. Once again, the culprit seems to be anger, as this swerve off-course is structurally apposite to Hamlet's earlier explosion. Moreover, it is notable that, just as at the beginning of the soliloquy, Hamlet's apostrophic 'Os' ('O, all you host of heaven! O earth!') served to denote the major loci of the memory theatre, at the end of the soliloquy another set of 'Os' serves to mark the images that will be deposited there. The irony is that these images are not what Hamlet intended to recall. He wanted his father's '*command*' to live 'all alone' in the 'book and volume of [his] brain'; however, triggered by the thought of his mother and uncle, Hamlet pulls out his writing tablets to scribble down some pithy yet shallow invective:

> My tables! Meet it is I set it down,
> That one may smile and smile and be a villain [...]
> So, uncle, there you are.
> *(I.5.107–11)*

As Wilder remarks, 'Hamlet's vow to remember reflects badly on his grasp of the principle of *divisio*. Rather than separating his vow to remember the Ghost from every other memorandum, Hamlet's 'tables' quickly become crowded with words that are not the Ghost's'.[19] In this way, Hamlet's 'tables' echo the same worry about confusion and mixture emblematized by the 'distracted multitude.' Whether we are talking about the 'book and volume' of Hamlet's brain, his 'tables,' or the 'distracted multitude,' the locus in question is too crowded and confused to serve as a fit repository for memory.

The most profound and far-reaching of the three 'globes' which Hamlet claims are distracted, though, is the third, the *orbis terrarum*, the theatre of the world. It is important to remember that Camillo's memory theatre was believed to draw its power from its resemblance to the world. The universe, in this view, was a highly various, superabundant structure, but ultimately one reducible to an orderly scheme. Moreover, the sources which Camillo drew upon for the theatre reflected this sense of order. Camillo knits together Classical, Christian, Neoplatonic, and Hermetic-Cabbalist traditions to create a model of the world that both draws on and transcends these traditions. The resulting memory theatre is undergirded not only by a faith in its value as a schematization of the world, but by a faith in the ability of the world to be so schematized. But what if the macrocosm itself is disordered? Then the fundamental assumption that underlies the entire project of the Renaissance memory theatre is threatened.

This is precisely what seems to be the case in Hamlet. Like Camillo's cosmology, the world of Hamlet is woven out of many sources—Classical, Anglo-Saxon, Catholic, Protestant. However, unlike in Camillo, it is not clear how these sources are knitted together. Instead they, and the cosmologies to which they belong, intersect and collide. These uncertainties crystallize around the figure of the Ghost. When he is first described by the night watchmen smiting 'sledded Polacks on the ice' (I.1.62), Hamlet's father sounds like a hero of Scandinavian legend, as in the Amleth story from which *Hamlet* is derived. When young Hamlet, the Renaissance courtier, remembers his father, he clothes him in the finery of classical mythology (III.4.54–55), as though he were a figure from the ancient world. When Hamlet's father appears in I.5, he comes like the ghost of a traditional Senecan tragedy, asking Hamlet to 'revenge his foul and most unnatural murder' (I.5.25). But then, when he describes his infernal torments, the Ghost seems to come from Catholic Purgatory (I.5.9–14). These various cosmological frames just don't sort. In this way, the Ghost is like an errant memory image—an *imagines agentes* without a locus—and this indeterminacy calls into question the sufficiency of the macrocosm which purports to contain him, like a newly discovered species that doesn't fit neatly into any classification system and therefore draws the sufficiency of the taxonomy itself into question.

We have already noted traces of this unplaceability in Hamlet's second soliloquy. Hamlet's question, 'And shall I couple hell?' appears to signal a shift in the prince's understanding of the world. 'What kind of memory theatre is this?' Hamlet seems to be asking; 'Does the Ghost belong *here*?' Despite this uncertainty, Hamlet initially seems prepared to take the Ghost at his word. However, this confidence doesn't last. Soon after Hamlet begins to suspect the Ghost's reliability (II.2.533–39), and in order to test the Ghost's word, he stages his own bit of memory theatre, 'The Mousetrap.' But the Mousetrap is unreliable a mechanism for sorting truth from fiction as the Ghost. Fusing the story of his father's murder with his own murderous fantasies against Claudius, and allowing his seething resentment at his mother's remarriage to infiltrate the play's representation of her guilt, the Mousetrap not only fails as a lie detector test, but reinscribes the very chaos and indeterminacy that it purports to sort out. By condensing several characters into each figure—Lucianus is both Claudius and Hamlet; Baptista is both Gertrude as she was and Gertrude as Hamlet wishes she were—The Mousetrap crowds too many memory images into the same locus. Like the tables that Hamlet allows to become overcrowded with words other than his father's, like the pit crammed with groundlings, like the Ghost himself, whose character is overloaded with competing cosmological signs, the 'theatre of the world' on which Hamlet attempts to model his memory theatre is confused.

The result of such overcrowding, the soliloquy tells us, is 'distraction,' the dis-integration of the mind's coordinated response. With every gesture Hamlet makes at organizing his memory, knitting together his thoughts as the soliloquy unfolds, those thoughts quickly unravel behind him, fracturing the mnemonic edifice he seeks to build. Hamlet then attempts to prop up these weaknesses, drawing on different forms of external aid. But the unreliability and variability of the mnemonic supports he turns to for assistance reinscribe the very disorder he sought to avoid. The ultimate effect of these cascading uncertainties is to sever the links that, in Camillo's theatre, connect microcosm and macrocosm. They open up a chasm between the Camillo-like ideal toward which the soliloquy reaches, and the actual materials of memory with which Hamlet has to deal. The result is alienation from self, other, and world.

Hamlet and Camillo's theatre

In the end, then, the differences between Camillo's memory theatre and Hamlet's 'distracted globe' are as important as the similarities. Indeed, we might think of Camillo's and Hamlet's theatres as standing on either side of an epochal divide. Camillo's theatre is a monument to metaphysical and epistemological confidence—it reflects the organization of a stable universe. Moreover, the contents of Camillo's theatre are stable. Once the mnemonist has forged the images and deposited them in their proper loci, they stay there. Camillo has figured out the organization of the world so you don't have to—a fact nicely illustrated by the history of the theatre's travels from Venice to Paris to a planned version for the French court.

The memory theatre that Hamlet constructs in his second soliloquy bears some important resemblances to Camillo's. Like Camillo's theatre, it possesses a stable external structure—a regular division into spheres and compartments—because the theatre that surrounds Hamlet does. Such structural constants, in turn, encourage certain patterns of memory work—speech after speech in early modern play texts reproduce the same spatial hierarchy of supernal, earthly, and infernal realms that we find in *Hamlet*. However, at this point the theatres diverge. Whereas Camillo's theatre was populated by an audience of fixed images, the audiences that flooded Shakespeare's Globe were famously variable. Moreover, the images that were entrusted to these audiences were variable, shifting with every scene and character. We can isolate one character, or even one speech, and unpack the significance of the images entrusted to this audience. But the memory theatre constructed by such verbal discourse is necessarily ephemeral, lasting only as long as the performance, or possibly even the scene. It is also radically subjective and partial. Unlike Camillo's mnemonist-magus, who peers down at creation like a god, the Shakespearean actor-mnemonist doesn't stand outside the theatre or above it, but *within* it. Shakespeare's memory theatre is a theatre for situated agents, situated not at the top of creation but in its midst.

The central tension of Shakespeare's 'distracted globe,' therefore, is the tension between its stable external structure—which promises a durable and identifiable framework for thinking about the world—and its variable contents, which give the lie to that framework by foregrounding how each character experiences his or her relationship to those surroundings differently. The 'theatre of the world' that surrounds Shakespeare's character thus becomes a locus of radically different meanings.

This phenomenon—how two characters can perceive the same thing and understand it differently—is a theme on which Hamlet broods incessantly. We see it in Hamlet's debate with Rosencrantz and Guildenstern about whether Denmark is a 'prison' ('We think not so, my lord.' 'Why, then, 'tis none for you.'); in his exasperation with Gertrude that she cannot see the difference between 'this fair mountain' and 'this moor' ('Have you eyes?'); in Hamlet's repartee with the Gravedigger about whether he is inside the grave or outside it ('You lie out on't, sir, and therefore it is not yours: for my part, I do not lie in't, and yet it is mine'); in his playful baiting of Osric on the subject of the weather ('I thank your lordship, it is very hot.' 'No, believe me, 'tis very cold').[20] It even happens within Hamlet himself. Only half-concealing the truth from his friends, Hamlet tells Rosencrantz and Guildenstern:

> I have of late—but wherefore I know not—lost all my mirth, forgone all custom of exercises; and indeed it goes so heavily with my disposition that this goodly frame, the earth, seems to me a sterile promontory, this most excellent canopy, the air, look you, this brave o'erhanging firmament, this majestical roof fretted with golden fire, why, it appears no other thing to me than a foul and pestilent congregation of vapours.
>
> *(II.2.294–302)*

Hamlet, as we remarked earlier, is possessed of a double vision. On the one hand, he can report on the beautiful features of the world: he admits that the earth is a 'goodly frame' and the sky a 'majestical roof.' The problem is that, to Hamlet, the world does not appear this way. Thus the images that the speech itemizes are quickly replaced by their thematic opposites: the 'goodly frame' becomes the 'sterile promontory,' the 'majestical roof' a 'pestilent congregation of vapours.' Of course, as in the second soliloquy, these descriptions take on a metatheatrical resonance—the 'goodly frame' is the Globe itself. To read this speech following Hamlet's earlier soliloquy is, then, to witness the refurbishment of Hamlet's memory theatre with a new set of images. Hamlet's 'distracted globe' is thus the ultimate embodiment of how the same locus can present multiple and conflicting images, not only for different people at the same time, but for the same person at different times, or even the same person at the same time.

For these reasons, Hamlet's 'distracted globe' is fundamentally a memory theatre for a shattered world—and this sense of shatteredness explains why, despite post-war predictions of *Lear* possibly taking its place, Hamlet will likely continue to hold pride of place in our cultural imaginary, the central position in our collective memory theatre. For the sense of the world that Hamlet articulates—of a universe no longer in possession of a clear overarching structure, but one crammed with the crowded and conflicting remnants of past structures—is still the predominant existential reality to this day, at least in the secular West. We too live in a shattered world, with the ruins of past epistemes all around us. There is no memory theatre that can put it back together again.

Notes

1 Bernard Richards, 'Hamlet and the Theatre of Memory', *Notes and Queries* 223 (1988), p. 53.
2 Ann Thompson and Neil Taylor's *Hamlet: Third Series* (London: Arden, 2006), I.3.95–97. Further references to this edition are given after quotations in the text.
3 Douwe Draaisma, *Metaphors of Memory: A History of Ideas About the Mind*, trans. by Paul Vincent (Cambridge: Cambridge University Press, 1995), pp. 43–44; Julie Stone Peters, 'Theater and Book in the History of Memory: Materializing Mnemosyne in the Age of Print', *Modern Philology* 102.2 (2004), pp. 179–206 (p. 198); Adele Davidson, *Shakespeare in Shorthand: The Textual Mystery of King Lear* (Newark: University of Delaware Press, 2009), pp. 49–50; Hester Lees-Jeffries, *Shakespeare and Memory* (Oxford: Oxford University Press, 2013), p. 30; Isabel Karremann, *The Drama of Memory in Shakespeare's History Plays* (Cambridge: Cambridge University Press, 2015), pp. 5–7. By far the most extensive discussion is Lina Perkins Wilder, *Shakespeare's Memory Theatre: Recollection, Properties, and Character* (Cambridge: Cambridge University Press, 2010), pp. 51–57.
4 I.A. Shapiro, 'Robert Fludd's Stage-Illustration', in *Shakespeare Studies* 2 (1966), 192–09; Wylie Sypher, 'Magical Mystery Tour' in *New York Review of Books*, 29 January, 1970, 23–25; see also Yates's reply and Sypher's rejoinder in the 12 March 1970 issue.
5 William West, *Theatres and Encyclopedias in Early Modern Europe* (Cambridge: Cambridge University Press, 2002); William Engel, *Death and Drama in Renaissance England: Shades of Memory* (Oxford: Oxford University Press, 2003); Katherine Rowe, '"Remember Me": Technologies of Memory in Michael Almereyda's *Hamlet*', in *Shakespeare the Movie II: Popularizing the Plays on Film, TV, Video, and DVD*, ed. by Richard Burt and Lynda E. Boose (New York: Routledge, 2003), pp. 37–55; *Forgetting in Early Modern English Literature and Culture: Lethe's Legacies*, ed. by Christopher Ivic and Grant Williams (New York: Routledge, 2004); Julie Stone Peters, *Theatre of the Book 1480–1880: Print, Text, and Performance in Europe* (Oxford: Oxford University Press, 2001) and 'Theater and Book' (2004); Garrett Sullivan, *Memory and Forgetting in English Renaissance Drama: Shakespeare, Marlowe, Webster* (Cambridge: Cambridge University Press, 2005); *Shakespeare, Memory, and Performance*, ed. by Peter Holland (Cambridge: Cambridge University Press, 2006); Evelyn Tribble, *Cognition in the Globe: Attention and Memory in Shakespeare's Theatre* (New York: Palgrave Macmillan, 2011); Wilder; Andrew Hiscock, *Reading Memory in Early Modern Literature* (Cambridge: Cambridge University Press, 2011); Catherine Richardson, *Shakespeare and Material Culture* (Oxford: Oxford University Press, 2011); Lees-Jeffries; Karremann.
6 On Hamlet's triplicate pun, see Richards; Anthony Dawson, 'The Arithmetic of Memory', in *The Culture of Playgoing in Shakespeare's England: A Collaborative Debate* by Anthony Dawson and Paul Yachnin (Cambridge: Cambridge University Press, 2001), pp. 161–81 (p. 177); Peters (2004), p. 198; Wilder, p. 113. The argument that follows about Hamlet's second soliloquy has been anticipated, in miniature, by Richards and Peters (2004), p. 199.
7 Peters, 'Theater and Book in the History of Memory', p. 192.
8 West, p. 1.
9 Ibid., p. 19.

10 Rowe, pp. 39–42; Wilder, pp. 51–58; Lees-Jeffries, pp. 30–31; Karremann, pp. 5–7.
11 Frances Yates, *The Art of Memory* (Chicago: University of Chicago Press, 1966), pp. 137–38.
12 Yates, pp. 140, 142.
13 Yates, foldout chart between pp. 144 and 145. Saturn Series, Fourth Grade.
14 Yates, p. 143.
15 Pico della Mirandola, 'The Dignity of Man', in *The Portable Renaissance Reader* (New York: Viking Press, 1953), pp. 476, 478.
16 Wilder, p. 107.
17 John Willis, *Mnemonica; or, The Art of Memory* (London, 1661), pp. 52–55.
18 Marius D'Assigny, *The Art of Memory* (London, 1699), pp. 27–28.
19 Wilder, p. 112.
20 1623: 3.2.248–49; 3.4.64–65; 5.1.115–16; 5.2.90–91.

2
SHAKESPEARE, MEMORY, AND PRINT CULTURE

Amanda Watson

'It's so full of quotations!'
(*Apocryphal theatergoer's reaction to* Hamlet)

Introduction

If writing is exteriorized memory (an association that stretches back at least as far as Plato's *Phaedrus*), then the printed word is exteriorized memory made reproducible on a large scale, and the history of the printing and reprinting of Shakespeare's works is at least in part a history of commemoration by an ever-widening set of editors, publishers, and readers. Print preserves texts by reproducing more copies of them than scribal transcription can, increasing their influence and their chances of survival. When Leontes greets Florizel in Act V of *The Winter's Tale*, he does so with a metaphor that links printing, paternity, and the continuance of the past:

> Your mother was most true to wedlock, prince;
> For she did print your royal father off,
> Conceiving you. Were I but twenty-one,
> Your father's image is so hit in you
> His very air, that I should call you brother,
> As I did him.
> (V.1.123–128)

For Leontes, printing signifies making a copy exact enough to trigger recognition. But Florizel also activates Leontes' memory, calling back Polixenes' 'image' and his 'very air' from the past; the faithful replica is also a mnemonic figure.[1] Leontes' print metaphor draws together his (and the play's) preoccupations with faithful reproduction and memorialization, suggesting that the printed word can stand for the latter as well as the former. Print commemorates, with varying degrees of exactness; it propagates both true representations and less-true ones, like the outrageous 'ballad[s] in print' that Autolycus sells to the gullible Mopsa and Dorcas (IV.4.261). Paulina uses the same printing metaphor to describe the infant Perdita as 'the whole matter | And copy of the father' even though 'the print be little' (II.iii.98–99). In so doing, she reminds us that print can change the appearance of a text even as it transmits the 'matter'.

In this chapter I ask how print culture helped Shakespeare's readers to remember him, and how the myriad printed versions of Shakespeare's works encouraged specific kinds of reading and remembering. My aim is to provide a brief survey of the intersection between Shakespeare studies and the history of the book, and to offer one set of answers to these questions in the form of a case study of nineteenth-century American readers of Shakespeare. By necessity, I focus on parts rather than wholes: the history of reading instead of the study of all of print culture, a particular time period and place instead of the entire global multi-century expanse of Shakespeare's influence. Nevertheless, I hope to furnish starting points for scholars with an interest in Shakespeare and print culture and suggest further directions for the history of reading.

Shakespeare scholars have been deeply involved in bibliography and textual studies for centuries. The earliest Shakespeare editors, in the eighteenth century, tried to establish authoritative texts of the plays, and editors and textual scholars have continued to do so into the present. A survey of textual scholarship on Shakespeare could (and does) fill entire volumes.[2] This chapter will focus, instead, on the more recent field of book history, which is often said to have begun with the publication of *L'apparition du livre* by Lucien Febvre and H.-J. Martin in 1958.[3] Book historians share an interest in what D.F. McKenzie called 'the sociology of texts,' including 'the human motives and interactions which texts involve at every stage of their production, transmission, and consumption.' Traditional bibliographers and textual critics, McKenzie argued, 'neglected' these factors or 'felt unable to denominate [them] as central to what we do.'[4] This expanded interest in the networks of social relationships and historical forces that underlie book production, transmission, and consumption informs the work of book historians into the present day.[5]

The study of the history of the book, as Robert Darnton wrote in 'What Is the History of Books?', one of the foundational essays for the field, occupies a 'no-man's land located at the intersection of a half-dozen fields of study,' embracing history, literature, sociology, and geography, among others.[6] It can be challenging to plot the relationships between all of these intersecting disciplines at once; Darnton attempted to do this by diagramming the life cycle of a printed book as a 'communications circuit.' Darnton's circuit connects authors, publishers, printers and their suppliers, shippers, booksellers, binders, and readers and readers' organizations, all with larger political, social, cultural, and economic influences operating in the background. Thomas R. Adams and Nicolas Barker proposed an alternate version of Darnton's circuit, which they call 'the whole socio-economic conjuncture,' focusing on 'five events in the life of a book—publishing, manufacturing, distribution, reception and survival,' putting the emphasis on the book itself rather than the people who produce, distribute, and consume it.[7] Adams and Barker's model highlights the ways in which the later end of the circuit, 'reception' and 'survival,' can extend the life of the text far beyond its author's lifetime.

If we imagine Shakespeare's plays and poems moving through Darnton's communications circuit, we can see how the study of print culture draws together a host of historical figures, objects, and influences involved with the creation and circulation of the texts. We can see that a book historian's approach to Shakespeare can encompass everything from the typographical conventions that helped to define sonnet sequences as a distinct print genre, to the evidence that particular bindings reveal about how plays were sold and read, to the effects of eighteenth-century copyright law on the publication of later editions of Shakespeare's works, to the ways in which women and working-class readers discovered the plays through informal libraries and reading clubs.[8] If we place Shakespeare within Adams and Barker's socio-economic conjuncture schema, we can see that the initial publication, manufacture, and distribution of the plays and poems forms part of a larger picture culminating with the endurance of works and individual copies into the future. Adams and Barker's concepts of 'reception' and 'survival' allow us to consider Shakespeare's long, varied, and ongoing afterlife in print: our collective memory of Shakespeare, as it were.

It is with this later collective memory that I am chiefly concerned. Much attention has been paid, with good reason, to Shakespeare's appearances in print during the sixteenth and seventeenth centuries. The publication of the 1623 First Folio was a key moment in Shakespeare's construction as an author, and the earlier texts of Shakespeare's plays and poems are more important from an editorial standpoint than the hosts of later editions. But the projects of canonizing and remembering Shakespeare have never stopped. We can learn a great deal from the ways in which Shakespeare's words found their way into print—and into the minds of readers—between the seventeenth century and the present day. David Scott Kastan reminds us that print, like memory, 'falsifies even as it recalls and records,' and that '[Shakespeare's] corpus is reconstructed by sets of motivations and practices that leave their marks upon the text, distorting it even as they preserve and set it forth.'[9]

In what follows, I trace the 'distorting' and 'preserving' reconstruction of Shakespeare through anthologies and schoolbooks, two print genres that fragmented Shakespeare's plays into memorable quotations. When editors presented Shakespeare as a source of quotations, they helped to shape how the wide audience for schoolbooks and anthologies understood his plays. Readers, as we will see, used these textual scraps in ways that seem both familiar and strange to modern eyes. As Roger Chartier writes,

> Readers [...] never confront abstract, idealized texts detached from any materiality. They hold in their hands or perceive objects and forms whose structures and modalities govern their reading or hearing, and consequently the possible comprehension of the text read or heard.[10]

The text/reader interaction, in other words, begins with particular material objects and generates meanings and understandings specific to those objects. To consider Shakespeare's massive presence in Anglo-American literary culture is to consider, among other things, the legacy of innumerable printed texts and the innumerable readings that these texts generate. This textual and interpretive legacy can show us our shared memory of Shakespeare at various stages in the process of its formation.

Remembering Shakespeare in anthologies

For much of the seventeenth and eighteenth centuries, copies of Shakespeare's plays were less accessible to readers than they later became. William St Clair has charted the history of markets for editions of Shakespeare, showing how the expensive First Folio and its successors moved Shakespeare 'upmarket' and how the dissolution of perpetual copyright in the late eighteenth century brought Shakespeare back into the public domain, leading to a proliferation of less expensive editions that a wider range of readers could afford. 'It had taken nearly 200 years for the minimum price of access to a Shakespeare play to fall back to what it had been in Shakespeare's day,' St Clair observes, but 'by about 1800, Shakespeare at last became available to readers of all classes and ages.'[11] A reader in early nineteenth-century Great Britain or the United States who wanted to discover Shakespeare's works had many options at her disposal. Plays were available singly and in various multivolume editions of the Complete Works. Editors also began to publish abridged and modified versions, aimed at wider audiences that included women and children—perhaps most infamously in the case of Thomas and Henrietta Bowdler's

Family Shakespeare (1807), carefully shorn of 'those words and expressions [...] which cannot with propriety be read aloud in a family.'[12]

Readers who lacked access to a multivolume set of Shakespeare's works, or to copies or adaptations of individual plays, could still find abundant quotations from Shakespeare in popular anthologies that reproduced passages from the plays.[13] The first of these, William Dodd's *Beauties of Shakespear*, first published in 1752 and reprinted nearly forty times during the eighteenth and nineteenth centuries, helped establish a vogue for books of selected quotations from a particular author or authors.[14] A host of poets got the 'Beauties' treatment during the eighteenth century, on both sides of the Atlantic.[15] Some critics scoffed at the superficial knowledge that these collections promoted. The poet and novelist Hannah More, for example, satirizing the fashion for 'Compendiums, Extracts, Beauties,' called anthologists

> literary cooks
> Who skim the cream of others' books,
> And ruin half an Author's graces,
> By plucking bons-mots from their places.[16]

Nevertheless, many readers used collections of beauties to familiarize themselves with the highlights of an author's work. The condensed format allowed access to a range of literature at a relatively low price.

Dodd began his *Beauties of Shakespear* with a preface explaining the relatively modest scope of his project. He originally intended, he writes,

> to have consider'd each play critically and regularly thro' all its parts, but as this would have swell'd the work beyond proper bounds, I was obliged to confine myself solely to a collection of [Shakespeare's] poetical *Beauties*: and I doubt not, every reader will find so large a fund for observation, so much excellent and refined morality, that he will prize the work as it deserves.

Dodd notes that he has had to omit passages whose beauties 'wholly depend' on 'the plot and characters' of the play in question and hence make less sense out of context.[17] Only the most easily decontextualized passages remain, ready for a reader to sample and reuse. Dodd, and many readers, nonetheless considered the collection a worthy introduction to his favorite author.

Dodd arranged his quotations by play, but titled each quotation descriptively and supplied 'a general index, digesting them under proper heads.' This organizational scheme allowed a reader to browse individual plays or to search for Shakespeare's thoughts on 'Dew in flowers,' or 'Wife's duty to her husband,' or 'King-killing, detestable' (to pick a few examples). Other collections of Beauties included similar subject headings and indexes.[18] So influential was Dodd's selection that, in the year after *Beauties of Shakespear* first saw print, Hugh Blair included a list of Dodd's 'beauties' at the beginning of his own edition of Shakespeare's complete works.[19]

Another highly influential Shakespeare anthologist was the educator Vicesimus Knox, whose series of *Elegant Extracts* in prose and poetry packaged a canon of English literature for a growing reading public. The *Elegant Extracts* were aimed at, and reached, a wide audience; according to St Clair, at least 23,000 copies were printed in England between 1796 and 1824.[20] In Jane Austen's *Emma*, both the farmer Robert Martin and the well-to-do Emma Woodhouse read from the *Elegant Extracts*, suggesting its appeal to multiple strata of society.[21] The 'Dramatic' section of *Elegant Extracts: or useful and Entertaining Pieces of Poetry* (first published in 1789) included many selections from Shakespeare borrowed from Dodd's collection.[22]

Knox's anthologies were intended, as the subtitle of the prose *Elegant Extracts* proclaimed, 'for the Improvement of Scholars at Classical and other Schools,' and other schoolbooks soon followed. Shakespeare quotations began appearing in textbooks in the late eighteenth century, a trend that continued into the twentieth century. Both British and American school readers used short passages from Shakespeare as examples of 'choice' sentences; elocution textbooks also included longer speeches from the plays for students to memorize and declaim.[23] In the United States, the widely used *McGuffey Readers* drew heavily on Shakespeare's plays for their selections for elocution and memorization.[24] A reader's first encounter with Shakespeare's works during this period was often mediated by a schoolbook. The writer and former factory worker Lucy Larcom, for example, first encountered passages from Shakespeare in John Pierpont's *The American First Class Book*, most memorably 'the pathetic dialogue between Hubert and little Prince Arthur [from *King John*], whose appeal to have his eyes spared, brought many a tear to my own.' To the poetry-loving Larcom, Shakespeare was an author she read 'from childhood, in a fragmentary way,' but did not read systematically until after she left school.[25]

Shakespeare in American commonplace books

I turn now to a brief case study of readers of Shakespeare whose engagement with the plays was shaped by the culture of anthologizing I have just outlined. Specifically, I will discuss the presence of Shakespeare in nineteenth-century American commonplace books, personal collections in which readers transcribed quotations from books they read. Commonplace books began as tools for humanist education, with contents organized under alphabetical subject headings. (Anthologies like Dodd's *Beauties*, with their descriptive titles and alphabetical subject indices, arise from this tradition.) The format became less structured over the centuries, but remained popular into the nineteenth century. Scholarship on commonplace books has emphasized their importance in the early modern period, but, with the exception of recent work such as David Allan's *Commonplace Books and Reading in Georgian England*, relatively few scholars have discussed the later history of the commonplace book.[26] Both earlier and later commonplace books form an important source of evidence for the history of reading. Although they reflect only a fraction of the texts a given person read, they can reveal the range of sources a person consulted and the active process of a reader's mind.

Readers first began commonplacing Shakespeare's plays and poems during his own lifetime, beginning in the late 1590s.[27] As several scholars have recently shown, seventeenth-century printers anticipated readers' needs by adding 'commonplace marks' (the forerunners of quotation marks) to the margins of printed plays, typographically signaling which lines were most worthy of being added to a commonplace book. As Margreta De Grazia observes,

> The quotation marks surrounding a passage now serve to fence in a passage as property of another; in earlier centuries, however, they served to advertise its appropriability. ... They marked material to be copied by readers in their copy-books or commonplace books, thereby assuring that the commonplaces would become more common still.[28]

In a similar vein, Zachary Lesser and Peter Stallybrass argue that the commonplace marks in the 1603 first quarto of *Hamlet* establish this version of the play not as a badly remembered playscript but as 'Shakespeare's first literary drama,' with extractable passages marked for the reader's benefit.[29] As Shakespeare moved more and more firmly into the canon of English literature, British commonplacers of the eighteenth and early nineteenth centuries continued to copy extracts from his plays into their collections. David Allan has found that a number of

Georgian-era readers engaged deeply with Shakespeare's plays in their commonplace books. In Allan's account, '[t]he evidence of commonplacing confirms that, by the end of [the Georgian] period, Shakespeare stood head-and-shoulders above all other writers in readers' esteem.'[30]

American readers of the same period also esteemed Shakespeare, though not, perhaps, to the same degree. As part of a larger project, I have been analyzing the contents of fifty American commonplace books of poetry, ranging from the 1810s to the early twentieth century and compiled primarily in the northeastern United States. Shakespeare is the only early modern author to appear in these collections with any regularity. Quotations from Shakespeare appear in 40% of the commonplace books in my sample, behind Lord Byron (48%) and Thomas Moore (54%), with a total of 125 distinct Shakespeare quotations. The most frequently quoted single play is *The Merchant of Venice*, with twelve quotations, followed by *Hamlet* and *Measure for Measure* with eight quotations each—a distribution that partly echoes the distribution of Shakespeare extracts in the *McGuffey Readers*, but not entirely. According to Jonathan Burton, the most quoted plays in the advanced *McGuffey Readers* were *Hamlet, King John, Othello, Julius Caesar, The Merchant of Venice,* and *Henry VIII*.[31] The compilers in my sample shared the *McGuffey* editors' enthusiasm for *Hamlet* and *The Merchant of Venice*, but they also repeatedly quoted comedies like *Measure for Measure, As You Like It,* and *The Two Gentlemen of Verona*. Anthologies such as Dodd's *Beauties*, available in the United States as imports and reprints, supplied some of these readers with passages from Shakespeare beyond what they would have found in their schoolbooks.

Indeed, anthologies (and other printed sources of short extracts) likely account for the occasional presence of lines from Shakespeare's least popular plays in readers' commonplace books. Annis Stockton of Princeton, New Jersey, copied three lines about mercy from *Titus Andronicus* (I.1.120–122) around 1821: 'Wilt thou draw near the mercy of the gods | Draw near then in being merciful | Sweet mercy is nobility's true badge.'[32] While a young woman like Stockton may have read this violent and gruesome play in its entirety, she more likely copied these lines from an anthology; indeed, all of the quotations in her commonplace book can also be found in Dodd's *Beauties of Shakspeare* or the *Elegant Extracts*. Similarly, the one quotation from *Timon of Athens* that I have found in an American commonplace book appears in a collection compiled by Julia Lippitt of Providence, Rhode Island: 'O Gold! thou dear divorce | 'Twixt natural son and sire! Thou bright defiler | Of Hymen's purest bed!' (IV.3.384–386).[33] These lines were copied as part of a sequence of selections from William Charles White's 1797 play *Orlando: or Parental Persecution, a Tragedy*, on whose title page the quotation from *Timon* is used as an epigraph.[34] Much like anthologized quotations, epigraphs lifted lines of verse out of context and brought them to the attention of readers who might not have encountered them elsewhere.

Short extracts from Shakespeare served the same purposes for these readers that short poems and other snippets of longer works did: they were used as samples of beautiful language, precepts to remember ('excellent and refined morality,' as Dodd would say), and words of guidance and consolation. Many of these readers could have read Shakespeare's plays in their entirety or seen them performed, given the popularity of Shakespeare in American theaters.[35] But if the quotations I have found in commonplace books are any indication, many American readers encountered their Shakespeare pre-extracted and pre-selected, and in a number of cases they clearly copied their selections from an anthology or a similar type of source. The result is that two Shakespeares distinct from Shakespeare the dramatist emerge from the commonplace book record: Shakespeare the proverbialist and Shakespeare the lyric poet. The detachable quotations in the printed sources these readers consulted encouraged exactly these responses to Shakespeare's words.

The conversion of lines from Shakespeare into proverbs is not a new phenomenon, and some nineteenth-century anthologists capitalized on it by producing collections of Shakespeare's 'aphorisms' and 'sayings.'[36] Compilers of commonplace books often gravitated toward aphoristic, memorable lines with the ring of proverbial wisdom. Polonius's advice to Laertes in *Hamlet*, for example, appears in two commonplace books, presented as universal advice. Maria Brockway of Newbury, Massachusetts, copied the lines 'The friends thou hast, and their adoption tried, | Grapple them to thy soul with hoops of steel' (I.3.62–63) around 1833, after a page of prose quotations about women's duty, education, and 'real religion.'[37] Edna Rhodes Gardiner of Providence, Rhode Island, wrote in one of her commonplace books in the 1890s, 'Polonius in "Hamlet" (Act I., Scene 3) says, "This above all: to thine own self be true, | And it must follow, as the night the day, | Thou canst not then be false to any man"' (I.3.78–80).[38] Neither Brockway nor Gardiner appears to care about the source or context of the advice. In this, they both follow a lead that began with the printers who added commonplace markers to this speech in the First Quarto.

Such decontextualization seems to have been widespread. Compilers treated Iago's more sententious speeches from *Othello* in the same way, quoting lines like 'Who steals my purse steals trash' and 'Good name in man and woman, dear my lord, | Is the immediate jewel of their souls' (III.3.158–160), unperturbed by the fact that one of Shakespeare's most notorious villains speaks these lines.[39] Some readers altered the meaning of their extracts from Shakespeare by juxtaposing them with other quotations. Sarah Hammond Palfrey of Boston, for example, copied Gertrude's lines from *Hamlet*—'All that lives must die, | Passing through nature to Eternity' (I.2.72–73)—without including Hamlet's sharp rejoinder.[40] Palfrey, who favored religious and elegiac poetry, copied these lines during a year (1847) in which she also transcribed hymns by John Wesley and Henry Ware, part of Elizabeth Barrett Browning's religious poem 'The Sleep,' and the line 'Sorrow and silence are strong, and patient endurance is godlike' from Henry Wadsworth Longfellow's *Evangeline*. Palfrey's favorite poems emphasize spiritual comfort in the face of death and suffering; in this context, the quotation from *Hamlet* becomes a maxim about the inevitability of death and the promise of 'eternity' beyond it.

Assembling a commonplace book often meant choosing extracts particularly relevant to one's own life. Anna L. Sweet compiled her first commonplace book while at school in Providence, Rhode Island, between the late 1830s and the early 1840s. She, or one of her friends, copied and condensed part of Helena's speech from *A Midsummer Night's Dream* (III.2.208–215):

> We grew together,
> Like a double cherry, seeming parted,
> But yet a union in partition:
> Two lovely berries moulded on one stem:
> So with two seeming bodies, but one heart,
> And will you rend our youthful love asunder?[41]

Like many commonplace books compiled by young women at school in antebellum New England, Sweet's collection shows signs of collaboration by a group of classmates: more than one hand transcribed the contents, friends' autographs appear in its pages, and the collection includes various poems about friendship.[42] In this context, the *Midsummer Night's Dream* quotation was likely chosen to emphasize not the quarrel between Hermia and Helena, but an idealized portrait of female friendship on the verge of separation—appropriate for schoolmates whose time together would inevitably end.

Anthologies and schoolbooks encouraged readers to select passages for their aesthetic, as well as their didactic, value. As Leah Price observes, anthologies of extracts from plays 'strip the dialogue away from soliloquies and songs to produce snatches of lyrical self-expression.'[43] And readers who filled their commonplace books with poetry tended to treat extracts from

Shakespeare like lyric poems. David Mariner of Portland, Maine, for example, transcribed twenty-seven quotations from Shakespeare into a collection he called 'Gems of Poetry.'[44] (For this he relied almost entirely on Dodd's *Beauties*, transcribing Dodd's titles along with his quotations.) Mariner's preference for the lyrical side of Shakespeare's plays can be seen in a sequence about a fifth of the way into the book. Seven quotations entitled 'Midnight,' 'The Same,' 'Moonlight,' and 'The Same' appear on two facing pages. The quotation titled 'Moonlight' is Lorenzo's speech from *The Merchant of Venice*, beginning 'How sweet the moonlight sleeps upon this bank' (V.1.54–65). The other quotations are from poems by John Blair Linn, Edward Young, James Thomson, Robert Southey, John Milton, and Elizabeth Carter. By embedding the *Merchant of Venice* quotation in a sequence of poems on night and moonlight, Mariner treats Lorenzo's speech as a poetic set piece.

Ironically, readers who transformed Shakespeare into a lyric poet quoted almost entirely from Shakespeare's plays, not his poems. Out of twenty commonplace books that quote Shakespeare, I have found only one quotation from the *Sonnets*, and none from the narrative poems. I suspect this reflects the anthologists' habit of providing extracts from the plays but not the poems, and the low critical opinion of the *Sonnets* during the eighteenth and early nineteenth centuries.[45] Both Dodd and Knox took their Shakespeare extracts exclusively from the plays.

Conclusion

I do not mean to suggest that nineteenth-century readers of Shakespeare never bothered to read an entire play, or that they never went to see one performed; far from it. But I do want to propose that textual fragmentation and decontextualization shaped a significant part of reader responses to Shakespeare from very early on, and particularly after Shakespeare anthologies began appearing in print in the eighteenth century. Editors, publishers, and printers facilitated this tendency in a number of ways: by signaling extractable passages (as in the case of the first quarto of *Hamlet*), by collecting Shakespeare's 'beauties' into anthologies and schoolbooks, and by pointing out these 'beauties' even in collected editions of the plays. The practice of commonplacing reveals how readers picked up on these cues and made use of the quotations that editors and publishers pointed out.

This fragmented Shakespeare, source of many quotable lines half-remembered from encounters out of context, may be a bigger part of 'Shakespeare' than we realize. Indeed, as Seth Lerer suggests, 'the history of reading may be a history not of books themselves but of excerpts'[46]—for no author, perhaps, more so than Shakespeare. Anyone who thinks this is a phenomenon of prior centuries should consider the persistence of quotation websites in our own time. Yesterday's commonplacer, transcribing 'How sweet the moonlight sleeps upon this bank!' into a personal collection, has a counterpart in today's user of a site like brainyquote.com, which includes over two hundred quotations from Shakespeare.

The readers I have discussed may at first seem like nothing more than bad students: at best failing to engage intellectually with the text, and at worst, dismembering more than they remember. Why, then, should we pay attention to them? I would argue that if we want to understand the construction of Shakespeare as a canonical author, we need to consider a broad range of responses to his works. If one is trained as a literary critic, it can be very easy to disregard the experiences of readers who are not, as Jonathan Rose puts it, 'members of the academic club.'[47] And yet these readers are part of the print history of Shakespeare's plays. Their habits and expectations helped to drive the market for the quotation collections that in turn shaped their responses to the texts. Attending to print (and manuscript) practices like the ones I have been describing allows us to see historical readers in action, and to understand the conditions that made their readings possible. One of the many ways in which the study of print culture can enrich our perspectives on literature is by defamiliarizing the familiar activity of reading, and by showing us historical aspects of the reading experience that our critical blinders may lead us to overlook.

Notes

1 'Print' here may mean stamping a seal in wax rather than impressing a page with characters; however, for an argument that the repeated printing metaphors in *The Winter's Tale* refer specifically to the printing press, see Aaron Kitch, 'Bastards and Broadsides in "The Winter's Tale"', *Renaissance Drama*, 30 (1999), 43–71.
2 For an outline of twentieth-century textual studies of Shakespeare's plays, see Gabriel Egan, *The Struggle for Shakespeare's Text: Twentieth-Century Editorial Theory and Practice* (Cambridge; New York: Cambridge University Press, 2010); for a history of editions of Shakespeare, see Andrew Murphy, *Shakespeare in Print: A History and Chronology of Shakespeare Publishing* (Cambridge: Cambridge University Press, 2003).
3 Lucien Febvre and Henri-Jean Martin, *The Coming of the Book: The Impact of Printing 1450–1800*, trans. by David Gerard (London: Verso, 1976). Brief and useful overviews of book history as a field include Robert Darnton, 'What Is the History of Books?', in *The Kiss of Lamourette: Reflections in Cultural History* (New York: Norton, 1990), pp. 107–35; Robert Darnton, '"What Is the History of Books?" Revisited', *Modern Intellectual History*, 4 (2007), 495–508; David Finkelstein and Alistair McCleery, *An Introduction to Book History* (New York: Routledge, 2005); and Leslie Howsam, *Old Books and New Histories: An Orientation to Studies in Book and Print Culture* (Toronto: University of Toronto Press, 2006).
4 D.F. McKenzie, *Bibliography and the Sociology of Texts* (Cambridge; New York: Cambridge University Press, 1999), p. 15.
5 Scholars sometimes use the terms 'book history' and 'print culture' interchangeably, though these terms are not synonymous (Finkelstein and McCleery, pp. 15–16). The category of print includes but is not limited to the book, since it also encompasses periodicals, ephemera, and other non-book uses of print. Similarly, both manuscript and print fall within the category of the book. My own focus here will be on the world of print, but the fact that the readers I discuss later in this essay kept handwritten books of quotations suggests some of the richness of the interplay between manuscript, print, and the book format, even in relatively recent history.
6 Darnton (1990), p. 108.
7 Thomas R. Adams and Nicolas Barker, 'A New Model for the Study of the Book', in *A Potencie of Life: Books in Society*, ed. by Nicolas Barker (London: British Library, 1993), pp. 5–43 (p. 15).
8 Marcy L. North, 'The Sonnets and Book History', in *A Companion to Shakespeare's Sonnets*, ed. by Michael Carl Schoenfeldt (Malden, Mass.: Blackwell, 2007), pp. 204–21; Aaron T. Pratt, 'Stab-Stitching and the Status of Early English Playbooks as Literature', *The Library*, 16 (2015), 304–28; William St Clair, *The Reading Nation in the Romantic Period* (Cambridge; New York: Cambridge University Press, 2004), pp. 140–57; Jonathan Rose, 'Rereading the English Common Reader: A Preface to a History of Audiences', *Journal of the History of Ideas*, 53 (1992), 47–70; Andrew Murphy, *Shakespeare for the People: Working-Class Readers, 1800–1900* (Cambridge; New York: Cambridge University Press, 2008); Katherine West Scheil, *She Hath Been Reading: Women and Shakespeare Clubs in America* (Ithaca, N.Y.: Cornell University Press, 2012).
9 David Scott Kastan, *Shakespeare and the Book* (Cambridge; New York: Cambridge University Press, 2001), pp. 15–16.
10 Roger Chartier, 'Laborers and Voyagers: From the Text to the Reader', trans. by J.A. González, *Diacritics*, 22 (1992), 49–61 (p. 50).
11 St Clair, p. 157.
12 See Murphy (2003), pp. 169–72; Leah Price, *The Anthology and the Rise of the Novel from Richardson to George Eliot* (Cambridge; New York: Cambridge University Press, 2000), pp. 77–90. On the Bowdlers' *Family Shakespeare* in the context of other adaptation of Shakespeare for young female audiences during the early nineteenth century, see Susan J. Wolfson, 'Shakespeare and the Romantic Girl Reader', *Nineteenth-Century Contexts*, 21 (1999), 191–234.
13 For a longer survey of Shakespeare's presence in anthologies from the seventeenth century to the present, see Kate Rumbold, 'Shakespeare Anthologized', in *The Edinburgh Companion to Shakespeare and the Arts*, ed. by Mark Thornton Burnett, Adrian Streete, and Ramona Wray (Edinburgh: Edinburgh University Press, 2011), pp. 88–105.

14 Margreta De Grazia, 'Shakespeare in Quotation Marks', in *The Appropriation of Shakespeare: Post-Renaissance Reconstructions of the Works and the Myth*, ed. by Jean I. Marsden (New York: St. Martin's Press, 1991), pp. 57–71 (p. 61); Price, pp. 80–81.
15 For longer discussions of the vogue for 'beauties' in the eighteenth and nineteenth centuries, see Barbara Benedict, 'The "Beauties" of Literature, 1750–1820: Tasteful Prose and Fine Rhyme for Private Consumption', in *1650–1850: Ideas, Aesthetics, and Inquiries in the Early Modern Era*, 1 (1994), pp. 317–46; Daniel Cook, 'Authors Unformed: Reading "Beauties" in the Eighteenth Century', *Philological Quarterly*, 89 (2010), 283–309. On 'beauties' in North America, see Robert A. Gross, 'Reading for an Extensive Republic', in *An Extensive Republic: Print, Culture, and Society in the New Nation, 1790–1840*, ed. by Robert A. Gross and Mary Kelley (Chapel Hill: University of North Carolina Press, 2010), pp. 516–44 (p. 539).
16 Hannah More, *Florio, a Tale, for Fine Gentlemen and Fine Ladies: And The Bas Bleu, Or, Conversation: Two Poems* (London: T. Cadell, 1786), pp. 8–9.
17 William Dodd, *The Beauties of Shakespear: Regularly Selected from Each Play* (London: Printed for T. Waller, 1752), pp. xv–xvi, xx.
18 Benedict, p. 321.
19 William Shakespeare, *The Works of Shakespear: In Which the Beauties Observed by Pope, Warburton, and Dodd, Are Pointed out*, ed. by Hugh Blair, 8 vols. (Edinburgh: Printed by Sands, Murray, and Cochran, for W. Sands [and 6 others], 1753).
20 Robert W. Uphaus, 'Vicesimus Knox and the Canon of Eighteenth-Century Literature', *The Age of Johnson: A Scholarly Annual*, 4 (1991), 345–61 (p. 350); St Clair, p. 540.
21 Susan Allen Ford, 'Reading Elegant Extracts in *Emma*: Very Entertaining!', *Persuasions On-Line*, 28 (2007).
22 Ibid.; Rumbold, p. 95.
23 Jean Ferguson Carr, Stephen L. Carr, and Lucille M. Schultz, *Archives of Instruction: Nineteenth-Century Rhetorics, Readers, and Composition Books in the United States* (Carbondale: Southern Illinois University Press, 2005), pp. 100, 115–16. On schoolroom recitation culture in nineteenth-century Britain and America, see Catherine Robson, *Heart Beats: Everyday Life and the Memorized Poem* (Princeton, N.J.: Princeton University Press, 2012); Joan Shelley Rubin, *Songs of Ourselves: The Uses of Poetry in America* (Cambridge, Mass.: Belknap Press, 2007), pp. 107–64.
24 Jonathan Burton, 'Lay On, McGuffey: Excerpting Shakespeare in Nineteenth-Century Schoolbooks', in *Shakespearean Educations: Power, Citizenship, and Performance*, ed. by Coppelia Kahn, Heather S. Nathans, and Mimi Godfrey (Newark: University of Delaware Press, 2011), pp. 95–111.
25 Lucy Larcom, *A New England Girlhood, Outlined from Memory* (Boston: Houghton, Mifflin, 1889), pp. 132, 237.
26 For overviews of the practice of commonplacing that extend past the early modern period, see Earle Havens, *Commonplace Books: A History of Manuscripts and Printed Books from Antiquity to the Twentieth Century* (New Haven: Beinecke Rare Book and Manuscript Library, 2001); David Allan, *Commonplace Books and Reading in Georgian England* (New York: Cambridge University Press, 2010), pp. 35–45.
27 Lukas Erne, *Shakespeare and the Book Trade* (Cambridge: Cambridge University Press, 2013), pp. 228–32.
28 De Grazia, pp. 58–59.
29 Zachary Lesser and Peter Stallybrass, 'The First Literary Hamlet and the Commonplacing of Professional Plays', *Shakespeare Quarterly*, 59 (2008), 371–420 (pp. 376–78).
30 Allan, p. 196.
31 Burton, p. 98.
32 Annis Stockton, '"Annis Stockton, 1819" (cover Title), Bound Volume', 1819, Princeton University Library. Stockton was the granddaughter of New Jersey coterie poet Annis Boudinot Stockton. I have written about this family and their commonplace books at greater length elsewhere (Amanda Watson, 'Shared Reading at a Distance: The Commonplace Books of the Stockton Family, 1812–40', *Book History*, 18 [2015], 103–33).
33 Julia Lippitt, 'Commonplace Books, April 26, 1814', 1814, Brown University, John Hay Library.
34 William Charles White, *Orlando: Or Parental Persecution, a Tragedy* (Boston, 1797).
35 Lawrence W. Levine, *Highbrow/Lowbrow: The Emergence of Cultural Hierarchy in America* (Cambridge, Mass.: Harvard University Press, 1988), pp. 16–18.
36 For an example of the proverbialization of a Shakespeare quotation, see Laura Estill, *Dramatic Extracts in Seventeenth-Century English Manuscripts: Watching, Reading, Changing Plays* (Newark: University of Delaware Press, 2015), pp. 201–23. On Shakespeare aphorisms in print in the nineteenth century, see Rumbold, pp. 97–98.

37 Maria Brockway, 'Commonplace Book, *ca.* 1833–1835', Brown University, John Hay Library.
38 Edna Rhodes Gardiner, 'Commonplace Book, [189?]', Brown University, John Hay Library.
39 Lippitt; David D. Mariner, 'Gems of Poetry', 1837, Brown University, John Hay Library.
40 Sarah Hammond Palfrey, 'Commonplace Book, Boston, *ca.* 1841–1876', Brown University, John Hay Library.
41 Anna L. Sweet, 'Commonplace Book, Providence, R.I., *ca.* 1837–1843', Brown University, John Hay Library.
42 For a discussion of young women's friendship albums (a format that overlaps with that of the commonplace book) and the school context in which they were created, see Catherine E. Kelly, *In the New England Fashion: Reshaping Women's Lives in the Nineteenth Century* (Ithaca, N.Y.: Cornell University Press, 1999), pp. 79–81.
43 Price, p. 81.
44 Mariner.
45 George Sanderlin, 'The Repute of Shakespeare's Sonnets in the Early Nineteenth Century', *Modern Language Notes*, 54 (1939), 462–66.
46 Seth Lerer, 'Epilogue: Falling Asleep over the History of the Book', *PMLA*, 121 (2006), 229–34 (p. 233).
47 Rose, p. 49.

3

SHAKESPEARE, MEMORY AND POST-COLONIAL ADAPTATION

Andrew J. Power

A Midsummer Night's Dream is a play that begins by remembering another canonical author from an earlier age (Chaucer), it dramatizes the (past) centre of Western cultural history (Athens) and it dramatizes the fringe, or the local, in the moment of performing the canonical in adaptation (Ovid, 'Pyramus and Thisbe') for an audience at the centre. In its focus on adaptation and revision, on language and translation, on the tension between the regional and the central, it dramatizes a number of the issues that are at the core of the study of Shakespearean adaptation. The patronization of, and the qualitative judgments offered to, the mechanicals' performances raise issues for the attitude of the academy towards performance and adaptation at the 'local' level by non-metropolitan companies.[1] Many of the same things can be said of its sister play, the collaborative *The Two Noble Kinsmen*, but that play also highlights something that is only briefly alluded to in the earlier *Dream*, the fact that Theseus is the ruler not just of a kingdom but of an empire, an empire that has colonized and subsumed the Amazon nation (for one) into its own political mass.[2] So when Hippolyta responds to the critique of the mechanicals' play she does so from the centre but not as the centre, she occupies a space at the centre of the empire as (imminent) wife to the emperor, but also still as foreign. Very few people can be argued to be of the centre anymore and the empire that Shakespeare was once a symbol of has crumbled,[3] and is moreover in danger of dividing even further in the wake of the 'Brexit' referendum to leave the European Union (in which Scotland and Northern Ireland seem to wish to remain).

The Two Noble Kinsmen begins by remembering roughly the same opening situation as *A Midsummer Night's Dream*, but it does so with an added request that Theseus colonize yet another realm (Thebes). The political duties of The King's Men are apparent in Palamon and Arcite's discussion of the competing loyalties to nation (under a tyrant king, Creon) and to honour (in response to a noble conqueror, Theseus). In their resolution of the discussion, Palamon determines that they must fight for Thebes against their sense of virtuous service:

> Let's to the King, who, were he
> A quarter carrier of that honour which
> His enemy come in, the blood we venture
> Should be as for our health, which were not spent,

> Rather laid out for purchase. But, alas,
> Our hands advanced before our hearts, what will
> The fall o'th' stroke do damage?
>
> *(I.2.107–13)*[4]

They choose nobly to remain loyal to their nation while desiring to be conquered by an honourable enemy. This is the ultimate fantasy of the colonizer, that the conquered would yield (like the once 'dreaded Amazonian' Hippolyta – *The Two Noble Kinsmen*, I.1.78) willingly to the conquering force, as Theseus expresses it: 'I wooed thee with my sword, / And won thy love doing thee injuries' (*A Midsummer Night's Dream*, I.1.16–17).

Both plays also contain a dramatic performance of questionable success. The mechanicals of *A Midsummer Night's Dream* perform an adaptation of something that they have very little understanding of, even in terms of the dramatic tradition that they vie to become a part of. However, there is an even more unusual disconnect between the rustics and what they play in *The Two Noble Kinsmen*.[5] Their dance recreates something that is both recognizable and recognizably native, but at the same time something whose origins are most probably foreign and exotic, a Moorish dance.[6] How much of this is recognizable to the critical and seemingly informed audience that they encounter in Athens is not easy to determine. In explaining some of the ways that adaptation works, Julie Sanders draws a theoretical line back through Julia Kristeva's intertextuality, noting that the networks that might form part of the systems of meaning that any new text might operate in or come from are not all literary.[7] How much must be recognizable for an audience to enjoy, or appreciate the work that they are presented is thus difficult to discern. In attempting to unravel some of the issues of power, control, ownership of text, nation, colonization, language and alienation that adhere to studies of Shakespeare in adaptation and in translation, this discussion will explore a number of different layers of Shakespeare's colonial legacy. From the preceding beginning in the explicit colonialism in *A Midsummer Night's Dream* and *The Two Noble Kinsmen* it moves to explore Shakespeare in a non-English context and a particular (and particularly problematic in terms of its treatment of intellectual disability) Spanish production of *A Midsummer Night's Dream*. From there it moves to a consideration of an actual and self-consciously English-colonial context in an adaptation of *Macbeth* in production in Dublin, before discussing another Dublin adaptation, again of *A Midsummer Night's Dream*. In this *Dream* the sensitive issue of disability is again revisited in that this production was by a cast constituted almost entirely of actors with intellectual disabilities. The critical discussion of these productions and adaptations, that develop parallel issues of language and difference, of power and authority, leads finally to a broader discussion of transcultural adaptations.

At a production of *Sueño de una Noche de Verano* (a Spanish language production of *A Midsummer Night's Dream*) in the Matadero in Madrid (Javier L. Patiño and Darío Facal, Metatarso, 2016) I found myself in the unusual position of not understanding very much of the text of a Shakespeare play for the first time in a number of years. It was a useful reminder of the difficulty that students have with plays in a language that is not familiar. I listened particularly hard for the line, 'Bless thee, Bottom, bless thee. Thou art translated' (III.1.105), but it eluded me. In the end what stood out was the foreign nature of the fairies (exemplified by Emilio Gavira in the role of Puck) and the hilarious stupidity of the mechanicals (most extreme in the performance of Oscar de la Fuente as Flute). However, these were not entirely unproblematic performances given that Gavira's dwarfism was played upon as part of his exotic appeal (he played as if regularly uncomfortable with the overly affectionate dandling, stroking and cradling that he received from Theseus) and that de la Fuente's performance as Flute seemed at times to emulate, insensitively, a person with an intellectual disability.[8] Thus, in some ways, these performances seemed to recall the uncomfortable sexuality of the mad Daughter of *The Two Noble Kinsmen*. There were also sexual overtones to this adaptation more generally (Alejandro Sigüenza, who doubled as Oberon and Theseus, was particularly libidinous in both roles and for both sexes, and Katia Klein's Helena was similarly lustful) playing as much, perhaps, with Madrid's reputation as a sexually liberated city as with the eroticism of Shakespeare's play. Like the 'babion with long tail and eke long tool' of *The Two Noble Kinsmen* (III.5.134), Bottom and the Indian Boy are, between them, the appealing (or desired) exotic and the feared monstrous of the cross-cultural encounter that is the essence of Said's 'other'. Indeed, Bottom (of the Mechanicals) and the Bavian (of the 'Moorish' dance) represent the rampant animalistic sexuality that is characteristic of the romantic entanglements of the two plays in terms of their desirability, but also in their disturbing and frightening difference. Lois Potter found that a production of *The Two Noble Kinsmen* at the Royal Shakespeare Company (RSC) (dir. Barry Kyle, Royal Shakespeare Theatre, London, 1986) 'connected the Daughter's experience of the morris with her later obsession about Palamon's sexual potency, emphasizing the sexuality of the dancers (especially the suggestively costumed Bavian) and their cavortings on their way home at the beginning of IV.1'.[9] Thus, both plays offer, in performance, and in the performance of performance, an interesting light on what can be most appealing and what is often off-putting in foreign appropriations of the canonical.

This discussion uses *A Midsummer Night's Dream* and even more so its sister play *The Two Noble Kinsmen* as a starting point to try to illuminate some of the ongoing issues in Shakespearean postcolonial adaptation, paying particular attention to the role that memory plays in the processes of adaptation and of interpretation. It begins from the position that *The Two Noble Kinsmen* dramatizes (as does *A Midsummer Night's Dream*), what Julie Sanders refers to as, 'a particular interest in margins: country settings and local, even regionalist, concerns'.[10] This process is played out against the background of a larger empire (in the process of expansion), acknowledging that language is one of the key problems (and perhaps opportunities) of adaptation, and that foreignness and/or otherness involves both attraction and repulsion (often both at once).

Empire

''erc'les vein, a tyrant's vein'
(A Midsummer Night's Dream, I.2.33)

When Theseus encounters the foreign Queens, the way that he finds to relate to them, to sympathize with their plight, is to remember Hercules' reaction to seeing one of them at her wedding: 'Hercules our kinsman – / Then weaker than your eyes – laid by his club. / He tumbled down upon his Nemean hide / And swore his sinews thawed' (I.1.66–9). His first instinct when he encounters the foreign warriors, Palamon and Arcite, is to admire the animalistic in them: 'I saw them in the war, / Like to a pair of lions smeared with prey, / Make lanes in troops aghast' (I.4.17–19). However, as he has grown to admire them more and more he again thinks back upon something familiar to him and can only make sense of Palamon's nobility by comparison again with the great Hercules: 'Surely the gods / Would have him die a bachelor lest his race / Should show i'th' world too godlike. His behaviour / So charmed me that, methought, Alcides was / To him a sow of lead' (V.5.116–20). This is one of the most prominent features of cross-cultural encounters, and as such of adaptation, that in order to make the strange comprehensible, the stranger must imagine the encountered as something familiar. Theseus must scan his memory for something that he imagines to be comparable to these newly encountered foreigners.[11] Conversely, Palamon and Arcite are in the curious predicament that they wish to reject or to forget their own culture, or at least their kinsman, the tyrant Creon and their country's recent history. Until word of Theseus' invasion had reached them, they had determined to 'leave his court that [they might] nothing share / Of his loud infamy' (I.2.75–6) and to escape beyond 'the echoes of his shames' (I.2.80).[12] The figures of Hercules (for Theseus) and of Creon (for Palamon and Arcite) loom large in the memories of both conqueror and conquered.

There are very few empires left in the world and very few colonies. On the morning that the British exit from the European Union (Brexit) was announced, Irish radio (discussing the potentially catastrophic effects that might ensue) declared that, prior to the opening of the Irish stock exchange, markets in Japan and Hong Kong had already significantly fallen.[13] On the other hand, that Scottish and Northern Irish politicians have been gaining popular feedback to assertions that it is better for these UK entities to remain in Europe than in the Kingdom is a sign of just how post- some former colonies of England now are. Memories are like monuments, and often stand awkwardly in the mind's eye-line when one would most like to forget. Even as one grand political alliance (if not empire) fell, Irish eyes gazed across from one former colony to two others (Japan and Hong Kong) and across at two current members (Scotland and Northern Ireland) as if to try and gauge, or to imagine, what might now ensue. The 2016 celebrations of Shakespeare's 400th Deathday stood in awkward relief with the 100th Anniversary of the birth, or at least conception, of the Irish Freestate. That 100 years later, as the UK leaves a political alliance to which Ireland remains integral, we shudder to be sundered from our erstwhile brutal conqueror says something of the political Stockholm Syndrome that is the postcolonial state. Two Irish productions of Shakespeare discussed below may be of particular interest here: one a professional, but decidedly fringe, production of *Macbeth* and the other an amateur production of an adaptation of *A Midsummer Night's Dream* with a particularly interesting twist.

Shakespeare's later, collaborative play, *The Two Noble Kinsmen* contains, alongside Palamon and Arcite's will to disengage themselves from a culture that has become distasteful to them, an idealized memory of an Amazon nation. Emilia recalls the love of her childhood friend Flavina and insists, upon Hippolyta's prompting, that she 'shall never, like the maid Flavina, / Love any that's called man' (I.3.84–5). The recollection is most often engaged as raising issues of gender and sexuality, and there is certainly something of the savour of the lesbian romance to the breathlessness of Emilia's retelling of this tale of perhaps not quite innocent love.[14] However, there is also something of the political lament for a culture (an all-female culture) now lost to the (male) conqueror. The resistance that she displays to the idea of a husband is, in this context, as much a political resistance as it is one of sexual preference, for to force her to choose a husband is to force her to relinquish the traditions of her own people. There is something of this resistance, and also of the anguished childhood memory, in the first Irish Shakespearean adaptation that I will discuss.

Pan Pan theatre company's *MAC-BETH 7* (dir. Gavin Quinn, Project Arts Theatre, Dublin, 2004) declared itself 'an unashamedly postcolonial interpretation of Shakespeare's *Mac Beth* [sic.]'. Play notes suggested a focus on language that jars with the realities of studying Shakespeare in our time, let alone in a post-colonial context. Quoting Oscar Wilde, it declared 'I am Irish by race but the English have condemned me to speak the language of Shakespeare'.[15] Quinn's innovation was to *localize* the play into an almost Beckettian Irish schoolroom where it seemed at times the play was recited (if not fully dramatized) on a daily basis. Thick Dublin accents (as opposed to those traditionally associated with Shakespearean performance in Ireland) jarred against the Shakespearean language in such a way that meaning became an extremely problematic experience. Macbeth's schoolroom bully was played off against Lady Macbeth's (aborted?)

teen pregnancy. Here, Shakespeare was a jarring and inappropriate symbol of a class, and one of a number of painful memories being played out on the stage. The additional layer of meaning so bluntly alluded to in the programme notes was that Shakespeare (language and all), as the ultimate symbol of Britishness, was one of the many traumatic events in the formative years of the Irish nation. That Shakespeare's play is effectively about civil war and the shadow of a usurping tyrant makes it all the more resonant when wrested to that purpose. In this type of adaptation Shakespeare is re-appropriated as the thing with which to strike back against its own original use. Here, the dominance of Shakespeare in an Irish school curriculum in the seventies and early eighties (during which Quinn would have been at school) is played off against the fact that the Irish language was banned from schools for centuries (the eighteenth and nineteenth primarily) and only survived in hedgeschools. In this conflation, Shakespeare becomes the thing that displaces the true language of the nation. This is the danger that the spread of Shakespeare has been seen to pose in the colonial world, and it continues to be at issue in the spread of a westernized Global culture. Of course, in opposition to Wilde's (and Quinn's) assertion, we learn that not even 'the English' speak 'the language of Shakespeare' anymore. An adaptation such as this sidesteps one of the most contentious issues with Shakespearean adaptation (that is fidelity to the text), because it does remain faithful to the original in having the actors speak it to a great extent as it is (questions of edition aside). However, the context of the performance, so at odds with the words spoken, highlights the problems inherent in that text, and moreover highlights the problems that that text poses for a generation of postcolonial subjects educated in a language that is not their own – a cultural history that is that of their recent forefathers' oppressors and murderers.

Following the Revolutions of 1989 as they have been popularly grouped (but that included revolutions in Poland, Hungary, and Bulgaria, and the fall of the Berlin Wall in 1989, the dismantling of the USSR in 1991, and the division of Czechoslovakia into two separate states in 1993), Eastern Europe (much of which is now more properly known as central Europe) became a site of intense interest for scholarship of Shakespearean appropriations. The Maastricht Treaty of 1993 turned the former EEC (European Economic Community) into the EU (European Union), so shaken in recent years by economic turmoil that has led, perhaps, to this moment of Brexit. In its wake, studies of European Shakespeares dominated Global Shakespeare scholarship.[16] Now, after the Arab Spring, it must be expected that some of the most intense adaptation scholarship will come from countries affected (or yet to be affected) by that seeming wave of revolution that has most recently swept our globe.

It is, perhaps, in this light that Stephen Greenblatt chose a visit to Tehran as the subject of his afterword to the Shakespeare Association of America Collection, *Shakespeare in Our Time*.[17] As has been characteristic of his work for much of his career, he began with an anecdote, a recollection that is not as clearly conscious of its own political history as one might expect from such a great scholar. Upon receipt of an invitation to act as keynote at a congress in Tehran, he found himself remembering an intended, but unrealized trip to Iran during his university days at Cambridge. He recalled the Persian wonders discovered in the British Museum, and he explains that he determined to accept the invitation despite difficulties over a visa and uncertainty over travel and, of course, fear for his own security: 'For Shakespeare has served for more than four centuries now as a crucial link across the boundaries that divide cultures, ideologies, religions, nations, and all the other ways in which humans define and demarcate their identities'.[18] It is difficult as an Irishman to stand, or even to remember standing, in the British Museum (awed all the same) and not ponder the violence that must have allowed for the acquisition of the artefacts on display. There is a cultural memory that many Irish share that makes it impossible to view British cultural institutions without recalling the violence done to our ancestors (on either side of the religious, political, cultural divide). In fact, the

Union Jack is a visual stimulus to fear among a certain strand of the Irish populace in much the same way that a balaclava or a burqa might subconsciously, subrationally inspire fear in others. Moreover, in spite of Greenblatt's magnanimity and will to partake in the great conversations that are ongoing in Global Shakespeare studies, to refer to the British Museum without irony in such a piece, to portray a visit to the University of Tehran as if it were a visit to the ultimate fringe, is telling of his own cultural place (even quite simply as someone who would be invited to address the Iranian Shakespeare Congress or to write the afterword to a book entitled *Shakespeare in Our Time*). For, of course, to assert that Shakespeare unites us across 'boundaries that divide cultures, ideologies, religions, nations, and all the other ways in which humans define and demarcate their identities' is Bardolatry at its most naive. Shakespeare *is* a dividing line. To pretend that he is anything else is to ignore culture, ideology, religion, nation, and all the other things that are important to human beings. In fact, sometimes that is the very utility of Shakespeare. If we cannot recognize that then we might as well say that Ronald MacDonald brings us together, deliver MacDonald's to Tehran, and leave it at that. In all honesty, Shakespeare very rarely serves the fringes, is never truly global (except perhaps in air miles and carbon footprint) because access to Shakespeare, even among the privileged, is limited by language. But there too there is opportunity for useful innovations in adaptation.

Nonetheless, Greenblatt's impulse is a helpful one and the same volume contains a really interesting section on 'Globalisation' (pp. 159–75) that concludes with a useful exploration of Shakespearean scholarship in India by Jyotsna G. Singh[19] that may help us get beyond the musical popularity of Bollywood appropriations.[20] Moreover, there is some equally important work focusing on political Shakespeares in the Arab world. Three years before the Arab Spring, *Critical Survey* devoted a volume to 'Arab Shakespeare' (19:3, 2007). Of course, Britain is not the only empire ever to have conquered significant portions of the globe and, perhaps less obviously, the experience of the Shakespearean colonial legacy is not exclusive to England. For instance, Shakespeare also becomes part of the French colonial legacy. As Khalid Amine explains, following Napoleon's invasion of Egypt (1798–1801), Shakespeare in French translation along with Molière became the staple of an incipient Egyptian theatre. Here, Shakespeare was not Shakespeare, but Shakespeare filtered through French translation into Arabic adaptation. However, it was also something else. In *Romeo and Juliet* (trans. Najib al-Haddad) subtitled *Martyrs of Love* (Shuhada' al-Gharam) audiences were reminded of *Quays and Leila*, a 'well-known love story in the Arab literature of the Umayyad period (pp. 661–750)'.[21] Shakespeare in this instance is a complicated cultural commodity (an imported (English) artefact of the western world), but not so much the thing itself as its echo through another western power (French), and in that a reminder of the conquered state of the producer.

Bottom's translation anxiety, Mowbray's fear of finding himself imprisoned within his own skull, is a fear of forgetting or of finding that there is nothing to remember. As if Hamlet's table full of 'trivial fond records' were indeed 'wipe[d] away' (1.5.99) rendering the search for meaning fruitless, pointless. His memory wiped clean, what meaning can emerge? Or, what can we do in the absence of the original cultural referents? Hamlet imagines the scenario in order to prioritize action, to make the act of vengeance live all alone in his mind. Early cinematic adaptations took this as their cue card, and the best cinematic adaptations still are marked by the ability to use the medium to make a picture tell a thousand words. The success of adaptations like *Throne of Blood* (1957) and *Ran* (1985) are a mark of the capacity for this sort of approach to make the most of a loss of language. However, of course, Akira Kurosawa is not just replacing words with action, or stripping bare Shakespeare to its essential narrative. He is also engaging his audiences in an act of social memory, replacing pre-Christian Scotland and Britain with the Samurai wars of medieval Japan and replacing early modern theatrical convention with recognizable ones from

Japanese Noh theatre. For a Japanese audience, this makes the foreign history of *Macbeth* and of *King Lear* recognizable, as the Mechanicals' rendition of Ovid relocates Pyramus and Thisbe to contemporary Athens (which, we may imagine, is strangely reminiscent of an early modern English town). For a western audience, this gives us a window into a foreign culture that we now have something from our own memories with which to compare and associate.

The RSC performance of *The Two Noble Kinsmen* of 1986 attempted to focus on the romance of the play. This was perhaps something beyond British cultural memory for most audience members, especially 'the sense of a warrior society': the director, Barry Kyle, opted not for the chivalric swords and steel that has now become so popular in the wake of *Game of Thrones*, but for imagery that was 'largely Japanese'.[22] Kyle here was responding (at the centre) to a particularly strong strand of Shakespeare adaptation and to studies of Shakespearean adaptation.

Language

> Have I said, 'thus let be', and 'there let be',
> And 'then let be', and no man understand me?
> (The Two Noble Kinsmen, III.5.9–10)

Dublin is hardly the fringe and Quinn's *Mac Beth 7* showed a critical awareness that betrayed a certain privilege that is not shared in other regions that are performing and adapting Shakespeare. In fact, it is something of an absurdity to suggest that, whatever the experiences of previous generations of Irishmen, 1980s Dubliners (with access to a relatively sophisticated critical read on Shakespeare and living through a 'Celtic Tiger' economic boom) were oppressed by very much of anything more than the odd, overzealous English teacher. Quinn's is sophisticated theatre. In fact, he is a brilliant adaptor and director, but it is not the theatre of the oppressed by any stretch of the imagination. A contemporaneous amateur production of an adaptation of *A Midsummer Night's Dream* offers a view from a far less privileged perspective and is enlightening for it. *By Moonlight* (dir. Declan Drohan) featured a cast (almost) entirely made up of actors with Down's Syndrome and of actors with other intellectual disabilities, working under the company name Quick Bright Things.[23] Their ingenious director, Drohan integrated with the play as part of the chaos of the forest outside of Athens, doubling up as one of the fairy entourage and as functional prompter, aiding his company with the difficult task of remembering their lines. One of the most difficult issues that attaches to adaptation is language and this production made clear that this is not just a matter of translation. The greatest energy of this performance lay in performance of the anguish caused by the language that Athenians use to each other in the forest.

In the play Bottom finds himself 'translated'.[24] Like his other malapropisms that reveal a linguistic inaccuracy to be one of his foibles, he finds himself transformed. However, his mistake highlights another of his difficulties. Though a native speaker, Bottom lacks the ability to use language accurately. Curiously, this does not limit his capacity to earn the admiration of his peers and even to profit by his performances to a sophisticated and critical audience. This is one of the essential difficulties in being the other in another place and language. The issue arises with Mowbray who fears being lost without it:

> The language I have learnt these forty years,
> My native English, now I must forgo,
> And now my tongue's use is to me no more
> Than an unstrengèd viol or a harp,

> Or like a cunning instrument cased up,
> Or, being open, put into his hands
> That knows no touch to tune the harmony.
> (Richard II, I.3.153–9)

Caliban utters this frustration from the other side, having learned a language not fully enough to express himself eloquently but just enough to curse, to vent anger at someone whose language puts him at an intellectual disadvantage: 'You taught me language, and my profit on 't / Is I know how to curse. The red plague rid you / For learning me your language!' (*The Tempest*, I.2.366–8). *The Tempest* is another play that Quick Bright Things and Declan Drohan produced with some success as *Tempest!* (2007). In this adaptation the play was transported to a mental space: 'A young woman [Miranda] struggles to retrieve her memory. In dreams, flashes and fragments she offers us glimpses of a nightmare world where ritual and symbol seem to hold actual power.'[25] This is where these adaptations are at their most brave and most effective/affective. These moments of lingual tension, of translation anxiety we might say, play off uncomfortably against the intellectual disabilities of the actors. Dirk Delabastita and Ton Hoenselaars deal with a number of passages that might fall into this category, 'examples [that] testify to the way in which early modern literature experienced multilingualism as a source of anxiety over disruption in inter-human communication'. However, in the same breath, they recognize the colonial impulse that followed hard upon this anxiety, 'the way in which, with some ease, this same anxiety could be (and in the course of the centuries actually was) successfully transformed into linguistic self-assertion, both at home and in the expanding world'.[26] At the Quick Bright Things production of *By Moonlight* there was no such colonial tension, rather the stated purpose of their work is to help with 'skill building, discipline and teamwork'. Though 'considered ancilliary' they admit to welcoming 'therapeutic or broader educational/learning outcomes'.[27] This is primarily an experimental theatre troupe, but one that uses the context of care as part of its experiment.

The difficulty that these actors must face in understanding the difficult language of Shakespeare's text (let alone remembering their lines) then is partially bridged over in these cases by the capacity to identify so much the better with the problems of language itself and the translation anxiety that these plays dramatize. There is also potential in an overly-keen dramatic irony here, where the audience may come to understand quite differently from the actors the nature of their disabilities. This can be a virtue of the performance, the discomfort of this recognition becoming one of the elements that highlights their plight for us, or it can be that which turns a production into one more ill-considered act of patronization against an already under-represented group within our communities.

Hamlet at home and abroad

> 'Remember me'
> (Hamlet, I.5.91)

In April 2014, Shakespeare's Globe commenced a two-year tour that would bring a production of *Hamlet* (dir. Dominic Dromgoole) to 'every country in the world'.[28] The performance (which I saw in the Canal Theatre in Madrid) played upon the idea that this was a travelling troupe. Their choice of *Hamlet* was a good one for a number of reasons. The Spanish woman who sat beside me mouthing whole speeches attested to how well known the text is internationally (or at least in Spain). Their set was thrown together out of a large travelling chest and shifted around by the actors (who doubled up roles as much as was possible) as the play developed. There were also diverse groups of ethnicities being staged, rendering the production 'global' in its investigations of questions of raison d'être, belonging and essence. Moreover, this is of course a play in which a travelling troupe performs for the court. The performance worked particularly well when in the play scene, which was the major innovation of this production: this scene hinged on the economical doubling of Claudius and Gertrude with the Player King and Queen. We see them seated for the play before Hamlet draws a curtain all the way across the stage and when he draws the curtain again the scene is changed to the dumb show of The Mousetrap. It ends and he draws the curtain again before revealing a puzzled, if not yet perturbed court. Turn and turn again (in theatrics not too far removed from the traditional magician's trick of sawing a woman in half) and we are shown The Murder of Gonzago, and then the angry reaction of the court and King. This is a travelling troupe which has (as troupes must in such situations) made a virtue of necessity. The effect was to shift our perspective as audience repeatedly. This is the essence of good adaptation and the great virtue of well-thought through local appropriation: at such moments, adaptation/appropriation can help to change your perspective, make you see the strange as familiar, and see anew what is long familiar. These, of course, are the players of the city, not the fringe. In the last number of years (and with the collaboration of King's College English Department) they have developed a strong reputation for authenticity as much as for innovation. The travelling Globe to Globe *Hamlet* grew out of their ambitious invitation of thirty-five theatre companies from around the world to perform thirty-seven plays in thirty-seven languages during the World Shakespeare Festival of 2012.

However, bringing the 'local' to the [Globe's] centre does not always work. A rather thoughtless example of this was the RSC *Hamlet* (dir. Simon Godwin, 2016) that used a mainly black cast in a misguided attempt to enliven Denmark with perceivedly tribal politics – to make the elective monarchy of Hamlet's state easier for a modern audience to appreciate by recreating it as a west-African military junta. The idea purportedly developed after Ghanaian-descended Paapa Essiedu was cast in the lead role. What failed here (although perhaps not for everyone) was that this was not a local reading of the most canonical western text, rather it was a cut-and-paste mapping of imported exoticism to appeal to the all-White audience of wealthy and privileged Stratford-upon-Avon. There was an attempt at self-parody in the casting of Rosencrantz and Guildenstern as white British tourists, exploring a postcolonial territory, but the joke was itself so half-aware as to be even more problematic. A nearly all white, all privileged audience in Stratford-upon-Avon (not the cheapest place in the world to visit) joined Rosencrantz and Guildenstern as tourists in a vaguely defined African world that had all the subtlety of a James Bond movie.[29] A third slice of *Hamlet* that I saw in between these two *Hamlet*s was *Hijos de Shakespeare* (dir. Juan Carlos Corazza).[30] Had it limited itself to daughters, this production (an anthology, in performance, of speeches and scenes that deal with parenthood/childhood from *Romeo and Juliet*, *The Merchant of Venice*, *Hamlet*, and *King Lear*) might have cohered beautifully. However, the temptation of the most canonical of speeches of Hamlet proved too much for Corazza and unbalanced what was otherwise an extremely innovative piece of adaptation. The explicit assertion was that we are all 'hijos' de Shakespeare (children of Shakespeare).

The players in *Hamlet*, though forced to travel, are 'the tragedians of the city' (*Hamlet*, II.2.316), they have court approval as 'the best actors in the world' (II.2.379), commonly play canonical material (in 'Aeneas' tale to Dido' (II.2.426–7)) and are comfortable in adapting their repertory to political agenda (or at least in accepting Hamlet's inserted 'speech' (II.2.518)). That is, unlike the mechanicals of *A Midsummer Night's Dream* or the rustics of *The Two Noble Kinsmen*, they are the sanctioned and as such central players of the realm.

Conclusion

> ... something to paint your pole withal.
> (The Two Noble Kinsmen, III.5.153)

In the end, whether Theseus travels to the woods outside Athens or the mechanicals come to him, it is he and his cohort who will judge. If Stephen Greenblatt travels to the Iranian Shakespeare Congress, or Dublin plays back from a fringe against a symbol of the centre, whether the tyrant sees himself in the murderous king with a poisonous vial or in the 'vile wall' that divides us, if Footsbarn brings its *Indian Tempest* to Shakespeare's Globe theatre, it is the centre that inevitably acts as judge.[31] Dissenting fringe voices who, like Hippolyta, have made (or married) their way to the centre can offer alternative voices, new perspectives, calls for different criteria of assessment, but in the end it is the centre that will judge. That centre effectively is our publishing industry and our classrooms (interrelated as they are).

Changes in the critical milieux mean that production history (including from the colonial/postcolonial fringes) now matters a great deal to us as scholars of Shakespearean drama almost, it sometimes seems, as much as critical histories do. So, for instance, the Arden Third Series now includes a significant section on performance history and New Cambridge Shakespeare's have an 'on stage' section. This comes, in part as a long effect of the 'death of the author' to the critical world. Now every reading matters and every production and adaptation is a reading worthy of scholarly examination. Two imminent publishing projects attest to the expansion of the area at the critical centre. The whole second half of *The Oxford Handbook of Shakespearean Tragedy*, is dedicated to adaptation with a 'Part' each on 'Stage and Screen', 'European Responses', and 'The Wider World'.[32] On the other side of the British publishing centre, Cambridge University Press has published a similarly massive two-volume set entitled *The Cambridge Guide to the Worlds of Shakespeare*, eds. Bruce R. Smith Katherine Rowe. The second volume, entitled *The World's Shakespeare, 1660–Present* contains a number of books that promise to be of interest to scholars of Shakespeare adaptation, not least those edited by Ton Hoenselaars ('International Encounters') and by Dirk Delabastita ('Translations'). The section editors for each of these are also jointly responsible for an edited collection, Ton Hoenselaars and Dirk Delabastita, eds. *Multilingualism in the Drama of Shakespeare and his Contemporaries* (Amsterdam: John Benjamins, 2015). The Routledge series, Reproducing Shakespeare: New Studies in Adaptation and Appropriation (now Palgrave-Macmillan) is another testament to how important this sector of Shakespeare studies has become in the traditional publishing world. It refers to the 'two decades of growing interest in the "afterlife" of Shakespeare'.[33] The series currently runs to eight volumes. Another feature of this critical trend in the last number of years is the inclusion in the second part of many critical works of an 'Afterlives' section. Sometimes this makes excellent sense and adds a coherent part to a whole exploration of a topic (as in Katie Knowles' *Shakespeare's Boys: A Cultural History*), but at other times it seems like a commissioning editor's instruction based in market trends.

There are also significant digital projects, the most significant of which for us is that run by Peter S. Donaldson (Director and Editor-in-Chief) and Alexa Huang (Co-Founder and Co-Director): the MIT Global Shakespeares Video and Performance Archive.[34] It currently houses collections from six regions of the globe (East and Southeast Asia, India, Brazil, Europe and the Arab World) and is a growing resource for a digital age, not quite such that one might say, 'they have all the world in their chamber' (*The Two Noble Kinsmen*, 2.1.26), but certainly it is developing into a really useful resource. *The Literary Encyclopedia* is also developing an extremely useful set of reviews of Shakespearean adaptation (mostly film at this point).[35] Smaller, regional, blogs and websites also prove to be invaluable local resources, like 'Shakespeare in Ireland' run by Derek Dunne, Emily O'Brien, and Edel Semple.[36] At one level we might, with Rory Loughnane in this volume (Ch., pp. 000–000), think of these growing resources as memory banks retaining particular performances and readings / interpretations of performances from a truly global Shakespeare. The more broad, and global, this memory bank becomes the more truly transcultural Shakespeare will actually become.

Notes

1 Working outward from Theseus' use of the word (5.1.17), Sonia Massai tangles helpfully with the term 'local' in the introduction to her edited collection *World-Wide Shakespeares: Local Appropriations in Film and Performance* (London and New York: Routledge, 2005), pp. 1–6.
2 This is also a dramatization of something past and, as is common to the romance tradition, it is in part a lament for a past empire.
3 Willy Maley, in observing how Shakespeare has been wrested to a number of political agenda, notes 'Shakespeare was certainly taught as a Tory for a long time, as a great symbol of Empire and Englishness'. See 'Recent Issues in Shakespeare Studies: From Margins to Centre', in Andrew Hiscock and Stephen Longstaffe (eds.), *The Shakespeare Handbook* (London: Continuum, 2009), pp. 190–205 (p. 191). Maley refers in this essay to the idea of a Black Hamlet. I shall return to this a little later in this chapter.
4 Quotations from Shakespeare's plays are from *The Norton Shakespeare*, eds. Stephen Greenblatt, Walter Cohen, Jean E. Howard and Katharine Eisaman Maus (London and New York: W.W. Norton & Co., 1997).
5 Such that it was for some time considered an irrelevant addition to the play.
6 Perhaps from the Spanish morisco tradition. For an exploration of the 'moorish' origins and resonances of the morris in this play see Sujata Iyengar, 'Moorish Dancing in *The Two Noble Kinsmen*', *Medieval and Renaissance*, 20.1 (2007) 85–107:

> Let me say at the outset that my claims about the collision of the domestic and the foreign owe more to the late Edward Said's definition of 'Orientalism' than to more recent arguments of contemporary postcolonial criticism. That is to say, I am more interested here in the morris dance and the Moorishness that informs it as indices to anxieties within early modern England, rather than in uncovering the material conditions of Moorishness and Moorish dancers in England.
>
> *(pp. 85–6)*

7 Julie Sanders, *Adaptation and Appropriation*. The New Critical Idiom (London: Routledge, 2006), p. 3. She deals particularly with Shakespearean appropriations in Chapter 3, "Here's a Strange Alteration": Shakespearean Appropriations', pp. 45–62.
8 I say more about theatre by actors with disabilities below.
9 Lois Potter, Introduction, *The Two Noble Kinsmen*, The Arden Shakespeare (London & New York: Bloomsbury, 2014), p. 87.
10 Julie Sanders, 'Mixed Messages: The Aesthetics of *The Two Noble Kinsmen*', Alan Dutton and Jean E. Howard (eds.), *A Companion to Shakespeare's Works, Vol. 4: Poems, Problem Comedies, Late Plays* (Oxford: Blackwell, 2003), pp. 445–61 (p. 446). Sanders here helpfully paraphrases an observation about *The Two Noble Kinsmen* that is made first by Gordon McMullan and Jonathan Hope (eds.) in their introduction to *The Politics of Tragicomedy: Shakespeare and After* (London: Routledge, 1992), p. 9. She continues to observe that beyond the opening and closing Chaucerian sections, 'The forest-based events of act 3 echo the setting of the romantic comedies such as *The Two Gentlemen of Verona* and *A Midsummer Night's Dream*' (Sanders, p. 448).
11 In some sense the Thebans are not as foreign as the play's rhetoric sometimes makes them seem, for they are (unlike Hyppolita and Emilia) also Hellenic.
12 Curiously, it is Creon's refusal of *remembrance* rites to the defeated party of a civil war at Thebes that is the main tyranny that Palamon and Arcite would rather forget. Those rites (including cremation) are clearly not intended to be Christian (I.1.43–50) though the Queens do wish to 'chapel' (I.1.50) their husbands' remains.

13 'Brexit Special', *Morning Ireland*, Radio Telefís Éireann, RTE1, June 24, 2016, 7am.
14 As Emilia concludes her 'rehearsal' of the 'true love 'tween maid and maid' that she shared with Flavina, Hippolyta observes, 'You're out of breath!' (I.3.78, 81–2).
15 Gavin Quinn, 'Programme notes', *Mac-Beth 7*, Project Arts Theatre, Dublin, 2004. http://dev.project artscentre.ie/archive/archive-p-detail/1005-macbeth-7 [accessed 7th October 2016].
16 On the history of Shakespeare in performance in Europe, Dirk Delabastita and Lieven D'Hulst (eds.), *European Shakespeares: Translating Shakespeare in the Romantic Age* (Amsterdam/Philadelphia: John Benjamins, 1993), and on modern appropriations of Shakespeare Michael Hattaway, Boika Sokolova, and Derek Roper (eds.), *Shakespeare in the New Europe* (Sheffield: Sheffield Academic Press, 1994).
17 Stephen Greenblatt, 'Afterword: Shakespeare in Tehran', in Dympna Callaghan and Suzanne Gossett (eds.), *Shakespeare in Our Time: A Shakespeare Association of America Collection*, The Arden Shakespeare (London & New York: Bloomsbury, 2016), pp. 343–52.
18 Greenblatt, p. 346.
19 Jyotsna G. Singh, 'The Bard in Calcutta, India, 1835–2014', *Shakespeare in Our Time: A Shakespeare Association of America Collection*, Dympna Callaghan and Suzanne Gossett (eds.), The Arden Shakespeare (London & New York: Bloomsbury, 2016), pp. 171–75.
20 Not to diminish their worth, but the popularity of the subgenre is in danger of eclipsing India's other engagements with Shakespeare. For a useful exploration of Shakespeare in Bollywood, see Craig Dionne and Parmita Kapadia (eds.), *Bollywood Shakespeares*, Reproducing Shakespeare: New Studies in Adaptation and Appropriation (London: Routledge, 2014).
21 Khalid Amine, 'Shakespeare's Tragedies in North Africa and the Arab World', in *The Oxford Handbook of Shakespearean Tragedy*, eds. Michael Neill and David Schalkwyk (Oxford: OUP, 2016), pp. 847–63.
22 Potter, p. 81.
23 Drohan provided an interesting biog of the company entitled 'By Moonlight: In the Light of Day' for *Frontline: The Irish Voice of Intellectual Disability*, 63 (June 12, 2005). http://frontline-ireland.com/by-moonlight-in-the-light-of-day/ [accessed October 10, 2016].
24 Although the in-play reality makes a literal reading of this impossible.
25 Declan Drohan (dir.), 'Show Information', *Tempest*, Project Arts Theatre, 2007. http://dev.project artscentre.ie/archive/archive-p-detail/114-tempest [accessed October 10, 2016].
26 Dirk Delabastita and Ton Hoenselaars, '"If But as Well I Other Accents Borrow That can My Speech Diffuse": Multilingual Perspectives on English Renaissance Drama', in Dirk Delabastita and Ton Hoenselaars (eds.), *Multilingualism in the Drama of Shakespeare and his Contemporaries* (Amsterdam: John Benjamins, 2015), pp. 1–16 (p. 7).
27 Declan Drohan, 'By Moonlight: In the Light of Day', *Frontline: The Irish Voice of Intellectual Disability*, 63 (June 12, 2005). http://frontline-ireland.com/by-moonlight-in-the-light-of-day/ [accessed October 10, 2016].
28 http://globetoglobe.shakespearesglobe.com. They visited 197 countries.
29 In fact the production had some of the savour of both *Live and Let Die* (1973) and of *Spectre* (2015), the latter perhaps influenced to some extent by the former. Particularly Hamlet's rather colourful 'inky cloak' which included a large skull on the back (perhaps to suggest that death was always following him) was suggestive of costumes worn by the voodoo practising villain Baron Samedi in *Live and Let Die* (some of which was filmed on the former British colony of Jamaica) or of the Mexican Day of the Dead celebrations that are a part of the opening sequence of *Spectre*.
30 Juan Carlos Corazza (dir.), *Hijos de Shakespeare*, Theatro de la Reunion (Conde Duque, Madrid), 2015.
31 I use the term 'plays back' in playful acknowledgement of the importance of Bill Ashcroft, Gareth Griffiths, Helen Tiffin's *The Empire Writes Back: Theory and Practice in Post-Colonial Literatures* (London: Routledge, 1989, 2002) in the field of post-colonial literary study. See especially, pp. 6–7 for an explanation of what it is to 'write back to the centre' (p. 6).
32 Michael Neill and David Schalkwyk (eds.), *The Oxford Handbook of Shakespearean Tragedy* (Oxford: Oxford University Press, 2016).
33 Thomas Cartelli and Katherine Rowe (ser. eds.), series note, in *Shakespeare and the Ethics of Appropriation*, eds. Alexa Huang and Elizabeth Rivlin, Reproducing Shakespeare: New Studies in Adaptation and Appropriation (New York: Palgrave Macmillan, 2014), p. ii. The note is reproduced in each volume of the series.
34 http://globalshakespeares.mit.edu/ [accessed October 10, 2016].
35 www.litencyc.com [accessed October 10, 2016].
36 https://shakespeareinireland.wordpress.com [accessed October 10, 2016].

4

SHAKESPEARE, MEMORY AND THE VISUAL ARTS

Shearer West

In considering the trio of Shakespeare, memory and the visual arts, we are immediately faced with three vast areas whose relationship is complex and by no means straightforward. Artists came to terms with Shakespeare's writing by producing paintings, engravings, sculptures, drawings and photographs, but this engagement did not emerge until the eighteenth century, at a time when England was beginning to portray Shakespeare as a national genius not least through other means, such as festivals and new editions of his plays. At the same time, this burgeoning of Shakespearean visual culture gave the English public a new way to think about and remember Shakespeare's plays that sometimes drew upon, and sometimes eschewed, contemporary theatrical portrayals. Teasing out the role of visual culture in memory studies helps provide us with a method of engaging with specific examples of the way in which Shakespeare and his plays were commemorated and remembered, from the Stratford Jubilee of 1769, the Boydell Shakespeare Gallery of 1789–1803, and the photographs of performances by Ellen Terry and Henry Irving that were produced in the 1870s and 1880s.

In the theoretical studies of memory published in the last few decades, the visual arts appear as either fundamental to how we remember or, more frequently, entirely absent in the way memory is discussed and conceived. It is worth beginning with Siobhan Kattago's useful, though by no means comprehensive, synthesis of what can be encompassed within memory studies: 'collective memory, mentalities, cultural memory, *lieux de mémoire*, monuments, museums, tradition, trauma, nostalgia, historical consciousness, forgetting, silence, commemoration, cosmopolitanism, narrative, mnemohistory, myth, event, modernity and hauntology'.[1] This list highlights the vast range of approaches within memory studies from the sociological to the psychological, but also potentially circumscribes visual culture to commemorative objects and institutions, as well as, more evocatively, to Pierre Nora's *lieux* or 'realms'.[2] Some of the most renowned scholars of memory studies give very little emphasis to the visual. Jacques Le Goff, for example, in his study of history and memory, is more concerned with psychological and biological elements of how people remember, and he puts memory firmly in the sphere of the textual: 'Memory, the capacity for conserving certain information, refers first of all to a group of psychic functions that allows us to actualize past impressions or information that we represent to ourselves as past.'[3] Mary Warnock has recognized that some philosophical writing rejects the significance of images in the process of remembering:

By no means all the writers who have understood and exploited the relation of memory to art have held, as Wordsworth did, that it was through images that the power of memory was experienced. Just as some philosophers have thought of memory as a particular kind of knowledge, not dependent upon images of any kind, so there have been writers who have thought of art as deriving from and seeking to articulate this kind of knowledge, to which images may be irrelevant, even an impediment.[4]

Hegel's observations on memory still cast a long shadow over the role of the visual arts in memory studies. Hegel's implicitly hierarchical distinction between *Erinnerung*, or recollection, which is a passive kind of memory triggered without effort, and *Gedächtnis*, which is more reflective and abstract, figures strongly in the literature on memory that consigns the visual image to a somewhat fraudulent role in the process of remembering.[5] This played out in Henri Bergson's highly influential *Matter and Memory*, which conceives of memory in terms of a combination of time and thought.[6] Maurice Halbwachs, in his intricate study of collective memory, recognizes the fundamental effect of monuments and festivals on how society collectively remembers events. Visual culture is of less interest to him than the ways in which societies use objects and events to understand and reconstruct their own history.[7]

However, the visual arts do appear in memory studies in several ways. On the most fundamental level, art has had a long and powerful role in the way in which memory and remembering have been understood and represented centuries before memory studies became fashionable. Frances Yates's magisterial work on memory highlighted the ancient world's fascination with the mnemonics of memory that was strongly correlated with a visual imagination.[8] Others, including Roland Barthes, have recognized the psychological power of images in triggering memories, whether true or false. The visual arts also have a much more specific place in memory studies, as one of several forms of mediation between historical 'truth' and individual and social understanding of what has happened in the past. Jan Assmann has expressed this most clearly: 'The concept of cultural memory comprises that body of reusable texts, images and rituals specific to each society in each epoch, whose "cultivation" serves to stabilize and convey that society's self-image';[9] or, as Aleida Assmann has noted, 'Because the media of memory provide the most important metaphors and models of memory, it is not surprising that human memory co-evolves with the technical progress of media history.'[10] In such studies as these, the visual art that is produced by particular societies affects how those societies remember, and how the objects trigger or shape a collective or personal memory. The agents for memory, according to Wulf Kansteiner are thus 'the visual and discursive objects of memory, memory makers and memory consumers.'[11] This is a helpful way to think about the visual arts, but we are faced with a vast field of enquiry that can include 'objects of memory' that range from miniature paintings to equestrian monuments; and 'memory consumers' who could be single individuals or entire populations.[12] Navigating this field requires a careful analysis of how various elements of visual culture can play different roles in generating, shaping and constructing both collective and individual memory.

If we introduce Shakespeare into this complex theoretical web, we have a case study that can provide us with a way of exemplifying the interactions between memory and the visual arts. There are numerous instances in Shakespeare's texts where memory, commemoration and remembering are powerful themes,[13] but I intend to look at Shakespeare and memory through the lens of art objects that represented him as an individual and visualized moments in his plays. Almost inevitably, these works of art were produced primarily in England. There were no representations of scenes from Shakespeare's plays before the early years of the eighteenth century, and in fact, apart from Martin Droeshout's engraved frontispiece to the First Folio of 1623, and the funeral monument to Shakespeare in Holy Trinity Church at Stratford-upon-Avon, there were no representations of the man himself either. However, by 1800 Shakespeare's plays were among the most popular subjects for artists working in England, and sculptural and painted commemorations of Shakespeare proliferated, despite the scant visual evidence that existed of what he looked like. This dramatic change in representational practice was in part driven by a greater professionalization of the art world in England, through the founding of the Royal Academy of Arts in 1768 and the popular annual exhibitions that followed from that event. However, the burgeoning of Shakespearean subject matter in art also served a chauvinistic need for a national genius to be re-invented, celebrated and remembered; and provided the public with ways of both remembering performances of his plays and re-imagining the character of his prose. The combination of Shakespeare and the visual arts became a locus for more individual memories of the plays themselves, both as they were read and as they were performed. As painting and engraving gave way more often to photographs of plays in the nineteenth century, the ways in which these images mediated memory became increasingly personal and emotional and less collective and national in character.

It is worthwhile to look first at the way in which Shakespeare himself became a focus for commemoration and, in fact, a *'lieu de mémoire'* in his own right. Following over a century of relative neglect after his death, there was a growing fascination with Shakespeare's writing throughout the eighteenth century, as indicated by a number of new editions of his plays and the increasing proportion of his works performed on London stages. These early signs of renewed interest came to a head in 1769 with the Shakespeare Jubilee held at his birthplace of Stratford-upon-Avon. Organized by the actor David Garrick, in collaboration with the Corporation of Stratford, the Jubilee was a three-day celebration of Shakespeare's genius, and a defining moment for memorializing the author, achieving his 'canonization', as Michael Dobson has so eloquently argued.[14] Interestingly, the Jubilee did not coincide with the anniversary of Shakespeare's birth, so either opportunism or a casual approach to the facts of history lay behind the decision to hold it in that year. The Jubilee took place between 6th and 8th September, and it attracted hundreds of people, largely from the elite of London. The event was much maligned in the London press, not least because it was claimed to be a cynical attempt to regenerate the economy of provincial Stratford, and because the numerous celebrations and activities that it comprised were plagued by heavy rain. However, metropolitan cynicism and the rain-soaked misery of the guests did very little to prevent the legacy of the Jubilee in establishing Shakespeare as a national star. As the *London Chronicle* put it:

> A Gentleman of the first rank in the literary world, speaking of the ill-natured, illiberal jokes thrown out on the Stratford Jubilee, observed that no occasion of festivity ever was or ever could be more justifiable than that of paying honours to the memory of so great an ornament to this country as the inimitable Shakespeare.[15]

The ways in which Shakespeare was remembered and celebrated were varied, and on one level, the visual arts played very much a back-seat role at the Stratford Jubilee itself. The events over the three days included a masked ball, cannon firing, a banquet, a procession of leading actors dressed as Shakespearean characters, fireworks, and an ode to Shakespeare recited by Garrick and set to music by Thomas Arne. None of Shakespeare's plays were performed, and the general tenor of the event was as sybaritic and playful as it was elegiac and commemorative. However, the build up to the Jubilee and the subsequent reverberations did much to establish a new national focus on Shakespeare and a resurrection of his reputation, as well as a creation of a new sense of collective memory.

While the Jubilee was processional and performative, rather than visual, its conception as well as its legacy was strongly dependent upon the visual arts. The very origin of the Jubilee was focused on a proposed statue of Shakespeare for the Stratford town hall. Garrick was approached by the local worthies of Stratford to help them raise money for this, and in the conversations that followed, the idea of a festival was spawned. Whatever may have motivated the mayor of Stratford to start with the idea of a commemorative sculpture, he most likely was aware of Scheemakers' monument to Shakespeare in Westminster Abbey (Figure 4.1) of 1740, John Michael Rysbrack's bust of Shakespeare of 1760, and Louis-François Roubiliac's life-size statue of Shakespeare for a temple in the garden of Garrick's house in Hampton of 1756—a work that was one of the first objects mentioned in Garrick's will.[16] The sculptor, John Cheere, was eventually hired to produce the monument for Stratford, and he relied on copying Scheemakers' sculpture in his design. These two monuments thus echoed each other and gave the figure of Shakespeare a symbolic presence amongst the principal funerary sculpture of the nation in Westminster Abbey and a civic role in his birthplace in Stratford, the latter of which subsequently became a site of tourism and collective memory. The significance of sculpture to the Jubilee is alluded to obliquely and playfully in Gainsborough's portrait of Garrick with a bust of Shakespeare (1766), painted in the lead up to the Jubilee. There is no real obeisance paid here to Shakespeare but rather a nod to Garrick's fundamental part in reviving his memory. In each of these instances, sculpture, as an art form that was inextricably associated with monuments and memorials, was the means of remembering and celebrating Shakespeare.[17] The sculptures were funerary (Westminster Abbey), celebratory (Stratford) and commemorative (Hampton), associated with both the death and the reinvention of one of England's most notable writers. The decisions that led so many top sculptors to produce these monuments helped give Shakespeare a new place in collective national memory.

Other visual legacies of the Jubilee had an almost religious feel about them, including the production of 'a medallion of Shakespeare, carved on a piece of the famous mulberry-tree, planted by the immortal poet's own hand, and richly set in gold.'[18] Garrick, as Steward of the Jubilee, wore this medallion, thus further consolidating his role as a purveyor and inheritor of Shakespeare's genius. The fact that Garrick himself was at the height of his career when he acted as Steward, and that Shakespeare was not yet at the height of his historic reputation, represents the meaningful role a contemporary celebrity could play in creating and shaping public perception around memorializing a figure from the past. Flourishes such as this, and the ritualistic processions and recitations of odes during the Jubilee itself, led some observers to condemn the event as 'papistical'.[19] Even in the cynical public response of the time, it was clear that the Jubilee was using ritual, procession, festival and relic to develop an aura around a historical figure who did not have anything like the reputation, significance or recognition that eventually led to Bardolatry.

So what was, in effect, a slightly vulgar and unsatisfactory event, held in a provincial town and mocked by metropolitan audiences, was accompanied by and associated with artistic objects of commemoration that served to create an aura of stability and gravitas around the memory of Shakespeare. Subsequent paintings and prints that referred implicitly or explicitly back to this event included George Carter's *Apotheosis of Garrick* (1782, Figure 4.2) and Caroline Watson's stipple engraving after Robert Edge Pine of Garrick reciting the Jubilee Ode (1784). Both of these works were produced over a decade after the Jubilee itself, but both refer back to that event as a formative episode in the elevation of Shakespeare to a national hero. Carter's work

Figure 4.1 Peter Scheemakers, monument to Shakespeare, 1740, Westminster Abbey.
© James Brittain/Bridgeman Images.

is particularly revealing in that it commemorated Garrick's death by showing him being carried up to heaven by angels, with recognizable fellow actors, costumed in the roles of various Shakespearean characters, lamenting his demise. Here, the procession of Shakespeare characters of the Jubilee is reinvented as a group that is mourning, rather than celebrating.

The Stratford Jubilee operated as a *lieu de mémoire*, in Pierre Nora's terms, that is: 'any significant entity, whether material or non-material in nature, which by dint of human will or the work of time has become a symbolic element in the memorial heritage of any community'—a place, site or realm that has a 'material, symbolic and functional' presence.[20] Before the Jubilee, it was not a matter of national interest or focus that Stratford was Shakespeare's birthplace. While the Jubilee itself was not wholly a success, the massive media publicity that surrounded it drew new attention to Shakespeare and generated a range of artistic and theatrical responses that continued to keep the Bard in the public eye long after the event was over. Garrick's recreation on the Drury Lane State of the procession from the Jubilee parade was performed 153 times

Shakespeare, memory and the visual arts

Figure 4.2 George Carter, *The Apotheosis of Garrick*, c. 1782.
© Royal Shakespeare Company Collection, Stratford upon Avon.

between 1769 and 1776, attesting to the significance of an event which captured public imagination and had a lingering place in collective memory. The Jubilee thus became what Halbwachs called a 'framework of social memory',[21] but it also served to create a new set of ideas as to what Shakespeare stood for in national historical consciousness.

While visual arts played a somewhat secondary role in the Jubilee in terms of bringing Shakespeare the poet, playwright and man, into national consciousness, they subsequently became a fundamental stimulus for the way in which the English public understood and remembered his plays. In 1787 Samuel Felton presciently wrote: 'The time is now come when Shakespeare's works will receive every embellishment of grateful art—when a temple will be erected to his memory—and where the productions of English artists will receive an eternal asylum.'[22]

Felton's *Imperfect Hints towards a New Edition of Shakespeare* was designed to recommend what a properly illustrated edition of his plays should comprise. He was drawing upon knowledge of several illustrated editions of Shakespeare's plays from that of Nicholas Rowe, published by Jacob Tonson in 1709 with 37 illustrations, to John Bell's edition of 1774 with 72 plates. Felton's pamphlet appeared at a formative moment after the foundation of the Royal Academy and shortly before the launch of the Shakespeare Gallery—a massive artistic enterprise drawing on the still fresh iconic status of Shakespeare. The Shakespeare Gallery, the brainchild of entrepreneur John Boydell and several Royal Academy artists, opened in

June 1789 at 52 Pall Mall in London with initially 34 paintings. The Gallery itself was only part of the full project, which also included two sets of engravings after the paintings: one to accompany George Steevens' new edition of Shakespeare's plays and the other to be a large stand alone folio set. The Gallery initially attracted enthusiastic reviews, but the collapse of the international print market due to war with France led to Boydell's bankruptcy and closure of the Gallery in 1803.[23] The Shakespeare Gallery served the notable function of focusing the minds of England's best artists on how to bring Shakespeare's works alive in a visual form. This was an especially challenging exercise, given the relative dearth of paintings and illustrations of Shakespeare up until that point.

By 1789, when the gallery opened, the commemorative impact of the Stratford Jubilee had become deeply embedded in public consciousness. Although the Shakespeare Gallery on one level was an extension of the myth creation and memorializing impetus of the Jubilee, the artists who contributed to the Gallery were also wrestling with some different issues. Attempting to tap the collective memory of audiences who were at once readers and theatregoers, and a literate public becoming increasingly interested in the accuracy and interpretation of Shakespeare's writings, the Shakespeare Gallery artists had few templates on which to draw. They therefore produced a variety of works that veered from the most extreme imaginative forays of Henry Fuseli to barely disguised references to contemporary theatre by James Northcote and Richard Westall. The Shakespeare Gallery was an extension of the memorializing and mythmaking that was the legacy of the Stratford Jubilee, but memory also played a role in how audiences collectively and individually came to terms with the representations of Shakespeare's plays exhibited in the Gallery.

The Shakespeare Gallery was founded on a chauvinistic desire to prove that English art was just as good, if not better, than that of other European nations. The mission statements of the Gallery thus drew upon what was becoming a commonly accepted idea of Shakespeare as an embodiment of English liberty, originality and imagination. The lack of unities of time and place in his plays and the ubiquity of supernatural scenes and characters, which so annoyed French writers such as Voltaire, began to be conceived of as the very things that made him an iconic English figure.[24] As Boydell wrote to MP John William Anderson:

> In the Shakspeare (sic) Gallery every Artist, partaking of the freedom of his country, and endowed with that originality of thinking so peculiar to its natives, has chosen his own road, to what he conceived to be excellence, unshackled by the slavish imitation and uniformity that pervade all the foreign Schools.[25]

What is notable here is how far the conception of Shakespeare's talents and contribution had evolved since the days of the Stratford Jubilee. Monuments to Shakespeare by Scheemakers, Roubiliac and others commemorated an individual who was thought to have made an important contribution to English literature; with the Shakespeare Gallery, the associations of Shakespeare with the very foundations of the English constitution was another step in the author's apotheosis.[26] Over the doors of the Shakespeare Gallery building was another monument by Thomas Banks, but this time Shakespeare was not represented as a simple figure but seated between the Dramatic Muse and the Genius of Painting 'Who is pointing him out as the proper subject for the Pencil.' While the Jubilee was a quotidian celebration, the Shakespeare Gallery was a solid building that was located in Pall Mall, at that time the very nucleus of London elite society. The locus of memorializing Shakespeare had therefore moved from a provincial town to the very heart of the capital, and the visual arts were a central, rather than peripheral part of constructing his historical image. History, memory and the visual arts came to a point of conflation here;

Shakespeare's imaginative conception of the past in his history plays became inextricably bound up with his iconic image. As Stuart Sillars has argued, 'Once Shakespeare is established as the essence of national identity, what is perceived as his version of history takes on a special kind of cultural truth.'[27]

While the Shakespeare Gallery as a project fuelled this sense of national pride, the paintings within the Gallery drew a range of responses from enthusiasm to bemusement. Each of the artists who contributed to the Gallery took a distinctive approach to realizing Shakespeare's plays for a literate audience familiar with the works from both reading and the stage. In some cases, they drew upon their individualistic and imaginative interpretations of the plays. We can see this, for example, in Henry Fuseli's fantastical portrayal of Titania and Bottom from *A Midsummer Night's Dream*, evoking the fairies Peaseblossom, Cobweb, Moth and Mustardseed; or in Joseph Wright of Derby's sublime landscape from *A Winter's Tale* that literally realizes the stage business of Antigonus being chased by a bear. Other paintings in the Gallery were more closely related to theatrical representation, and in these cases both the experiences and the memories of the Gallery audiences were key. The relationship between the paintings and the theatre was a particularly problematic one, as critics were keen to see representations of Shakespeare that diverged from theatrical performance, while the artists themselves often referred implicitly or explicitly to celebrated contemporary actors. At the opening of the Gallery in 1789, some critics expressed relief that the paintings did not merely illustrate stage performance:

> There was some reason to fear that our painters would have sought for and gathered their ideas from theatre, and given us portraits of the well-dressed ladies and gentlemen [of the stage] ... There was some reason to fear that extravagance of attitude and start which is tolerated, nay in a degree demanded, of the playhouse.[28]

However, in paintings such as James Northcote's *Meeting of the Princes* from *Richard III* (Figure 4.3) or Richard Westall's depiction of Lady Macbeth in the letter scene, we see barely disguised references to the actors John Philip Kemble and Sarah Siddons; in the former case, Northcote actually altered the painting to introduce Kemble's visage in the character of Richard III.[29] As one reviewer wrote of William Hamilton's painting of Act IV, scene 1 from *Much Ado About Nothing*: 'Few people will need an explanation of this subject. The play is frequently acted; and the characters not only speak for themselves, but are habited in some measure as we are used to see them on the stage.'[30]

The way in which art visualizes retrospectively a theatrical performance is worth considering here. Portraits of actors playing Shakespearean roles were frequently evoked in eighteenth- and nineteenth-century theatrical biographies, although it is not always clear whether the biographers were aware of how much prints and paintings influenced their memories of what happened on the stage. For example, Hogarth's famous portrait of Garrick in the tent scene of *Richard III* (1745, Figure 4.4) seems to have coloured the descriptions of many biographers who recalled Garrick's performance as Richard waking up from his dream exactly in that way, with his hand outstretched and his face in a mask of horror. John Bell, in his edition of Shakespeare, claimed to provide frontispieces that showed plays 'as they are now performed', but included actors in roles which they had never performed as well as plays that had not been performed in living memory.[31]

One can question the extent to which descriptions of actors performing Shakespearean roles were genuine memories of performance or memories sparked by a famous and evocative image. The Shakespeare Gallery was filled with depictions of scenes from plays that were acted on the London stage, at a time when the performances of celebrity actors such as Kemble and Siddons

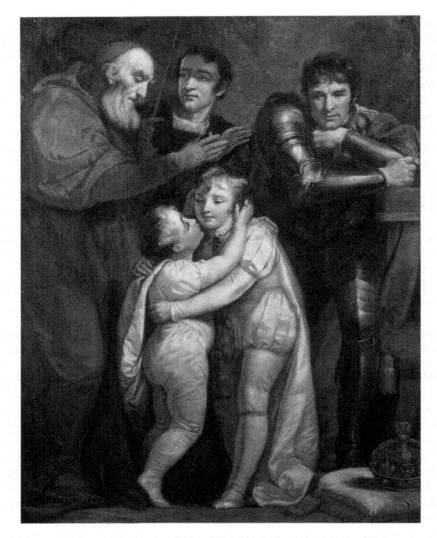

Figure 4.3 James Northcote, *The Meeting of Edward V and his brother Richard, Duke of York, contemplated by King Richard III*, 1799.
National Trust, Petworth House. NT486168 © National Trust Images/Derrick E. Witty.

received critical scrutiny equal to the works of art in the gallery itself. While many people were eager to recall these outstanding performances, there were others who found that the visualizing of Shakespeare was a threat to their own imaginative reading of his work, rather than a way of remembering. When the Gallery was first announced, for example, Horace Walpole wrote to Lady Ossory:

> Mercy on us! Our painters to design from Shakespeare! His commentators have not been more inadequate. Pray who is to give us an idea of Falstaff, now Quin is dead? And then Bartolozzi, who is fit only to engrave for the Pastor-Fide, will he give us a pretty enameled fan mount of Macbeth?[32]

Figure 4.4 William Hogarth, *David Garrick as Richard III*, 1745.
© Walker Art Gallery, National Museums Liverpool/Bridgeman Images.

And Charles Lamb, looking back on the phenomenon of the Shakespeare Gallery retrospectively, opined:

> What injury (short of the theatre) did not Boydell's 'Shakespeare Gallery' do me with Shakespeare, light-headed Fuseli's Shakespeare, heavy-headed Romney's Shakespeare, wooden-headed West's Shakespeare ... deaf-headed Reynold's (sic) Shakespeare, instead of my and everybody else's Shakespeare. To be tied down to an authentic face of Juliet! To have Imogen's portrait! To confine the illimitable![33]

In contrast to the ways in which Shakespeare became part of national pride and collective re-imagining of history, the works in the Shakespeare Gallery divided public views about the how the plays themselves were both imagined and remembered. Alexandre Dessingué, writing about Halbwachs' ideas of collective memory, argues for the links between the individual and the collective memory: 'The "we" becomes the global framework within which and through which the individual has the opportunity to rebuild their own souvenirs from the perspective of the others who surround them.'[34] A certain quality of this collective memory appears in the work of biographers who demonstrated their memory of plays through reference to paintings and prints of actors in role. However, part of the ambivalence around the critical response to the Shakespeare Gallery no doubt lay in the fact that the disparate works represented there—while tying Shakespeare firmly to a national agenda of liberty and freedom—did not provide a consistent enough view of the plays themselves to link individual artistic interpretation with collective memory.

And indeed in terms of collective memory, the nineteenth century represented a period in which responses to visual representations of Shakespeare became increasingly atomized, even while his place as a national icon was consolidated. One reason for this was the proliferation of visual representations of Shakespeare's plays in a variety of media. The paintings and prints that were privileged by the Boydell Shakespeare project were supplemented by new and faster printings techniques, including lithography, which could provide many more copies to an ever-larger consumer base, and photography, which eventually supplanted painting and engraving as the primary means of capturing theatrical performance. The increasingly individualized responses that surrounded the relationship between Shakespeare, memory and the visual arts can be tested in the critical reactions to representations of Henry Irving and Ellen Terry at the Lyceum Theatre. They consciously drew upon art to provide souvenirs for their theatrical audiences. The critic William Archer, in his biography of Henry Irving, expressed most poignantly the unrequited desire of audiences to remember the details of plays they had seen:

> A critic of sculpture, of painting, of music, of poetry, can have ever before him the masterpieces from which his critical canons are generalized. He can go to work both inductively and deductively. He evolves from his inner consciousness the idea of what art *should* be: he looks backward through the centuries and learns what art *has* been: and a compromise between the two gives him his standard of what art *can* be under existing conditions … With the critic of acting the case is different. Each individual, or at any rate each generation, has to form a new ideal, unaided by the ideals and achievements of the past. Suppose that all the paintings then in the world had suddenly faded at the beginning, say, of this century: suppose our whole knowledge of Italian, Spanish, German, and Flemish art … had to be gathered from printed descriptions; how empiric would our art criticism be, how utterly given over to individual mood and whim![35]

Archer here was recognising something that many audiences felt: an impulse to preserve their memory of an exciting or moving performance, and the frustrating inability to do more than recall it in the most general terms. I have already mentioned how biographers of actors would use prints to jog their memory of a theatrical performance—however fictional the prints may have been—but by the late nineteenth century, actors and managers themselves worked to capture and preserve their performances for their audiences. The Lyceum Theatre is a particularly useful case study here, as Irving and Terry deliberately cultivated an artistic approach to their productions, and Shakespeare figured strongly in their repertoire. Despite the relative sophistication of photography in his lifetime, Henry Irving continued to rely on an artist, Bernard Partridge, to sketch the sets and performances of plays produced in the Lyceum, and Partridge's sketches were used to illustrate the 'souvenirs' that were sold in the theatre. However, by the 1860s, there were many fewer representations of Shakespeare's plays in public exhibitions than there were at the time of the Shakespeare Gallery,[36] and increasingly Irving and his lead actress, Ellen Terry, used professional photographers to capture the moment of performance.

This attempt to use visual arts to bottle memory for the delectation of audiences is most fully exemplified in Ellen Terry's performances as Lady Macbeth. Here there are a number of inter-generational considerations that show how legacy and memory were inextricably tied up with visual representation. Terry was fascinated by the character of Lady Macbeth, and in the early twentieth century gave lectures on Shakespeare, making deliberate and thoughtful references to an essay by Sarah Siddons on the same character, published in Thomas Campbell's biography of that actress nearly 70 years before.[37] So here we see the way in which a reflection on a Shakespearean character provides a chain of association among different generations of actors whose performances could not have been remembered or recorded in any other way than through verbal description or visual arts. Terry's vivid portrayals of Lady Macbeth attracted John Singer Sargent (Figure 4.5) to paint his bravura portrait of an intimidating dominatrix Terry with her beetle wing dress holding the crown that Macbeth so coveted, described evocatively by Graham Robertson in *Time Was*: 'long plaits of deep red hair fell from under a purple veil over a robe of green upon which iridescent wings of beetles glittered like emeralds, and a great wine-coloured cloak, gold embroidered, swept from her shoulders.'[38]

Figure 4.5 John Singer Sargent, *Ellen Terry as Lady Macbeth*, 1889. London © Tate Gallery.

Sargent's vivid reminiscence of Terry's performance was at odds with her description of the role, that paid homage to Siddons' view that Lady Macbeth was 'an astonishing creature ... fair, feminine, nay, perhaps, even fragile'.[39] The critic, William Archer, saw the troubled relationship between theatre and memory that was mediated by Sargent's painting. Archer attacked Max Beerbohm's assertion that people should stop reviving Shakespeare's famous plays because everyone remembers what they are like. He wrote:

> I can assure Mr. Beerbohm that when I saw *Macbeth* a second time, I found I had forgotten almost all the details of the first performance, not three weeks earlier. As for comparing Mr. Robertson with Sir Henry Irving or Mrs. Campbell with Miss Ellen Terry, I could as easily compare them with John Kemble and Mrs. Siddons. Of course I know Sir Henry Irving's and Miss Ellen Terry's methods, and I remember generally how these methods, as applied to Macbeth and Lady Macbeth, affected me; but I search my memory in vain for a single detail of elocution or of action ... With some aid from Mr. Sargent, I remember the picture presented by Miss Terry in her wonderful green gown; but as to her performances—well, Mrs. Siddons's Lady Macbeth stands much more vividly before my mind's eye.[40]

Thus the memory of Terry performing Lady Macbeth was emotional and ineffable, and Sargent's work served to provide both a memento and a new stimulus for fans who struggled to recall those details of their heroine's performance. Charles Hiatt, another admirer of Ellen Terry, found too that his memories were catalyzed by art:

> I have before me a reproduction of the wonderful portrait of [Terry] by Mr. Sargent ... and, by the side of it, a print of Westall's portrait of Mrs. Siddons as Lady Macbeth. The latter represents a woman who is simply 'fearsome,' without a touch of dignity or beauty. That Mrs. Siddons, who inspired Sir Joshua and Gainsborough so happily, looked at all like the woman in this picture, I absolutely decline to believe. If she did, and was still able to impress her audiences, her genius, so far from being exaggerated, has been absurdly underestimated. But we know that Mrs. Siddons was a magnificent woman and Westall a very mediocre painter, so that there is little doubt that this pretended counterfeit presentment is scarcely better than a burlesque of the woman who sat to Reynolds for the Tragic Muse.[41]

Such reflections on Terry's performance as Lady Macbeth, its legacy in the lost memories of Sarah Siddons' acting, and its fuelling by Sargent's portrait were further complicated by photography. Sargent's portrait created an image of Lady Macbeth that registered with the English public and provided much more fodder for re-imagining her performance than the many photographs of her in role, which were decidedly more posed and empty of emotion than the portrait painting itself (Figure 4.6).[42] Lindsay Smith, writing about the early years of photography, has highlighted the distinctions 'between memory of visual phenomena and memory mediated specifically by photographic representation'.[43] When looking at the rather flat photograph of Terry in the role that Sargent so vividly brought to life, we need to consider Barthes' view that a photograph is both an 'agent of death' and a 'substitute for life': 'not a memory, an imagination, a reconstruction ... such as art lavishes upon us, but reality in a past state: at once the past and the real.'[44]

Figure 4.6 Ellen Terry as Lady Macbeth, Window & Grove platinum print, 1888. Published 1906, London © National Portrait Gallery.

Barthes' view reveals the same sort of iconophobia that characterized Hegel's rejection of *Erinnerung* in favour of *Gedächtnis*. When one considers the configuration of Shakespeare, the visual arts and memory, this ambivalence about the role of visual culture is sharply surfaced in a national narrative that sees Shakespeare's works as too sublime to be memorialized or remembered by the specificity of the visual arts.

Notes

1 Siobhan Kattago, 'Introduction', *The Ashgate Research Companion to Memory Studies* (Farnham: Ashgate, 2015), p. 2.
2 Pierre Nora, *Realms of Memory: Rethinking the French Past*, volume 1, ed. Lawrence Kritzman, trans. Arthur Goldhammer (New York: Columbia University Press, 1996).
3 Jacques Le Goff, *History and Memory* (New York: Columbia University Press, 1992), p. 51.

4 Mary Warnock, *Memory* (London: Faber & Faber, 1982), p. 89.
5 Gerhard Richter, 'Acts of Memory and Mourning: Derrida and the Fictions of Anteriority', in Susannah Radstone and Bill Schwarz (eds.), *Memory: Histories, Theories, Debates* (New York: Fordham University Press, 2010), pp. 157–8.
6 Henri Bergson, *Matiere et mémoire* (Paris: F. Alcan, 1900 2nd edn. 1st pub. 1896).
7 Ina Blom argues that contemporary video art challenges Halbwachs' theory of art as monument; however the subject of this essay is confined to art before the moving image was adopted by artists. Blom, 'The Autobiography of Video: Outline for a Revisionist Account of Video Art', *Critical Inquiry*, 39:2 (winter 2013), 276–95.
8 Frances Yates, *The Art of Memory* (Chicago: University of Chicago Press, 1966).
9 Jan Assmann, 'Collective Memory and Cultural Identity', trans. J. Czaplicka, *New German Critique*, 65 (spring/summer 1995), p. 132.
10 Aleida Assmann, *Cultural Memory and Western Civilization: Functions, Media, Archives* (Cambridge: Cambridge University Press, 2011), p. 137.
11 Wulf Kansteiner, 'Finding Meaning in Memory: A Methodological Critique of Memory Studies', *History and Theory*, 41 (2002), 179–97.
12 See, for example, Jay Winter, *Sites of Memory, Sites of Mourning: The Great War in European Cultural History* (Cambridge: Cambridge University Press, 1998); and Hanneke Grootenboer, *Treasuring the Gaze: Intimate Vision in Late Eighteenth-Century Eye Miniatures* (Chicago: University of Chicago Press, 2013).
13 For example, Lina Perkins Wilder, *Shakespeare's Memory Theatre: Reflections, Properties and Character* (Cambridge: Cambridge University Press, 2010); and Hester Lees-Jeffries, *Shakespeare and Memory* (Oxford: Oxford University Press, 2013).
14 Michael Dobson, *The Making of the National Poet: Shakespeare Adaptation and Authorship 1660–1769* (Oxford: Clarendon Press, 1992), p. 134.
15 *London Chronicle*, 31 August 1769.
16 Old Comedian, *The Life and Death of David Garrick, Esq, the Celebrated English Roscius* (London: J. Pridden, et. al., 1779), p. 33.
17 Shearer West, 'The Visuality of the Theatre', in Michael Cordner and Peter Holland (eds.), *Players, Playwrights, Playhouses: Investigating Performance, 1660–1800* (Basingstoke: Palgrave Macmillan, 2007), pp. 271–93.
18 Old Comedian, *Garrick*, p. 6. See also the *Public Advertiser*, 17 August 1769: 'A few days since was finished the Bust of Shakespeare, elegantly carved (on Part of the Mulberry Tree) by Mr. Davies, and designed to be set in Gold and worn by Mr. Garrick, as Steward of the Jubilee.'
19 *Garrick's Vagary; or, England run mad, with particulars of the Stratford Jubilee* (London: S. Bladon, 1769), p. 4.
20 Nora, *Realms of Memory*, p. xvii.
21 Maurice Halbwachs, *On Collective Memory*, ed. and trans. Lewis Coger (Chicago and London: University of Chicago Press, 1992).
22 [Samuel Felton], *Imperfect Hints Towards a New Edition of Shakespeare* (London: Logographic Press, 1787), p. ii.
23 See Winifred Friedman, *Boydell's Shakespeare Gallery* (New York: Garland, 1976); Sven Bruntjen, *John Boydell 1719–1804: A Study of Art, Patronage and Publishing in Georgian London* (New York: Garland, 1985); and Walter Pape and Frederick Burwick, eds, *The Boydell Shakespeare Gallery* (Bottrop: Peter Pomp, 1996).
24 See, for example, Elizabeth Montagu, *An Essay on the Writings and Genius of Shakespear, compared with Greek and French dramatic poets, with some remarks on the misrepresentations of Mons de Voltaire* (London: J. Dodsley, 1769).
25 John Boydell in *A Collection of Prints from Pictures Painted for the Purpose of Illustrating the Dramatic Works of Shakspeare*, vol. 1 (London: John and Josiah Boydell, 1803), preface.
26 See Rosie Dias, *Exhibiting Englishness: John Boydell's Shakespeare Gallery and the Formation of a National Aesthetic* (New Haven, Conn., and London: Yale University Press, 2013); and Hildegard Hammerschmidt-Hummel, 'Boydell's Shakespeare Gallery and Its Role in Promoting English History Painting', in Pape and Burwick, *Shakespeare Gallery*, pp. 33–44.
27 Stuart Sillars, *Painting Shakespeare: The Artist as Critic 1720–1820* (Cambridge: Cambridge University Press, 2006), p. 17.
28 *Public Advertiser*, 6 May 1789.
29 Shearer West, *The Image of the Actor: Verbal and Visual Representation in the Age of Garrick and Kemble* (London: Pinter, 1991), p. 117.

30 Humphry Repton, *The Bee, or a Companion to the Shakespeare Gallery* (London: T. Cadell, [1789]), p. 19.
31 For example, the actress Miss Younge was represented as Cleopatra, though *Antony and Cleopatra* had only been performed in Dryden's much altered version during the eighteenth century. See West, *Image of the Actor*, pp. 53–7.
32 W.S. Lewis (ed.), *Horace Walpole's Correspondence*, vol. 33 (Oxford: Oxford University Press, 1983): p. 547 (15 December 1786).
33 Percy Fitzgerald (ed.), *The Life, Letters and Writings of Charles Lamb*, vol. 3 (New York: Cosimo, Inc, 2008), p. 62.
34 Alexandre Dessingué, 'From Collectivity to Collectiveness: Reflections (with Halbwachs and Bakhtin) on the Concept of Collective Memory', in Kattago, *Ashgate Companion to Memory Studies*, p. 96.
35 William Archer, *Henry Irving: Actor and Manager* (London: Field and Tuer, 1883), pp. 14–16.
36 Ross Anderson (ed.), *A Brush with Shakespeare: The Bard in Painting 1780–1910*, exhibition catalogue (Montgomery Museum of Fine Arts, 1986).
37 Thomas Campbell, *The Life of Mrs. Siddons*, 2 vols. (London: Effingham Wilson, 1834): vol. 2, pp. 10–34; and Ellen Terry, *Four Lectures on Shakespeare*, ed. Christopher St. John, (London: Martin Hopkinson, 1932). See Shearer West, 'Roles and Role Models: Montagu, Siddons, Lady Macbeth', in Elizabeth Eger (ed.), *Bluestockings Displayed: Portraiture, Performance and Patronage, 1730–1830* (Cambridge: Cambridge University Press, 2013), pp. 164–86.
38 W. Graham Robertson, *Time Was* (London: Hamish Hamilton, 1931), pp. 150–1.
39 Campbell, *Life of Siddons*, vol. 2, pp. 10–11.
40 William Archer, *Study and Stage* (London: Grant Richards, 1899), pp. 105–6.
41 Charles Hiatt, *Ellen Terry and Her Impersonations* (London: George Bell and Sons, 1898), pp. 214–15.
42 Nina Auerbach, *Ellen Terry: Player in her Time* (London: J.M. Dent and Sons, 1987), p. 194: 'It is impossible … to recreate that powerful figure [Terry] today; her stage presence elicited abstract rhapsodies, not precise descriptions. She is celebrated most consistently as a picture … She is magnetic but not quite real. She had been groomed for stardom in a theater that took its identity from painting.'
43 Lindsay Smith, *Victorian Photography, Painting and Poetry: The Enigma of Visibility in Ruskin, Morris and the Pre-Raphaelites* (Cambridge: Cambridge University Press, 1995), p. 88.
44 Roland Barthes, *Camera Lucida*, trans. Richard Howard (London: Flamingo, 1984), p. 82.

5

SHAKESPEARE, MEMORY, FILM AND PERFORMANCE

Sarah Hatchuel and Nathalie Vienne-Guerrin

Shakespeare is deeply inscribed in the table of filmic memory. From the early days of cinema, his plays have been performed for the screen and this has contributed to keeping their memory alive, constituting what is now considered an on-going *history* of Shakespeare on screen.[1] This history includes several ages, from the age of silence to the digital age, through the Olivier, Welles and Branagh eras or the *fin de siècle* moment, and from a UK/US and European scale to a global scope.[2] Shakespeare inspired several hundred silent films in the USA[3] and in Europe at the beginning of the twentieth century, when cinema strove for artistic legitimacy by exploiting the playwright's cultural status. Paradoxically, in those days, transforming Shakespeare plays into filmic objects consisted in overlooking and, in fact, forgetting his texts. From the silent movies, which Judith Buchanan has called back to collective memory by reconstituting the conditions of their production and performance and by making them accessible,[4] to Justin Kurzel's recent *Macbeth* (2015) which inscribes flashback, trauma and memory at the heart of the play, the history of Shakespeare on screen invites researchers to interrogate the complex relationship between Shakespeare, memory, film and performance at a time when digital Shakespeare fosters forms of both hypermnesia and amnesia. On the one hand, we have – or will soon have – access to every single Shakespeare film that has been released worldwide as well as to ever more numerous film recordings of live theatrical performances, which will allow us to remember everything; on the other hand, the digital age precisely allows spectators *not to* remember by making all filmic materials available online or on DVD, meaning there is no *need* to remember them, since we have them at our fingertips. As Katherine Rowe documents the complexities of the relationships between technology, memory and film, she rightly asserts that 'The communications and storage of media we depend on to shore up the past, also ruin it'.[5]

Compared with the theatre, which is conventionally perceived as ephemeral[6] and can be remembered only through prompt books, programmes, photos, anecdotes and reviews,[7] cinema appears as the medium of permanence, as one can view the same film again and again *ad libidum*. To become fixed in time, a theatre performance needs to turn into something that it essentially *is not*, a film, in an age of media hybridity. Yet, films too constitute a world of evanescent remembrance of Shakespeare's plays, especially if one considers how cinema cultivates allusion and conveys the spectral presence of Shakespeare in films that are not explicitly labelled 'Shakespearean', so much so that it is no longer possible to say when Shakespeare stops being present (or even absent) on film. As Richard Burt asserts, 'Like the continuum between strong

Shakespeare adaptations and weak Shakespeare citations, there is a continuum between strong and weak examples of the Shakespeare-play-within-the-film genre'.[8] This ghostly presence of Shakespeare on screen in world cinema contributes to the calling back of his works to memory, suggesting that Shakespeare is forever rooted in our collective psyche.

Shakespeare on film, Shakespeare forever?

One could easily believe that, thanks to film recording, Shakespearean performances have become eternal. Filmic technology undeniably contributes to preserving the memory of Shakespeare's plays.[9] Among the main providers of Shakespeare's filmed plays we find National Theatre Live (performances are filmed in public and broadcast live or not), the Royal Shakespeare Company (some productions are available on DVD, suggesting that films are the best way of preserving the trace and memory of a theatrical performance) and Digital Theatre Live (with downloads subject to a subscription). Thomas Jolly's recent 18-hour-long three-part *Henry VI*, which was performed on stage at the Avignon theatre festival before touring all over France, was released on DVD in 2015, thus allowing spectators all over the world to watch the production and inscribing the theatre venture in a logic of preservation. Indeed, the entire trilogy was recently shown in a major cinema in Paris, thus turning a theatrical experience into a cinematographic one. This is just one example of the trend of transforming theatre shows into hybrid films that can be viewed on DVD or in cinemas. The 'Shakespeare's Globe On Screen' initiative also promises to offer 'spellbinding performances' and 'an unforgettable cinema experience'.[10] Yet the permanence of Shakespeare in our memory through film is to be questioned. In his book on Shakespeare and world cinema, in which he analyses seventy-three Shakespearean adaptations produced outside Anglophone mainstream cinema, Mark Thornton Burnett suggests that memory requires *work* because 'Shakespeare and world cinema products are potentially perishable commodities'.[11] If no one preserves these Shakespearean films by analysing their conditions of production, distribution and translation, they could disappear and be forgotten.

Shakespeare on film certainly does not mean Shakespeare forever – and this remains even more the case because some of Shakespeare's plays are very rarely put on screen and thus tend to be relegated to a world of oblivion. Cinema does not take care of the Shakespeare heritage evenly. Some plays prove more attractive to film directors than others. More often adapted to film than comedies, histories or romances, the tragedies seem to be more central in spectators' memory and constitute greater *lieux de mémoire*.[12] Like Shakespearean scholars around the world, we contribute, through writing, to the memory of these films and, beyond them, of Shakespeare. The work that is currently being done to excavate and reconstitute old silent films shows that early films are perishable. In 1917, Theda Bara, the silent-screen star (who became known as 'The Vamp'), played Cleopatra in a film directed by J. Gordon Edwards and produced by William Fox productions which appropriated the Orientalist pageantry and theatricality of the Cleopatra story. Theda Bara, an anagram of 'Arab Death', was publicized as the ultimate Oriental *femme fatale*, embodying all the fears linked to the mysterious and dangerous otherness of Egypt and womanhood. Yet no prints of the film appear to have survived and it is only thanks to the research work of Robert Hamilton Ball[13] that we know the film focused on its star (in extravagant dress and undress) and featured many spectacular scenes displaying magnificent costumes, the elaborate reconstruction of Rome and Alexandria, and dozens of galleys burning during the battle.

Even more recent films have proved perishable. In our research on the French TV films (known as the 'dramatiques') broadcast on television from the early fifties to the late seventies,[14] we discovered that the Inathèque, an independent collection inside the building of the

Bibliothèque Nationale de France (which holds the French Television Archive), had started digitizing a great part of the collection in a lengthy and on-going process aimed at preserving the heritage of French television in a lasting form of storage. New digital technologies certainly serve the preservation of films of the past, but also make for a highly different viewing experience, which demands some effort from the viewers if they want to try and recapture the initial viewing conditions. But the archaeological nature of this research meant that we sometimes only discovered mere fragments of Shakespearean plays. For example, we could only find a ten-minute excerpt from the 1957 *Twelfth Night* with the famous actress Annie Girardot as Viola/Cesario while the final minutes of the 1962 *Twelfth Night* were missing.[15] As Burnett suggests, filmic objects that would seem to be eternal are in fact fragile and easily forgettable, and so 'Shakespeare film can all too often stumble at the first hurdle and quickly disappear from view'.[16]

Memorable Shakespeare on film

If films are a way of preserving the Shakespearean heritage and of making it live, this form of afterlife would remain relatively limited if Shakespearean scholars did not keep this memory alive through reviews and analyses. Few Shakespearean films have been blockbusters and thus the remembrance of Shakespeare through films relies perhaps more on their large number through the ages than on the success of any particular one. Paradoxically, the memory of Shakespeare on film depends to a great extent on the written words that prolong the films' lives. Shakespearean films are kept vivid in collective memory by exterior agents. Without the pioneering work of Kenneth S. Rothwell, who would remember that the first Shakespearean talking movie was *The Taming of the Shrew* shot in 1929 and featuring Mary Pickford and Douglas Fairbanks as Katharina and Petruchio? This first Shakespearean 'All talking, All Laughing'[17] film was itself a fragmented and hybrid memory of the play, both forgetting and remembering Shakespeare's work, since it borrowed words from Garrick's eighteenth-century adaptation, *Catharine and Petruchio* (London, 1756) and is known for the textual additions written by its director, Sam Taylor.

Shakespeare's plays were obviously considered too cumbersome to be entirely digested. In 1935, Max Reinhardt and William Dieterle released a version of *A Midsummer Night's Dream* with James Cagney as Bottom, Mickey Rooney as Puck and Olivia de Havilland as Hermia. If the film remains memorable, it is probably due as much to the music of Felix Mendelssohn to its visual features. The fairy world of the play is conveyed through many dream-like visual effects, with fairies dancing on clouds and Puck metamorphosing into variously a dog, a boar or a little flame. The film remains famous, however, for its soundtrack, Mendelssohn seeming to come to Shakespeare's rescue to ensure better remembrance.

As Lisa S. Starks suggests, referring to Freud's theorizing, 'memory is constituted by loss and fragmentation'.[18] To be better remembered, it seems, Shakespeare needs to be reconfigured. The history of Shakespeare on film is also the history of his loss. If, as Starks notes, 'moving pictures were first seen as the storehouse of memory providing a material record that promised immortality',[19] this immortality depends on recurrent 'murders' of Shakespeare which introduce creative gaps in his memory.

Some other Shakespearean films remain in collective memory thanks to their directors or actors. In 1936, George Cukor adapted *Romeo and Juliet*, with Leslie Howard and Norma Shearer playing the parts of the eponymous heroes. Eleven years later, Cukor directed *A Double Life* (1947) based on *Othello*, a film for which Ronald Colman won an Oscar for his role as a theatre actor who is psychologically disturbed by the part of Othello he is playing on stage. The film thus dramatizes the journey of an actor whose memory is haunted by a

Shakespearean part. This actor's and director's obsession with Shakespeare seems to be a recurrent phenomenon even in the non-fictional world, if we consider how some cinematographic careers are literally fostered by the playwright – so much so that one may wonder whether actors and directors make Shakespeare memorable or whether it is Shakespeare who makes some actors and directors famous.

Every age creates its own Shakespearean filmmaker. Laurence Olivier's film career was mostly built around Shakespeare's works. His patriotic *Henry V*, released in 1944, just before the Normandy Landings, is remembered as the first Shakespearean colour movie. Olivier also adapted *Hamlet* in 1948 and *Richard III* in 1955. The three films oscillate between theatrical performance – with artificial *décors* and long theatrical sequences – and filmic sequences, as if Olivier could not forget his life as a stage actor and wanted cinema to be both an archive for his theatrical performances and a means for Shakespearean reinterpretation and recreation.

This resistance of a theatrical world both to and within the filmic medium is also evident in Joseph Mankiewicz's 1953 *Julius Caesar*, featuring Marlon Brando as Mark Antony. If Olivier feared there might not be enough cinema in his films, Mankiewicz, in contrast, seemed to fear there may not be enough theatre in his cinematographic adaptation, and thus included long theatrical takes in his Shakespearean 'sand-and-sandals' adaptation.[20]

Orson Welles, too, created his own Shakespeare by directing and playing in three Shakespearean films: *Macbeth* (1948), *Othello* (1952) and *Chimes At Midnight (Falstaff,* 1965), the latter combining the two parts of *Henry IV* and *The Merry Wives of Windsor*. Welles's films are all about forgetting Shakespeare: the texts are cut; verse transformed into prose; the order of scenes changed; soliloquies reduced, and lines redistributed. Memory is here not synonymous with artistic constraints, but with creative freedom. Welles reconfigures Shakespeare's plays and adapts Shakespeare to his personal cinematographic style, well-known for its quick cutting, chiaroscuro effects, oblique shots, low or high angle shots and its conspicuous depth of field. In *Othello*, for example, Welles chose to give great prominence to the metaphor of the net used by Iago: the film is 'enmeshed' in images of nets and grids, thus creating echoes between text and image. Interestingly, Welles's aesthetic choices found echoes in Claude Barma's 1962 French television film where the obsessive presence of objects and effects creating a net visually can also be found.[21]

Similar questions about 'original' source are raised in the film *Saptapadi* (1961), Ajoy Kar's interracial love story set in Bengal in pre-Independence India. *Saptapadi* features a stage performance of Othello murdering Desdemona, but the scene appears more as a film-within-the-film than as a play-within-the-film. The on-film audience is never shown in the same shot as the stage actors and does not seem to belong to the same environment. The stage performance also looks to Welles, strongly recalling his *Othello* with the same chiaroscuro lighting and whistling wind. As Richard Burt has analyzed, this postcolonial performance of *Othello* is thus disrupted by an already mediatized, cinematic Shakespeare, displacing Shakespeare's 'centre' from the English theatre to American film.[22] Shakespearean films such as Welles's leave their trace in collective memory and become, in their turn, canonical performances which can be quoted, imitated or transformed.

Franco Zeffirelli's Shakespearean films bear the marks of his former career as a stage designer by showing an interest in building the right *décor* for the creation of a naturalistic world. His *Taming of the Shrew* (1966), featuring Elizabeth Taylor and Richard Burton as Kate and Petruchio, uses the tempestuous story of the two lovers to blur the limits between fictional and real worlds. In his *Romeo and Juliet* (1968), the director reconstructed the Renaissance city of Verona. In 1990, his *Hamlet* is located in the twelfth century, following the legend of Prince Amleth as told by Saxo Grammaticus, one of Shakespeare's sources. Elsinore thus becomes a real medieval castle located in Scotland, recalling the claustrophobic atmosphere conveyed in

Olivier's *Hamlet*. Again, a Shakespearean filmmaker creates a legacy which constitutes a web of remembrance, Shakespearean films dialoguing with one another.

This dialogue may involve homage or confrontation. At the end of the sixties, Peter Hall and Tony Richardson, for instance, rebelled against former ways of filming Shakespeare. In his 1968 film of *A Midsummer Night's Dream*, Hall eschewed magical effects and fairy-tale landscapes in order to emphasize the muddy forest in which the lovers lose their illusions, thus giving life to Jan Kott's dark vision of the play.[23] Richardson set his 1969 *Hamlet* on the stage of the Round House Theatre in London, insisting more on the characters' faces and emotions than on the creation of a realistic environment.

A Shakespearean film encapsulates the memory of the specific historical and material conditions which gave it shape. The social and cultural movements of the 1960s and 1970s encouraged irreverence towards the 'Bard' of Stratford. Peter Brook's *King Lear* and Roman Polanski's *Macbeth* – both released in 1971 – are located in cruel and pagan worlds between the Neolithic and the Middle Ages where the natural elements – water, earth, fire – dominate. These elements are also pivotal in Russian director Grigori Kozintsev's *Hamlet* (1964) and *King Lear* (1971), which both appropriate Shakespeare in order to lead an ideological fight for freedom of expression in the context of the Brezhnev regime. Akira Kurosawa's adaptations – *Throne of Blood* in 1957; *Ran* in 1985 – are similarly embedded in their cultural environment, rewriting Shakespeare for Japan and its devotion to the memory of its samurai warriors.

In the 1970s and 1980s, adaptations for the cinema became rarer while Shakespeare invaded the small screen. Television asserted itself as a memorial vessel through the British Broadcasting Company (BBC) which endeavoured from 1978 to 1985 to 'can' the canon[24] or 'box the Bard'[25] for posterity by filming every single play, as complete and unabridged as possible. As Susan Willis[26] narrates the 'history of the BBC Shakespeare Series', she preserves the memory of a memorizing enterprise. For Holderness, the series was 'produced in the image of the Corporation itself: a classical monument of national culture, an oppressive agency of cultural hegemony'.[27] This 'solidify[ing]'[28] project of creating a so-called definitive version of Shakespeare or, at least, 'a library of Shakespeare video-productions',[29] did not decide clearly what was its target audience and hesitated between producing a pure Shakespeare (by keeping every word from every play) and good TV drama (by restructuring the text). As Michèle Willems points out, the BBC series' adaptation strategy oscillated between three modes: realistic, pictorial and stylized. The realistic mode favoured the 'authentic' reconstruction of places, filming on location, the reconstitution of Elizabethan life and naturalistic sequences with, for instance, 'Hollywood style' battles, while the pictorial mode involved setting the productions within the atmosphere of famous Renaissance paintings by Rembrandt, Veronese or Caravaggio.

Both these representational strategies conjured visual memories that raised the question of their significance in relation to Shakespeare's text. Later productions came to adopt a more stylized and metonymic mode which proclaimed the artificiality of the sets and recalled theatrical conventions, supporting the text rather than competing with it. Ironically, the BBC project of 'encapsulating' Shakespeare may have ended up showing that the memory of the plays is better preserved when the spirit of theatre is carefully nurtured or the text boldly tampered with, as another BBC project successfully demonstrated in 2005. Aptly named *ShakespeaRe-Told*, this new series included four plays each adapted by a different writer, rewritten in modern English and relocated to the present day.

At the end of the 1980s, Kenneth Branagh started to revive Shakespeare on the big screen through a twofold act of remembrance. His films of *Henry V* (1989), *Much Ado About Nothing* (1993), *Hamlet* (1996), *Love's Labour's Lost* (2000) and *As You Like It* (2006) captured, first, the *mises-en-scène* of former stage productions in which Branagh was involved as an actor. Yet, second, they also recycled the Hollywood film genres with which audiences were familiar. *Henry V* became a Vietnam war film; *Much Ado About Nothing*, a screwball comedy; *Hamlet*, an epic thriller; *Love's Labour's Lost*, a musical. These screen adaptations may thus be viewed as both embodying an actor-turned-director's memory of his previous stage work and a personal encyclopaedia of favourite films.

The influence of Branagh's films may be felt in the wave of Shakespearean adaptations in the 1990s, as documented in Samuel Crowl's *Shakespeare at the Cineplex: The Kenneth Branagh Era*.[30] Like Branagh's, Oliver Parker's *Othello* (1995), Richard Loncraine's 1995 *Richard III*, Trevor Nunn's 1996 *Twelfth Night*, Baz Luhrmann's 1996 *Romeo + Juliet* or Michael Hoffman's 1999 *A Midsummer Night's Dream* include numerous references to other films and interpolate segments revealing what the characters imagine, dream or remember. Through flashbacks and mental images, the Shakespeare films of the 1990s reflected on the construction of memory as a *mise-en-abyme* of what they achieved; indeed, according to Mark Burnett and Ramona Wray, these *fin-de-siècle* films 'glance[d] to the future as much as they look[ed] back', using a 'constructed "now" to negotiate what [was] to come' and 'raise questions about things past' in a nostalgic, romantic movement.[31]

Contrasting with this wave of Hollywoodian films, *avant-garde* directors such as Peter Greenaway, Christine Edzard or Adrian Noble found new ways of doing Shakespeare, thereby prolonging the experimental trends of the sixties and seventies. In 1991, Peter Greenaway directed *Prospero's Books*, a film that constantly reminds us that it is a film and is an eminently meta-filmic version of *The Tempest* where the density of visual signs prevails over the story. The obsessive presence of the book and the emphasized materiality of ink in the film led Rothwell to describe *Prospero's Books* as a 'post-post modernist adaptation'[32] and 'A Finnegans Wake of visual art'[33] and suggests that memory depends on the written word. In a world where Prospero (John Gielgud) inherits the words of all the other characters, the enduring presence of the Italian Renaissance can be felt in the image of Prospero's study, reminiscent of the cell in Antonello da Messina's painting *St Jerome in His Study*.[34] If books stand for the memory of Shakespeare's scripts, the act of drowning them takes on a highly symbolic value and suggests that one must forget or 'kill' Shakespeare in order to, perhaps, regenerate him or regain artistic freedom. The visual abundance orchestrated by Greenaway seems to be embedded in a crucial paradox of memory: drowning Shakespeare under layers of artistic artefacts contributes to burying him, but the obsessive presence of books throughout the film questions the very possibility of forgetting Shakespeare.

If Greenaway's film conveys a profusion of signs, Edzard, on the other hand, cultivates minimalism. Her adaptation of *As You Like it* in 1992 situates the story in an urban environment at the end of the twentieth century. The Forest of Arden becomes a suburban wasteland inhabited by outcasts from capitalist society. The gap created between the film's setting of derelict buildings and the dialogues' references to Nature questions the concept of cinematographic verisimilitude. Shakespeare is this time buried under layers of concrete leaving little space for the pastoral world of the play. In *The Children's Midsummer Night's Dream* (2001), Edzard again chooses to get rid of layers of memory by having the parts played by budding young actors, whose minds are not yet encumbered by centuries of Shakespearean films and performances.

Realism is again brought into question in Adrian Noble's 1996 *A Midsummer Night's Dream*, based on a production Noble directed for the Royal Shakespeare Company in 1994. The whole film is in fact a dream made by a young boy who watches each scene with wonder and who sometimes intervenes in the course of events by, for instance, making the moon rotate or by pulling the curtains open for the play of *Pyramus and Thisbe* to begin. The young boy thus becomes a *doppelgänger* of the director, pulling the strings of his own creative dream. In *Titus*, her 1999 adaptation of *Titus Andronicus*, Julie Taymor uses the same kind of device, by having a young boy (played by the same actor, Osheen Jones) attend the spectacle from the beginning to the end of the film. Youth becomes, therefore, both the means of escaping memory and the repository of Shakespearean remembrances.

Memorizing Shakespeare on screen seems indeed to rest paradoxically on processes of erasure and forgetfulness. Mid-way between Hollywood and *avant-garde* trends, Al Pacino's 1996 *Looking For Richard* explicitly aims to get rid of a burdensome Shakespearean legacy, materialized by a large book too heavy for the actor to hold and which he chooses to replace with a handy paperback. In his quest for Richard, which takes the hybrid form of a documentary film of a theatrical performance, Pacino shows that very little of Shakespeare remains in the memory of those he interviews on the streets, the play being reduced in collective consciousness to the famous 'A horse, a horse, my kingdom for a horse'. The film precisely suggests that Shakespeare naturally tends to be forgotten and that the meaning of his texts is to be preserved and constantly 'looked for'.

Looking for Shakespeare

Shakespeare films prolong the memory of the Elizabethan and Jacobean playtexts and testify to the cultural debates on-going at the time of their making, but can also be re-experienced and revisited, generating new criticism and reviews that, in their turn, become reminders of particular moments of spectatorship. If Taymor's *Titus* (1999) may have been made to preserve her acclaimed Off-Broadway production with its spectacular tableaux of stylized violence, the film's gender and sexual politics have been reconsidered over time. In her essay 'Julie Taymor's *Titus* (1999), ten years on',[35] Elsie Walker recalls her first experience of the film – 'I confess that I was blindsided by the sheer extravagance of the film. I wrote about it, ten years ago, with almost unqualified excitement' – to address more disconcerting ideological aspects of the film which only appeared to her as time went by and as more and more essays were written about the production.

A quarter of a century after the 'Branagh era' started, we seem to have entered a post-'Shakespearean-blockbuster' phase. Shakespeare's plays are still vitally filmed, appropriated, quoted and revisited all over the world, but screen adaptations are now generally produced on lower budgets and scales and/or channelled through secondary, albeit transnational and digital, circuits of distribution. This is the case, for example, with the recent adaptation of *Cymbeline* by Michael Almereyda (2014), which was released in France only on DVD under the non-Shakespearean title *Anarchy*, a title reminiscent of *Sons of Anarchy*, a Hamlet-inspired TV series which, like Almereyda's version, is set among a community of bikers. The trailer describes the film as 'a bold new vision of the undiscovered masterpiece by William Shakespeare'[36], but one may doubt whether this version will implant this romance play in collective memory.[37]

As analyzed by Maurizio Calbi, Shakespeare is now remembered through the experimental dissemination of the plays in multi-layered, multi-mediatized afterlives on film, TV and the web.[38] Nevertheless, with the birth of social networks (such as Facebook in 2004 or Twitter in 2006) and new media platforms (such as YouTube in 2005), with the development of videogames and TV series as prominent aesthetic and narrative forms, the Shakespearean films of the 1990s are now fragmented, quoted and deconstructed not only in other films, but in a variety of media, by institutions such as theatre companies or broadcasting networks, or by individuals who interact parasocially[39] and performatively with the materials to create videos that become new sites of cultural negotiations.[40] The films are 'poached' (Henry Jenkins's expression, borrowed from Michel de Certeau's notion of 'braconnage'[41]) as if they have become as canonical as Shakespeare's plays, as if they have actually *replaced* Shakespeare's plays in our collective memory. The various elements of which the films are made – characters, soundtracks, images, actors – are being mined as if they have become fully autonomous and can be freed from the original film. They are recomposed creatively in ways that defy categories and genres.[42] In the animated film *Gnomeo & Juliet* (Kelly Asbury, 2011), the balcony scene features, for instance, a swimming pool, hinting at Lurhmann's original take on the lovers' meeting in the 1996 *Romeo + Juliet* and contributing to the setting, through parody, of a new trend for staging the famous scene.[43]

As the Shakespearean films of the 1990s are dismembered and recycled, cited and parodied, imitated and disseminated, 'original' Shakespeare (in both meanings of the term) continues to be produced through the very acts of iteration, adaptation and mediatization. The films always *re*-appear and stand as surrogate for an ever elusive, evanescent and unstable 'original Shakespeare' that is always-already mediatized. The 1990s wave of Shakespearean films is still spreading ripples that make Shakespeare both present and absent, producing the idea of an 'original' and erasing it at one and the same time.

Rehearsing, memorizing and ... forgetting Shakespeare on screen

Considering the intricate links between Shakespeare, film, memory and performance, it is not fortuitous that so many films should embed the very processes of rehearsing, memorizing and forgetting Shakespeare in their own story worlds. Many films, such as *Dead Poets Society* (Peter Weir, 1989), *In the Bleak Midwinter* (Kenneth Branagh, 1995), *Shakespeare in Love* (John Madden, 1999) or *Caesar Must Die* (Paolo and Vittorio Taviani, 2012) reveal the processes of rehearsing and memorizing Shakespeare's parts. What Rothwell classifies as 'mirror' films[44] dramatize the journeys 'of the actor to the role, and of the role across the duration of the play'.[45] In this genre, backstage and onstage worlds interact with each other. The actors explore their inner and past feelings to identify with the roles and playing the parts helps them solve their personal issues. Though they generally convey an authoritative and universalist view of Shakespeare, these journeys reflect the stories that mainstream theatre people construct among (and for) themselves, and which audiences want to discover as being about the productions' behind-the-scenes work-in-progress. In this way, rehearsals-within-the-film generally reveal the kind of subtext audiences expect to be told about the reasons why (and the ways in which) Shakespearean performances are internalized by the actors and produce powerful emotions and memories among the public.

Rehearsals-within-the-film is a staple of a long tradition of films about the production of shows,[46] revealing how memorizing Shakespeare comes with forgetting or misquoting the lines. In Branagh's *In the Bleak Midwinter*, amateur actors mount a production of *Hamlet* in a disused church. The 'camp' rehearsal sequences play on the actors' faulty memory, which ends up queering Shakespeare's lines – Gertrude's 'Good Hamlet, cast thy nighted colour off' (1.2.68)[47] becoming 'Cast your coloured nightie off'. In *Shakespeare in Love*, a young Shakespeare creates *Romeo and Juliet* while in the throes of love himself. During the opening performance, the actor who plays the Chorus has such a strong stutter that the inset audience, as well as the spectators in the cinema, fear he might 'dry up' in the middle of a sentence, as if Shakespeare's lines could be forgotten when being uttered for the first time. The actor eventually succeeds in delivering his speech, a sign that the Shakespearean show always goes on.

Actual 'drying up' is what happens to the character of Granville Thorndyke (Alan Mowbray), an itinerant 'ham' actor in the western *My Darling Clementine* (John Ford, 1946). Forced to recite Hamlet's 'To be or not to be' soliloquy atop a saloon table, Thorndyke wavers out of fright. Amongst the saloon audience, Doc Holliday (Victor Mature) then takes up the speech, momentarily mesmerizing Marshal Wyatt Earp (Henry Fonda) with his Shakespearean knowledge.

Holliday only falters at 'thus conscience does make cowards of us all' when he suffers a tubercular coughing fit. The film seems to suggest that the memory of Shakespeare's texts circulates among actors and audiences alike – a shared treasure which, in the context of a western, symbolizes the advent of 'civilization' in the wilderness and the American longing to claim a part of the Shakespeare tradition.

Shakespearean excerpts at one and the same time legitimize and challenge the memory of canonical Shakespeare. They can be nostalgic acts preserving 'high' culture and classical values, or they can be audacious acts of deconstruction, questioning our assumptions about artistic originality and the capitalist notion of ownership that thrives on supposed uniqueness. As forms of appropriation, translation and adaptation that quote and misquote Shakespeare, the different ranges of plays-within-the-film at one and the same time acknowledge Shakespeare as 'a repository of symbolic power and knowledge'[48] and challenge the cultural authority surrounding his plays and persona. Some Shakespearean excerpts seem to function as tokens that can be transacted freely, no longer connected to any kind of fixed cultural standard or stable meaning. Yet they still allow us to reflect upon what Shakespeare signifies or engenders, how Shakespeare circulates and is recalled in our postmodern contemporary culture and how he ultimately remains in our 'memory locked'.

Notes

1 See Kenneth S. Rothwell, *A History of Shakespeare on Screen: A Century of Film and Television*, second edition (Cambridge: Cambridge University Press, 2004 [1999]). See Samuel Crowl, *Shakespeare and Film: A Norton Guide* (New York and London: Norton, 2008) in which he relates 'a brief history of Shakespeare on screen' (p. 3).
2 See Mark Thornton Burnett, *Shakespeare and World Cinema* (Cambridge: Cambridge University Press, 2013).
3 See Judith Buchanan, *Shakespeare on Silent Film: An Excellent Dumb Discourse* (Cambridge: Cambridge University Press, 2009).
4 See her on-going project: 'Silents now': http://silents-now.co.uk [accessed 15 December 2015].
5 See Katherine Rowe, '"Remember me": Technologies of memory in Michael Almereyda's *Hamlet*', in *Shakespeare The Movie II: Popularizing the Plays on Film, TV, Video, and DVD*, ed. by Richard Burt and Lynda E. Boose (London: Routledge, 2003), pp. 37–55 (p. 37).
6 See Robert Shaughnessy, 'One piece at a time', in *New Directions in Renaissance Drama and Performance Studies*, ed. by Sarah Werner (Houndmills, Basingstoke: Palgrave Macmillan, 2010), pp. 15–29. In the same section of the volume entitled 'working with the ephemeral', William N. West, in his article 'Replaying early modern performances' (pp. 30–50) writes that 'a crucial quality of performance is that it disappears' (p. 30).
7 See Barbara Hodgdon, *Shakespeare, Performance and the Archive* (London and New York: Routledge, 2016), a work that analyzes how a performance survives as a cluster of different stories and images; see also Paul Menzer, *Anecdotal Shakespeare: A New Performance History* (London: Bloomsbury, 2015), which explores the anecdotes surrounding productions – another way of documenting the lingering memory of a performance.
8 Richard Burt, 'All that Remains of Shakespeare in Indian film', in *Shakespeare in Asia: Contemporary Performance*, ed. by Dennis Kennedy and Yong Li Lan (Cambridge: Cambridge University Press, 2010), p. 89.
9 See W.B. Worthen, 'Fond records: Remembering theatre in the digital age', in *Shakespeare, Memory and Performance*, ed. by Peter Holland (Cambridge: Cambridge University Press, 2006), pp. 281–304.
10 http://onscreen.shakespearesglobe.com [accessed 6 December 2015].
11 Burnett, *World Cinema*, p. 233.
12 See Pierre Nora, 'Between Memory and History: Les Lieux de Mémoire', *Representations* 26 (Spring 1989), pp. 7–25.
13 Robert Hamilton Ball, *Shakespeare on Silent Film: A Strange Eventful History* (London: George Allen and Unwin, 1968), p. 253.

14 See, for instance, Sarah Hatchuel and Nathalie Vienne-Guerrin, 'Remembrance of things past: Shakespeare's comedies on French television', in *Television Shakespeare: Essays in Honour of Michèle Willems*, ed. by Sarah Hatchuel and Nathalie Vienne-Guerrin (Rouen: Presses des Universités de Rouen et du Havre, 2008), pp. 171–97.
15 At the time of writing, the Inathèque has still not been able to find those missing minutes.
16 Burnett, *World Cinema*, p. 233.
17 See the poster of the film at www.imdb.com/media/rm2967784704/tt0020479?ref_=tt_ov_i [accessed 15 December 2015].
18 Lisa S. Starks, '"Remember me": Psychoanalysis, Cinema, and the Crisis of Modernity', *Shakespeare Quarterly* 53 (2002), pp. 181–200 (p. 183).
19 Starks, p. 184.
20 See Francis Bordat, 'Table ronde sur Shakespeare et le cinéma', in *Shakespeare et le cinéma, Actes du Congrès 1998 de la Société Française Shakespeare*, ed. by Patricia Dorval and Jean-Marie Maguin (Paris: ENS, 1998), p. 197. Quoted and translated by Sarah Hatchuel, *Shakespeare: From Stage to Screen* (Cambridge: Cambridge University Press, 2004), pp. 20–1.
21 See Sarah Hatchuel and Nathalie Vienne-Guerrin, '"O monstrous": Claude Barma's French 1962 TV *Othello*', in *Shakespeare on Screen in Francophonia* (2010–), ed. by Nathalie Vienne-Guerrin and Patricia Dorval, Montpellier (France), University Montpellier III, Institut de Recherche sur la Renaissance, l'Âge Classique et les Lumières (IRCL), 2014, www.shakscreen.org/analysis/barma_othello [accessed 30 November 2015].
22 Burt, pp. 73–108.
23 Jan Kott, *Shakespeare Our Contemporary*, translated by Boleslaw Taborski; preface by Peter Brook (London: Methuen, 1967, sd. ed.), pp. 171–90.
24 See Stanley Wells, 'The Canon in the Can', *Times Literary Supplement*, 10 May 1985, p. 522.
25 Graham Holderness, 'Boxing the bard: Shakespeare and television', in *The Shakespeare Myth*, ed. by Graham Holderness (Manchester: Manchester University Press, 1991), pp. 173–89.
26 Susan Willis, *The BBC Shakespeare Plays Making the Televised Canon* (Chapel Hill, London: The University of North Carolina Press, 1991), chapter one.
27 Holderness, p. 181.
28 Ibid.
29 Michèle Willems, 'Verbal-visual, verbal-pictorial or textual-televisual? Reflections on the BBC Shakespeare series', in *Shakespeare and the Moving Image: The Plays on Film and Television*, ed. by Anthony Davies and Stanley Wells (Cambridge: Cambridge University Press, 1994), pp. 69–85 (p. 73).
30 Samuel Crowl, *Shakespeare at the Cineplex: The Kenneth Branagh Era* (Athens: Ohio University Press, 2002).
31 Mark Thornton Burnett and Ramona Wray, 'Introduction', in *Shakespeare, Film, Fin-de-Siècle*, ed. by Mark Thornton Burnett and Ramona Wray (Houndmills, Basingstoke, and London: Macmillan, 2000), p. 4.
32 Rothwell, p. 208.
33 Rothwell, p. 209.
34 Mentioned by Rothwell, p. 211. On this film, see also *Peter Greenaway's* Prospero's Books: *Critical Essays*, ed. by Christel Stalpaert (Ghent: Academia Press, 2000).
35 In *Shakespeare on Screen: The Roman Plays*, ed. by Sarah Hatchuel and Nathalie Vienne-Guerrin (Presses des Universités de Rouen et du Havre, 2009), pp. 23–65.
36 See the trailer at this address: www.youtube.com/watch?v=AUVFoktNATY [accessed 14 December 2015].
37 On this film, see Douglas Lanier, 'Michael Almereyda's *Cymbeline*: The end of teen Shakespeare', in *Shakespeare on Screen: The Romances*, ed. by Sarah Hatchuel and Nathalie Vienne-Guerrin (Cambridge: Cambridge University Press, 2017), pp. 232–50.
38 Maurizio Calbi, *Spectral Shakespeares: Media Adaptations in the Twenty-First Century* (Houndmills, Basingstoke and London: Macmillan, 2013).
39 Paul Booth, *Digital Fandom: New Media Studies* (New York: Peter Lang, 2010).
40 Matt Hills, *Fan Cultures* (New York: Routledge, 2002).
41 Henry Jenkins, *Textual Poachers: Television Fans & Participatory Culture* (New York: Routledge, 1992); Michel de Certeau, *L'Invention du quotidien, I: Arts de faire* (Paris: Union Générale d'Éditions, 1980).
42 See numerous examples of this trend in Sarah Hatchuel, 'The Shakespearean films of the 90s: Afterlives in transmedia in the 21st century', in *Shakespeare 450*, Actes de la Société Française Shakespeare, April 2015, http://shakespeare.revues.org/2945 [accessed 15 December 2015].

43 See the excerpt here: www.youtube.com/watch?v=D6HpUndEtP8 [accessed 15 December 2015].
44 Rothwell, '[T]he second kind (mirror movies) will meta-cinematically make the movie's backstage plot about the troubled lives of actors run parallel to the plot of the Shakespearean play that the actors are appearing in', p. 209.
45 Cary M. Mazer, 'Sense/Memory/Sense-memory: Reading Narratives of Shakespearian Rehearsals', *Shakespeare Survey*, 62 (2009), pp. 328–48 (p. 348).
46 See, for instance, Russell Jackson, *Theatres on Film: How the Cinema Imagines the Stage* (Manchester: Manchester University Press, 2013).
47 *Hamlet*, ed. by Ann Thompson and Neil Taylor (Arden, London: Thomson Learning, 2006).
48 Mark Thornton Burnett, 'Parodying with Richard', in *Shakespeare on Screen: Richard III*, ed. by Sarah Hatchuel and Nathalie Vienne-Guerrin (Rouen: Presses des Universités de Rouen et du Havre, 2005), pp. 91–112 (p. 104).

6

SHAKESPEARE, MEMORY, AND NEW MEDIA

Rory Loughnane

Search engine optimization (SEO) now plays a significant role in online research. All academic publishers know this, of course, which is why authors must supply a list of 'keywords' to help direct web traffic to the publisher's site. It goes almost without saying that the name of Shakespeare carries much greater online weight than any other early modern author.[1] Shakespeare was the third-most searched for author, early or otherwise, in 2015.[2] The SEO process only helps shed a light on what we already know about Shakespeare's predominance in literary studies. Shakespeare sells. And connecting Shakespeare to any study of the early modern period makes it instantly more attractive to publishers, who are safe in the knowledge that such work can potentially reach a wider group of readers. That readership already exists, of course, and early modern literary criticism has always been weighted in an imbalanced way towards Shakespeare. All that has changed is the way in which the reader is directed towards what they might read.

So it is, and has been for several centuries, that even when Shakespeare does not write directly about a subject, his works still regularly emerge disproportionately in critical discussions of such subjects in research about the early modern period. This is certainly the case with the Art of Memory, in which critical interest has blossomed since the mid-twentieth century, and in which Shakespeare's works loom large in several recent studies.[3] This is despite the fact that Shakespeare never makes direct reference to the 'Art of Memory', unlike his fellow dramatists Thomas Nashe, Ben Jonson, and John Webster. Yet it has been persistently claimed that the precepts underlying the art of memory enlivened his artistic practice.

The *Ars Memorativae* is a practice to aid memorization derived principally from classical texts about the fourth canon of rhetoric. Students of the Art of Memory use a technique of *imagines* (images) and *loci* (places) to deposit and store information that they wish to retrieve later for public oratorical use. They labour to construct a series of *loci* in their mind's eye at which they can deposit evocative *imagines* which enable them to recall associatively what they wish to retrieve. The series of *loci* were often recalled from a real public space (such as a temple in the classical period, or a monastery in the medieval period). The *loci* (such as a statue, or window, or corner) should be neither too close nor too far apart. The mnemonic technique relies upon the ease with which the student can move between *loci*, the strict order to the *loci* and *imagines* to be recalled, and the memorability of the *imagines* at each *locus*. There are many fine introductions to the Art of Memory and its historical evolution, so outlining the principles of the technique need not detain us further.[4]

The present discussion is concerned with information storage and retrieval, modern and early modern. There is, of course, an obvious analogy to be made initially between web-based search-and-retrieval and the Art of Memory.[5] Both are information technologies for extending memory reliant upon method and order. Both use prompts, keywords or visualized cues, to retrieve the information sought. The memory student relies upon their ability to utilize networks of coded associations to remember; the Internet is itself a network of networks, while the web is the software that enables you to access and navigate the Internet. Indeed, it is not too tenuous to assert that the organizing principles underlying the Art of Memory—ordered, coded associations enabling the user to retrieve the information necessary to carry out a sequence of operations—also underlie modern computing. Microsoft Windows, as well as the operating system(s) for Apple, might be compared to an imaginary set of rooms (folders) in which recallable items are stored. In these ways, it might be useful to think of the Art of Memory as a sort of pre-history to the computer and Internet age. Especially in the sense that the mnemonic technique was formulated as a practice in oral culture; its remediation into modern times traces a path from written to print to digital culture.[6] In lieu of other means of storing and retrieving information in the pre-modern period, the Art of Memory offered a practical, if cumbersome, way to do so.

New print technologies emerged in the early modern period that easily surpassed the Art of Memory in practicality and utility for information storage and retrieval. So, too, in the modern period new technologies regularly emerge that help us find improved ways with which to preserve or identify the information we want to be retrievable. For students of early modern literature, the advent of electronic digital databases of early modern writing over the past two decades has increased access to texts that were otherwise often only consultable with considerable effort. Such databases (primarily, *Early English Books Online* and *Literature Online*) are now widely used by early modern researchers. There can be little doubt as to the importance of these databases, though their considerable limitations (in both content and search function) are sometimes less well understood. This discussion, building upon several recent excellent articles about database limitations, investigates how new media can be utilized to better understand the cultural resonance in early modern England of that most remediated of methods, the Art of Memory.

We will begin with a brief overview of Shakespeare, memory, and New Media, more generally, before turning to the intersection of two emergent technologies, one early modern and one modern. The former is the printing press. The latter is the database technology that provides online access to some of what is extant from that early English print culture. In a pleasingly meta way, the subject emergent in English print culture that we will trace is the Art of Memory; that is, the subject's whose emergence we will investigate through the use of modern technologies is that same subject whose principles underlie that modern technology. It has been asserted that Shakespeare knew the Art of Memory, that he understood the technical aspects of this method. What we can glean from his works to support this assertion is more ambiguous. Using *Early English Books Online*, both the most heavily used and most heavily criticized database, we will track (within certain parameters) the emergence of writing about the Art of Memory in early English print culture and gauge its wider cultural resonance from these (and comparative) results.

Shakespeare and new media

The years 2014 and 2016 saw a veritable explosion of interest in Shakespeare and his works. Instead of picking between celebrating the 450th anniversary of the poet's birth and commemorating the 400th anniversary of his death, Shakespeareans worldwide, professional and amateur, were minded to honour both. Conferences and symposia (e.g. Shakespeare 450 in Paris, 2014, and the World Shakespeare Congress in Stratford and London, 2016) and special events and performances (e.g. Shakespeare 400 at Chicago and Shakespeare 400 at the Globe, and the British Council's programme of events 'Shakespeare Lives') were organized across the world to memorialize the poet's life and achievements. Three new editions of the Complete Works were also launched in this two-year period: the Bedford Shakespeare (2014), the Norton Shakespeare (2015), and the New Oxford Shakespeare (2016–). Coinciding with such public interest and research events were several new online initiatives. These included, for example, shakespearedocumented.org, an online exhibition of primary-source materials related to the life of Shakespeare and bymewilliamshakespeare.org, a primary source exhibition with a digital component (as part of the overall shakespeare400.org project run out of King's College London). Both the Norton and New Oxford Shakespeare editions have a prominent digital component. Most of these new initiatives include some form of social media (Twitter, Facebook, YouTube, etc.) to inspire public interest in Shakespeare's works.[7] These accounts add to the growing number of prominent (and less so) Shakespeareans who operate on social media, and call attention to Shakespeare-related events. Indeed, there are two 'William Shakespeare' avatars on Twitter operating with varying success.[8] The one-off events in this two-year period helped sustain and embellish Shakespeare's legacy; the new online resources made accessible primary source materials, literary and non-literary, in unprecedented ways. Memorializing Shakespeare, as all these events and initiatives attest, is big business.

The harnessing of New Media to Shakespeare studies is an unsurprising development. From Michael Best's *Shakespeare's Life and Times* (available on floppy disk in 1988) to Donald Foster's promised (but undelivered) *Shaxicon* in the early 1990s, to the online resources we see today, including the *Internet Shakespeare Editions* (internetshakespeare.uvic.ca, which grew out of Best's initial project), *Oxford Scholarly Editions Online*, the British Library's *Shakespeare in Quarto* (www.bl.uk/treasures/shakespeare/homepage.html), and *The Shakespeare Quartos Archive* (www.quartos.org), Shakespeareans have been quick to adopt increasingly sophisticated technologies to support research. Other online resources, only in part related to Shakespeare, such as the *Oxford Dictionary of National Biography* and *British History Online*, complement such research activities. More specifically theatre-oriented resources include the *Lost Plays Database* (www.lostplays.org) and Catherine Richardson's forthcoming digitization of Martin Wiggins's *British Drama 1533–1642: A Catalogue*. The online databases of *Early English Books Online* and *Literature Online* will be discussed below.

In the context of the present discussion's interest in information retrieval, one project merits special mention. The *Six Degrees of Francis Bacon* project (sixdegreesoffrancisbacon.com, now in Beta mode) data-mines the searchable database of the *Oxford Dictionary of National Biography* to attempt to construct a 'social network' of early moderns, tracing the personal relationships between individuals in the period. Many personal relationships can be easily established—spouse, relative, employer, patron, collaborator, etc.—but the project promises to be most useful in recording hitherto unrecognized (probable or possible) relationships in the period. Tracing the exposure of individuals to an idea, a concept, is less easy.

In lieu of other absent resources (unrecorded private and public discourse; unsearchable, unavailable, lost, or destroyed, manuscripts and printed materials) we must make do with what we can search readily. If an author makes mention of or discusses in writing an idea current in that period, and if that writing is extant in manuscript or print, and can be firmly attributed to that author, then we can establish that that author was familiar (more or less) with that certain concept. Let us say that this author only ever makes mention of this concept once in his extant writing. If we can then date the piece of writing with some accuracy, that can help us establish the latest date in which that author became familiar with this idea. This is the basic principle behind using allusions to contemporary events to date texts. As the speculative references to Essex's triumphant return from the Irish wars (in 1599) in one of the Chorus's speeches in *Henry V* (first printed in the 1623 Folio) make clear (5.0.30–34), topicality can quickly become out-dated or invalid. But it helps to establish the time-line for this piece of writing—November 1598 to a time closer to Essex's departure on 27 March 1599—and reveals to us what were some of Shakespeare's preoccupations (and his presumptive audience) at the moment in time.[9] He could not have written these lines one year earlier (when Essex's campaign was unknown) or one year later (when Essex's campaign had failed). The printed record, though post-dating the events by some twenty-four years, thus memorializes the cultural resonance of that idea (that Essex will return triumphant) at that moment in time. The Irish wars obviously constitute a very specific series of events and the allusion in *Henry V* is well known. But how might we apply some of the same principles to track the cultural resonance of an idea across an entire period?

Online database resources such as *Early English Books Online* (*EEBO*) and *Literature Online* (*LION*) allow for the possibility of tracking chronologically the emergence of certain key words and phrases in print across the period. However, as we will see, this process is not without its flaws and shortcomings. Our focus here will be *EEBO*, an early experiment in digitization which has since become a standard research tool.[10] The 'use and misuse' of *EEBO*, in Ian Gadd's phrase, has inspired much recent scholarship. *EEBO* is a set of bibliographical records for all English books printed before 1700 (over 125,000 predominantly English texts), plus digital pictures of these books. Most of what is on *EEBO* is not searchable (only the bibliographical records; digital pictures are not searchable, of course), and a project is ongoing, the *Text Creation Partnership* (*TCP*), to make available some 70,000 of the texts on *EEBO* in searchable, digitally encoded electronic editions. *TCP* is a set of transcriptions of the words in the books in EEBO, initially (Phase One) 25,000 transcriptions and then (Phase Two) a further 45,000 transcriptions to make the total of 70,000 transcriptions. Being typed-up transcriptions, these files are by definition full-text searchable. Currently *TCP* is nearing the completion of Phase Two. If an institution subscribes to both *EEBO* and *TCP*, its version of *EEBO* is enhanced to make *EEBO-TCP*, although nothing on the *EEBO* search engine shows this except the option (in the drop-down "Limit to:" field) to search "Items with keyed full text". As Phase Two of *TCP* progresses, batches of keyboarded full texts from *TCP* are added to *EEBO-TCP* as they become available, and currently there are 60,000 searchable full texts in *EEBO-TCP* because of this. TCP has released all of Phase One into the public domain, available as one download of 25,000 transcription files from the *TCP* websites in the UK and US and also searchable within the *TCP* websites. As such, any use of *EEBO-TCP* to search for key words and phrases is thereby limited within the constraints of the digitized materials available. The transition from microfilm to digital to searchable texts is slow, and each remediation introduces the possibility of the introduction of further errors, oversights, and omissions. Caveats thus abound when using *EEBO* and *EEBO-TCP*, and that is before one even considers the limits of print as a record. Manuscripts are not close to being gathered into a searchable text—if they ever could be—and the networks they represent are even more complex than those represented in print. *The Catalogue of English Literary Manuscripts, 1450–1700* (www.ies.sas.ac.uk/research/current-projects/catalogue-english-literary-manuscripts-1450-1700-celm) and *Scriptorium: Medieval and Early Modern Manuscripts Online* (http://scriptorium.english.cam.ac.uk/) are invaluable resources but neither seeks to provide searchable transcriptions (which would, of course, be subject to error). And even manuscript has limits. The influence of an individual in a prominent position (as we will note for a teacher like Alexander Dicsone in the case of the Art of Memory) may have as much to do with the currency of an idea or concept as would the existence of a more robust print and manuscript record.

Thus, while many obstacles prevent or temporarily delay our efforts at retrieval, what is searchable within the databases of early English print currently offers a useful if treacherous path forward. Better technologies continue to emerge, but much material is inevitably and irretrievably lost.

What remains, and what is readable and searchable within what remains, offers only a partial insight into the cultural currency of certain ideas and concepts. The remainder of this discussion will consider both qualitative and quantitative approaches to establishing the resonance of certain ideas within a culture.

Mnemonics and the Shakespearean stage

Frances A. Yates made a daring claim in *The Art of Memory* (1966) that caused a sensation within intellectual circles of her day, though the dispute itself has since been largely forgotten. In chapter 16, tucked away after her largely careful explication of the history of the Art of Memory from antiquity to the early modern period, Yates asserted that the layout of Robert Fludd's memory theatre was modelled upon the Globe Theatre. She based this claim upon an engraving of a physical theatre space in Fludd's *Utriusque Cosmi . . . Historia*. Yates's monograph was instantly heralded as an important work upon its publication. However, some critics, including Frank Brownlow, Glynne Wickham, and I.A. Shapiro, thought the specific connection to Shakespeare's Globe tenuous and unsupported by any evidence.[11] Shapiro argued that the illustration was based upon the Blackfriars stage instead. Within a year of publication and following several incredulous reviews, Yates doubled-down in an article in *The New York Review of Books* and (in her gentle but firm way) responded specifically to Shapiro's counter-argument in *Shakespeare Studies*, concluding that Fludd's illustration 'presents . . . with absolute reliability the arrangement of entrances, upper chamber, and terrace on the stage wall of the Globe theatre'.[12] Three years later, Yates published a book-length study, *The Theatre of the World* (1970), in an attempt to lend further basis to her claim about the architectural layout of the Globe. Yates's expanded thesis was that there was a Vitruvian revival in late Elizabethan England (broadly influenced by the writings of John Dee, and later Fludd and Inigo Jones), and that this revival influenced the architectural design and structure of James Burbage's The Theatre (and, later theatres such as the Globe and New Globe), literally and symbolically denoting that 'all the world's a stage'.

It is certainly true that writings about Vitruvian design were available when The Theatre was built, and Burbage (and others involved in theatre construction) might have read Dee's 'Mathematicall Praeface' to Henry Billingsley's English translation of Euclid's *Elements* (1570) where such material is in part discussed. Nonetheless, the degree of influence upon Elizabethan playhouse design is contestable at best—so, too, the degree to which the early modern theatrical space can be recovered from Fludd's illustration. Moreover, we are on even less solid ground again when discussing how such architectural symbolism might have altered Shakespeare's own conception of the purpose and principles of drama, or how this relates specifically to the Art of Memory. Yet, as many scholars have noted, a formalized approach to memorization may be found frequently in Shakespeare's plays, from the fallen building that might 'leave no memory of what it was' in *The Two Gentlemen of Verona* (5.4.10) to Richard Plantagenet's 'book of memory' in *1 Henry VI* (2.4.101) to Hamlet's tables and Ophelias rosemary 'for remembrance' (4.5.175).[13] Shakespeare could have first heard of the Art of Memory when studying rhetoric as a schoolboy in Stratford; the canonical works of the Art of Memory—the anonymous *Rhetorica Ad. C. Herennium*, Cicero's *De Oratore* and *De Inventione*, and, possibly, Quintilian's *Institutio Oratoria* (though the latter may have been unsuited to class-work)—were part of the *de facto* Tudor core curriculum.[14] The presence of (albeit indirect) references to formal techniques for memorization in Shakespeare speaks to, but does not prove that the author was thoroughly familiar with the concept of the Art of Memory. It also suggests a degree of awareness of the subject for at least some audience members in the period.

To qualify and better understand this general degree of awareness, let us first consider an exchange in John Webster's added 'Induction' scene to John Marston's *The Malcontent*:

SINKLO   Nay, truly, I am no great censurer, and yet I might have been one of the college of critics once. My cousin, here, hath an excellent memory indeed, sir.
SLY   Who, I? I'll tell you a strange thing of myself, and I can tell you, for one that never studied the art of memory, 'tis very strange too.
CONDELL   What's that, sir?
SLY   Why, I'll lay a hundred pound I'll walk but once down by the Goldsmith's row in Cheap, take notice of the signs, and tell you them with a breath instantly.
LOWIN   'Tis very strange.
SLY   They begin as the world did, with Adam and Eve. There's in all just five and fifty. I do use to meditate much when I come to plays too.

(Induction, 95–108)[15]

Several particulars of the 'Art of Memory' are articulated by Sly: first, the architectural mnemonic approach is clearly established, with Sly stating that he needs only walk down the street in Cheapside once and memorize the signs as he goes which he will later be able to recall; second, the distinct order of the signs, as Sly moves from one shop to the next; third, the shop-signs described, with their images, recalling the use of evocative or associative images in such mnemonic schema; fourth, the reference to *Genesis*, implicitly suggesting that the micro design of the mnemonic schema relates to a macro divine play; and, fifth, Sly's (otherwise unexplained) use of this architectural mnemonic technique when he attends plays to presumably memorize the lines he hears. The Art of Memory is here emphasized as a fantastical technique, perhaps lending itself towards fraudulent activities. Sly brags audaciously about what he can remember, a fact that may be obvious to the audience; John Stow's *Survey of London* (1598) records that Goldsmith's Row 'continueth in number, tenne faire dwelling houses, and fourteene shops, all in one frame vniformely builded, foure stories high, bewtified towards the stréete' (sig. L4ᵛ). But there may be more to the swindle: before Sly has even completed that *one* walk, he is already telling the others about one of the signs, indicating that he has already memorized them. In this comic passage, is the Art of Memory something that is itself intrinsically humorous or worthy of ridicule? It may all be in jest, yet Webster is still careful to indicate that he understands its principles. Any joke will surely be lost to the audience (and later readers) if they have little understanding of what the 'Art of Memory' means. Webster may be gently poking fun at the technique and, moreover, the pretensions of those who claim to use it (or claim not to use it to perform feats of memory), yet the elementary success of this comic exchange relies upon the author's belief that his audience will at least grasp the basic principles of the mnemonic technique.

Textual Memory *I*

The Malcontent is well known and often read, and Webster's allusion to the Art of Memory appears in almost all studies of the subject. But how might we use electronic databases to better understand the context within which the allusion appears? Using *EEBO* to guide our study (by which I mean from henceforth the searchable texts generated via *TCP*), let us attempt to measure quantitatively the proliferation of references to the 'Art of Memory' in the period. It is certainly an imprecise measure for the cultural resonance of the Art of Memory but we must begin somewhere. If we begin by inputting 'Art of Memory' to our search box (ticking both variant spelling and variant form) and search chronologically from 1473–1699, it will turn up a reading list of 308 texts (the phrase occurs 435 times within these texts). This high number, as we will see, is misleading on several counts.

If we examine each use of the phrase, we would note that there is much duplication in the various forms of reprint. We would also note that the bookseller Nathaniel Brookes seems to have a quasi-monopoly on late seventeenth century texts that include references to the 'Art of Memory'. This is because Brookes includes a catalogue of books to be sold at his shop in many of his publications, and this advertisement includes Richard Saunders's (Sanders) writings about the Art of Memory. Having checked each instance for duplication and advertisements and removed these from our count, we would be left with the first occurrence of discursive uses of the phrase in extant searchable texts. These number 217 texts, stretching from Laurence Andrewe's 1527 additions to William Caxton's printing of Gossuin of Metz's *Image du Monde* (*The myrrour: dyscrypcyon of the worlde*) to the anonymous 'A funeral oration; as it was delivered at Darby-House: The 6 of Feb. 1648' in *The Maze* (dated 1699 on *EEBO*). Andrewe's text is not transcribed on *EEBO*; the 'hit' derives from the transcribed title page that describes the 'many meruaylles' of the world, including 'rethorike with the arte of memorye'. (We will also see below that Hugh Plat's un-transcribed *Jewel House of Nature* is excluded from our set of search results even though it includes a section about the subject.) However, Andrewe's text does actually include a subject-specific discussion of the *Ars Memorativa* as the fourth canon of rhetoric and a description of its principles (tildes are marked with a ~ sign):

> Memory Artyfycyall is that which men cal Ars memorativia/ The crafte of memory/ by which craft thou mayste wryte a thynge with y mynde/ & set it in thy mynde as euydely[16] as thou mayst rede and set the wordes whych thou wrtyest with inke upon parcheme~t or paper. Therefore in this arte of memory thou muste haue laces . . .
>
> (sig. D3^{r-v})

Frustratingly, if 'Art of Memory' had not been in the title, a search of *EEBO* using these parameters would not have delivered this earliest hit. The author of the later 'funeral oration' from *The Maze* feels no need to explicate the meaning of the phrase; it is now, we might assume, a familiar reference:

> I have many times heard him maintain it (to the gallantry of his spirit be it spoken) that it was one of his ambitions to learn perfectly the Art of Memory, to the end he might receive a sense of his injuries the better.
>
> (sig. I2^{r-v})

But when is 'now'? *EEBO* dates *The Maze* to 1699, but the title page dates it to 1659. The mark of the '5' in the date is corrupt and vaguely resembles a '9'. *EEBO*, therefore, records the work's date incorrectly. This means that the text would be excluded from any searches restricted by date to, say, the decade of the work's first composition and publication. The actual latest references to the 'Art of Memory' in extant print of the seventeenth century as digitized by *EEBO* are to be found in these four texts from 1697, one a dedicated memory treatise: these are the anonymous *An Apology for the Parliament*, Ezekiel Polsted's *Kaloz Telonesantai or, The Excise-man*, William Berkeley's *Diatribae discourses moral and theological* and Marius D'Assigny's dedicated study of the subject, *The Art of Memory*.

Another difficulty with establishing a chronology is with references to the 'Art of Memory' in plays and other performance pieces that were printed much later than when they were first performed (or formed part of a repertory). For example, consider the case of John Fletcher's *Father's Own Son*, first performed c.1615, but only printed in 1639.[17] The primary source for the play itself was Honoré d'Urfé's *Astrée*, published in 1610. The title-page to the later edition notes performances at Blackfriars. *Father's Own Son* appears to be the earlier playing title, while *Monsieur Thomas* is a revised later version of that play.[18]

> *Cell[ide]*. What losse of youth,
> What everlasting banishment from that
> Our yeares doe only covet to arive at
> Equall affections and shot together:
> What living name can dead age leave behind him
> What art of memory but fruitlesse doating?
> *Fra[ncis]*. This cannot be.
>
> (sig. F2ʳ)

In our working chronology, should we note the date of first performance or publication? Similar issues occur for Philip Massinger's *The Bashful Lover*, unprinted until 1655 (in octavo with two other Massinger plays), but first licensed and performed at Blackfriars in 1636. In such uses of the phrase 'Art of Memory', I have opted to include the likely date of authorship/first performance instead of publication. My goal here is to attempt to establish the wider cultural resonance of the 'Art of Memory' in Shakespeare's lifetime and thereafter. In the case of performance pieces, specifically, it seems unlikely that an author would include a passing reference to the 'Art of Memory' if they thought their audience could not (even vaguely) understand it. Perhaps the same case could be made for uses of the phrase in sermons, though these would have reached a much wider readership in print than as occasion pieces.

Taking these caveats, alterations, and corrections into account, we can now track the use of this phrase in 217 searchable *EEBO* texts between 1473 and 1699. These findings are shown in Figure 6.1. While it is necessary to recognise the fact that many more texts were printed in, and are extant from, the seventeenth century, a general sense of the emergence of the phrase in print can be determined. While only 13 texts directly refer to the 'Art of Memory' by 1579, the phrase occurs in 65 texts between 1580 and 1639. The vogue for use of the phrase reaches an apex between 1640 and 1659, during the time of the Civil War and Interregnum, where it occurs in 67 texts; a period that created, in a sense, a rupture in the country's national memory, culminating in the passing, and fall-out to, Charles II's Acts of 'Indemnity and Oblivion.' References to the 'Art of Memory' thereafter decline, though the frequency of occurrence still greatly exceeds any period in the sixteenth century.

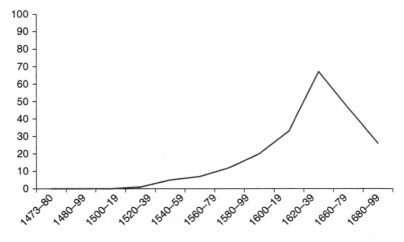

Figure 6.1 References to the 'Art of Memory' in searchable *EEBO* texts 1473–1699.

widely renowned for his medical writings—after all, the section discussing the Art of Memory is only part of his greater work—and particularly his writings about alchemy, including his collection, *Verae alchemiae artisque metallica* (Basel, 1561).

    Outlines of the general principles of the technique do occur, however, in various sixteenth-century texts. We have noted above that Laurence Andrewe's discussion of the Art turns up in our *EEBO* search because the title-page refers to the 'Art of Memory'. However, other discussions of the Art of Memory are excluded from our count because (a) the author never uses the trigram 'Art-of-Memory' or (b) the work has not yet been transcribed. We will consider one notable example of each type.[19] Stephen Hawes' *The Pastime of Pleasure* (1509) appears to be the first printed English text that discusses the Art of Memory, or, as he labels it in his poem, 'memorial art'. The work was first printed in 1509 though only fragments of that printing are extant. The following originates in John Wayland's 1554 reprinting of the poem, where Hawes discusses 'the retentife memory / Whiche is the fift, must euer aggregate / All matters thought':

> If to the oratour, many a sundry tale
> One after other, treatably be tolde
> Then sundry ymages, in his closed male
> Eche for a matter, he dothe then well holde
> Like to the tale, he doth then so beholde
> And inwarde, a recapitulation
> Of eche ymage, the moralization
> Whiche be the tales, he grounded priuely
> Upon these ymages, signification
> And when time is, for him to specifye
> All his tales, by demonstration
> In due order, maner, and reason
> Then eche ymage, inwarde dyrectly
> The oratour, dothe take full properly
> So is enprynted, in his propre mynde
> Euery tale, with whole resemblaunce
> By this ymage, he dothe his matter finde
> Eche after other, withouten variaunce
> Who to this arte, will geue attendaunce
> As therof to knowe, the perfectnes
> In the Poetes schole, he must haue intresse
> Then shall he knowe, by perfect study
> The memoriall arte . . .
>
>   (sig. F2^v–F3^r)

Hawes outlines the basic principles of the art and its function—private meditation, use of images in 'due order', enabling the orator to deliver his speech—though the reader would find it difficult to put this technique into practice. A much more detailed explication of the specifics of the Art appears in Sir Hugh Plat's *The Iewel House of Art and Nature* (1594). Plat's 'Jewel House' is an eclectic collection of various techniques, recipes, and quasi-scientific practices. For example, near to the section about the Art of Memory is advice upon 'Howe to know when the Moon is at the full by a glasse of salt water' and a how-to guide for making 'parchment cleere and transparent, to serue for diuers purposes'. In the section about the Art of Memory, Plat expresses particular displeasure with the Scotsman Alexander Dicsone (Dickson), a disciple of

Giordano Bruno when the latter spent time in England in the 1580s. Plat notes that Dicsone has been teaching the subject 'of later yeres in England, and whereof he hath written a figurative and obscure treatise', meaning *De umbra rationis et judicii* (1583). Plat dismisses Dicsone as a money-grabbing charlatan, his students as card-cheats who use the Art of Memory to gain an unfair advantage, and decries their willingness to 'turne an honest and commendable invention into meere craft and cousenage' (sig. N3ʳ). What precedes this is a careful, but plain explication of the architectural mnemonics of places and images using sets of ten (decades) in each case.

It is not difficult to empathize with the pragmatic Plat; the Art of Memory is for him a fundamentally practical, useful art, and seemingly far removed from the esoteric strains Yates describes in the continental tradition, stretching from Lull to Camillo to Bruno. English mercantile culture does not make an easy bed partner with the more mystical elements in the evolution of the Art of Memory. One of the more tedious engagements with mnemonics in seventeenth-century writing is Thomas Willsford's 'Art of Memory' table in *The Scales of Commerce of Trade* to be used to memorize the correspondence between weights and measures and shillings, groats, and pence. Far removed from any classical Art of Memory originating in Rhetoric, here is a representative example of one 'benefit of this Table . . . to ease the Art of Memory' (sig. H6ᵛ):

> If one pound of Cheese cost 3 ¾ D, what comes the Weigh unto? This properly belongs to a certain quantity of Wooll and Cheese, consisting of 32 Cloves, whereof one contains 8 lb, so the Weigh is 256 lb. which having found in the table, I seek it in the colume of pence, and find 1 L 1 sh 4 D. and in the row of farthings 5 sh 4 D. the summe 1 L 6 sh 8 D. and being that there was 3 times so much to be imposed in either denomination, the summe is 4 L for the Weigh at the rate propounded.
>
> (sig. H7ʳ)

It is a little more taxing to gauge earlier English interest, and investment, in the subject. And, more specifically for this discussion, to gauge the type of exposure Shakespeare would have had to the subject beyond his time at grammar school. Though there has been a recent outpouring of interest in Shakespeare and Memory, as this book attests, Shakespeare and the Art of Memory remains a contested subject to a large extent. Jonas Barish was an early dissenter, insisting that Shakespeare did not 'show any curiosity about the so-called *artes memorativae*, that weird melange of mnemotechnics and occultism that dazzled so many Renaissance philosophers and scientists'.[20] Garrett A. Sullivan, who records Barish's complaint, sought in his monograph study about memory and forgetting to 'correct a critical overemphasis on artificial memory evident since at least the groundbreaking work of Frances Yates'.[21] What is undeniable, as all commentators note, is that Shakespeare is deeply preoccupied with issues surrounding memory. Connecting the formal mnemonics of the Art of Memory to Shakespeare, whether in the vein of Bruno and his disciples or the blunt pragmatism of many sixteenth-century English writers as typified by Plat and earlier writers about the study of rhetoric, remains in dispute and perhaps impossible to prove. Nonetheless, we can at least begin to establish some of what he could have known.

Adding Hawes and Plat to our list, Table 6.1 consists of forty-five English texts printed before or during Shakespeare's lifetime that mention in passing or at length the Art of Memory, as gleaned from, and expanding slightly upon, our *EEBO* trawl (with modernized titles).

This list is certainly incomplete; as noted above, *EEBO* cannot lay claim to comprehensively representing all extant printed materials from the period. The Art of Memory is alluded to in other texts in the period, such as George Puttenham's *The Art of English Poesy* (1589) and Francis Meres's *Palladis Tamia* (1598), both texts we might assume Shakespeare knew. However, narrowing our list to direct references to the 'Art of Memory', or specific

Table 6.1 Shakespeare's potential reading in the Art of Memory

Stephen Hawes	The Pastime of Pleasure	1509
[Laurence Andrewe]	The Mirror and Description	1527
Peter of Ravenna (trans. Robert Copland)	The Phoenix	1545
Polydore Vergil (compiled by Thomas Langley)	De Inventoribus Rerum	1546
Richard Sherry	A Treatise of Schemes and Tropes	1550
Thomas Wilson	The Art of Rhetoric	1553
Thomas Pecke	Advice to Balam's Ass	1558
Guglielmo Gratarolo (trans. William Fulwood)	The Castle of Memory	1562
Etienne Pasquier (trans. Geoffrey Fenton)	Monophylo	1572
Lodowick Lloyd	The Pilgrimage of Princes	1573
Guglielmo Gratarolo	A Direction for the Health	1574
Levinus Lemnius	Touchstone of Complexions	1576
Raphael Holinshed	Chronicles	1577
Francesco Petrarch (trans. Thomas Twyne)	Physic against Fortune	1579
Pierre Viret (trans. Thomas Stocker)	The Cautles, Canon and Ceremonies	1584
William Webbe	A Discourse of English Poetrie	1586
Abraham Fraunce	The Lawyer's Logic	1588
Thomas Nashe	Strange News	1592
Thomas Nashe	The Unfortunate Traveller	1594
Juan Huarte (trans. R.C. Esquire)	Examination of Men's Wits	1594
Hugh Plat	Jewel House of Art and Nature	1594
Philip Sidney	Apology for Poetrey	1595
Miles Mosse	Arraignment and Conviction of Usury	1595
Richard Greenham	Propositions	1597
Thomas Playfere	The Pathway to Perfection	1597
Ben Jonson	The Case is Altered	1597
Robert Albott	Wit's Theatre of the Little World	1599
Lodowick Lloyd	Stratagems of Jerusalem	1602
James Godskall	The Ark of Noah	1604
John Webster (Induction scene)	The Malcontent	1604
Francis Bacon	Advancement of Learning	1605
John Brinsley	The True Watch	1606
Gervase Markham	Cavelrice	1607
John Denison	A Three-fold Resolution	1608
Alexander Craig	Epitaph' for Dickson	1609
Cesar De Plaix	Anti-Coton	1611
Joseph Hall	Contemplations	1612
Benvenuto (trans. Mr. King)	Passenger	1612
Lewis Bayly	The Practice of Piety	1613
Robert Dallington	Aphorisms	1613
John Hoskins	A Sermon'	1615
John Fletcher	Father's Own Son	'c.1615
Pierre D'Avity (trans. Edward Grimstone)	Estates, Empires and Principalities	1615
Sampson Price	Ephesus Warning	1616
Robert Anton	The Philosopher's Satyr	1616

discussions about the subject, helps us to establish some grounds for the textual circulation of writings about this subject before and during Shakespeare's lifetime. If Shakespeare wished to read about the Art of Memory beyond his Latin classwork, the most complete accounts were to be found in the corrupt translation of Ravenna's *Phoenix*, the dedicated chapter in

The Castle of Memory, and Hugh Plat's *Jewel House*. The subject of memory training is discussed briefly in Hawes's *The Pastime of Pleasure*, Wilson's *Art of Rhetoric*, Lloyd's *The Pilgrimage of Princes*, Sidney's *Apology for Poetry*, and Bacon's *Advancement of Learning*. These other references to the 'Art of Memory' would make Shakespeare familiar with the phrase, though inform him little about the technique. These additional references, frequently but not necessarily more casual in nature, give us a sense of general cultural resonance of the phrase 'Art of Memory', and what it implies, in the period.

Textual Memory *II*

To achieve a better sense of the textual circulation and cultural resonance of such key phrases as the 'Art of Memory' in the period, let us compare another memory-related phenomenon found frequently in early modern English writing. A cognate of the Art of Memory that is also trackable chronologically across the period is the use of the Latin-originating phrase *Memento Mori*. Like the Art of Memory, it has its own pagan foundation myth. It means, literally, 'remember to die' (as the infinitive of the verb form), but the phrase carried with it a great store of associated meanings. As the *OED* records, it could mean 'remember death' or 'remember that you must die'. The faithful had not only to remember their own mortality, but also to be mindful of what occurs at the moment of one's death. Death, mortality, the cessation of life on this earth, the separation from those still living, only partially represents what was to be recalled. The action of recollecting an inevitable future death also informed how the faithful were to act in the present. Similar to the inclusion of the mnemonic arts under the banner of the Cardinal Virtue of Prudence, as advocated by scholastic theologians following Cicero, the *Memento Mori* tradition, similarly Christianized, was concerned with habitual Christian behaviour. Its edifying lesson—remember one's mortality—aided the faithful in keeping to the path towards salvation, directing them away from the road to sin and damnation. Nonetheless, by the sixteenth century, *Memento Mori* could simply invoke the iconographic tradition of the use of a skull or timepiece to indicate the relentless march of time and the transience of life (most famously depicted in *vanitas* paintings of the European Renaissance). In England, the *Memento Mori topos* became almost a shorthand for 'death's head' (skeletal remains of the skull) and vice versa, in the sense that the presence of skulls, cadavers, bones, clocks and other time-pieces in a painting or sculpture was an iconographic shorthand for the phrase (and connoted meaning of) *Memento Mori*.

Unlike the 'Art of Memory', Shakespeare does refer directly to '*Memento Mori*', juxtaposing it with 'a death's head' and marking the contemporary practice of using such symbolic imagery for meditative purposes.

[BARDOLPH] Why, Sir John, my face does you no harm.
[SIR JOHN] No, I'll be sworn; I make as good use of it as many a man doth of a death's head, or a *Memento Mori*. I never see thy face but I think upon hell-fire and Dives that lived in purple—for there he is in his robes, burning, burning.

(III.3.2732)[22]

Sir John (Falstaff) here makes 'good use' of Bardolph's ruddy face as a reminder of the ceaselessly burning fires of hell and thereby his own mortality. Yet the comparison is nuanced by the sinful activity implicated by Bardolph's 'burning' redness—venereal disease. The further comparison to the biblical figure of Dives—a rich man (*dives* literally means 'rich man') sent to damnation for his maltreatment of Lazarus (*Luke* 16.19–31)—assures us that what Sir John sees in Bardolph is a reminder of hell and eternal punishment specifically.

Let us begin our search by employing the same parameters as with 'Art of Memory', taking account of the likely performance date (*Monsieur Thomas*, for instance, also occurs in these results) for plays, and excluding reprints and duplications. Several new issues affect our search results. The first is that certain iconography without any textual accompaniment is para-textually recorded in some *EEBO* transcriptions. This means that if there is an image of a skull or bones, etc., but there is no use of the phrase '*Memento Mori*' then a description of the iconography might (or might not) be included, recording in square brackets: [Memento Mori . . .]. This occurs, for example, in the search results for Josuah Sylvester's *Lachrimae Lachrimarum* (1612), Thomas Wentworth Strafford's *The Two Last Speeches* (1641), Anon. *Great Britain's Warning-Piece* (1689) and Anon. *A Poem on the Death of the Queen* (1694). It could be protested that '*Memento Mori*' is implicitly (or even explicitly) present here, but as with the 'Art of Memory' we are only tracking uses of the phrase textually. The second issue is related to the first. From the mid-1660s on there was a vogue for including images of skulls, bones, etc., adorned with the phrase '*Memento Mori*' in the printing template for elegies, and this accounts for a significant number of the references to *Memento Mori* in the latter half of the seventeenth century. In fact, some fifty-one separate texts in *EEBO* (1665–1699) included '*Memento Mori*' in this way. I have elected to exclude these fifty-one texts from the overall results, because although they represent a significant textual trace of the phrase, it is essentially duplicative and non-discursive.[23] Finally, 'death's head' sometimes, but not always acts as a synonym for '*Memento Mori*', and there could be grounds for similarly tracking the use of that much more widely used phrase as simultaneously representing the emergence of this concept. However, sometimes a skull is just a skull. In addition, the Latin phrase *Memento Mori* was essentially amalgamated into English; Elisha Coles glossed the phrase in his *An English Dictionary* (1677) as of Latin origin and to mean 'remember dying'. For these reasons, I have chosen to focus simply on the use of '*Memento Mori*', as represented by Figure 6.2 (set to the same scale as Figure 6.1). By excluding some subsets of the *Memento Mori* tradition, it might seem as if the data has been skewed to draw the sets of results closer together, but my treatment of it concurs with the treatment of the earlier phrase 'Art of Memory' (and, for the purposes of this discussion, makes little difference to the findings for texts printed before or during Shakespeare's lifetime).

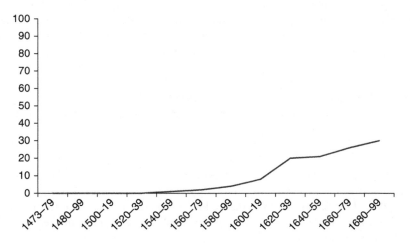

Figure 6.2 References to '*memento mori*' in searchable *EEBO* texts 1473–1699.

Table 6.2 Shakespeare's potential reading about *memento mori*

David Lindsay	*Dialogue*	1554
Richard Day	*Christian Prayers*	1569
Anon.	*Palace of Private Pleasures*	1579
John Carpenter	*Remember Lot's Wife*	1588
William Rankins	*The English Ape*	1588
John More	*A Lively Anatomy of Death*	1596
Thomas Nashe	*Summer's Last Will and Testament*	1600
John Hanson	*Time is a Turncoat*	1604
William Birnie	*The Blame of Kirk-Burial*	1606
Samuel Rowlands	*A Terrible Battle . . . Time and Death*	1606
Thomas Walkington	*Solomon's Sweet Harp*	1608
Stephen Jerome	*Moses His Sight of Canaan*	1614
John Fletcher	*Monsieur Thomas*	1615

Shakespeare may make reference to '*Memento Mori*', but there are many more (extant and searchable) individual texts that make use of the distinct phrase 'Art of Memory'. Indeed, only the following (again, extant and searchable) texts before or during Shakespeare's lifetime refer to '*Memento Mori*' in our *EEBO* search (titles are once more modernized) (Table 6.2 above).[24]

These results should not make us seriously doubt the wider cultural impact of the *Memento Mori* tradition; it is plainly of crucial importance to our understanding of early modern English funereal and mourning practices. Richard Day's *A Booke of Christian Prayers* is one of the most important in the period and '*Memento Mori*' occurs forty-nine times in that text alone. However, by the time Shakespeare wrote *1 Henry IV* (c.1598), there were only six other English texts (as per the outcome of our search) where the phrase occurred. In comparison, by the time of Shakespeare's death, when he had not once referred directly to artificial memory, there were (at least) forty-five printed English texts that referred to the 'Art of Memory'.

New directions

There was no *EEBO* or *LION* or any other digital database to aid Frances Yates when she set out to write about *The Art of Memory*. She drew on the resources of the Warburg Institute, her home institution, the London library, the British Museum, and major holding libraries at Oxford and Cambridge, while also conducting further research at libraries in Florence, Milan, Rome, Venice, and Paris (pp. xiv–xv). We can only speculate about what scholars of her generation might have done had they had access to such modern search technology. Despite the flaws and limitations of our various searches above, these new technologies enable scholars to identify in an expedient manner the occurrence of certain words and key phrases within a database's searchable transcribed texts. The format is still evolving, what is searchable in the databases is still expanding, and the search mechanisms are still improving. As we have seen at various points in this discussion, it is of vital importance that we assess our findings qualitatively as well as quantitatively. Many immensely popular works have been lost, while other works that were probably obscure and barely read when first written have survived the passage of time and are now fully searchable in online databases. However, by way of a conclusion to this discussion, I think we can begin to make some tentative statements about the cultural resonance of the Art of Memory in Shakespeare's England.

Shakespeare did not choose to refer directly to the Art of Memory, though it is implausible to suppose that he was entirely unaware of the practice. A sudden increase in printed references to the 'Art of Memory' beginning in the late Tudor period strongly suggests that the phrase itself became a part of the greater English early modern cultural lexicon during Shakespeare's lifetime: from eight references before Shakespeare's birth to a further thirty-seven references over Shakespeare's lifetime to another 122 references between 1617 and 1659. For some young people, including Shakespeare most likely, their first encounter with the Art of Memory would have been through their education in the classical texts of Rhetoric. They need not have fully understood its precepts or principles, but their class-work would have introduced them to the basic concept of memory training using places and images. It may well have seemed (and been discussed as) a cultural oddity from antiquity. Those who entered higher education at Oxford, Cambridge or the Inns may have been familiar with the debates surrounding the Art of the Memory in the 1580s (e.g. between Dicsone and William Perkins). Bruno's notoriety (and execution in 1600) could have contributed to a rise in general awareness of the subject, though we need not assume this. Erasmus's condemnation of the practice might also have been known. The upwardly mobile of English society might have read about the technique in Plat's *Iewel House* or in any of the dedicated studies of the subject such as Gratarolo's, or, less plausibly, Ravenna's: each work emphasizes the utility of the technique in a wide range of professions. For the uneducated, the 'Art of Memory' probably became a relatively familiar reference to an obscure practice about whose application they had little idea.[25] The phrase itself might have more broadly conveyed some type of secret or hidden knowledge, with writers of the period frequently implying that practitioners of the Art used it for fraudulent or dubious purposes.

With the advent, and continuous update, of digital databases we now have access to an unparalleled abundance of searchable material with which we can perform acts of recall that would have seemed like witchcraft to early moderns like Shakespeare, and like science fiction to mid-twentieth century scholars like Yates. How we act upon these latest innovations in memory and recall will be what distinguishes our own practices with memory as scholarship from parlour trick.

Acknowledgements

I am grateful to Gabriel Egan, William E. Engel and Andrew J. Power who provided invaluable feedback upon an earlier version of this essay.

Notes

1 Search Engine Optimization refers to the process whereby webmasters employ frequently searched for 'keywords' to maximize web traffic for their sites.
2 He trailed after Harper Lee, in second place, who published a 'new' book for the first time in 55 years, and Martin Luther King. http://jmediagroup.net/top-10-most-searched-authors-of-2015/ (Accessed June 2016). As of May 2016, Google Trends records that 'William Shakespeare' has been in the top 10 most searched for authors for the past 149 months. A Google search for 'William Shakespeare' produces some 144 million results. By comparison, a search for 'Christopher Marlowe' produces 435,000 results (both June 2016). https://www.google.com/trends/topcharts#vm=cat&geo=US&date=201510&cid
3 See Rebeca Helfer's chapter in the present collection.
4 See, for example: W.S. Howell, *Logic and Rhetoric in England, 1500–1700* (Princeton, NJ: Princeton University Press, 1956); Walter J. Ong, *Ramus, Method, and the Decay of Dialogue: From the Art of Discourse to the Art of Reason* (Cambridge, MA: Harvard University Press, 1958); Paolo Rossi, *Logic and the Art of Memory: The Quest for a Universal Language*, trans. Stephen Clucas (London: Athlone Press, 2000). First published as *Clavis Universalis* in 1960; Frances A. Yates, *The Art of Memory* (London: Routledge and Kegan Paul, 1966); Mary Carruthers, *The Book of Memory: A Study of Memory in Medieval Culture* (Cambridge: Cambridge University Press, 1990); Mary Carruthers, *The Craft of Thought: Meditation,*

Rhetoric, and the Making of Images, 400–1200 (Cambridge: Cambridge University Press, 2000); Mary Carruthers and Jan M. Ziolkowski, eds., *The Medieval Craft of Memory: An Anthology of Texts and Paintings* (Philadelphia, PA: University of Philadelphia Press, 2002); Janet Coleman, *Ancient and Medieval Memories: Studies in the Reconstruction of the Past* (Cambridge: Cambridge University Press, 1992); Lina Bolzoni, *The Gallery of Memory: Literary and Iconographic Models in the Age of the Printing Press*, trans. by Jeremy Parzen (Toronto: University of Toronto Press, 2001); Lina Bolzoni, *The Web of Images: Vernacular Preaching from its Origins to Saint Bernardino da Siena* (Aldershot: Ashgate, 2004); Jocelyn Penny Small, *Wax Tablets of the Mind: Cognitive Studies of Memory and Literacy in Classical Antiquity* (London: Routledge, 1997); Anna Maria Busse Berger, *Medieval Music and the Art of Memory* (Berkeley and Los Angeles: University of California Press, 2005); Michael T. Clanchy, *From Memory to Written Record 1066–1307*, 2nd edn. (Oxford: Blackwell, 1993); and Raphael Samuel, *Theatres of Memory, Vol. 1: Past and Present in Contemporary Culture* (London: Verso, 1994).

5 A connection between modern technologies for remembering and early modern practices of memorization has been made before. Peter Stallybrass *et al.*, discussing the use of erasable writing tables in the period, suggested that they served a similar function as a Palm Pilot 'recording dates, addresses, accounts'. However, the authors warned that 'Renaissance tablets ... shaped and were shaped by a structure of memory different from our own. In particular, they were part of a pedagogical system that emphasized the gathering of commonplaces, their organization under topical headings, and their redeployment as the materials of one's own writing' (410–411). Now, of course, the Palm Pilot has given way to the increased functionality of the tablet computer and the smartphone. Peter Stallybrass, Roger Chartier, John Franklin Mowery, Heather Wolfe, 'Hamlet's Tables and the Technologies of Writing in Renaissance England', *Shakespeare Quarterly*, Vol. 55, No. 4 (Winter, 2004), 379–419.

6 For printing as the 'first truly major practice of remediation', see John Guillory, 'Genesis of the Media Concept', *Critical Inquiry*, 36.2 (2010), 321–362 (esp. 324).

7 For YouTube as a platform for teaching and learning about Shakespeare, and for Shakespeare and New Media more broadly, see Stephen O'Neill's excellent account, *Shakespeare and YouTube: New Media Forms of the Bard* (London: Bloomsbury Arden, 2014).

8 See @Wwm_Shakespeare and @Shakespeare. Interestingly, while Shakespeare has more cultural capital, Chaucer and Marlowe have arguably more interesting Twitter avatars: see Chaucer Doth Tweet, @LeVostreGC and @Marlowe_Society.

9 For the date and authorship of *Henry V*, see Gary Taylor and Rory Loughnane, 'The Canon and Chronology of Shakespeare's Works', in Gary Taylor and Gabriel Egan, eds. *Shakespearean Authorship: A Companion to the New Oxford Shakespeare* (Oxford: Oxford University Press, 2017), pp. 526–527. Richard Dutton suggests that this Chorus (and the others) are 'later additions', and proposes that the passage alludes to the return of Lord Mountjoy after victory in Kinsale in 1601 (*Shakespeare, Court Dramatists* (Oxford: Oxford University Press, 2016), 182). Stylistic tests, however, support an earlier date of 1599 (Taylor and Loughnane, p. 527).

10 For various accounts and critiques of the use of *EEBO* in scholarship, see: Kichuk, Diana. 'Metamorphosis: Remediation in *Early English Books Online (EEBO)*', *Literary and Linguistic Computing*, 22.3 (2007), 291–303; Ian Gadd, 'The Use and Misuse of *Early English Books Online*', *Literature Compass*, 6.3 (2009), 680–692; Bonnie Mack, 'Archaeology of a Digitization', *Journal of the Association for Information Science and Technology*, 65.8 (2014), 1515–1526; and Martin Mueller, 'The EEBO-TCP Phase I Public Release', *Spenser Review*, 44.2.36 (Fall 2014).

11 I.A. Shapiro, 'Robert Fludd's Stage-Illustration', *Shakespeare Studies* 2 (1966), 192–209.

12 Frances Yates, 'The Stage in Robert Fludd's Memory System', *Shakespeare Studies* 3 (1967), 163 (138–166).

13 All references to Shakespeare's works are derived from *William Shakespeare: The Complete Works*, ed. Stanley Wells, Gary Taylor, John Jowett, and William Montgomery (Oxford: Clarendon Press, 1986).

14 For Shakespeare's reading in rhetoric, and the broader Tudor curriculum, see: T.W. Baldwin, *William Shakspere's Smalle Latine and Lesse Greeke* 2 volumes (Urbana: University of Illinois Press, 1944), and Peter Mack, *Elizabethan Rhetoric: Theory and Practice* (Cambridge: Cambridge University Press, 1996).

15 All references are to John Marston, *The Malcontent*, ed. Bernard Harris (London: Ernest Benn Limited, 1967).

16 'idly' or, perhaps, 'readily'.

17 Martin Wiggins gives a date range of 1613-19, but his 'best guess' is 1615. See *British Drama: A Catalogue*, Vol. VI: 1609-1616 (Oxford: Oxford University Press, 2015). (Wiggins, 1788)

18 The comic story is of a love triangle between Francesco, Valentine and Cellide. Valentine is an older man, betrothed to Cellide, and when he returns from travels abroad he brings home Francesco, a much younger man. Francesco immediately falls ill – we later discover the cause of his ailment to be lovesickness; he has fallen in love with Cellide. Valentine cedes all interest in Cellide to the younger man. And in a twist in the finale, we discover that Valentine is actually the long-lost father of Francesco. In the scene from which this passage is excerpted, Valentine overhears a private exchange between Cellide and the sickly Francesco. Cellide's presence and possible kiss seems to cure Francesco, but then he is wracked by guilt because of his strong feelings of friendship for Valentine. Cellide attempts to justify the action, saying Valentine wants him to be cured.

19 Two other notable discussions of memory composed after Shakespeare's death, but not appearing in our search, merit special mention. William Basse's *A Helpe to Memory and Discourse* (1620) discusses the value of 'pretious' memory to discourse, and briefly introduces the subject of the Art of Memory (without using that specific three-word phrase):

> in this Artificiall memory distinguished by places, the places are as it were paper leaues, the *Ideas* or Images, letters, the disposition of the Images in their places, the method for reading, all which are a charge to the memory, yet the Authors in this Art say, this is done more by the vnderstanding then the memory: The helpes whereof by this Art *memoratiue*, they would proue to be as effectuall, by these conceiued fictions in the eye of the mind, as those we remember by the visible eye of the body.
>
> (sig. B5ʳ⁻ᵛ)

Another is the private correspondence about mnemonics between John Beale, Samuel Hartlib and others between 1661–1663. *EEBO* has film of these manuscripts, though they are not yet available in transcription.

20 Jonas Barish, 'Remembering and Forgetting in Shakespeare', in *Elizabethan Theater: Essays in Honor of S. Schoenbaum*, ed. R.B. Parker and S.P. Zitner (Newark: University of Delaware Press, 1996), pp. 214–221 (p. 219).

21 Garrett A. Sullivan, Jr., *Memory and Forgetting in English Renaissance Drama: Shakespeare, Marlowe, Webster* (Cambridge: Cambridge University Press, 2005), p. 5.

22 The 1986 Oxford edition changes the surnames 'Falstaff' to 'Oldcastle' and 'Bardolph' to 'Russell'.

23 Please contact me to request to see an alternate graph with these results included.

24 I have excluded the use of the phrase in Edward Vaughan's *A Method, or Briefe Instruction* (1590), where it is to be found in a Latin passage.

25 In modern terms, compare the concept of 'Cloud Computing' for those without any knowledge of how information is stored and shared online. A casual reference to, or joke about, 'the Cloud' does not demand any great insight into the technicalities of this practice.

Figure 7.1 Image courtesy of Zoe Bramley, author of *The Shakespeare Trail: A Journey into Shakespeare's England* (Amberley Publishing, 2015).

7

SHAKESPEARE, MEMORY AND CONTEMPORARY PERFORMANCE

Shakespeare in Shoreditch

Sarah Dustagheer

At the end of New Inn Broadway in Shoreditch, East London, a building site is covered with graffiti: 'Here is where the original Globe Theatre stood in 1599'. It is an improvised and inaccurate memorial to what lies behind the wooden white hoardings. In 2008 Museum of London archaeologists discovered the remains of the Theatre, a playhouse which staged some of Shakespeare's earliest works. It was this venue that Shakespeare's company the Chamberlain's Men dismantled, taking its timbers across the river Thames to use in the construction of the Globe. The contemporary street art conflates these two related early modern playhouses into one with the misnomer, the 'Globe Theatre'. This graffiti and the remains of the Theatre are insubstantial traces of sixteenth century playing in Shoreditch. Yet since the discovery of the remains of the Theatre, and

The extent to which the Art of Memory is discussed varies greatly in each of these texts. To give a representative sample of well-known authors who use the phrase, it occurs in the poetry of John Taylor and Robert Herrick, the plays of Philip Massinger and John Dryden, the sermons of Sampson Price, John Donne, and Thomas Manton, the historical works of Raphael Holinshed and William Howell, the philosophical writings of Francis Bacon and Robert Boyle, Robert Burton's writings on melancholy, John Melton's writings against astrology, Charles Cotton's erotica and writings about games, and Thomas Vaughan's discussion of the Rosicrucians. Though references to the 'Art of Memory' are ubiquitous, book-length studies dedicated to improving memory (naturally and artificially) are actually quite rare. Only six are printed in the period: Peter of Ravenna's *The Art of Memory, that otherwyse is called the Phenix*, trans. Robert Copland (1545), Guglielmo Gratarolo's *The Castel of Memorie*, trans. William Fulwood (1562), John Willis's *The Art of Memory* (1621), Henry Herdson's *Ars Memoriae* (1651), Richard Saunders's *Art of Memory* (1653) and Marius D'Assigny's *The Art of Memory* (1697).

We notice immediately that only the first two of these works were printed in English before or during Shakespeare's lifetime. Commentators discussing the Art of Memory in Shakespeare's works often make mention of Copland's translation of Ravenna's *Foenix* (Venice, 1491) as though it was quasi-canonical in the period. The truth is that it was printed (poorly) once and the text is extremely difficult to follow. Here is a representative sample from the beginning of the book (tildes are marked with a ~ sign, but otherwise the original orthography is retained):

> THe fyrste conclusyon shalbe suche. This arte is, and consysteth of places and magnytudes The places be as cardes or scrolls or other thynges for to wrytte in. The ymages be ye symylytudes of the thynges that we wyll retayne in mynde. Than I wyl fyrst p~pare my carde wherin we may colloke & ordre ye ymages in places. And for the foundacion of this fyrst co~clusyon I wyll put foure rules. THE fyrste is this. The places are the wyndowes set in walles, pyllers, & anglets, with other lyke. THE .ii. rule is. The places ought nat to be to nere togyther nor to fare a so~der. For the nerenesse trouble greatly the naturall memory, by the opposytion of thynges for yf ye places were to fare dystaunt. We wyl recyte with a lytel leaser the thynges that shalbe gyuen to places, where by they shalbe of meane dystaunce. And that shalbe done whan one is. vi. fote fro ye other.

The reader must dive in headfirst at the deep-end, intuiting for her or himself that these rules for 'places and magnytudes' refer to the proper order and form for the *loci* to be used in creating one's memory space, converting a physical space into a psychic one. Yates proposed that Ravenna 'laicised and popularized memory and emphasized the purely mnemotechnical side' (pp. 113–14); this may be true on the continent (about which Yates was writing primarily), but I have found no evidence to support the same conclusion in England. Yates readily admits that in Ravenna's original there is a 'good deal of unexplained confusion and curious detail'. Such difficulties are not alleviated in the version of the text printed in England; doubly removed, the 1545 text is a weak translation of an unacknowledged French translation of Ravenna's text. Fulwood's translation of Gratarolo's *De Memoria Reparanda* (Basel, 1553) is much better and far more thorough. *The Castle of Memory* was first printed in 1562 and reprinted in 1563 and 1573. In *A Consolation for our Grammar Schooles* (1622), John Brinsley advises the use of two books 'for the helpe of Memorie' beyond those lessons learned in the 'Grammar schoole and others': chapter 6 of Gratarolo's '*Castle of Memorie*', wherein one would find 'diuers good rules and precepts for memorie' and 'Maister Willies his book of Memorie' called *Mnemonica siue Reminiscendi* (already translated in 1621 as *The Art of Memory*) (sig. L4^{r-v}). However, we should still be cautious about over-stating the influence of either translation. Gratarolo was more the remains of another early modern playhouse the Curtain in 2012, artists in this unique area of London have made attempts to remember, revive and respond to histories of Shakespeare in Shoreditch. Drawing on interviews with these artists, in what follows I seek to complicate current critical conversations about cultural memory and performance through practitioner testimony, and to examine the political dynamics of Shakespeare and memory in contemporary theatre-making.

The Theatre's remains and its graffiti sign appear to confirm Peggy Phelan's belief that 'Perhaps the only way to confront memory, especially performance memory, heavy with betrayals and forgetting, is to begin with its loss'.[1] Phelan's now seminal argument seems apt for the small segment of red brick foundation which marks where an entire playhouse stood, and for a makeshift memorial that forgets the real name of the venue (the Theatre) and confuses it with another (the Globe).[2] Notably writing in response to the excavations of another sixteenth century playhouse (the Rose in 1989), Phelan highlighted the ways in which such remains revealed much about our attitudes to buried bodies and loss; and in doing so she stood in contrast to theatre historians that argued the Rose might allow access to 'truths' about early modern theatre.[3]

Yet several critics have challenged Phelan's view of the finality and impermanence of performance. For Joseph Roach and Diana Taylor, rather than forgetting and loss, performance is deeply bound up with memory and constructing ideas of the past.[4] Roach argues that

> the memories of some particular times and places have become embodied in and through performances [...] The social processes of memory and forgetting, familiarly known as culture, may be carried out by a variety of performance events, from stage plays to sacred rites, from carnivals to the invisible rituals of everyday life.[5]

It is possible, I will suggest, to see the theories of Phelan, Roach and Taylor played out through Shakespeare's contemporary cultural reimagining in Shoreditch. The work of artists in this area reveals much about the meaning and nature of cultural memory and the role of performance in the construction of the theories of the past, as this chapter will demonstrate. I begin by establishing the history of early modern theatre in Shoreditch and the meaning and operation of cultural memory in the area; the next section analyses who and what 'Shakespeare' is in Shoreditch and the ways memories of the playwright are tied up with artistic identity. The chapter concludes by examining the political, social and cultural function of Shakespearean history in East London. Before beginning it is necessary to outline some detail about the three companies under consideration, and the individuals who kindly gave up their time for interviews: Tom Chivers of London Word Festival, Felix Mortimer, Joshua Nawras and Francesca Duncan of the Shakespeare in Shoreditch Festival and Ben Blyth of The Malachites.[6] All interviewees are under 35 and had worked in the area for between two and six years.

London Word Festival (LWF) was an annual three-week festival of poetry, spoken word, performance and music events that took place in East London, which ran from 2009–2011. In its first year the founders Tom Chivers, Marie McPartlin and Sam Hawkins produced an event called 'Shakespeare in Shoreditch'.[7] On 11 March 2009 in an underground bar situated just off Curtain Road, novelists/spoken word artists Siddhartha Bose, Joe Dunthorne, Jean Hannah Edelstein, Salena Godden and Lee Rourke performed their reinterpretations of five different Shakespeare plays, set in contemporary Shoreditch in mind. For example, Dunthorne turned King Lear into singer/songwriter/producer and Shoreditch resident Ridley Truck – his debut album carrying the title 'I Named My Daughters After STDs' – and Lear's daughters into Ridley's biggest fans, Errol, Regina and Delia. All five writers were accompanied by projected live drawings from Mustashrik, the illustrator behind the Manga version of *Julius Caesar*.[8]

The Shakespeare in Shoreditch Festival (SSF) spans 2014 to 2016, the two years between the 450th anniversary of the playwright's birthday and the 400th anniversary of his death.[9] For ten days in October 2014 creative producers Felix Mortimer and Joshua Nawras, with producer Francesca Duncan curated a series of events including commissioning ten playwrights to reinterpret Shakespeare's characters in relation to contemporary Shoreditch. In the same way as LWF, writers were encouraged to re-think Shakespeare through this specific London location. The results included Thomas McMullan's *Three Loose Teeth*, a meditation on sleeplessness and jealousy based on *Macbeth* and performed along an alley way in Hoxton; *The Best Pies in London*, a re-telling of *Titus Andronicus* by Abi Zakarian set in a pie and mash shop; and Tobias Wright's *Heir to the Throne*, a family feud in a hair salon based on *King Lear*. The Festival also saw writer-in-residence Annie Jenkins produce 1,000 short plays (some only one line) over ten days from a shed at the Rose Lipman building.[10] In addition, SSF involved a series of workshops on playwriting from writers and performers involved in the project, screenings of Shakespeare-inspired films and a discussion panel with Shakespearean academics.

Finally, The Malachites are an East London-based theatre company committed to performing what they call the 'Shoreditch 19', the 'works written by Shakespeare while he was living in Shoreditch, some of which premiered at Shoreditch's two Elizabethan theatre venues: the Theatre (New Inn Yard) and the Curtain (Hewitt St, off Curtain Road)'.[11] The Malachites perform at sites associated with the early modern theatre industry: several of their productions have taken place in St Leonard's Church, the place where Shoreditch resident Shakespeare may well have worshipped in the sixteenth century. In addition, the company staged *A Midsummer Night's Dream* on the roof of Rockwell House, just above the site of the Curtain; and they have produced *King Lear* and *Macbeth* for the Rose Bankside.

Shoreditch history and cultural memory

Shoreditch was the location for the start of Shakespeare's career, as well as the first place he lodged at in the city. 'This area,' I have suggested elsewhere, 'was a highly representative part of London for a newcomer to the city like Shakespeare to choose, packed with immigrants, a range of trades, people of differing ages, and differing degrees of affluence, from the rich to the very poor indeed'.[12] For sixteenth-century moralists, Shoreditch was notorious for 'Theatres' and its 'Kissing booths [brothels], Bowling alleyes and such places where the time is so shamefully mis[s]pent', leading to 'the corruption and utter destruction of youth'.[13] In making East London his home, Shakespeare joined other members of the theatre community in choosing to live in this seemingly illicit area, outside the jurisdiction of the City of London. They included Chamberlain's Men actor Richard Burbage, comic actor Richard Tarlton, playwrights Christopher Marlowe, Robert Greene and actor Gabriel Spenser, who was buried at St Leonard's Church after being murdered by Ben Jonson in a duel. Shoreditch was a hub of theatrical activity; as home to the Theatre and the Curtain it witnessed the first performances of *Romeo and Juliet* and *Henry V*. It was also the location for what we shall see has become an infamous occurrence in the Elizabethan theatre industry. In December 1598 the Chamberlain's Men fell out with their landlord Giles Allen and dismantled their Theatre and recycled the materials to build the Globe in Southwark – this was seen as an act of theft by Allen and a court case enthused, which is the main source of knowledge about the incident.[14]

It is the rich history of Shakespeare in Shoreditch that Ben Blyth of The Malachite Theatre Company feels 'lies forgotten in public consciousness'. His company aims 'to reconnect Shakespeare with Shoreditch' for its audiences. Similarly, SSF producers introduce the Festival which 'celebrates' the playwright's works by pointing out that 'Shakespeare's life in Shoreditch is far from the public consciousness'.[15] For Tom Chivers of LWF, 'Shakespeare was a part of Shoreditch's history, an important part of it, maybe an overlooked part of it, and even now you'll walk through the streets of Shoreditch and you'll find little evidence of Shakespeare's existence'. LWF's Shakespeare in Shoreditch event was, he suggests, 'a very small part of a much broader cultural awakening' about this 'overlooked' past. All three companies figure their work in the context of a Shakespearean history that has been 'forgotten' and 'overlooked' and that can be 'reconnected' and 'reawakened' in the public conscious. There is very much a cultural, even political, imperative here as these artists feel a sense of urgency that Shoreditch is not part of the vast public knowledge of Shakespeare. The language of remembrance they use (forgetting, consciousness, 're'-words) also alerts us to the operation of cultural memory, a term which requires some exposition.[16]

French sociologist Maurice Halbwachs first argued that memories were socially created and constructed; ideas of the past were shared together in families, social classes, political and religious groupings.[17] Building on this work, critics such as Paul Connerton, Pierre Nora, and Aleida and Jan Assmann began to consider past occurrences beyond society's living memory that are preserved through shared cultural practices and events.[18] Their far-ranging enquiries considered the social mechanisms (Connerton especially), the places (key for Nora), the cultural structures and the actions (the Assmanns) through which society shares memory. In a synthesis of this scholarship, Astrid Erll defines the somewhat 'multifarious notion' of cultural memory as 'the interplay of present and past in socio-cultural contexts'.[19]

Often this interplay is prompted by an anxiety about loss or forgetting; Nora suggests that 'We speak so much about memory because there is so little of it left'.[20] This seems to be true of artists in Shoreditch who have created work in response to the loss of Shakespeare's history in the 'public consciousness'. Of particular relevance to performance, I suggest, is the notion that cultural memory is 'the media, institutions and practices by which social groups construct a shared past'.[21] Interpreted in the context of cultural memory theory, performance – and by extension arguments about its endurance put forth by Roach, Taylor and others – forms one of the media and practices by which social groups construct a sense of their past. As Colin Counsell notes, performance is 'an essentially *constructive* medium' and '[h]owever and wherever they appear, bodies and their actions are shaped by, given form *to*, figures drawn from cultural memory'.[22] Placing Shakespeare back in Shoreditch through staging of the plays or performances of creative adaptations of his work, these companies seek to construct a historic presence for the playwright in East London; a presence that has a very specific identity.

Who is 'Shakespeare' in Shoreditch?

The term 'construction', used throughout criticism on cultural memory, is key here as it is very much selective narratives and ideas about Shakespeare's experiences in Shoreditch with which these artists engage. Specifically, it is one narrative that keeps emerging: 'We, very arrogantly, saw ourselves as a young Shakespeare coming to Shoreditch and doing his most radical work and being involved in building theatres, and taking them across the river and stealing wood'. In this comment, Felix Mortimer of SSF considers the inception of the Festival and why he found the history of Shakespeare in Shoreditch compelling. He notes the way in which his identity as an artist is reflected in a memory of Shakespearean past. The 'stealing' of the timbers of the Theatre also emerges in Joe Dunthrone's reflections on his involvement in the LWF's Shakespeare in Shoreditch event. He writes:

Nowadays, Shoreditch is too expensive for most artists and writers; even in Elizabethan times, they had problems keeping hold of their workspace. Burbage's landlord wanted to reclaim the space on which The Theatre was built (for live/work apartments?!) and so kicked out Shakespeare's company, the Lord Chamberlain's Men. According to theatre legend, however, Burbage had a cunning plan: in the dead of night on Christmas Eve, he and his stage carpenter carried the theatre – piece by piece – across the frozen Thames, and gave it a new location on the south of the river. They called it The Globe.[23]

Writer and novelist Dunthorne uses his words carefully here. Recalling a 'theatre legend' and 'cunning plan' (perhaps a reference to the BBC sitcom *Blackadder*, which offered comic pastiches of history), Dunthorne seems playfully aware that he is invoking myth and even hyperbolic interpretation, echoed in his own dramatic language ('in the dead of the night', 'piece by piece'). Yet, in a similar way as Mortimer, he connects Shakespeare's difficulties as an emerging playwright to contemporary artists in Shoreditch, both struggling to keep hold of their 'workspaces' in the face of greedy landlords. Reviewing the LWF event, blogger Guilia Merlo also recalls that same mythical dismantling of the Theatre and makes the link between the story and modern Shoreditch culture explicit, arguing 'The story teaches us [...] that young kids in skinny jeans haven't discovered anything new in terms of cultural vibrancy: Shoreditch was always where it's at'.[24]

The performances created in Shoreditch, then, do not solely seek to foster memory of the playwright. For these contemporary East London artists the recollection and reiteration of a version of the Shakespearean past also forms part of the construction of their identity. Writing 'radical' work, struggling to secure workspace and willing to take risks for his art, this 'Shakespeare' fits right into contemporary culture in Shoreditch. This process – the remembering of the 'timber myth' by Mortimer, Dunthorne and Merlo and the similar interpretation of its meaning – exemplifies the link between cultural memory and identity formation, as noted by many memory theorists. 'The series of iconic and symbolic events and myths become a core part of cultural knowledge of the community, such that distant memory plays an important role in its identity,' writes Siobhan Brownlie about the history of the Norman Conquests in the UK.[25] Her words, though, are applicable too to the process occurring in Shoreditch. The Shakespearean 'timber myth' has been incorporated into a wider sense of identity for artists in a particular location. Recalling their 'Shakespeare' links a contemporary artistic community to that of Elizabethan theatre-makers, both groups struggling to survive in a distinct locale of London.

We are familiar with analysing links between identity and interpretations of Shakespeare's plays. According to Terence Hawkes, we *use* them [the plays] in order to generate meaning' such that 'In the twentieth century, Shakespeare's plays have become one of the central agencies through which our culture performs this operation'.[26] Alongside a range of literary scholars, even memory theorist Aleida Assmann has drawn on the playwright's work, particularly the history plays, to discuss theories of remembrance and national identity.[27] In the case of productions in Shoreditch, though, it is Shakespeare's biography not his plays – his (unproven) role in the dismantling of the Theatre – that forms the basis of identity-making. This phenomena reflects a strong trend in Shakespeare studies over the last fifteen years. As Graham Holderness noted in 2009, 'the quest for the life that precedes the works has become again a legitimate object of inquiry' with biographies of Shakespeare by Peter Ackroyd, Katherine Duncan-Jones, Stephen Greenblatt, Bill Bryson, Charles Nicholl, James Shapiro, Stanley Wells and Michael Wood, to name a few, achieving varying degrees of popular success.[28] What we see in the performance work on Shakespeare in Shoreditch is the trickle-down effect of this trend, with theatre-makers similarly turning their attention to the playwright's life for creative inspiration. If the biographer, as Holderness asserts, 'creates a narrative consistent with the documentary facts, and with the emotional truths embedded in the hearts of both biographer and subject', so then, do the artists of Shoreditch: it is their 'emotional truth' of being young, struggling artists in East London.[29]

For it is a focus on a particular time in Shakespeare's biography – when he was a young and developing playwright in Shoreditch that influences the work that all three companies produce. The Malachites write explicitly of interpreting Shakespeare's plays 'from the perspective of the young writer as he grows up in East London' and discovering 'instances of Shakespeare finding his feet'.[30] Similarly, Dunthorne argues that Shoreditch was the place where 'Shakespeare honed and perfected his skills, as both an actor and a playwright'. Both LWF and SSF have put new writing at the centre of their creative response to Shakespeare and thus seek to remind audiences of the playwright as a young, aspiring and fresh voice in the early sixteenth century. In this context, playwright Anne Jenkins, commissioned to write 1,000 new plays for the SSF, was 'cast as this modern day Shakespeare' by the Festival producers; a comparison that is not aggrandising if one is imaging Shakespeare at the beginning of his career as a work-in-progress. Again, these young aspiring writers and theatre makers project their own identity onto Shakespeare. In addition, remembering Shakespeare as 'finding his feet' and 'honing his skills' neutralises any reverence for and intimidation by the playwright that might inhibit creative engagement and response to the plays. Thomas McMullan, who wrote *Three Loose Teeth* for the SSF, describes Shakespeare as the 'albatross round the neck of pretty much every playwright' and writing for the Festival as an 'opportunity to beat up Shakespeare'.[31] The memory of Shakespeare in Shoreditch as an emerging playwright forms part of this process.

The 'Shakespeare' constructed through cultural memory in Shoreditch is not only of a developing young writer, but also one who was 'radical' (Mortimer, SSF) and produced work 'about debauchery', as noted by writer Siddhartha Bose who took place in the LWF event.[32] 'Embodied performance,' Taylor argues, 'makes visible an entire spectrum of attitudes and values', and thus we see this version of Shakespeare, and the attitudes and values it underpins, in the work staged.[33] SSF producers sought writers to '*radically* reinterpret Shakespeare's characters' (my emphasis), the word associated with the playwright's actions in the sixteenth century deployed again to described work inspired by him.[34] We begin to see what the term 'radical' might mean to these artists in the plays produced. Engaging with contemporary controversial politics of Shoreditch, particularly concerns about property development and homelessness, the SSF plays might be read as radical because of their liberal tone that sought to provoke thoughts about Shoreditch's inequality from audiences.[35]

At the LWF event, Bose's adaptation of *Othello* also foregrounded the liberal, dirtier and debauched nature of the location: 'Shoreditch burns from a beer can crack. Floodwater remains of piss-stench. Chipshop fried chickenwings waft, gambolled. Cityboy transformers stalk the high street, slurping outta strip bars that constellate round kebab zero singularity'.[36] In this atmosphere the Venetian soldier and courtly lady are transported and adapted: '

> Sipping whisky, he saw her for a month, in underground afterparties … the tanks of her body rolling to the spin of Tokyo DJs. She watched him watch her watch the mirrors of eyes refracted, the heave of her sweat morphing to pure electricity in his scentbreath.

Bose's prose does not shy away from the sordid nature of East London (piss-stench, strip bars) and creates a visceral and sensual 'Othello' and 'Desdemona', leering and sweating in underground bars. Bose's Shoreditch might, like the sixteenth century location, be seen as a site for 'the corruption and utter destruction of youth'.[37] It is clear that a particular version of 'Shakespeare' has been remembered by artists in Shoreditch, but what is its purpose?

Shakespeare and the battle for the soul of Shoreditch

Political theorist Kevin Bruyneel, examining cultural memory of Martin Luther King Jr. in the US, argues that 'actors, institutions and discourses speak for and shape the meaning of the past through the construction of histories and memories' and that there 'are serious stakes here, because the relationship of a people to its past is critical to defining the political imperatives of the present and the future'.[38] The remembering of Shakespeare as a radical timber-stealing young man has an important contemporary political purpose in the urbanscape of Shoreditch. The work of SSF, LWF and The Malachites takes place within a wider context of a 'battle for the "soul of Shoreditch"' as property developers seek to capitalise on unused land in 'the heart of the East End's most vibrant community'.[39] There is a sense that the creative and artistic community which make up parts of the area will be pushed out by luxury flats and skyscraper offices. The sites of the Theatre and the Curtain are a notable location in the battle for Shoreditch's identity. It has taken seven years and three years, respectively, for stable plans for the Theatre and Curtain to emerge.[40] Blyth of the The Malachites expresses some frustration about this wait: 'Two sites which are lying decrepit, are highly vulnerable and at the mercy of the city'.

In this context, it is little wonder that the memory of Shakespeare in Shoreditch at the forefront of artists is that of the young playwright battling a landlord and reclaiming property for theatrical endeavours. Cultural memory blends here with a political imperative to resist the gentrification of Shoreditch. Indeed, the SSF producers note the importance of raising awareness in those who 'had no idea about the history of their neighbourhood'. The heavy weight of Shakespeare as a cultural icon gives an authority to this resistance, and gives a longevity and history to Shoreditch's current identity that is vulnerable to current commercial interests.

SSF producers were keen to assert a link between sixteenth and twenty-first century Shoreditch as they asked their commissioned writers to imagine 'a stream running through Shoreditch from 1500s to now'; 'We do believe,' Mortimer notes, 'in this cultural ley line that runs through Shoreditch and tapping into that'. Similarly, Chivers discussing the atmosphere of the LWF night described 'a suburb of sin feeling'. I asked him to elaborate on this somewhat early modern sounding term; 'it's the idea that people call Shoreditch the suburb of sin, and they say it in a way of trying to connect the early modern to the modern, there is connective tissue between these two time periods'. The 'stream', 'ley line' and 'tissue' linking Shakespeare to contemporary Shoreditch gives a legitimacy to a marginalised political and economic group. The images all three companies used for the links between then and now denote tangible, material and real-world connections (the water of stream, the ley line that links landmarks, the tissue that constitutes fabrics and/or bodies); their word choice suggests a strong will to make visceral and concrete the tie between sixteenth and twenty-first century London.

Alongside spatial-economic background, constructions of the playwright's history in Shoreditch takes place within a wider cultural context of Shakespearean performance. Bose argued that the LWF event was successful because 'it took place in a basement of a bar which is kind of like a dive and it had that rock 'n' roll atmosphere more than a National Theatre atmosphere'. Bose does not state what a National Theatre 'atmosphere' is but we can infer that it is the opposite of debauched, perhaps more conservative and staid. Like Bose, SSF producer Mortimer also describes his work by placing it in opposition to older and more established theatres. He notes that on the Southbank at the Globe there's an incredible mausoleum recreation that has its merits and is really interesting to a lot of people. And then the RSC has a very distinct and very protective feeling over Shakespeare's work. And we wanted in a small way to oppose those forces.

Mortimer's use of the word 'mausoleum' makes clear the perceived contrast between his work and that of the Globe's. The Southbank theatre is certainly a form of cultural memory, but one that is dead, archaic even (all bound up in the meanings and associations of 'mausoleum') as contrasted with memory work happening in Shoreditch; linked as it is with a young Shakespeare and a re-awakening of a lost history.

Similarly, Blyth of The Malachites describes a desire for a permanent performance venue in relation to the Globe and RSC when he points out 'there is a tradition in Southbank and in Stratford so established, I would like an earlier, more intimate, smaller space to produce Shakespearean work in Shoreditch'. Cultural memories offer 'versions of the past according to present knowledge and needs' and the radical and young Shakespeare remembered through work in Shoreditch serves to delineate these artists from the established and traditional institutions of Shakespearean performance.[41] Shakespeare as a cultural icon and constructions of his history are the terrain on which contemporary creative productions and responses to his work are played out. LWF, SSF and The Malachites are companies who are not regularly funded by the State (the National Theatre and RSC) and who do not enjoy immense commercial success (the Globe); in this light, it is unsurprising they focus on the historical moment where Shakespeare was also in financial hardship. Their 'Shakespeare' is different from the royal patronised and wealthy playwright who made investments in London property and brought the biggest house in Stratford upon Avon. Indeed, Mortimer of SSF notes 'We want to celebrate the time when Shakespeare wasn't the richest man in Stratford'.[42]

The companies under discussion here assert a difference between their work and that of more established theatres which centres around cultural memories of Shakespeare in Shoreditch. In terms of memory, there is also a big variance in terms of the remembering and archiving of performance. Taylor alerts us to the difference between 'the archive of supposedly enduring materials (i.e. texts, documents, buildings, bones)' and 'the so-called ephemeral repertoire of embodied practice/knowledge (i.e. spoken language, dance, sports, ritual)'.[43] Certainly performances at the Globe, National Theatre and RSC are embodied practice; yet this repertoire is surrounded and supported by an extensive archive. All three have physical collections of recordings, costumes, props, prompt books, scripts and, in the case of the Globe, interviews with practitioners. Notably, the majority of scholarly work on Shakespeare, memory and contemporary performance has focussed on these three institutions.[44] In contrast, the SSF, LWF and The Malachite Theatre Company have no such archiving structures in place. The material I have used here and this chapter itself forms an (albeit incomplete) archive; this chapter is, in fact, a memory of their work and my interviews with them. We might acknowledge that performance is ephemeral and embodied, and that there is a difference between the archive and the repertoire. However, it is equally important to recognise that in twenty-first century Shakespearean performance, economic and cultural differences mean that the balance between archive and repertoire is uneven from company to company. In some well-established institutions performances are recorded, incredibly successfully documented and in some cases have been 'livecast'. Such practices blur archive and repertoire and raise questions about liveness and embodiment with which scholars are just beginning to grapple.[45] As recorded or 'livecast' theatre increases for more well-established and wealthier establishments, what affect might this have on smaller avant-garde theatre-makers within the broadest spectrum of contemporary Shakespearean performance? This question, I suggest, is one that we need to begin to answer as part of a debate about livecasting.

The theatre makers I interviewed all, to some extent, articulated a concern about Shakespeare's time in Shoreditch being forgotten, and even the 'vulnerability' of the remains of his playhouses being 'at the mercy' of the ever-changing city. There is, therefore, certainly a sense of an ephemerality of performance, that nothing remains. And yet they all recognised the power of their own work to remind and ignite a memory of the playwright in Shoreditch. In this way it is apparent that their performances lie somewhere in between ephemerality and remembrance. Chivers of the LWF expressed this duality in discussing his 'Shakespeare in Shoreditch' night. For the audience, he noted, 'you remember for a moment and you forget again, that's what art does – that event made a moment, there was a real buzz, it was an act of remembrance but it is also ephemeral'. The practitioner testimony examined in this chapter offers a way through the potential dichotomy offered by Phelan, on one hand, and critics such as Roach and Taylor on the other. Ultimately though interpreting performance as memory enables us to see the cultural and political implications at work in any given event. Shakespeare in Shoreditch allows us to look at the playwright as cultural icon in a very different setting to that of the Southbank and Stratford-upon-Avon. From the viewpoint of this location, we see memories of the playwright utilised in the identity-formation of young up-and-coming theatre makers, and also in the context of economic urban landscapes. 'Shakespeare', both his biography and plays, remains a negotiated and culturally charged entity used for political purposes.

Notes

1 Peggy Phelan, *Unmarked: The Politics of Performance* (London: Routledge, 1993), p. 148.
2 The full report of the archaeological remains of both playhouses is yet to be released. However, the most up to date accounts can be found in Julian Bowsher, *Shakespeare's London Theatreland: Archaeology, History and Drama* (London: MOLA, 2012), pp. 55–67 and Bowsher, 'Shakespearean Playhouse Development', *Theatres Magazine* 35 (Spring, 2013), pp. 18–21.
3 Phelan, 'Playing Dead in Stone, or When Is a Rose not a Rose?', in *Performance and Cultural Politics*, ed. Elin Diamond (London and New York: Routledge, 1996), pp. 65–88. Phelan writes in response to theatre historians Andrew Gurr and John Orrell, 'What the Rose Can Tell Us', *Antiquity* 63.240 (September, 1989): 421–429.
4 Joseph Roach, *Cities of the Dead: Circum-Atlantic Performance* (New York: Columbia University Press, 1996) and Diana Taylor, *The Archive and the Repertoire: Performing Cultural Memory in the Americas* (Durham, NC: Duke University Press, 2003).
5 Roach, *Cities of the Dead*, p. xi.
6 All quotes from these artists are from my interviews with them, unless stated otherwise in endnotes.
7 Pictures of the event can be viewed at: http://londonist.com/2009/03/london_word_festival_shakespeare_in.php?showpage=5#gallery-1 and a short video https://vimeo.com/8116764; accessed October 2016.
8 *Manga Julius Caesar* (London: Self-Made Hero, 2008).
9 For further details see the Festival website: www.shakespeareinshoreditch.in/; accessed October 2016.
10 Anne Jenkins, *Annie's 1000 Plays: Volume One* (London: Shakespeare in Shoreditch, 2015). Also available at: www.annies1000plays.com/; accessed October 2016; The Rose Lipman building is a 'creative community art space' in Haggerston, www.themillcoproject.co.uk/spaces/the-rose-lipman-building/; accessed October 2016.
11 www.themalachites.co.uk/#!shakespeares-shoreditch/c1nsx; accessed October 2016.
12 Hannah Crawforth, Sarah Dustagheer and Jennifer Young, *Shakespeare in London* (London: Arden Shakespeare, 2014), pp. 7–8.
13 T.F, *News from the North* (London, 1579), F4r.
14 For further details, see Glynne Wickham, Herbert Berry and William Ingram, eds., *English Professional Theatre, 1530–1660* (Cambridge: Cambridge University Press, 2000), pp. 330–387.

15 www.shakespeareinshoreditch.in/; accessed October 2016.
16 I offer a short one here but for more in-depth introduction, see Anne Whitehead, *Memory*, The New Critical Idiom Series (London: Routledge, 2008), pp. 123–152 and Astrid Erll, *Memory in Culture*, trans. Sara B. Young (Basingstoke: Palgrave Macmillan, 2011), pp. 13–36.
17 Although originally published in 1925, Halbwachs works were translated, partially and posthumously, into English much later: *The Collective Memory*, trans. Francis J. Ditter, Jr and Vida Yarzdi Ditter (New York: Harper & Row, 1980) and *On Collective Memory*, trans. Lewis Coser (Chicago: Chicago University Press, 1992).
18 Paul Connerton, *How Societies Remember* (Cambridge: Cambridge University Press, 1989); Pierre Nora, eds., *Les lieux de mémoire* (Paris: Gallimard, 1984–1992). In English: *Realms of Memory: The Construction of the French Past*, 3 volumes, ed. Lawrence D. Kritzman, trans. Arthur Goldhammer (New York: Columbia University Press, 1996–1998) and *Rethinking France*, trans. Mary Trouille (Chicago: University of Chicago Press, 2001–2006). Jan and Aleida Assmann have published widely in German; key English translations include: Jan Assmann, 'Collective Memory and Cultural Identity', trans. Jogn Czaplicka, *New German Critique* 65 (1995): 125–133 and Aleida Assmann, *Cultural Memory and Western Civilization: Functions, Media, Archives* (Cambridge: Cambridge University Press, 2011).
19 Erll, 'Cultural Memory Studies: An Introduction', in Erll and Ansgar Nünning, eds. with Sara B. Young, *Cultural Memory Studies: An International and Interdisciplinary Handbook* (Berlin: Walter de Gruyter, 2008), pp. 1–15 (pp. 1–2).
20 Nora, 'Between Memory and History: Les Lieux de Mémoire', *Representations* 26 (Spring, 1989): 7–24 (7). Increasingly memory theorists have argued that 'forgetting, *considered in all its complexity*, desires to be taken seriously', Whitehead, p. 156.
21 Erll, 'Cultural Memory Studies', p. 5.
22 Colin Counsell 'Introduction', in Counsell and Roberta Mock, eds. *Performance, Embodiment and Cultural Memory* (Newcastle-upon-Tyne: Cambridge Scholars Publishing, 2009), pp. 1–15 (p. 8).
23 Joe Dunthorne, 'This Week in Books', *The Guardian*, 28 February 2009, www.theguardian.com/books/2009/feb/28/shakespeare-shoreditch-roberto-bolano-smiths; accessed October 2016. All further quotes from Dunthorne are taken from this article.
24 Guilia Merlo, 'Shoreditch Was Always Where It's At', *Cultural Wars*, 18 March 2009 www.culturewars.org.uk/index.php/site/article/shoreditch_was_always_where_its_at/; accessed October 2016.
25 Siobhan Brownlie, 'Does Memory of the Distant Past Matter? Remediating the Norman Conquest', *Memory Studies* 5.4 (2011): 360–377 (367).
26 Terence Hawkes, *Meaning by Shakespeare* (London and New York: Routledge, 1992), p. 3.
27 A. Assmann, *Cultural Memory*, pp. 53–78; see also Hester Lees-Jeffries, *Shakespeare and Memory* (Oxford: Oxford University Press, 2013), pp. 61–89.
28 Graham Holderness, '"Author! Author!": Shakespeare and Biography', *Shakespeare* 5.2 (April, 2009): 122–133 (123).
29 Holderness, p. 131.
30 www.themalachites.co.uk/#!shakespeares-shoreditch/c1nsx; accessed October 2016.
31 Shakespeare in Shoreditch: Three Loose Teeth, www.youtube.com/watch?v=wlbVh5zzjZA; accessed October 2016.
32 Bose speaking on the short video about the event, https://vimeo.com/8116764; accessed October 2016. All further quotes by Bose are from this video, unless stated otherwise.
33 Taylor, *Archive and Repertoire*, p. 49.
34 www.shakespeareinshoreditch.in/; accessed October 2016.
35 See Brad Birch, *Pit of Clay*, www.youtube.com/watch?v=jWu1IH1CfYc&list=UUz0RHBDoE4n3EVRr6gdfE5Q&index=54; Sabrina Mahfouz, *Disnatured*, www.youtube.com/watch?v=1d9GB029GXc&index=52&list=UUz0RHBDoE4n3EVRr6gdfE5Q; Thomas McMullan, *Three Loose Teeth*, www.youtube.com/watch?v=wlbVh5zzjZA; accessed October 2016.
36 Excerpts from Bose's adaptation taken from personal correspondence with the author, 22 July 2015.
37 T.F, *News from the North*, F4r.
38 Kevin Bruyneel, 'The King's Body: The Martin Luther King Jr. Memorial and the Politics of Collective Memory', *History and Memory* 26.1 (Spring/Summer, 2014): 75–108 (76).
39 Jonathan Prynn, '800million Development will Kill the Soul of Shoreditch', *Evening Standard* 23 January 2015, www.standard.co.uk/news/london/800m-development-will-kill-the-soul-of-shoreditch-9998504.html; accessed October 2016. For further press on campaign against Shoreditch development see www.hackneygazette.co.uk/news/mayor_of_hackney_launches_save_shoreditch_campaign_1_3968575;

www.independent.co.uk/news/uk/home-news/shoreditch-skyscrapers-home-of-the-hipsters-is-under-threat-from-development-plans-10070591.html; http://hackneycitizen.co.uk/2014/07/30/campaign-launches-against-skyscrapers-planned-for-bishopsgate-goods-yard/; accessed October 2016.

40 The Belvedere Trust's development plans for the Theatre site, as submitted to Hackney Council, can be viewed here http://idox.hackney.gov.uk/WAM/doc/Design%20and%20Access%20Statement-377424.pdf?extension=.pdf&id=377424&location=VOLUME1&contentType=&pageCount=1; and plans for the Curtain site, 'The Stage' development by Pringle, Brandon, Perkins and Will can be viewed here http://uk.perkinswill.com/news/the-stage-shoreditch-development-planning-permission.html; accessed October 2016.
41 Erll, 'Cultural Memory Studies', p. 5.
42 Quoted in Nell Frizell, 'Pop Up Plays at Rift's Shakespeare in Shoreditch Festival', http://now-here-this.timeout.com/2014/10/08/pop-up-plays-at-rifts-shakespeare-in-shoreditch-festival/; accessed October 2016.
43 Taylor, *Archive and Repertoire*, p. 19.
44 For example, Peter Holland, ed. *Shakespeare, Memory and Performance* (Cambridge: Cambridge University Press, 2006) contains essays on the National Theatre, RSC and Globe.
45 Questions of 'liveness' of performance were covered extensively in debate between Phelan and Auslander (see *Liveness: Performance in a Mediatized Culture* (London and New York: Routledge, 1999). However the rise of recorded and live broadcast theatre in cinemas since 2006 is only just being examined in detail by scholars: see Robert Shaughnessy, 'The Shakespeare Revolution Will not Be Televised: Staging the Media Apparatus', in *Shakespeare, Memory and Performance*, pp. 305–328; Martin Baker, *Live to Your Local Cinema: The Remarkable Rise of Livecasting* (Basingstoke: Palgrave Macmillan, 2013); Steven Purcell, 'The Impact of New Forms of Public Performance', in *Shakespeare and the Digital World*, ed. Christie Carson and Peter Kirwan (Cambridge: Cambridge University Press, 2014), pp. 212–225.

PART II

Tragedy

8

'THE RAVEN O'ER THE INFECTIOUS HOUSE'

Contagious memory in *Romeo and Juliet* and *Othello*

Evelyn Tribble

'He lies like an eyewitness—Russian proverb'
(Julian Barnes, Talking It Over*)*

Early modern actors and playwrights were skilled in manipulating audience attention and memory. Perhaps the most comic example can be found at the conclusion of Ben Jonson's *The Alchemist*, a play that hinges upon how laughably easy it is to misdirect attention and to manipulate memory, both of the on-stage characters and the audience. The ease with which this can be done is structured into the plot, of course: con games only work when marks are eager to deceive themselves, and Jonson's marks are hungry to be duped. But Jonson widens his aim to include spectators and bystanders (and, by implication, the audience itself) in this web of delusion. In 5.1 and 5.2, Lovewit returns and is surrounded by the neighbours telling tales of the constant resort of citizens' wives, ladies and gentlewomen, knights, coaches, oyster-women, gallants, sailor's wives, and tobacco men to his house[1] (5.1.1–5). The apparent disappearance of Jeremy prompts the Fifth Neighbour to wonder if he has 'slipped away,' which the Sixth converts immediately to the prospect that he has been 'made away,' which in turn prompts him to confabulate having heard a 'doleful cry [...] like unto a man / that had been strangled for an hour, and could not speak.' This vivid, if implausible image moves the second neighbour to recall that 'I heard it too, just this day three weeks, at two o'clock in the morning' (5.1). When Jeremy opens the door to deny the report, as proof he displays the keys that 'have been / in this my pocket now above twenty days.' The sight of the keys, although utterly irrelevant to the actual facts of the situation, seem to operate something like Desdemona's handkerchief in attracting attention as apparently solid evidence of Jeremy's innocence. The cognitive dissonance generated by the butler's 'honest' presence causes the neighbours' memories to melt away: 'Good Faith, I think I saw a coach,' says the First Neighbour, a weak avowal that sparks the Second Neighbour to place the event in the conditional past: 'And I too, / I'd ha' been sworn.' (35). By the time the Third Neighbour arrives back with his tools, Jeremy's story has slipped into fact: 'He's had the keys / And the door has been shut these three weeks.' Lovewit's disgust with the 'changelings' (43)—'Fine rogues, to have your testimonies built on!'—underscores the instability of memory and perception in the theatrical world. Here, Jonson stages what an influential school of contemporary cognitive psychologists have deemed the 'misinformation effect': the 'distorting effects of misleading post-event information on memory for words, faces, and details of witnessed events.'[2] The comic resolution of Jonson's play limits the dangers of such manipulation. Within a tragic context, however, such moments are ripe for exploitation.

One of the key findings of research about memory in the last few decades has been its fundamental constructedness. Memories are not pre-existing objects or events stored in the brain for later; rather, each act of memory retrieval is also an act of reconstruction.[3] In the experimental cognitive psychology tradition, these studies have produced a large body of research on the susceptibility of autobiographical memory to the shaping of other minds. Much of this work has had as its focus high-stakes forensic contexts: for example, the very robust evidence for the fundamental unreliability of much eye-witness testimony has shown that witnesses are highly suggestible to post-event information, especially if provided by authority figures.[4] The work of Elizabeth Loftus and others on 'the impairment in memory for the past that arises after exposure to misleading information' has repeatedly shown the ways that episodic memory (memory for events) can be moulded by later experiences.[5]

Loftus and the cognitive psychologists in her tradition tend to view the 'misinformation effect' suspiciously, no doubt because of the forensic context in which their research originated. Yet this tradition has blind spots: for one, it tends to view memory—in ideal cases—as individually bounded. As Sutton et al. note, 'research on "false memory" has focused on malign forms of influence [...] The unsullied individual memory appears as the gold standard, and social influence as a primarily negative intrusion.'[6] Sutton argues that constant social shaping is a condition of the fundamental constructedness of memory itself. Although our memories feel to us as profoundly 'ours,' they are also co-created with others. For these reasons, Kourken Michaelian suggests distinguishing between the normal malleability and social shaping of memory and potentially malign high-stakes misinformation; assimilating inaccurate post-event testimonial information should be referred to as 'harmful incorporation'.[7] He points out that since post-event information may be true as well as false, this phenomenon is better seen as an 'information' effect rather than the more sinister 'misinformation effect,' with its implication of contamination or taint:

> The pervasiveness of construction, together with the frequency with which testimony is received, suggests that incorporation cannot be rare: given that retrieval normally involves drawing on whatever stored information is accessible in order to produce a best guess about the relevant event, and given that much testimonial information is stored, the representations produced by retrieval will often incorporate testimonial information—many perfectly ordinary cases of episodic remembering involve incorporation.[8]

Indeed, the process of attending to theatre involves a constant process of memory creation, incorporation, and revision, as audiences react and reformulate their attitudes as the events flow on before them. At times memory construction and revision is effortless and silent—simply a product of attending to complex narratives unfolding in real time. At other times, however, plays foreground and call attention to the fragility and malleability of memory, exploiting the 'information effect' to destabilize perception, both on and off the stage.

In these ways, players and playwrights have designs upon their audience's memory. In this they are similar to magicians and conjurers, who exploit the slipperiness of memory and its susceptibility to suggestion. Stephen Macknik and Susana Martinez-Conde, cognitive psychologists who have trained as amateur magicians, write that a crucial element in the magician's tool-kit is the way that the story is told.[9] Slight inaccuracies in describing how a trick was supposedly done invisibly shape the memories of participants and spectators alike, producing the effect of 'magic':

> supple human memory combines events seen with legends only heard. We reshape our memories with each retelling of them, which means that along with your willingness to be misdirected, your memory is an easy target for magicians to exploit in the countless tricks of their trade.[10]

As Donald Hedrick has shown, magicians employ a similar set of sleights and tricks as actors and playwrights.[11]

Players, the characters they inhabit, and audiences are all involved in the co-creation of a theatre of memory. In her important book on the subject, Lina Wilder describes the tension between the supposedly orderly habits of memory that underpinned classical and early modern theories, and the chaotic and unpredictable acts of memory performance that inhabit Shakespeare's plays.[12] One of the mechanisms Shakespeare employs to explore such tensions is retrospective story-telling. In this dramaturgical device, used extensively in *Romeo and Juliet* and *Othello*, a character recounts action that the audience has just seen performed. Such moments are never simple repetitions; often, they add new information, provide vivid descriptions, and modify and reinterpret staged events. Retrospective storytelling is particularly significant in the light of psychological understandings of the malleability of memory discussed above. In Shakespeare's plays these malleable memories become contagious, affecting other characters, moulding the shared experience of the events of the play both for the other characters and for the audience's unfolding perception of it. The 'information effect' is thus is a key device in the actors' and playwright's tool kit.

Romeo and Juliet

Romeo and Juliet's preoccupation with malleable memory sets up what we might call the grammar of tragic mnemonics that is later fully exploited in *Othello*. As Wilder has noted, *Romeo and Juliet* repeatedly stages 'recapitulation and reportage' and is characterized by a 'habit of retrospection': 'the art of recollection in this play is diseased.'[13]

The prologue or chorus emphasizes a clear binary logic: 'two households'; 'two foes'; 'a pair of star-crossed lovers' will mark the 'two hours traffic' of the play. But the events of the play belie this neat formula. The play famously begins in a whirl of action, an escalating fight that quickly draws all the characters into its vortex. This is an unusually eventful first scene for Shakespeare's plays: possibly only *The Tempest* begins more abruptly. For its first audience, even after having heard the Prologue, it would have been difficult to track the narrative: the quarrel between the servants, the fight between Tybalt and Benvolio, the entrance of '*three or four Citizens with clubs or partisans*'; the comical attempted brawl between Old Capulet and Montague, as they are restrained by their wives; and the final attempt by the Prince to quell his subjects.

In the wake of these chaotic events, which inevitably divide and fracture the attention of the audience, Shakespeare uses the technique of post-action exposition to mould the audience's memory. The retrospective narration is prompted by Montague's question: 'Who set this ancient quarrel new abroad'?[14] Benvolio recounts:

> Here were the servants of your adversary
> And yours, close fighting ere I did approach.
> I drew to part them; in the instant came
> The fiery Tybalt, with his sword prepar'd,
> Which, as he breath'd defiance to my ears,
> He swung about his head and cut the winds,
> Who nothing hurt withal, hiss'd him in scorn.
> While we were interchanging thrusts and blows
> Came more and more, and fought on part and part,
> Till the Prince came, who parted either part.
> *(1.1.106–115)*

Benvolio's account embellishes the action implied by the dialogue; especially relevant is the reference to Tybalt's fancy swordplay and his bravado showmanship with his rapier. This description functions as a retrospective stage direction to the actors, giving an unusually detailed account of the stage action, but it is also a key way of shaping the audience memory for the events just seen. Only Tybalt—who is named for the first time in this narrative—is described in vivid terms. In contrast, the other characters are described generically; then 'came more and more, and fought on part and part.' The prominence of Tybalt in Benvolio's story narration casts focus upon that character, causing him to stand out amidst the general backdrop of disorder that marks the opening scene.

This technique of retrospective narration is again employed in the aftermath of the slaying of Mercutio. Like the fight that opens the play, the fracas among Mercutio, Tybalt, and Romeo in 3.1. unfolds rapidly and chaotically. Indeed, the action moves so quickly that the characters themselves are unable to fully comprehend what has happened. This bewildering suddenness of Mercutio's fatal injury is in keeping with contemporary accounts of rapier duels, in which the young men squared off with deadly razor sharp weapons: victory was often more a matter of sudden chance than superior skill.[15] The language of the Folio sheds little light on the stage action at the key point. As Mercutio and Tybalt begin to fight, Romeo intervenes:

> ROMEO—Draw, Benvolio, beat down their weapons.
> Gentlemen, for shame, forbear this outrage.
> Tybalt, Mercutio! The Prince expressly hath
> Forbid this bandying in Verona streets.
> Hold, Tybalt! Good Mercutio!
> A FOLLOWER—Away, Tybalt.
> MERCUTIO—I am hurt.
> *(3.1.85–91)*

Just before Tybalt's exit, almost all editions of the play here include some version of the stage direction that appears only in the Quarto: *Tibalt under Romeos arme thrusts Mercutio, in and flyes.*[16] However, the action itself and the consequences are ambiguous even to the characters themselves. Neither Benvolio nor Romeo realize the gravity of Mercutio's wound; only Mercutio himself knows that he is 'worm's meat.'

As in the first scene, retrospective narration is a key technique for imposing coherence upon the chaotic events. In this case, however, Benvolio's narrative is decidedly more interested. He carefully exploits the 'information effect,' using post-event information to shape the memory of the other characters and the audience. Benvolio's reply minimizes Romeo's culpability and emphasizes Tybalt's aggression: Romeo's pleas for peace 'uttered / With gentle breath' are spurned by Tybalt's 'unruly spleen,' which causes him attack:

> With piercing steel at bold Mercutio's breast,
> Who, all as hot, turns deadly point to point [...]
> Romeo, he cries aloud
> 'Hold, friends! Friends, part!' and swifter then his tongue
> His agile arm beats down their fatal points
> And 'twixt them rushes; underneath whose arm
> An envious thrust from Tybalt hit the life
> Of stout Mercutio, and then Tybalt fled;
> But by and by comes back to Romeo,
> Who had but newly entertain'd revenge,
> And to't they go like lightning: for, ere I
> Could draw to part them, was stout Tybalt slain,
> And, as he fell did Romeo turn and fly.
> This is the truth, or let Benvolio die.
>
> *(3.1.153–182)*

There are numerous discrepancies between Benvolio's narrative and the events as they unfolded before the audience. Romeo's refusal to respond to Tybalt's challenge was made in terms that are deliberately mysterious to the other characters. He does not invoke 'the high displeasure' of the Prince until the fight is already engaged, when he cries that 'The Prince expressly hath / Forbade this bandying in Verona streets' (3.1.87–88). Thus, Benvolio either conflates the two instances or confabulates when facing the displeasure of the Prince himself. The more obvious post-event shaping of the narrative, however, is the erasure of Mercutio's culpability. It was Mercutio who displayed 'unruly spleen,' challenging Tybalt out of disgust with Romeo's 'calm, dishonourable, vile submission.' Tybalt in fact seems somewhat surprised by Mercutio's demand to 'walk': 'What wouldst thou have with me?' (3.1.75). Benvolio's retrospective account casts Tybalt as the aggressor—'tilt'[ing] / With piercing steel at bold Mercutio's breast'—and the Mercutio as the defender. Similarly, the fatal blow from Tybalt is described as 'an envious thrust,' implying a dishonourable victory rather than a response to an attack. Furthermore, Benvolio implies, although does not say, that Tybalt challenged Romeo upon his return, suggesting that Romeo had 'but newly entertain'd revenge' and that their fight was a sudden altercation: 'to't they go like lightning.'

This retrospective shaping of the event throws up the way that revenge feeds upon contested memory. Lady Capulet offers up her own version of the events:

> He is a kinsman to the Montague.
> Affection makes him false. He speaks not true.
> Some twenty of them fought in this black strife
> And all those twenty could but kill one life.
> I beg for justice, which thou, Prince, must give.
> Romeo slew Tybalt. Romeo must not live.
>
> *(3.1.177–182)*

Lady Capulet's demand for justice equates Tybalt's life with Romeo's and in effect erases Mercutio from the economy of the play. Indeed, following this scene Mercutio is virtually forgotten by all the characters and is mentioned again in the play only at the end, when Romeo describes Paris as 'Mercutio's kinsmen'.

Thus, an element of the retrospective shaping of the play is to mould and remould it into the binary categories outlined in prologue. It is this impulse that helps to explain the most famous and seemingly most gratuitous act of retrospective narration: the Friar's account at the close of the play. As James Black argues, this moment is structured very similarly to Benvolio's two retrospective narratives, save that the elderly Friar substitutes for Benvolio, who has mysteriously disappeared.[17] Wilder refers to the Friar's retelling as an example of 'calcified remembrance,' and certainly it adheres closely enough to the events that the audience, though not the onstage characters, have witnessed that it is often cut from production.[18] The speech is framed by references to the Friar's venerable age: he reminds the Prince of his 'short date of breath' (5.3.229) in the opening line and concludes by inviting him to 'let my old life / Be sacrificed some hour before his time' (5.3.267–268). His 'tedious tale' is structured not by analysis but by temporal markers: 'Then she comes to me [...] Then gave I her [...] 'Meantime I writ [...] Then all alone [...] But when I came. [...] But then, a noise did scare me from the tomb' (5.3.229–279 passim). The tale is sequential: one event succeeds the other. The paratactic structure gives the effect of numbing length, and the absence of explicit grammatical markers of causality may function as a way of avoiding responsibility for events, masking numerous points at which his judgement might be questioned. The Friar's speech thus is structured as a series of bizarre contingencies, papering numerous questionable decisions, including his panicked exit from the tomb.

These contingencies and discrepancies are ignored in favour of the binary shaping of the play as it is remembered from the prologue. Mercutio's final words reassert that structure—'a plague o' both your houses'—despite the fact that it is his own code of honour rather than the 'ancient quarrel' that provokes the fight with Tybalt.[19] Drawing upon James Black's work, Jill Levenson remarks that 'these summary narratives counterpoise strong, contradictory visual impressions: tableaux of a chaotic fight scene and of the bodies of dead youth that betray passions and ironies of which the words take no account.'[20] Here, the persistent patterning and the visual and iconic links among the scenes—the Prince mediating the feuding families—helps to reduce and simplify the trajectory of the play into the binary narrative that ends with the erection of gold monuments to the young lovers—a kind of cultural misinformation effect that has resulted in the longstanding reception of the play as the tragedy of young love rather than contingent circumstances, accidents, and masculinist codes of honour.

Othello

The tragic mnemonics sketched in *Romeo and Juliet* dominate *Othello*. Iago is a canny and skilled mnemonist, well aware of the susceptibility of memory to retrospective manipulation. Within the play, Iago sets up a memory laboratory, testing and probing the limits and possibilities of retrospectively shaping memory, creating a virus that infects not just Othello but the other characters as well.[21]

Iago's ability to manipulate memory is a key reason for his well-known skill in improvization. This ability is put to the test in the aftermath of the quarrel scene in Othello (2.3). This scene is in many ways a reprise of two quarrels in *Romeo and Juliet*, save of course that Iago himself manufactures the confusion that will allow him to shape both the event itself and his retelling of it. Iago creates a complex, fast-moving scene, full of noise and chaos that quickly escalates. As in *Romeo and Juliet*, the attempt by Montano to quell the battle simply creates more confusion, and Iago quickly capitalizes on the chaos to escalate the event into a 'mutiny' (2.3.142). This cry triggers the ringing of the bell, which continues throughout Othello's entry, until some fifteen lines later he commands it to stop. Like Benvolio, Iago is called upon to retrospectively narrate events that the audience has witnessed but that remain opaque to the characters. Othello demands: 'Honest Iago, that looks dead with grieving, / Speak: who began this? On thy love I charge thee!' (2.3.168–169).

Iago's first reply casts the quarrel in general terms: 'I cannot speak / Any beginning to this peevish odds' (2.3.176). Such demurrals of course are key elements in Iago's general strategy of apparent reluctance. Othello's resulting anger raises the stakes so that the eventual retrospective narration carries more salience than it might otherwise have:

> Touch me not so near.
> I had rather have this tongue cut from my mouth
> Than it should do offence to Michael Cassio,
> (2.3.212–214)

Iago's recounting of the event mentions Montano only once and refers to Roderigo as 'the crying fellow.' In contrast, he calls Cassio by name five more times; the repetition of the name reinforces his culpability and of course belies Iago's disingenuous reluctance to cast blame. This crucial moment in his plan is successful not only because of his ability to manipulate events themselves, but also because of his ability to shape and mold memory for the event: to turn a chaotic and confusing episode into a clearly defined narrative casting blame upon Cassio.

Iago's insight into ways of manipulating post-event information is demonstrated particularly clearly when he and Othello see Cassio making a hasty and embarrassed farewell from Desdemona:

> IAGO—Ha, I like not that.
> OTHELLO—What dost thou say?
> IAGO—Nothing, my lord; or if—I know not what.
> OTHELLO—Was not that Cassio parted from my wife?
> IAGO—Cassio, my lord? no, sure, I cannot think it
> That he would steal away so guilty-like
> Seeing you coming.
> (3.3.34–39)

The literature on the ease of manipulating eyewitness testimony is of particular relevance to this passage. Researchers have repeatedly shown that the language with which questions are formed or events are described have a powerful effect on witness memory. Indeed, this moment bears striking resemblances to experiments on eyewitness testimony. In such experiments, an event is witnessed (usually via photographs or video); after some time passes, the subject is prompted to recall the event in terms that are misleading or slanted in some way; later, he or she is often found to have incorporated the misleading information into his or her own memory of the event. In a classic example, a subject might be shown a video of a car driving through a yield sign; she is asked 'how fast was the car going when it went through the stop sign?'; later, when asked to recall the event, the subject is likely to mistakenly recall that the driver sped through a stop sign.[22] While this near-ubiquitous characteristic of memory is liable for routine exploitation by actors and playwrights, in *Othello* and in *Romeo and Juliet* it becomes explicitly thematized. Cassio walks through a yield sign when bidding farewell to Desdemona; Iago recasts the event they have both witnessed as running a stop sign, 'guilty-like.'

This framing is part of a pattern in which past events are shaped and molded to fit the narrative that Iago relentlessly peddles. And because the narrative, sadly, works along well-worn misogynistic tracks, it is particularly compelling. The tendency of narrative and memory to revert from the unusual or the idiosyncratic—in this case the 'improbable' love of a young Venetian gentlewoman for a Moorish warrior—is attested by Frederick Bartlett's foundational work on remembering. Bartlett told a number of acquaintances at Cambridge a story adapted from F.C. Boas entitled 'The War of the Ghosts,' which contained a number of odd and disconcerting elements. He conducted his research by simply asking his friends to recall the story whenever he encountered them. As time went on, features of the story that did not conform to conventional (for this group) norms were abandoned, and the story began to more closely take on a standard form. Bartlett termed these processes familiarization, rationalization, and conventionalization:

> Both familiarisation and rationalisation are, in fact, results of a common tendency to change all presented material into such a form that it may be accepted without uneasiness, and without question. The influence of this tendency is exerted upon absolutely all material which is received into and preserved within a mental system. Sometimes the effect is that specific reasons are evolved to account for the form of given material; sometimes, even when such reasons are lacking, the form of the material is changed into something which can be readily accepted simply because it is familiar.[23]

A key example of the phenomena Bartlett describes is Iago's statement that 'I know our country disposition well— / In Venice they do let God see the pranks / They dare not show their husbands' (3.3.204–206). This comment works as a kind of 'familiarization effect,' attempting to assimilate the stereotypical mismatch between elderly husband and young wife into a familiar cuckoldry narrative.[24] Having established this well-worn narrative, Iago uses it to retrospectively shape Othello's memory of Desdemona's account of the wooing: 'She that so young could give out such a seeming / To see her father's eyes up, close as oak— / He thought 'twas witchcraft (3.3.212–214). As Michael Neill observes, this recounting of the Council scene subtly modifies Brabantio's witchcraft accusation: 'Iago's well-timed paraphrase cunningly transfers the charge of "witchcraft"' from Othello to Desdemona, just as it reassigns the imputation of blindness from the bewitched daughter to the deceived husband.'[25]

This retrospective shaping of Desdemona's character of course above all is instantiated in the handkerchief, which becomes irrevocably stained with Iago's slanders. Othello's confession to Desdemona's murder takes the object as a given its solidity as evidence of infidelity:

> 'Tis pitiful; but yet Iago knows
> That she with Cassio hath the act of shame
> A thousand times committed. Cassio confessed it,
> And she did gratify his amorous works
> With that recognizance and pledge of love.
> Which I first gave her: I saw it in his hand,
> It was a handkerchief, an antique token
> My father gave my mother.
>
> *(5.2.210–217)*

This moment of crystallization unravels the plot: Emilia recognizes the true significance of the handkerchief as well as her own complicity in acceding to Iago's 'solemn earnestness' to steal it. This moment also marks a disruption to the relentless time-pressure of the play and its oppressive dyadic structure that allows Iago to shape Othello's perception and memory so tragically. Like *Romeo and Juliet*, the play concludes by re-rehearsing events that the audience knows all too well—and indeed events that the main character, Othello, has actually experienced, albeit as Iago's dupe. Having presented an economical if horrifying narrative arch that ends with Desdemona's death, the play then proliferates endings and explanations, clumsily documenting events that have already been performed on stage. One example is the strange multiplicity of Othello's weapons: the sword with which he wounds Iago and which is 'recovered' from him by Montano; the weapon that he brandishes before Gratiano; and the dagger with which he stabs himself.

The multiplicity of weapons is mirrored by the multiple forms of exposition that conclude the play, when most of the remaining characters, including 'Cassio in a chair', arrive to rehash the events. Iago has off-stage made some sort of confession, but he refuses to speak more: 'what you know, you know' (5.2.303). Othello's wish to see himself as 'an honourable murderer' is undermined by the creaky ludicrousness of the revelation of the machinations of the plot. As Alan Stewart notes, 'Lodovico finds no fewer than three letters in Roderigo's pockets,' a device that infuriated Thomas Rymer as well as, Stewart notes, Ann Pasternak Slater, who argues that 'the dead Roderigo is pressed into posthumous postal service.'[26] Lodovico tells Othello:

> Sir, you shall understand what hath befallen,
> Which, as I think, you know not. Here is a letter
> Found in the pocket of the slain Roderigo,
> And here another: the one of them imports
> The death of Cassio, to be undertook
> By Roderigo
> […]
> Now here's another discontented paper
> Found in his pocket too, and this, it seems
> Roderigo meant t'have sent this damned villain
> But that, belike, Iago in the nick
> Came in, and satisfied him.
>   *(5.2.306–311; 313–317)*

In addition to confirming the off-stage confession of Iago that the handkerchief was deliberately dropped in his room, Cassio also reveals a letter explaining that Iago 'made him / Brave me upon the watch' (325–326). These revelations confirm and repeat what has already been seen and said. So, on the one hand, they are redundant, but on the other they destabilize audience memory for the events of the play—Roderigo does not seem like much of a letter-writer, and Iago has throughout the play been so careful and cunning with insinuation that it is difficult to imagine him committing his plots to the written word, and especially to so unreliable a character as Roderigo. Stewart argues that both this scene and *Romeo and Juliet* use letters to end in 'what seems to be a horribly untheatrical manner.'[27] Neill concurs that this moment can 'easily seem very clumsy in performance […] In so far as the [revelatory letters] belong to a predominantly comic convention, the effect is to emphasize the ironies of Othello's deception by underlining the grossly theatrical and mechanical nature of Iago's plotting.'[28]

Having the play's denouement handled by so ridiculous a character, and a dead one at that, momentarily shifts the frame of the play from tragedy to comedy. The happy endings of comedy depend upon forgetting; characters such as Malvolio who refuse to forget are excluded from the comic reconciliation. Both *Romeo and Juliet* and *Othello* have quasi-conclusions that take the events out of the tragic frame and unbundle them, momentarily distributing memory across a variety of characters and devices, such as letters and retrospective narratives. The Friar's testimony and the letters of the dead Roderigo are often cut in production; they seem redundant and invite the audience to 'misremember,' to re-evaluate the tragic mnemonics as comedy. The actual endings—the monuments to the young lovers and Othello's self-regarding narrative of the 'service' he has done to the state—reinstate the economies of memory that underpin the tragedy, inviting tragic memory at the expense of comic forgetting.

Notes

1. Ben Jonson, *The Alchemist*, in *Cambridge Complete Works of Ben Jonson*, vol. 3 ed. David Bevington et al. 7 vols (Cambridge: Cambridge University Press, 2012), pp. 541–710.
2. Steven J. Frenda and others, 'Current Issues and Advances in Misinformation Research', *Current Directions in Psychological Science*, 20.1 (2011), 20–23 (pp. 20–1).
3. There is a vast literature on the constructedness of memory; Daniel Schachter provides some very useful popular surveys of the research in *Searching for Memory* (New York: Basic Books, 1995). See also Daniel Schachter and Joseph T. Coyle, *Memory Distortion: How Minds, Brains, and Societies Reconstruct the Past* (Cambridge, MA: Harvard University Press, 1997).
4. Elizabeth F. Loftus, 'Planting Misinformation in the Human Mind: A 30-Year Investigation of the Malleability of Memory', *Learning and Memory*, 12.4 (2005), 361–6.
5. Loftus, p. 361.
6. John Sutton, and others, 'The Psychology of Memory, Extended Cognition, and Socially Distributed Remembering', *Phenomenology and the Cognitive Sciences*, 9.4 (2010), 521–60 (p. 544).
7. Kourken Michaelian, 'The Information Effect: Constructive Memory, Testimony, and Epistemic Luck', *Synthese*, 190.12 (2013), 2429–56.
8. Michaelian, p. 2444.
9. Stephen L. Macknik, Susana Martinez-Conde, and Sandra Blakeslee, *Sleights of Mind: What the Neuroscience of Magic Reveals about our Everyday Deceptions* (New York: Macmillan, 2010).
10. Macknik et al., p. 113.
11. Donald Hedrick, 'Distracting Othello: Tragedy and the Rise of Magic', *PMLA*, 129.4 (2014), 649–71.
12. Lina Wilder, *Shakespeare's Memory Theatre: Recollection, Properties, and Character* (Cambridge: Cambridge University Press, 2010).
13. Wilder, p. 25.
14. Unless otherwise indicated, all quotations from Shakespeare's plays are taken from *The Arden Shakespeare Complete Works*, ed. by Richard Proudfoot, Ann Thompson, and David Scott Kastan (London: Methuen Drama; Bloomsbury Publishing, 2011); subsequent references are given within the text.
15. See Ian Borden, 'The Blackfriars Gladiators: Masters of Fence, Playing a Prize, and the Elizabethan and Stuart Theater', in *Inside Shakespeare: Essays on the Blackfriars Stage*, ed. Paul Menzer (Selinsgrove, PA: Susquehanna University Press, 2006), pp. 132–46; Charles Edelmen, *Brawl Ridiculous: Swordfighting in Shakespeare's Plays* (Manchester: Manchester University Press, 1992); George Silver, *Paradoxes of Defence* (London, 1599).
16. Lukas Erne, The First Quarto *Romeo and Juliet* (Cambridge; New York: Cambridge University Press, 2006).
17. James Black, 'The Visual Artistry of *Romeo and Juliet*', *SEL*, 1500–1900 15.2 (1975), 245–56. Benvolio's death is reported in Q1.
18. Wilder, p. 60.
19. This point is made by Raymond Utterback, 'The Death of Mercutio', *Shakespeare Quarterly*, 24.2 (1973), 105–16.
20. Jill Levenson, *Romeo and Juliet: Shakespeare in Performance* (Manchester: Manchester University Press, 1987), p. 6.

21 See Hedrick for a discussion of the range of conjurer's tricks Iago employs.
22 See Loftus (2005).
23 F.C. Bartlett, 'Some Experiments on the Reproduction of Folk Stories', *Folk-Lore*, 31 (1920), 30–47 (p. 37).
24 The best discussion of the intersection of racism and misogyny in the play remains Karen Newman, '"And Wash the Ethiop White": Femininity and the Monstrous in *Othello*', in *Shakespeare Reproduced: The Text in History and Ideology*, ed. Jean E. Howard and Marion F. O'Connor (London and New York: Routledge Press, 1987).
25 Michael Neill, ed., *Othello* (Oxford: Oxford University Press), p. 144.
26 Alan Stewart, *Shakespeare's Letters* (Oxford: Oxford University Press, 2008) pp. 293–4.
27 Stewart, p. 292.
28 Neill, p. 394.

9

'LEST WE REMEMBER ... OUR TROY, OUR ROME'

Historical and individual memory in *Titus Andronicus* and *Troilus and Cressida*

Jesús Tronch

Shakespeare's earliest tragedy, *Titus Andronicus* (ca. 1594), and his most satirical play, *Troilus and Cressida* (ca. 1601), exhibit similarities that are opportune for exploring the functions of memory.[1] A basic premise for this exploration is that memory is essential to the construction of identity, to one's sense of continuity of the self over time and space, and to one's relationship with society; and that memories and identities, as John R. Gillis has argued, are 'representations or constructions of reality' that are subjective, selective and changing, since 'we are constantly revising our memories to suit our current identities'.[2] For the Elizabethans, memory was one of the faculties of the human soul, together with imagination and reason,[3] and was, as Andrew Hiscock stresses, 'intimately bound up with an understanding of how their everyday selves were constructed'.[4] Affective bonds tying the individual to other individuals are formed through memory[5] as are the moral and legal relationships established within a given social order, so that forgetting these bonds entails a departure from social normative pressures, often expressed as 'forgetting oneself'.[6] In the early modern period, memory was also at the centre of identity constructions based on lineage and reputation. Remembrance of one's lineage was often invoked in order to require a particular behaviour and to seek legitimation of one's acts. Fame and honour, as acquired by one's behaviour through memorable acts, especially heroic deeds, ensured that one was remembered and respected by others and that one's memory lived on after death. Similarly, the collective identity of cities and nations was moulded by ways in which citizens remembered their past. They invested history with meaning in order to define the present, often appropriating the past in the interest of specific political agenda.[7]

Both plays under study in this discussion refer to a classical past in rather opaque terms: an ahistorical Rome during the late and declining imperial period in *Titus Andronicus*,[8] and the legendary Trojan war of *Troilus and Cressida* which was known through a host of various narratives. In effect, the unresolved nature of the past in these Shakespearean narratives links directly with the plays' demythologization of what remembering Rome and Troy would entail for many Elizabethans: an evocation of a glorious civilization; heroic militarism; chivalric virtue; and a historical legitimation of their present, fostered by the notion of 'translation of empire'[9] – a notion that had London imagined as a new Troy, and Britain as created by Brute, a descendant of Aeneas, the Trojan founder of Rome.[10] As Heather James has pointed out, both plays question such a celebratory remembrance of the past, and therefore the 'political program invested in transporting imperial authority' from the past to Elizabethan England,[11] while, at the same time, both, in Hester Lees-Jeffries' terms, 'demonstrate the fallibility of memory' and how 'memory of the classical past in particular is fragmentary, fractured, ruined'.[12] However, it remains in no doubt that for the Elizabethans, the remembering or alluding to Virgil's *Aeneid* engaged with the political valences of its imperial ideology to which the Tudor monarchy remained richly sensitive, while, equally importantly, remembering Ovid's 'counter-epic' *Metamorphoses* evoked critiques concerning the founding of empire.[13]

One of the ways in which Shakespeare's plays seek to demythologize the classical past is by constructing their protagonists as fractured individuals. The discussion which follows explores how memory operates in this process through a close reading of those moments when characters remember and forget (including remembering and forgetting themselves), are remembered and forgotten, or allude to acts of remembrance and forgetting.[14]

Titus Andronicus

Personal and social practices of memory can be seen to define the titular hero of *Titus Andronicus*. The revenge hero paradoxically shows, on the one hand, a resistance or inability to forget the wrongs he has suffered (as if an act of forgetfulness would destroy the avenger's identity)[15] and, on the other hand, he acknowledges the necessity to forget normative behaviour and allegiances to social order in order to pursue revenge.[16] Remembrance of injustices committed against one's relatives involves the strengthening of affection, or perhaps the demonstration of loyalty or obligation towards that affection, while forgetting social norms in favour of private revenge entails a disaffection with (a disloyalty towards) the existing order.

Titus first appears in the play as remembered by his brother Marcus in terms that cast him as an example of Roman virtue (I.1.23–38).[17] By hailing him as 'surnamed Pius', Marcus recalls Pius Aeneas as described in Rome's foundational epic *The Aeneid*.[18] Remembrance (either implicit, as in this case, or explicit) of the classical authorities of Virgil's national epic and later of Ovid's *Metamorphoses* becomes a structural device for the tragedy. Indeed, for Heather James, these allusions 'perform a critique of imperial Rome on the eve of its collapse and, in doing so, glance proleptically at Elizabethan England as an emergent nation' (p. 42). Titus's first physical appearance is at a processional 'triumph', which, like all social rituals, is, as Isobel Karremann underlines, 'formally and functionally associated with memory', turning individual members into 'an imagined community' and helping to establish 'continuity and collective identity'.[19] In his first speech, Titus remembers his sons killed in war against the Goths (I.1.74–98) in a publicly uttered remembrance that is both a homage to the slain and a personal expression of affliction.[20] The presence of the 'tomb' on stage (whether in the so-called discovery space or in the trap-door) reinforces the public and social dimensions of this act of remembering the dead. Later in the scene, Titus calls it a 'monument' where 'none but soldiers and Rome servitor's / Repose in fame' (I.1.355, 357-8), thus bringing together in one reference the notions of reputation and of a commemorative architectural structure.[21]

As the tomb is opened, Titus associates the values of 'virtue and nobility' (I.1.96) with the monument, but also invests in it his affections as a father: 'O sacred receptacle of my joys' (95). As the coffin is laid in the tomb (152), with a ceremonial flourish of trumpets, Titus repeats 'In peace and honour rest you here, my sons' (153, 159):[22] their burial ritual is sanctified with the wish that they be remembered. Acknowledging the collective memory of the warrior culture of which he has become an epitome, Titus turns his private suffering into public mourning, and so he aptly recalls King Priam of Troy as a model – a warrior-father with many of his sons killed during the war (I.1.83). This reference to Troy might immediately remind the audience of 'the familiar typology Troy-Rome-London (Troynovant)'.[23] However, the funerary rites to 'welcome' Titus's dead sons 'to Rome' (150) are juxtaposed onstage with the 'Roman rites', as Lucius terms the human sacrifice of Tamora's son Alarbus (146). This juxtaposition strikes a discordant note. Titus's and his surviving sons' affliction is thus satisfied ('revenged') by means of a socially circumscribed ritual involving the dismemberment and cremation of the perceived antagonist. Interestingly, Titus invokes this sacrifice in the name of religion: 'Religiously they ask a sacrifice' (128) – that is, in its etymological sense, of the bonds that tie humans to the divine order. In the knowledge, as Jonathan Bate points out, that 'Rome prided itself on not allowing human sacrifice',[24] one may suspect that this acclaimed Roman general is forgetting a determinant cultural code in pursuit of private gratification. This act of forgetting sparks the first suspicion that the play intends to question the values associated with the ancient city-state.[25] Indeed, when Chiron exclaims 'Was never Scythia half so barbarous!' (134) on Lucius's command to dismember Alarbus, the opposition between the civilized Romans against the barbaric Goths is placed under severe interrogation.[26]

In this dramatic narrative, honour (construed as memory for the dead) is soon replaced by fame (construed as memory for the living). Titus's repeated phrase 'In peace and honour' is taken up by Lavinia as she greets her father with 'In peace and honour, live Lord Titus long: / My noble lord and father, live in fame!' (I.1.160–161). More generally, the wish to be remembered, expressed in terms of fame, recurs obsessively in the first scene: Titus replies with a wish that his daughter outlive not only him but also 'fame's eternal date' (171); Marcus welcomes his dead nephews as those 'that sleep in fame' (176), and later describes his nephew Mutius, just killed by his father, in terms of living 'in fame' (395). The remembrance of Titus's famous deeds lies at the heart of the social obligations the Roman emperor Saturninus assumes towards him and towards Rome. After Titus decides on Saturninus as new emperor and delivers his sword and prisoners to him, Saturninus replies, 'How proud I am of thee and of thy gifts, / Rome shall record, and when I do forget / The least of these unspeakable deserts, / Romans forget your fealty to me' (I.1.258–261). In this way, the emperor expresses his bond and affection towards Titus in terms of a public record in the city's annals (something worthy to be remembered by the Romans) and, significantly, the hypothetical breakdown of such an obligation in terms of forgetting: if Saturninus fails to remember the merits ('deserts') he has received from Titus, then the Romans will be free to 'forget', to neglect their obligation of loyalty ('fealty') towards the emperor.

Before the extended first scene concludes, the tragic hero commits a second act of oblivion and, at the same time, is figured as a victim of acts of forgetting – all in such quick succession that they seem to challenge radically his sense of self-hood. Whereas Titus had remembered his dead sons at the opening of the play, he soon forgets the affective ties that bind together parents and children when he kills his own son Mutius (I.1.295) for rebelling against his decision to give the hand of his daughter Lavinia to the newly crowned emperor Saturninus. For Titus, such intolerably rebellious behaviour on the part of Mutius brings 'dishonour' upon the father (300). In this surprising situation of conflicting loyalties towards family and a social superior, Titus opts for the latter, only to learn swiftly that his social superior has forgotten him: Saturninus does not need Lavinia, or her father, or any of his sons any more (304–312) and chooses to make Tamora his empress (324–325). Titus is left 'dishonoured' (345) by his emperor, feeling like a forgotten wedding guest ('I am not bid to wait upon this bride', 343), and 'dishonoured' (350 and 390) by his surviving sons and brother. His sense of wounded honour (370), of having his social and familial status humiliatingly neglected, traumatises him to such an extent that his second son declares that his father 'is not with himself' (373). From this bitter experience of marginalisation and scorn, Titus begins to reconstitute his sense of selfhood by re-investing in the sanctity of kinship, as he agrees to his brother's and sons' pleas to inter Mutius in the family tomb. He curtly concedes, 'Well, bury him, and bury me the next' (391): to bury his son is to remember him properly, but metaphorically to bury himself is to forget his notion of self-hood that has been so tortured by recent events. However, as the hero of a revenge tragedy, this investment in the contrary motions of remembering and forgetting can only continue to unsettle and excite the development of the intrigue. It becomes clear that the hero's sense of self-worth needs to be reconstituted before he can fashion himself as a victim of the wrongs that will trigger his ultimate revenge. This process of emotional and political reconstitution is set in motion with the emperor's gesture of reconciliation – a dissembling tactic advised by Tamora. The emperor's words and looks now 'infuse new life' in Titus (466). The next time Titus is onstage he is the jovial host of a royal hunt (II.1): to all intents and purposes, he seems to have *forgotten* the affronts caused by the emperor, his sons, or by his brother.

However, the hero's cheerfulness and self-assuredness collapse when Tamora's own revenge plot[27] has his sons, Quintus and Martius, accused of having murdered the emperor's brother. Kneeling again before Saturninus, Titus offers himself as security for his sons and supports his appeal to the emperor by vowing on his 'fathers' reverend tomb' (II.2.296). The Andronici's funerary monument had remained centre-stage metaphorically (and probably literally) in the play's first scene. However, it also inhabits a strategic place in Titus's growing mental and emotional sense of self. The monument is inextricably associated with the values of heroic militarism which Titus has demonstrated in his campaigns in the service of the state. In the event, Titus pleads in vain. Saturninus denies Titus's plea (II.2.299).

As II.2. draws to a close with public demonstrations of Titus's apparent resignation and submission to imperial authority, there arises the possibility that the hero's apparently vain attempts at commemoration occasion yet another crisis of purpose. This is confirmed in Titus's next appearance when he vehemently asks the tribunes to have mercy on his condemned sons heading towards '*the place of execution*' (III.1.0.3). In his appeal, he resorts firstly not only to the evidence of his old age and of his tears, but also to the judges' remembrance of his military past at the service of Rome (III.1.2–4). Titus has built his personal and social identity on his soldierly exploits, which remain the key shaping influences on his reputation and honour, but these are now, it seems, at stake. Again, in this encounter with the tribunes, Titus remains unsuccessful. Without uttering a single word, the tribunes '*pass by him*' as Titus '*lieth down*' (III.1.11.1), and so the father and general, now feeling his grief 'at the height' (as he later explains in III.1.71), finds himself addressing the 'reverend tribunes' (23) in vain.

The realisation that recalling his military service to the country is futile serves to exacerbate Titus's crisis of his self-worth and shakes his sense of purpose to the core. The profound nature of his disorientation is witnessed as he now refers to the imperial city as 'a wilderness of tigers' (III.1.54): Rome is no longer remembered as the epitome of civilisation, but as a place that devours its sons. Furthermore, this crisis is inevitably rendered even more acute with the appearance of the brutally maimed Lavinia (III.1.58), whom her uncle Marcus compares to Philomela as raped by Tereus in *Metamorphoses* (II.3.26–43).[28] The agony of the aged father is communicated in his reply to Marcus, that if the sorrow his brother brings will destroy him, he will submit to it: 'Will it consume me? Let me see it then' (III.1.62). In a culture wholly obsessed with processes of commemoration, the hero can now envisage the utter loss of self in anguish and oblivion.

The sight of his 'handless' daughter turns 'hands' into the focus of Titus's overbearing grief. His wish to chop them off expresses his desire to put an end to a grief that overflows like the river Nilus (III.1.72). As if unable to forget that he 'fought for Rome, and all in vain' (74), Titus makes his hands the subject of the action he painfully remembers. At the same time, they are the subject of the more personal dimension of his identity: his parental care. In an outpouring riddled with contending memories, Titus remembers that his hands 'nursed' his daughter, feeding her life only to bring her to 'this woe' (75); and he remembers that his hands had been 'held up' in 'bootless prayer' (76), and served him to 'effectless use' (77). Titus's troubled meditations continue as he reassures Lavinia that it is well that she has no hands, 'For hands to do Rome service is but vain' (81). He concludes his speech of intense misery with a reference, again, to his hitherto unwavering sense of social and patriotic obligation. In lines 99–103, the hero recalls and recounts the accumulated grief that overburdens his memory and undermines his very sense of self.[29] Among them, Lavinia is 'the greatest spurn' (102) which leads his mind to inquire about forms of suffering that 'may do [her] ease' (122). Titus's accumulation of imagined miseries (including self-mutilation of hands and tongues), expressed in rhetorical questions, leads him to a new resolution: 'Let us that have our tongues / Plot some device of further misery / To make us wondered at in time to come' (III.1.134–136). Here, Titus fashions a new, superlative identity through which his family may be remembered in the future as those supremely afflicted with suffering.

Continuing this examination of the play's figurative and physical concern with hands, Aaron brings the emperor's offer to ransom Titus's sons in exchange for a chopped hand of their relatives. The worth of Titus's hand is measured by the remembrance of its military exploits in the service of Rome, as Lucius recalls in III.1.164–165, and as Titus bids Aaron to remind Saturninus (194–196).[30] After the messenger returns Titus's 'good hand' (236) and the heads of his sons Quintus and Martius, Titus expresses his suffering as a terrible sleep from which he wishes to awake.[31] His brother Marcus replies that this cycle of suffering is indeed real by reminding Titus that he does not sleep, and by pointing to the severed heads of Titus's sons, his 'warlike hand', his 'mangled daughter', and his 'other banished son' (255–257). The common association of sleep with oblivion continues to structure Marcus's responses: he wants to prevent Titus from forgetting his misery and so points out to him tokens of remembrance. These become the foundations of Titus's new identity as an avenger. Despite the backdrop of indecorous laughter ('Ha, ha, ha!', 265), Titus now vows to seek vengeance (expressed in terms of finding 'Revenge's cave' (271, 280)) and the vow commits Titus to an obligation which involves maintaining in his memory the 'wrongs' he has sworn to 'right' (279).[32]

The following scene, probably a later addition and only printed in the Folio volume of 1623,[33] confirms Titus and his family as revengers.[34] Yet, these new identities are not without striking challenges which continue to be viewed through the lens of memory at a personal and public level. The first symptom of the tremendous strain of this newly assumed identity is Titus's fit of insanity (what Marcus calls 'ecstasy' in IV.1.125).[35] Titus even acknowledges (and boasts of) his insanity when he replies to Marcus's reproach that he is teaching his daughter Lavinia how to kill herself (III.2.21–22).[36] If, in the first scene of the play, Titus had forgotten the affective bonds between parent and child when he killed his son Mutius (I.1.295), this 'first' scene of the play's second half[37] has Titus equally oblivious of these ties, but the difference now is that this act of oblivion can be explained by a fit of madness.[38] Another difference can be seen in the fact that Titus gives instructions to others for the killing, instead of carrying out the action himself – although these instructions may be seen as an anticipation of Titus's actual slaughtering of his daughter at V.3.46.

The following nine lines in Titus's speech (III.2.25–33) are illustrative of the way memory plays a role in the tense inner life of the revenger. He reproaches his brother Marcus for using the words 'violent hands' (22), which renew the awareness of suffering, and thus act as painful prompts to the memory of their maimed condition. In the interventions which follow, Titus recalls the classical story of Aeneas and Dido in the *Aeneid*: Marcus's naming of hands re-members their 'miserable' (28) state in a manner similar to that of Aeneas' retelling of 'How Troy was burnt' (28) renewed his own woe. Titus tries to avoid additional suffering tied to the operations of memory. Initially, he wishes not to remember ('Lest we remember', 30), as if oblivion might mitigate pain, but soon realises the futility of such a desire: it is but mere wishful thinking to believe that they can forget they have no hands if Marcus does not 'name the word of hands' (33). Subsequently, Titus's mood transforms into a lament concerning his role as interpreter of Lavinia's speechless signs (35–45), and then into anger at his brother's killing of a fly (54–66). Interestingly, Marcus cuts short his brother's reprimand by turning the fly into a reminder of 'the empress' Moor' (69). Significantly, remembering Aaron throws Titus into another fit of insanity in which 'He takes false shadows for true substances' (80).

The opening scene of Act IV stages the revelation of 'the damned contriver' (36) of Lavinia's rape and mutilation, which is brought about by using a memory device: the book of 'Ovid's *Metamorphoses*' (42) containing the 'tragic tale of Philomel' (47).[39] Memory also comes to the fore when Titus remembers Tarquin's rape of Lucrece as he thinks of Saturninus (63–64), and when, reacting to the revelation that Chiron and Demetrius raped Lavinia, he remembers and draws upon the phrasing from Seneca's tragedy *Hippolytus* (also known as *Phaedra*) and from his *Moral Epistles* in an appeal to the gods' sense of justice (81–82).[40] The next step one would expect the revengers to take would be to commit themselves formally to their task. However, it is not clear whether the hero participates in a swearing ritual, conducted by Marcus, in which the whole family (including Lavinia and Lucius's son) is asked to kneel down and vow to 'prosecute .... Mortal revenge' (IV.1.92–93). Interestingly, in the next speech (95–106) Titus adopts an attitude of caution. After pointing out Tamora's shrewdness and Marcus's inexperience, he advises to 'let alone' (i.e., leave off) any direct approach to revenge and 'lay it by' (101, 104) until a more propitious time or until revenge 'can be carried out more subtly'.[41] Yet, postponing revenge runs the risk of forgetting about it. One recognised recourse against forgetfulness is writing, and so Titus resolves, 'I will go get a leaf of brass / And with a gad of steel will write these words' (102–103). At this point, there are two aspects to Titus's inscription worth pointing out: it is on a 'leaf' (which suggests the prophetic character of supernatural inscriptions usually made on leaves) and it is on 'brass', that is, on a more durable material than sand (as suggested in line 105). Scene IV.3, where kinsmen attempt to soothe the distracted Titus, highlights the social and political dimensions of the revenge story. However, from the beginning of the scene, the hero is intent upon foregrounding the notion that justice has forsaken the world:

> *Terras Astraea reliquit*: be you remembered, Marcus,
> She's gone, she's fled. [...]
> Happily you may catch her in the sea;
> Yet there's as little justice as at land.
> *(IV.3. 4–5, 8–9)*

This assertion is later repeated and expanded to include the underworld: 'sith there's no justice in earth nor hell' (50). Interestingly, at line 4, two acts of remembering are being performed: Titus recalls in Latin a phrase from Ovid's *Metamorphoses* (I.169–170)[42] and enjoins his brother to remember it, as if binding themselves to a new course of action. The Latin phrase refers to the legendary virgin goddess of justice, Astraea, leaving the earth during the Iron Age, the fourth and last age of Mankind.[43] By remembering the *Metamorphoses*, Titus gives expression to the revengers' recurring condemnation of the absence of justice in this fallen, Roman world.[44] Inevitably, if there is no justice on earth, the logic of the avenger leads him to seek it elsewhere: Titus exhorts his kinsmen to look for justice in 'Pluto's region' (IV.3.13), once he has realised that sending them to 'the ocean' (6) is of no purpose.[45] Titus focuses his complaint on 'ungrateful Rome' (17), which causes him painfully to remember – at IV.3.18–20 – how he helped Saturninus become a 'wicked emperor' (23). Remembrance here not only brings about feelings of sadness and regret to the deranged avenger, but also a sense of guilt concerning the social and political ills of Roman society. It is also worth highlighting here that Titus calls Rome 'ungrateful' (and later Marcus also denounces the ingratitude of Rome at IV.3.34), which implies the Roman authorities' forgetting about the merits and services of the Andronici.

At this point in the play, Titus seems to have forgotten any imperative for private revenge, in contrast to his brother Marcus, who remains steadfast to the hope that the war with the Goths will bring about 'vengeance on the traitor Saturnine' (IV.3.35) and on Rome for its ingratitude.[46] Yet, as the tragedy draws to its catastrophe, Titus carries out his first act of revenge in killing Chiron and Demetrius at the end of scene V.2. The event unfolds in a slow, ceremonious, almost ritualistic manner: Chiron and Demetrius are bound and gagged, Titus and Lavinia enter with a knife and a basin respectively; and before Titus cuts their throats, he delivers a thirty-two line address in which he reminds Tamora's sons of their crimes (V.2.169–179), of their forthcoming execution and how he will bake a pasty with their bones and blood for the feast he is giving to Saturninus and Tamora (180–203). In his detailed explanation, Titus resorts to Ovid's *Metamorphoses* twice, first to remember the story of Philomel and Procne (194–195), and secondly to the story of the 'Centaurs' feast' (202–203). Both references recall banquets that were notorious for their savagery.[47]

The Ovidian stories Titus remembers serve as precedents with which to compare Chiron and Demetrius's crimes and the extreme rigour with which he plans to carry out his revenge at the banquet, which even surpasses these models: 'For worse than Progne I will be revenged' (V.2.195).[48] Remembering Philomel also reinforces his sense of duty to keep in mind the wrongs that caused the revenge. In both the Philomel story and in *Titus Andronicus*, the cook is also the slayer of the mythical heroine and of the Shakespearean hero's offspring respectively, while in each case the royal authorities are tricked into the cannibalistic eating of their children. Remembering Procne anticipates Titus's slaughtering of Lavinia in the last scene (V.3.46) during the banquet that he offers the Roman authorities and the Goth warriors. In direct comparison with his killing Tamora's sons, Titus resorts to the recollection of another story, that of the Roman centurion Virginius, who slew 'his daughter with his own right hand, / Because she was enforced, stained and deflowered' (V.3.36–37). For Titus, remembering Virginius has an added purpose, as compared to his recalling of Philomel and Procne: it provides not only an example, but also an authorisation or 'conclusive proof'[49] which validates the immediate action of killing his own daughter.[50]

In contrast to the legendary character of Procne, Virginius's story is recorded in several historiographic sources, among them Livy's history of Rome *Ab Urbe Condita*.[51] Yet, it is not only its factual character that renders it a 'lively warrant' for Titus, but also the fact that Saturninus approves of, and gives reasons for, Virginius's behaviour (V.3.40–41).[52] Two concepts here are key to a discussion of memory. Lavinia's sacrifice is a matter of reputation, of how the family will be remembered. The Roman code urges the cleansing of dishonour by death, and Lavinia's mutilated body is a continuous reminder of such a dishonour. At the same time, Lavinia's existence reminds her father of his own grief caused in part by her 'shame'. It should be pointed out that Titus's declarations and the killing of Lavinia are performed in full view of the onstage audience. Titus is dealing with the outward dimension of his parental identity as patriarch of the Andronici. Nothing is related concerning his inner feelings as a father. Titus's logic here is that if Lavinia is alive in her shameful state, he is unable to forget the affliction brought about by the experience of dishonour (V.3.45–46).[53] His unnatural action recalls the slaughtering of his son Mutius in the first scene of the tragedy. In both situations, Titus forgets the affective ties and moral bonds involved in parent–child relationships. The first action was 'rash', the fatal reaction of a fit of anger or of a habit deeply ingrained in a warrior; Lavinia's killing is premeditated, the result of a conscious decision made by a divided self in whom the public and social dimensions of identity prevail over the private and personal ones.

After the murder of Titus at the close of the play,[54] all that remains is to remember him both privately and publicly. First, Titus is remembered in the private sphere of his family, when his son Lucius, his brother Marcus and his grandson 'shed obsequious tears' upon his corpse and kiss it (V.3.151), but in full view of the onstage audience. Lucius even reminds his son of the tenderness Titus bestowed on him as a grandfather. Public remembrance is linked both to the burial rites (not mentioned in the play) and the place of burial. Lucius's reference to the Andronici's 'household's monument' (192) creates another connection with the first scene that underpins a dramatic and thematic symmetry which lies at the heart of Shakespeare's play. Titus will be remembered in his proper place at 'his fathers' grave' (191). This burial at the monument is in sharp contrast to the burying of Aaron alive, and to the absence of burial for the other avenger of the tragedy, Tamora. The play's very last lines are devoted to explaining how Tamora's corpse will be disposed of with no funeral rite – her body thrown 'forth to beasts and birds of prey' (197) in the same manner as executed criminals in Shakespeare's England.[55] Lucius reminds the onstage and offstage audience that she was 'beastly and devoid of pity' (198), and uses that memory to justify his pitiless disposal of her body. The audience may well remember that Lucius and his family pitilessly dismembered Tamora's son when she arrived in Rome. At the end of the play, the glorious ancient Roman civilisation that Elizabethans were 'nostalgic' about has proved to be uncivilised and inglorious.

Troilus and Cressida

Strikingly, memory is also put to the test in a play like *Troilus and Cressida* whose characters and combined stories (like those in *Titus Andronicus*) bring to the fore a sense of anguished fracturing and implicitly a nostalgia for or painful remembrance of a lost wholeness.[56] This fracturing is integral to the play's deflationary and satiric treatment of the classical past.[57] In contrast to *Titus Andronicus*, the stories of war and love in *Troilus and Cressida* might be well 'remembered' by educated sections of the Elizabethan audience.[58] As Stanley Wells remarks, 'Shakespeare capitalizes on his knowledge that his audience would know the end of the stories'.[59] Indeed, the play's satirical mode depends on the addressee's remembrance of the object of satire.[60] Among the major characters in *Troilus and Cressida*, Thersites is the only one the audience might have difficulty in recalling because he only appears once in Book II of the *Iliad*.

In general terms, Shakespeare seems to have drawn upon Chapman's translation and this is manifested in many verbal echoes throughout the play.[61] Interestingly, Chapman's negative characterisation of Thersites as a scolder of his superiors is emphasised by the addition of 'and thus himself forgot.'[62] This phrase, added to rhyme with 'throat' to complete the fourteener, reveals the narrator's unfavourable judgment of Thersites, making explicit the notion of insubordination in terms of forgetting one's position in the social hierarchy.[63] Shakespeare appropriates the railing, insolent and authority-challenging traits of the Homeric character and expands his presence to several scenes in Act II and Act V where he often comes to dominate the stage with his satiric observations.[64] At such dramatic moments, Thersites is often turned into a fool (much like Feste and Touchstone) assuming the privileges of speaking without restraint,[65] as well as into a choric commentator on the action, exposing the follies and stupidities of the other characters and diminishing their lofty sense of heroic greatness.[66] Thus, Thersites acts as a reminder to the audience that the play is a satire of war and of the chivalric ideals of valour, honour and love.[67]

In contrast to Thersites, Achilles was widely remembered as the greatest warrior among the Greeks. This received knowledge appears in the play's first mention of him, when Cressida remarks that he is a better man than Troilus (I.2.238). However, the play's deflationary emphasis is soon shown to be at work with Pandarus's immediate reply that he is 'a drayman, a porter, a very camel' (240). The warrior-hero is mentioned for the second time in Ulysses's set speech on Achilles in I.3, describing the latter's refusal to fight in the war and how he lies lazily on his bed laughing at his friend Patroclus's sarcastic mocking of the Greek commanders. The context is the Greeks' discussion about the low morale in their army and their failure to achieve their military objectives after seven years. Ulysses explains that the cause lies in their forgetting ('neglecting') the exercise of authority and sense of hierarchy (I.3.78–184), and uses Achilles's attitude as an instance of this. Indeed, Ulysses's description undermines any positive memory that offstage addressees may have of Achilles. At the beginning of his speech, Ulysses summarises the received image of the warrior: 'The great Achilles, whom opinion crowns / The sinew and the forehead of our host' (142–143), but then he identifies the nature of the problem in the fact that Achilles has 'his ear full of his airy fame' (144). Ulysses insists that the hero, like any other, is defined by his reputation, his public 'opinion'.[68] If Achilles's ear is full of fame, he is constantly reminded by word of mouth of his heroic deeds. The adjective 'airy' brings together the meanings 'insubstantial' or 'evanescent'[69], thus anticipating his lecturing of Achilles in III.3, and 'dependent on mere words'[70], which continues the image of Achilles's fame being remembered in the commentaries of others. In any event, if Achilles's reputation is on everybody's lips, the warrior is also mindful of it and grows 'dainty of his worth' (I.3.145) – the adjective 'dainty' in the sense of 'fastidious', very attentive, or 'careful, chary'.[71] Achilles's memorial formulation of his glorious past has made him a presumptuous and self-opinionated man. This excess of 'self-remembrance' could be placed in stark contrast with what the offstage audience might remember from Book I in the *Iliad*: Agamemnon's humiliation of Achilles concerning the damsel Briseis whom the latter had taken as prisoner.

Ulysses's later descriptions of Achilles as swollen with pride (I.3.316–318),[72] and 'too insolent' (370) agree with Homer's characterisation, but in Shakespeare these traits appear to be motivated by Achilles actively desiring remembrance by others: as Ulysses also explains, Achilles 'broils in loud applause' (380), that is, is overheated by others' praise.[73] If, in the *Iliad*, Achilles is primarily moved by honour, by the zeal to ensure that men will remember his name, in Shakespeare's play excessive self-remembrance hinders the hero's need to perform further deeds of glory.[74] For Ulysses, the solution to Achilles's problem, the way to spur him back into action, lies in forgetting about him. The Greek commanders are called upon to feign that they are not interested in Achilles ('As if he were forgot' (III.3.40)) as they walk past his tent; they return a 'negligent and loose regard upon him' (41).[75] Their neglectful attitude sows a crisis of identity in Achilles.[76] Moreover, in order to wound Achilles's pride more acutely, Ulysses resorts to a book (a mnemonic tool) he is reading (III.3.93) about how one's qualities are not valued 'but by reflection' (100) – that is, only when they are seen or remembered by others. This book prompts the ensuing conversation between Ulysses and Achilles on vanity, on the mutability of Fortune and on the virtue and merit needed to be remembered by others, which finally leads Achilles to wonder: 'What, are my deeds forgot?' (III.3.145). Ulysses replies by resorting to Time's proverbial ingratitude and forgetfulness:[77]

> Time hath, my lord, a wallet at his back,
> Wherein he puts alms for oblivion,
> A great-sized monster of ingratitudes.
> Those scraps are good deeds past, which are
> Devoured as fast as they are made, forgot
> As soon as done.
>
> *(III.3.146–151)*

The familiar image of oblivion as a devouring monster is combined with Shakespeare's apparently original personification of Time as carrying a sack with heroic deeds, qualified as mere 'alms'. The sense of forgetting is reinforced in this instance by the traditional and emblematic image of the sack being worn over the shoulder:[78] not seeing its contents contributes to their being easily forgotten. Then, Ulysses underscores his argument about the futility of heroic glory achieved only in the past and the transience of fame by means of the image of a 'rusty mail' (a suit of armour) that hangs on the wall in 'monumental mock'ry' (III.3.154), like a 'mocking trophy of forgotten noble deeds'.[79] Ulysses goads Achilles even more by suggesting that he will be remembered for winning one of Hector's sisters, Polyxena, and not for overcoming the great Hector, who will be defeated by his rival Ajax (III.3.209–215). To this, Patroclus reminds Achilles that his 'great love' for him (223) is one of the reasons 'They think' (222) the great warrior has withdrawn from the war. In this way, Achilles has been made strategically to realise that his 'reputation is at stake' and that his 'fame is shrewdly gored' (229–230).

From this point on, Achilles resumes his expected warrior identity and maintains it when the Trojans visit the Greek camp (IV.5). However, his resolution to take up arms again is thwarted when he is reminded of his promise not to fight by a letter from Queen Hecuba and by a token of remembrance sent by his beloved Polyxena (V.1). Achilles decides to keep his promise, but the death of Patroclus in battle (V.5.17) turns him into an irate avenger, eager to confront Hector (V.5.46). The climatic moment of Hector's death does not coincide with what the audience remembers from Book XXII in the *Iliad*. Here, Shakespeare 'forgets' the narrative sources[80] and demythologises this narrative moment: rather than facing Hector in single combat as in Homer, Achilles forgets the chivalric code and has his Myrmidons unfairly attack Hector when the latter is unarmed (V.9.9–10). This debunking of Achilles is made more forceful when the audience remembers that a few scenes earlier (in V.6.14–20) it was Hector who had chivalrously let him go unharmed. Moreover, the Greek prince orders his Myrmidons to proclaim 'Achilles hath the mighty Hector slain!' (V.9.14), a proclamation confirmed by Diomedes (V.10.4): Achilles has secured his memory as the slayer of Hector, but for the offstage audience this memory does not correspond to the dishonourable act they have witnessed.

Troilus first appears in Shakespeare's play as an impatient, suffering, sighing, love-sick gallant whose instability is also interestingly expressed in memorial terms.[81] As he chides Pandarus for making him wait too long and compares himself to the goddess Patience, Troilus calls to mind – and mentions for the first time – the name of Cressida:

> At Priam's royal table do I sit,
> And when fair Cressid comes into my thoughts –
> So, traitor! 'When she comes'! When is she thence?
>
> *(I.1.27–29)*

This self-interruption remains telling. The prince cuts himself short when he remembers Cressida and berates himself as 'traitor' – for remembering his love entails the possibility that he, the faithful lover, has momentarily forgotten her.[82] When next onstage, Troilus is not the impassioned love idealist, but the strenuous warrior upholding the ethos of heroic militarism. In the debate over Helen's release to the Greeks (II.2),[83] in which Hector favours giving her back because 'she is not worth what she doth cost / The holding' (51–52), Troilus voices the opposite attitude. The young prince questions Hector's sense of 'worth' and invoking honour and fame instead, Troilus resorts to two uses of memory. First, he reminds the Trojans that everyone agreed on Paris's abduction of Helen as an act of revenge on the Greeks for holding Priam's sister captive (72–80). Secondly, after Hector has unexpectedly reversed his own commitment to this decision, Troilus brings the debate to a close by adducing that keeping Helen is a stimulus for the Trojans to 'beat down' the Greeks and be remembered in the future for this heroic exploit (199–202).[84]

In the initial presentation of Cressida in scene I.2, the use of memory is not expressed in explicit terms, but, significantly in the light of the broader concerns of this discussion, it will be later connected to her sense of fractured self. The heroine's conflicted sense of purpose is already in evidence in the way she hides her true feelings for Troilus, first in the witty dialogue with her uncle Pandarus and then in her soliloquy that closes the scene in whose last couplet she clearly states her strategy of pretence. A similar demeanour can be identified in her next appearance (scene III.2), the first real encounter of the lovers. After the initial conversation with Troilus in which she still feigns a resistance to his charms, Cressida's revelation of her love in line 110 launches a series of hesitations and interruptions that denote a tormented self, to the point of acknowledging a kind of self-division:

> I have a kind of self resides with you,
> But an unkind self that itself will leave
> To be another's fool. Where is my wit?
> I would be gone. I speak I know not what.
> *(III.2.143–145)*

These words reveal what Anthony Dawson terms 'a kind of nostalgia for wholeness'[85] and articulates a longing for her past ability to use her wit in her own defence (as was witnessed in her conversation with Pandarus in I.2).[86] Scene III.3 culminates in a triple act of memory (at the turning point of the intrigue),[87] with Troilus, Cressida and Pandarus anticipating how they will be remembered in the future: as faithful gallant, unfaithful female lover, and go-between respectively. Troilus postulates himself as a model of truthfulness that future poets will remember (III.2.168–169).[88] Then, Cressida lays her constancy to the judgment of memory, but she employs the opposite notion of falsehood introduced by a conditional clause:

> If I be false, or swerve a hair from truth,
> When time is old and hath forgot itself,
> When waterdrops have worn the stones of Troy,
> And blind oblivion swallowed cities up,
> And mighty states characterless are grated
> To dusty nothing, yet let memory,
> From false to false, among false maids in love,
> Upbraid my falsehood!
> *(III.2.179–186)*

In contrast to Troilus's declarative mode, that of the conditional in Cressida's speech anticipates her infidelity and increases the dramatic irony of that moment, as the audience remembers that she will prove unfaithful. Furthermore, in contrast to Troilus's invocation of poets, Cressida sets higher stakes by introducing the all-encompassing idea of history ('memory' in line 184) as the agent that may upbraid her unfaithfulness. While Troilus simply refers to the future with the indefinite phrase 'the world to come', Cressida extends the time-span in a four-part hyperbole that culminates in an almost apocalyptic vision of 'cities' and 'mighty states' devastated. In this vision, Cressida uses the proverbial notion of time's ingratitude and forgetfulness (anticipating Ulysses's use, seen above). The 'states' that are 'characterless' have their recorded history destroyed. By invoking time's powerful forgetting, Cressida emphasises the remembrance of her putative falsehood: time may destroy, but history will remember her, if she 'be false'.

In the parting scenes (IV.2 and IV.4), Troilus's all too quick acceptance of Cressida's departure (IV.2.71–73) has been interpreted as an indication that he has almost forgotten her because he has already fulfilled his sexual desire (as Cressida suspected in I.2.278–286 referring to men in general). By contrast, Cressida struggles during this separation from Troilus by arguing that she has a new identity involving the forsaking of the affective ties with her father: when Pandarus informs her 'Thou must to thy father, and be gone from Troilus', Cressida replies with 'I will not go' and 'I have forgot my father' (IV.2.92, 95 and 97). This investment in erasing her identity as a daughter, together with the social pressures inherent in being a child, is necessary for her re-constitution of her new identity as a lover. The new connections of 'kin', 'love', and 'blood' she acknowledges are only those belonging to her 'sweet Troilus' (IV.2.100). This fracturing of her identity is directly linked to this decision to forsake her past status as dutiful daughter, to query her role in the present as Troilus's, and that of the future which will be characterised by 'falsehood' (100–102).[89]

Interestingly, when the parting lovers exchange tokens of remembrance in scene IV.4 – Troilus's 'sleeve' (69) and Cressida's 'glove' (70) – he insists on her being 'true' rather than on remembering him or not forgetting him, as would be conventionally expected. This insistence on faithfulness is part of the play's ironic exploitation of the audience's memory of the legendary inconstancy of this female lover. The tokens are invoked again in the scene (V.2) confirming Cressida's unfaithfulness towards Troilus. Her inconstancy is shown not only by the fact that she participates in a kind of sexual dealing with her Greek protector, Diomedes, but also through her changeable behaviour. An enigmatic act of remembrance initiates the episode.[90] As Troilus is puzzled by Cressida's familiarity with Diomedes, he listens to this exchange:

DIOMEDES Will you remember?
CRESSIDA Remember? Yes.
DIOMEDES Nay, but do, then,
          And let your mind be coupled with your words.
                                              (V.2.14–17)

Bearing in mind that unfaithfulness is associated with forgetting, Cressida's inconstancy is made more poignant because she is first seen in her second new identity formulating acts of remembering: she will remember, 'Yes' (with the implication that she has forgotten Troilus); and she is made to remember again: 'What did you swear you would bestow on me?' (V.2.27). What Diomedes asks Cressida to remember is never made clear, but most critics suggest it is the promise (an 'oath', V.2.28) of a sexual favour.[91] Depending on the attitude and intonation employed, Cressida's line 'I prithee, do not hold me to mine oath' may be perceived as an attempt to untie herself from such a unspecified pledge or as an intentional provocation (as Thersites interprets in his aside 'A juggling trick: to be secretly open', V.2.26). Similarly enigmatic is Diomedes's 'But will you, then?' (60), engaging Cressida in remembering her promise in the future. In any case, remembrance entails obligation for the new lovers as they are developing their new relations. In order to ratify this new commitment, Diomedes asks for a token (62) to which Cressida agrees by delivering Troilus's sleeve (68). This token of remembrance, which excites the eavesdropping Thersites ('Now the pledge, now, now, now!' V.2.67) and makes Troilus exclaim 'O beauty, where is thy faith' (69), eventually fulfils its role when it reminds Cressida that Troilus loved her (73), and prompts her to put a stop to Diomedes's wooing.

> O pretty, pretty pledge!
> Thy master now lies thinking on his bed
> Of thee and me, and sighs, and takes my glove,
> And gives memorial dainty kisses to it –
> (V.2.83–86)

The sleeve makes Cressida imagine Troilus in two acts of memory: remembering her and the absent sleeve he gave her; and kissing the other token (her glove) in an act of loving remembrance. The choice of 'memorial' is significant here. The word only appears three times in the Shakespeare canon: twice as a noun in Sonnet 74, line 4, and in Thersites's 'oblique memorial' (V.1.54) in the sense of a 'monument';[92] and once as an adjective in this case, which carries nostalgic overtones of a commemoration for someone who is no longer present. It is a subtle trick of dramatic irony that Cressida imagines Troilus absent, when in fact he is watching her.

Troilus's sleeve is handed back and forth from Cressida to Diomedes between lines 66 and 96, thus functioning as the visual materialisation not only of her expected desertion but also of her changeable conduct and divided self. Cressida's last speech in the play epitomises this situation and consummates her legendary betrayal of Troilus: 'Troilus, farewell! One eye yet looks on thee, / But with my heart the other eye doth see' (V.2.113–114). The phonetic wordplay on 'eye/I' brings to the fore her sense of divided self: one 'I' still remembers Troilus with the eyes of her mind in what Dawson calls a 'regretful nostalgia',[93] while the other 'I' follows her heart's inclination towards Diomedes. For the deserted lover, the whole disappointing episode causes such a destabilising effect that he needs time in order to assimilate and register it: 'To make a recordation to my soul' (V.2.122). The imaginary mnemonic device is expressed through an unusual word of Latin origin, 'recordation', with the sense of 'commemorative account'.[94] To a certain extent, Cressida no longer exists for Troilus, at least the Cressida he once knew and now remembers. Troilus's inner struggle to come to terms with Cressida's identity reverberates with the heroine's sense of self-division and finds expression in his paradoxes and in his speech on 'Bifold authority' (151). Fragmentation is forcibly communicated when in the first line of this speech Troilus inquires 'This she?' and acknowledges 'No, this is Diomed's Cressida' (143), and later, 'This is and is not Cressid' (153), to acknowledge finally in defeat that 'The fractions of her faith [...] are bound to Diomed' (165, 167).[95]

Henceforth, Troilus casts off his lover persona and assumes that of the enraged warrior, eager to fight in the battle.[96] When he receives a letter from Cressida, whose contents the audience is not allowed to know, he tears it up and throws the scraps to the wind (V.3.109) – a gesture that signals his forgetting her as a necessary condition in order to confirm his reconstitution as a warrior. Troilus's final act of memory is to remember Achilles's ignominy in dishonouring Hector's corpse (V.11.4–5) with a view to committing the Trojans to 'Hope of revenge' (V.11.31). With the audience remembering the tragic ending that the play declines to show, Troilus's hope of revenge foreshadows an endless story of retaliations in which the warriors are unable to forget their wrongs until they meet their death.

Concluding thoughts

As was indicated at the beginning of this discussion, *Troilus and Cressida* and *Titus Andronicus* have different chronological relations to the classical past they demythologise: the former is contemporary with the legendary events of the Trojan war, while the latter, set in the decline of the Roman empire, looks back to the ancient glories of both Trojans and Romans. Given this temporal framework, it seems fitting that Shakespeare's Agamemnon should signal both the past (marked by bellicose enmity) and the future (whatever it may be in their present war) in 'oblivion' in his expression of welcome to the Trojans: 'What's past and what's to come is strewed with husks / And formless ruin of oblivion'[97] (IV.5.167–168). The conventional image of oblivion in terms of 'husks' and 'formless ruin' suggests that the past is one of decayed greatness and that 'the future will be strewed with such ruins as well'.[98]

Agamemnon's image gives expression to the play's broader debunking of the legendary past. However, equally significantly in the context of this discussion, the anonymous Roman lord at the end of *Titus Andronicus* asks Marcus to explain the events by drawing upon a comparison with Aeneas, whom he calls 'our ancestor' (V.3.79), narrating the fall of Troy to Dido, and by juxtaposing Rome and Troy: 'who hath brought the fatal engine in / That gives our Troy, our Rome, the civil wound' (V.3.85–86). The Roman lord recalls Rome's past lineage in Troy in an attempt to bring back a sense of unity and meaning to the social collapse he is witnessing around him. Certainly, 'our Rome', the one the Roman lord invokes and the one shown in *Titus Andronicus*, is not identical to the Rome of Augustus, and neither is 'our Troy' identical to the legend represented in many stories, including Shakespeare's.

In both plays contained in this discussion, Shakespeare invites the audience not to remember Rome and Troy in conventional ways, but to engage with heroes and heroines torn apart by acts of remembering and forgetting, offering thus an 'oblique memorial' of an unexpected classical past.

Notes

1 This study was supported by the Research Project GVAICO2016-094, funded by *Generalitat Valenciana*.
2 John R. Gillis, 'Memory and Identity: The History of a Relationship', in *Commemorations: The Politics of National Identity*, ed. by John R. Gillis (Princeton, NJ: Princeton University Press, 1994), pp. 3–26 (p. 3). See also Jonas Barish, 'Remembering and Forgetting in Shakespeare', in *Elizabethan Theater: Essays in Honor of S. Schoenbaum*, ed. by R.B. Parker and S.P. Zitner (Newark: University of Delaware Press, 1996), pp. 214–221 (p. 218); and Garrett Sullivan, *Memory and Forgetting in English Renaissance Drama* (Cambridge: Cambridge University Press, 2009), p. 21. For a complex discussion of the role of memory in individual identity, see Eric T. Olson, 'Personal Identity', in *The Stanford Encyclopedia of Philosophy* (Spring 2016 Edition), ed. by Edward N. Zalta, http://plato.stanford.edu/archives/spr2016/entries/identity-personal/ [accessed 28 March 2015].
3 A notion ultimately derived from Book Three of Aristotle's *On the Soul* (Περὶ Ψυχῆς), and omnipresent in early modern authorities, e.g. George Puttenham, *The Arte of English Poesie* (1589), I.xix.
4 Andrew Hiscock, *Reading Memory in Early Modern Writing* (Cambridge: Cambridge University Press, 2011), p. 10.
5 Barish, pp. 216, 221; Sullivan, p. 55.
6 Grant Williams and Christopher Ivic, 'Introduction: Sites of Forgetting in Early Modern English Literature and Culture', in *Forgetting in Early Modern English Literature and Culture*, ed. by Christopher Ivic and Grant Williams (London: Routledge, 2004), pp. 1–17 (p. 4); and for the meanings of 'to forget oneself', see pp. 4–5.
7 Gillis, pp. 3–4. As Terry Eagleton remarks, '"Our" Homer is not identical with the Homer of the Middle ages, [...] it is rather that different historical periods have constructed a "different" Homer [...] for their own purposes', *Literary Theory: An Introduction* (1983; Oxford: Blackwell, 2008), p. 11.

8 Although portraying no exact historical figure among the Romans and the Goths, *Titus Andronicus* seems to be set in the late fourth century CE, at a time near the collapse of the Roman empire. Geoffrey Bullough (ed.), *Narrative and Dramatic Sources of Shakespeare*, vol. 6 (London: Routledge and Kegan Paul, 1966), pp. 1–33.
9 English national histories since Geoffrey of Monmouth's twelfth-century account of the kings of Britain, *Historia Regum Britanniae*, domesticated the medieval notion of *translatio imperii* (the 'genealogical' transmission of power from Troy to imperial Rome to later European civilizations or rulers), which in sixteenth-century England served the nationalist agenda of the Tudor monarchs. See Frances A. Yates, *Astraea: The Imperial Theme in the Sixteenth Century* (London: Routledge & Kegan Paul, 1975).
10 In *Shakespeare's Troy: Drama, Politics, and the Translation of Empire* (Cambridge: Cambridge University Press, 1997), Heather James analyzes these plays (as well as *Antony and Cleopatra*, *Cymbeline* and *The Tempest*) as dramatizing the 'translation of empire' in a critique of political and cultural authority (pp. 1–41).
11 James, p. 85.
12 Hester Lees-Jeffries, *Shakespeare and Memory* (Oxford: Oxford University Press, 2013), p. 59.
13 James, pp. 13–40, and for Ovid's *Metamorphoses* as a 'counter-epic', p. 44.
14 For surveys of various functions of remembering and forgetting, see Leo Salingar, 'Memory in Shakespeare', *Cahiers Élisabéthains*, 45 (1994), 59–64, and Barish, pp. 214–221.
15 How remembrance incites vengeance in Elizabethan revenge tragedies is studied by John Kerrigan in '"Remember Me!": Horestes, Hieronimo, and Hamlet', *Revenge Tragedy: Aeschylus to Armageddon* (Oxford: Clarendon Press, 1996), pp. 170–92. In *Issues of Death: Mortality and Identity in English Renaissance Tragedy* (Oxford: Clarendon Press, 1997), Michael Neill states that revenge tragedy is about the 'murderous legacies of the past' (p. 244), 'the destructive grip of the past upon the present' (p. 291) and 'the terrible power of memory' (p. 244), so that 'revenge drama shows vengeance to be no more than memory continued by other means' with the revenger's role being 'essentially that of a "remembrancer" [...]: he is both an agent of memory and one whose task it is to exact payments for the debts of the past' (p. 247). Vengeance, then, becomes 'a form of remembering' (Sullivan, p. 22).
16 Neill describes the revengers' situation in terms of their relation to the dead relatives that inhabit their memories: revenge heroes are 'Alternately disabled by their inability to forget, and driven by their violent compulsion to remember', and 'must wrestle to redeem their dead from the shame of being forgotten, even as they struggle to lay these perturbed spirits to rest, and thereby free themselves from the insistent presence of the past' (pp. 245–246).
17 References to the text of *Titus Andronicus* are keyed to the edition by Jonathan Bate, The Arden Shakespeare (London: Routledge, 1995). In *Shakespeare's Rome* (Cambridge: Cambridge University Press, 1983), Robert Miola discusses the role of the *Aeneid* in the construction of Titus's character, who, in Act I, 'represents Rome in all its greatness and barbarity' (p. 75).
18 James, p. 51.
19 As Isabel Karremann explains in 'Rites of Oblivion in Shakespeare's History Plays', *Shakespeare Survey*, 63 (2010), 24–36 (p. 24).
20 'To ears trained by Vergil,' James points out, 'Titus' military acts against the Goths and their Queen recall Rome's ancient wars with Carthage, the enemy civilization founded by another queen' (p. 51).
21 See *Oxford English Dictionary* [henceforth *OED*] *n.* 2. The term 'monument' ultimately derives from the Latin verb *monere*, that is, 'to remind'. As Brian S. Osborne explains, monuments anchor '"collective remembering" in material sites' that serve as 'rallying point for a shared common memory and identity', 'Landscape, Memory, Monuments and Commemoration: Putting Identity in its Place', *Canadian Ethnic Studies*, 33.3 (2001), 39–77. http://search.proquest.com/docview/215637580?accountid=14777 [accessed 28 March 2016].
22 Repetition is one of the bases of ritual, as Karremann explains (p. 24).
23 Andrew Hadfield, *Shakespeare and Renaissance Politics* (London: Methuen, A & C Black, 2004), pp. 129–130.
24 Bate, p. 135.
25 Alternatively, the human sacrifice of Alarbus can be seen as part of Roman civilization together with the ritual burying of soldiers in the family tomb, but these acts 'are also an intimation of the latent barbarity by which this civilization will be consumed' (Neill, p. 290).
26 Titus's act of forgetting will prompt Tamora's and her children's revenge in a sequence of wrongs that in turn will lead to Titus's vengeance. At this point, Demetrius resorts to remembering the queen

of Troy's 'sharp revenge / Upon the Thracian tyrant' (I.1.140–141), narrated in Ovid's *Metamorphosis* (XIII.615–688), as a precedent for his family's revengeful desire to 'massacre' the Andronici (I.1.455).

27 As an avenger, Tamora invokes the act of revenge in terms of memory: 'Remember, boys, I poured forth tears in vain / To save your brother from the sacrifice' (II.2.163–164).

28 This is a striking visual image that, following Engel's argument, would make *Titus Andronicus* evoke and even become a melancholy memory palace or memory theatre itself, as other English tragedies that used stunning silent spectacles: William E. Engel, *Death and Drama in Renaissance Drama: Shades of Memory* (Oxford: Oxford University Press, 2002), p. 53. For James, this marks the play's 'turning point from the imperial epic of Vergil to the counter-epic of Ovid' (p. 44). From the memory-related perspective of emblem studies, Lavinia's entrance is an emblematic display of the mythological mutilated Philomel absent from emblem books of the period, Agnès Lafont, 'Mythological Reconfigurations on the Contemporary Stage: Giving a New Voice to Philomela in *Titus Andronicus*', *Early Modern Literary Studies* (2013). https://extra.shu.ac.uk/emls/si-21/11-Lafont_MythologicalReconfigurations.htm [accessed 28 March 2016] (para. 11).

29 This is vividly expressed in the image of a castaway standing 'upon a rock' (III.1.94) watching how the growing tide will 'swallow him' (98).

30 'Good Aaron, give his majesty my hand. / Tell him it was a hand that warded him / From thousand dangers, bid him bury it'. In 'Dismembering and Forgetting in *Titus Andronicus*', *Shakespeare Quarterly*, 45 (1994), 279–303 (pp. 290–291), Katherine Rowe insightfully points out that Titus's hand is construed as a *memento mori* by the messenger, and 'plays the role that ghosts typically inhabit in the revenge tradition'.

31 'When will this fearful slumber have an end?' (III.1.253).

32 The scene ends with a soliloquy by the banished Lucius, another avenger of the play, who will seek the Goths to 'raise a power, / To be revenged on Rome and Saturnine' (300 -301). Interestingly, his banishment is expressed in terms of living 'in oblivion' (III.1.296). Lucius must forget his country, his loyalty to Rome, in order to reconstitute Rome again in terms of greater justice.

33 W.W. Greg, *The Shakespeare First Folio* (Oxford: Clarendon Press, 1955), pp. 204–205; Bate, pp. 117–118.

34 Right from the beginning of this scene, without any hesitation as to their animus, Titus exhorts his relatives sitting at the banquet to 'eat no more / Than will preserve so much strength [...] As will revenge these bitter woes' (III.2.1–3).

35 This Folio-only scene seems to serve the same purpose the 'additions' to the 1604 quarto of *The Spanish Tragedy* do: to provide 'additional testimony to (and witty performance of) the protagonist's madness' (Bate, p. 118).

36 'How now, has sorrow made thee dote already? | Why, Marcus, no man should be mad but I' (III.2.23–24).

37 For the two-part (and three-part) structuring of the play, see Giorgio Melchiori, *Shakespeare: Genesi e struttura delle opere* (Roma: Editori Laterza, 2003), pp. 40–41.

38 For connections between memory and insanity, see Jerome Mazzaro, 'Madness and Memory: Shakespeare's *Hamlet* and *King Lear*', *Comparative Drama*, 19, no. 2 (Summer 1985), 97–116.

39 For books as memory tools, see Mary Carruthers, *The Book of Memory: A Study of Memory in Medieval Culture* (Cambridge: Cambridge University Press, 1990), p. 16; and Lina Perkins Wilder, *Shakespeare's Memory Theatre: Recollection, Properties, and Character* (Cambridge: Cambridge University Press, 2010), pp. 25–32.

40 Bate, pp. 30 and 166.

41 Bate, p. 217.

42 'And Ladie Astrey, last | Of heavenly vertues, from this earth in slaughter drowned past', from *Ovid's 'Metamorphoses': The Arthur Golding Translation 1567*, ed. by John Frederick Nims (Philadelphia: Pau Dry Books, 2000).

43 This Iron Age is dominated by 'all mischief' and 'Craft, Treason, Violence, Envie, Pride and wicked Lust' replaced 'Fayth and Truth', as Ovid sings in Golding's 1567 translation (I.146–149).

44 See, for instance, Hieronimo in *The Spanish Tragedy*: 'Though on this earth justice will not be found, / I'll down to hell, and in this passion/Knock at the dismal gates of Pluto's court' (III.13.107–109). Thomas Kyd, *The Spanish Tragedy*, ed. by Clara Calvo and Jesús Tronch (London: Bloomsbury, 2013).

45 In the case of Hieronimo, it is the ancient Greek realm of the underworld. From this legendary place, Hieronimo imagines his son Horatio returned to ask for justice (III.13.1301), and charges him to go back because 'here's no justice [...] For justice is exiled from the earth' (III.13.136–137).

46 Even when Publius names 'Revenge' when, by way of humouring Titus's maddened state, he simulates that he brings word from Pluto that Titus shall have revenge from hell if he wants to, as he will have

to wait for a while if he expects 'Justice' (4.3.38–42), Titus keeps focussed on 'Justice for to wreak our wrongs' (52). Then, in his attempt to solicit the gods for Justice, Titus commands that arrows loaded with petitions be shot at the heavens (4.3.54–65), while his brother Marcus gives the order to aim at court in order to 'afflict the emperor and his pride' (63).

47 Progne (usually spelt Procne) was Philomel's sister and served food to her husband, King Tereus, made from the flesh of their son. In *Metamorphoses*, Ovid recounts the story of Philomela in VI.540–855, and that of the Centaurs in XII.246–599. The Centaurs, at the wedding banquet of the Lapith King Pirithous, tried to abduct the bride and other women, which triggered off the famous battle between Centaurs and Lapiths.

48 Katharine Maus correlates this pattern of surpassing the model to Shakespeare's way of exceeding his sources, which brings about the memorable events for which the play is famous, in '[Introduction to] *Titus Andronicus*', in *The Norton Shakespeare: Third Edition*, ed. by Stephen Greenblatt, Walter Cohen, Suzanne Gossett, Jean E. Howard, Katharine Eisaman Maus, and Gordon McMullan (New York: W.W. Norton, 2015), pp. 491–498 (p. 403).

49 Bate, p. 267.

50 As Titus himself remarks, it is 'A pattern, precedent, and lively warrant / For me, most wretched, to perform the like' (V.3.43–44).

51 Holger Norgaard, 'Never Wrong but with Just Cause', *English Studies*, 45 (1964), 137–141.

52 'Because the girl should not survive her shame, / And by her presence still renew his sorrows' (V.3.40–41).

53 'Die, die, Lavinia, and thy shame with thee, / And with thy shame thy father's sorrow die' (V.3.45–46).

54 After revealing the contents of the pasty Tamora and Saturninus have just eaten, Titus finally fulfils his revenge by killing Tamora (V.3.46) in an attack during which he is slain by Saturninus, who, in turn, is killed by Lucius (V.3.62–65). In most revenge tragedies, the avenger is not allowed to survive and dies violently: the same happens with Titus. As the target of his revenge is formed by the prominent political figures of state, his vengeance has the political consequences of cleansing the state of its tyrants and bringing about a new order.

55 Neill points out that behind this contemptous treatment of Tamora and Aaron's bodies lies the belief that happiness in the afterlife depended on having had a proper burial, a belief that has been traced back to pagan superstitions and that also 'animates the bitter quarrel ... over Mutius' right to proper interment in the family tomb' at the beginning of the play (p. 266).

56 References to the text of *Troilus and Cressida* are taken from the edition by David Bevington, The Arden Shakespeare (Walton-on-Thames, UK: Thomas Nelson, 1997). See especially his sections on skeptical deflation of Trojan honour and chivalry, pp. 29–33, and fragmentation of the divided self, pp. 76–87. The sense of nostalgia is also linked to 'longing for an imagined medieval, orthodox and chivalric past' that offered 'the illusion at least of a God-given wholeness and immutability' (Bevington, p. 78).

57 Gilbert Highet includes *Troilus and Cressida* in his discussion of 'stage satire' and defines it as a 'satirical burlesque', in *Anatomy of Satire* (Princeton, NJ: Princeton University Press, 1962), pp. 14 and 123.

58 In '*Troilus and Cressida*, 1609', *The Library*, 4th series, 9 (1928–29), 267–286, Peter Alexander proposed that the play was performed before the educated and sophisticated audience of the Inns of Court, a hypothesis upheld by many critics but ultimately 'unprovable' (Bevington, p. 89). In his New Cambridge Shakespeare edition of the play, Anthony Dawson is skeptical about Shakespeare having written the play *ad hoc* for this private audience. See William Shakespeare, *Troilus and Cressida*, ed. Anthony Dawson (Cambridge: Cambridge University Press, 2003), p. 8.

59 Stanley Wells, *Shakespeare: A Life in Drama* (New York: W.W. Norton, 1997), p. 218.

60 One can apply to satire what Linda Hutcheon describes regarding adaptation, that 'as audience members, we need memory in order to experience difference and similarity', *A Theory of Adaptation* (New York: Routledge, 2013), p. 22.

61 Bevington, p. 378.

62 Chapman's translation as reproduced in Bullough, p. 120. In the Homeric epic, Thersites is described as one that, 'rashly and beyond all rule used to oppugn the lords', was 'laughed at mightily', chid Achilles and Ulysses 'eagerly', dared to 'upbraid the General' Agamemnon, and was rebuked and even whipped by Ulysses.

63 See, for instance, Agamemnon's 'rank Thersites' (I.3.73) and Nestor's 'A slave whose gall coins slanders like a mint' (I.3.193).

64 Shakespeare's expansion of this railer 'proves that the play has much in it of the "comical satyre" fashionable between 1598 and 1603' (Bullough, p. 110).

Historical and individual memory

65 As Achilles states in II.3.55. In his insolence towards superiors, Thersites even commands Jupiter to forget his identity as Olympian god (that is, to lose his divine powers) if he does not dispossess Ajax and Achilles of their little intelligence (II.3.9–13): 'O thou great thunder-darter of Olympus, forget that thou art Jove [...] if ye take not that little, little, less than little wit from that they have!'

66 To provide just one example, when Thersites remarks 'He'll tickle it' (V.2.184) referring to Troilus's ranting that his sword will fall on Diomedes, he 'deflates Troilus' high passion of rage' (Bevington, p. 325).

67 The only act of forgetting that Thersites carries out appears in scene II.3, in the context of his bitter complaints against Ajax and Achilles, when Patroclus exhorts him to come to their tent. To this, Thersites replies: 'If I could ha' remembered a gilt counterfeit, thou wouldst not have slipped out of my contemplation; but it is no matter' (II.3.23–24). The 'gilt counterfeit' refers both to a fake coin (also called a 'slip') or 'glittering falsehood' (Dawson, p. 128), which Thersites relates to Patroclus. The latter's words 'come in and rail' prompt Thersites to remember that he has forgotten Patroclus when cursing Ajax and Achilles, and chides himself for that slip of memory.

68 Later Nestor concurs with Ulysses in describing Achilles as someone 'Who [...] opinion crowns / With an imperial voice' (I.3.186–187).

69 Bevington, p. 166; Dawson, p. 102.

70 Dawson, p. 102.

71 *OED adj.* 5a and 5b respectively.

72 Ulysses's words are: 'the seeded pride / That hath to this maturity blown up | In rank Achilles' (I.3.316–318); and 'His crest that prouder than blue Iris bends' (381).

73 Dawson, p. 112.

74 In scene II.3, this demythologized view of Achilles is recalled again by Agamemnon, as 'over-proud' (121), 'in self-assumption greater / Than in the note of judgement' (122–123), and overestimating himself (131).

75 Again there is a connection between negligence and forgetting, as in Ulysses's speech on 'degree' in I.3.

76 For James's discussion of Achilles's crisis of identity, see pp. 1–2, 34, 39, and chapter 3, pp. 85–118.

77 R. W. Dent, *Shakespeare's Proverbial Language: An Index* (Berkeley: University of California Press, 1981), I66.1.

78 See discussion at III.3.145 in William Shakespeare, *Troilus and Cressida*, New Variorum, ed. Harold N. Hillebrand and T. W. Baldwin (Philadelphia: J. B. Lippincott, 1953).

79 Bevington, p. 251.

80 Shakespeare's act of forgetting here is understood as a creative act, following Stephen Orgel in his 'Shakespeare and the Art of Forgetting', in *Shakespeare and Renaissance Literary Theories: Anglo-Italian Transactions*, ed. by Michele Marrapodi (Farnham, UK: Ashgate, 2011), pp. 25–35 (p. 25).

81 His first words denote inner struggle, as he finds 'cruel battle' inside him and a womanish weakness compared to the fierce Greeks (I.1.3, 7–12), strives to hide his lovesickness (32–37), and finally confesses 'I am mad / In Cressid's love' (48–49).

82 Line 29, as edited and punctuated in many modern editions, with two exclamations and a self-indicting question, indicate a more unstable and angry lover than printed in the early quarto and folio texts: 'So (traitor) then she comes, when she is thence'. This statement reveals Troilus's becalmed recognition that he remembers her ('then she comes') because he treacherously forgets her ('she is thence'). Alternatively, as Bevington explains, it may mean that 'Cressida is bodily absent but remains constantly in Troilus's thoughts, tormenting him with an unfulfilled love' (Bevington, p. 133).

83 Forgetting about the damage caused by the war is what Nestor proposes to the Trojans if they hand over Helen. The phrase he uses implies an inscribed list of grievances that 'Shall be struck of' (II.2.7), as if by the stroke of a pen, thus suggesting the ease with which those 'damages' can be committed to oblivion.

84 'She is a theme of honour and renown, / A spur to valiant and magnanimous deeds, / Whose present courage may beat down our foes / And fame in time to come canonize us'. The verb 'canonize', glossed by Dawson as 'memorialize', suggests an inscription 'in the calendar of (secular) saints' and therefore the achievement of 'eternal glory' (p. 126).

85 Dawson, p. 29.

86 Jonathan Dollimore remarks that 'The discontinuity in Cressida's identity stems not from her nature, but from her position in the patriarchal order', in *Radical Tragedy* (Brighton: Harvester, 1984), p. 48. Among the feminist critics noting Cressida's self-division and inability to maintain her integrity, see Gayle Greene, 'Shakespeare's Cressida: "A Kind of Self"', in *The Woman's Part: Feminist Criticism of Shakespeare*, ed. by Carolyn Ruth Swift Lenz, Gayle Greene, and Carol Thomas Neely (Urbana: University of Illinois

Press, 1980), pp. 133–149 (p. 136–140); and Claire Tylee, 'The Text of Cressida and Every Ticklish Reader: *Troilus and Cressida*, The Greek Camp Scene', *Shakespeare Survey*, 41 (1989), 63–76.

87 Melchiori, p. 440.

88 'True swains in love shall in the world to come / Approve their truth by Troilus' (III.2.168–169).

89 'O you gods divine, / Make Cressid's name the very crown of falsehood | If ever she leave Troilus' (IV.2. 100–102).

90 The episode is cast in a double game of eavesdropping, with Troilus and Ulysses spying on Cressida and Diomedes while Thersites furtively observes these two groups. The audience's point of view is thus fragmented into three, 'an inventive theatrical metaphor for the breaking down not only of faith but of reality itself as Troilus laments in his great speech' at 144–167 (Dawson, p. 206).

91 Dawson, pp. 206–207.

92 *OED n.* 2a. In Sonnet 74, 'memorial' is glossed as 'a reminder' and 'a monument' by John Kerrigan in his edition, *The Sonnets and A Lover's Complaint*, The New Penguin Shakespeare (Harmondsworth: Penguin Books, 1986), p. 267.

93 Dawson, p. 210.

94 *OED* 3. As in Shakespeare's other only use of 'recordation' in *Henry IV Part Two*, 2.3.61, with Lady Percy recalling her dead husband.

95 Greene, p. 135.

96 As Richard Wheeler pointed out, 'Troilus, hopelessly divided within himself when he loses the identity he thinks he has found in his love for Cressida, will attempt desperately to exorcise that part of himself based on relations to the feminine', *Shakespeare's Development and the Problem Comedies* (Berkeley: University of California Press, 1981), p. 200.

97 Lines 166–171 only appear in the Folio version.

98 Bevington, p. 297.

10

FOOLING WITH TRAGIC MEMORY IN *HAMLET* AND *KING LEAR*

Kay Stanton

Memories, in retention, suppression, erasure, and overlap, are fraught with complexities of scientific, personal, and archetypal dimensions, and in *Hamlet* and *King Lear*, Shakespeare 'fools' with those issues' interaction in the tragic domain. Prince Hamlet, already troubled over the insufficiently honoured memory at the court of his father, Denmark's recently deceased king, experiences a crisis when the revenant of that memory, in the form of his father's ghost, appears, relates the account of his murder, charges Hamlet to revenge it, and entreats him to 'Remember me' (I.5.91).[1] In response, the prince, incredulous over the plea for remembrance, vows that 'from the table of my memory / I'll wipe away all trivial fond records', including 'all pressures past / That youth and observation copied there': the entreaty 'all alone shall live / Within the book and volume of my brain, / Unmix'd with baser matter' (I.5.98–101, 102–4). Hamlet does not, cannot hold to this hyperbolic oath.

Among the memories unrelated to his king-father that he later easily recalls are those of Yorick, the court's long-departed jester. As we learn that Hamlet at the point of encountering the jester's skull is thirty years old (V.1.161) and that Yorick had died twenty-three years prior (V.1.171–2), the prince had been a seven-year-old child at the time of Yorick's death. However, evidently the 'pressures past'—impressions on his psyche—as an observant youth were not so easy to 'wipe away', even though, because related to a fool, such 'records' would seem to be 'trivial', even if 'fond'. Hamlet's vivid, detailed memories of Yorick are full of humour, enjoyment, and mutual affection—qualities entirely lacking in those recalling King Hamlet. In fact, it is not his king-father-ghost, but fool Yorick who becomes the play's iconic *memento mori*. Yorick assumes this mnemonic function because his skull emerges when his grave is dug up to make a place for the newly deceased Ophelia, who thus in a sense 'replaces' Yorick. In *King Lear* the Fool similarly 'replaces' the banished Cordelia, and the equation of the two characters is particularly evident in Lear's ambiguous lament near the play's end that 'my poor fool is hanged' (V.3.304). When present, the Fool insistently reminds Lear of his daughter Cordelia and the tragedy of the king's misjudgment of her. Thus, in both *Hamlet* and *King Lear*, Shakespeare employs a fool character in a complex relationship between tragedy and memory, one that ultimately takes the protagonists from their personal memories into the realm of 'collective memory' inhabited by the archetypes of the Fool, Hero, King, and Princess.

Although Hamlet's erasure intention is most hyperbolically stated, memory modification is a recurring issue in Shakespeare's works. As Jonathan Baldo notes, citing Hamlet's remarks on wiping his 'table' of memory, 'Remembering often entails displacement in critical or crisis moments in Shakespeare', such as Hamlet's encounter with the ghost, yet 'even the most ordinary demands upon memory in Shakespeare's later histories and tragedies inevitably produce some degree of displacement or divestiture within the domain of memory'.[2] In other words, 'There needs no ghost' 'come from the grave' (I.5.131) to displace memories, and, as suggested above, some memories resist divestment, even with intentional effort. Early modern memory theory, as Lina Perkins Wilder states, generally 'adheres to the Aristotelian idea that memory has two "motions": the retentive function (*memoria* or *mnesis*) and the searching function, *reminiscentia* or *anamnesis*, which is usually translated as "remembrance" in early modern England'.[3] Contemporary theory of memory scientifically complicates, though does not negate in metaphoric value, these representations in Shakespeare of displacement, memory 'table', and retentive and searching functions.

According to memory researcher and scientist Larry R. Squire, although still 'relatively little' is known 'about how the brain learns and remembers', 'remarkable progress has been made' with study being performed by 'psychologists, neurologists, biologists, mathematicians, and computer scientists'.[4] Currently, Squire highlights, memory 'is presumed to depend on the cooperative participation of assemblies of neurons, which reside in cortical and subcortical brain systems, and which are specialized to process different kinds of information', with each specialized system having 'its own specific, short-term, working-memory capacity and also the capacity to retain in long-term memory specific features or dimensions of information', and with each specialized system storing 'the product of its own processes'. Long-term memory 'of even a single event depends on synaptic change in a distributed ensemble of neurons, which themselves belong to many different processing systems, and the ensemble acting together constitutes memory for the whole event'.[5] Thus, a memory is registered within various segments of the central nervous system in a 'cooperative' manner, and yet studies suggest that 'representations of events in memory are subject to competition and dynamic change', because the 'strengthening of some connections within an ensemble occurs at the expense of other connections'. These 'dynamic changes' are 'the synaptic reflections of rehearsal, relearning, normal forgetting, and perhaps the passage of time alone', and 'they result in a resculpting of the neural circuitry that originally represented the stored information'.[6] In this way, memories can and do 'compete' for space over the compartmentalized 'table' of brain system elements, particularly in order to move from short-term to long-term storage, so Hamlet's metaphoric representation is scientifically consistent. In fact, as another memory researcher, George Christos, states, most theoreticians now accept the notion of a 'palimpsest model', by which some older memory is partially erased in order to rewrite new memory.[7] Such erasure happens by 'an evolutionary process' of 'intense pruning' that 'keeps only the most important connections'; though how it happens is still 'a mystery', most of 'this rapid development of the brain takes place during infancy and childhood', the 'periods of most intense learning'.[8] Since memory development occurs with most concentrated focus during early childhood, for Hamlet that would have been the period when Yorick was still alive.

Conditions operating while long-term memory is being instituted are significant. Squire states that the 'establishment of long-term memory in any of the brain systems specialized for different kinds of information processing can be influenced by, and depends on, a number of other brain systems', such that particular 'hormones and transmitters influence the strength of learning and can modulate memory if given close to the time of learning', and some of these 'effects may involve the action of mechanisms that subserve attention or reinforcement', and 'Peripherally released hormones can also modulate memory, perhaps by influencing the level of stress or arousal that follows an event'.[9] As numerous studies have shown, 'Humorous material tends to be recalled at higher rates than non-humorous material'.[10] Thus, it is reasonable to believe that memories laid into the child Hamlet's mind accompanied by humour and other emotions, predominantly of affection, would be particularly durable, especially if the case were that Yorick was his frequent playfellow. This is strongly suggested by the memories of the court jester that the prince reports to Horatio upon viewing Yorick's skull: the latter was 'a fellow of infinite jest, of most excellent fancy' who 'hath borne' the young prince 'on his back a thousand times' and whose 'lips' he had 'kissed' he 'know[s] not how oft' (V.1.182-4, 186-7). In this scene we also learn that, as 'Every fool can tell', Prince Hamlet had been born on the very day, thirty years prior, that 'King Hamlet o'ercame Fortinbras' the elder (V.1.145, 143). As King Hamlet had been a warrior king, it seems likely that he had been absent not only on the day of his son's birth, but also for much of the prince's childhood, such that young Hamlet had had more direct interaction with Yorick than the king. Such regal affectionate familiarity with a jester has an historical basis: Beatrice Otto reports that in Europe and elsewhere during the medieval and early modern periods, the court jester was often so integrated into royal households that he was included in their family portraits.[11] In addition, Lear's Fool is well acquainted with the royal family, understanding the characters of the king's daughters better than the king himself does.

An image provided by memory researcher Christos is helpful in this context: 'the way that memory is stored in the brain is similar' to 'how flowing water cuts out a network of trenches and rivers': during rain, 'the water will preferably flow along the same paths that were previously scoured out of the land'. Thus, in the brain, 'when a particular channel between two neurons is used often, this channel normally becomes "enlarged" so that it is even more accessible in the future, and conversely if a particular channel is not used, it diminishes in its capacity'. This is the manner by which 'learning takes place in a nervous system': by 'directing the flow of electricity through the same channels as before, the brain is able to reinitiate (or recall) the same electrical patterns, or memory states, that caused this change in the first place'.[12] Besides its being 'known that emotions and moods play a prominent role in learning, or the process of laying down memories', the more frequently that 'something is presented to us or encountered, the greater is the tract of that memory', such that 'something may need to enter consciousness a few times' 'before it enters long-term memory'.[13] For the child Hamlet, his learning and memory channel of Yorick's humorous techniques would probably have become enlarged by his frequent interaction with the court fool. To all intents and purposes, the prince seems to have learned the wit of the jester better than warfare mentality of the king.

As noted briefly above, memories are currently thought to be stored in the brain in a distributed manner, but, according to Christos, they lodge 'in semispecific areas'.[14] However, 'a complete memory may contain aspects that are stored in a number of modules in different areas of the brain', with 'each module storing a particular feature of that memory, such as its color, shape, size, an associated emotion, and a time'.[15] For retrieval, a memory 'is recalled when all of these modules', 'relevant to that particular memory, are simultaneously activated'. Furthermore, both neurons and modules can 'correct each other'; if a person inputs 'only some of the features of a memory (each of which is stored in a different module)', then 'the modules in the correct firing pattern (corresponding to that stored memory) will excite the modules that are initially not in the correct configuration for the memory'.[16] If 'a sufficient number of modules are in the correct state for a particular memory, they will work together to excite the other modules that carry the other features of that memory, and the complete memory will be recalled', so 'features of memories help to collectively excite each other'.[17] Thus, memories will overlap, because 'Particular module configurations can be shared among different memories, just as different memories, or memory features, can share the same neurons', and memories that 'share common module states may either be in competition with each other (if their overlap is small) or they may excite each other (if their overlap is large)'.[18] This overlapping feature of memories, as will be discussed below, has demonstrable impact on the mental states of both Hamlet and King Lear.

The brain system's distributed storage arrangement 'facilitates the recall of memory from incomplete cues or partial information'[19], because 'neurons in the correct firing mode for a particular memory will activate the other neurons that are initially not activated by the input', thereby piecing together the memory correctly.[20] Thus, 'When the brain is presented with an input that closely resembles a stored memory but is not identical to it (like the faces of our family and friends, which change from day to day), the majority of the neurons that are in the correct firing mode will help to excite those neurons in the memory that are inappropriately quiescent', and 'improperly firing' neurons 'will also be quelled by the general inhibition and lack of support they will subsequently receive from the neurons that continue firing'.[21] In this way, 'When we want to recall something, a piece of knowledge or an episodic memory, we normally put some cues (or clues) concerned with the sought-after memory into our mind and let the brain search its memory store for the most appropriate memory corresponding to that input'[22]— i.e. there is a searching function, as early modern interpretation of Aristotle on memory function suggested. Furthermore, 'similar memories are probably stored in the same general area or alongside each other, as this enables the brain to "compare" them easily'.[23] Thus, Hamlet's childhood memories of both his father and Yorick were probably stored near each other, so comparisons between them could easily have been made.

Although these distributed but overlapping and collaborating systems allow memory to be robust and to regenerate particular memories from incomplete cues, there is a 'natural consequence' to this type of storage, which is that, along with intentionally stored memories, 'the brain generates its own sets of memories, so-called spurious memories'.[24] These inauthentic 'memory states' are 'comprised of combinations of features of the stored memories' and 'were not intentionally stored in the brain'.[25] Spurious memories 'may explain why we cannot remember certain things at certain times, why our memories become distorted with time, and how "false memories" arise'.[26] Because 'Simple mathematical neural network models suggest that without some sort of intervention', spurious memories 'can reach catastrophic proportions, and the network will eventually be unable to retrieve any of the stored memories'[27], spurious memories have been considered at least a 'nuisance' and potentially a 'problem'. As a consequence, 'much theoretical work has been concerned with finding ways to limit their number and influence on intentionally stored memories'.[28] Christos holds that some forms of madness, like schizophrenia (a mental disease that commentators have frequently diagnosed in Hamlet), could be the result of spurious memory assuming too great an influence upon the subject.[29]

However, new theorizing on spurious memory suggests that with 'suitable control', spurious memories may be a 'blessing in disguise', in that they may be 'responsible for our creative ideas'.[30] Because spurious states are 'made up of combinations of features of stored memories', a brain network 'can make a mistake by selecting a spurious state that is similar to one of the stored memories', but these 'mistakes' may be 'important in making associations between memories', assisting the brain to 'generalize and categorize'.[31] Without such 'mistakes', 'we would just recall and relearn what we already know', but, 'since creative ideas generally combine different aspects of memories by putting bits and pieces of information together to arrive at a new way of doing something', spurious memories may be 'the basis of creativity (or new ideas)', so 'required to learn something new'.[32] Christos notes that the 'fine line between genius and madness' may be dependent upon adjustment in the brain system's neurochemistry (perhaps by trauma), which could increase creativity but also 'result in confusion'[33], a description quite appropriate to the creative but sometimes confused and mad Hamlet.

Evidence that Hamlet, even before encountering the ghost, indulges a tendency to adopt spurious memory relating to his father (and mother) as true is present even in his first soliloquy, in I.2, during which, within a few lines, he reduces the time-span between his father's death and his mother's remarriage. His initial statement, 'But two months dead—nay, not so much, not two' (I.2. 138), makes the true time-span likely to have been about eight weeks, but it becomes 'within a month' (I.2 145) seven lines later, and he twice reiterates that modification, with 'A little month, or ere those shoes were old / With which she follow'd my poor father's body, / Like Niobe, all tears' (I.2. 147–9) and with 'Within a month [. . . / . . .] / She married' (I.2.153–6). Between the statement about nearly two months to the first 'within a month', he had exclaimed, 'Heaven and earth, / Must I remember?' (I.2. 142–3), suggesting that the trauma of the true memory provokes his chosen acceptance of the spurious one. James Hirsh, arguing that in Shakespeare's plays 'a soliloquy does not represent the "innermost thought" or essential being of a character' but rather 'a form of behavior, a particular role, that a character adopts at a particular time and place', states that 'The role Hamlet plays for himself at a given moment may differ from any of the roles he plays for others, but he still plays roles when he is alone and sometimes catches himself doing so'.[34] In this instance, while alone, Hamlet not only moves to accept his own spurious memory, but also creatively adorns it with the literary allusion to Niobe and the witty comment on his mother's shoes; he will carry forward a similar technique in conversation with others. Thus, in the soliloquy, through combining both the positive and negative potentials of spurious memory, he is rehearsing and playing the role of artist, using 'poetic license' to deal with his pain.

After Horatio and the guards enter the scene, when Horatio, shortly before telling him of the ghost-sighting, agrees with him that the queen's remarriage 'follow'd hard upon' the king's death (I.2.179), Hamlet replies with an extremely witty version of the spurious memory: 'Thrift, thrift, Horatio. The funeral bak'd meats / Did coldly furnish forth the marriage tables' (I.2.180–1). Later, just before the performance of the play *The Mousetrap* is to begin, in response to Ophelia's comment that he is 'merry' (III.2.124), Hamlet replies, 'What should a man do but be merry? For look you how cheerfully my mother looks and my father died within's two hours' (III.2.127–9). When Ophelia corrects him that 'Nay, 'tis twice two months, my lord' (III.2.130), he insists on halving her account: 'O heavens, die two months ago and not forgotten yet!' (III.2.132–3). By this point, locked within a diminishing time-span, spurious memory holds a more tenacious grip on the prince's mind than the real one. In addition, his wit has even more fully embraced 'merriment' as a coping strategy with which to confront not only his father's death and mother's remarriage, but also the ghost's command. His 'merriment' at this moment comes from his joyous anticipation that his 'creative' tactic for proving the ghost's accusation true, developed in II.2. within soliloquy after his encounter with the actors—'The play's the thing / Wherein I'll catch the conscience of the King' (II.2.606–7)—is about to bear fruit, though not in the manner that he hopes.

However, within this same soliloquy in II.2 in which he happily hits upon the strategy of the play, Hamlet also articulates his doubts about the ghost: 'The spirit that I have seen / May be a devil, and the devil hath power / T'assume a pleasing shape', so 'perhaps' 'Abuses me to damn me' by manipulating his 'weakness' and 'melancholy' (II.2.600–3, 605). By deciding that he should have 'grounds' for acting against King Claudius 'More relative than' the word of a ghost that might be the devil (II.2.605–6), Hamlet 'resculpts' his memory of the ghost and its demands on him. With his creativity engaged in an idea that allows him to pursue his own artistic interests rather than rushing headlong into violence, Hamlet gains some temporary freedom from paternal authority, a tension for him evident even directly after the memory of the ghost was first imprinted.

Hamlet habitually but not invariably resists authority, as his father when alive probably knew. As Wilder observes, 'In *Hamlet*, controlling memory is a means of subordination', particularly by fathers over sons,[35] and King Hamlet's ghost certainly puts much effort into strongly impressing himself upon his son's memory and thereby subordinating him to his will during their interaction in I.5. The ghost mysteriously appears on the battlements in 'warlike form' (I.1.50) to the guards three times—the last of which includes Hamlet's friend Horatio among the witnesses. On these occasions and in the presence of his son, the ghost deliberately evokes the image of himself as heroic warrior-king, dressed in the 'very armour he had on' (I.1.63) during his victory over Fortinbras the elder, which remains well-remembered in Denmark. Those stunning appearances seem calculated to provoke Hamlet's movement to *his* territory (battlements, sites evocative of his power and warlike authority) and the strategy works. Hamlet first views him in front of these fellow witnesses, preventing him from later believing that he had merely imagined it—in another instance of seeing his father 'in [his] mind's eye' (I.2.185). After the ghost succeeds in separating Hamlet from his companions by beckoning him to 'a more removed ground' (I.4.61), he begins by telling of the 'sulp'rous and tormenting flames' to which he must soon return. He then hints at the horrifying 'secrets of [his] prison house' that, if revealed to his son, 'Would harrow up [his] soul' (I.5.3, 14 16), before slamming him (as King Lear will do to his daughters) with a manipulative love-test: 'If thou didst ever thy dear father love', 'Revenge his foul and most unnatural murder' (I.5.23, 25). In relating the grisly details of his death by poison poured into his ear by his brother, in order to extract the promise of revenge by Hamlet, the ghost succeeds in poisoning his son's mind towards violence with the memory of this stressful encounter.

This combination of deliberately evoking stress in Hamlet, through narrated gory details, hinted horrors, and the love-test with the entreaty to 'Remember me' (I.5.91), seems to constitute a strategic plan by the ghost to lay down the memory of this encounter in the strongest possible manner. Memory researcher Squire states that hormones released during stress 'may participate in the formation of peculiarly vivid recollections, those that develop when a stressful event punctuates an experience': they have been termed '"flashbulb" memories' to denote their unusual character and vividness'.[36] The current hypothesis about them is that 'peripheral hormones play a role in establishing particularly vivid memories because a stress-producing and hormone-releasing signal often follows events that will later be well remembered'—which, as Squire acknowledges, does not, however, explain why non-stress-related memories, such as the basic facts of a casual conversation, may be remembered almost as well[37]—hence, Hamlet's inability to 'wipe away' all other memories (I.5.99), even very shortly after the ghost has delivered his demand.

Initially, Hamlet is so overwhelmed by the ghost's tale that he intends to 'sweep to [his] revenge' (I.5.31) by accepting the offered 'hero role'. However, what Harold C. Goddard calls his 'unadmitted doubts' begin to manifest themselves shortly thereafter, because in 'the depths of his nature, or rather on its heights, there are forces making against revenge'.[38] Goddard posits that although Hamlet's 'fantastically ideal portrait' drawn of his father may be 'based on his boyish ideal', such that he 'exaggerates the virtues of his father' and vows to 'embrace his mission' with 'furious joy',[39] in this way, he 'is trying to force himself to obey orders from his father to do something that his soul abhors', since 'he hates with equal detestation those who issue orders and those who obey them, particularly fathers and children'.[40] In Hamlet's vow to remember the ghost 'whiles memory holds a seat / In this distracted globe' (I.5.96–7), Goddard prioritizes the word 'distracted', as 'in a single adjective or stray phrase the truth escapes'.[41] Thus, Hamlet subconsciously *wants* to be distracted from becoming the ghost's instrument for violent revenge. That desire, Goddard indicates, is particularly demonstrated when, in having Horatio and the guards swear by his sword never to reveal what they have seen that night, Hamlet shifts ground three times, because the ghost, from below their changing place of stance, tries to participate by speaking 'Swear' (I.5.157, 163, 169). This literal movement, Goddard continues, represents 'a prophecy and microcosm of the rest of the action', because 'Hamlet's delay is a perpetual shifting of ground in an attempt to get away from the ghost'.[42]

Having thrice failed to escape the ghost's participation in the oath, Hamlet then has the group shift ground yet once more. This time without involving the sword in their vow (removing the instrument of violence), he again entreats Horatio and the guards to swear. In this last instance, however, he adds his personal choice of strategy for proceeding, which his companions must vow not to comment upon—he will 'put an antic disposition on' (I.5.180). Although the ghost chimes in with 'Swear' once again (I.5.189), Hamlet is calmer in this last instance, when he has augmented the oath with his personalized tactic: one that will allow him range not only for investigation, but also for his creativity and anti-authoritarianism. At this critical moment, under such intense pressure from his commanding warrior-king-father to take up the role of violent, avenging 'hero', he remembers and decides to play the role of his childhood 'subversive' playfellow, the fool.

In his study of 'thinking space', Andrew Hiscock asserts that because 'space is not a neutral, fixed, passive container, but socially constructed and constantly in process', the play *Hamlet*'s 'preoccupation with divergent human engagements with representations of space points up its significance as one of the primary axes through which we attempt modes of self-definition'— such that meaning is produced 'through the occupation of mental and geographical spaces'.[43] Though Hiscock does not discuss the ground-shifting incident, it precisely illustrates his thesis that in this play 'environments and landscapes are "produced" by those who occupy them and the subjectivities of those occupants are in turn "produced" by the spaces they inhabit'.[44] Thus, the ghost of King Hamlet 'produced' the battlements (which had 'produced' himself as warrior-king) as the space to bring Prince Hamlet physically and mentally to violent revenge— to 're-produce' him in his 'heroic' image—and the Prince tries to 'produce' his own mental and physical response space. Hiscock continues that the play depicts 'the endeavours of dramatic subjects to locate themselves through spatial productions and practices with myths of belonging, promoting various physical, cultural and psychological "homes"'. However, 'difficulties emerge when it becomes evident that these homes' later 'prove only to be provisional in nature'.[45] Such is the case with Hamlet's chosen 'space' of his adopted 'antic disposition', a mental space rich in various 'myths' that provide him a personalized 'home' that he eventually must abandon.

The phrase that Hamlet chooses to describe his stance, 'antic disposition', involves a wide range of attributes bound together in the historical, theatrical, and mythic/archetypal meanings comprising the 'space' of the fool. Several critics over the years have noted ways in which Hamlet becomes the 'fool' character of the play, and Robert Barrie summarizes these characteristics as follows: 'an association with the devil, improvisational wit, special speech and body languages, an association with music and dancing, cynicism regarding women, and roles as Presenter, Chorus, plotter, and swordsman', such that the prince 'recalls the Fool/Vice figures of earlier popular drama in all of their playful, anarchic, diabolic, topsy-turvy functions'.[46] In addition, Hamlet employs the association with lunacy and/or mental deficiency in the historical development of the fool role.

As Enid Welsford details, at various times in diverse civilizations, persons who were physically abnormal, mentally challenged, or regarded as insane were taken into the households of the rich and powerful to serve as combination mascot and scapegoat, partly because 'an over-sophisticated society' is often 'prone to revert to the most primitive superstitions',[47] including the idea that such persons could function as a kind of lightning rod for the visitations of evil so were allowed a 'license' for their often socially unconventional remarks that could be politically dangerous for others to voice. Otto states that although 'the fool as simpleton, the natural, was laughed at and whipped', he was 'also held in awe as a potential mouthpiece for God', so it is 'perhaps this perceived link with a higher authority' that led to the idea of fools as prophets.[48] Indeed, Lear's Fool, who is repeatedly threatened with whippings (I.4.108, 1.4.175–81), states a 'prophecy' before going to the hovel, adding that it is one that 'Merlin shall make, for I live before his time' (III.2.80, 95–6). As he is alone on stage when he speaks the 'prophecy', which seems banal or nonsensical, he is thereby asserting to the audience that he has a kind of supernatural wisdom. Otto notes that the early modern drama's 'court jester or clown was often a bridge between the characters in the play and the audience', such that he 'belonged to the play and often had a central role in it, but he was also detached, and his asides could make it seem he was more aware of the presence of the audience than any of the other characters'. In this manner, he reflected 'what court jesters did in real life—they could be at the nub of the action and then suddenly stand outside it with their dispassionate observations'[49]—a technique that Hamlet attempts, but overplays, during the performance of *The Mousetrap*. In his Jungian analysis of the fool type, William Willeford posits that the fool is 'relatively independent of our time and of the modes of conscious thought and action dependent upon it', having a 'permanence in the sense that he seemingly has an intimate connection with the future from which meaning and nonsense, often combined or annulling each other, are disclosed to us'[50], an observation relevant to the reference to Merlin and living before his time made by Lear's Fool.

Lear's Fool has sometimes 'fooled' critics into believing him a 'natural', but he is very much a professional, whereas Hamlet is an amateur with a divided purpose that eventually leads to his abandonment of the role in its competition with the 'hero role'. As Robert Goldsmith notes, in the medieval period 'The merging of the professional jester with the licensed fool gave rise to a new species—the artificial fool or court jester',[51] also called the 'wise fool', who pretended the stance and societal position of the natural fool and thereby assumed his uncivilized, irrationalized, unsocialized freedom, or 'license', to speak truths through wit to his social superiors. Within Shakespeare's canon, besides the professional jesters like the Fool of *King Lear*, there are several characters who serve fool-like functions for their peer group. Among them, in this context, Jaques of *As You Like It* is most relevant, as he, like Hamlet, wishes to adopt the wise fool role, but Duke Senior realizes that he would abuse the position in chastising others for sins that he too has committed and so disallows it.

The best description in Shakespeare's canon of the artistry of the wise fool is provided in *Twelfth Night*, by Viola, who, disguised herself, can well appreciate Feste's masking of his wit in folly: 'This fellow is wise enough to play the fool, / And to do that well, craves a kind of wit', as 'He must observe their mood on whom he jests, / The quality of persons, and the time' in performing 'a practice / As full of labor as a wise man's art' (III.1.60–5). Lear's nameless Fool, who, like Feste, 'wear[s] not motley in [his] brain' (I.5.52–53), self-consciously links himself to Feste by singing a stanza (III.2.74-7) from the song that Feste sings as epilogue in *Twelfth Night* (V.1.381–400). This song occurs just before he delivers his 'prophecy' and goes to the hovel with Lear, suggesting that he either *is* Feste, has access to his folly 'material'—or, most probably, that he is the archetypal Fool.

As has been explored at length in studies of history, psychology, and myth, there definitely is such a thing as a fool 'type'. In her comprehensive study of the fool throughout history and around the world, Otto notes that the fool 'is very much a universal character, more or less interchangeable regardless of the time or culture in which he happens to cavort—the same techniques, the same functions, the same license'.[52] Thus, as has been confirmed by psychologists Seymour and Rhoda L. Fisher, there are identifiable features that differentiate the talents required to become a successful professional fool from those in evidence in figures like Jaques and Hamlet, who are merely 'ambitious for a motley coat' (*As You Like It* II.7.43). The Fishers have performed extensive research on professional comedians, using professional actors, amateur comedians, and persons not connected at all to entertainment as control fields. Although they recorded much variety in professional comedians' personalities, the Fishers found a striking consistency of pattern, 'not easily duplicated out of common elements'[53] and not present even in amateur comedians or professional actors. In this way, psychological research substantiates the idea that there is demonstrably a fool type, and the work of Willeford on the Fool's archetypal significance, particularly in relation to accompanying archetypes, helps to clarify the role.

Extrapolating from Carl Jung's theories on archetypes, Willeford notes that a 'symbol contains an element that is ahistorical and transcendent', which is 'the source of its deepest effect on us': 'In forming a concept of something that has an archetypal effect we are drawing a distinction between what it is as a fact that may be known objectively and what it is as a content of subjective, personal experience'.[54] Thus, for Hamlet, Yorick was a fool with whom he had factual experience, as Lear has with his Fool. However, Yorick and Lear's Fool both also function archetypally for both protagonists, each of whom additionally understands himself in an archetypal role. Lear was a king and thereby embodied (and post-rule continues to believe himself as embodying) the King archetype; Hamlet as prince and ghost-designated avenger is called to the Hero archetype, which does to some degree resonate with him, though his psychic preference is for that of the Fool. The archetypal role of the Princess is held by Cordelia, and, in as much as Ophelia is Hamlet's love-object, it is a role also projected upon her. The role of the archetypal Hero is to win the Princess and ultimately become the King. The King's archetypal role, as societal fount of power, is parodied by the Fool, whose bauble satirizes the King's sceptre. In both tragedies, psychic memories of the Fool's archetypal meanings profoundly influence the outcome.

The tarot card deck provides further information as to the Fool's archetypal significance. As David Conford states, the origin of the tarot remains unknown, but the 'earliest reference' to the cards 'dates from 1442 at Ferrara, Italy'; over the centuries they have 'played a part in the Western world's cultural history',[55] with the Tarot Fool identified as the 'most influential figure in the deck'—and Jung saw the cards as representing archetypes.[56] Whether Shakespeare knew of tarot cards or not, the symbolism of the tarot Fool card aligns with the characteristics that he assigns the Fool of *King Lear*. The Tarot Fool is associated with 'both journeys and homecoming', indicating the travels of the unconscious mind, particularly through circularity, reflected in the card's number being zero: 'the great mystery, the attempt to express the inexpressible'[57] links the archetypal Fool with 'nothing' as the concept develops in *King Lear*. When, in the play's first scene in response to her king-father's 'love-test', Cordelia (unlike Hamlet) says 'Nothing' (I.1.86), Lear replies that 'Nothing will come of nothing' (I.1.89), meaning the loss of her potential 'fortunes' (I.1.194). The king and princess have entirely different understandings of 'nothing': for Cordelia it represents what should be self-evident truth of love; for Lear it is the absence of the something he desired (praise) and the consequent absence of things for Cordelia of material value that he in his role as king has the power to bestow. In subsequently disowning and banishing the only daughter who truly loves him, Lear in his next scene (I.4) begins his journey into his 'thinking space' of folly, where he will be accompanied by the Fool, who will ask him, 'Can you make no use of nothing, Nuncle?' (I.4.128–9). The Fool recognizes before Lear does that the king's 'thinking space' will be that of the fool and that his expanded understanding of 'nothing' will be his task of psychic redemption.

Willeford notes that the fool 'lives in a no-man's land in several senses, one of which is his connection with the area of consciousness into which hunches, intuitions, and interesting but not quite meaningful images and ideas emerge'.[58] For Lear's Fool, this preconscious territory particularly involves memory, specifically that of Cordelia. In their respective archetypes, the Fool and the Princess, Willeford states, have an affinity, a 'secret bond'; although he is 'beneath the woman he yearns for, she often enigmatically seems to belong to him'.[59] When Lear asks for the Fool in I.4, a knight tells him that since Cordelia has gone to France, 'the Fool hath much pined away', and Lear replies that he has 'noted it well', but wishes to hear 'No more of that' (I.4.71–3). However, when the Fool does finally appear, he continually assaults Lear with the folly of his banishment of Cordelia and his foolishness in trusting in Goneril and Regan, in attempts to 'resculpt' Lear's memories. What seemed to have happened in I.1 was that, although Lear had remembered his own love of Cordelia, his love of the idea of a grand bestowal of land and power as he stepped down as king produced a 'spurious memory' of her as one who would play an appropriate role in effusively praising him, as her sisters had done. His true and imaginary memories produced the unfortunate memory overlap that led to her banishment. Although Kent tried to counsel him against his folly, Lear had banished him as well, leading to his disguised reappearance as Caius, whom Lear is hiring when the Fool appears in I.4. The Fool immediately tries to hire him too, indicating a similarity in their 'employment'.

In attempting to hire Caius/Kent, the Fool offers him his coxcomb, a traditional accoutrement of the fool's costume (which is meant to represent the 'cock's comb') and he then offers it to Lear as well. Willeford suggests that this element arose via legend that 'the cock calls the day into being'. Since 'Symbolically the day is the time of consciousness', as 'the cock expresses the coming dawn', so 'the fool often expresses an incipient consciousness still in the darkness of the unconscious'.[60] Indeed, the Fool does not appear in the play until after Lear has said, 'Where's my Fool, ho? I think the world's asleep' (I.4.47). Furthermore, the Fool will not appear in the play again following Lear's crazed 'arraignment' of Goneril and Regan at the height of his madness, when he says, as his last line, 'And I'll go to bed at noon' (III.6.83). With his time in the play's action thus bookended by these references to sleep, the Fool may be seen to operate on Lear's mind, and memory, in the hazy subconsciousness of a sleep-like state that will eventually lead to his healing through his actual deep, and dreaming, sleep later.

Before Lear will enter his healing sleep, he experiences escalating loss of the material trappings of the role of king and increasing insistence from the Fool that he too is a fool: 'All thy other titles thou hast given away; that thou wast born with' (I.4.146–7). The Fool, however, has the self-consciousness that Lear lacks of being a fool, as he tells the king, 'now thou art an O without a figure. I am better than thou art now; I am a Fool, thou art nothing' (I.4.18–91). When Lear perceives that because of his foolishness, he has nothing, he begins to see himself *as* nothing, which insight pushes him into true madness, the historical attribute of the natural fool that Hamlet feigns in his stance as wise fool.

As noted above, memory overlap and spurious memories, though probably helpful for creativity, may lead to madness if they are in overabundance, and such becomes the case for both Hamlet and Lear. After adopting his 'antic disposition' and its associated memories, Hamlet frequently utilizes the role in ridiculing Polonius, father of Ophelia, whom he resents as an authority over her and whom he believes and often says is a 'fool'—though he means a 'natural' fool, not a 'wise' fool as he, the prince, strives to be. Hamlet's employment of the wise fool role, however, becomes manic at the performance of *The Mousetrap*. Though he had counselled the actors against letting their clowns speak 'more than is set down for them', especially when 'some necessary question of the play be then to be considered', a practice that is 'most pitiful ambition in the fool that uses it' (III.2.40, 43–4), he himself becomes such a pitifully ambitious fool during the play's performance. His 'merry' excitement over combining his father's charge to be avenging hero with his creativity and adoption of the wise fool role leads him to subvert art's power by his excessive choric commentary, interruptions, bawdy remarks, and jesting.

As I have elsewhere noted, 'Hamlet whores his love of the theatre to his revenge' and 'employs the play as his "cue" for revenge in a virtually pornographic way, as it seems to provide the erotic charge to stimulate the blood-lust of his behavior in Gertrude's closet'.[61] While there, hearing a voice, he bungles the roles of both avenging hero and wise fool by his folly in acting, for once, without thinking, stabbing through the arras in the hope that his target is the king, but it is instead Polonius, whom he then identifies as a 'wretched, rash intruding fool' (III.4.31). Hamlet has become a fool in madly killing a fool and bequeathing madness to Ophelia as a result, ruining a potential future with her. In the murder's aftermath, while chastising his mother for remarrying, he calls Claudius a 'king of shreds and patches' (III.4.102)—a jester—jumbling up the true and spurious memories and archetypal associations of fool Yorick, father-fool Polonius, murderer King Claudius, 'heroic' King Hamlet, and himself. As the ghost of King Hamlet then appears, to him alone, the hallucination seems to have resulted from this memory overload. The phantasm's part in this memory hodge-podge is to 'whet [Hamlet's] almost blunted purpose' and to admonish him 'Do not forget' (III.4.110–11). According to Gertrude, the 'mad' Hamlet has been seeing, hearing, and speaking to 'Nothing' (III.4.106, 133, 135).

Overload of jumbled true and spurious memories calls forth madness too in Lear. His rage intensifies over his 'heart-strook injuries' (III.1.17) as his 'wits begin to turn' (III.2.67) to the madness that reaches its zenith when he is in the farmhouse in III.6, accompanied by a seeming madman (Edgar in disguise as Poor Tom), the Fool, and his servant Caius/Kent. With those characters symbolically reinforcing his mental condition as being served by folly and madness, Lear looks upon nothing and 'sees' an arraignment of Goneril and Regan, conjured up by his stressed state. In his next appearance, in IV.6, dressed in flowers (as is Ophelia in her madness) he encounters Gloucester, and in their interaction, as Welsford observes, Lear 'has something of the wit, the penetration, the quick repartee of the court-jester'.[62] Otto states that the 'story of a king's being forced to become a jester to teach him humility was widely known in the Middle Ages' but 'its origins go back further'.[63] Though Lear initially tells Gloucester that he is 'every inch a king' (IV.6.107), he is now a king who recognizes himself as 'The natural fool of Fortune' (IV.6.189), and as such, he shares the general condition of humanity: 'When we are born, we cry that we are come / To this great stage of fools' (IV.6.180–1). Unlike Hamlet, who deliberately attempts to become a 'wise fool' and instead unwittingly becomes a 'natural fool', Lear has been prodded by the wise Fool to understand himself as a 'natural fool' and thereby briefly himself becomes a 'wise fool'. With this recognition accomplished, Lear can benefit from his healing dream-sleep.

Twentieth-century discoveries that during dreaming the brain activates its most 'ancient' sections in terms of evolution, the limbic regions, suggest that Jung had been correct in theorizing that 'Just as the human body represents a whole museum of organs, each with a long evolutionary history behind it, so we should expect to find that the mind is organized in a similar way'. Thus 'It can no more be a product without history than is the body in which it exists'.[64] So, he asserted, each person has both a personal and a collective unconscious, and dreams and archetypes play in both territories. Christos states that 'Most theorists believe that the brain is engaged in some sort of internal processing of memory during dream sleep', in which phase 'the brain is extremely active'[65], adding that one function of dreams may be to 'unlearn' some information to make room for new information garnered in the future. This 'reverse learning' may involve 'the weakening of obsessional states, the gradual forgetting and degradation of old memories, the elimination of daily trivial memories, and the weakening of strong fantasies'.[66] Lear, with his mind diseased, is in need of such weakening of obsessions, and his dream sleep will provide it. As he awakens in the company of Cordelia, his initial remarks indicate that he has been dreaming, and, as he returns to consciousness, he demonstrates that his memory has been 'resculpted' by telling her, 'your sisters / Have, as I do remember, done me wrong: / You have some cause, they have not' (IV.7.73–5). Marjorie Garber states that 'The awakening of Lear reaches out to unify more than inner man and outer world—for a moment it unifies time itself, obliterating the differences between death and life, this world and the next'.[67] Although Lear will die near the play's end, the king has found redemption for his folly, through the reconciliation of himself with his loving daughter that will bond them into the afterlife. The mystical connection between the Fool and Princess seems to have manifested between her and the King through his recognition of himself as Fool.

For Hamlet there is no such healing dream-sleep for his unconscious mind, though he wants and needs it and does regard it as a unifier between life and death. In the 'To be or not to be' soliloquy, he considers that if to die is to sleep and thereby 'end / The heart-ache and the thousand natural shocks / That flesh is heir to', it would be 'a consummation devoutly to be wished', but if death does parallel sleep, it would include not only oblivion, but periods as well of 'dreams', corresponding to a possible afterlife of hell (III.1.61–4, 66). The 'space' for him to 'resculpt' memories and connect life and death is instead the graveyard. When he encounters Yorick's skull, though it calls forth his personal fond memories of the living jester that almost certainly was his model for his wise fool role, it is also an archetypal *memento mori*, as the 'death's-head and skeleton are traditional emblems of the fool in the sense that death makes a fool of life's joys and purposes'.[68] Furthermore, the sensory disgust that the skull evokes in him 'gives physical form to unwilled recollection', as Wilder notes,[69] and he recognizes that not just fools, but also a heroic king-figure like Alexander or Caesar or a lady 'to this favour' 'must come' (V.1.192). When he learns that it is the lady Ophelia that will replace fool Yorick in the grave, the consequences of his foolish murder of her father manifest themselves, and he attempts to reassume the Hero role by fighting Laertes to claim the 'Princess' as his own. If he 'unlearns' some of his obsessive memory in the space of the graveyard, he also anticipates his future, as his fight with Laertes takes place in the grave, the 'space' in which he, the Hero/Fool, and the 'Princess' will soon ultimately unite.

A memory of *Hamlet* that remains in the minds of audiences and readers is the image of the prince with the skull of the dead fool Yorick, and for *King Lear* a comparable memory is of the repentant former king carrying the dead princess and lamenting, ambiguously, that his 'poor fool is hanged' (V.3.304). Folly, however, is never dead; foolish vanities and choices by all of us continue, but so does looking into the abyss of literature's and life's tragedies with the fool's perspective, seeing absurdity and humour, and attempting to make creative 'use of nothing' (*King Lear* I.4.128–9) as we proceed through our psychic journeys. Thus, the fool endures, to assert even more powerfully than does the ghost of King Hamlet, 'Remember me' (*Hamlet* I.5.91).

Notes

1. All quotations from Shakespeare in this essay are from R. Proudfoot, A. Thompson, and D.S. Kastan, eds., *The Arden Shakespeare: Complete Works*, 3rd series, rev. ed. (London: Arden, 2001).
2. J. Baldo, *Memory in Shakespeare's Histories: Stages of Forgetting in Early Modern England* (New York: Routledge, 2012), p. 36.
3. L.P. Wilder, *Shakespeare's Memory Theatre: Recollection, Properties, and Character* (New York: Cambridge UP, 2010), p. 13 (Wilder's emphases).
4. L.R. Squire, *Memory and Brain* (Oxford: Oxford University Press, 1987), p. viii.
5. Squire, *Memory and Brain* p. 241.
6. Ibid.
7. G. Christos, *Memory and Dreams: The Creative Human Mind* (New Brunswick, NJ: Rutgers University Press, 2003), p. 67.

8 Christos, *Memory and Dreams*, p. 5.
9 Squire, *Memory and Brain*, p. 243.
10 K.A. Carlson, 'The Impact of Humor on Memory: Is the Humor Effect about Humor?' *Humor: International Journal of Humor Research* 24.1 (2011): 21–41 (p. 21).
11 B.K. Otto, *Fools Are Everywhere: The Court Jester Around the World* (Chicago: University of Chicago Press, 2001), p. 48.
12 Christos, *Memory and Dreams*, p. 3.
13 Christos, *Memory and Dreams*, p. 40.
14 Christos, *Memory and Dreams*, p. 43.
15 Christos, *Memory and Dreams*, p. 44.
16 Ibid.
17 Christos, *Memory and Dreams*, pp. 44–45.
18 Christos, *Memory and Dreams*, p. 45.
19 Christos, *Memory and Dreams*, p. 5.
20 Christos, *Memory and Dreams*, p. 43.
21 Ibid.
22 Ibid.
23 Ibid.
24 Christos, *Memory and Dreams*, p. xi.
25 Christos, *Memory and Dreams*, p. 5.
26 Christos, *Memory and Dreams*, p. 41.
27 Christos, *Memory and Dreams*, p. 5.
28 Christos, *Memory and Dreams*, pp. 5–6.
29 Christos, *Memory and Dreams*, p. 93.
30 Christos, *Memory and Dreams*, pp. 6, 42.
31 Christos, *Memory and Dreams*, p. 6.
32 Christos, *Memory and Dreams*, p. x.
33 Christos, *Memory and Dreams*, pp. 92–93.
34 J. Hirsh, *Shakespeare and the History of Soliloquies* (Cranbury, NJ: Associated University Press, 2003), p. 28.
35 Wilder, *Shakespeare's Memory Theatre*, p. 107.
36 Squire, *Memory and Brain*, pp. 53–54.
37 Squire, *Memory and Brain*, p. 54.
38 H.C. Goddard, *The Meaning of Shakespeare*, 2 vols. (Chicago: University of Chicago Press, 1951): I. 352.
39 Goddard, *The Meaning of Shakespeare*: I. 350, 352.
40 Goddard, *The Meaning of Shakespeare*: I. 356.
41 Goddard, *The Meaning of Shakespeare*: I. 352.
42 Goddard, *The Meaning of Shakespeare*: I. 354.
43 A. Hiscock, *The Uses of this World: Thinking Space in Shakespeare, Marlowe, Cary and Jonson* (Cardiff: University of Wales Press, 2004), pp. 15, 17.
44 Ibid. p. 17.
45 Ibid.
46 R. Barrie, 'Telmahs: Carnival Laughter in *Hamlet*', in M.T. Burnett and J. Manning (eds.), *New Essays on Hamlet* (New York: AMS, 1994), pp. 83–100 (p. 83).
47 E. Welsford, *The Fool: His Social and Literary History* (Garden City, NY: Anchor, 1961), p. 61.
48 Otto, *Fools Are Everywhere*, p. 33.
49 Otto, *Fools Are Everywhere*, p. 230.
50 W. Willeford, *The Fool and His Scepter: A Study of Clowns and Jesters and Their Audience* (Evanston, IL: Northwestern University Press, 1969), p. 71.
51 R.H. Goldsmith, *Wise Fools in Shakespeare* (East Lansing: Michigan State University Press, 1955), p. 7.
52 Otto, *Fools Are Everywhere*, p. xvi.
53 S. & R.L. Fisher, *Pretend the World is Funny and Forever: A Psychological Analysis of Comedians, Clowns, and Actors* (Hillsdale, NJ: Lawrence Erlbaum, 1981), p. 200.
54 Willeford, *The Fool and His Scepter*, p. xvii.
55 D. Conford, 'The Tarot Fool', in V.K. Janik (ed.), *Fools and Jesters in Literature, Art, and History: A Bio-Bibliographical Sourcebook* (Westport, CN: Greenwood, 1998), pp. 453–58 (p. 453).
56 C.G. Jung, *Man and His Symbols* (Garden City, NJ: Doubleday, 1964), p. 455.
57 Conford, 'The Tarot Fool', pp. 456–57.

58 Willeford, *The Fool and His Scepter*, p. 71.
59 Willeford, *The Fool and His Scepter*, p. 188.
60 Willeford, *The Fool and His Scepter*, p. 4.
61 K. Stanton, '*Hamlet*'s Whores', in M.T. Burnett and J. Manning (eds.), *New Essays on* Hamlet (New York: AMS, 1994), pp. 167–88 (p. 184).
62 Welsford, *The Fool*, p. 266.
63 Otto, *Fools Are Everywhere*, pp. 49–50.
64 Jung, *Man and His Symbols*, p. 67.
65 Christos, *Memory and Dreams*, p. xii.
66 Christos, *Memory and Dreams*, p. 147.
67 M. Garber, *Dream in Shakespeare: From Metaphor to Metamorphosis* (New Haven, CT: Yale University Press, 1974), p. 124.
68 Willeford, *The Fool and His Scepter*, p. 199.
69 Wilder, *Shakespeare's Memory Theatre*, p. 128.

11

FATAL DISTRACTION

Eclipses of memory in *Julius Caesar* and *Antony and Cleopatra*

Jonathan Baldo

For the Middle Ages, a strong memory was held to be a sign of moral virtue and a strong and necessary guide to an individual's ethical behaviour, so that, according to Mary Carruthers, 'prodigious memory is almost a trope of saints' lives'.[1] In what follows I will examine two of Shakespeare's Roman plays that challenge the assumption that a strong memory, or at least a strong allegiance to memory, breeds virtuous behaviour. Both *Julius Caesar* (1599) and *Antony and Cleopatra* (1606–8) enact a clash of values associated with memory. Memory holds no more stable sway in Shakespeare's Rome than does the recently assassinated Pompey the Great or the soon-to-be-assassinated Julius Caesar. Objects and devices that ordinarily serve to reinforce and stabilize memories—the calendar, images, statues, and monuments—often become distractions in these two plays and wear the mantle of forgetting as often as that of memory. Shakespeare's staging of the death of Caesar, the would-be ruler over time and memory, reveals the fluid and uncertain nature of historical memory and the provisional and insecure nature of any rule over the past. Rather than an anchor to the past, memory in Shakespeare's Rome is revealed to be a present performance, one requiring repeated restaging, and bearing all the uncertainty of a performance, including a variable and sometimes unpredictable effect on a public.

Brutus is the character most closely associated with the idea of memory as a foundation of moral virtue, but by the end of *Julius Caesar* it is no longer a reliable one. In fact, the example of Brutus raises questions that haunt the rule of memory in Rome. Is steadfastness a sign of superior memory, or perhaps the reverse: of a memory so narrowly selective as to appear deficient? Does unwavering adherence to a single principle or fixed course of action issue from a firm, unwavering memory, or the willful suppression or forgetting of alternate, conflicting demands and imperatives? Does the superior memory commit to a fixed course of action or does it strive to hold contradictory demands in a kind of equilibrium?

Both Brutus in *Julius Caesar* and Octavius Caesar in *Antony and Cleopatra* embody a particular type in the Roman plays that I would call the indistractible self. One meaning of 'distraction' was a 'diversion of the mind or attention' (*OED* 2a), its predominant meaning today. But 'distraction' held other, less familiar meanings as well, including temporary madness. Distraction for the early modern period was a form of forgetfulness, one that caused a dispersion and disintegration of the self. Remembrance, by contrast, could act as a restorative, returning the self to wholeness. As Carol Thomas Neely writes, 'Thomas More exemplifies the period's view when he says of one who recovered from distraction that he "gathered hys remembraunce

149

to hym and beganne to come agayne to hym selfe'".[2] To be 'distracted' was to be divided from oneself. Another prominent early modern definition of the word, however, brings it closer to common experience, including the experience of theatregoers. Indeed, this definition sounds very much like a description of the effects of Shakespeare's stagecraft on audiences: 'The fact or condition of being drawn or pulled (physically or mentally) in different directions by conflicting forces or emotions' (*OED*, 3a); or, in its adjectival form, 'mentally drawn to different objects; perplexed or confused by conflicting interests; torn or disordered by dissension or the like' (*OED*, 3). Brutus and Octavius, by contrast, embody a type that I would call the indistractible. They seek to thwart internal division and diversion by memory and fixed principles in the case of Brutus, or by an equally fixed drive for power in that of Octavius. Both Brutus and Octavius resist what had long been considered a danger of the theatre, a mainstay of antitheatrical diatribe 'from classical Athens through the Reformation period: that the actor's mimicry is intrinsically harmful to himself and others because it involves duplicity and change rather than unity and permanence'.[3] Brutus and Octavius, in other words, resist the fundamental conditions of their own existence as theatrical characters. The Roman model of selfhood forbids, or seeks to keep at bay, 'distractedness' in all these forms. That model begins to unravel in *Julius Caesar*, in Mark Antony's funeral oration, and the process accelerates in *Antony and Cleopatra*, a play that might be described as a study in distraction.

An older association between a steadfast memory and virtue is still visible in both plays, though memory must beware of plots and encroachments against it by its rivals, forgetting and distraction. Over the course of the playwright's career, the values associated with remembering and forgetting were undergoing, if not a sea-change, at least a shake-up, owing largely to pressures associated with a rising nationalism and with the English Reformation. Religious reformers looked askance on those who harboured a nostalgia for the old religion and the festive calendar associated with it. Remembering England's past became a divisive issue for inhabitants of early modern England, and forgetting, a plausible path to national unity. As Ernest Renan famously noted in his analysis of nation-building in a lecture at the Sorbonne, 'Forgetting, I would even go so far as to say historical error, is a crucial factor in the creation of a nation'.[4] *Julius Caesar* reveals forgetting to be the stronger basis of Rome's political life. The ascendance of Caesar at the beginning of the play depends upon Pompey's having been forgotten, as the tribune Murellus complains. Subsequently, Mark Antony will exploit the Roman people's, as well as Shakespeare's audiences', forgetfulness and the pliability of their memory in order to achieve and consolidate his power, while Brutus adheres faithfully and fatally to an older and unquestioning adherence to memory as a stable source of value and virtue.[5] *Antony and Cleopatra* takes the earlier play's skepticism toward memory still further, exploring as it does both the moral and aesthetic superiority of what I would call the distracted self.

The calendar as palimpsest

As Shakespeare would have known both from Plutarch and from a controversy over the calendar in his own time that underscored the religious divisions in early modern Europe, Julius Caesar sought to make his mark on time and history in more ways than one: not merely as a conquering hero whose name would outlast time, but also as master of time itself. In 44 BC, the year in which Shakespeare's play is set, Caesar established himself as a reformer of the calendar. The instituting of the Julian calendar provoked resentment by conservatives who, according to Sigurd Burckhardt, 'felt it to be an arbitrary and tyrannical interference with the course of nature'.[6] A similar controversy, Burckhardt reminds us, informed Shakespeare's own time: namely, that between the Julian calendar, favoured by Protestants across Europe, and the newly reformed Gregorian calendar, introduced in 1582 and named for Pope Gregory XIII. The adoption of the Gregorian calendar was to be a bitter and divisive issue in the 'politico-religious struggles of the age'.[7] Dubbed the 'New Style', it was adopted by most Catholic European countries in 1582, though Protestant countries resisted and remained loyal to the 'Old Style' calendar. The Book of Common Prayer and most Protestant editions of the Bible 'opened with pages from the Julian calendar',[8] and many of the popular calendars and almanacs of Shakespeare's day included explanations of the controversy and the resulting confusion.[9] Indeed, England would not fully adopt the new calendar until 1752. Burckhardt has shown how Brutus's question and command to his servant Lucius, 'Is not tomorrow, boy, the first of March? . . . Look in the calendar and bring me word' (II.1.40, 42) link Caesar's controversial reforms with the recent impositions by another Roman, Pope Gregory.

In his introduction to the Arden Third Series edition of the play, David Daniell maintains that the opening of the play also refers to the controversy over the adoption of the Gregorian calendar. The second line of the play, the tribune Flavius's 'Is this a holiday?' Daniell suggests, 'could well have produced a powerful response', not only by the London City fathers who staunchly opposed the practice of playgoing that made working days effectively into holidays for those in attendance, but also by those Protestants who resisted Pope Gregory's reform of a system of keeping time that they regarded as 'that of Christ's revelation'. Daniell notes how this controversy has been largely papered over in editions of the play, ever since Lewis Theobald in his 1733 edition emended 'the first of March' in Brutus's question to Lucius to 'the Ides of March,' on the grounds that Brutus could not be so far off on his dates, especially with such an important task looming. Theobald's 'emendation' of the supposed error has been adopted by most editors since.[10]

The opening of the play, I want to suggest, evokes yet another calendrical controversy in early modern England. The old ecclesiastical calendar was in the process of being rewritten as a series of national celebrations of Protestant deliverance, David Cressy has shown, with Queen Elizabeth's accession day and the anniversary of the Gunpowder deliverance representing key dates in the new, reformed calendar. During the reigns of Queen Elizabeth and King James, certain reforms of the calendar took place that shifted its traditionally ecclesiastical focus to a dynastic one. The number of holy days was reduced, and in partial compensation Queen Elizabeth's government 'encouraged prayer and festivity on 17 November, the anniversary of the queen's accession' and 'the first annual concert of bells that was not tied to the Christian year'.[11] 'The day of remembrance of her highness' coronation', as it was sometimes referred to, jostled with other commemorative intentions, for 17 November happened to fall on the saints' day of Bishop Hugh of Lincoln, one of the few English saints in the canon. 'In some parts [of England],' Cressy writes, 'the festivity [on 17 November] was taken to perpetuate the memory of Hugh of Lincoln'.[12]

The confusion of these two dates proved advantageous not only to the crown but also to adherents of the old faith. The overlapping festivals of St. Hugh and Queen Elizabeth allowed recusants and so-called 'cold statute Protestants'[13] to fulfill their duties to one of England's most popular saints, while appearing to honour the Protestant monarch of the realm: 'The national dynastic observance was conveniently grafted on to a regional custom, and the ringing [of bells] could simultaneously satisfy conservative religious instincts and honour the Protestant queen'.[14] The persistence of a desire to honour the memory of Bishop Hugh of Lincoln in parts of England belonged to a more general pattern: 'The old saints' days were fondly preserved in the popular memory, governing traditional farming practices and days of markets and fairs'.[15] Furthermore, these overlayings of the calendar were reversible. Burdened by the public memory of his predecessor, King James would later do away with the observance of Elizabeth's Accession Day.

The King James Bible (1611) marks November as the saint's day of Hugh of Lincoln, with no mention of the former Queen, the popular memory of whom haunted him in the early years of his reign.

The people of early modern England would have immediately recognized the confusion at the beginning of *Julius Caesar*, about whether it is a holiday or working day, as their own, and not simply with respect to their opposition to European Catholic powers' adoption of the Gregorian calendar but also with respect to their own internal calendrical reforms. Told to disperse and get back to their houses by the tribunes, the working men of the opening scene have come out to witness the triumphal return of Caesar. Shakespeare makes Caesar's triumph coincide with the Feast of the Lupercal, a religious festival designed to ensure fertility and cleanse the city of evil spirits, held in honour of Lupercus, the god of shepherds, and Lupa, the she-wolf who suckled the infants Romulus and Remus. The working men of the city, however, have come out to witness what appears to be a celebration of state power, Caesar's victory in 45 BC in Munda, Spain, against Pompey's sons and his triumphal processional entry into Rome in October of that year: 'But indeed, sir, we make holiday to see Caesar and to rejoice in his triumph' (I.1.31–2).

A religious observance coincides with a state celebration, as it did when the older ecclesiastical calendar was overwritten by 'the new providential-commemorative calendar of Protestant England'.[16] That the older holiday has been only partially eclipsed becomes evident in Caesar's own remarks. His first words, directing his wife Calphurnia to stand 'directly in Antonio's way', reference a Lupercalian practice described in Shakespeare's principal source for the play, Plutarch's *Life of Caesar*: 'for our elders say, / The barren touched in this holy chase / Shake off their sterile curse' (I.2.3, 7–9).[17] By telescoping the two events—the feast of the Lupercal took place on February 15, and Caesar's triumphal entry in October—Shakespeare achieved just the convergence that was familiar to English audiences of the day.

Like the calendar controversy, the medieval cult of images that came under increasing attack in the reigns of Edward VI and Elizabeth hovers like Caesar's ghost over the play. For most medieval writers, the image played an important role as aide-mémoire, as it had in the classical memory arts.[18] The image was an effective means of focusing the memory, although occasionally a dissenting voice like that of Bernard of Clairvaux would complain about the distracting effect of images: how 'other people's images, presented in programs of sculpture and murals and book illuminations, not only may promote spiritual laziness and *curiositas* among those too adept to require them any longer, but also promote the vice of pride'.[19] There was widespread agreement, however, on the evils of distraction. Bernard himself warned against curiosity as a source of distraction, which in turn inhibits 'the concentrated inner "seeing"', and the richly sensory, emotional, and fully experiential recreation of 'things,' that profound memory work requires'.[20] So do Caesar's adorned images, ostensibly in the service of memory, seem to hold the power to distract from the religious observance taking place at the beginning of the play.

Caesar's statues seem to be objects of near-religious reverence, as the word 'images' would have suggested to an early modern audience. Flavius uses the word twice and Casca once in reporting on the tribunes having been 'put to silence' for 'pulling scarves off Caesar's images' (I.2.284–5). The word would have had vivid associations for an audience for whom the Reformation's attack on images was still either a painful memory or a cause célèbre: in either case, a deeply divisive issue. Especially likely to have been remembered was the fierce debate over so-called 'abused images': that is, images that became objects of pilgrimage and offerings and that were often associated with 'feigned' or false miracles. As Matthew Milner writes, 'Abuse was characterized as veneration and belief an image affectively mediated grace'.[21] The early stages of the Reformation witnessed 'a concerted campaign against abused images.

The vanity of those images which had been worshipped as idols was to be publicly exposed before the people they had deceived'.[22] The distinction between abused images and those that were not abused was maintained in earlier injunctions by Henry VIII, though the distinction was not easy to sustain:

> Sorting out abused images for removal from those who merely taught the faith, was a slippery affair. The objects of the cult of the saints, relics and votive offerings like the jewels and cloths placed on images had no didactic value and were not authentic.[23]

In 1548, the Council effectively put an end to trying to sort out abused from non-abused images, ordering all images to be removed from churches of the realm. Many venerated images deemed as belonging to the 'abused' category were 'adorned with elaborate mantles, beads and silver rings'.[24] Flavius instructs his fellow tribune Murellus, 'Disrobe the images, / If you do find them decked with ceremonies' (I.1.65–6); that is, remove any decorations adorning Caesar's statues (diadems and laurel crowns, according to Plutarch). His fellow tribune Murellus asks, 'May we do so? / You know it is the feast of Lupercal' (I.1.67–8), in an apparent non sequitur, since the Lupercal has quite another purpose than honouring Rome's rulers. Flavius seems to recognize this in his response, 'It is no matter. Let no images / Be hung with Caesar's trophies' (I.1.69–70). The question, both unasked and unanswered, is whether the decoration of 'images' or statues of Caesar or their removal would have been more inappropriate for the Lupercal. The tribunes do not seem to object to the celebration of state power on the occasion of a religious festival. Rather, it is the memory of a previous ruler, Pompey, whose eclipse they resent.

Flavius's command would have borne sharp memories of the attack on images, particularly 'abused images', which had not ended with the Elizabethan Settlement. As Patrick Collinson[25] and others have shown, the English Reformation was an ongoing process whose local and regional effects were still being carried out late in Elizabeth's reign and even into James's. The Edwardian and Elizabethan Injunctions ordered that all images be removed 'so that there remain no memory of the same in walls, glasses, windows, or elsewhere within their churches or houses'.[26] As the wording of the Injunctions indicates, the assault upon images was part of a broader attempt to reform and to control the popular memory. Alexandra Walsham writes, 'In a world in which the art of remembering was primarily an art of mental visualization, the reformers recognized that removing physical reminders of popish error was vital to the task of transforming mentalities'.[27] Eamon Duffy writes of the elements of the traditional faith that were discarded by the Reformation, 'Like the silencing of the bede-rolls, the removal of the images and petitions of the dead was an act of oblivion, a casting out of the dead from the community of the living into a collective anonymity'.[28] The work of revisionist historians like Duffy and Christopher Haigh has made it abundantly clear that the English Reformation's broader enemy was, in Peter Marshall's words, 'the hold of the past, and of past dead generations, on the present and the living'.[29]

Following the more violent decades of the English Reformation, the landscape of the British Isles came to resemble a series of palimpsests: effaced monuments, statues, and buildings were like manuscript pages on which the original writing had been effaced, but of which visible traces remained. The calendar shared this quality with landscapes of the early modern period as a result of Elizabethan and Jacobean reforms. Just as Elizabeth's Accession Day partly effaced the saint's day of Hugh of Lincoln in such a way as to leave traces of the original feast day behind, so does the celebration of Caesar's triumph only partly efface or overwrite the Feast of the Lupercal. Mary Carruthers details how a similar process of 'overlay and remapping' of pagan ceremonies and places characterized the world of early Christians, who practised a species of 'communal forgetting': 'not through some variety of amnesia, but by applying carefully the mnemotechnical principles of blocking one pattern of memories by another through "crowding" or overlay, and by intentional mnemonic replacement'.[30] In a world in which the calendar, a signal tool for organizing and controlling the national memory, was being overwritten, the past tends to become a ghost that stalks the present: never entirely erased, the past continues to remind the present of its future return. 'I shall see thee again?' Brutus asks Caesar's ghost in his tent while encamped near Sardis. 'Ay, at Philippi,' the ghost answers (IV.3.282). So does the past invariably answer the present: the past shall rise again, not only at Philippi but also on countless other battlegrounds of memory.

Statues and ghosts

Caesar's ghost's promise to Brutus to return doubles as a promise to Shakespeare's audience, which will hear of, if not see, Caesar's ghost again in subsequent productions at the Globe. Marjorie Garber notes how 'the prowess of "Julius Caesar, / Who at Philippi the good Brutus ghosted"' (*Antony and Cleopatra* II.6.12–13) ghosts the young men of the succeeding generation in *Antony and Cleopatra*'.[31] Sarah Hatchuel describes the 2008 Shakespeare Theatre Company's productions of *Julius Caesar* and *Antony and Cleopatra* in Sidney Harman Hall in Washington, DC, as part of a 'Roman Repertory', in which 'thematic links were constructed through the doubling of roles, creating ghosting effects between the productions':[32] for instance, the actor who played Julius Caesar in the earlier play returns as Enobarbus in the later one, adding to the pathos of Antony's desertion by his most loyal soldier. 'Yet of all Shakespeare's plays,' Garber writes, 'it is perhaps in *Hamlet* that we feel most the ghostly, dislocated presence and pressure of Julius Caesar'.[33]

Garber's word 'dislocated' is germane to the ending of *Julius Caesar*. Because of the Ghost's promise in Act IV, we anxiously anticipate his return at Philippi. Shakespeare, however, never allows us the frisson of the ghost's second return. Caesar's ghost returns only in the still ghostlier demarcations of language: specifically, Brutus's apostrophe in Act 5, scene 3, 'O Julius Caesar, thou art mighty yet. / Thy spirit walks abroad and turns our swords / In our own proper entrails' (V.3.94–6), and his report in Act V, scene 5, in which he confirms to Volumnius that the ghost has appeared to him a second time, 'The ghost of Caesar hath appeared to me / Two several times by night: at Sardis once, / And this last night, here in Philippi fields: / I know my hour is come' (V.5.17–20). Caesar's ghost has been 'dislocated', appearing with ghostly imprecision in report, not bodied forth by an actor, and that dislocation makes his presence and influence even more pervasive because diffused. Seeming to be flawed and vulnerable while alive, as a revenant and a memory he seems to actually achieve the power that when alive he was accused of pursuing.

Caesar's is not the only ghost that haunts Rome in the course of the play. In fact, the play begins with a species of haunting. The memory of Pompey the Great, whose forces Caesar defeated at the Battle of Munda and who was eventually murdered in Egypt by an officer of Ptolemy XIII, hovers over much of the play. During the events leading up to the assassination, he is a word, a memory. Not even his embodied memory in the form of his son Sextus Pompeius, who will appear in *Antony and Cleopatra*, will materialize in the course of the earlier play. After his assassination, Caesar moves into Pompey's role as revenant. But in addition to a memory and a name, Pompey is known to the audience as a statue. Caesar dies at the foot of Pompey's statue, the river of blood issuing from Caesar's body being likened by Mark Antony in a private moment to Lethe, the river of forgetfulness: 'And here thy hunters stand / Signed in thy spoil and crimsoned in thy lethe' (III.1.205–6). Privately, Mark Antony worries that

Caesar's virtues and triumphs will be forgotten, but publicly he will don the mantle of memory: 'You all do know this mantle. I remember / The first time ever Caesar put it on' (III.2.168–9), on the eve of Caesar's much celebrated triumph over the Nervii. Antony proceeds to make Caesar's wounds into memorials to each conspirator's individual malice—Cassius's, Caska's, and Brutus's 'most unkindest cut of all' (III.2.181)—thereby undoing Brutus's efforts to put the interests of Rome before that of any individual. The speech proceeds from Caesar's mantle, to his wounds, to yet another memorial, Pompey's statue, at whose base Caesar dies, so that even his former enemy seems to bleed for him: 'Even at the base of Pompey's statue, / Which all the while ran blood, great Caesar fell' (III.2.186–7). Recalling Flavius's command to 'disrobe the images' at the beginning of the play, this image of Pompey appears to have been re-robed, and in his former rival's blood.

Caesar's collapse at the feet of Pompey's statue has the qualities of an emblem, but one that seems as open to contested interpretations as the corpse of Caesar itself. It may signify Pompey's revenge against his former rival. Since both were victims of assassination, the image might suggest the tendency of revenge to recoil against the avenger. As Michael Neill writes, 'Because the revenger can free himself from his burden of deadly obligation only by an action that precisely counteracts the original offense, revenge drama is characterized by a relish of witty symmetries'.[34] In this case, not one but two such symmetries are visible: that between two deadly rivals, Caesar and Pompey, and that between memory and forgetting itself. The river of blood characterized as Lethe at the base of Pompey's memorial might imply that Caesar was destined to meet the same fate as his enemy: namely, oblivion. As Pompey was forgotten, eclipsed by Caesar at the beginning of the play so that the people, according to the tribunes, do not seem to recall their former leader, so will Caesar dissolve in the waters of the people's wavering memories. Mark Antony's characterization of Caesar's blood as Lethe suggests an ironic conjunction of statuary, presumably intended to fix and stabilize the public memory of a notable figure, and forgetfulness. Perhaps, the tableau suggests, a people erects public memorials like the statue of Pompey to keep the past at bay: not so much to make its memory of the past imperishable, but rather to forestall its being troubled or haunted by the past. Statues may memorialize our desire to forget, to bury the past once and for all so that it no longer haunts the present: to so ossify a living memory that it becomes stationary and therefore manageable and harmless, unlike the mobile and unpredictable ghost that haunts Brutus.

The thinking behind the party's slogan in George Orwell's futuristic Oceania in *Nineteen Eighty-Four*, 'Who controls the past . . . controls the future: who controls the present controls the past',[35] also animates Mark Antony's manipulation of popular memory in his funeral oration. He begins with an implicit denial of the hold of the past over the present: 'The evil that men do lives after them: / The good is oft interred with their bones' (III.2.76–7). The lines cast the dead as victims of their survivors, who selectively keep alive in memory the worst aspects of the departed. He then builds, through a careful orchestration of his audience's memory, to a virtual sanctification of Caesar that places his memory beyond the reach of further questioning. For Mark Antony, the past is as pliable as his audience, never hardening into anything as fixed, unvarying, and immobile as a statue. He implies that in death Caesar has been drained of all power: 'But yesterday the word of Caesar might / Have stood against the world. Now lies he there, / And none so poor to do him reverence' (III.2.119–21). But he knows better. Like the material Shakespeare found buried alive, as it were, in Thomas North's Plutarch, the corpse of Caesar lies ready to be awakened and exploited by those among the living most able to manage it. Like the power vacuum in Rome left by the death of Caesar, the past, too, stands waiting to be ruled by a survivor skilled enough to command the often unruly legions of the dead.

In his oration, Antony's opportunistic manipulation of the crowd's memory builds through a reference to the Lupercal, linking Caesar's memory to a religious observance (when 'I thrice presented him a kingly crown,' III.2.97); to producing a cloak that serves as the material memory of Caesar's victory over the Nervii, now linked to a personal reminiscence 'I remember / The first time ever Caesar put it on,' III.2.168–9); to the conversion of Caesar's wounds into visible memorials of betrayal and infamy ('Look, in this place ran Cassius' dagger through: / See what a rent the envious Caska made: / Through this, the well-beloved Brutus stabbed,' III.2.172–4). This series of vivid remembrances is also distracting in the very manner of a theatrical performance, causing his audience to forget what touches them most nearly: 'You have forgot the will I told you of' (III.2.231). Orchestrating the people's memory by reminding them of what they have managed to forget, what he has compelled them to forget through his own distracting rhetoric—namely, everything Brutus had said in his own oration—Antony predicts that all who hear the reading of the will 'would go and kiss dead Caesar's wounds, / And dip their napkins in his sacred blood, / Yea, beg a hair from him for memory' (III.2.135). He anachronistically projects a sainthood for Caesar, appearing to place his memory beyond reach, even while contriving to manipulate it as cunningly as Shakespeare's Henry V will manage to do with the public memory of his own actions, from the same stage and in the same theatrical season (1599). By placing Caesar's memory beyond further question or debate, Antony grants the illusion of stability to the memory of Caesar, something he knows to be volatile and as pliable as the Roman plebeians' affections.

Beginning with public acts of memory linking religious observance and state power, the play moves toward a mnemonic vacuum. By the middle of the play, Antony knows that rule over the past, like rule in Rome itself, stands ready for the taking. By contrast, Brutus stands for what the play represents as an outmoded understanding of memory and reverence for a past regarded as a stable and reliable guide to judgement and ethical action. In repeated comparisons of Brutus to his ancestors and a plebeian's suggestion, following his oration, that he be given 'a statue with his ancestors' (III.2.50), Brutus embodies the idea of memory as a conservative and stabilizing principle. Even after the assassination, in quarreling with Cassius over the accusation that Lucius Pella took bribes, Brutus invokes the recent past as guide: 'Remember March, the Ides of March, remember: / Did not great Julius bleed for justice' sake?' (IV.3.18–19)

In the course of the play Caesar undergoes what appears to be a two-stage process of dissipation: from stone, to flesh (of whose weaknesses the play repeatedly reminds us), to air. Whereas a statue is a reified public memory, a ghost is private and unsettled, and unsettled in more ways than one: unsettling the one visited by the ghost, having unsettled business, and also having not settled into any fixed, official, public memory, like a statue. Statue and ghost: together these two images suggest two orders of memory, and two distinctly different relations between past and present. Whereas statues might suggest a stable past whose visitations are more or less orderly and governed by the present, expressed in forms of festive celebrations and regular calendrical observances, the ghost represents a past whose returns are far less predictable and potentially more disturbing: an unruly past that refuses to be subdued and ruled by the present. The calendar in *Julius Caesar* acts more like a ghost than a statue, destabilizing memory where it should help to regulate an orderly and predictable relation between past and present.

It is no accident that the play begins with statuary and ends with a ghost. This shift in imagery signals a change in the status of memory. No longer a reliable ally of and guide to behaviour, it becomes, in the competing eulogies of Brutus and Mark Antony, as uncertain as performance itself, and more servant than master and guide to present interests. Brutus's final lines, spoken after running upon his sword, suggest a broader desire to 'still' the past, to make the ghost the equivalent of a statue, in the imagery of the play: 'Caesar, now be still. / I killed not thee with half so good a will' (V.5.50–1). The play as a whole demonstrates, however, that there are no statutory limits to the past. It might very well have reminded early modern audiences of the power of Republican Rome to continue to haunt the monarchs of a divided Europe in the Renaissance, in which monarchies existed side by side with small republics like Venice, Genoa, and Florence, states controlled by commercial rather than landed elites; and perhaps, in the tribunes opening command to strip statuary of adornments, of the ways on which England in 1599, at the end of a turbulent century of religious division, conflict, and reform, continued to be haunted by its pre-Reformation self.

Fatal distraction

In Shakespeare's day, the theatres were under frequent attack as sources of distraction from worship and work. Puritans regarded playgoing 'as a dangerous distraction from their all-important call to repentance, and a distraction that all too often led the people further into sin'.[36] Oddly enough, Parliament used the same word often wielded as a weapon against the theatres to describe the condition of the nation when banning the performance of plays in 1642. Referring to the 'distressed estate of Ireland, steeped in her own blood, and the distracted estate of England, threatened with a cloud of blood by a civil war', Parliament's 'An Ordinance concerning Stage Plays' of 2 September, 1642 held that 'public sports do not agree with public calamities, nor public stage-plays with seasons of humiliation'. It recommended that the English people seek out, in lieu of public entertainments, 'profitable and seasonable considerations of repentance, reconciliation and peace with God'.[37] In an otherwise superb discussion of the closing of the theatres, Christopher Hodgkins misquotes the parliamentary ordinance by conflating its characterizations of Ireland and England to yield 'the distressed state of England'.[38] The difference between 'distressed' and 'distracted,' however, is key. The meaning of 'distracted' in the phrase 'distracted estate of England' hearkens back to the senses cited earlier: of 'divided', 'pulled (physically or mentally) in different directions by conflicting forces or emotions', or 'perplexed or confused by conflicting interests; torn or disordered by dissension or the like' (*OED*). It is curious indeed that Parliament should have applied the same word to the nation that was often leveled at the theatres, but the redundancy is most likely deliberate and not simply the result of an unwitting transference of properties from the theatre to the nation as a whole. The wording of the ordinance implies that an already distracted or divided nation does not need further distraction in the form of theatrical entertainments, but rather a concentration of attention that it associates with worship, one that will presumably restore unity—not only unity with God but also internal unity—to a divided nation.

The Roman model of selfhood forbids 'distractedness' in all its forms. That model begins to unravel in *Julius Caesar*, and the process accelerates in *Antony and Cleopatra*, a play that might be described as a study in distraction. *Julius Caesar* and *Antony and Cleopatra* are linked not only by their Roman content and characters, but also by their interest in what Umberto Eco has called an *ars oblivionis*, an art of forgetting.[39] In particular, both show an interest in the temporary form of forgetting known as distraction. In *Julius Caesar,* distraction is represented as a destructive force, one that results in Portia's death: 'she fell distract, / And, her attendants absent, swallowed fire' (IV.3.153–4). Brutus regards distraction as a defect, even though he is the very model of the 'distract' self in the sense that he is pulled simultaneously in two directions, divided by his twin loyalties to Caesar and to the Roman Republic. The distracted self is the microcosm of civil strife, as Brutus famously observes when he imagines the 'genius' or 'guardian spirit which conceives and controls action'[40] challenged by 'mortal instruments', which results in an individual's equivalent of civil strife: 'the state of man, / Like to a little kingdom, suffers the / The nature of an insurrection' (II.1.67–9). By contrast, distraction frequently acts as an enabling and liberating force in *Antony and Cleopatra*. Ultimately, it points towards underlying connections between the Mark Antonys of the two plays.

The apparent discontinuities between the Antony of *Julius Caesar*, concerned above all with achieving and consolidating power, and his passionate, pleasure-seeking counterpart in *Antony and Cleopatra* have often been remarked. A less apparent connection between the two is their shared disregard of memory as a guide to conduct. The Antony of *Julius Caesar*, who manipulates the collective memory of the Roman populace through carefully orchestrated acts of remembering and forgetting, bears much in common with the older Antony who is content to indulge in the pleasures of oblivion in Egypt and who refuses to honour and respect ancestry and memory of the dead in the Roman way.

Antony and Cleopatra is as fragmented and divided as its male protagonist. Scenes change as rapidly as Cleopatra's moods. Like its female protagonist, it is a study in the appeals of distraction. In its mixed mode of tragicomedy, the play exhibits a 'well-divided disposition', as Cleopatra says of Antony; that is, it encourages us to regard its hero and heroine's capacity for distraction as a virtue as well as a flaw. If it is a hallmark of Shakespeare's theatre to reproduce in its audience 'well-divided dispositions' like Antony's, to distract us not only in the sense of to divert but also in the more strenuous sense of to draw or pull '(physically or mentally) in different directions by conflicting forces or emotions' (*OED*, 3a), then the Egyptian setting of *Antony and Cleopatra*, where Antony allows himself to be 'distracted' in multiple senses, resembles nothing so much as the Globe Theatre itself.

Shakespeare's ultimate embodiment of the allures of distraction, Cleopatra, asks that 'the memory of my womb' (III.13.167) dissolve, 'Together with my brave Egyptians all, / By the discandying of this pelleted storm, / Lie graveless, till the flies and gnats of Nile / Have buried them for prey!' (III.13.168–71), if she has indeed mistreated her Roman lover. Cleopatra imagines the dissolving of memory itself, as she envisions Egypt as becoming a country without graves or monuments, and without the trace of an obligation to remember. Of course, Egypt as we experience it in the play is already a region without monuments or any apparent attachment to or reverence for its past. Deploying the language of the constant lover, she is characteristically inconstant in the sense of untrue to herself; that is, she is paradoxically untrue to her salient characteristic, her non-self-identity, deriving from the manifold attractions of forgetting that she exhibits and the fluid possibilities and freedom of her Egyptian 'well-divided disposition'.

Antony establishes Egypt as a site of distraction in the very first scene. Antony's extravagant vow to find out 'new heaven, new earth' suggests that Egypt pays homage to the present as a seat of pleasure and to the future as a place of imaginative play and possibility, but decidedly not to the past and to its reminders of ongoing responsibility. He proceeds to propose a programme of diversion to Cleopatra: 'No messenger but thine, and all alone / Tonight we'll wander through the streets and note / The qualities of people' (I.1.52–4). Characteristically untrue to herself, this queen of distraction takes on the role of a chiding or carping memory throughout this scene, repeatedly reminding Antony to hear the Roman messengers and to recall his pledges to his wife Fulvia. The excessive repetition of Fulvia's name causes it to become a comic signature of memory itself, which, like Fulvia, is unceremoniously buried in the laughter of this scene (I.1.19f., 42f.). Unlike the more historically minded Rome, Egypt is a place of epicurean excess leading to pleasurable oblivion. The prospect of so great a monument to the human spirit as Rome dissolving in the solvent of present pleasure, a kiss or an embrace ('thus'), brings forth not a whisper of regret:

> Let Rome in Tiber melt and the wide arch
> Of the ranged empire fall! Here is my space.
> Kingdoms are clay; our dungy earth alike
> Feeds beast as man. The nobleness of life
> Is to do thus, when such a mutual pair
> And such a twain can do't—in which I bind,
> On pain of punishment, the world to weet
> We stand up peerless.
>
> *(I.1.35–42)*

Instead of opportunities to be seized for heroic exploits of enduring memory (I.1.45–9), minutes become couches of pleasure, and hours, female servants attending Venus.

In the second scene in Alexandria, Charmian, Iras, and Alexas seek diversion by having their futures told by a soothsayer, in turn diverting us from the main plot lines of the play. The Roman preoccupation with honour, by contrast, causes it to dwell largely on the past, as Antony bitterly observes: 'Our slippery people, / Whose love is never linked to the deserver / Till his deserts are past' (I.2.178–80). Ironically, Antony's departure from Egypt makes it more Roman, transforming it from a place of 'Lethe'd dullness' (II.1.27) to a site of memory. According to Cleopatra, her lover's 'remembrance lay / In Egypt with his joy' (I.5.60–1). She will not 'forget to send to Antony' (I.5.67). Although she is more frequently the agent of forgetting, here she elects to play the role of its victim: 'O, my oblivion is a very Antony, / And I am all forgotten' (I.3.91–2). In Antony's absence, however, she becomes herself again, calling upon a series of distractions in quick succession: music, billiards, and angling. Rather than having the desired effect of helping her to forget Antony, however, these distractions eventually lead to her recollection of an occasion when 'I drunk him to his bed; / Then put my tires and mantles on him, whilst / I wore his sword Philippan' (II.5.21–3); a characteristically Egyptian memory, since it is a recollection of divided identities and of identities put under erasure, as in a theatre.

Antony and Cleopatra seems ultimately divided as to the very nature of division itself. A mark of breadth or enlargement in Egypt and of an incoherent and unstable identity lacking integrity in Rome, the divided or distracted self, 'drawn or pulled (physically or mentally) in different directions by conflicting forces or emotions' (*OED*), in turn divides its spectator, causing her to be of two minds about division. Antony expresses something like a universal principle of distraction when he muses, 'What our contempts doth often hurl from us, / We wish it ours again' (I.2.120–1). Although his is an unusually distracted self—'He was disposed to mirth, but on the sudden / A Roman thought hath struck him' (I.2.77–8)—he pretends to possess a Roman unity, an integral self, overlooking his inner faction as he relates to Cleopatra the civil wars in Italy and arguing his need to return to Rome:

> The strong necessity of time commands
> Our services awhile, but my full heart
> Remains in use with you. Our Italy
> Shines o'er with civil swords; Sextus Pompeius
> Makes his approaches to the port of Rome;
> Equality of two domestic powers
> Breed scrupulous faction.
>
> *(I.3.42–8)*

Answering Cleopatra's anxious question about Antony's disposition in Rome, whether he was 'sad or merry,' Alexas reports, 'Like to the time o'th'year between the extremes / Of hot and cold, he was nor sad nor merry' (I.5.53–5). In response, Cleopatra praises Antony's 'well-divided disposition', its 'heavenly mingle' of moods (I.5.56, 62). In Egypt as in a theatre, a well-divided disposition is the measure of scope and breadth, flexibility and variety, complexity and completion.

In Rome, unlike Egypt, distraction in the sense of 'being drawn or pulled (physically or mentally) in different directions by conflicting forces or emotions' is regularly construed as debilitating. Like a distracted nation, a distracted self looks like a weakened one from the Roman point of view. An intoxicated Lepidus fights 'the greater war between him and his discretion' (II.7.5–9). His love for and allegiance to both Octavius and Antony further divides Lepidus (III.2.7f.), just as love for her brother and her husband divides Octavia, resulting in an internal paralysis that makes her unable to speak: 'Her tongue will not obey her heart, nor can / Her heart inform her tongue—the swansdown feather / That stands upon the swell at the full of tide, / And neither way inclines' (III.2.47–50). The Roman view holds an internally distracted self to be a feminine and attenuated one, by virtue of being pulled by conflicting forces or emotions. In Egypt, by contrast, periodic distraction may seem a source of strength, producing a sturdier selfhood that is able to withstand division and bear buffeting by violent extremes. Shakespeare's ultimate creature of extremities asserts in an apostrophe to Antony, 'Be'st thou sad or merry, / The violence of either thee becomes, / So does it no man else' (I.5.62–4). In this respect Antony resembles the play that contains him, a tragicomedy that itself exhibits the violence of extremes that Cleopatra attributes to Antony. Unlike *Julius Caesar*, which harbours a residual nostalgia for a moral life based upon memory and continuity with the past, and for public memory as the basis of political action, *Antony and Cleopatra* advances an implicit argument for the moral claims of a theatre of distraction.

Although Octavius complains about Cleopatra's distraction of Antony throughout the play, he learns from her and ultimately defeats his rival by distracting him. Maecenas urges Octavius Caesar to 'make boot of [Antony's] distraction' (4.1.9), and Enobarbus counsels Antony not to engage the enemy by sea at Actium, for 'you therein . . . Distract your army' (III.7.41, 43). Soon we learn that Octavius Caesar has cunningly divided his own army in order to distract his enemy's scouts: 'While he was yet in Rome / His power went out in such distractions / As beguiled all spies' (III.7.75–7). Octavius triumphs by distracting an already highly distracted opponent: the very conditions of which Parliament would complain in their 1642 ordinance. Although Octavius wins the battle against his rival, he loses the greater one for the audience's sympathies by virtue of his very indistractibility. The eminently distractible Antony seems more like ourselves, the divided denizens of 'this distracted globe' that Shakespeare's dramaturgy has taught us to be.

Octavius Caesar's final words project onto the lovers a Roman identity, shrouding them in the language of monumental history:

> No grave upon the earth shall clip in it
> A pair so famous. High events as these
> Strike those that make them; and their story is
> No less in pity than his glory which
> Brought them to be lamented. Our army shall
> In solemn show attend this funeral,
> And then to Rome. Come, Dolabella, see
> High order in this great solemnity.
> *(V.2.353–60)*

Forgotten in Octavius's eulogy are the earlier lessons of the play, which taught the ways in which monumental history is erected on the sands of forgetting. Octavius now imitates the common people's fickle memory, which he has taunted so often. Public, monumental memory is built on the slippery foundation of the vagaries of 'this common body' for whom 'the ebbed man, ne'er loved till ne'er worth love, / Comes deared by being lacked' (I.4.43–4), since Antony and Cleopatra themselves become deared by being lacked at the end of the play. The Egyptian word 'come' haunts the edges of Octavius's eulogy (V.2.359), suggesting that audiences' apparently fixed and monumental memory of the becoming lovers and lovers of becoming will resemble the shifting sands of the Egyptian desert more than the marble of Rome. If, as both Antony and Octavius have asserted, lack and loss cause a thing to become dear, and if memory is predicated on absence or loss, then recollection is necessarily bound up with desire, including all the Egyptian vagaries and shifts of desire. The experience of loss, in other words, makes Egyptians of us all. Cleopatra's retreat for safety within her monument is the ultimate irony of the play: a volatile figure of distraction placed within a symbol of memorial culture that she challenges with every fibre of her being. A monument is no protection against future acts of re-membering, as Shakespeare's mixed treatment of the lovers attests. Indeed, a monumental memory is the least probable myth in this mythogenic play, as the early modern theatres repeatedly demonstrated to their audiences with their divergent retellings of well-known histories.

Antony and Cleopatra vividly and sometimes gaudily displays the advantages of distracted and therefore more flexible and receptive minds like Antony's and Cleopatra's. By virtually personifying swift change and distraction in the sense of temporary forgetting, Cleopatra exemplifies the allure of the theatres that a significant number of Shakespeare's contemporaries deplored as sites of distraction from more sombre pursuits. But the play does not ask us to wholly embrace distraction. Instead, I would propose that it is ultimately divided on the subject and constructed in such a way as to produce division in its spectators. The play as a whole may be taken to imply that an apparently unified self like Octavius Caesar is needed in order to unify an empire; at least that is one of the implications of the play's ending and its ultimate prophesy of the *pax romana*, the 'time of universal peace' (IV.6.5). The play is asymmetrical, however, in regard to its stance on distraction. If it is designed to make its audience distracted—'perplexed or confused by conflicting interests; torn or disordered by dissension or the like' (*OED*, 3)—about distraction itself, then perhaps we must conclude that the dominant sensibility of the play is more Egyptian than Roman. The play, that is, moulds us into 'distracted' Egyptians, divided about the very value of its own Egyptian dividedness. Causing us to suspend our judgements between Egypt and Rome, Antony and Octavius, the highly distracted and the indistractible, *Antony and Cleopatra* poses, even if it does not answer, a question about both the aesthetic and the moral advantages of distraction. It constitutes a powerful if volatile, fluid, and changeable monument to those selves who practise the play of remembering and forgetting with formidable passion.

Notes

1. M. Carruthers, *The Book of Memory: A Study of Memory in Medieval Culture* (Cambridge: Cambridge University Press, 1990), p. 12.
2. C.T. Neely, *Distracted Subjects: Madness and Gender in Shakespeare and Early Modern Culture* (Ithaca, NY: Cornell University Press, 2004), p. 3.
3. C. Hodgkins, 'Plays Out of Season: Puritanism, Antitheatricalism and Parliament's 1642 Closing of the Theatres.' In *Centered on the Word: Literature, Scripture, and the Tudor-Stuart Middle Way*, ed. D.W. Doerksen and C. Hodgkins (Newark: Delaware University Press, 2005), pp. 298–318 (p. 306).

4 E. Renan, 'What is a Nation?', trans. Martin Thom. In *Nation and Narration*, ed. Homi Bhaba (London: Routledge, 1990), p. 11.
5 See C. Guéron, 'Forgetful Audiences in *Julius Caesar'*, Actes des congrès de la Société française Shakespeare 30 (2013): *Shakespeare et la mémoire*. https://shakespeare.revues.org/1959?lang=en
6 S. Burkhardt, *Shakespearean Meanings* (Princeton, NJ: Princeton University Press, 1968), p. 6.
7 Burckhardt, *Shakespearean Meanings*, p. 6.
8 See: W. Shakespeare, *Julius Caesar*, Arden Third Series, ed. D. Daniell (Walton-on-Thames, Surrey: Thomas Nelson and Sons, 1998), p. 17; R.C. Hassel, R.C. Jr., *Renaissance Drama and the English Church Year* (Lincoln: University of Nebraska Press, 1979), p. 8.
9 S. Sohmer, *Shakespeare's Mystery Play: The Opening of the Globe Theatre 1599* (Manchester and New York: Manchester University Press, 1999), pp. 20–1.
10 Shakespeare, *Julius Caesar*, ed. Daniell, p. 17.
11 D. Cressy, *Bonfires and Bells: National Memory and the Protestant Calendar in Elizabethan and Stuart England* (Berkeley: University of California Press, 1989), p. 50.
12 Cressy, *Bonfires and Bells*, p. 51.
13 A. Walsham, *Church Papists: Catholicism, Conformity and Confessional Polemic in Early Modern England* (Woodbridge, UK: The Boydell Press, 1999), p. xv.
14 Cressy, *Bonfires and Bells*, p. 51.
15 Cressy, *Bonfires and Bells*, p. 15.
16 Cressy, *Bonfires and Bells*, p. 30.
17 Plutarch, *Lives*, vol. 7. *Demosthenes and Cicero, Alexander and Caesar*, trans. Bernadotte Perrin, Loeb Classical Library 99 (Cambridge, MA: Harvard University Press, 1919), p. 585.
18 Bartlovà; Hagen.
19 M. Carruthers, *The Craft of Thought: Meditation, Rhetoric, and the Making of Images, 400–1200* (Cambridge: Cambridge University Press, 1998), p. 87.
20 Carruthers, *The Craft of Thought*, p. 84.
21 M. Milner, *The Senses and the English Reformation* (Aldershot, UK: Ashgate, 2013), p. 243.
22 S. Brigden, *London and the Reformation* (Oxford: Clarendon Press, 1989), p. 289.
23 Milner, *The Senses*, p. 243.
24 R. Whiting, 'Abominable Idols: Images and Image-breaking under Henry VIII.' *Journal of Ecclesiastical History* 33 (1982): 30–47 (p. 32).
25 P. Collinson, *The Birthpangs of Protestant England: Religion and Cultural Change in the Sixteenth and Seventeenth Centuries* (Basingstoke: Macmillan Press, 1988), p. ix.
26 W.H. Frere and W.P.M. Kennedy (eds.), *Visitation Articles and Injunctions. Vol. 3: 1559–1575* (London: Longmans, Green and Co., 1910), p. 16.
27 A. Walsham, 'History, Memory, and the English Reformation', *The Historical Journal* 55 (2012): 899–938 (p. 907).
28 E. Duffy, *The Stripping of the Altars: Traditional Religion in England 1400–1580* (New Haven, CT: Yale University Press, 1992), p. 494.
29 P. Marshall, *Beliefs and the Dead in Reformation England* (Oxford: Oxford University Press, 2002), pp. 89–90.
30 Carruthers, *The Craft of Thought*, p. 54.
31 M. Garber, *Shakespeare's Ghost Writers: Literature as Uncanny Causality* (New York and London: Methuen, 1987), p. 71.
32 S. Hatchuel, *Shakespeare and the Cleopatra/Caesar Intertext: Sequel, Conflation, Remake* (Madison, NJ: Fairleigh Dickinson University Press, 2011), p. 59.
33 Garber, *Shakespeare's Ghost Writers*, p. 59.
34 M. Neill, 'English Revenge Tragedy.' In *A Companion to Tragedy*, ed. Rebecca Bushnell (Oxford: Blackwell, 2005), p. 334.
35 G. Orwell, *Nineteen Eighty-Four* (London: Penguin Books, 1990), p. 37.
36 Hodgkins, 'Plays Out of Season', p. 305.
37 Hazlitt, W.C., *English Drama and Stage Under the Tudor and Stuart Princes: Documents and Treatises* (London: Roxburghe Library, 1869), p. 63.
38 Hodgkins, 'Plays Out of Season', p. 304.
39 Eco, U. and M. Migiel, 'An Ars Oblivionis? Forget It!', *PMLA* 103 (1988): 254–61 (p. 254).
40 Shakespeare, *Julius Caesar*, ed. Daniell, p. 201.

PART III

History

12
HANDLING MEMORY IN THE HENRIAD
Forgetting Falstaff

William E. Engel

> FLUELLEN As Alexander killed his friend Clytus, being in his ales and his cups, so also Harry Monmouth, being in his right wits and his good judgements, turned away the fat knight with the great-belly doublet: he was full of jests, and gipes, and knaveries, and mocks; I have forgot his name.
>
> (*H5* 4.7.44–49)

The Falstaff perplex

Few characters loom as large in the popular imagination as Falstaff. Once encountered, he is hard to forget. And yet this apparently is what Shakespeare asks the audience to do: to forget Falstaff. He must be sent packing so the young king can get on with ruling and England can get on track for the destined, glorious reign of Elizabeth. In much the same way the fool in *King Lear* must be off stage by the end of act three so the remainder of that tragedy can accede to the gravitas it warrants, Falstaff must be out of sight for the final play of the Henriad.[1]

As if anticipating audience resistance to letting this most prodigious of his creations slip from mind, Shakespeare devotes two scenes early in *Henry V* to Falstaff's death. The play also is peppered with references that recall Falstaff's former presence as the Prince's carousing companion, going so far as to have one character need to be reminded of his name (the epigraph to this essay). Gower's ready reply, 'Sir John Falstaff' (*H5* 4.7.50), as if invoking a demon by using its proper name, is enough to raise the familiar spirit—not on stage but in the mind's eye. Isabel Karremann points out that the scene 'both mimics the King's deliberate forgetfulness and prompts the memory of the audience' reminding them to 'resort to their own historical and theatrical memory in order to withstand the force of nationalist oblivion.'[2] This *aide-mémoire* encoded in the Henriad portrays in broad strokes the figure of a clown; as Lina Perkins Wilder explains: 'Fluellen recalls Falstaff's mnemonically charged physicality, but he forgets Falstaff's name.'[3] Other less explicit conjurations of Falstaff crop up as well, keeping him from sliding irretrievably into oblivion. These memory traces leading back to and in effect tethering us to the after-image of the exuberant if corpulent knight are, this essay contends, emblematic of how memory—historical, dynastic, and national—is handled in the Henriad. Recovering and analyzing some of the more prominent of these traces and thematic echoes brings into focus the extent to which Shakespeare used the principles, techniques, and tropes associated with the memory arts.[4]

Falstaff's prospective absence

Shakespeare was well aware that historical figures carried a host of received, sometimes competing, representations, requiring that he mold and alter them to fit his projection of dynastic integrity.[5] His attention to memory images, drawing on key physical characteristics and outward signs to show the inner character, left lasting impressions that could overwrite other previous portraits.[6] Henry IV thus contrasts his own cunning self-presentation to that of deposed Richard II by way of chiding Hal, comparing him to 'the skipping King', a caricature that sums up what Shakespeare wanted recalled from the Henriad's first play: 'The skipping King, he ambled up and down | With shallow jesters and rash bavin wits, | Soon kindled and soon burnt; carded his state, | Mingled his royalty with cap'ring fools' (*1H4* 3.2.60–63). Likewise Falstaff's egregious silhouette makes the carefree rascal so memorably amusing in the opening acts of *1 Henry IV*. The stakes are raised, however, when Falstaff shamelessly acknowledges his self-serving materialism as endangering the lives of the rag-tag troops he musters, 'good enough to toss' on the end of a pike, 'food for powder' (*1H4* 4.2.64–65). What is merry in the tavern, though, is inappropriate in the wider world, especially the field, as Hal makes clear in his rebuke to Falstaff for his witty quip at the Shrewsbury parlay: 'Peace, chewet, peace' (*1H4* 5.1.29).

Earlier in the same play, in the second movement of the tavern skit, when Falstaff assumes the role of the Prince defending the reprobate knight to his father being played by Hal after having 'deposed' Falstaff, the true place of Falstaff in the realm is churned up from within the burlesque, the satire acquiring more bite with each invective.

> PRINCE Why dost thou converse with that trunk of humours, that
> bolting-hutch of beastliness, that swollen parcel of dropsies, that
> huge bombard of sack, that stuffed cloak-bag of guts, that roasted
> Manningtree ox with the pudding in his belly, that reverend Vice,
> that grey Iniquity, that father Ruffian, that Vanity in years?
> (*1H4* 2.4.436–42)

In his defense Falstaff, half-hoping Hal (whom he is playing here) will echo the same when questioned by the King, responds in a way that sets up an easily retrievable memory cluster, based on a seriatim catalogue and bolstered by anaphora (or calculated repetition) such as aspiring humanist orators might practice.[7]

> FALSTAFF No, my good lord, banish Peto, banish Bardoll, banish
> Poins, but for sweet Jack Falstaff, kind Jack Falstaff, true Jack
> Falstaff, valiant Jack Falstaff, and therefore more valiant,
> being, as he is old Jack Falstaff, banish not him
> thy Harry's company, banish not him thy Harry's
> company. Banish plump Jack and banish all the world.
> (*1H4* 2.4 461–67)

While the Prince's reply, 'I do; I will' (*1H4* 2.4.468), remains the subject of on-going interpretation, the breaking of the frame of the play-within-the-play signals Hal's understanding that this is to what things must come. And as the Henriad unfolds, Falstaff, denounced as the 'tutor and the feeder of' the newly crowned King's former 'riots', is banished 'on pain of death', along with his other 'misleaders' (*2H4* 5.5.62–64).

A different fate awaits Poins who, perhaps even more than Falstaff, would have distracted attention away from Hal's assuming his proper station. He disappears from the narrative by the end of the second act owing to his knowledge of the Prince's having been 'so lewd', his partner in crime and 'second brother' (*2H2* 2.2.58, 63). Unlike Hal's relationship to Falstaff, his to Poins is one of shared secrets and conspiratorial jests, most notably the robbing of the robbers (*1H4* 1.2.152–58). Poins is responsible for further Boar's-Head hijinks when he convinces the Prince to join him, disguised as tapsters, to overhear and surprise Falstaff with Doll Tearsheet (*2H4* 2.2.164–65 and 2.4 279ff.) in retaliation for Falstaff's letter warning Hal that Poins aims to marry his sister to the Prince (*2H4* 2.2.120ff.). Poins is similar in kind but different in degree from the feckless Falstaff. And Bardolph, with his oft-remarked-on red nose (*2H4* 2.4.333) and face that Falstaff says he would use 'as many a man doth of a death's head, or a *memento mori*' because 'I never see thy face but I think upon hell fire' (*1H4* 3.3.30–31), will be hanged by order of the King for looting a church during England's campaign in France (*H5* 3.6.100). Mistress Nell scarcely receives a full line describing her syphilitic death (*H5* 5.1.82). But Falstaff's exit from the Henriad is all the more poignant for his not appearing on stage. This way of handling Falstaff's death—including the reported memories of his having passed from the world—reveals Shakespeare's careful attention to mnemotechnic principles (which also make for good theatre), such that the deadbed scene is orchestrated to supply a series of lingering memory images in the audience's mind's eye.

The treatment reserved for Falstaff provoked J. Dover Wilson to question what exactly makes him 'the most conspicuous' and 'most fascinating character in *Henry IV*'; and Harold Bloom saw him as unrivaled in the Shakespearean canon as a character study in 'authentic freedom'.[8] He is unforgettable as much for his actions as for his distinctive bodily presence,[9] to the extent that he exceeds the boundaries of the literary types he is meant to evoke. These types include, from the Latin comic tradition, the *buffone*, who amuses others by his indecorous behavior; the *miles gloriosus* or braggart soldier; and also the *puer senex* who insists on the privileges both of youth and of age. As Rosalie Colie observed of the literary types rolled into Falstaff: 'we recognize in him (as does the English Hal) the Vice of the morality play, *Mundus* with his *Infans*, Gluttony, Appetite, Riot, and the rest of the temptations besetting this important prodigal son; we recognize in him the Lord of Misrule and Carnival of folkish and medieval festivals'.[10]

We easily can visualize Falstaff playing the roles of those homegrown English allegorical types mentioned in Hal's description of his dissolute companion: 'that reverend Vice, that grey Iniquity, that father Ruffian, that Vanity in years' (*1H4* 2.4.441–42). Merely naming these well-known stock figures suffices to set up a resonant memory image of Falstaff's embodiment of them. Shakespeare's reliance on conjuring up established dramatic types already ensconced in his audience's imagination, to which then might be added particularized features betokening 'Falstaff' as part of this mnemotechnic background image, is one of the chief ways 'that stuffed cloak-bag of guts', otherwise known as 'sweet Jack Falstaff', attains an extended frame of reference.

Falstaff's signature corpulence thus features prominently in the criticism of the Henriad. Terry Eagleton proposed that within 'the single figure of Falstaff, both body and language are pressed to a self-parodic extreme' such that his 'reductive materialism and verbal license' situate him squarely within the 'carnivalesque'.[11] C.L. Barber saw Falstaff as contrasted to Hal in terms of 'the holiday-everyday antithesis'.[12] He later emphasizes that it is not a question of whether Hal will be good or bad, 'but whether his holiday will become his everyday, whether the interregnum of a Lord of Misrule, delightful in its moment, will develop into the anarchic reign of a favorite dominating a dissolute king'.[13] Falstaff, in body and word, up-ends the decorum of the chivalric code and relations of fealty upon which so much of the political trajectory of the Henriad depends: 'What is honour? A word. What is in that word "honour"? What is that "honour"? Air. A trim reckoning! [...] Therefore I'll none of it. Honour is a mere scutcheon. And so ends my catechism' (*1H4* 5.1.133–35, 139–40). As an extravagant Lord of Misrule, we would expect no less from Falstaff and yet, because he would play that role not just for a day but at all times and in all places including the battlefield, he must be sacrificed, as part of a purgative rite, to England's dynastic and national destiny.[14]

Prince Hal must rid himself of the stain both of his tavern father, Falstaff, as well as his own father, Henry IV, a successful usurper.[15] The latter point concerns Henry IV deeply, as he confesses on his deathbed to Hal: 'By what by-paths and indirect crook'd ways | I met this crown' (*2H4* 4.5.184–85). It surfaces as a point of contention among the rebel lords who helped him win the crown from Richard II based on an oath and promises which Worcester charges the King has forgotten (*1H4* 5.1.158). Such passages anticipate Hal's putting his tainted fathers behind him, enabling him to blaze as brightly as he projects he is capable: 'I'll so offend to make offence a skill | Redeeming time when men think least I will" (*1H4* 1.2.206–07). This monologue beginning with the ominous 'I know you all, and will awhile uphold | The unyoked humour of your idleness' (*1H4* 1.2.185–86), sets up a parallel expression of Hal's closely-held self-knowledge echoed later in his 'I do; I will' already discussed (*1H4* 2.4.468). Falstaff's reported deathbed farewell effectively overwrites the memory of Falstaff as the Henriad takes its decisive turn toward the redeemed Prince exhibiting kingly virtues. 'Monarch, play, and nation,' Jonathan Baldo observes, 'all stand in need of "reformation," a constant theme of the Prince Hal material.'[16] And yet for all of this work to wipe away Falstaff's presence and influence, his after-image casts a long shadow over the Henriad, as well as the Shakespearean cultural inheritance.

In death Falstaff becomes, as Baldo points out, 'a kind of theatrical shorthand for a more youthful England for which nearly everyone in *2 Henry IV* waxes nostalgic' (p. 89) (Figure 12.1).

Prince Hal's roustabout relationship with 'sweet Jack Falstaff' (*1H4* 2.4.462–63) undoubtedly helps pave the way for 'A little touch of Harry in the night' (*H5* 4.0.47), as a man of the people—his people: 'But now behold, | In the quick forge and working-house of thought, | How London doth pour out her citizens [...] To welcome him! Much more, and much more cause, | Did they this Harry' (*H5* 5.0.22–24, 34–35). For the Henriad to reach its satisfying if revisionist conclusion of triumphant nationalism, Falstaff not only must be denied access to court and shown no longer to hold a place in Harry's affections (*2H4* 5.5.63), but also must leave the world altogether. The careful staging of the scenes involved in Hal's former band of tavern-dwellers learning of Falstaff's illness and the subsequent narration of his off-stage death (*H5* 2.1 and 2.3) indicates Shakespeare recognized that handling Falstaff's memory was as fundamental to his larger plan for the Henriad as it was tricky to pull off—as the popularity of *The Merry Wives of Windsor* attests, a spin-off that revives Falstaff for another bout of comic misadventures.

With Falstaff safely redirected from the battlefield to the suburbs, this citizens' comedy portrays the lusty knight as mostly harmless, past his prime but refusing to acknowledge his waning appeal to the opposite sex. With its domestic setting and narrative arc of the trickster-tricked,

Handling memory in the Henriad

Figure 12.1 Francis Kirkman, *The Wits, or sport upon sport* (London, 1662), frontispiece.
Reproduced with permission of the Folger Shakespeare Library. The first 'drollery' in the collection, 'The Bouncing Knight or the Robbers Rob'd' (pp.1–13), although unidentified, is *1H4* 1.2.

Merry Wives has been described by Baldo as an antidote to the disease of nostalgia 'from which so much of England suffers in *2 Henry IV*' (p. 90). It is the fictive world of 'merry old England' that the aging knight conjures up and which his soliloquized reminiscences so longingly recall, a world surviving at best within the self-contained and freestanding comedy. Satisfying a desire for what was felt to be absent, replete with disguises and faerie-land chastisement and forgiveness of the misguided knight, *Merry Wives* is fit matter for the stage. Nostalgia reigns supreme, as we once again welcome, overthrow, and allow back into our lives the festive Lord of Misrule. This is what makes *Merry Wives* such a remarkable moment in Shakespeare's canon; even as it is for Giuseppe Verdi who, at 80, chose this setting of Falstaff for his final opera, a wistful and synoptic farewell to a world and way of life charmingly cast as a vital memory of things past.[17]

In what follows I want to pursue this notion of bidding farewell with respect to how Shakespeare managed, handled, and shaped audience responses to Falstaff. There are three distinct moments of such farewell when Falstaff takes his leave, each presented with increasing intensity though none achieving absolute closure. The first comes at the end of the Battle of Shrewsbury, when the Prince allows the pretense of Falstaff's insistence on having killed Hotspur to play out howsoever it might: 'For my part, if a lie may do thee grace | I'll gild it with the happiest terms I have' (*1H4* 5.4.157–58). There is a hope of Falstaff reforming himself, but even were he to do so it would not undo the memory of his previous riot and misrule involving the Prince: 'for I'll purge and leave sack and live cleanly, as a nobleman should do' (*1H4* 5.4.164–65). Much hinges on this 'should do' for were Falstaff to act on this precept and become other than his true nature, it would be tantamount to banishing 'all the world' (*1H4* 2.4.467). His demeanor and habits in the next play indicate he has not done as he 'should do'. Consequently the Prince's farewell to Falstaff takes the form of a public announcement, 'I know thee not, old man', having 'turn'd away my former self', adding 'I banish thee' (*2H4* 5.5.47, 58, 63). The precise wording of this decree however, reminiscent of the end of the previous play's farewell to Falstaff, leaves room for the possibility of redemption: 'And as we hear you do reform yourselves, | We will, according to your strengths and qualities, | Give you advancement' (*2H4* 5.5.67–69). In Falstaff's appeal to Justice Shallow, though, we catch a hint of desperation: 'Do not you grieve at this; I shall be sent for in private to him. Look you, he must seem this to the world. Fear not your advancements; I will be the man yet that shall make you great' (*2H4* 5.5.77–80). The third and final farewell—with neither Henry nor Falstaff in sight—is an account of Falstaff's deathbed agony. His not being on stage but being conjured back to mind consigns him to a kind of meta-theatrical limbo, his remnant spirit stored away for further fleeting glimpses in *Henry V*. Accordingly none of these three farewells aims to impose an end to the fictive, festive world that Falstaff inhabits and emblematizes, giving thereby a peculiar ring of truth to his inadvertently prophetic words: 'Banish plump Jack, and banish all the world' (*1H4* 2.4.466–67). Such a world, however, must be made to appear as having receded from the work-a-day world of England, a nation-state free from civil strife and united by a legitimatized dynasty.

But to remove Falstaff from the main plot without comment (as with Poins who, already discussed, simply was written out of the Henriad) would be tantamount to falling prey to the mistaken belief that the repressed somehow will not return, transfigured in another guise and asserting its sway by other means. Falstaff takes the form of an egregious memory image and, as with any already-set-in-place figure within a Memory Theatre, must be kept in check, brought under control and, as needed, redirected toward a different end. Writers on contemporary mnemotechnics, such as Giordano Bruno, clarify that when one has finished using a set of values associated with a particular memory image, the *locus* (or place-holder within the mnemotechnic scheme) can be made to signal some other referent if 'separated, and reused after the insertion of a number of distinct, different actions, implications, and in different relationships'.[18] Such is Shakespeare's approach to handling Falstaff in *Henry V*, for there is no possibility of absolute erasure once the image of 'that reverend Vice, that grey Iniquity, that father Ruffian, that Vanity in years' (*1H4* 2.4.441–442) has been so firmly fixed in the audience's memory.

This applies not just to Falstaff but also to the role of memory itself within the Henriad; the great 'grey Iniquity' instantiates how memory is handled in the two tetralogies. In the second, memory largely is a private issue, whereas in the first, as Baldo has argued, memory is a 'slender thread that ties the English soldiers in France to their identities as Englishmen'; in the Henriad it is 'recalcitrant, rebellious, scattered and difficult to subdue to the purposes of the nation-state' (p. 177, n.87). Accordingly the final section of this essay identifies specific strategies Shakespeare used to activate and buttress the memory of Falstaff as that which shades off into a kind of intimated oblivion, and traces the mnemotechnical implications of his dramaturgically necessary death. His corporality is a means by which memory is registered and set up to be handled, in every sense of the term—negotiated, traded, and exchanged. In such a critical formulation of his presence and projected absence in the Henriad, Falstaff becomes an index to a very particular end in Shakespeare's economy of memory—historical, dynastic, and national.

Falstaff's ineluctable presence

Although speaking about Prospero's 'memorial labours' at the beginning of *The Tempest* (to enlighten his daughter, servants, and the new arrivals), Andrew Hiscock's assessment of what underlies the determination 'to renew power relationships' by 'stressing the burdens that his accounts of the past impose', applies equally well to Prince Hal on his way toward proving himself worthy of kingship—including the turning out of Falstaff.[19] The impact of his rejection by Hal marks, according to his tavern comrades, the beginning of Falstaff's end. The Hostess laments: 'The King has killed his heart' (*H5* 2.1.88).[20] The audience both on-stage and in the theatre, as Hiscock argues, cannot help but be impressed with "the very fragility of the social network that they inhabit—a network that requires constant renewal through acts of memory'.[21] As a result Henry, making the transition from Prince to noble warrior to King in fulfillment of his long-range master plan, like Shakespeare's Prospero, shores up 'the collapsing limits of memory with spectacular acts of violence'.[22] A telling example in this regard is the hanging of Scrope (*H5* 2.2.166-82), decreed in the scene following hard upon the reported death of Falstaff. On the one hand Falstaff is dying because, as reported by Nell, the King betrayed him; whereas Scrope, another former confidant of Harry's, is condemned for betrayal, having 'conspired against our royal person' (*H5* 2.2.167).

The juxtaposition of these two announced deaths reinforces the lengths to which Henry recognizes he must go to ensure stability, which includes bracketing off any pleasant memories of relationships with those from his tavern days. The memory of such associations cannot be allowed to endure, and yet the acts of violence that sever these ties in fact fix them more firmly in the mind's eye. Such episodes of attempted eradication therefore become emblematic of how such associations (and the memories they previously conjured) only can be crossed out and over-written, hardly an erasure of the text that is Henry's personal history and thus that of England. Sparing Scrope and showing clemency would imply weakness of character and compromise his effort to secure an unassailable basis upon which to build a stable regime. The personal and private in the Henriad are sublated into the public and national.

The way Falstaff is removed from Henry's life—but not altogether from the Henriad—is made clear by the Dancer's parting speech:

> If you be not too much cloyed with fat meat, our humble author will continue the story, with Sir John in it [...] where, for any thing I know, Falstaff shall die of a sweat, unless already 'a be killed with your hard opinions.
>
> (*2H4 epilogue 26–31*)

As already indicated, it is only through the re-inscription of Falstaff into *Merry Wives* that he makes his return, carefully circumscribed in a world decisively not that of the epic chronicle. Garrett Sullivan notes that Falstaff's slips into slumber (symbolizing obliviousness to social decorum and moral responsibility) 'are central both to the romance episodes at the heart of the *Henry IV* plays and to the articulation of the romance alternative'.[23] It is the highway robbery of the King's exchequer that precipitates an early intimation of Falstaff's eventual banishment (*1H4* 1.2), for Hal would believe—and must convince himself—that he is, as Sullivan shows, 'at an ethical remove from the tavern world'.[24] This opens up the possibility, Sullivan continues, of a more complicated construction of Falstaff, not so much 'the malign influence Hal must banish in order to restore his epic identity' as 'the figure upon whom Hal's own implicatedness in the romance world of the tavern is projected'.[25]

Hal understands well enough, as expressed in his soliloquy beginning 'I know you all' (*1H4* 1.2.185), that Falstaff cannot make the transition with him to court.[26] The very appearance of Falstaff is for Hal a *memento mori* reminding him of his end; if not spiritually then certainly politically and dynastically. This memory device of the death's head circulates freely within the Henriad, remaining fresh in the audience's mind. Falstaff alludes to it when mocking Bardolph's face, as already discussed (*1H4* 3.3.30); and uses the same conceit later with Doll Tearsheet when the Prince and Poins, disguised as tapsters, overhear him: 'Peace, good Doll, do not speak like a death's-head, do not bid me remember mine end' (*2H2* 2.4.231–32). The mere sight of Falstaff is a reminder to Hal of his own end, pricking his conscience and goading him to make proper provision. Whereas a traditional *memento mori* associated with a skeletal death's head reminds one to reflect on to what all must come, the superabundant fleshy face of Falstaff is a mirror to Hal of his own past 'riot and dishonour' with which his father specifically charges him (*1H4* 1.1.84). The personal as well as political implications for Hal's much anticipated reformation, the hope for which he pledges to 'redeem all this on Percy's head' (*1H4* 3.2.132), are closely linked to the larger social concern that deviant behavior, as Paul Bouissac observes, 'can always become normative, for the simple reason that merely demonstrating the possibility of such actions can lead to their generalization and usher in chaos'.[27]

Among the many tropes and conventions rolled into the body and character of Falstaff, albeit with a subversively carnivalesque stamp, is that of Moriens, the penitent supplicant in the *ars moriendi* tradition, the art of dying well.[28] Nowhere is this presented more literally than in his reported last moments. The *moriendi* drama is set up throughout the *Henry IV* plays with Falstaff's profanely parodic oaths and frequent protestations of his fear of damnation; specifically, his being corrupted by Hal, 'able to corrupt a saint' (*1H4* 1.2.88). But Falstaff opts for the *ars vivendi*, or art of living well, though not in the sense intended by preachers who saw this as the penitential result of lessons gleaned from pious mediation on one's end: 'But to counterfeit dying when a man thereby liveth is to be no counterfeit but the true and perfect image of life indeed. The better part of valour is discretion, in the which better part I have saved my life' (*1H4* 5.4.116–20). Isabel Karremann likewise sees Falstaff in this passage as 'a figure for the theatre' and, furthermore, points out that his 'resurrection from a pretended state of death provides a metatheatrical comment by staging the contemporary view of the theatre's mnemonic role'.[29]

A key part of the *ars moriendi* involves enumerating and confessing one's sins, and, although nothing ever gets amended, Falstaff does this throughout the earlier plays almost as a verbal tic. The recurring acknowledgements of his own repulsive habits follow the form but not the spirit of one seeking salvation: 'I must give over this life, and I will give it over. By Lord, an I do not, I am a villain. I'll be damned for never a king's son in Christendom' (*1H4* 1.2.92–94). This is one of the many roles Falstaff subversively plays in the Henriad, thereby subsuming and refracting a range of dramatic conventions. As such he embodies and recapitulates key moments in the history of drama, especially the recognizable stage types of folly and self-indulgence, consistent with the classical dictum that art holds a mirror to nature. Shakespeare's Hamlet voices this commonplace in his advice to the players: 'the purpose of playing, whose end, both at the first and now, was and is, to hold as 'twere the mirror up to nature: to show virtue her feature, scorn her own image, and the very age and body of the time his form and pressure' (*Hamlet* 3.2.21–25). If ever a figure showed 'the very age and body of the time his form' it is Falstaff.

In addition to playing at Moriens, Falstaff embodies (as already observed) the sacrificial scapegoat, the classical braggart soldier, the medieval figure of Vice and its various allegorical incarnations. Moreover Falstaff richly conforms to the traits and properties associated with a properly constituted placeholder in a typical Memory Theatre. Early modern treatises on memory record that the more grotesque and outlandish the tagged image, the more easily recalled and hence the more efficacious:

> Again you shall not forget that in placing or setting of the images or figures in their places the thing is always to be placed with a merry, a marvelous, or cruel act, or some other unaccustomed manner: for merry, cruel, injurious, marvelous, excellently fair, or exceedingly foul things, do change and move the senses and better stir up the Memory.[30]

Early modern playwrights readily applied such principles in the development of their most dramatically significant characters,[31] and Shakespeare's Falstaff can be seen as having been drawn in accordance with the Art of Memory's axiom of egregiousness. Moreover, once brought onto the stage of this communal and national Memory Theatre of England's chronicles, the Henriad recalibrates the audience's apprehensions about the reigns of Henry IV and Henry V using Falstaff as an emblematic foil. A lesson learned with laughter is a lesson learned and less likely soon to be forgotten, especially when it is the image of Falstaff that stays in one's mind long after having left the theatre.

Another way this evanescent presence of Falstaff as a lingering after-image is reinforced concerns the rhetorical trope and poetic convention of the *blason*. This term (in English, blazon) originally derives from French heraldry to signify either the codified description of a coat of arms or the coat of arms itself. Adapted to amatory poetry as popularized by Petrarch, it became the *sine qua non* of literally thousands of sonnets of the period. Shakespeare sports skillfully with the device, for example, in sonnet 130: 'My mistress' eyes are nothing like the sun'. The blazon describes the blazonneur's 'face-to-face encounter with his or her beloved' and, Grant Williams continues, 'blazons consistently rely upon implicit and explicit comparisons to make corporeal alterity known to the reader'.[32] Typically applied by the poet-lover to the face and body of the object of desire, this staple of erotic verse is used by the Hostess to describe moribund Falstaff, thus combining the conventions for expounding upon the desires associated with love and death, respectively the *blason* and the *ars moriendi*.

> HOSTESS Nay, sure, he's not in hell; he's in Arthur's bosom, if ever man went
> to Arthur's bosom. 'A made a finer end, and went away an it had been any
> christom child. 'A parted even just between twelve and one, even at the
> turning o'th' tide. For after I saw him fumble with the sheets and play
> wi'th' flowers, and smile upon his fingers' ends, I knew there was but
> one way; for his nose was as sharp as a pen, and 'a babbled of
> green fields. 'How now, Sir John!' quoth I, 'what, man! be o'
> good cheer.' So 'a cried out 'God, God, God!' three or four times.
> Now I, to comfort him, bid him 'a should not think of God; I hoped there
> was no need to trouble himself with any such thoughts yet. So 'a
> bade me lay more clothes on his feet. I put my hand into the bed and
> felt them, and they were as cold as any stone. Then I felt to his knees,
> and so up'ard and up'ard, and all was as cold as any stone.
>
> (H5 *2.3.9–25*)

Her malapropisms and double entrendres (such as 'stone', slang for testicle),[33] give the whole scene a comic atmosphere befitting Sir John, who himself ever mixed high and low. Instead of detailing the features of the subject of the blazon to evoke a sense of wondrousness by virtue of incomparable beauty, here we find (typical of all things that touch Falstaff) those same conventions applied to the grotesque mortification of the body of the beloved—and from the bottom-up. In the topsy-turvy world of which Falstaff is the avatar in the Henriad, love still remains a guiding sentiment of the scene. This is especially the case given Falstaff's endearing if villainous qualities. The subversive rhetorical use of the blazon in its evocation of death recalls as well the erotic context, for 'death' was an early modern by-word for sexual ecstasy. While Petrarchan lovers can wax eloquent about how being denied the object of their desire is a kind of living-death, here we find a prose expression of the death of one around whom a world indeed has turned, in this case the tavern. The loss encompasses all that nostalgically was imagined and coded as embodying the 'good old days' of which Falstaff is an emblem.

Falstaff's stage presence previously had held in its gravitational pull all that symbolized the holiday spirit, now sublated into the orderly state ruled by the no-longer waggish Prince. Shakespeare keeps this announcement of Falstaff's death within the subversive world of the tavern, whose spokesperson fittingly is the Hostess. This site of Falstaff's death also brings within its orbit the commonplace conceit of the world being an inn.[34] The name of the Hostess, Mistress Nell, originally known as Dame Quickly before her betrothal to Nym and marriage to Bardolph, bespeaks both life ('the quick and the dead') and liveliness, with a double entendre on sexual activity. All of these implications travel around with her whenever she is on stage and serve to heighten the dramatic import of blazoning Falstaff's body in death, translated not to the bosom of God but the quintessential figure of English romance, Arthur. The vernacularizing of Falstaff's final resting place as Avalon rather than the Christian Heaven or Hell is all part of the way the memory of Falstaff is managed in the Henriad. This accords with what Grant Williams has observed about Shakespeare's regular use in his comedies of Petrarchan poets and their conceits, as supplying 'a much needed cultural reference point for the reassessment of the blazon's ideological import', insofar as any 'ideological analysis of early modern poetry must take into account the imaginary event of the birth of national consciousness induced by the development of European vernaculars'.[35] Setting up the inversion of a Petrarchan blazon, this reference to Arthur allusively re-places Falstaff in the English mythopoeic homeland whence he originates. As already suggested, he comprises and conjures up so many earlier stock types that, in the end, he is something of a pastiche of the homegrown English literary imagination. It is wholly in keeping with his character then that such a creature should rest in the bosom of England's Arthur.

Tellingly, though, there is more to be remembered here and it is closely encrypted within Falstaff's off-stage deathbed scene. At stake is a re-writing of the rationale for Hal's having banished Falstaff both from his presence and the newly emerging official court memory: 'Presume not that I am the thing I was; | For God doth know, so shall the world perceive, | That I have turn'd away my former self' (*2H4* 5.5.56–58). Falstaff's expulsion from the projected royal narrative that Henry is setting in place need not imply (as already observed) his passing from the Henriad (*2H4* 5.5.68); and the Epilogue to *2 Henry IV* likewise reassures the audience that Falstaff is not necessarily banished from the world of the theatre. All the same, Shakespeare thought better of having Falstaff take the stage in *Henry V* for the next we hear of him is his reported death.

In some fundamental way Falstaff belongs to everyone, a theme symbolized by each person at the tavern having something personal to relate about him after his passing. Shakespeare has us imagine a ritualized space for speaking him back into remembrance set in motion by the Hostess's inverse blazon of the much beloved reprobate.[36] As if deferring to let him slip from mind everyone has something more to say, urging the Hostess further to 'remember' this or that detail—including episodes in previous plays, such as Falstaff calling Bardolph's face a *memento mori* (*1H4* 3.3.30–31). The conjuring up of this past event, like previously articulated reminiscences of Falstaff's youth (*2H4* 3.2.24–25),[37] creates a *mise en abîme* in the Henriad such that what is being remembered itself becomes an emblem of remembrance. Moreover the whole scene parodically is contextualized as an ekphrastic portrait of Moriens from the *ars moriendi*:

NYM	They say he cried out of sack.
HOSTESS	Ay, that 'a did.
BARDOLPH	And of women.
HOSTESS	Nay, that 'a did not.
BOY	Yes, that 'a did, and said they were devils incarnate.
HOSTESS	'A could never abide carnation, 'twas a colour he never liked.
BOY	'A said once the devil would have him about women.
HOSTESS	'A did in some sort, indeed, handle women; but then he was rheumatic and talked of the Whore of Babylon.
BOY	Do you not remember 'a saw a flea stick upon Bardolph's nose and 'a said it was a black soul burning in hell-fire?
BARDOLPH	Well, the fuel is gone that maintained that fire; that's all the riches I got in his service.

(*H5* 2.3.26–42)

This scene also mirrors in miniature the constructed and contentious nature of the sweeping historical narrative of Henry's kingship, much discussed outside the playhouse. Everyone has his or her own take on what exactly happened. Ambiguous or contested recollection of the past is a hallmark of Shakespeare's filling the Henriad with different views of what happened, ranging from Hotspur's account of why he did not turn his prisoners over to the 'certain lord' who flitted onto the battlefield 'neat and trimly dressed, | Fresh a bridegroom' (*1H4* 1.3.33–34), to the wooing of Katherine of France by Henry, a prospective bridegroom, who 'would have her learn, my fair cousin, how perfectly I love her, and that is good English' (*H5* 5.2.280–81). Along the same lines, as a commentary on conflicting representations of the past, Shakespeare adds digressive self-serving tales told by Falstaff whose own historical origins, as Gary Bouchard argues, 'are controversially ambiguous, and whose gross and obvious lies in his attempt to conceal his folly, parody the crafted remembrances wrought by the play's historical figures.'[38] For all his professed love of the 'sweet wag' Hal, it is sack he calls out for in his final moments. Misruled Hal is quite forgot; indeed he left the Henriad long ago.

A final, quite remarkable, memory strand leading back to Falstaff remains still to be retrieved: the boy. His very presence on stage evokes the former presence of his long-time patron. Falstaff's young attendant, who now must shift for himself, goes to the wars in search of a new master. Groomed by Falstaff, and thus directly connected to the tavern world (though somehow becoming fluent in French along the way), the boy provides a post-Falstavian trajectory for the audience to follow. As such he too is a resonant memory image, embodying and conveying a particular point of reference in Shakespeare's larger historical Memory Theater that is the Henriad, which contributed so fulsomely to the establishment of England's early modern national consciousness. The boy thus becomes a particular means toward accomplishing this end.

We find him with what remains of his tavern family on the battlefield, where Bardolph mimics the heroic lines just spoken in the previous scene by their former tavern denizen, now the King: 'Once more unto the breach, dear friends, once more, | Or close the wall up with our English dead' (*H5* 3.1.1–2). Pausing in the heat of battle, the alehouse longingly is invoked as they slide back into their accustomed Boar's-Head banter and momentarily take solace in an improvised barroom song.

> BARDOLPH On, on, on, on, on, to the breach, to the breach!
> NYM Pray thee, Corporal, stay; the knocks are too hot, and, for mine own part I have not a case of lives. The humour of it is too hot, that is the very plain-song of it.
> PISTOL The plain-song is most just, for humours do abound.
> Knocks go and come; God's vassals drop and die,
> And sword and shield
> In bloody field
> Doth win immortal fame.
> BOY Would I were in an alehouse in London! I would give all my fame for a pot of ale and safety.
> PISTOL And I.
> If wishes would prevail with me
> My purpose should not fail with me,
> But hither would I hie.
> BOY As duly –
> But not as truly –
> As bird doth sing on bough.
>   *Enter* FLUELLEN
> FLUELLEN [*Beats them.*]
> Up to the breach, you dogs! Avaunt, you cullions!
>   (*H5* 3.2.1–13, 21–22)

The boy's lines sound a lot like something Falstaff, 'who could wish this tavern were my drum' (*1H4* 3.3.205) might say; and indeed did say in the pitch of battle, exhibiting tavern behavior in the field, bottle in hand, for which the Prince berates him (*1H4* 5.3.40–56). Notwithstanding his associative link to Falstaff, there is also something of Hal recognizable in the boy for, like the Prince, he knows his companions well. He sums up their characters with damning if jocular precision, and resolves to leave them (*H5* 3.2.28–53). His lines though are cast in prose as befits his station, unlike the blank verse of Prince Hal's 'I know you all' soliloquy (*1H4* 1.2.185–207). For the boy it is a matter of just getting away from the 'three swashers' (*H5* 3.2.28–29). Hal's situation is more complicated, for he presumes to have deep knowledge of others.[39] He displays the same sense of self-conscious theatricality toward others as to himself, for example in his response to Poins regarding his father's grave illness, acknowledging that to show signs of grief among his companions from tavern days, who know him too well, only would make him appear a hypocrite (*2H4* 2.2.50–60).

The boy, for a time, stakes his fortune with Pistol, and acts as a translator; indeed, he is the translator *par excellence* in the play, moving with ease from one register of speech to another even as he symbolizes the translation from tavern life to the battlefield, where he facilitates prisoner negotiations. While a frail vessel, he resonates amply throughout this play, especially given the meta-theatrical reference in the following speech that comments incisively on the terrifyingly real truth of the situation and goes on with grimly ironic prescience to foretell his own death:

> BOY Bardolph and Nym had ten times more valour than this roaring devil i'th' old play, that every one may pare his nails with a wooden dagger, and they are both hanged, and so would this be if he durst steal any thing adventurously. I must stay with the lackeys with the luggage of our camp; the French might have a good prey of us if he knew of it, for there is none to guard it but boys.
>
> (*H5* 4.4.69–76)

And die he must, this diminutive echo of right reason and counter-echo of Falstaff for, like his former master, he too must be wiped from the play, his sacrifice preparing the foundation for England's emerging nationalist memory. Gower relates the incident which subsequently results in Henry's resolve to show no mercy and cut the throats of the prisoners: ''Tis certain there's not a boy left alive, and the cowardly rascals that ran from the battle ha' done this slaughter' (*H5* 4.7.5–7).

Amidst the many reverberating echoes of lives once lived under the magnetic pull of Falstaff, the boy's off-stage death becomes a pathetic reminder of Falstaff's own view of honor as a 'trim reckoning' (*1H4* 5.1.135). The slaughter of the English stragglers shows there are more forms of dishonor than Falstaff ever was capable of displaying in his unquestionably dishonorable life. It is with the exchange between Fluellen and Gower about the slaughter of the boys and their ensuing quibble over 'Harry of Monmouth' that the name of Falstaff is prompted and spoken at the very moment when he is most in danger of being forgotten by the audience (*H5* 4.7.50). Thus is Falstaff remembered, even as is the name of the place where the historic victory occurred and shortly thereafter will be memorialized, recreating as it were an originary point of memory in the English national consciousness. The King asks Mountjoy 'What is this castle called that stands hard by', to which he replies, 'They call it Agincourt' (*H5* 4.7.87–88). Repeating the name reminds Shakespeare's audience to see in this place a site of memory within England's grand Memory Theatre: 'Then call we this the field of Agincourt, | Fought on the day of Crispin' (*H5* 4.7.89–90). With the death of the boy (followed by one last glance back to 'Sir John Falstaff' for the audience), the young King is riveted into action, victory attained, his own name redeemed and reputation secured.

Other tokens of remembrance and honor are slotted into the play as well, such as when Henry gives a badge signifying his royal cognizance (as part of a larger plan he has to confront and forgive Williams): 'Here, Fluellen, wear thou this favour for me and stick it in thy cap' (*H5* 4.7.151–52). This is but one of many mnemonic tokens circulating throughout the Henriad in the service of furthering the narrative, similar in kind but different degree from the *memento mori* allusions. Such memory devices contribute significantly to the overall sense of the play as a vast Memory Theatre. In much the same way as Shakespeare uses the Hostess to have us imagine both the steady movement up the topography of Falstaff's body and the sequence of events conducing to his death, the Chorus calls our attention to the very act of imagination which *Henry V* demands.[40] Most notable in this regard is the mnemonic itinerary suggestively dictated to the audience, moving sequentially from place to place until we arrive at the siege of 'Harfleur'; the speech that begins, 'Thus with imagined wing our swift scene flies | In motion of no less celerity | Than that of thought. Suppose that you have seen', and concludes 'Still be kind, | And eke out our performance with your mind' (*H5* 3.0.1–3, 33–35).

It is one thing to paint in words the scene for the audience to visualize in one's mind's eye, 'playing with' our 'fancies' (*H5* 3.0.7), and another to be asked to excise the memorable image of Falstaff, 'the fat knight with the great-belly doublet' (*H5* 4.7.47), once he already has been so indelibly rendered and fondly recalled. And yet both approaches show complementary aspects of the playwright's skill at managing and handling memory in the Henriad. Each is fundamental to the dramatist's art involved in fashioning England's national history as a mnemonic backdrop against which to project all manner of memorable wonders—and certainly among the most wondrous of them all remains 'that stuffed cloak-bag of guts', 'that father Ruffian', 'plump Jack' Falstaff.

Acknowledgement

Christopher Bryan, John Gatta, James Ross Macdonald, and Kelly Malone provided helpful comments on early versions of this essay.

Notes

1. On *RII*, *1H4*, *2H4*, and *H5* as a coherent 'epic', see Alvin Kernan, '*The Henriad*: Shakespeare's Major History Plays', in *Modern Shakespeare Criticism*, ed. by Alvin B. Kernan (New York: Harcourt, 1970), pp. 245–75 (p. 245).
2. Isabel Karremann, *The Drama of Memory in Shakespeare's History Plays* (Cambridge: Cambridge University Press, 2015), p. 151.
3. Lina Perkins Wilder, *Shakespeare's Memory Theatre: Recollection, Properties, and Character* (Cambridge: Cambridge University Press, 2010), p. 100.
4. On the memory arts and early modern drama, see William E. Engel, *Death and Drama in Renaissance England: Shades of Memory* (Oxford: Oxford University Press, 2002), pp. 48–53; on physical and social properties—the materials of theatre—encouraging mnemonic instruction and recollection, see Wilder, pp. 1–23, *passim*.
5. Nicholas Grene, *Shakespeare's Serial History Plays* (Cambridge: Cambridge University Press, 2002), pp. 191–245.
6. Cf. Karremann, p. 29.
7. Heinrich F. Plett, *Rhetoric and Renaissance Culture* (Berlin: Walter de Gruyter, 2004), pp. 14–16.
8. J. Dover Wilson, *The Fortunes of Falstaff* (Cambridge: Cambridge University Press, 1943; repr. 1979), p. 17; Harold Bloom, 'Introduction', in *Falstaff*, ed. by Harold Bloom (New York: Chelsea House, 1992), pp. 1–4 (p. 4).
9. Hester Lees-Jeffries, *Shakespeare and Memory* (Oxford: Oxford University Press, 2013), p. 66.
10. Rosalie Colie, *Shakespeare's Living Art* (Princeton, NJ: Princeton University Press, 1974), p. 19.
11. Terry Eagleton, *William Shakespeare* (Oxford: Blackwell, 1986), pp. 15–16.
12. C.L. Barber, 'The Saturnalian Pattern in Shakespeare's Comedy', *The Sewanee Review*, 59.4 (1951), 593–611 (p. 607).
13. C.L. Barber, *Shakespeare's Festive: A Study of Dramatic Form and Its Relation to Social Custom* (Cleveland and New York: Meridian, 1959), pp. 6–14.
14. Cf. René Girard, *Violence and the Sacred*, trans. by Patrick Gregory (Baltimore, MD: Johns Hopkins University Press, 1972), p. 86.
15. Kenji Yoshino, 'The Choice of the Four Fathers: Henry IV, Falstaff, the Lord Chief Justice, and the King of France in the *Henriad*', *Yale Journal of Law and the Humanities*, 22.2 (2013), 417–439 (p. 433).
16. Jonathan Baldo, *Memory in Shakespeare's Histories: Stages of Forgetting in Early Modern England* (New York: Routledge, 2012), p. 89.
17. Burton D. Fisher, *Falstaff* (New York: Opera Journeys, 2004), p. 22.
18. Giordano Bruno, *De Umbris Idearum et Ars Memoriae*, trans. Scott Gosnell (New York: Huginn, Muninn, 2013), p. 88.
19. Andrew Hiscock, *Reading Memory in Early Modern Literature* (Cambridge: Cambridge University Press, 2011), p. 6.
20. On this passage, interpreted as problematizing the presentation of kingship on the early modern stage, see R. Scott Fraser, '"The king has killed his heart": The Death of Falstaff in *Henry V*', in *Sederi*, 20 (2010), pp. 145–157.
21. Hiscock, *Reading Memory*, p. 6.

22 Ibid.
23 Garrett A. Sullivan, Jr., *Sleep, Romance and Human Embodiment: Vitality from Spenser to Milton* (Cambridge: Cambridge University Press, 2012), p. 81.
24 Sullivan, *Sleep*, p. 85.
25 Ibid.
26 Harry Berger, Jr., *Harrying: Skills of Offence in Shakespeare's* Henriad (New York: Fordham University Press, 2015), pp. 71–82.
27 Paul Bouissac, *The Semiotics of Clowns and Clowning: Rituals of Transgression and the Theory of Laughter* (London: Bloomsbury, 2015), p. 177.
28 Paul M. Cubeta, 'Falstaff and the Art of Dying', *Studies in English Literature*, 27.2 (Spring 1987), pp. 197–211.
29 Karremann, p. 87.
30 William Fulwood, *The Castel of Memorie* (London, 1562), sig. H6; quoted from *The Memory Arts in Renaissance England: A Critical Anthology*, eds. William E. Engel, and others (Cambridge: Cambridge University Press, 2016), p. 64.
31 Engel, *Death and Drama*, pp. 49–50.
32 Grant Williams, 'Early Modern Blazons and the Rhetoric of Wonder', in *Irigaray and Premodern Culture*, ed. by Theresa Krier and Elizabeth D. Harvey (London: Routledge, 2005), pp. 126–137 (pp. 129, 132).
33 Cf. *MW* 1.4.107–109.
34 See, for example, Francis Quarles, *Divine Fancies* (London, 1633), sig. N3^v: 'The World's an *Inn*; and I, her *Guest*. | I eat; I drink; I take my Rest: | My *Hostess*, Nature, does deny me | Nothing, wherewith she can supply me: | Where, having stayed a while, I pay | Her *lavish bills*, and go my way.'
35 Grant Williams, 'Double Exposure: Gazing at Male Fantasy in Shakespearean Comedy', in *Staging the Blazon in Early Modern English Theatre*, ed. by Deborah Uman and Sara Morrison (Burlington, VT: Ashgate, 2013), pp. 13–24 (p.14).
36 For further implications of this '*anti*-blazon', see Joseph M. Oritz, 'By the Book: Blazoning the Subject in Shakespeare's History Plays', in *Staging the Blazon in Early Modern English Theatre*, ed. by Deborah Uman and Sara Morrison (Burlington, VT: Ashgate, 2013), pp. 125–136 (p.133).
37 Alexander Leggatt, *Shakespeare's Political Drama: The History Plays and The Roman Plays* (New York: Routledge, 1988, repr. 1989), p. 90.
38 Gary Bouchard, 'Unforgiving and Wasted Memory in *2 Henry IV*' (unpublished paper, p.4). On the latent memory of proto-Protestant martyr Sir John Oldcastle overwritten by Falstaff, see Baldo, p. 52; and Karremann, pp. 115–122.
39 Lina Perkins Wilder, '"My Exion is Entered": Anatomy, Costume, and Theatrical Knowledge in *2 Henry IV*', *Renaissance Drama*, 41.1–2 (2013), 57– 84 (p. 72).
40 Richard Lanham, *The Motives of Eloquence: Literary Rhetoric in the Renaissance* (New Haven, CT: Yale University Press, 1976), p. 191.

13

HENRY VI TO *RICHARD III*
Forgetting, foreshadowing, remembering

Nicholas Grene

Critical debates on the *Henry VI–Richard III* plays have largely centered on issues of design. Were they planned as a sequence or only assembled as such in the First Folio after a more adventitious theatrical creation? Were the *Henry VI* plays written in chronological order, 1,2,3, or was *1 Henry VI* a prequel to the earlier diptych *First part of the Contention* and *True Tragedy of Richard Duke of York*? Was the series planned and written by Shakespeare alone or in collaboration with others? There have been fashions and trends in this scholarship as in everything else, which can be charted in the successive Arden editions of the *Henry VI* plays. The first Arden editor, H.C. Hart, in 1909 was a disintegrationist, attributing much of *1 Henry VI* to Shakespearean collaborators, while by 1962 Andrew Cairncross argued strongly for a solo-designed integrated series of Wagnerian *Ring* proportions. Both Edward Burns and Ronald Knowles, editors respectively of the third-series Arden editions of *1 Henry VI* and *2 Henry VI*, followed the lead of the Oxford editors, Stanley Wells and Gary Taylor, in returning to the concept of concept of collaborative authorship and 2,3,1 order of composition. I have advanced my own position elsewhere and do not intend to rehearse here again my reasons for believing that the plays were written in chronological order and, even if *1 Henry VI* was a collaborative work, the structural design for the series was Shakespeare's.[1] My most controversial conviction is that, whatever their origins, the four plays, once written, would have been played by Shakespeare's company as a sequential series and that it is to this that the Epilogue of *Henry V* gestures with the reference to the disastrous reign of Henry VI 'which oft our stage hath shown'.[2] In so far as this essay is based on such an assumption, I need to comment briefly on why scholars have been so unwilling to entertain that possibility.

It has been repeatedly claimed as unthinkable that the three parts of *Henry VI* and *Richard III* should have been performed on successive days in the early modern theatre. Thus Ric Knowles remarks (without giving any reason) that 'the plays of the tetralogy were presumably not performed together in Shakespeare's lifetime'.[3] Similarly, Burns in his Introduction to the Arden 3 edition of *1 Henry VI* claims that '*Henry VI* would be unique if conceived as a three-parter, and at no point could the dramatists have envisaged performances of the plays in sequence'.[4] This is affirmed in spite of the evidence from Henslowe's *Diary* showing that two-part plays were often, if not always, played successively in this way.[5] The main reason why scholars are so sceptical is that there are so few multi-part play sequences in the period and none for which there is production evidence.[6] But the early references to the *Henry VI* plays, the first signs of

Shakespeare's activity in the theatre, testify to their remarkable popularity and the backward glance of the *Henry V* Epilogue is consistent with a well remembered theatrical triumph.[7] The sequence may indeed have been unique, as Thomas Pendleton maintains commenting on the deliberately unfinished action in each of the three *Henry VI* plays: 'The result is a narrative that is not just continuous from play to play but that is "to be continued," and no one else, not even Shakespeare himself in the Second Tetralogy (which is the closest approach), ever does this again'.[8]

In this textually interconnected sequence of four plays, what was an audience asked to remember, what were they allowed to forget, and how were future events in the action anticipated? We can answer these questions better if we look at the ways the chronicle sources were given dramatic shaping, compare Shakespeare's practices of construction with that of his contemporary playwrights, as well as looking at modern productions of the plays that have been deliberately planned as integrated series. One of the aims of this chapter, in fact, will be to show the distinctiveness of Shakespeare's sort of seriality in the *Henry VI–Richard III* plays both in terms of his own time and of ours. By looking at what is forgotten, what is foreshadowed, and what is remembered across the four plays we can better understand the principles of design that bind them together.

Forgetting

One of the arguments for regarding *1 Henry VI* as prequel has been the lack of allusion to the action of that play in *2* and *3 Henry VI*. In particular, the fact that Talbot, hero of the first play, fails to get so much as a mention has been regarded as a clinching piece of evidence. So Ronald Knowles follows John Dover Wilson, the Cambridge Shakespeare editor, in commenting on 'the absence of any mention of Talbot in *1 Contention* or *2 Henry VI*, particularly in Gloucester's early speech [in I.1.75–100].' He concludes: 'It is very hard to believe that if *1 Henry VI* preceded *2 Henry VI* Shakespeare would not, at some point, have capitalized on its success, particularly by having Gloucester recall such patriotic self-sacrifice'.[9] It is worth quoting at length the speech in question to probe the reasons why Talbot should not be remembered here. King Henry has just exited to have his newly married bride Margaret of Anjou crowned Queen, and Gloucester is protesting to his fellow council members about the shamefulness of the marriage and its conditions:

> What! did my brother Henry spend his youth,
> His valour, coin and people, in the wars?
> Did he so often lodge in open field,
> In winter's cold and summer's parching heat,
> To conquer France, his true inheritance?
> And did my brother Bedford toil his wits,
> To keep by policy what Henry got?
> Have you yourselves, Somerset, Buckingham,
> Brave York, Salisbury and victorious Warwick,
> Received deep scars in France and Normandy?
> Or hath mine uncle Beaufort and myself,
> With all the learned council of the realm,
> Studied so long, sat in the council house
> Early and late, debating to and fro
> How France and Frenchmen might be kept in awe,

>   And had his highness in his infancy
>   Crowned in Paris in despite of foes?
>   And shall these labours and these honours die?
>   Shall Henry's conquest, Bedford's vigilance,
>   Your deeds of war and all our counsel die?
>   (I.1.75–94)

It is clear in the context of the scene what Gloucester is seeking to do in this well-wrought rhetorical appeal. He is trying to draw together all those present to share his sense of indignation at the Henry/Margaret marriage, which has yielded up the gains of so many hard-won victories against France. To do that he balances the contributions of those like Henry V who have actually fought in France – Somerset, Buckingham, York, Salisbury and Warwick – and the councillors like his dead brother Bedford, 'mine uncle Beaufort and myself'. Included here are deadly political opponents: Gloucester and Beaufort, Cardinal Winchester, are long-term antagonists, as are the Lancastrians Somerset and Buckingham against York, Warwick and Salisbury. But Gloucester, as a statesman, is here appealing across partisan divisions to a sense of shared patriotism.

The appeal, as one might expect, gets him nowhere. Before long they are at what Gloucester calls their 'ancient bickerings' (I.1.141) again. And the rest of the scene shows the political fission by which all of those named in Gloucester's speech pair off in separate conspiratorial alliances leaving the stage finally to the arch-conspirator York. The scene establishes the story arc for the play as a whole: Duke Humphrey of Gloucester will try to uphold the interests of the common good but will be destroyed by the self-interested factions who will finally leave the field open for the rebellion of York, beginning the actual Wars of the Roses. The action of *2 Henry VI* is continuous with *1 Henry VI*. In *1 Henry VI* V. 2, Suffolk takes Margaret prisoner on the battlefield, dreams up the scheme for satisfying his desire for her, while at the same time winning court power, by marrying her off to King Henry, and is prepared to give up the provinces of Maine and Anjou to her father Reignier to achieve his goal (V. 2. 175-80). *2 Henry VI* starts with the accomplishment of that aim and Gloucester, who has opposed the match from the start, is appalled at the surrender of the French provinces. But each of the plays has its own thematic centre. The principal subject of *1 Henry VI* was the war in France with Talbot and Pucelle the main antagonists. *2 Henry VI* is concentrated on the struggle for power within England. In that context, Talbot is yesterday's hero and there is no particular felt need to recall him.

The comparable case of the absence of Gloucester from *3 Henry VI* may be used to make the point. Duke Humphrey is without doubt the central figure of *2 Henry VI*. The plotting against him is the main subject of the action of the first two acts; his downfall and murder occupy the third act, and retribution for his death follows for his murderers – Winchester (III.3), Suffolk (IV.1) and Somerset (V.2). The one time when we see King Henry take decisive action it is to banish Suffolk for his part in the murder (III.2.29ff.). Yet in *3 Henry VI* the king never acknowledges his failure to support Gloucester as one of the causes of the civil war he witnesses, even though he devotes a long hand-wringing speech to just this theme in *2 Henry VI*, III.1.198–222. When Richard resists being made Duke of Gloucester, because 'Gloucester's dukedom is too ominous' (*3 Henry VI*, II.6.107), he appears to be thinking about a general superstition attached to the title going back to Thomas of Woodstock, murdered in the reign of Richard II.[10] The death of Humphrey of Gloucester, centerpiece of the previous play, is not mentioned. The story has moved on by *3 Henry VI* to the full-scale, fratricidal wars of York and Lancaster for the crown, and Gloucester, the one figure who tried to stem that tide in the previous play, has no role there, any more than Talbot, hero of *1 Henry VI* had in *2 Henry VI*.

If we compare some contemporary examples of history plays by other playwrights – and quite few of them survive – the extraordinary level of narrative coherence and integrity that obtain in the *Henry VI–Richard III* sequence will be obvious. Thomas Heywood's two part *Edward IV* is typical of the sort of 'hybrid history' that seems to have been the norm. The full title suggests its eclectic subject matter and form: 'The First and Second Parts of King Edward the Fourth. Containing his merry pastime with the Tanner of Tamworth; as also his love to fair Mistress Shore, her great promotion, fall, and misery, and lastly the lamentable death of both her and her husband'.[11] Produced in the autumn of 1599, after the staging of *Henry V*, the last in Shakespeare's history plays cycle, Heywood seemed to have worked on the basis of picking over the available materials Shakespeare left out. So, much of the first half of *1 Edward IV* is devoted to a city-stirring account of the attack on London by the Bastard Falconbridge, while a good deal of the second is taken up with King Edward's invasion of France, chronicle material for which Shakespeare found no room in *3 Henry VI*. This is eked out with the sentimental melodrama of Jane Shore, Edward's mistress who is alluded to several times in *Richard III* but famously never appears, and a ballad story of Edward incognito meeting with the merry Tanner of Tamworth wrapped up at the end of Part I. There is no consistent characterization of Edward, who seems never to be blamed for his seduction of Jane, and whose death is merely reported late in Part II, by which time the action has switched to the villainous actions of Richard of Gloucester, who appears first unheralded in Part II, scene 11, and who fills out the rest of the play with an obvious rip-off of *Richard III*. It is similar with what we have of *The Life of Sir John Oldcastle*, planned as a two-part play by Antony Munday, Michael Drayton, Robert Wilson and Thomas Hathway. The authors sought to make capital of Shakespeare's controversial use of the name Sir John Oldcastle for his comic fat knight in *1 Henry IV*, presenting instead the real Oldcastle, Lollard hero of the reign of Henry V:

> It is no pamperd glutton we present,
> Nor aged Councellor to youthfull sinne,
> But one, whose virtue shone above the rest,
> A valiant Martyr, and a vertuous peere.[12]

But not far into the play, there is a comic thieving parson Sir John who has a whore called Doll, and incidental reminiscences of Falstaff and the Gadshill robbery. Shakespeare's series of history plays dominated the market in the 1590s, set standards of structural integrity that his imitators could not begin to meet.

In expecting certain sorts of narrative continuity we are influenced by modern modes of seriality reflected in productions of the *Henry VI–Richard III* plays. So, for example, Talbot by no means disappeared from the later plays in Michael Boyd's 2000 staging of the *Henry VI* trilogy for the Royal Shakespeare Company, revived again in 2006 for the full history cycle. Instead the dead warrior and his son kept coming back as ghosts or zombies in their bloodied battledress as they had died at Bordeaux in *1 Henry VI*, IV.4. In *2 Henry VI* they played the Spirit that speaks the deceptive prophecies to the Duchess of Gloucester, a demon that prevented Winchester from making a sign of deathbed repentance, and the Captain and Walter Whitmore who killed Suffolk. Most strikingly of all, they returned as the Father who has killed his son and the Son who has killed his father in the nightmare tableau witnessed by the King in *3 Henry VI*, II.5. As Stuart Hampton-Reeves and Carol Chillington Rutter comment, 'by doubling Talbot and his son with other fathers and sons, Boyd tied their story emblematically to the biggest ideas the trilogy staged'.[13] It is certainly true that the heroic and self-sacrificing solidarity of the Talbots is the exemplary antitype of the father and son who have killed their own kin in battle who represent the extreme of degenerative disorder brought on by civil war.

Yet there is no evidence that Boyd's sort of significant doubling was a feature of early modern theatre, and it is likely that if there was a serial production of the plays in Shakespeare's time, Talbot would hardly have been remembered by *3 Henry VI*, so many battle scenes later.

From the time of nineteenth-century serialized fiction through to twentieth-century TV soaps and series, we expect that all characters will be accounted for in the story, whether in the wrap-up final chapter of a Dickens novel or the convenient car crash that takes out a character when the actor's contract has come to an end. It was not so for Shakespeare. The Fool can disappear from *King Lear* without explanation. In the second half of *Julius Caesar*, all the conspirators bar Brutus and Cassius have gone, replaced by a completely new cast of loyal Republicans we have never met before. Shakespeare is simply following Plutarch with no thought of the sort of continuity of personnel that we as modern readers and viewers expect. Through the *Henry VI–Richard III* series he created through narratives for several of his key characters; Queen Margaret appears in all four plays, quite unhistorically and implausibly returning as a vengeful Fury in *Richard III*; Richard of Gloucester himself already figures at the Battle of St Albans in *2 Henry VI* when in actuality he would have been three years old. But the playwright is content to fill up his minor parts with names collected from the chronicles that can appear in a scene or two before vanishing for ever. And in the case of major characters, such as Talbot or Humphrey of Gloucester, they can dominate the action of one play and be forgotten in the next.

Foreshadowing

Edward Hall's chronicle, Shakespeare's principal source for the *Henry VI–Richard III* plays, is a teleological narrative emphasized in its very title *The Union of the Two Noble and Illustre Famelies of Lancastre and York*. In so far as the history looks forward to that union with the coming of the Tudors, it is full of proleptic commentary on the ways future events are foreshadowed. So, for example, there is Henry VI's prophecy about the young Richmond:

> Lo, surely this is he, to whom both wee and our adversaries levyng the possession of all thynges, shall hereafter geve rome and place. So this holy man shewed before, the chaunce that should happen, that this erle Henry so ordeined by God, should in tyme to come (as he did in deede) have and enjoye the kyngdome, and the whole rule of the realme.[14]

Shakespeare follows Hall in making of this a moving moment in *3 Henry VI* when the King gives his blessing to the boy:

> Come hither, England's hope.
> *Lays his hand on Richmond's head.*
>   If secret powers
> Suggest but truth to my divining thoughts,
> This pretty lad will prove our country's bliss.
>   (IV.6.68–70)

The King, mutating from inept ruler to inspired prophet, ordains his true successor. Yet not all Shakespeare's foreshadowing scenes in the plays, whether drawn from Hall or invented, are designed to support this sort of providentialist narrative.

The most famous of such scenes, which even the most committed disintegrators attribute to Shakespeare, is *1 Henry VI*, IV.4, the dispute in the Temple Garden. This gathers together the cast of principal characters in the wars to come, York, Warwick, Somerset and Suffolk, in a young men's quarrel over no-one ever quite knows what legal question. The retreat into the garden – 'Within the Temple Hall we were too loud' (II.4.3) – the plucking of the red roses or the white as tokens of allegiance, the quite incidental blowing up of the question of the status of York when the bad loser Somerset insults him as a 'yeoman' (II.4.81), all make this appear the most natural thing in the world. What looms beyond is spoken by Warwick in lines that move an audience forward through the next two plays:

> And here I prophesy: this brawl today,
> Grown to this faction in the Temple Garden,
> Shall send between the red rose and the white
> A thousand souls to death and deadly night.
> *(II.4.124–7)*

The rights and wrongs of the dynastic question are not even at issue yet; instead what is forecast is the grim, inevitable progression from brawl through faction to all out war.

This is a major narrative prolepsis, like the opening scene of *1 Henry VI* which charts the wholesale loss of France to come with a series of disaster-bearing messengers even at the moment of Henry V's funeral. But there are also what you might call characterological prolepses. York is given one such at the first scene of *2 Henry VI* when his long-term strategy for claiming the crown is revealed in full, a strategy only to be achieved by the end of the play (I.1.211–56). In a similar vein, but much more striking is the revelation of character of Richard of Gloucester at the dead centre of *3 Henry VI*, III.2.124–95. The Richard we have seen up to this point has been merely the most committed and aggressive of the loyal sons of York. The figure who steps out from the shadows here is the fully-formed villain of *Richard III*: the hunchback made loveless by his deformation – 'Why Love foreswore me in my mother's womb' (III.2.153) – the Machiavel – 'Why, I can smile, and murder whiles I smile' (III.2.182) – the fantasist made desperate by overcompensating ambition. It is no wonder that star actors from Colley Cibber to Laurence Olivier cannibalized this speech for their roles in *Richard III*. As with Hal's soliloquy early in *1 Henry IV*, 'I know you all and will a while uphold | The unyoked humour of your idleness' (I.2.190ff.), the complete unfolding of the character is made manifest to an audience well in advance of its gradual revelation in the narrative.

Most of the foreshadowing in *Henry VI–Richard III*, however, is much more local and relatively short-term in what it prefigures. Take, for example, the prophecies conjured up by Margery Jourdain for the Duchess of Gloucester in *2 Henry VI*, I.4. The conjuring is interrupted by York and Buckingham who arrest the Duchess and her magical assistants. It has struck some editors as surprising that it is York who leads here, given that it is his deadly enemies Suffolk and Winchester who set up the plot to entrap the Duchess (I.4.40.1n.). But the irony is to have him read out the prophecy that tells his own fortune:

> The duke yet lives that Henry shall depose,
> But him outlive, and die a violent death.
> *(I.4.59–60)*

York immediately sees the deliberate ambiguity in this and cited the classical analogue: 'Aio te, Aiacada, Romanos vincere posse' (I.4.62), the riddling prophecy of the Pythian Apollo to Pyrrhus, alternatively, 'I tell you, descendant of Aeacus, you can conquer the Romans' or alternatively 'the Romans can conquer you' (I.4.62n). The formulation is devised to mislead the Duchess into thinking that it is her husband Duke of Gloucester who will depose Henry but of course it is York who the audience will see depose the King in *3 Henry VI*, the play in which Henry survives York only to die violently in the Tower. The other two prophecies are similarly deceptive, predicting the death of Suffolk 'by water' and warning Somerset to 'shun castles' (I.4.65, 67). We see these fulfilled later in the play when Suffolk is killed by Wa(l)ter Whitmore (IV.1.144), and Somerset dies in battle under an inn-sign 'the Castle in Saint Albans' (V.2.68). There is a basic pleasure for the audience in seeing these cryptic clues being solved in action.

Revisions to this scene in modern productions illustrate the projection of a different sort of narrative arc. In the John Barton and Peter Hall adaptation of the plays, *The Wars of the Roses* for the RSC in the 1960s, it is Suffolk not York who interrupts the conspirators and the central prophecy is re-written:

> The King shall be depos'd by that great Duke
> Who this same hour doth wait upon his presence.

Suffolk sees this as a blank cheque to be used against any duke he wants. More immediately incriminating for the Duchess and her husband, however, but intended to be more sinister for the future, is the additional invented response to Eleanor's enquiry as to 'Gloucester's house': 'Why, Gloucester shall be king, ah, Gloucester, King!'[15] The 'ah' of terror makes it clear that it is the coming of Richard of Gloucester that is predicted here. In Adrian Noble's 1988 adaptation of the series as *The Plantagenets* a similar change was made, with Barton's added line retained: 'Why Gloucester shall be king, Gloucester king'.[16] Audiences in the 1960s or the 1980s will have been much more familiar with Shakespeare's Richard III and the horrors of his reign than with the troubled times of Henry VI, so Hall or Noble could be confident that they would pick up the prediction of the story's endgame with the coming of Richard of Gloucester. The original texts, even if they were planned as a series and do point the way forward with foreshadowing tropes, do not shape up this sort of grand narrative.

Remembering

What sort of things do characters remember across the four plays? Primarily, these are injuries that provide motives for revenge; the series constitutes one extended revenge tragedy.[17] So Talbot's vow of vengeance on the French who have killed Salisbury is only the first of many:

> Hear, hear, how dying Salisbury doth groan:
> It irks his heart he cannot be revenged.
> Frenchmen, I'll be a Salisbury to you.
> *(1 Henry VI, I.4.103–5)*

York's primary impetus for his actions is the revenge for the slight on him by Somerset in the Temple Garden scene, though it is given much more substantial grounds by his interview with

Mortimer revealing his claims to the crown (II.4–5). The level of ferocity is increased with the killing of Old Clifford in *2 Henry VI*, V.2, producing Young Clifford's declaration of merciless vengeance:

> My heart is turned to stone, and while 'tis mine
> It shall be stony. York not our old men spares;
> No more will I their babes
>
> *(V.2.51–2)*

What follows in the next play is the killing of young Rutland and the subsequent torture of the captured York, two events that will be recalled again and again through *3 Henry VI* and *Richard III*.

However, in *Richard III* there comes a change of tone in the recollections. In Clarence's dream, when he imagines himself drowned in an underworld afterlife, two figures appear to accuse him:

> The first that there did greet my stranger-soul
> Was my great father-in-law, renowned Warwick,
> Who spake aloud, 'What scourge for perjury
> Can this dark monarchy afford false Clarence?'
> And so he vanished. Then came wandering by
> A shadow like an angel, with bright hair
> Dabbled in blood, and he shrieked out aloud:
> 'Clarence is come, false, fleeting, perjured Clarence,
> That stabbed me in the field by Tewkesbury.
> Seize on him, furies! Take him into torment!'[18]

Clarence's changing of sides first to the Lancastrians, cemented by his marriage to Warwick's daughter, followed by his reversion to his brother Edward of York, was all in the day's work of the conscienceless politics of *3 Henry VI*. Here it produces real guilt particularly for the oath-breach involved, urged against him by the Second Murderer later in the scene: 'Thou didst receive the sacrament to fight | In quarrel of the house of Lancaster' (I.4.202–3). Edward, Lancastrian Prince of Wales, was stabbed to death at the battle of Shrewsbury by all three York brothers – just one more bloody incident in a bloody war. In Clarence's dream he appears as a 'bright angel' whose brutal murder will condemn the killer to eternal damnation. It is as though from the *Henry VI* plays to *Richard III* we have been moved from a shame culture, where honor, power, prestige and their opposites are the only occasions of action, to a guilt culture in which retribution is visited on sinners.

There is a newly prominent religious dimension to this, but not one that is uniformly Christian in tone. Queen Margaret, responsible directly or indirectly for some of the most vicious atrocities of the civil wars is untouched by remorse, even when the murder of the innocent Rutland – 'that peevish brat' (I.3.193) – and the torture of York are vividly recalled. And yet through the play she is the agent of nemesis, a system of retribution that goes beyond the local tit for tat killings of the *Henry VI* cycle. It is her curses that are visited upon the heads of those who stood by when her son Edward was stabbed, and each of them, Grey, Rivers, Hastings, remembers her execration as they face death. The most solemn such recollection is that of Buckingham on All Souls' Day when he is about to be executed, with Margaret's warning of him against Richard repeated word for word,

> This is the day which, in King Edward's time,
> I wished might fall on me when I was found
> False to his children and his wife's allies.
> This is the day wherein I wished to fall
> By the false faith of him whom most I trusted.
> This, this All Souls' Day to my fearful soul
> Is the determined respite of my wrongs [...]
> Thus Margaret's curse falls heavy on my neck:
> 'When he', quoth she, 'shall split thy heart with sorrow,
> Remember Margaret was a prophetess'.
> (V.1.13–27)

As he acknowledges the bitter truth of the Queen's prediction, he penitently accepts his own guilt.

Something is gathering to a head in *Richard III* which would make any audience watching the play as a series realize it was being brought to a close. There are the gruesome reminders of the past in the recollections of the deaths of Rutland, York, Edward of Lancaster, Henry from the previous play. There is the growing choric threnody of mourning women, lamenting their lost men. And finally there are the ghosts of those whom Richard has killed appearing to curse him, bless Richmond, on the eve of Bosworth. But there is also a new element in the dramatization of memory; Shakespeare does not limit himself to events that have been played out earlier in the series. One example, the opening of Clarence's dream, may serve as illustration:

> Methoughts that I had broken from the Tower,
> And was embarked to cross to Burgundy;
> And in my company my brother Gloucester,
> Who from my cabin tempted me to walk
> Upon the hatches. There we looked toward England,
> And cited up a thousand heavy times,
> During the wars of York and Lancaster,
> That had befall'n us.
> (I.4.9–16)

Shakespeare here draws upon a detail from the chronicles not used in the *Henry VI* plays, when the Duchess of York, after the defeat of the Yorkists at Wakefield and the death of her husband, for safety 'sent her. ii. yonger sonnes, George & Richard, over the sea, to the citie of Utrechte in Almayn: where they were of Philippe, duke of Bourgoyne, well receyved and fested'.[19] While the dream is premonitory – Richard 'tempted' his brother to walk on the hatches and will accidentally on purpose push him into the sea – what is conjured up in the dreamscape here is a glimpsed moment of a shared past. It is similar when Edward, remorseful for the death of Clarence, executed as he supposes on his own orders, reproaches those who failed to plead for his brother by reminding him of Clarence's past services:

> Who told me in the field at Tewkesbury,
> When Oxford had me down, he rescued me
> And said, 'Dear brother, live, and be a king'?
> Who told me, when we both lay in the field,

> Frozen almost to death, how he did lap me
> Even in his garments, and did give himself,
> All thin and naked, to the numb-cold night?
> *(II.1.112–18)*

Within the increasingly fated chain of action of the concluding play of the series, Shakespeare contrives these sort of freehand sketches of past lives that overspill the characters' narrative-bound roles.

Conclusion

There is a design to the *Henry VI–Richard III* series – such has been the burden of my argument – a design figured in the interconnection of the several parts which relies on the memory of the audience looking back and looking forward. Resistance to the idea of such a series has been based, at least in part, on a misconception of what might have been involved, influenced by modern conceptions of seriality. Shakespeare was certainly not a Wagner, pre-planning a four-part *Ring*. Whether or not he had collaborators in *1 Henry VI*, the series grew organically under what by the later plays would be generally agreed was his own hand. The style changes from the Marlovian bragadoccio of the early plays to the Seneca-heavy mode of *Richard III*. Allowing for such a developmental trajectory, the sequence of four plays has an astonishing degree of narrative coherence, certainly in comparison with the surviving work of contemporary playwrights. The fact that Talbot disappears from the story after *1 Henry VI* is no sign of 'unconformity' in the later plays, to use Kristian Smidt's term, any more than the failure to mention Humphrey of Gloucester in *3 Henry VI*.[20] In this sort of sequence, unlike a modern soap opera, the action moves on and earlier heroes can be forgotten. Elsewhere, however, memory is used strategically both to shape the trajectory of the drama to come and to build the escalating pattern in which each remembered act of violence will be outtopped by its avenging counterpart. *Richard III* brings that pattern to a climax and a conclusion by the enactment of a belated retributive justice for all those who have died. Yet Shakespeare introduces into the play, also, moments of individual memory that bespeak a new sort of independent interiority, and memory will come to be a key element in the intricate weave of his later drama. In the *Henry VI–Richard III* plays it provides linear threads for an audience in a series unlike anything Shakespeare subsequently wrote.

Notes

1. Nicholas Grene, *Shakespeare's Serial History Plays* (Cambridge: Cambridge University Press, 2002), pp. 12–24.
2. *Henry V*, Epilogue, 13. The quotation here and for all passages cited in the essay other than the *Henry VI* plays and *Richard III* is taken from *The Arden Shakespeare Complete Works*, ed. Richard Proudfoot, Ann Thompson and David Scott Kastan (London: Arden Shakespeare, 2002), with references cited parenthetically in the text.
3. Ric Knowles, 'The First Tetralogy in Performance', in Richard Dutton and Jean E. Howard (eds), *A Companion to Shakespeare's Works*: vol II *The Histories* (Oxford: Blackwell, 2003), pp. 263–86 (p. 267).
4. *King Henry VI, Part I*, ed. Edward Burns, Arden Third Series (London: Thomson Learning, 2000), Introduction, p. 72. This is the edition of the play used throughout, hereafter cited parenthetically in the text.
5. For the evidence, see Grene, p. 23.
6. There are references in Henslowe's *Diary* for 1598–9 to a four-part sequence by Dekker and Drayton on the *Civil Wars in France* but no texts have survived: see R.A. Foakes and R.T. Rickert (eds), *Henslowe's Diary* (Cambridge: Cambridge University Press, 1961), pp. 98–103.

7. Tara L. Lyons provides an interesting sidelight on the spin-off publishing market for serial histories in this period in 'Serials, Spinoffs, and Histories: Selling "Shakespeare" in Collection before the Folio', *Philological Quarterly*, 91.2 (2012), 1–37.
8. Thomas A. Pendleton (ed.), *Henry VI: Critical Essays* (New York and London: Routledge, 2001), Introduction, p. 15.
9. *King Henry VI, Part II*, ed. Ronald Knowles, Arden Third Series (Walton-on-Thames: Thomas Nelson, 1999), Introduction, p. 115. This is the edition of the play used throughout the essay, with references cited parenthetically in the text. Knowles in fact gives the reference for the lines of Gloucester as '2.2.175–100' but this is clearly a mistake for 1. 1. 175–100.
10. *King Henry VI, Part III*, ed. John D. Cox and Eric Rasmussen, Arden Shakespeare, Third Series (London: Arden Shakespeare, 2001), II. 6. 103–4n. This is the edition used throughout this essay, cited parenthetically within the text.
11. Thomas Heywood, *The First and Second Parts of King Edward IV*, ed. Richard Rowland, Revels Plays (Manchester: Manchester University Press, 2005), p. 79.
12. *The Life of Sir John Oldcastle* (1600), Malone Society Reprint (Chiswick: Charles Whittington, Chiswick Press, 1908), A2r.
13. Stuart Hampton-Reeves and Carol Chillington Rutter, *The Henry VI Plays* (Manchester and New York: Manchester University Press, 2006), pp. 194–5.
14. Geoffrey Bullough, *Narrative and Dramatic Sources*, vol. III (London: Routledge and Kegan Paul, 1960), p. 195.
15. John Barton with Peter Hall, *The Wars of the Roses* (London: BBC, 1970), *Henry VI*, scene 20, p. 57.
16. William Shakespeare, *The Plantagenets* (London: Faber, 1989), *Henry VI*, Act Two, scene 4, p. 63.
17. On this aspect of the *Henry VI* plays, see Harry Keyisham, 'The Progress of Revenge in the First Henriad', in Pendleton, pp. 67–77.
18. *Richard III*, Arden third series, ed. James R. Siemon (London: Bloomsbury Arden Shakespeare, 2009), I. 4. 48–57. This is the edition used throughout the essay, cited parenthetically in the text.
19. Bullough, III, 180.
20. Kristian Smidt, *Unconformities in Shakespeare's History Plays* (London and Basingstoke: Macmillan, 1982).

14

RUMOUR'S HOUSEHOLD

Truth, memory, fiction, history in *2 Henry IV* and *All Is True*

Ed Gieskes

> Methinks the truth should live from age to age,
> As 'twere retail'd to all posterity,
> Even to the general all-ending day.
>   (Shakespeare, *Richard III*)

Retailing, retelling, and remembering are all involved in the theatrical representation of the past. The *OED* cites Prince Edward's speech as the first example of retail as a verb meaning 'recount or tell again in detail; to repeat to others.' There is also a pun on selling since the play is a product for sale and the truth the Prince refers to might be contained in books available for sale. When the young prince makes this remark to his uncle Richard of Gloucester, he expresses a wish of a historian in an episode that itself lacks the kind of historical truth that he wishes would be told over until the 'all-ending day.' Even the fate of the princes themselves remains debatable despite the play's unambiguous representation of their murders at the hands of Richard's men. It is a commonplace that the image of Richard produced by this play has a stronger hold on cultural memory than almost any properly historical image of the king. The fictions of the play secure and shape whatever truth is 'retail'd to all posterity.' Retailing might not be exactly the same as remembering, but they are deeply engaged with each other. For a 'truth' to be remembered, the Prince suggests, it must be retailed over and over through time. History plays make claims to truth, but at the same time are dependent on the tools of fiction in order to retail their truths to theatrical and literary posterity. Theatre's contribution to historical memory lies in the force and vividness of its narratives. *2 Henry IV*, by opening under the sign of Rumour, and *Henry VIII,* or *All is True*, with its choric invocation of 'chosen truth,' make explicit the importance of fiction to the production of memorable theatrical histories.

Composed sometime before 1590, George Puttenham's *Art of English Poesy*, echoing and synthesizing other thinkers, takes up the matter of historical poetry and its important role in relation to memory:

> ... the poesy historical is of all other—next the divine—most honorable and worthy, as well for the common benefit as for the special comfort every man receiveth by it, no one thing in the world with more delectation reviving our spirits than to behold as it were in a glass the lively image of our dear forefathers... which, because we are not able otherwise to attain to the knowledge by any of our senses, we apprehend them by memory.[1]

As Puttenham goes on to say 'the present time and things so swiftly pass away, as they give us no leisure almost to look into them' (129), but the past, being fixed in memory, can be looked at in depth. Memory, for Puttenham, offers the only way to gain any knowledge of the past and poesy is tied to the cultivation and preservation of historical memory.

What is remembered about the past is often a product of theatrical and other fictions, and memories derived from theatre often substitute for what might more conventionally be thought of as 'historical knowledge.' Indeed, much of the response to the recent exhumation of what is apparently the body of Richard III from a parking lot alludes directly to Shakespeare's play. Not only does the fictional image of Richard occupy a major part of historical memory, but so too do figures like Falstaff, the other inhabitants of the Eastcheap tavern world, and Justice Shallow. Theatre retails these 'truths' to posterity both as things told over and as things offered for sale. This process of retailing generates memories at least as powerful as those that are created by the records that the prince thinks will preserve the truth from age to age.

That this episode from *Richard III* is created from whole cloth and is also about how truths are remembered points to the complicated relationship between the fictional and the historical in the context of the theatrical retailing and remembering of truth 'from age to age.' This chapter addresses this relationship in two of Shakespeare's plays, one from the second tetralogy and the other from the end of Shakespeare's career. *2 Henry IV* is a play obsessively concerned with report. These reports take many forms and are of varying reliability, but all come on 'many tongues' and are accessible to everyone. In this, as Rumour points out, report is like the theatre. Rumour offers a description of *2 Henry IV*'s intervention into the writing and representation of 'history'. Rumour's many tongues are the voices heard in the history play as much they are of history understood more broadly: many-voiced, contradictory, and demanding response from the audience. History, understood as narratives about the past, particularly as represented in the drama, is a multivocal dialogue with past events and whatever is remembered of that past is carried by those voices.[2] Rumour, as prologue to a history play, stands as an embodiment of the inevitably unreliable nature of historical representation.

When Rumour asks what need it has to anatomize itself before its 'household,' it refers specifically to the theatre in which the play is being performed. That household also includes the whole of the country since Rumour's reach extends to anywhere there are people. Rumour links history and theatre in explicit and implicit terms and the play goes on to show the inevitability of this connection in the production of 'history'. Rumour's fictions run before, alongside, after, and with whatever truths the play carries and often seem truer than the truth. When Shakespeare returns to history in collaboration with John Fletcher in *All is True* the play's title itself raises the question of veracity and accuracy in a play that owes as much to romance as it does to 'history.' In both plays, Rumour's household, the theatrical audience, is the space where history emerges out of the varied, contradictory, true (and false) voices of the past to be 'retail'd through all posterity.'

'Why is Rumour here?'

RUMOUR: The posts come tiring on,
And not a man of them brings other news
Than they have learn'd of me: from Rumour's tongues
They bring smooth comforts false, worse than
true wrongs.[3]

The 'smooth comforts false' brought on Rumour's tongues might be 'worse than true wrongs' but they are welcomed by characters in the play and, as Rumour asserts, by the audience in the playhouse. They are, moreover, the only news that is being delivered; there is no post other than Rumour's. The audience will go forth to retail both the false comforts and true wrongs of the play since it too is part of Rumour's household. This particular iteration of the 'history play' opens under the sign of Rumour, and if the play contributes to the construction of some version of historical memory it is one that is inextricably entwined with the 'lies' of fiction. Unlike Marlowe's *Edward II* or some of the more clearly tragic plays on history, *2 Henry IV* does not promise a single story focused on a character's fate or even that of the Crown. Instead it presents a tissue of smaller stories, only some of which can be thought of as conventionally 'true' but nevertheless all bring news. Like theatre itself, the truth of the account lies in the interaction between the characters and events represented onstage and the response of audiences. Rumour offers a collaborative vision of history and that collaboration depends as much on the effect of Rumour's 'smooth comforts' as it does on the 'true wrongs' of history. In turn, what is recalled both in the play and by the audience derives from this collaboration.

At least since the publication of Hayden White's work on narrative and historiographical theory, clear distinctions between what 'true wrongs' and the 'smooth comforts' Rumour associates with fiction (and 'lies') have been difficult to maintain.[4] Historical representation makes use of the tools of narrative to produce meaning out of the rush of events, meaning that is not fictional. White argues that to imagine that 'history' is transparently true is just as mistaken as to imagine that fiction only lies. Shakespeare's historical drama produces its effects in the space between some imaginary absolute truth and the notional untruth of fiction. That some of the most memorable truths of the plays emerge from fiction only underscores the importance of the collaboration of fiction and history.

In the 2004 Shakespeare Theatre production of *2 Henry IV*, Rumour was represented not by a single figure wearing a cloak covered in tongues, nor by a group of actors in stage blacks, but by a group of actors seated at a long table who divided the speech among themselves as table conversation. Staging Rumour as a conversation made its project explicitly a social interaction and underscored ways in which history, here (everywhere?), depends on both conversational transmission of stories and the sifting of those stories for truth content. Rumour was quite literally the product of a collaboration between voices. These actors, if memory serves, also populated the play as members of the ensemble. Literally polyglot, Rumour thus became presenter and presented, a visible 'wav'ring multitude,' literalizing the position of self-address it speaks to in the lines cited above. Rumour speaks with many tongues, embodying the heteroglot nature of speech and of history. Full of conflicting accents, Rumour is a kind of icon for Bakhtin and Voloshinov's ideas about language. Literally many-tongued, the kind of history put forth by Rumour is polyvocal. Bakhtin and Voloshinov both argue that meaning arises out of verbal interactions of the sort that Rumour describes throughout its prologue.[5]

Rumour is here introducing a play that spends far more time with report, reminiscence, and memory than actual action, and is the wholly appropriate presenter for a play whose effect (and memorability) as history depends at least in part on its status as theatrical fiction.[6] Rumour's household, its addressee here, is comprised of the audience as well as the acting company acting as Rumour's tongues. In addition, Rumour's words circulate throughout the play's England:

> through the peasant towns
> Between that royal field of Shrewsbury
> And this worm-eaten hold of rotten stone,
> Where Hotspur's father, old Northumberland,
> Lies crafty-sick. The posts come tiring on,
> And not a man of them brings other news
> Than that they have learnt of me.
> (Ind. 33–38)

The household thus extends wherever speech extends and Rumour's work infiltrates any effort at the reporting of events—all news comes through Rumour, true or not. The social and spatial inclusivity of Rumour and its household is striking here, ranging from royal field to peasant town to worm-eaten castle. At the same time, the speech continually alludes to the theatrical framework within which this particular set of rumours is being communicated. For example, it references the previous play's events and as it describes Northumberland's castle as 'worm-eaten' reminds us of the fate of Hotspur. It also reminds audience members of Northumberland's characterization in *1 Henry IV* as a politic figure even as it suggests a new reading of Northumberland's illness in that play. Much of the speech makes such overt and covert allusion to either *1 Henry IV* or to theatre more generally. Such back-references to the earlier play run through all of *2 Henry IV*. Loren Blinde argues that Rumour represents a 'signal' of Shakespeare's engagement in questions of historiography. Specifically, 'by embodying the conflict between narrative and display, Rumour transcends the split between aural and visual epistemologies in order for Shakespeare to argue that history is fundamentally imaginative.'[7] To take this a step further, Rumour, like the Chorus of *Henry V*, argues that history is also fundamentally theatrical. Rumour is both more confident than the *Henry V* Chorus and less committed to a more or less unified narrative. Rumour's 'lies' operate in the ears of the audience, in contrast to *Henry V*'s choric invocation of 'imaginary forces' in the minds of its hearers.[8]

Rumour opens the play commanding its audience to listen and then immediately asserts that that command is unnecessary because it cannot imagine any ears that would not open to its speech:

> Open your ears; for which of you will stop
> The vent of hearing when loud Rumour speaks?
> ...
> Upon my tongues continual slanders ride,
> The which in every language I pronounce,
> Stuffing the ears of men with false reports.
> (Ind. 1–3, 5–8)

A. R. Humphries' second-series Arden edition of the play cites John Dover Wilson's note to Rumour's unfolding 'the acts commenced' as being in 'the theatrical sense,' and the whole of the speech engages with theatrical representation. When Rumour asks this opening question, it is assured of obedience not only because everyone listens to rumours, but also because it is speaking as the prologue to a play whose audience has come to hear it. It can assume that it will get a hearing because it is in its house—the theatre. Theatre commands the hearing of its audience while filling the ears of the audience with 'continual slanders' and 'false reports.'[9] Rumour's pejorative descriptions of its 'language,' of theatrical fiction, are given the lie by the way that truths emerge from them. Veracity and falsity operate less as opposites in the play than as necessary complements, in much the same way that memory and forgetting operate.[10]

When Rumour describes its project here it does not merely offer an account of its audience's desire for its reports; it delivers that description in language that derives from the drama it introduces, analogizing historical report with theatrical fiction:

> I speak of peace, while covert enmity
> Under the smile of safety wounds the world.
> And who but Rumour, who but only I,
> Make fearful musters, and prepared defence,
> Whiles the big year, swoll'n by some other grief,
> Is thought with child by the stern tyrant War?
> And no such matter. Rumour is a pipe
> Blown by surmises, Jealousy's conjectures.
> *(Ind. 8–16)*

Rumour speaks of deceitful smiles of safety that hide enmity, like those of Richard of Gloucester or any number of theatrical villains, and of the way imagined threats produce real reactions, like the responses that Hamlet will expect from his theatrical threat in a play shortly to be composed. Rumour's surmises, the suppositions of jealous or fearful imaginations, are the stuff of theatre and, as the play demonstrates, part of history. The effect of historical drama derives precisely from this combination of history and imagination. Rumour mixes true and false report about the outcome of the Battle of Shrewsbury, mimicking the confused nature of historical report which strives to sift fact from fiction but inevitably confuses them.[11]

Rumour runs before historical truth, carrying tales that Henry IV 'hath beaten down young Hotspur and his troops,' reporting this fact before returning to its normal function of noising the false story 'abroad that Harry Monmouth fell | Under the wrath of noble Hotspur's rage' (Ind. 24, 29–30). The many-voiced nature of Rumour's reports resembles that of a theatre purporting to present 'real' events, but only ever produces a series of simulacra. Responding to this problem, the Chorus in *Henry V* explicitly addresses the failure of a theatre to adequately present the events it strives to put forth. The inadequacy of the 'wooden O' requires the imagination and forbearance of the audience to supplement the sketch offered by the action onstage. In *2 Henry IV*, Rumour seems unworried about this problem. Instead, it relies on what it suggests are the natural effects of rumour to fill in gaps and do the work of *Henry V*'s 'imaginary forces.'[12] The first scene of the play enacts this process as Northumberland sifts through the conflicting reports that come to him regarding the disaster at Shrewsbury. Asking Lord Bardolph for news, Northumberland shows the effect of Rumour's tongues:

> Every minute now
> Should be the father of some stratagem;
> The times are wild; contention, like a horse
> Full of high feeding, madly hath broke loose,
> And bears down before him.
> *(I.i.7–11)*

The times, like Rumour's post-horses, prompt wild ideas and stratagems based on the unsettled nature of events. 'Contention,' Northumberland says, bears down all before it in much the same manner that Rumour outpaces true report. As many critics have noticed, this speech and many others in the play show a deep awareness of time and its vicissitudes. Time, Rumour, and History are all linked and all three are inflected by the specifically theatrical mode that Rumour represents.

Lord Bardolph answers Northumberland's question, acting as one of Rumour's posts, and fills Northumberland's ears with smooth comforts about Hotspur at Shrewsbury, saying that there has been no similar victory 'since Caesar's fortunes!' (I.ii.24). Northumberland seeks verification, asking if Bardolph saw the battlefield himself and the conversation exemplifies the process of Rumour's work:

> How is this deriv'd?
> Saw you the field? came you from Shrewsbury?
>
> LORD BARDOLPH
> I spake with one, my lord, that came from thence,
> A gentleman well bred and of good name,
> That freely render'd me these news for true.
>
> NORTHUMBERLAND
> Here comes my servant Travers, whom I sent
> On Tuesday last to listen after news.
>
> *Enter TRAVERS*
>
> LORD BARDOLPH
> My lord, I over-rode him on the way;
> And he is furnish'd with no certainties
> More than he haply may retail from me.
> (I.ii.23–32)

Bardolph's news comes from the words of another 'gentleman' of unspecified good name who 'render'd' his information for 'true.' Both men have been listening 'after news,' in Northumberland's words, and both hear and retail the kind of news provided by Rumour (see Prol. 38). Tellingly, perhaps, Bardolph's certainties are something that can be retailed in the several senses of the term. Shakespeare's use of the word here recalls the context of its use in *Richard III* and while Bardolph's certainties might be retailed, they are far from the truths that the young Prince appeals to.

Bardolph's 'certainties' begin with untruths having more to do with wishful thinking than the facts about the result of the fighting at Shrewsbury. Memory of these events is mediated through these fragmented and contradictory reports and that characters respond to them in specifically theatrical terms indicates the play's interest in the imbrication of history, theatre, and memory. To look back to *Richard III* one more time, when the Prince asks about whether Caesar built the Tower he wants to know if it is 'upon record, or else reported | Successively from age to age, he built it?' (3.1.72–73). Both *Richard III* and *2 Henry IV* undermine the security of his opposition between record and report, implicitly arguing that that memory of the past depends on both. This is not, perhaps, surprising given that Shakespeare's dramatic history is a product of the blending of report, record, and stories.

Later in the scene Northumberland makes the theatrical connections more explicit. When Morton enters, Northumberland addresses him saying 'Yea, this man's brow, like to a title-leaf, | Foretells the nature of a tragic volume' (I.i.60–61), using the same kind of language as characters in Marlowe's *Edward II*.[13] He may also allude to Hieronimo's lamentations in one of the additional scenes in Kyd's *Spanish Tragedy* when he refers to Priam's hearing about Troy's burning:

> Even such a man, so faint, so spiritless,
> So dull, so dead in look, so woe-begone,
> Drew Priam's curtain in the dead of night,
> And would have told him half his Troy was burnt:
> But Priam found the fire ere he his tongue,
> And I my Percy's death ere thou report'st it.
> This thou wouldst say, 'Your son did thus and thus;
> Your brother thus: so fought the noble Douglas'—
> Stopping my greedy ear with their bold deeds:
> But in the end, to stop my ear indeed,
> Thou hast a sigh to blow away this praise,
> Ending with 'Brother, son, and all are dead.'
> *(I.i.70–81)*

Shakespeare's scene likely alludes to one of the scenes added to *The Spanish Tragedy* where Hieronimo discusses how to paint a murderer with the painter Bazardo.[14] The reference indicates the usefulness of a specific variety of stage rhetoric in creating representations of grief. In the scene, Hieronimo is speaking to Bazardo, who also has a murdered son. As part of the conversation, Hieronimo asks if Bazardo can 'draw a murderer' (Fourth addition, 130). He goes on to imagine a painting of his entry in II.v, quoting II.v.4 and describing a possible staging of that scene—like Northumberland here. Northumberland's turn to the kind of grief that is repeatedly displayed in the play strengthens the connection. In Addition 4, after Hieronimo refers to Priam, the Painter asks 'is this the end' prompting Hieronimo to complain that 'O no, there is no end: the end is death and madness!' (l. 159) When Northumberland shifts into a mode of loud lament that closes with a wish that 'the rude scene may end' with darkness and death, he thus resembles both Hieronimo in the added scene and the Portuguese Viceroy. His 'strained passion' (I.i.161), as Lord Bardolph calls it, is in the vein of a certain kind of theatre. While Lord Bardolph attempts to steer Northumberland away from what he thinks of as unproductive and self-indulgent 'passion,' this vocabulary nevertheless links Northumberland to other members of Rumour's Household.

Characters in the subplot belong to what Rumour calls 'the blunt monster with uncounted heads, the still-discordant wavering multitude' that comprise its household. Pistol comes out of this multitude and his speeches are built out of a particular mode of theatre that helps define the outlines of Rumour's household. The kind of theatricalized, story-driven, history produced in the play likewise depends on the same kind of theatre. Specifically, a significant portion of Pistol's speech is constructed out of the dramatic language of other playwrights. That language was designed to be memorable, and Pistol, if he does anything, demonstrates that it was memorable. Pistol's specific variety of polyvocality blends earlier fictions into something new and distinctive. The tags he retails seem designed to be remembered and his fragmented recall of other plays comments on how both history and memory operate through a kind of uneasy synthesis of recalled stories, some more true than others.

While he is a fiction, his career through the second tetralogy is tied to Shakespeare's historiographic project. Pistol is introduced as a 'swaggerer,' and enters speaking a language that lifts from the bombast of *Tamburlaine* and imitators of Marlowe's play. His allusions are, moreover, to historical drama. In II.iv, Pistol speaks in a mixture of quotations from plays, familiar proverbial tags, and speeches from Eliot's *Ortho-epia Gallica* (1593):

> These be good humours indeed! Shall pack-horses,
> And hollow pamper'd jades of Asia,
> Which cannot go but thirty mile a day,
> Compare with Caesars and with Cannibals,
> And Troyant Greeks? Nay rather damn them with
> King Cerberus, and let the welkin roar.
> *(II.iv. 160–165)*

Beyond his reference to 'humours,' Pistol's whole speech is laden with dramatic allusion. When Pistol talks about 'Caesar,' 'Cannibals,' and 'Troyant Greeks,' he is making historical references that are at the same time theatrical. *Tamburlaine*, though not generally acknowledged to be a 'history play' in the way that *2 Henry IV* is, still offers a dramatic representation of putatively historical events.[15] This can also be said of other plays Pistol alludes to (Peele's *Battle of Alcazar*, etc.). Like Shakespeare's history plays, these dramas retail 'history' to their audiences, offering a mixture of truth and fiction in much the same way as Rumour does.

Pistol's allusions also participate in the kind of 'passionate' theatrical discourse deployed by figures like Northumberland when preemptively lamenting the death of his son in I.i. Arguing with Doll Tearsheet, Pistol characteristically uses language far in excess of the concrete situation:

> To Pluto's damned lake, by this hand, to th'infernal deep, with Erebus and tortures vile also! Hold, hook and line, say I! Down, down, dogs! Down, faitors! Have we not Hiren here?
> *(II.iv. 153–157)*

Commentators have suggested many specific sources for the references here—from Peele's *Battle of Alcazar* to Kyd's *Spanish Tragedy*—but they all partake in what the Arden 2 editor terms the 'dramatic rant of the early 1590s.'[16] The plays Humphries sees Pistol referring to include Greene's *Alphonsus of Aragon* (1589, Q1594), Peele's *Battle of Alcazar* (1589?, Q1594), Kyd's *Spanish Tragedy*, *Locrine* (1594?, Q1595), and the lost *Turkish Mahomet and Hiren the Fair Greek* (1589?). Notably, most of these plays deal with historical or pseudohistorical events and deploy the tools of a more or less Marlovian dramaturgy. Pistol's irrepressible rant attests to the memorable nature of this stage language. If he does not wear Rumour's cloak, he speaks with Rumour's many tongues. His polyvocality ties him to multiple voices that make up history. This quality of the speech makes Pistol (and other Eastcheap figures) stand out, regardless of their lack of historical 'reality.' Humphries' 'dramatic rant' is also the language of Northumberland's lamentation and, significantly, of Hotspur in the early scenes of *1 Henry IV*. The stage rhetoric of these contemporary plays provides much of the language of Rumour's household and its speakers are from across the whole spectrum of rank.[17]

As Giorgio Melchiori notes in his New Cambridge edition of the play, *2 Henry IV* participates at least tangentially in the comedy of humours most closely associated with Ben Jonson.[18] Early title pages of both parts describe the plays as containing 'humours' (the 'humourous conceits' of Falstaff alone in the 1598 quarto of *1 Henry IV* and the 'humours' of Falstaff and 'swaggering' Pistol in the *2 Henry IV* quarto of 1600). Links to humours comedy and city comedy have long been recognized but not the relation of such comedy and such dramatic language to Rumour's household and to the kind of history Shakespeare's play is working to produce. The tavern scenes in both parts of *Henry IV* occupy a social space more akin to that of later city comedy than the courts of princes or the battlefields of the first tetralogy. Pistol's kinship to other *miles gloriosus* figures in plays like the roughly contemporary *Every Man in His Humour* seems clear: he and Bobadill occupy a very similar social space—the tavern, the ordinary, the street. Jonson's Bobabill offers comic colour and a certain kind of realism to both versions of *Every Man In*. Pistol and his Eastcheap cohort perform a similar function in the *Henry IV* plays.

Like the tavern scenes in *1 Henry IV*, the tavern and London street scenes along with the Gloucestershire scenes serve as a kind of temporal or historical bridge between the imagined past of the play and the lived present of the audience. As Jonathan Baldo has argued, characters like Shallow demonstrate nostalgia for the 'merry world' of *1 Henry IV*, a nostalgia that almost by definition recognizes that world as lost.[19] Baldo points out how this nostalgia is:

> everywhere belied by the ubiquitous sense that so much of what transpires in the play echoes a prior speech or scene from *1 Henry IV*. Even as Shallow regards with bittersweet pleasure a past beyond recuperation, we witness the past everywhere returning before our eyes and ears, much like a play with its rounds of rehearsals and performances.[20]

The rehearsals and performances that comprise the voices heard in the streets of London and in Gloucester are both theatrical and anachronistic. The historical anachronisms serve twin representational agendas. First, they make the image of the past 'lively,' to quote Nashe, by evoking recognizable and vibrant figures to populate the past imagined in the play. Second, that same vibrancy carries over to other to characters whose representation is less free from the demands of historical accuracy, making them appear more real by association with the fiction. The lie of the representation—its anachronism and patent theatricality—thus creates the impression of historicity that accounts for the plays' status as 'history' and at the same time points to the necessary distance between the reality of the past and its representation. The images bodied forth in the theatre, regardless of their literal 'truth,' have a powerful impact on how the past is recalled.

'Every third word a lie': staged memory

> FALSTAFF: I do see the bottom of Justice Shallow. Lord, Lord, how subject we old men are to this vice of lying! This same starved justice hath done nothing but prate to me of the wildness of his youth and the feats he hath done about Turnbull Street and every third word a lie, duer paid to the hearer than the Turk's tribute.

Like city comedy, the tavern scenes and the Gloucester scenes offer an image of 'everyday life' to the audience, but the apparent realism of these scenes in both parts of the play is constantly undercut by their insistence on their status as fiction. Falstaff's statement that 'every third word' of Shallow's tales of his youth is a 'lie' at the end of III.ii can just as easily apply to Falstaff himself and to the play as a whole. 'We old men' are subject to the vice of lying, audience members enjoy the consumption of these lies, and the theatre is in the business of generating them. Shallow's lies about his connections to John of Gaunt as well as his youthful amorous adventures are rumours as much as they are memories, both subject to assessment and revision, much as any of the rest of the events and information provided in the play. Even Falstaff's own status is in the border space between history and fiction. The Epilogue to *2 Henry IV* evokes a desire for the next play and addresses the Falstaff-Oldcastle identification:

> One word more, I beseech you. If you be not too much cloyed with fat meat, our humble author will continue the story, with Sir John in it, and make you merry with fair Katharine of France: where, for any thing I know, Falstaff shall die of a sweat, unless already a' be killed with your hard opinions; for Oldcastle died a martyr, and this is not the man.
>
> *(Epilogue 26–34)*

Falstaff is here both identified with and distanced from Oldcastle—placing him both inside and outside of actual history since this seems like to have been delivered with a wink and a nudge. The story does continue, of course, but Falstaff is all but absent from *Henry V*, his actual reappearance is delayed until *Merry Wives*, and that play takes place in a fictive, comic, world whose connection to the historical lies only in the characters it shares with *1* and *2 Henry IV*. If *2 Henry IV*'s status as history somehow depends on scenes such as the tavern or Gloucestershire scenes and on this epilogue, the kind of history it presents is one that comes to us very much under the sign of Rumour.[21]

Both the tavern scenes and the Gloucestershire scenes develop a particular kind of historicity, one that depends on reminiscence, allusion, and the representation of what might be called daily life. At the same time, those reminiscences are shown to be lies, the allusions are to bombastic and theatrically distorted versions of exotic history, and the figures who populate both locations find themselves increasingly marginalized as the play moves towards its end. The extra- or para-historical quality of figures like Pistol or Shallow includes them in Rumour's household. At the same time, however, characters in the main and more ostensibly historical plot of the play use the same kind of theatrical language and, at times, offer the words of Rumour as truths. This shared vocabulary indicates that characters of high status (and who have 'real' past existences) belong as much to Rumour's household as a figure like Pistol does. Audiences and readers of the play too have 'heard the chimes at midnight' that Falstaff recalls and those chimes, despite never being actually played on the stage, still ring in our collective ears.

Characters consistently remind each other of the events in the play's first part—examples range from the Lord Chief Justice's remembering that Falstaff was in 'question for the robbery' (I.ii.60) at Gadshill to the Archbishop remembering 'young Hotspur's case at Shrewsbury' (I.iii.26) when Lord Bardolph argues for caution about 'aids incertain' (I.iii.14) like those promised by Northumberland—and these reminders refer to both true events and their fictional representations.[22] Combined with the constant back reference to events as represented in *1 Henry IV*, the anachronistic commoner characters serve as an implicit argument about how history works by producing a complicated tissue composed of truths, rumours, lies, and memories that owe as much to fiction as they do to facts. To answer Rumour's question from the prologue, Rumour is here because it is the proper presenter of a play that necessarily mingles the true and the false, the fictional and the real, the theatrical and the historical. Combined with the repeated and insistent way that the play recalls *1 Henry IV*, Rumour's presence points to the close connection between theatrical fiction and something like 'history' as well as to how difficult it can be to distinguish the two. As Rumour says, 'the posts come tiring on, | And not a man of them brings other news | Than they learnt of me' (Ind. 36–39). That news is history—the product of Rumour's household. The careful deployment of theatrical fiction to support the 'reality' of the history presented in these plays is one of the central innovations of the play.

'Chosen truth'

A little more than a decade after the first performances of *Henry V*, Shakespeare, in collaboration with John Fletcher, produced another play on English history, turning to a recent monarch and one far closer to living memory. Shakespeare and Fletcher's play has a complicated place in scholarship about the 'history play.' Its deployment of pageant-like dream visions, elements reminiscent of tragicomedy, tonal and structural links to dramatic romance, as well as its date of composition have all contributed to a critical distancing of the play from the history play. To take a seminal example, Ribner argues that *Henry VIII* fails 'to embody an overall consistent philosophical scheme such as makes cohesive unities out of all of Shakespeare's earlier histories, including *King John*.'[23] Ribner's idea that that the 'history play' must express some unifying philosophy of history works to exclude a whole range of plays.[24] Arguing that *Henry VIII* is not really a history play runs strangely counter to his argument that Shakespeare (Ribner refers to the play as only by Shakespeare) 'follows his sources with a greater fidelity than he had ever before observed in an English history play, but with a strange unawareness of the basic inconsistencies within his sources.'[25] Aside from it being difficult to see precisely what he means by this, the play's use of inconsistent sources *is* consistent with earlier plays and Shakespeare's willingness to alter events for dramatic effect. It also can be argued to participate in the kind of historical writing that Annabel Patterson describes as typical of Holinshed—a mode where accounts are presented to the judgement of the reader/audience—and of the chronicle tradition more generally.[26]

When Shakespeare and Fletcher came to write *Henry VIII* or *All Is True* in 1612 or early 1613, they entered a field rich in representations of Tudor monarchs. From the first words of the Chorus, the play sets out quite deliberately to distinguish itself from the others—especially those reprinted between 1611 and 1613—making claims for the play's distinctiveness but those claims at the same time depend on tying it to earlier historical drama. The specifics of the Prologue's tactics give insight into the play's efforts at defining the field. In a position-taking tied to the immediate conditions of the theatrical field, the playwrights stake a claim to seriousness, high-mindedness, and noble concerns:

> I come no more to make you laugh: things now
> That bear a weighty and a serious brow,
> Sad, high and working, full of state and woe,
> Such noble scenes as draw the eye to flow,
> We now present.
> *(Prol. 1–5)*[27]

The Prologue, in keeping with many others, differentiates the play from others and makes a claim for the special distinction of what it offers. Precisely what the comments about laughter refer to remains unclear, though the comic business of Rowley's play seems the most logical reference.

The Prologue moves quickly to describing sections of the audience in terms of the affects and desires they bring to the theatre. The Prologue divides the audience into several probably overlapping groups all of whose expectations (save one) will be met. The interests of the first two follow directly from the 'weighty and serious' matter promised in the Prologue's first lines:

> Those that can pity here
> May, if they think it well, let fall a tear:
> The subject will deserve it. Such as give
> Their money out of hope they may believe
> May here find truth too.
> *(Prol. 5–9)*

The 'working' parts of the play will permit those inclined to pity to weep and the 'state and woe' of the subject will speak to those looking for truth. Just what those truths might be is left open to question and, not unlike *2 Henry IV*, some of the most arresting and memorable moments in the play (like, say, Queen Katherine's vision, or Cranmer's Virgil-inflected prophecy about the infant Elizabeth) are more matters of belief than they are truths. The chorus figures pity and truth as objects of potential audience interest—to be hoped for—rather than self-evident aspects of the play. Even such as only want 'a show or two' will 'see away their shilling | Richly in two short hours' (12–13). 'Only they':

> That come to hear a merry, bawdy play,
> A noise of targets, or to see a fellow
> In a long motley coat guarded with yellow,
> Will be deceived.
> *(Prol. 13–17)*

These auditors, looking for noise and jokes, will be deceived by their expectations, expectations conventionally held to have been established by Rowley's play.[28] One of the distinctive features of the play is its distance from and revision of the 'bluff King Harry' tradition that was important to the stage and remains a substantial part of how Henry VIII is remembered—killing his wives or munching a turkey leg and drinking.[29] The idea that Rowley's play is what the Prologue refers to has a great deal to recommend it, but it also echoes claims of seriousness found in prologues at least as far back as Marlowe's *Tamburlaine*.[30] Typically, such choric claims represent efforts to locate the play they introduce in the dramatic field and to separate it from a less serious common run of theatre. *Henry VIII*'s opening is no different in its effort to locate the play in the field, but it makes claims about the play's particular kind of veracity that separate it from choric introductions to historical plays like *2 Henry IV* or *Henry V*.

The Chorus goes on in an almost Jonsonian vein as it appeals to the gentleness of the play's proper audience. The first line tells the 'gentle hearers' to 'know' that:

> To rank our chosen truth with such a show
> As fool and fight is, beside forfeiting
> Our own brains and the opinion that we bring
> To make that only true we now intend,
> Will leave us never an understanding friend.
> *(Prol. 18–22)*

Opening with an emphasis on knowledge underscores that the play is concerned with truth. This 'chosen truth' combines attention to the historical subject matter and a serious approach to that matter. The play's truth is connected to the 'high and working' elements promised to the understanding audience and distinct from the implicitly lower kinds of pleasures that some in the audience might expect or prefer. The Chorus also deploys the language of distinction both to excuse the action and to assert its superiority to the 'fool and fight' that the Chorus rejects as a debasement of truth despite the expectations of ignorant and ungentle understanders. To set the 'chosen truth' of the play with such plays would betray both the 'brains' of the writers and the intention to make the play 'only true.' 'Rank' here plays on multiple senses of the word. The players will not line up 'fool and fight' with the serious matter of their play, nor do they see the current work as having similar status to such a play.[31] Trading on and asserting the stature of the acting company presenting the play, whose work makes its hearers the 'first and happiest hearers' (Prol. 24) of the town, encourages the audience to take what they are about to see seriously—to remember it. The 'gentle hearers' are reminded that were the actors to lower themselves to 'fool and fight,' they would betray both their 'own brains' and their reputation for presenting plays that are 'true.' Moreover, since the people in the theatre *are* the 'first and happiest hearers,' they ought to respond properly to the sad, high, and working truths that the play presents.

The final move the Chorus makes adds detail to how the audience is to respond in language that links it to Shakespeare's *Henry V*. Repeated invitations to 'think' deliberately echo that earlier Chorus who places much of the obligation for the play's success with the audience and its 'imaginary forces,' but this Chorus seems more confident than its predecessor: 'Think ye see | The very persons of our noble story | As they were living' (Prol. 25–28). This Chorus is more hortatory than plaintive, better accustomed, perhaps, to command than request by this point. And this Chorus also makes explicit the play's connection to earlier plays about history even as it makes a claim for the play's distinction in the immediate theatrical context.

The Epilogue recapitulates some of the positions taken in the Prologue addressing the tastes and expectations of the audience and dismissing those who get it wrong and appealing to better understanders. Before detailing bad sorts of audience members, it tells us that "Tis ten to one this play can never please | All that are here' (Epilogue 1–2). The Epilogue assumes that a substantial part of the audience will dislike, ignore, misunderstand, or be disappointed by the play that has just concluded. Those that have come for a nap might be alarmed and woken up by the trumpets and so criticize the play, others looking for anti-citizen plays will be disappointed, leaving only the 'good women' of the audience to appreciate the toil of the actors. Critics have noted the appeal to female audience members and that such appeals are not uncommon, but less attention has been paid to how the Epilogue, like the Prologue, locates the play in relation of other kinds of drama.[32] It is not a play for the inattentive who will be scared by trumpets and it will not please an anti-citizen audience which leads the Epilogue to fear that 'all the expected good' the company 'is like to hear | For this play at this time is only in | The merciful construction of good women' (10–12). The charity of 'good women' will be called forth because the play has represented a good woman as a kind of gesture of solidarity. The question of which woman is being referred to here remains an open one. McMullan's edition calls this 'probably a deliberately ambivalent reference to one or all of Katherine, Anne and Elizabeth, though generally taken to refer only to Katherine.'[33] The salient point here is that this good woman—whoever she is—was *shown* to the audience and their recollection of her representation is the key to the play's being appreciated.

The play marks Katherine and Elizabeth as 'good women' through visions and prophecies that are substantially the stuff of theatrical fiction. Neither Katherine's vision nor Cranmer's prophecy about the upcoming Elizabethan Golden Age have clear 'historical' sources. Instead, both draw on dramatic, poetic, and political traditions whose force (or truth) does not derive from historical fact. Katherine's vision may draw on a report in Holinshed of one of Anne Bullen's dreams and as McMullan may also refer to Princess Elizabeth's vision in Heywood's *If You Know Not Me, You Know Nobody*.[34] This kind of repetition of theatrical fiction has at least a double effect—that of associating Katherine with the other 'good women' Elizabeth (and Anne) and of subtly pointing to a play about Tudor monarchs recently (1610 and 1613) reprinted (and possibly revived on stage)—and is akin to what Shakespeare does in *2 Henry IV*. Moments like this ready the ground for the Epilogue's elision of the differences between Katherine, Anne, and Elizabeth and broaden the range of figures that the 'good women' in the audience can see as making the play worth smiles and applause.

To take a final example before concluding, Cranmer's prophecy, though lacking authority from the chronicles, does have a series of sources that contribute to its power both as prophecy and as theatre. Cranmer prefaces his prophetic speech with a claim that no one should think his words 'flattery, for they'll find 'em truth' (V.ii.16) before moving on to describing Elizabeth as a 'pattern to all princes' (V.ii.22). The speech is an instance of political prophecy that alludes to the Bible and to Virgil's fourth eclogue, which predicts a return to a pastoral golden age.[35] Cranmer tells his onstage audience that:

> she shall be—
> But few now living can behold that goodness—
> A pattern to all princes living with her,
> And all that shall succeed.
>
> *(V.iv.20–23)*

Most of those hearing his prophecy onstage will not live to see its fulfillment, but the princess will become a pattern for both contemporary and later princes. The audience in the playhouse is in a position to remember her and this fictional prophecy seems designed to create a kind of Elizabethan nostalgia and to place Elizabeth's reign into an historical succession from her father down to James. Cranmer's words fabricate a memory of Elizabeth's reign, a memory no less evocative or meaningful than the material derived from the chronicles despite it being fiction.

Conclusion

This chapter has attempted to indicate some ways that Shakespeare's historical drama deploys the tools of fiction in grappling with the problem of memory and its relation to history. Rumour, as presenter of *2 Henry IV*, incarnates the problematic connection between truth and fiction and memory with its 'smooth comforts false, worse than true wrongs.' Its words carry both truths and lies and, sometimes, the lies are more forceful and memorable than the truths (even if they are 'worse'). In a period that was increasingly interested in the production of more reliably 'true' accounts of the past, dramatic representations of history make an important contribution to how history is remembered. Thomas Nashe's description of the effect of Talbot's stage resurrection (and, more importantly, his death 'fresh bleeding') in *1 Henry VI* registers the power of stage representations in the commemoration of a heroic historical figure. Nashe's is only one example of the power attributed to stage representations. That power works as well for fictions as it does for truths and Shakespeare's plays make conscious use of this in both explicit and implicit ways. The more or less constant reference to *1 Henry IV* that run through its sequel is one aspect of this—audiences are encouraged to remember history as represented by the plays—as are repeated references to rumour, imagination and supposition.

When Shakespeare turns to the reign of Henry VIII late in his career, he collaborates on a play whose prologue declares that its truth is 'chosen,' intended, and at least asserted to be believable. The play presents elements that draw heavily on reliable chronicle material—especially for the pageantry of the trial and coronation scenes—but it also stages dream visions and prophetic effusions without any 'true' antecedents. Sir Henry Wotton's well-known letter gives the play the title *All is True* and offers one example of the play's truth. In his letter, he writes that the play depicted:

> some principal pieces of the Reign of Henry 8. which was set forth with many extraordinary circumstances of Pomp and Majesty, even to the matting of the stage; the Knights of the Order, with their Georges and Garter, the Guards with their embroidered Coats, and the like: sufficient in truth within a while to make greatness very familiar, if not ridiculous.[36]

Wotton sees the truth of the representation as sufficient to make 'greatness very familiar'—memorable. The play's chosen truth depends as much on the adequacy of visual spectacles that have chronicle sources as on those that are explicitly fictions.

That truth is sufficient due to its accurate bodying forth of an imagined spectacle—the 'extraordinary circumstances of Pomp and Majesty.' Theseus's disparagement of the imagination in *A Midsummer Night's Dream* might serve as a critique of historical drama but Hippolita's response offers a counter-account, one that speaks more adequately to the work of these plays:

> all the story of the night told over,
> And all their minds transfigured so together,
> More witnesseth than fancy's images
> And grows to something of great constancy;
> But, howsoever, strange and admirable.
> (V.i.23–27)[37]

History is as much something 'told over' as *Midsummer's* 'story of the night' and, as I hope to have suggested, is of a similar constancy. These plays suggest that the 'something of great constancy' that grows out of story is history—a chosen truth—whose claim on memory derives as much from truth as fiction.

Notes

1 George Puttenham, *The Art of English Poesy*, ed. by Frank Whigham and Wayne Rebhorn (Ithaca, NY: Cornell University Press, 2007), 129.
2 See Annabel Patterson's *Reading Holinshed's Chronicles* (Chicago: University of Chicago Press, 1994) for a discussion of the multivocality of chronicle history.
3 I quote from the Arden text of A.R. Humphries (New York: Methuen, 1966).
4 See, for example, the essays collected in *The Content of the Form: Narrative Discourse and Historical Representation* (Baltimore, MD: Johns Hopkins University Press, 1990).

5 See Bakhtin's *The Dialogic Imagination* (Austin: University of Texas Press, 1981) and Voloshinov's *Marxism and the Philosophy of Language* (Cambridge, MA: Harvard University Press, 1986).
6 Rumour's gender has been the subject of much debate in the critical history of the play. See Frederick Kiefer, 'Rumor Fame and Slander in *2 Henry IV*', *Allegorica* 20 (1999), 3–44, and Harry Berger, 'Sneak's Noise or Rumor and Detextualization in *2 Henry IV*', *The Kenyon Review*, N.S. 6 (1984), 58–78.
7 Loren M. Blinde 'Rumored History in Shakespeare's *2 Henry IV*', *ELR*, 38:1 (2008), 35.
8 Nashe's comments about Talbot's reanimation in *1 Henry VI* point to this theatricalization of history as well. Brian Walsh's *Shakespeare, the Queen's Men, and the Elizabethan Performance of History* (Cambridge: Cambridge University Press, 2009) offers an excellent account of the Nashe passage and how it indicates an early modern awareness of the role of fiction in historical memory.
9 As one example, the change of name from Oldcastle to Falstaff derives from perceptions of slander, a slander retailed by the theatre that falsely reported him to be the fat knight dismissed in this play. Anti-theatre polemic uses these terms as well.
10 See Garrett Sullivan's *Memory and Forgetting in English Renaissance Drama: Shakespeare, Marlowe, Webster* (Cambridge: Cambridge University Press, 2005). Paul Ricoeur's *Memory, History, Forgetting* (Chicago: University of Chicago Press, 2004) engages with these questions in ways that have influenced my thinking.
11 Thomas Blundeville, like other writers of *ars historica*, talks about this problem but has more faith in the sifting than Rumour does. See his *True Order and Method of Writing and Reading Histories* (STC 3161. London, 1574). Shakespeare repeatedly returns to scenes dramatizing the sifting of conflicting reports—*Hamlet* and *Othello* are only two of the best known examples of this interest.
12 By conflating Rumour with the acting company, the production referred to above underscores this reliance.
13 This sort of language also links Northumberland to historical poetry like Drayton's, which makes use of the same imagery of writing for the stage.
14 The scene with the Painter appears in the 1602 quarto and was probably on the stage in early 1597. Humphries argues that the *Jeronimo* that Henslowe records as 'ne' on January 7, 1597 was probably this version of Kyd's play ('renovated with editions' (11)). If we can accept that Northumberland's lines refer to *The Spanish Tragedy*, they suggest how Shakespeare draws on a distinct dramatic tradition in order to enhance the effect of his play and to characterize Northumberland by linking him to a tradition of rhetorical bombast (to which Hotspur is also connected).
15 See Kewes' 'The Elizabethan History Play: A True Genre?' (Richard Dutton, et al. eds. *A Companion to Shakespeare's Works: The Histories* (London: Blackwell, 2003), pp. 170–93). As part of her argument about the problematic boundaries of the 'genre', she discusses a number of plays about 'foreign' history including several alluded to by Pistol.
16 Arden 2 73. It is also worth considering how this resembles parodic versions of Hotspur's 'drowned honor' speech in *1 Henry IV* which itself has this kind of theatrical and literary antecedents.
17 If these speakers have anything in common it is that they are marginal figures—either historically (being on the losing side) or socially.
18 William Shakespeare, *The Second Part of Henry IV*, ed. by Giorgio Melchiori (Cambridge University Press, 1989), pp. 18–19.
19 Jonathan Baldo, *Memory in Shakespeare's Histories: Stages of Forgetting in Early Modern England* (New York: Routledge, 2012), pp. 87ff. Baldo's chapter on *2 Henry IV* is fascinating and his interest in ways that the play 'shows history to be a process of continual reinvention, no more authorized than Rumour itself' (p. 89) is complementary to my own focus on the role of fiction in the production of historical memory.
20 Baldo, p. 92.
21 Critical associations of Falstaff with Rumour derive from a recognition of this tie. See, for example, David Bergeron's 'Shakespeare Makes History: *2 Henry IV*', *SEL*, 31(1991), 231–45.
22 It is not coincidental that Lord Bardolph, a bearer of false rumor in 1.1, here reminds the Archbishop about Shrewsbury.
23 Irving Ribner, *The English History Play in the Age of Shakespeare* (2e., Princeton, NJ: Princeton University Press, 1965), p. 288.
24 See Chapter 9 of *The English History Play* ('The History Play in Decline') for an extended discussion of how these plays are either signs of a decline or that they are not 'history plays'. For Ribner, 'romance history' is not history at all.
25 Ribner, p. 289.
26 See Patterson's *Reading Holinshed's Chronicles*.

27 I cite from Gordon McMullan's Arden edition of the play (London: Arden Shakespeare, 2000).
28 See for example, the Arden 3 edition's notes and introduction.
29 For a discussion of both the tradition and *Henry VIII* as a rupture with it, see Eckhard Auberlen '*King Henry VIII*: Shakespeare's Break with the "Bluff King Harry" Tradition', *Anglia*, 98 (1980), 319–47.
30 For a still-useful discussion of the genre, see Franklin B. Williams, Jr. 'Commendatory Verses: The Rise of the Art of Puffing', *Studies in Bibliography*, 19 (1966), 1–14.
31 Rank could mean both 'to arrange or draw up people' (OED 'rank' v.3 1b) and 'to give a certain position in a sequence, series, or hierarchy to (a person or thing)' (OED 'rank' v.3 3b).
32 On appeals to women in the theatre, see Richard Levin, 'Women in the Renaissance Theatre Audience', *Shakespeare Quarterly*, 40:2 (Summer, 1989), 165–74.
33 Note to line 11 of the epilogue in McMullan's edition.
34 McMullan, *Henry VIII*, 437.
35 See McMullan's notes for the biblical references and for the Virgilian echo see Heather James' *Shakespeare's Troy* (Cambridge: Cambridge University Press, 2013), p. 13.
36 Sir Henry Wotton, quoted in R.A. Foakes, ed. *Henry VIII* (London: Methuen, 1968), p. 180.
37 Quoted from the Arden edition of Harold Brooks (New York: Routledge, 1979).

15

CULTURAL MEMORIES OF THE LEGAL REPERTOIRE IN *RICHARD III* AND *RICHARD II*

Criticizing rites of succession[1]

Anita Gilman Sherman

Both *Richard II* and *Richard III* evoke memories of coronation rites, although no coronation is ever staged. Richard II uncrowns himself in a climactic scene, deposed by Henry Bolingbroke. In *Richard III*, Edward, Prince of Wales, talks of his imminent coronation (III.1.62), but ends up murdered by his uncle, Richard, Duke of Gloucester, whose subsequent coronation we never see. If the course of true love never did run smooth, as Lysander laments in *A Midsummer Night's Dream*, seldom does the transfer of power run smooth in Shakespeare. *Richard II* and *Richard III* are no exception, their focus on troubled royal succession amounting to what Ronald L. Grimes calls ritual criticism. 'Ritual criticism,' as Grimes defines it, 'is the interpretation of a rite or ritual system with a view to implicating its practice'.[2] Why might one engage in ritual criticism? Grimes lists several reasons, among them, 'to enable the revision and construction of more effective rites' and 'to protect oneself from exploitation by ritual means'.[3] This chapter argues that *Richard II* and *Richard III* implicate the practice of monarchical succession with a view to inviting audiences and readers not only to protect themselves from exploitation, but also to revise and construct more effective rites.

Shakespeare's staging of royal ritual has long inspired controversy, especially regarding the effects on audiences of counterfeiting sacred ceremonies. In 1613 Sir Henry Wotton observed of *Henry VIII*'s ceremonial scenes that they made majesty 'very familiar, if not ridiculous'.[4] More recently Stephen Greenblatt has argued that *King Lear* presents 'evacuated rituals'.[5] Brian Cummings attacks this view for resuscitating a Weberian narrative of disenchantment whereby formerly meaningful social and religious practices are 'emptied out'. Cummings claims instead that many staged rites occupy a middle ground between mimesis and representation such that audiences are both participants and spectators, enjoying the 'pleasure of the boundary'.[6] He defends the idea of a contact zone where ritual participation and theatrical spectatorship blend, yet he polarizes this phenomenological issue when he construes skeptical playgoers as viewing theater's counterfeit rituals with ironic detachment or anxiety. I contend that skeptical playgoers may respond with as much passion as pious ones. Shakespeare's success proves that playgoers participate feelingly in maimed rites, not despite their skepticism, but because of it. The creative inversions performed in ritual criticism may reveal secularization at work, yet it does not follow that secularization evacuates ritual power. Rather, ritual criticism demonstrates ritual's continuing hold, as it seeks to incite reform.

Ritual taps into cultural memory, bringing the past into the present through language and gesture.[7] Jan Assman considers cultural memory the domain of tradition and other social practices going far back in time. He distinguishes it from communicative memory, which goes back no more than three generations. Communicative memory is like Maurice Halbwachs's notion of collective memory; it involves conversation and story-telling within a social group. Assman explains, 'If we think of the typical three-generation cycle of communicative memory as a synchronic memory-space, then cultural memory, with its traditions reaching far back into the past, forms the diachronic axis'.[8] Diana Taylor adds a further distinction within cultural memory. Borrowing the term 'archive' from Michel Foucault to designate written records, Taylor contrasts it to more ephemeral knowledge practices that she calls the 'repertoire'. By repertoire, she means embodied behaviors like 'performances, gestures, orality, movement, dance, singing' that transmit 'communal memories, histories, and values from one group/generation to the next'.[9] The relation between archive and repertoire 'is not a binary', Taylor tells us, because it is neither sequential nor temporal 'nor true versus false', although it does overlap with the orality/literacy divide.[10] Both modes of social practice store and transmit knowledge, and both involve embodied action, existing in productive tension. Taylor also resists the dichotomies following from Pierre Nora's distinction between *milieux* and *lieux de mémoire*. She believes that Nora's terms map too readily onto other binaries: memory/history, past/present, archaic/modern, real/mediated. Archive and repertoire, by contrast, 'usually work in tandem' and 'in a constant state of interaction', neither one more valid than the other. The performance of cultural memory in the present, Taylor points out, 'belongs to the strong as well as the weak; it underwrites de Certeau's "strategies" as well as "tactics", Bakhtin's "banquet" as well as "carnival"'.[11] In *Richard III* and *Richard II* both the strong and the weak perform dazzling maneuvers that shuttle between the archive and repertoire, drawing on cultural memory to question rites of succession. The weak often mime their dissent, while the strong subvert and improvise rites to register their criticism.

Taylor introduces a third term, 'scenario', to describe how cultural memory is transmitted in performance. Taylor explains that 'scenarios' are 'culturally specific imaginaries—sets of possibilities, ways of conceiving conflict, crisis, or resolution—activated with more or less theatricality'.[12] She also describes them as 'formulaic structures that predispose certain outcomes and yet allow for reversal, parody, and change'.[13] At once inherited and flexible, these scenarios are more than codes because they reimagine modes of behavior handed down the generations, capturing the political dynamic of social relations. Scenarios thus have a contestatory dimension absent in what critics like Janette Dillon and Louise George Clubb have dubbed 'scenic memory' or 'theatergrams'. Dillon's 'scenic memory' reveals the 'iconicity' of certain theatrical tableaux, showing how they are evoked and repeated across time, while Clubb's 'theatergram' denotes a stock episode or dramatic meme that can be recombined. Taylor's scenarios, by contrast, are flexible and politically charged. They encompass not only theatrical traditions, but also embodied memories from other social spheres. These scenarios become the vehicles for Ronald Grimes's ritual criticism.

In considering scenarios for the transfer of royal power, Shakespeare taps into multiple, overlapping reserves of cultural memory drawn from several social spheres. He remembers prior plays, his own and those of others. He appropriates liturgical memories of ritual sacrifice and martyrdom.[14] With respect to jurisdictional battles, he draws on a reservoir of legal gestures gathered from venues such as the guildhall, the courts, Parliament, and the church. This chapter attempts to recover some of the bodily vocabulary alive in the cultural memory of Shakespeare, his actors and his audience. It argues that Shakespeare's political criticism is subtle insofar as he mobilizes this gestural choreography obliquely in his scenarios of succession.

While both plays take for granted a supine Parliament, swayed by the powerful, neither play can stage the transfer of power without the commons' tacit approval. In both plays the rites confirming the king's legitimacy occur in the presence of a silent majority whose witnessing of the transfer serves to ratify it. With respect to the weak, the plays feature citizens who are coopted, passive and fearful. Intimidated by the powerful, these citizens hang back, allowing their country to devolve into civil war. With respect to the strong, the plays feature monarchs who manipulate ritual vocabulary and legal traditions to redress or protest rites of succession. Taking its cue from Thomas More's *History*, *Richard III* stages the legal protocols required for effecting the appearance of legitimacy, going so far as to jog a dormant memory of royal election, while *Richard II* dramatizes the king's deliberate disenchantment of his office through a mnemonic parody of a both legal and sacred rite—what Harry Berger, Jr. calls the discoronation (46).[15] Because the scenarios of royal succession activate memories of the legal repertoire, they remind audiences of legal tools at their disposal. While *Richard III* and *Richard II* are famous for chronicling the rise or fall of their charismatic title characters, this chapter shows how Shakespeare conjures memories of the legal repertoire to question rites of succession.

The legal repertoire of the commons

Richard III boasts more citizens voicing their opinions than *Richard II*. Ordinary Londoners appear in several scenes, commenting on political events and expressing their fears and hopes, while occasionally hiring themselves out as hitmen, despite their tender consciences. Their prominence is owed partly to the fact that Gloucester needs their support in order to become Richard III, whereas Richard II has long ignored them. Even so, critics have observed that Shakespeare mutes the role of the commons in *Richard II*, lessening the agency given to them in the chronicles. By contrast, *Richard III* explores their physical participation in a range of legal scenarios.

We can access the gestures of the commons when these are cued in the lines, as happens in II.3 when one citizen hails another, saying, 'Whither away so fast?' The actor is most likely moving quickly, but whether he is darting across the stage, looking behind him anxiously, marching forthrightly or scurrying in avoidance is open to improvisation. Improvisation designates a space of freedom where actors and director can respond creatively to the unscripted moment, introducing an element of surprise. In other scenes, however, the citizens' opposition to infringements of law becomes apparent thanks not to improvisation so much as to a gestural repertoire pertaining to governance.

In III.6, for example, the Scrivener enters holding a legal document, and, taking the audience into his confidence, expresses amazement at Richard's brazen manipulation of the laws even while complying with their outward forms. Does this moment of downstage complicity with the audience constitute what Diana Taylor calls a scenario? Robert Weimann might argue that by occupying the *platea* and chatting up the groundlings, the Scrivener is embodying attitudes associated with medieval popular theater. The Scrivener's posture aligns him with a histrionic tradition transmitting skepticism about norms. The prop he holds in his hand, however—a record soon to form part of the 'archive' legitimating Richard's rise to power—complicates the scenario with overtones of alienated labor and self-conscious historiographical suspicion about the interplay between orality and literacy. Brandishing it, the Scrivener confides:

> Here is the indictment of the good Lord Hastings,
> Which in a set hand fairly is engrossed,
> That it may be today read o'er in Paul's.

> And mark how well the sequel hangs together:
> Eleven hours I have spent to write it over,
> For yesternight by Catesby was it sent me;
> The precedent was full as long a-doing;
> And yet within these five hours Hastings lived,
> Untainted, unexamined, free, at liberty.
> Here's a good world the while. Who is so gross
> That cannot see this palpable device?
> Yet who so bold but says he sees it not?
> (III.6.1–12)

The Scrivener is proud of his 'set hand' and penmanship. He boasts about the magnitude of his task and the many hours he was busy copying. Evidently the prop is no flimsy broadside. When he tells us to 'mark how well the sequel hangs together', perhaps he unspools a scroll or riffles through a quire of pages hanging upside down and held by the spine.[16] This slightly manic performance engages a gestural repertoire about hefty legal documents that taps into a shared experience of bureaucratic hassle. Yet, the Scrivener knows that he is complicit in a whitewash, fabricating records for an archive that will represent Richard and his cronies as complying with the law. He feels no shame about his role, only amazement at Richard's boldness. He illustrates how the employees of the King's Council have been coopted—charming rascals (like their boss) who produce paper trails to legitimize the behavior of the ruling class. His gestural repertoire evokes a cultural memory of legal fraud.

The next scene also features citizens attesting to legal fraud, but this time their conduct is reported in Buckingham's flashback. This should resolve the ambiguities of their body language, as the descriptive flashback preempts physical improvisation. Yet the Duke of Buckingham asserts that the crowd's behavior mystifies him. Buckingham tells Richard that he has just returned from the Guildhall and despite his best oratorical efforts to advance Richard's claim to the throne, the citizens remain unpersuaded. The scene opens with Richard asking, 'How now, how now, what say the citizens?' He needs their consent. Buckingham replies, 'The citizens are mum, say not a word' (III.7.3). Richard presses him to recite the arguments that elicited their resistant silence. Buckingham runs through them, concluding, 'And when my oratory drew toward end, | I bid them that did love their country's good | Cry, "God save Richard, England's royal king!"' (III.7.20–23). He initiates a speech-act that, to be completed, requires a sign of what John Austin calls 'uptake'. This speech-act is meant to set in motion what he hopes will be a ritualized scenario of call and response. 'And did they so?' Richard asks, incredulous that they will not play along. 'No', Buckingham explains, 'they spake not a word, | But like dumb statues or breathing stones | Stared each on other and looked deadly pale' (24–26). Buckingham's dehumanizing simile relays the crowd's performed behavior: silence, stillness, pallor, and mutual stares. Buckingham adds, 'Which when I saw, I reprehended them | And asked the Mayor what meant this willful silence?' (27–28). Faced with behavior he purports to find baffling, Buckingham calls upon interpreters. He asks the Mayor to translate the citizens' gestural repertoire. It's his way of refusing to acknowledge the performance of incipient dissent.

Hijacked into this mediating role, the Mayor is evasive, saying 'the people were not used | To be spoke to but by the Recorder' (29-30). The Recorder was a legal advisor and spokesman for the Mayor and Alderman, among other duties.[17] His position captures the dual aspect of legal advocacy with its oral repertoire and its documentary archive. Tasked by the Mayor with interpreting the people's 'wilful silence', the Recorder parrots Buckingham. Why? Unlike the Scrivener's impromptu confession that has no analogue in the chronicles, in this scene

Shakespeare compresses and dramatizes events related in various histories, most likely Holinshed (1587) and Edward Hall (1548).[18] Both Hall and Sir Thomas More (whose history Hall uses) have the Mayor describe the Recorder as 'the mouthe of the citee'. Both name him as one 'Fitz Wyllyam, a sadde man and an honeste, which was but newly come to the office, and never had spoken to the people before, and loth was with that matter to begyn'.[19] In the chronicles, the stonewalling of the citizens prompts a series of repetitions both on Buckingham's part and the Recorder's, 'but all this no chaunge made in the people, which alway after one stoode as they had been amased'.[20] Shakespeare abbreviates this byplay, but retains the portrait of the Recorder as an unwilling mouthpiece who 'nothing spoke in warrant from himself' (33). He also retains the portrait of the people as an obdurate collective, aware that laws are being violated and therefore withholding the assent required for Buckingham's speech-act to have uptake.

The confrontation in the Guildhall is defused once a claque of Richard supporters infiltrates the crowd. Their gestural repertoire trumps the citizens' silence, constituting the uptake Buckingham requires—a set of formulaic cries, leaps and hat-tossings that he finds legible without assistance:

> When he had done, some followers of mine own
> At lower end of the hall hurled up their caps,
> And some ten voices cried, 'God save King Richard!'
> And thus I took the vantage of those few:
> 'Thanks, gentle citizens and friends,' quoth I;
> 'This general applause and cheerful shout
> Argues your wisdom and your love to Richard.'
> (III.7.34–40)

In Buckingham's report, his followers save the day, overwriting the inhibited repertoire of dissent with the flashy repertoire of acclaim. Shakespeare has polarized More's account, which attributes the intervention not only to 'a bushement of the dukes servants and Nashfeldes and other longing to the protectour', but also to 'some prentises and laddes that thrust into the hal amonge the prese'.[21] These apprentices and lads are absent in Buckingham's flashback perhaps because their support for Richard is independent of the Duke's sphere of influence, perhaps because it blurs the line the play draws between a skeptical populace and opportunistic camp followers.

In *Richard II* the people have even less legal standing. No cultural memories surface of complicit scrivening or stony silence. York describes them as fickle and contemptuous, transferring their allegiances from the King to Bolingbroke out of boredom (V.2.23–40). When we meet them, York turns out to be wrong. The few commoners who appear on stage are loyal to the King, but irrelevant to the ruling families and their jockeying for power. Whether it is the groom who finds his way to Richard's cell in his last hours of life or the gardener and his men who 'talk of state' (III.4.27), the commoners in *Richard II* have no access to the legal repertoire, only to the repertoire of service and labor.

Charades of legal compliance

Each play stages a rite to mark the transfer of power in a scenario involving the commons; yet, each play criticizes that rite by evoking cultural memories, not only of the legal repertoire, but of religious ceremonies. In *Richard III* the strong devise a scenario echoing episcopal investiture to coerce a petition from the citizens. In *Richard II* the beleaguered King performs a charade of legal compliance, challenging parliamentary procedure by professing to erase a memory of coronation. Both scenarios star manipulative strongmen soliciting popular complicity in rites of succession. Confronted with embodied ritual criticism, audiences are encouraged to search their own memories of political participation in evaluating the plays' events. In a typically Shakespearean strategy, audiences are invited to develop skeptical judgment and to cultivate the imagination of political alternatives.[22]

In *Richard III* the citizens ratify the new regime in a scene that ridicules popular petition even as it keeps alive the cultural memory of that form of legal redress. In lieu of a coronation scene, Buckingham improvises a rite designed to secure the consent of Londoners. Playgoers are asked to understand themselves, not merely as spectators, but as participants in the irregular transaction. We blend in with the crowd milling around Baynard's Castle where we witness the spectacle of Richard's pretended reluctance to receive the citizens' petition that he accept the crown, even as Buckingham and London's Lord Mayor thrust it upon him. In an encounter scripted by Buckingham, we see Richard, 'a book of prayer in his hand' (III.7.97) and between two bishops, as he protests too much, saying no, but meaning yes to the citizens' 'entreaties' (III. 7.114). The legal 'rite' of petition may be exhuming a memory trace of the 1484 Act of Settlement whereby Parliament 'elected' Richard to the throne.[23]

More's history, while conceding the 'mockish eleccion' stage-managed by Richard's party, claims that the rite of solicitation was widely acknowledged as a legal charade.[24] Annabel Patterson describes More's take on this scene as 'a sceptical account of the connection between state ritual and ideology, offered as evidence for the sceptical penetration of ritual and ideology by ordinary citizens'.[25] More describes the reactions of these ordinary citizens after departing from Baynard's Castle, noting how they were 'talking diversly of the matter every man as his fantasye gave him'. Fantasy suggests free speech, as if on going home, the citizens might exchange unbuttoned views of Richard's irregular accession. On the contrary, by fantasy More means the continuation of the phony performance of political enfranchisement:

> But much they talked and marveiled of the maner of this dealing, that the matter was on both partes made so straunge, as though neither had ever communed with other thereof before, when that themself wel wist there was no man so dul that heard them, but he perceived wel inough, yt all the matter was made betwene them. Howbeit somme excused that agayne, and sayde all must be done in good order though. And menne must sommetime for the manner sake not bee a knowen what they knowe.

Lest these remarks be confusing, More clarifies them with two analogies that bear upon Shakespeare's cultural memory of the legal repertoire:

> For at the consecracion of a bishop, every man woteth well by the paying of his bulles, yt he purposeth to be one, & though he paye for nothing elles. And yet must he bee twise asked whyther he wil be bishop or no, and he muste twyse say naye, and at the third tyme take it as compelled there unto by his owne wyll. And in a stage play all the people know right wel, that he that playeth the sowdayne is percase a sowter. Yet if one should can so lyttle good, to shewe out of seasonne what acquaintance he hath with him, and calle him by his owne name whyle he standeth in his magestie, one of his tormentors might hap to breake his head, and worthy for marring of the play. And so they said that these matters bee Kynges games, as it were stage playes, and for the more part plaied upon scafoldes. In which pore men be but ye lokers on. And thei yt wise be, wil medle no farther. For they that sometyme step up and playe wt them, when they cannot play their partes, they disorder the play & do themself no good.[26]

The ritual of a bishop's consecration, according to More, involves a little stage play in which the candidate is invited three times to take the position, but which he must pretend to refuse twice. Moreover, 'good order' means following this protocol 'for the manner sake'. To disrupt it would be as foolish as breaking the fourth wall and calling out an actor starring as the sultan and exposing him as a cobbler or rude mechanical in real life. The citizens, in More's history, reconcile themselves to their walk-on roles as extras for the sake of self-preservation and also because it behooves them as wise men not to 'medle'.[27] Their performance of cooptation amounts to a survival strategy under tyranny: bodily practices with theatrical histories recognizable to an audience schooled in political looking.

In Shakespeare's adaptation of this scene, he secularizes a cultural memory of episcopal investiture to accentuate Richard's chicanery. Shakespeare recalls the religious origins of Buckingham's ad hoc ritual by having Richard appear 'aloft, between two bishops' as if he had just been interrupted in the midst of 'meditation' (72) and 'zealous contemplation' (93)—a performance of piety absent from More's account of the interchange at Baynard's Castle. More's rite of episcopal investiture is unmoored from its religious framework and repurposed. As Buckingham quips, 'Play the maid's part; still answer nay, and take it' (50). The secular ritual that he improvises (to borrow Sally Moore and Barbara Myerhoff's term) carries within it a cultural echo of the gestural repertoire involved in investiture. While William C. Carroll might see this transposition as part of 'Richard's relentless and, in every sense, fruitless, assault on ritual and order', I see the scenario of petition as a palimpsest, revealing the secularization of religious ritual, and hence as evincing an attenuated, if strategic, attachment to ceremonial traditions. Despite Richard's future-oriented plotting, his 'concern for legal niceties' shows his understanding that some traditional protocols must be followed, however cynically.[28]

While Carroll is surely right that Richard 'has contaminated everything' by showing the audience 'that these rituals [marriage, birth, death, lineal succession, and law] can be emptied out and made arbitrary', it is still the case that Richard cannot think his way past or around the legal repertoire.[29] When Richard invokes emergency powers to justify his execution of Hastings before London's Lord Mayor, his claim that circumstances license an exception to 'form of law' shows that even tyrants must pay lip service to legal traditions. 'What!' Richard exclaims in response to the Mayor's timid query,

> Think you we are Turks or infidels?
> Or that we would, against the form of law,
> Proceed thus rashly in the villain's death,
> But that the extreme peril of the case,
> The peace of England, and our persons' safety,
> Enforced us to this execution?
> *(III.5.41–6)*

His rationale that a state of emergency permits a quasi-sovereign exception shows that Richard acknowledges 'the form of law' as a set of customs honored in the breach.[30] He knows he must observe legal forms pertaining both to the written archive and to the gestural repertoire at least some of the time, if he is to secure the throne. But it is not enough to co-opt scriveners and lawyers. His title to the crown is so flimsy that he has to shore up all routes to legitimacy, not only strengthening his lineal inheritance by eliminating his rivals and securing dynastic alliances through marriage, but also by rigging a petition and popular election. He needs to obtain the appearance of the citizens' ratification—hence the scenes at the Guildhall and Baynard's Castle with the Mayor, the Aldermen, and their entourage. As Carroll remarks, 'No sooner has he emptied them [rites] of all cultural force, turned them inside out, than he tries to crawl back inside them himself,' unable to subsist without 'the empty shell of ritual'.[31] Richard depends on ritual even as he subverts it, displaying that mix of reverence and iconoclasm characteristic of ritual criticism.[32]

In *Richard II*, by contrast, the king has no use either for the laws or for popular approval. The play may be more ceremonial than *Richard III*, given its stately sequence of interrupted chivalric rituals, yet as a leader, Richard II shows less respect for legal ceremony than Richard III. Perhaps because he never doubts his legitimacy as God's anointed, Richard II feels no need to acknowledge the form of law or to be seen as complying with it.[33] Borrowing from Pierre Nora's work, one might say that Richard behaves for the first two acts as if he embodied in his person a *milieu de mémoire*, possessing 'an integrated, dictatorial memory—unselfconscious, commanding, all-powerful, spontaneously actualizing, a memory without a past that ceaselessly reinvents tradition, linking the history of its ancestors to the undifferentiated time of heroes, origins, and myth'.[34] As a *milieu de mémoire* in himself, Richard has no need to articulate his status as God's deputy protected by phalanxes of angels. Part of the journey he travels is discovering, not just that the king has two bodies, but also two memories, the second requiring effort and recitation.[35] This does not mean that Richard experiences a fall into history, realizing that he is only a congeries of 'sifted and sorted historical traces', what Nora calls *lieux de mémoire*. It means rather that he feels compelled to articulate a memory of majesty that he previously took for granted. He transmits the cultural memory of majesty in the embodied acts and language of ritual criticism, challenging the legal framework of his overthrow by devising a failed rite of succession.

As Richard II feels his power ebbing, he starts to perform his majesty, reviving the choreography of legitimacy available in cultural memory. Only then does he activate the gestural repertoire sustaining his royal identity. Tellingly, he is most engaged in performing the repertoire of kingship when he himself ceases to believe in the role—his theatricality rising as his conviction wanes. Richard's performances of ebbing majesty in III.2, III.3, and IV.1 draw on the resources of both the archive and the repertoire, defying neat categorization. They tap into a cultural reservoir of kingly gestures, patterned movements, symbolic codes, and story-telling mannerisms that help him rehearse his identity. But the more he insists on his majesty, the more skeptical doubt besets him. These performances constitute what Stanley Cavell calls a skeptical recital: an enunciation of conditions, criteria, and tests whereby 'the passive skeptic' tries to make himself known to others and to himself.[36] Richard's skepticism toward his majesty culminates in his theatrical parody of the coronation rite. Unlike Richard III, whose gleeful mockery of the rites of succession propels his meteoric rise, Richard II levels his ritual criticism in a mood of vindictive despair.

In lieu of a coronation, the play offers an exquisitely manipulative counter-ritual whereby Richard uncrowns himself before his own Parliament, saying yes, but meaning no to the transfer of power. 'Seize the crown', Richard snarls at the climax of the play, orchestrating its most emblematic gesture: 'Here, cousin, | On this side my hand, and on that side thine' (IV.1.182–83). He lifts the crown high, offering it to Bolingbroke, perhaps retracting it so as to make his cousin reach for it, teasing him. Then, with the two men clasping the crown—a gesture fraught with tension since with the slightest jerk of the hand, their bodily poise threatens to devolve into a tug of war—Richard dilates the moment with a cascade of chiastic similes and metaphors, most famously the image of two buckets, one rising, the other falling. How long the actors hold that position with the crown between them, perhaps aloft, is a matter of choice. Perhaps Bolingbroke lets go of the rim sooner rather than later, recognizing the unseemliness of the posture into which Richard has maneuvered him. But we know Richard has resumed possession of the crown by the time he utters, 'I give this heavy weight from off my head' (204), a gesture that may require both hands given the heaviness (whether metaphorical or real) of the prop.

Between these two emblematic gestures lies space for physical improvisation. Because the bodies of the actors are not scripted, improvisation permits both the weak and the strong to develop tactics and strategies. In this scenario, Richard's tactics—however they manifest themselves physically—contest the legality of his deposition. Bolingbroke says, 'I thought you had been willing to resign', and moments later repeats, 'Are you contented to resign the crown?' (190, 200). Richard chokes on the word, resign, responding with a set of aural puns and chiastic figures that capture his indecision and self-division: 'Ay, no. No, ay; for I must nothing be. | Therefore, no "no", for I resign to thee' (201–02). The 'ay' may register as both 'I' and 'aaiiee', while the 'no' may register as 'know', creating a tongue-twister synchronized with improvised gestures relating to the crown. In a memorable performance Michael Pennington cradled the prop possessively, made as if to relinquish it, then drew it to his chest again, all the while swaying and shaking his hulking head from side to side. But whatever an actor chooses to do here, the freedom to improvise the power transfer is dangerous—reason alone for the scene to have been omitted from the first three Quarto editions.

The improvisational body language developed in response to the crown as a prop shifts in tone during the next sequence when Richard taps into the collective memory of royal coronations and consecrations. Harry Levin calls it 'a ritual [...] uniquely improvised, a coronation in reverse, wherein every intimate gesture reinforces an attitude of widening detachment from his consecrated grandeur'.[37] But unlike the immediately previous improvisation, with the two contenders dancing around the crown, this sequence depends on a scripted, even archival, order of events. Richard relies not merely on the putative memory of his own coronation as an eleven-year-old in 1377, but on a shared cultural memory of coronation rituals to produce the hallucinatory effects of his discoronation. Holinshed writes of the historical Richard in 1377: 'The archbishop came unto him, and tearing his garments from the highest part to the lowest, stripped him to his shirt'.[38] However he is costumed upon arriving at Westminster, the theatrical Richard now undresses himself, peeling off one symbolic garment after another in a reversal of investiture. 'Now mark me how I will undo myself,' he begins. 'I give this heavy weight from off my head, | And this unwieldy sceptre from my hand' (203–05). To whom does he turn over the crown and scepter? Robert M. Schuler assumes that Richard 'takes each semisacred object from the Officers and hands it' to Bolingbroke who must 'awkwardly put it aside, demonstrating that he is *unable, unauthorized* to wear Richard's crown or hold his scepter'.[39] Schuler follows Charles R. Forker in speculating that these ritual objects are presented on a 'ceremonial pillow' carried by an 'Officer'.[40] But the text stipulates neither pillow nor officers any more than it stipulates the person to whom Richard hands these objects. If the idea is to stage a faithful undoing of the coronation rite, then the recipient of these props should be the Archbishop of Canterbury, but he is absent from Shakespeare's play. The disjunction between whoever receives the props and the Archbishop foregrounds the invented quality of this counter-ritual.[41] As Grimes observes, invented rituals often arise in response to troubled rituals and their infelicitous performances. Grimes adapts John Austin's speech-act theory in his taxonomy of ritual infelicities.

Richard is engaged in an illocutionary act, to borrow Austin's terms, inasmuch as his language enacts his undoing in the very moment of utterance. While this speech-act may derive from a memory of a ritual formula—Walter Pater says it comes from 'the Roman Pontifical, of which the order of Coronation is really a part'[42]—it is repurposed in hopes of shaming his enemies. If its performance is felicitous, not only will he uncrown himself, but he will expose the fraudulence of the Lancastrians' judicial process. Richard's divestiture therefore shifts into a more abstract register, mingling symbolic props with less material tokens of sovereignty:

> With mine own tears I wash away my balm,
> With mine own hands I give away my crown,
> With mine own tongue deny my sacred state,
> With mine own breath release all duteous oaths.
> All pomp and majesty I do forswear;
> My manors, rents, revenues I forgo;
> My acts, decrees and statutes I deny.
> (IV.1.207–13)

The anaphora of the first four lines and the caesurae give this passage a ritualistic pacing. The parallelism between "manors, rents, revenues" and "acts, decrees, and statutes" reveals Richard's continuing view of the law as a personal instrument of power. Michael Pennington spat out the lines, incredulous that he had been reduced to uttering them and yet determined to coil his verbal magic around his enemies and strangle them.

Richard's ritualized denial of the law prompts Northumberland to come forward with paperwork. 'Read o'er these articles', he tells Richard, warning him that unless he 'read[s] o'er this paper', 'the commons will not then be satisfied' (243, 269, 272). What sort of prop does he thrust at Richard? Might the 'paper' resemble the Scrivener's? Northumberland insists that Richard confess his crimes 'against the state and profit of this land' so that 'the souls of men | May deem [him] [...] worthily deposed' (225–27). David Norbrook defends Northumberland, arguing that 'in the deposition scene he is more keen than Bullingbrook to keep attention on constitutional issues as opposed to Richard's personal emotions'. But while Norbrook may be right that Northumberland offers 'the audience a perspective' related to 'a discourse of the aristocratic, and occasionally of the common good' which mitigates 'any simple dualism between Richard and Bullingbrook', surely Northumberland also offers a perspective into yet another form of ritual improvisation, this time involving the archive.[43] Like Buckingham in *Richard III*, Northumberland is concerned with securing the appearance of legitimacy in the transfer of power. He understands the importance of manufacturing a paper trail in achieving that end. As in *Richard III*, the paper trail preserved in the archives, clearing the new regime of usurpation, invokes the Commons' demands for reform.

Richard defers the legitimizing spectacle involved in reading Northumberland's articles by requesting a looking-glass, a prop which produces the play's second most emblematic *coup de théatre*. Richard's tactics with the mirror marshal an array of cultural memories. His gestural repertoire is barely retrievable, but it doubtless tapped into an iconography of vanity well represented in morality plays, paintings, books of hours, church sculptures and bas-reliefs, not to mention classical mythology as relayed, for example, in Ovid's *Metamorphoses*. Perhaps audience and actors retained some memory of Lucifer's preening before a mirror in the York Corpus Christi play; perhaps they remembered the mirror proffered by Sensual Suggestion in the Protestant morality play, *The Conflict of Conscience*. Richard's lines, however, give us one certain point of repair. When addressing his reflection in the mirror and asking, 'Was this face the face | That every day under his household roof | Did keep ten thousand men? Was this the face | That like the sun did make beholders wink?' (281–84), the actor, Richard Burbage, may well have mimicked Edward Alleyn's impersonation of Marlowe's Doctor Faustus. Perhaps

Burbage held the mirror before him in a pose designed to evoke Faustus's words to the ghost of Helen of Troy ('Was this the face that launched a thousand ships?'). Certainly his performance of Richard's self-division, with its mingling of self-love and self-hate, would have called up a memory of Faustus's last hurrah before his descent to hell. These satanic echoes militate against the Christological imagery Richard invokes in an effort to paint himself as martyr and victim, producing a cognitive dissonance inviting skepticism.[44]

The dissonant symbology and complex performative genealogies of these ritualizing scenarios confirm Grimes's point that 'criticism is not only of rites but by rites'.[45] Rites themselves enact criticism thanks to their reflexivity. As Grimes explains in terms both Richards would understand, the ritualizing body is 'creative, cognitive, critical'[46]; therefore, 'ritual has its edge, its ways of judging, of saying Yea and Nay'.[47]

Places of memory

Given that the art of memory is activated by the ordering of places, *loci*, to what extent does place incite cultural memories of the legal repertoire in *Richard II* and *Richard III*? The Tower of London, for example, functions in both plays as a terrifying locus of incarceration, the last stop before execution. In *Richard II* Queen Isabel calls it 'Julius Caesar's ill-erected tower' (V.1.2), while in *Richard III* young Prince Edward says, 'I do not like the Tower, of any place' (III.1.68). He is resisting his uncle's sinister suggestion that he stay there. Never mind that the Tower was thought to offer protection to royal incumbents prior to their coronations or that it was part of the ritual to start the coronation procession at the Tower which ended at Westminster Abbey.[48] In early modern drama, Kristen Deiter argues, the Tower became such a potent symbol of violence that theater audiences brought a collective memory of 'the Tower plays' to any given performance. Shakespeare addresses these memories when he has Prince Edward ask Buckingham about Caesar's supposed building of the Tower. Their conversation raises the question of the origins of cultural memory—understood here in Jan Assman's sense of the *longue durée*. Cultural memories of the Tower's origins, it transpires, emerge from a patchwork of rumor and report, archive and repertoire combined. The overall effect of the exchange induces a healthy skepticism about memory, including *loci memoriae*.

It is all the more significant, then, that Shakespeare departs from his sources and shifts the scene of Richard II's resignation from the Tower, where it in fact occurred, to Westminster Hall, the locus of Parliament. Jean-Christophe Mayer claims that the change of venue sends 'discreet political or even confessional signals', enhancing 'the oppositional discourses' that 'like powerful undercurrents' traverse the scene. Mayer suggests that Shakespeare may have been 'following Stow's version of events', noting that John 'Stow is unique among the chroniclers in the stress he appears to lay on the deciding role of Parliament and on the notion of "election"'.[49] Patterson, however, believes that Holinshed also 'did everything he could to imply that "Parliament", kingless or not, was in fact the scene, the spirit, and the instrument of the deposition'.[50] In my view, Shakespeare makes this change because he wants to foreground the legal setting and the legal repertoire set into motion by the deposition. Locating the deposition in Westminster permits Richard's ferocious play on the word, 'convey', his parting shot as Bolingbroke orders him conveyed to the Tower (IV.1.315–16). The shift in venue also makes the audience, standing in for the Commons, complicit in Northumberland's request that Richard read the articles aloud. The people are thus reminded of their role in ousting Richard and of the powers wielded in their name. Once more, Shakespeare may be signaling the commons' timidity and failure to influence events.

If Shakespeare had staged the scene in the Tower, the coercive nature of Bolingbroke's usurpation would have been emphasized. This, in turn, would have diminished the mysterious psychology of Richard's surrender and upset the delicate balance between the two antagonists. It would also have brought out the oligarchic nature of the coup. By setting the scene in Parliament, Shakespeare insists on the legality of the power transfer—or rather on the Lancastrian need for the appearance of legality. As Bolingbroke puts it, 'Fetch hither Richard, that in common view | He may surrender; so we shall proceed | Without suspicion' (IV.1.155–56).

The shift in venue, furthermore, helps Shakespeare put political and dramaturgical distance between himself and Marlowe's handling of the deposition scene in *Edward II*. Edward II, in Killingworth Castle, also plays dilatory games with his crown, donning and doffing it, when he is asked to resign. Sir William Trussel impatiently repeats, 'My lord, the Parliament must have present news, | And therefore say, will you resign or no?' (V.1.84–85). This prompts the stage direction, 'The King rageth', recalling perhaps memories of Herod raging in the streets in the York mystery play. Edward recovers enough to retort, 'Elect, conspire, install, do what you will', as if election, conspiracy, and installation were interchangeable 'treacheries' (V.1.88–89). If Shakespeare could not hope to overreach Marlowe's murder scene of Edward, he could overtop the deposition scene. Moving it to Westminster Hall where audiences might imagine themselves as the assembled estates of the realm formed part of his strategy.

Brian Cummings has recently challenged the view that 'counterfeit rituals'—that is, rituals performed on stage—are a sign of secularization. These staged ceremonies, Cummings argues, have a mimetic quality that complicates any binary pitting ritual participation against theatrical spectatorship. This mimetic relation means that audiences are, as Diana Taylor insists, forced to situate themselves in relation to the scenario. It does not follow that audiences are cool or dispassionate, as if secularization involved an evacuation of feeling. When Richard II reverses the order of the coronation, undoing himself with sarcastic panache even while describing himself as betrayed like Christ, he seeks to kill belief in the legality of Bolingbroke's takeover, exposing it as usurpation. Yet we pity his losses, awed by the brilliant fireworks of his self-destruction. Our experience of 'disillusion' about his sanctity is not cerebral but tumultuous, manifested in 'complex feelings of mourning and loss' about leadership and legitimacy.[51] Likewise, our disillusion with London's citizens in *Richard III* inspires emotion: exasperation and pity, followed by individual and communal resolve. Ritual criticism thus demonstrates ritual's continuing power. 'Enchantment is held in constructive tension with disenchantment,' Grimes observes[52], such that 'a highly reflexive, largely aesthetic consciousness' can coexist with 'second naïveté', a phrase Grimes borrows from Paul Ricoeur.[53] Ritual criticism thus enriches ritual practice.

That said, the creative inversions performed in ritual criticism may well reveal secularization in action. In writing about the funeral procession at the start of *Richard III*, Cummings observes that 'what is represented is not so much a funeral as a deliberate travesty of one'.[54] Surely this is as true of Richard III's election as of Richard II's deposition. We witness a travesty of a rite, that is, a fictional performance of a historical ceremony designed to elicit doubt about the legality of the power transfer. In each case, the invented rite is modeled on an older religious one that it parodies in a daring—and secular—act of overwriting: a bishop's investiture and a coronation. The cultural memory of these religious ceremonies accompanies the counterfeit rites, surfacing in a gestural repertoire that both recalls and mocks their antecedents. That repertoire extends to others in the legal drama, including the commons who perform their disenfranchisement with disarming nonchalance. Ritual criticism, Ronald Grimes reminds us, seeks to instigate reform and resist exploitation. By criticizing rites of succession, perhaps Shakespeare hoped that playgoers would leave the theater alive to their civic responsibilities, aware of the legal avenues at their disposal, ready to make their political voices heard. By conjuring cultural memories of the legal repertoire and cultivating the audience's skeptical judgment, he may have hoped to spark the imagination of new political rites.

Notes

1 Thanks to Theodore Leinwand and Deborah Payne for their comments and suggestions on a prior version of this paper.
2 Ronald L. Grimes, *Ritual Criticism* (Columbia: University of South Carolina Press, 1990), p. 18.
3 Ibid., p. 1.
4 Sir Henry Wotton, *Life and Letters of Sir Henry Wotton*, ed. by Logan Pearsall Smith, vol. II (Oxford: Clarendon Press, 1907), pp. 32–33.
5 Stephen Greenblatt, *Shakespearean Negotiations* (Berkeley: University of California Press, 1988), p. 127. Brian Walsh goes further, suggesting that the history play as a genre solicits 'an acceptance that can never fully "take" and thus produces a suspension of absolute belief or absolute skepticism toward history and the possibilities of historical knowledge'. See Brian Walsh, *Shakespeare, the Queen's Men, and the Elizabethan Performance of History* (Cambridge: Cambridge University Press, 2009), p. 208.
6 Brian Cummings, '"Dead March": Liturgy and Mimesis in Shakespeare's Funerals', *Shakespeare*, 8 (2012), 368–85 (p. 370).
7 Recent studies of *Richard III* and *Richard II* have emphasized mourning rituals and the role of ceremony in the post-Reformation period (e.g. Cummings, Döring, Goodland, Kerremann, Marche). Some take a Benjaminian approach and view Richard II as a tyrant/martyr typical of a Baroque *Trauerspiel* (e.g. Baldo, Lorenz, Luis-Martinez, Donovan Sherman). Others investigate the plays' negotiations with collective memory, focusing on group identities across time rather than traumatic rupture (e.g. Aleida Assmann, Dawson, Ivic, Schwyzer). Of course, mourning rituals cannot be disentwined from collective memory, but in recent scholarship these approaches have tended to diverge.
8 Jan Assman, *Religion and Cultural Memory* (Stanford, CA: Stanford University Press, 2006), p. 8.
9 Diana Taylor, *The Archive and the Repertoire: Performing Cultural Memory in the Americas* (Durham, NC: Duke University Press, 2003), pp. 20–21.
10 Ibid., p. 22.
11 Ibid., p. 23.
12 Ibid., p. 13.
13 Ibid., p. 31.
14 See René Girard, *Violence and the Sacred*, 1972, trans. by Patrick Gregory (Baltimore, MD: Johns Hopkins University Press, 1977) and Naomi Conn Liebler, 'The Mockery King of Snow: *Richard II* and the Sacrifice of Ritual', in *True Rites and Maimed Rites: Ritual and Anti-Ritual in Shakespeare and His Age*, ed. by Linda Woodbridge and Edward Berry (Urbana and Chicago: University of Illinois Press, 1992), pp. 220-29.
15 Harry Berger, Jr, *Imaginary Audition: Shakespeare on Stage and Page* (Berkeley: University of California Press, 1989), p. 46.
16 Cf. 'In the famous fifteenth-century pictures of the law courts which hang in the Library of the Inner Temple, the clerks are shown holding membranes' (Thornley, xxvii) cited in W.F. Bolton, 'Ricardian Law Reports and *Richard II*', *Shakespeare Studies*, 20 (1988), 53–65 (p. 54). More describes the 'proclamacion' of Hasting's death as a 'parchment' (54).
17 Lawrence Verney, 'The Office of Recorder of the City of London', *Transactions of the Guildhall Historical Association*, 8.9 (2000), 1–7. www.guildhallhistoricalassociation.org.uk/docs/The%20Office%20of%20Recorder%20of%20the%20City%20of%20London.pdf [accessed 6/22/2015] (3).
18 *Narrative and Dramatic Sources of Shakespeare*, ed. by Geoffrey Bullough, 8 vols (London: Routledge and Kegan Paul, 1957–75) III (1960), p. 226.
19 Bullough, III, 274 and Thomas More, *Complete Works*, 15 vols (New Haven, CT: Yale University Press, 1963), II: *The History of Richard III*, ed. by Richard S. Sylvester, p. 75.
20 Bullough, III, 275.
21 More, II, 76.
22 See Anita Gilman Sherman, *Skepticism and Memory in Shakespeare and Donne* (New York: Palgrave Macmillan, 2007), pp. 122–41.

23 See David Weil Baker, 'Jacobean Historiography and the Election of Richard III', *HLQ*, 70 (2007), 311–42. Baker explains,

> the Parliament of Richard III had ratified a pre-coronation petition urging Richard III to take the throne by 'lawful election' of the 'three states assembled' as well as by 'inheritance'. But there were problems with this petition, the text of which was included in the parliamentary act. For as the act itself acknowledged, the assembly of the three estates, which had petitioned Richard to become king in 1483, was an irregular one, not 'in form of parliament', and this irregularity had led to 'divers doubts, questions, and ambiguities'. Hence, it was necessary for Parliament to ratify the petition, in order to make 'most feithe and certaine' and to remove 'occasion of all doubts' about Richard's succession.
>
> *(p. 313)*

While Shakespeare would not have known about the Act, 'one of the more remarkable discoveries' published by William Camden in the 1607 edition of *Britannia*, Baker notes that 'More knew of the Act of Settlement' (313–14). I suggest that More's repeated use of the word election caught Shakespeare's attention and helped shape the contours of III.7.

24 More II, 82.
25 Annabel Patterson, *Reading Holinshed's* Chronicles (Chicago: University of Chicago Press, 1994), p. 208.
26 More II, 80–81.
27 Bradin Cormack, *A Power to Do Justice: Jurisdiction, English Literature, and the Rise of Common Law, 1509–1635* (Chicago: University of Chicago Press, 2007), pp. 88–90.
28 William C. Carroll, '"The Form of Law": Ritual and Succession in *Richard III*', in *True Rites and Maimed Rites*, ed. by Woodbridge and Berry, pp. 203–19 (pp. 204–05).
29 Ibid., p. 215.
30 See Giorgio Agamben, Homo Sacer: *Sovereign Power and Bare Life*, 1995, trans. by Daniel Heller-Roazen (Stanford, CA: Stanford University Press, 1998) and Carl Schmitt, *Political Theology*, 1922, trans. by George Schwag (Chicago: University of Chicago Press, 2005).
31 Carroll, p. 210.
32 Grimes, p. 137.
33 See Edna Zwick Boris, *Shakespeare's English Kings, the People, and the Law* (New Jersey: Fairleigh Dickinson University Press, 1978); Donna B. Hamilton, 'The State of Law in *Richard II*', *Shakespeare Quarterly*, 34 (1983), 5–17; William O. Scott, 'Landholding, Leasing, and Inheritance in *Richard II*', *SEL*, 42 (2002), 275–92.
34 Pierre Nora, 'Between Memory and History: *Les Lieux de Mémoire*', *Representations*, 26 (1989), 7–25 (p. 8).
35 Ernst H. Kantorowicz, *The King's Two Bodies: A Study in Medieval Political Theology* (Princeton, NJ: Princeton University Press, 1957), pp. 24–41.
36 Stanley Cavell, *The Claim of Reason: Wittgenstein, Skepticism, Morality, and Tragedy* (Oxford: Oxford University Press, 1979), pp. 444–47.
37 Harry Levin, 'Sitting upon the Ground (*Richard II*, iv.i)', in *Shakespeare's Universe: Renaissance Ideas and Conventions; Essays in Honor of W. R. Elton,* ed. by John Mucciolo (Aldershot, UK: Scholar Press, 1996), pp. 3–20 (p. 14).
38 Raphael Holinshed, *Holinshed's Chronicles*, ed. by Henry Ellis, 6 vols (London: J. Johnson, 1807–08), II, 713.
39 Robert M. Shuler, 'Magic Mirrors in *Richard II*', *Comparative Drama*, 38 (2004), 151–81 (p. 159).
40 Ibid., p. 157.
41 Richard's deposition occurred over three days. Three delegations—the first two headed by Northumberland, the last by Bolingbroke—visited him in the Tower until he agreed to resign. On 30 September 1399, in Richard's absence, Parliament, led partly by Thomas Arundel, the Archbishop of Canterbury, approved the resignation, thereby deposing the King. See Nigel Saul, *Richard II* (New Haven: Yale University Press, 1997), pp. 420–22.
42 See Walter Pater, *Walter Pater: Three Major Texts*, ed. by William E. Buckler (New York: New York University Press, 1986), p. 515.
43 David Norbrook, '"A Liberal Tongue": Language and Rebellion in *Richard II*', in *Shakespeare's Universe*, ed. by Mucciolo, pp. 37–51 (p. 46).
44 Compare Schuler.
45 Grimes, p. 228.
46 Ronald L. Grimes, 'Reinventing Ritual', *Soundings*, 75 (1992), 21–41 (p. 32).

47 Grimes, *Ritual Criticism*, p. 233.
48 Kristen Deiter, *The Tower of London in English Renaissance Drama: Icon of Opposition* (New York: Routledge, 2008), pp. 38, 44.
49 Jean-Christophe Mayer, 'The "Parliament Sceane" in Shakespeare's *King Richard II*', *XVII–XVIII, Bulletin de la société d'etudes anglo-americaines des XVIIe et XVIIIe siècles*, 59 (2004), 27–42 (pp. 33, 43).
50 Patterson, p. 114.
51 Cummings, pp. 377, 382.
52 Grimes, 'Reinventing Ritual', p. 32.
53 Grimes, *Ritual Criticism*, pp. 97, 135.
54 Cummings, p. 373.

PART IV

Comedy

16

MEMORY AND SUBJECTIVE CONTINUITY IN *AS YOU LIKE IT* AND *ALL'S WELL THAT ENDS WELL*

Erin Minear

When Rosalind discovers Orlando's poems scattered about the forest, she remarks wryly, 'I was never so berhymed since Pythagoras' time that I was an Irish rat, which I can hardly remember' (III.2.172–73).[1] Pretending belief in the theory of metempsychosis, Rosalind imagines her soul having transmigrated from body to body over millennia, from a time so distant that she has almost—but not quite—forgotten it. Her memory thus stretches back far beyond her identity as 'Rosalind' (or 'Ganymede', as the case may be). She's joking; but the joke is peculiarly apt given the questions about memory and identity swirling through *As You Like It*. In Rosalind's fancy, her sense of herself as 'I' goes back to the time when 'I was an Irish rat': a time when 'I' was someone else (and something else) entirely. No one in the play undergoes metempsychosis, but many undergo transformations almost as complete. There are ways of being someone else without being reborn as a rat. In this play, a transmigration from one age to another, one guise to another, can be quite as transformative. Any sense of subjective continuity depends on memory, but memory can also make us uncomfortably aware of how different we once were.

Garrett Sullivan has argued that while social identity in many early modern texts is constructed by 'remembering' one's fixed place and the proper behaviors said to go with it, self-forgetfulness 'makes possible the production of a distinctive interiority, a subjectivity outside of ideology'.[2] To forget oneself is to reject propriety for desire. Sullivan observes that, while in tragedy the crises of identity brought about by self-forgetting almost always end in catastrophe, a certain amount of forgetfulness is salutary, even necessary, in a comedy. In *As You Like It*, forgetfulness and desire ultimately lead to the recuperation of the social order, as Zackariah Long suggests. Rosalind may learn to forget a banished father in her love for Orlando, but she is also aware when she falls in love that her own father loved Orlando's father 'as his soul' (I.2.24).[3] In *All's Well That Ends Well*, Helena's forgetfulness of father and social position also leads to the perpetuation of the social order when she is finally gathered into Bertram's family (though *All's Well That Ends Well* stretches to the limit the ability of audiences and characters to forget).[4]

While social identity and a 'forgetful' subjectivity clash only to come to an uneasy alliance in both these plays, the two dramas also explore the problem of subjective continuity. After all, the act of remembering may involve more than recalling one's proper place in the world. We also remember or forget our own actions of the day before, and how we felt when we performed them. Reconciling yesterday's emotions with today's can be just as difficult as reconciling desire with social identity, as Demetrius discovers in *A Midsummer Night's Dream*. Trying to make sense of the transfer of his affections from one woman to another, he offers a somewhat contradictory explanation of the night's events:

> But, my good lord, I wot not by what power—
> But by some power it is—my love to Hermia,
> Melted as the snow, seems to me now
> As the remembrance of an idle gaud
> Which in my childhood I did dote upon,
> And all the faith, the virtue of my heart,
> The object and the pleasure of mine eye
> Is only Helena. To her, my lord,
> Was I betrothed ere I saw Hermia.
> But like in sickness did I loathe this food;
> But, as in health come to my natural taste,
> Now I do wish it, love it, long for it,
> And will for evermore be true to it.
> *(IV.1.161–73)*

At first he compares his vanished love for Hermia to a childhood fancy, melted as naturally and inevitably as the snow in the changing of the seasons at his growth to maturity. But then, he emphasizes that his love for Helena predated the attraction to Hermia; and in his new comparison he returns, after an interim of inexplicable illness, to his 'natural taste'. He struggles, in other words, with two different ways of understanding and remembering his own history. In one version, child-Demetrius at some point, mysteriously, becomes adult-Demetrius, and looks back in confusion at the 'idle gaud[s]' that once enraptured him, remembering that he found them attractive, but unable to remember why. In the other version, which he seems to find more satisfying, his story is one of consistency, broken by one bizarre aberration. He projects this consistency into the future, promising that his desires 'now' will remain true 'for evermore', and Theseus suggests a triple wedding ceremony.

Demetrius's experience is hardly unique. Comedies are driven by what Northrop Frye describes as 'constant change, the principle of giddiness in life which enables people to take up and discard their moods, their attitudes, their prejudices, and their affections'.[5] The typical comic plot is shaped by the demands of the form, rather than by a need for consistent characterization, in what David Scott Kastan calls 'a logic of comedy rather than of character'.[6] In a further twist, Shakespeare's comedies often show how consistency of character bends before social demands, the expectation for people to play certain parts: the lover, the soldier; the maiden, the wife. Such consistency also suffers internal pressures, the demands of inconsistent, contradictory passions. Nevertheless, even the most puppet-like characters in Shakespeare's comedies will attempt to explain their actions and passions in terms of a coherent, consistent selfhood, insisting on subjective continuity despite all evidence to the contrary. From his act four perspective, Demetrius invents the best story he can in order to go on seeing himself as essentially coherent. In other plays, the audience may be constructing similar stories. After all, in order for us to perceive a comedic ending as satisfactory, we must be able to accept the closing marriages as permanent satisfactions of desire. On some level, both characters and audience must believe that the final pairings will last 'for evermore'.

As You Like It and *All's Well That Ends Well* place particular pressure on questions of memory and identity. Both plays ask: how much do our memories of our personal past, our experience, shape who we are? Both also assume that this question cannot be answered without determining to what degree memories are truly 'past' at all. To what degree is remembering like experiencing? Does memory connect you with your past self or alienate you from a past self that had different interests and desires? In these 'comic' narratives, such questions are important not just because of what the answers imply about the possibilities for lasting happiness, but because any connection between two characters, or between audience and characters, depends upon some sharing of emotional experience. It is a truism that to know, or think you know, what others feel, you must have felt what they are feeling. Such a seemingly simple equation is complicated, though, if that 'you' in the past is, in fact, someone else, and not at all the 'you' in the present. Through narratives like Demetrius's, it gradually becomes clear that to make sense of one's self requires as much imaginative reconstruction as to make sense of someone else, for the simple reason that the past self often *was* 'someone else'. In As You Like It, selves can seem alarmingly discontinuous; but in the best cases, understanding or at least tolerance—even transformation— are possible when memory is used as the basis for imagining the experience of strangers, whether these strangers be former selves or other people. In *All's Well That Ends Well*, however, acts of recollection and acts of imagination become too close for comfort.

"Twas I, but 'tis not I'

A play that begins 'As I remember, Adam' immediately focuses our attention on memory. Strikingly, however, the words are at odds with the stage picture: a young man and an old man enter together, the latter's elderliness underlined by his name, but it is the *young* man who is unfolding his memory to the old. Orlando's speech is a transparent device to provide the audience with the back-story, but it also sets up a series of elements: the young and the old and their relationship to one another, the connection between memory and identity, and the continuity of the past with the present. Oliver threatens this continuity by neglecting his father's wishes and mistreating the brother whom old Adam addresses, 'O you memory / Of old Sir Rowland' (II.3.3–4). The play explores questions of continuity in familial and generational terms, as Orlando's memory of his father and his sense of his father within himself create a tension with his social position as the younger son.[7] But the story also focuses on the continuity, or discontinuity, of past and present *within* the self.

The play appears to set up an emblematic encounter when Rosalind announces, 'Look you, who comes here—a young man and an old in solemn talk' (II .4.15–16). Rosalind does not yet know these characters by name, and so has no more specific way to refer to them; nevertheless, her line sets up an encounter between Youth and Age, rather than between two individuals. And indeed, their conversation appears to represent general perspectives: the passion of the young lover, and the detached wisdom of experience.

> SILVIUS O Corin, that thou knew'st how I do love her!
> CORIN I partly guess; for I have loved ere now.
> SILVIUS No, Corin, being old thou canst not guess,
>   Though in thy youth thou wast as true a lover
>   As ever sighed upon a midnight pillow.
>   *(II.4.20–24)*

Silvius's desire for another to know his experience, from the inside, re-emerges later in Rosalind's exclamation to Celia: 'O coz, coz, coz, my pretty little coz, that thou didst know how many fathom deep I am in love! But it cannot be sounded' (IV.1.193–95).

Part of the humor of the exchange lies in Silvius's insistence that no one ever loved as he does, couched in the same terms everyone uses to insist that no one ever loved as they do. As the perfect pattern of the Young Shepherd in Love, there is nothing unique about him. Silvius considers it a foregone conclusion that Corin cannot understand his feelings; furthermore, despite beginning with the wish that Corin could 'know' how he loves Phoebe, he doesn't wish anything of the kind, as Corin's knowledge would make his own experience less singular. So far, so predictable. But the exchange also opens up a series of questions about knowledge, experience, and subjectivity. Corin can only know how Silvius loves if Corin himself has felt the same emotion. The old shepherd has 'loved ere now', and so can 'partly guess'. But Silvius abruptly changes the terms of the discussion. Not only can Corin not know, he cannot guess: he's old. Silvius's objection is hardly an original one, but it raises troubling possibilities. Corin thinks he can know Silvius because of his past experience; but Silvius claims that no matter what Corin's experience was—even if he was 'as true a lover / As ever sighed on midnight pillow'—he can neither know nor guess anything of Silvius's current state, because he is not experiencing love *now*. Corin claims a continuous identity that builds upon itself, recalling past experiences in order to weigh and understand new events and other people. But as far as Silvius is concerned, current Corin and mythical young Corin are two completely different people.

Silvius, however, goes on pushing at the idea of likeness between himself and Corin, if only to close down its possibility.

> But if thy love were ever like to mine—
> As sure I think did never man love so—
> How many actions most ridiculous
> Hast thou been drawn to by thy fantasy?
> CORIN Into a thousand that I have forgotten.
> SILVIUS O, thou didst then never love so heartily.
> If thou rememberest not the slightest folly
> That ever love did make thee run into,
> Thou hast not loved.
>
> *(II.4.25–33)*

Corin's sense of continuous identity is untroubled—perhaps even reinforced—by forgetting. He remembers enough to know that he *has* forgotten a thousand follies. And indeed, he speaks in order to emphasize his authority and knowledge: he's done so much for love it is impossible to remember everything. In response, Silvius undercuts his own previous argument. He has just claimed that memory is an insufficient way for Corin to truly understand what he, Silvius, is now experiencing, even if Corin was once an equally true lover. Now he claims that Corin could never have been such a true lover if he *cannot* fully remember the experience. Before, memory was inadequate to comprehend passion; now memory is the measure of passion. (And of course, Silvius has no way of knowing if he will remember the details of his passion for Phoebe when he reaches Corin's age.) Silvius blurs the distinction between remembered and immediate feeling: to allow any distance from the present state is to forget and to forget is to be a different person.

While Silvius may find an insufficiently empathetic audience in Corin, he is overheard by two other characters whose responses further develop the scene's attention to memory and subjective experience. 'Alas, poor shepherd,' exclaims Rosalind, 'searching of thy wound, / I have by hard adventure found mine own' (II.4.41–42). Rosalind is not a passive listener; she describes her eavesdropping as active investigation, a searching of Silvius's wound, which turns out, in a startling moment of identification, to be her own. She does 'know' how Silvius loves; or at least, she is able to imagine, based on his words, that he loves as she does. Then

Touchstone chimes in:

> And I mine. I remember when I was in love I broke my sword upon a stone and bid him take that for coming a-night to Jane Smile, and I remember the kissing of her batlet, and the cow's dugs that her pretty chapped hands had milked; and I remember the wooing of a peascod instead of her, from whom I took two cods, and giving her them again, said with weeping tears, 'Wear these for my sake.' We that are true lovers run into strange capers. But as all is mortal in nature, so is all nature in love mortal in folly.
>
> *(II.4.43–52)*

Touchstone immediately blurs the distinction between being in love and remembering having been in love. His first words suggest that he, too, is wounded like Rosalind and Silvius, but his next sentence—'I remember when I was in love ...'—places this wound firmly in the past. He appears to be riffing on Silvius's claim that one who has truly loved will not forget even 'the slightest folly' acted in love's service, as he catalogs a whole list of absurdities: 'I remember ... and I remember ... and I remember'. This series of recollections thus justifies his inclusion in the category of 'we that are true lovers'. Yet he remembers these follies with evident irony, and implicitly takes a more dubious view of passion than the forgetful Corin. Silvius has overlooked the possibility of looking back sardonically, finding a younger self ridiculous and yet claiming that younger self—if indeed that is what Touchstone is doing when he speaks of 'we that are true lovers'.

An old shepherd and a young engage in a similar, if much lengthier, dialogue in Thomas Lodge's *Rosalynde*, Shakespeare's main source. Suggestively, however, *As You Like It*'s emphasis on memory and empathetic knowledge is absent. The two characters are more starkly opposed, and even more firmly rooted in the limited identities of 'a young man and an old'. While Shakespeare's Corin adopts a pragmatic approach, pointing out that Silvius's behavior will only make Phoebe continue to scorn him, Lodge's Coridon takes an admonitory stance, as he urges his companion to 'follow mine arreede, / (Whome age hath taught the traynes that fancie useth) / Leave foolish love; for beautie wit abuseth'.[8] For his part, Lodge's young lover shows no interest in the question of the old man's possible memories.

> Ah Coridon, though manie be thy yeares,
> And crooked elde hath some experience left;
> Yet is thy mind of judgement quite bereft
> In view of love, whose power in me appears.
>
> The ploughman little wots to turne the pen,
> Or bookeman skills to guide the ploughmans cart,
> Nor can the cobler count the tearmes of Art,
> Nor base men judge the thoughts of mightie men;
>
> Nor withered age (unmeete for beauties guide,
> Uncapable of loves impression)
> Discourse of that, whose choice possession
> May never to so base a man be tied.
>
> But I (whom nature makes of tender molde,
> And youth most pliant yeeldes to fancies fire)
> Doo builde my haven and heaven on sweet desire,
> On sweete desire more deere to me than golde.[9]

Experience is useless, because an old man has no more judgment in affairs of love than a cobbler has in the arts. Such lack is physiological; an old man is 'uncapable of loves impression', while a youth of 'tender molde' is pliant and yielding. The language suggests images often associated with memory: the impression in the mind, the need for yielding material in which to make the impression. But Lodge's lover makes no claim about Coridon's memory. His age cannot take impressions, and therefore he cannot have any sense of love. The question over whether *past* love may have left an impression from his youth never arises. Each of Lodge's speakers speaks from a fixed position. Shakespeare's characters, on the other hand, are in dynamic relation, both approaching one another and withdrawing. Corin is wryly amused, claiming knowledge and understanding, but also pointing out that he has forgotten more about love than Silvius has experienced. Silvius wishes Corin could *know*, but insists that he can't know; wants to know what he remembers, but insists on measuring all experiences in love by his own.

Lodge's young shepherd sees men at different ages of life not only as physiologically different, but as if drawing on entirely different wells of experience. The fact that an old man was young once, while the average ploughman was never a scholar, does not impinge upon his view of the world. Such a conception of ages is not terribly different from the one set forth by Jaques in his famous speech.

There is no continuity to the figure who passes through the seven ages of man, and the lack is emphasized by the theatrical metaphor, the emphasis on costume. Each 'part' is characterized by certain clothing, props, or stereotyped gestures, as Jaques 'describes behaviour, but not experience.'[10] The schoolboy has his 'satchel / And shining morning face,' the lover marks his identity by 'sighing like a furnace', and the soldier is 'full of strange oaths and bearded like the pard' (II.7.146–47, 151). The justice has a 'round belly' and 'beard of formal cut' (155, 156), while the sixth age is the most extravagantly costumed of all:

> the lean and slippered pantaloon,
> With spectacles on nose and pouch on side,
> His youthful hose well saved, a world too wide
> For his shrunk shank.
> *(II.7.159–62)*

The detail about the youthful hose is especially telling. On the one hand, it is the only detail that suggests any kind of continuity between one stage of life and another. Yet this connection is undermined not only by the fact that the hose no longer fit the old man, but by the fact that this age of life derives its comedic potential from this very lack of fit. Similarly, the pantaloon's 'big manly voice, / Turning again towards childish treble' (162–63) suggests continuity only to deny it: the big manly voice no longer exists; and while the man's voice may return to childhood, his experience of himself does not, as he passes into 'second childishness and mere oblivion' (165). But the entire pageant, save for the detail of the saved hose, is characterized by 'mere oblivion', as no age seems to have any awareness of an earlier one.

This effect is not the inevitable result of the 'ages of man' trope. In fact, other versions of the trope illuminate what is unusual in Jaques's conception, offering a less deterministic account of man's life, and suggesting continuity and growth rather than changes of costume.[11] In *The History of the World*, Sir Walter Raleigh finds the seven ages to correspond with the seven planets:

> Whereof our Infancie is compared to the Moone, in which we seeme onely to live and growe, as Plants; the second age to *Mercurie*, wherein we are taught and instructed; our third age to *Venus*, the dayes of love, desire, and vanitie; the fourth to the *Sunne*, the

strong, flourishing, and beautifull age of mans life; the fifth to *Mars*, in which we seeke honour and victorie, and in which our thoughts travaile to ambitious ends; the sixth age is ascribed to *Jupiter*, in which we begin to take accompt of our times, judge of our selves, and grow to the perfection of our understanding; the last the seventh to *Saturne*, wherein our dayes are sad and over-cast, in which wee finde by deer and lamentable experience, and by the losse which can never be repaired, that of all our vaine passions and affections past, the sorrow onely abideth.[12]

Here the focus is not on how 'man' behaves in each age, but on what 'we' seek and desire. The final age, while grim, is not 'mere oblivion,' but a reckoning of the past; and in the penultimate age, 'we begin to take accompt of our times, judge of our selves, and grow to the perfection of understanding'. Accounts like Raleigh's illuminate Jaques's cynical world-view, in which men change, but never learn anything. Jaques's story of man's life confirms Silvius's sense that an old man and a lover are different creatures. Nevertheless, Raleigh's old man likely would appear much the same to Silvius as Jaques's old man, the one's accumulated memories offering no more vantage for empathy than the other's senility. 'Dear experience' teaches Raleigh's man what it teaches Lodge's Coridon: all passions are transitory and vain. The mind in the seventh age, looking back, does not re-experience recollected emotion. In the sixth age, at the 'perfection of our understanding', the understanding of the past is purely objective.

Raleigh's account of a judging and judgmental memory, a memory offering a lofty vantage from which the reason may evaluate past actions and values, resonates with Pierre de la Primaudaye's account of the relationship between reason, memory, and judgment:

> For as we have need of such a Judge as reason is ... so it is requisite, that the conclusion and definitive sentence should be registered in *Memory*, as it were in a roll or booke of accompt, that it may always be ready and found when need requireth. For what good should we get by that, which imagination, fantasie, and reason conceive and gather together, if it shoulde all vanish away presently through forgetfulnesse, and no more memorie thereof should remaine in man, then if nothing at all had bene done?[13]

We recall our reasoned judgments; and, presumably, look back over the roll of memory with an eye to judgment and analysis. We do not re-experience what we remember. In his *Confessions*, Augustine marvels over the way in which we recollect feelings without feeling them.

> [H]ow is it that when I, being happy, remember my past sadness—so that the mind contains happiness and the memory contains sadness—the mind is happy because of the happiness in it, but the memory is not sad because of the sadness in it? ... [T]he memory must be, as it were, the stomach of the mind, and happiness and sadness like sweet and bitter food, and when they are committed to the memory it is as though they passed into the stomach where they can be stored up but cannot taste. A ridiculous comparison, perhaps, and yet there is some truth in it.[14]

Augustine articulates exactly what Silvius finds objectionable about Corin's memory. If Corin can look back and remember how he felt when he loved, but not feel that *now*, then he doesn't 'know' anything. Corin, on the other hand, thinks he knows more, for the very reason that he has had a chance to apply judgment to his memories of emotion. It seems clear that a person can become someone new by forgetting. But can they stay the same person by remembering? Augustine seems to think so: he marvels over the fact that one can remember feeling an emotion without feeling it again, but his comparison suggests that the feeling person and remembering person are still one and the same, just as the person who digests food is the same as the one who tasted it. Nevertheless, his analysis suggests an unsettling possibility for disjunction. 'I, being happy' can remember an 'I' who was sad; but the empathetic connection, the experience of sadness, is gone. For Silvius, such an 'I' would be useless, uncomprehending.

Rosalind and Silvius are not the only characters in *As You Like It* to search for others with experiences similar to theirs. Certain moments even suggest that the empathy generated from such shared experiences may make social bonds possible, as when Orlando hopes that the seemingly savage inhabitants of the forest may once have 'know[n] what 'tis to pity and be pitied' (II.7.114). But the play also conveys the sense that people are fundamentally discontinuous. Even if they remember their previous experiences and feelings, their next actions may not be informed by them. Rosalind picks up on this idea when she warns Orlando of the dangers of wedlock: 'Say "a day" without the "ever". No, no, Orlando, men are April when they woo, December when they wed. Maids are May when they are maids, but the sky changes when they are wives' (IV.1.136–39).[15] Rosalind faces similar possibilities with less equanimity when Celia casts doubt on Orlando's faithfulness.

> ROSALIND Not true in love?
> CELIA Yes, when he is in, but I think he is not in.
> ROSALIND You have heard him swear downright he was.
> CELIA 'Was' is not 'is'.
> (III.4.24–27)

Seen from this angle, sincerity becomes meaningless, as the truth of one moment may no longer be relevant to the next.

The possibilities for sudden transformation become positive, however, in the cases of Oliver and Duke Frederick. Oliver in particular becomes a shining example of the virtues of 'was is not is'. Rosalind and Celia, he says, will learn 'Some of my shame, if you will know of me / What man I am' (IV.3.94–95). Here, his identity seems singular and intact, if shameful. As he goes on, however, this identity becomes extraordinarily complicated. Oliver is able to remember his former self as if that self were a different person; but he seems able to undergo such a transformation only by seeing his old self through another's eyes.

Oliver's narrative turns upon not one, but two key revelations: the first when he reveals the identity of the ragged man that Orlando finds sleeping under a tree; the second when he reveals that this man is, or was, himself. For over twenty lines, he tells the tale from Orlando's point of view, describing how the young man discovered 'a wretched, ragged man, o'ergrown with hair, / [...] sleeping on his back' (IV.3.105–06), threatened by a snake and a lioness. Oliver has a fine sense of the dramatic: 'This seen, Orlando did approach the man / And found it was his brother, his elder brother' (118–19). The play audience, which has presumably recognized Orlando's elder brother when he entered, now must realize, as Rosalind and Celia do not, that the speaker is talking about himself in this strangely alienated way: describing his sleeping self through his brother's eyes. The recognition is Orlando's recognition. Oliver then gravely agrees with Celia's comments on the elder brother's character, 'For well I know he was unnatural' (123). The audience, knowing well that the speaker is Oliver himself, is in a position to appreciate the complexity of his position. Does Oliver have the best or worst perspective on his own unnaturalness? If best, at what point does he gain this perspective? The play suggests that the unnatural man is unlikely to know his full unnaturalness until he can know himself from the outside, as someone else, looking back at what he was. This is the first time Oliver has used the first person since he offered to tell 'what man I am' (95). The distinction between 'I' and 'he' comes to dramatic life when he concludes the account of Orlando's battle with the lion by suddenly emerging in his own story: 'in which hurtling / From miserable slumber I awaked'.

> CELIA   Are you his brother?
> ROSALIND Was't you he rescued?
> CELIA   Was't you that did so oft contrive to kill him?
> OLIVER   'Twas I, but 'tis not I. I do not shame
>   To tell you what I was, since my conversion
>   So sweetly tastes, being the thing I am.
>   (IV.3.130–36)

Oliver is at last, climactically, recognized—or not. The man standing before the ladies *is* Orlando's brother, but he is *not* the man who 'so oft contrive[d] to kill him'. Oliver here reverses his initial claim that they will learn something to his shame if they learn his identity. Over the course of the story, he manages to separate the 'man I am' from 'what I was'. Did this separation in fact occur with the literal and metaphorical awakening from 'miserable slumber'? Or is it the telling of the story that makes such a separation possible? Oliver claims not only to remember what he was, but to find sweetness in remembering—presumably because he can enjoy the stark contrast between was and is. But he does not tell of his unregenerate self as if he can remember what it was like to be inside that person. As much as he can, he borrows Orlando's perspective, and for the rest, imagines his own prior existence as a kind of allegory. It is as if a new Oliver only becomes possible when Oliver sees himself—or imagines what it would be to see himself—through his brother's eyes.

It is important to point out that the audience has no way of knowing, when Oliver enters in Act 4, that they are seeing a New Man. We learn of his conversion only as he describes it; and our belief in it depends on the success of the speech, and vice versa. *We* recognize Oliver three times: first when he enters; then in his story, through Orlando's perspective, when the younger brother recognizes the ragged man under the tree; and then with Rosalind and Celia, when Oliver declares, 'I awaked'. But who are we recognizing at any given time? At Oliver's entrance, the audience likely mistakes him for the old, villainous Oliver; when Orlando recognizes the ragged man under the tree, we recognize that villain again; but is this recognition correct? We are never informed about the sleeper's state of mind. Had Oliver already begun to experience a change of heart, or did he only become a new person at the moment he awoke and discovered he had been rescued by Orlando? (The only change of heart *described* is Orlando's, when he considers abandoning Oliver to the lioness, but then resolves to save him.) What is it like to experience becoming another person? Oliver cannot tell us, despite his long narration. The multiple recognitions of Oliver—or of someone who once was Oliver—make it impossible to tell just when the moment of transformation occurs, the moment when 'I' becomes 'not I'. Or perhaps, such magical conversion can occur only in recollection; Oliver, like Demetrius, tries to make sense of himself through narrative.

Oliver's story reaffirms the necessity of memory to obtain deeper knowledge of self and others by turning the usual narrative inside out. Instead of understanding another person by remembering still-resonant emotions, Oliver recognizes his former, 'unnatural' self by remembering through another's perspective. Instead of this knowledge depending on subjective continuity, it makes a discontinuity possible: ''Twas I but 'tis not I'. Empathy, interpersonal understanding, and self-knowledge do not require a continuous identity: a discontinuity, producing a new perspective, may be necessary for true recognition. Oliver remembers the meeting in the forest as if he were someone else, because he *was* someone else. And looking back at a past self, and understanding that self, may at least serve as practice for trying to understand others. The self is often little less foreign.

If there is always an element of fantasy in attempting to think and feel as another person, there may be the same element of fantasy in remembering past experience. *As You Like It* shows how such productive creativity can yield a greater understanding of self and others. Yet such imaginings can collapse into delusion and an ultimate lack of self-knowledge. This is the story of *All's Well That Ends Well*.

'He knows himself'

'Our rash faults', says the gloomy King of *All's Well That Ends Well*, 'Make trivial price of serious things we have, / Not knowing them until we know their grave' (V.3.60–62).[16] In this odd formulation, nothing is truly known (or appreciated) until it is gone; which raises the question of how something absent can be known at all. 'Knowing' becomes an increasingly uncertain endeavor as the final scene wears on. The verb is used to refer to subjective assurance that is objectively false. Diana in particular quibbles with the word as she taunts Bertram: 'He knows I am no maid, and he'll swear to it; / I'll swear I am a maid, and he knows not' (V.3.284–85). In fact, she returns obsessively to Bertram's supposed knowledge: '[He] hath abused me as he knows himself— / Though yet he never harmed me'; 'He knows himself my bed he hath defiled, / And at that time he got his wife with child' (292–93; 294–95). Her unsettling reiteration—'He knows himself'—suggests both certainty and severe limitation. Bertram cannot deny the truth of her accusations, as he knows himself that they are true; knowledge is an entirely subjective matter, and Bertram can only know what he thinks he knows. From Bertram's perspective, what he 'knows himself' *is* true, which is why 'he's guilty, and he is not guilty'. In his head, things happened a certain way, and until he can see things from another perspective, that's the only way that they happened. This understanding of knowledge, which makes Diana's riddles possible, further undermines the play's conclusion, as Bertram states his condition: 'If she, my liege, can make me know this clearly / I'll love her dearly, ever, ever dearly' (V.3.309–310). If knowledge is such a subjective matter, how can Helena make Bertram know anything, clearly or not? Even more troublingly, the callow Bertram doesn't know himself. What he himself 'knows' makes such self-knowledge impossible. But in fact, the whole play is built on such an untrustworthy substrate of things known through the memory.

In *All's Well*, 'That's good that's gone' (V.3.60), a line that could stand in for much of the play's discussion of the past. But the King's line suggests two possible, if entangled, readings. Is the good gone because it cannot survive in these degenerate times; in other words, is it gone because it is good? Or does the past merely seem good because it is gone? The past exists only in the memory, and can be reshaped, which is exactly what most of the characters are trying to do, not only in the final scene, but throughout the play.

According to the King, we only 'know' something when we remember it in its absence; or rather, when we know its grave. The implication of this odd metaphor is that we may know the grave rather than the thing itself, whatever it might have been. To know a grave, as the play's obsession with monuments suggests, is to know a memorial; or, the act of 'knowing' is the act of memorializing. After all, it is only through such eulogies that the audience knows Bertram's father, the man the King idealizes as one who 'might be a copy to these younger times / Which followed well would demonstrate them now / But goers-backward' (I.2.46–48). The King himself, in a different sense, is a 'goer-backward', as he devotes all his attention to the past. Bertram's polite response underlines the connection between memory and monument:

> His good remembrance, sir,
> Lies richer in your thoughts than on his tomb.
> So in approof lives not his epitaph
> As in your royal speech.
>
> *(48–51)*

These courtly words are ambiguous. By 'approof,' does Bertram mean proof or approval? Likely both, though the doubleness may not be so ironic as it will be in the next act, when Bertram claims Parolles to be 'of very valiant approof' (II.5.2). Parolles is one who has been proven valiant, and who receives approval for being valiant; in fact, the only proof lies in Bertram's approval. Here the King's praise provides Bertram's father with more approbation than appears in his epitaph. His words also confirm the Count's 'good remembrance', prove his value. Bertram's father may well have been the paragon the King describes, but the audience has no way of knowing. More insidiously, the play suggests that the King has no way of knowing either. This is also how Bertram 'knows' Diana when he sleeps with Helena: 'so lust doth play / With what it loathes, for that which is away' (IV.4.24–25).[17] In this play, to know is to remember a fantasy.

Although Helena appears to have replaced her dead father's memory with the living reality of Bertram, her first soliloquy suggests that she has merely replaced a memory with a memory. 'I have forgot him', she says flatly. 'My imagination / Carries no favour in't but Bertram's' (I.1.80–81). Memory and imagination, closely related functions in any case, here blur together. Helena's father is not banished by the distraction of a physical presence, but by an image that occupies her mind to the extent of blocking out all else. In Bertram's absence, she misses the bittersweet experience of being near him:

> 'Twas pretty, though a plague,
> To see him every hour; to sit and draw
> His arched brows, his hawking eye, his curls,
> In our heart's table—heart too capable
> Of every line and trick of his sweet favour.
> But now he's gone, and my idolatrous fancy
> Must sanctify his relics.
>
> *(I.1.90–96)*

In drawing Bertram in her heart's table, Helena impresses his image in her memory.[18] Indeed, the workings of the memory were often figured as tables, such as those in which Hamlet sets down the Ghost's precepts. Helena distinguishes sadly between Bertram's physical presence and his 'relics'; but what she actually describes is not *him*, but the image in her heart. This image also is, inevitably, a kind of relic, but a relic that is in considerable danger of replacing the real thing, judging by the startling gap between Helena's idealized version of Bertram and the unprepossessing reality.

The final scene emphasizes the failures of both memory and oblivion. Helena cannot be forgotten successfully; and yet the person who re-emerges is recognized and known in the same way that the King knows Bertram's father: she has been idealized and sanctified by her 'death'. In her turn, Helena quotes a significantly revised version of Bertram's letter. She cannot show him 'a child begotten of [her] body that [he is] father to'; but fortunately, the letter now requires her merely to be 'by [him] with child, &c' (III.2.57–58; V.3.307). At the beginning of the scene, the characters are not so much disposed to forget the past as to remember it differently. The King gives Bertram his cue: 'Not one word more of the consumèd time; / . . . You remember / The daughter of this lord?' (V.3.38, 42–43). Bertram is quick to seize his opportunity: 'Admiringly, my liege' (44). The audience, of course, has no recollection whatsoever of Lafew's daughter, who has not been mentioned until this moment. Nevertheless, we learn from Bertram that his preexisting love for this lady led him to reject Helena, an action which he now regrets.

Bertram's speech here is not unlike Demetrius's (another character with an uneasy relationship to a stubborn Helena).[19] The young count is excusing himself more than trying to make sense of himself; but the effects are similar as he explains how his first love for Maudlin shifted to Helena only after it was too late:

> At first
> I stuck my choice upon her, ere my heart
> Durst make too bold a herald of my tongue;
> Where, the impression of mine eye enfixing,
> Contempt his scornful perspective did lend me,
> Which warped the line of every other favour,
> Stained a fair colour or expressed it stolen,
> Extended or contracted all proportions
> To a most hideous object. Thence it came
> That she whom all men praised and whom myself,
> Since I have lost, have loved, was in mine eye
> The dust that did offend it.
>   (V.3.44–55)

Bertram's syntax is appropriately convoluted, as he both declares and denies agency. He assertively 'stuck [his] choice' upon Maudlin (whose name we are yet to learn), but his heart did not yet dare order his tongue to speak; the impression of his eye was fixed, and then the scornful perspective loaned by contempt distorted and warped the images of all other ladies. The phrase, 'where, the impression of mine eye enfixing', fails to clarify who is doing what to whom. Is Bertram saying that he actively fixed his eye upon Maudlin? Or did her impression on his eye enfix her in his heart? Despite its vagueness, the phrase recalls the operations of memory, which was typically described in terms of sense impressions that are stamped or 'fixed', as in a wax tablet. The image thus appropriately follows the King's question: 'You remember / The daughter of this lord?' Bertram goes so far as to suggest that his memory of the sight of Maudlin distorted every other impression received through the same channel. Interestingly, according to this version of events, he could only appreciate Helena when she too became a memory. While he could see her, she was offending dust; so how could Bertram love her, lost, when he had never received an accurate impression of her while she was present? Helena was not merely a distorted vision to him, but an active distorting agent, dust offending his eye, assaulting and blurring his sight. Maudlin's absence from the preceding four acts must lead the audience to believe that Bertram, at the King's suggestion, is here rewriting the past. His story is nevertheless, in the context of this play, disturbingly accurate in its account of the distortions of memory.

Memories in *All's Well*, then, are full of fantasies: dubious idealizations of the dead or supposedly dead; images of the beloved that eclipse present reality; revisions and idolatry. There is only one instance of recollection in the play that leads to actual knowledge. Significantly, in this moment, a character remembers something that is past, but not buried. The Countess recognizes signs of passion in Helena by remembering a younger self who is gone, but not quite dead:

> Even so it was with me when I was young.
> If ever we are nature's, these are ours; this thorn
> Doth to our rose of youth rightly belong;
> Our blood to us, this to our blood is born:
> It is the show and seal of nature's truth,
> Where love's strong passion is impress'd in youth.
> By our remembrances of days foregone,
> Such were our faults, or then we thought them none.
> (I.3.123–30)

The Countess's memory of her own youthful passions causes her to empathize with Helena. As she remembers, she experiences both powerful identification and a sense of distance. The simple intensity of 'Even so it was with me when I was young' combines the two responses: she recognizes in Helena not what she feels now, but what she once felt; still, she seems to remember quite clearly how it felt to feel that way. Her next lines, though sympathetic, set her further apart from the experience, as she both begins to speak in more general terms and insists on the essentially youthful nature of love. She recognizes that love is not a unique and individual experience; it has been shared not only by herself and Helena, but by all who are subject to nature. Yet although love belongs rightly to 'our rose of youth', the Countess's language suggests that the experience is so strongly imprinted in the memory that the old *can* 'know' what it is to love. Love does not simply belong to youth; its 'strong passion is impressed in youth'. The Countess's following reference to 'our remembrances of days foregone' confirms the implication that passion creates an impression in the memory, and a strong one, too.

The final line shows a delicate balance between the Countess's current perspective and her memory of her youthful perspective: 'Such were our faults, or then we thought them none'. In her age, she appears to perceive the symptoms of love as faults, but then remembers that they didn't seem that way to her younger self. Her words do not necessarily validate the mature perspective. She doesn't say, '*though* then we thought them none', or '*but* then we thought them none'. The 'or' seems to balance the two halves of the sentence, the two perspectives, as two equal alternatives; '*or*' suggests that the Countess cannot quite recollect, or know, how young people think. Those were our faults, unless we didn't think of them as faults . . . so they weren't faults? The present Countess and the youthful one—though likely she was not a Countess then—seem continuous, but this continuity evades absolute identification.

The Countess may not know her past self or her present self fully, nor can she fully know Helena. But she knows enough for the purpose, accurately recognizing Helena's love-struck state and sympathizing with her situation. Her clarity of vision, in a play in which memories and fantasies are all too closely related, may stem from her refusal either to identify completely with her past or to disown it. She thus avoids the tendency to place too much value either on her youth or on her current perspective. In sensing how much she shares with Helena, while admitting the limits of that sharing, she forms a bond stronger and more selfless than any other in the play. The Countess's form of empathetic recognition likely would not convince Silvius that the old can know the feelings of the young. Nevertheless, she manages as well as anyone could, given what Shakespeare depicts as the unavoidable otherness of past selves.

Notes

1. The play is cited parenthetically from William Shakespeare, *As You Like It*, ed. by Juliet Dusinberre, The Arden Shakespeare Third Series (London: Thomson Learning, 2006).
2. Garrett A. Sullivan, *Memory and Forgetting in English Renaissance Drama* (Cambridge: Cambridge University Press, 2005), p. 48.
3. Zackariah Long, '"Unless you could teach me to forget": Spectatorship, Self-forgetting, and Subversion in Antitheatrical Literature and *As You Like It*', in *Forgetting in Early Modern English Literature and Culture: Lethe's Legacies*, ed. by Christopher Ivic and Grant Williams (London: Routledge, 2004), pp. 151–64 (p. 160).
4. Sullivan, pp. 54, 63.
5. Northrop Frye, *A Natural Perspective: The Development of Shakespearean Comedy and Romance* (New York: Columbia University Press, 1965), p. 140.
6. David Scott Kastan, '*All's Well That Ends Well* and the Limits of Comedy', *ELH*, 52 (1985), pp. 575–89 (p. 577).
7. See Louis Montrose, '"The Place of a Brother" in *As You Like It*: Social Process and Comic Form', *Shakespeare Quarterly*, 32 (1981), 28–54 (p. 37).
8. Thomas Lodge, *Rosalynde* (London, 1590), sig. F1^r.
9. Lodge, *Rosalynde*, sig. F1^v.
10. Frederick Turner, *Shakespeare and the Nature of Time* (Oxford: Clarendon Press, 1971), p. 34.
11. See Alan Taylor Bradford, 'Jaques' Distortion of the Seven-Ages Paradigm', *Shakespeare Quarterly*, 27 (1976), pp. 171–6; and Michael J.B. Allen, 'Jacques against the Seven Ages of the Proclan Man', *Modern Language Quarterly*, 42 (1981), pp. 331–46.
12. Sir Walter Raleigh, *The History of the World* (London, 1614), sig. D4^r.
13. Pierre de la Primaudaye, *The Second Part of the French Academie* (London, 1594), p. 160.
14. *The Confessions of St. Augustine*, trans. by Rex Warner (New York: New American Library, 1963), pp. 223–4.
15. For the changefulness and inconsistency of Rosalind/Ganymede, see Lina Perkins Wilder, 'Playing Sodomites: Gender and Protean Character in *As You Like It*', in *Shakespeare's Sense of Character: On the Page and From the Stage*, ed. by Michael W. Shurgot and Yu Jin Ko (Farnham, UK: Ashgate, 2012), pp. 189–207.
16. The play is cited parenthetically from William Shakespeare, *All's Well That Ends Well*, ed. by G.K. Hunter, The Arden Shakespeare Second Series (London: Methuen; Cambridge, MA: Harvard University Press, 1966).
17. For Shakespeare's metaphorical fusion of 'the sexual act with the act of understanding', see James L. Calderwood, 'Styles of Knowing in *All's Well*', *Modern Language Quarterly*, 25 (1964), pp. 272–94 (p. 276).
18. For the metaphoric use of 'heart' for memory, see Mary Carruthers, *The Book of Memory* (Cambridge: Cambridge University Press, 1990), pp. 48–9.
19. See Susan Snyder, '*All's Well that Ends Well* and Shakespeare's Helens: Text and Subtext, Subject and Object', *ELR*, 18 (1988), pp. 66–77.

17

VEILED MEMORY TRACES IN *MUCH ADO ABOUT NOTHING, PERICLES,* AND *THE WINTER'S TALE*

Lina Perkins Wilder

In an often-cited passage, St. Augustine describes remembering as a search through a treasure-chamber. The search requires innumerable agents whose eagerness may, for a time, obscure the object being sought:

> And I come to the fields and spacious palaces of my memory, where are the treasures of innumerable images, brought into it from things of all sorts perceived by the senses. There is stored up, whatsoever besides we think, either by enlarging or diminishing, or any other way varying those things which the sense hath come to; and whatever else hath been committed and laid up, which forgetfulness hath not yet swallowed up and buried. When I enter there, I require what I will to be brought forth, and something instantly comes; others must be longer sought after, which are fetched, as it were, out of some inner receptacle; others rush out in troops, and while one thing is desired and required, they start forth, as who should say, 'Is it perchance I?' These I drive away with the hand of my heart, from the face of my remembrance; until what I wish for be unveiled, and appear in sight, out of its secret place. Other things come up readily, in unbroken order, as they are called for; those in front making way for the following; and as they make way, they are hidden from sight, ready to come when I will. All which takes place when I repeat a thing by heart.[1]

As these 'peremptory [memory] traces'[2] present their treasures one after another, they coalesce with the treasure they bring, until the object that Augustine is trying to remember emerges on its own, 'unveiled', 'from its secret place'. Seventeenth-century divine John Willis, the author of a treatise on the memory arts as well as several shorthand manuals, imagines memory traces which are even more active: in a disorderly memory, 'though an Idea negligently reposited, cannot be found when it is sought, yet at another time when a Notion reposited in the cell of Memory near it, is excited, that also of its own accord discovereth itself'.[3] Artificial memory is meant to be orderly, and its orderliness is gendered, 'linked to an idealized conception of masculinity'.[4] In constructing mnemonic tableaux, the memory arts arrange the rest of the world as the mnemonic objects and memorial architecture of the male rememberer's mind, and in so doing repeat and valorize patriarchal hierarchy. When veiled memory traces themselves speak and remember, this hierarchy is drawn into question.

Like the workings of a disorderly memory, Shakespeare's comic endings depend on the improbable, last-minute, and frequently illogical return of desired persons and objects. Their relationship to mnemonic practices is emphasized by the presence of objects consonant with the practices of the memory arts: Shakespeare's comedies and late plays contain such mnemonic devices as striking objects of different kinds, boxed treasure, formal memorial markers, ordered pillars and interior spaces, and seas and oceans. The three plays I will examine contain another mnemonic device, veiled women. In fact, Shakespeare's comedies are littered with the paraphernalia of memory, although the apparatus is not always put to use. As Erin Minear argues in the previous chapter (Chapter 16), Shakespeare's comedies often appeal to memory only to draw attention to the discontinuities between present and past. One might expect such troubled comic plots as Shakespeare's to advise forgetfulness, but in fact this is rarely the case. Even a formal renunciation of the past (like Prospero's at the end of *The Tempest*) nonetheless returns what has supposedly been renounced to mnemonic circulation: Prospero's staff may be 'bur[ied] ... certain fathoms in the earth', but one need only visit *Hamlet*'s graveyard (or any sixteenth- or seventeenth-century graveyard) to be reminded that burial is impermanent; and his book may be 'drown[ed]', but as the rest of the play demonstrates, the sea is as likely to return as to retain the objects placed in it. While Shakespeare's comedies require us to recognize the past and the present as different places (and, as Minear argues, to recognize that past and present selves are *not the same*), the comedies also insistently return to the idea of memory. The engagement with mnemonic objects and places is particularly intense in the late plays. Simultaneously an engagement with mnemonics and an imperative to forget, the return of figures like Hero, Thaisa, and Hermione is a paradox, an allegory of remembering which nonetheless requires forgetfulness.

In this chapter, I examine the reappearance of three veiled or covered women who are not quite, or not entirely, mnemonic objects: Hero in *Much Ado About Nothing*, Thaisa in *Pericles*, and Hermione in *The Winter's Tale*. In all three cases, there is tension between the functionality of the veiled woman as a mnemonic prompt (particularly, although not exclusively, for men) and the woman's own relationship to the past.[5] Hermione's transition from object to person is the most obvious illustration of this tension, but the conclusion of *The Winter's Tale* requires re-reading based on the larger pattern of mnemonics in other plays. In all three cases, the degree to which women's inner lives—and thus their sexual desires—exist and can be controlled remains a central question. Reappearing as both objects and persons, Hero, Thaisa, and Hermione indicate that this issue is far from resolved. As mnemonic objects and remembering subjects whose presence evokes anxieties about female sexuality,[6] Hero, Thaisa, and Hermione recall the beautiful women controversially deployed as memory objects by Peter of Ravenna.[7] Rather than operating solely according to men's desires and as images of their mental processes, however, these women also operate to differing degrees as desiring, remembering agents. More broadly, memory operates in these plays not as a teleological device producing the revelations, lost information, or self-knowledge which might enable a different kind of comic plot to conclude, but as a faculty which submits only partially and incompletely to external control. Aligned structurally with the giving of a woman in marriage—a woman who has drawn or will draw into question the power dynamic of this gendered exchange—the return of the veiled woman creates an analogy between marriage and memory, and the loose ends left by this device trouble both institutions.

Mnemonic therapy in *Much Ado About Nothing*

It is safe to say that the first wedding in *Much Ado About Nothing* is a failure. Egged on by his companions, the bridegroom accuses the bride of infidelity and leaves her collapsed on the ground and apparently dead. The Friar offers an elaborate solution designed not to exonerate Hero but to act on Claudio's memory:

> For so it falls out
> That what we have we prize not to the worth
> Whiles we enjoy it, but being lacked and lost,
> Why, then we rack the value, then we find
> The virtue that possession would not show us
> Whiles it was ours. So will it fare with Claudio:
> When he shall hear she died upon his words,
> Th'idea of her life shall sweetly creep
> Into his study of imagination,
> And every lovely organ of her life
> Shall come apparelled in more precious habit,
> More moving, delicate and full of life,
> Into the eye and prospect of his soul
> Than when she lived. Then shall he mourn—
> If ever love had interest in his liver—
> And wish he had not so accused her;
> No, though he thought his accusation true.
> *(IV.1.217–233)*[8]

Drawing on faculty psychology and evoking St. Augustine's eager memory traces, the Friar describes an intellectual process in which, in the absence of sense information, the memory produces a stored 'idea' or image which is then brought forward to internal contemplation. 'Th'idea of [Hero's] life', the memory trace that remains in his brain once Hero herself is removed from his sight, will make the journey forward from the ventricle of memory and present itself to his 'study of imagination', a phrase that combines the faculties of understanding and fantasy. Because Claudio will no longer be able to *see* Hero, his past impression of her will replace the negative impressions he received from Don John and during the wedding ceremony and will cause him to repent his actions. Making a memory trace of Hero relocates the action to Claudio's mind and has the effect both of dehumanizing Hero and of making the audience uncomfortably aware that Claudio's feelings may not stand the test to which the Friar puts them.

Like St. Augustine's memory traces, the 'idea' of Hero is to some degree independent of Claudio's will. Its reappearance is a love-test. The therapy will only work 'if ever love had interest in his liver', if Claudio's body has actually been transformed by his passions. Whether he has been so transformed is far from certain. The contrived plotting that brings together Beatrice and Benedick can make it easy to overlook the flimsy justification that Claudio gives for his love for Hero. He praises Hero, conventionally, to Benedick, as 'the sweetest lady that ever I looked on' (1.1.177–178), but when he discusses the subject with Don Pedro, he seems more interested in Hero's financial status. Having learned that Hero will inherit her father's property, when Don Pedro asks whether he 'affect[s]' the old man's 'only heir' (1.1.277, 276), Claudio adds:

> O my lord,
> When you went onward on this ended action
> I looked upon her with a soldier's eye,
> That liked, but had a rougher task in hand
> Than to drive liking to the name of love.

> But now I am returned, and that war-thoughts
> Have left their places vacant, in their rooms
> Come thronging soft and delicate desires,
> All prompting me how fair young Hero is,
> Saying I liked her ere I went to wars.
> (I.1.277–286)

Again suggesting St. Augustine's memory traces, the 'soft and delicate desires' crowding into the places left by departing 'war-thoughts' act independently and cause Claudio to recall what he never knew, that he 'liked' Hero before the war began, even if his mind was too busy to allow him to recognize the fact. By describing his current state of mind as continuous with his earlier thoughts (even if unconsciously so), Claudio claims that his love for Hero is real and not simply a reaction to the news that she is Leonato's heir. He retains some anxiety on this point, however: 'But lest my liking might too sudden seem, / I would have salved it with a longer treatise' (I.1.295–296). The 'longer treatise' is left to Don Pedro to create, since it is he who woos Hero on Claudio's behalf.

In fact, the entire discourse of love in *Much Ado About Nothing* suggests that love fractures the past from the present. To be a lover, both Don Pedro and Benedick suggest, is to adopt a new persona at odds with a previous one. Noting that Claudio has 'become the argument of his own scorn by falling in love', Benedick mocks both the changes in Claudio's vocabulary, as does Don Pedro (having spoken 'plain and to the purpose' in the past, Benedick complains, Claudio now 'turn[s] ortography' [2.3.18, 19–20]), and other effects that Benedick also contrasts with the behavior of Claudio's previous persona as a soldier. While there is some continuity in Beatrice's and Benedick's behavior before and after they each accept the proposition that the other is in love, they also describe their transformation as just that: 'Doth not the appetite alter?' (2.3.229), Benedick asks; less metaphorically, Beatrice apostrophizes, 'Contempt, farewell; and maiden pride, adieu' (3.1.109). The play's hints about a previous love affair between Beatrice and Benedick do not give secure grounds for thinking of their love as long-standing or internally motivated.[9] It may be just what it seems, a reaction to circumstances which prompts an unreasoned self-transformation.

All this gives reason to suspect that skepticism is justified. Can love exert force on the brain (or liver) if it is a calculated decision (Claudio) or a whim (Beatrice and Benedick)? Hero's status among these lovers is even less clear. Silent until Act 2 and until then only an object to be 'note[d]' by Claudio (I.1.154), she does not directly respond to the advice about marriage given either by her father and uncle or by her cousin regarding marriage, not deigning to say whether she will marry 'as it please me', as Beatrice advises (II.1.49), or whether she will follow her father's instructions (II.1.44–45, 58–60). Her brief flirtatious exchange with Don Pedro—the man her father has told her to accept—notwithstanding, Hero's first avowal of love occurs privately, 'in [Claudio's] ear' (II.1.289) and is reported by others, and he does not become 'my dear Claudio' until after their engagement (III.1.93). Her love for Claudio is given no other point of origin than his avowal of love for her, and until he declares his love, she is given almost nothing to say (and little after). In other words, until Claudio rejects and slanders her, Hero neither has a past nor expresses desire. Her testimony at that point—'I talked with no man at that hour, my lord' (IV.1.86)—is twisted by Don Pedro (who suggests that her statement means that she did something other than 'talk') and disregarded by Claudio and by her father. Having emerged briefly from her status as an object to be 'noted' and passed between men, Hero is firmly returned to that status by the Friar, who even suggests that, if their ploy is unsuccessful (and Claudio's liver is judged to be unaffected by love), she may simply be put away: 'you may conceal her, / As best befits her wounded reputation, / In some reclusive and religious life, / Out of all eyes, tongues, minds, and injuries' (IV.1.240–243).

The Friar's therapeutic intervention does not, in the end, produce the results that he anticipates. On hearing the news of Hero's death, Claudio has no response, and until Hero's innocence is unequivocally revealed, he continues to jest with Don Pedro and even attempts to do the same with the newly serious Benedick. Not until Borachio confesses his and Don John's plot against Hero does Claudio respond in a way that suggests that his memory is affected: 'Sweet Hero! Now thy image doth appear / In the rare semblance that I loved it first' (V.1.241–242). The Friar had theorized that, '[i]f ever love held interest in his liver', Claudio would be so strongly affected by the mental image of Hero that he would repent his actions, even if he still considered her guilty as charged. Claudio fails the Friar's love-test. The mental image of Hero is not so strongly fixed in his memory that it overcomes his sense of injury or his loyalty to his male companions.

Arranged by Leonato, the play's second wedding scene replays Claudio's memory of Hero as external rather than internal drama. Like a good memory-arts practitioner, Leonato first banishes a bevy of women to 'a chamber by [them]selves' (V.4.10), and then calls them forth masked. The masculine control over this scene would be total, were it not for the fact that (apparently unprompted) Hero speaks:

CLAUDIO:	Give me your hand before this holy friar.
	I am your husband, if you like of me.
HERO *[Unmasks.]*:	And when I lived I was your other wife;
	And when you loved, you were my other husband.
CLAUDIO:	Another Hero!
HERO:	Nothing certainer.
	One Hero died defiled, but I do live,
	And surely as I live, I am a maid.
DON PEDRO:	The former Hero! Hero that is dead!
LEONATO:	She died, my lord, but whiles her slander lived.
FRIAR:	All this amazement can I qualify,
	When after that the holy rites are ended,
	I'll tell you largely of fair Hero's death.
	Meantime, let wonder seem familiar,
	And to the chapel let us presently.

(V.4.58–71)

Hero's own speech, glossing her return, is bracketed by Claudio's, Don Pedro's, Leonato's, and finally the Friar's responses. Claudio describes what he sees as 'another Hero', as if he still believes that he is to marry someone else, the cousin who is supposed to resemble Hero so closely. Don Pedro's exclamation ('The former Hero! Hero that is dead!') looks backward, but makes no attempt to reconcile his memory with the current reality. Hero herself does not reconcile her past self with her present existence: she agrees with Claudio that she is 'another Hero' and describes herself as two: 'Nothing certainer. / One Hero died defiled, but I do live, / And surely as I live, I am a maid'. Neither Claudio nor Pedro jumps to what one might expect, given their love of gulls and tricks, to appear to them the obvious (and, as it happens, true) explanation, that they have been tricked. They respond to Hero as if she is the remembered image described by

Claudio earlier, a re-virginated Hero 'in that rare semblance that I loved her first'. Nor do they express the remorse, nor Hero offer the forgiveness, that the moment demands. The surprise of Hero's reappearance is pushed away by the Friar, who urges his company, until he can explain what happened, to 'let wonder seem familiar'.

Hero's uncertain relationship with temporality, desire, and identity in the last four of her very few lines never receives resolution. She speaks of a time 'when [she] lived', as if she speaks from beyond the grave, and then she says that someone else died, and that she is alive. None of this is resolved or explained. A final reconciliation between Beatrice and Benedick diverts attention, and the play ends—as many of Shakespeare's comedies do—by delaying the reckoning that will truly resolve the plot. Indeed, in this play, the conventional dance that ends the play functions further to delay the marriages which have already been delayed by Don John's plot and the Prince's and Claudio's gullibility. The messenger who announces the recapture of Don John offers a scapegoat for the Prince and for Claudio, whose repentance has been solemnized by the promise of a 'yearly' ritual that will continue for the rest of his life. Presumably, since Hero is not dead, he will no longer mourn at her tomb. Whether Don John's 'brave punishments' (V.4.126) can provide a substitute for this ritual of repentance is not clear. Hero does not ask for repentance; she turns the attention instead to herself, proclaiming, as she did in the earlier scene, her virginity. Even this point is left somewhat undetermined, since Hero predicates her maidenhood on the fact that she now lives, and Don Pedro, as if compelled and unable to absorb the new information, answers with the antithesis: she 'is dead'. Just as before, Hero's words are not accepted but drawn into question. She says, 'I live'; Don Pedro responds, 'Hero . . . is dead'. The play invites us to remember, displays the 'Hero that was dead', 'the former Hero', but then offers 'another Hero' in her place, substituting for the ethical work of remembering the surprise and pleasure of *peripeteia*.

Along with their masks, the fact that Claudio refers to the group of masked women as 'other reckonings' (V.4.52) suggests another way of understanding the riddle of Hero's reappearance.[10] Claudio, Benedick, and Don Pedro have been engaged in one kind of reckoning, the exchange of jests which demands either equal or greater impact from each succeeding contribution. This ongoing exchange is about to give way to a more permanent reckoning: the word suggests both the Day of Judgment and the end of a term of pregnancy in childbirth. (The Friar uses the childbirth metaphor earlier when he describes the progress of his plot [IV.1.213], and as Hester Lees-Jeffries points out in reference to *The Winter's Tale*, for Shakespeare's audiences, 'a figure awaking from the apparent sleep of death would be a herald of doomsday'.[11]) This play does not look so far forward as to offer us 'another Hero' in the form of a child. However, the play's more than usually frequent recourse to cuckold jokes is a reminder that procreation was one of the central purposes of marriage.

Among the intertexts for the masked woman in *Much Ado About Nothing* is Lucina, the aspect of the Renaissance tripartite Diana who is responsible for childbirth and who in at least one frequently-consulted source is depicted with her face covered. In the English translation of Vincenzo Cartari's *Le imagini degli Dei Antichi*, with Lucina's intervention, 'from the moisture and humiditie of the Moone . . . the woman receiueth speedier deliuery, and the child easier euacuation'. Cartari reports Cicero's description of

> a Statue or Picture of Diana, which he brought out from a temple in Cicilia, and he saith that it was of wonderous heighth, and huge demension, hauing the whole bodie circumcinct with a thin vaile or couerture, the face of it a most youthful and virgineall aspect, holding in her right hand a liuely burning torch, and her left an yvorie bow, with a quiver of siluer-headed arrows hanging at her back.[12]

An edition of Cartari's treatise printed in Venice in 1609 includes an image of the three aspects of the tripartite Diana, in which Lucina is covered entirely by a 'thin vaile or couerture'.[13] Like this version of Lucina, women undergoing the churching ceremony after giving birth were conventionally veiled, and veils were also associated with prostitutes (due primarily to the story of Judah and Tamar) and other penitents.[14] Associated with childbirth, the veil represents both privacy and knowledge denied. While the women in *Much Ado About Nothing* are wearing masks, not veils, the fact that their faces are covered may associate them with Lucina and her mysteries and with the practice of churching and the female communities it evokes, and it certainly alludes to the play's larger concerns with truth, falsehood, and inwardness. In accusing Hero of being a 'rotten orange' (IV.1.30), Claudio invokes a different understanding of opaque surfaces, claiming that Hero's unreadability can only be deceptive and casting the interior of the female body as a space of decay and disease, not fecundity. The masked women in the final scene recall this image of deceptive surfaces, and in fact their concealed faces do allow Leonato to substitute a different woman than the one promised to Claudio. Through this set of associated images, the audience is cued to remember the crimes against Hero, but only obliquely. One might expect Hero's reappearance to be a moment for forgetting what's past, but she reminds us of that past, albeit while describing her past as (in one way or another) discontinuous with her present, and even with her person.

Memory adrift in *Pericles*

Hero's reappearance is orchestrated by men, and as an act of remembering it is embedded in the hierarchy of heterosexual marriage. The fact that she speaks represents a small but significant rebellion against their control over her person and the uses to which it is put. Like Hero, Thaisa in *Pericles* returns after an absence, apparently wearing a veil, although her face may or may not be covered. More emphatically than Hero, Thaisa cannot be reduced to a figure in someone else's mnemonic tableau. When she and Pericles are united, the recognition is mutual, and Thaisa is not a virginal girl 'in that rare semblance that [Pericles] loved her first'; nor does Marina step into this role, since, as in *The Winter's Tale*, Shakespeare sidesteps the possibility of incest and avoids the moment when the unrecognized daughter might take her mother's place. Thaisa may be a memory trace, but she is a memory trace belonging to no particular person, and the allegory leaves trails that cannot be folded into the central metaphor. Moreover, the type and quality of memory allegorized is unclear. Releasing Thaisa's body into the sea suggests forgetfulness, but it also suggests the contingency of a disorderly memory, one in which a memory trace may 'of its own accord discove[r] itself'.

Thaisa is only one among many memory images in *Pericles*.[15] The play abounds in mnemonic objects: Gower, the Chorus; the heads of slaughtered suitors read by Pericles as a *memento mori* (I.0.40, I.1.42–47); the 'casket' of a 'Daughter' whose only act is to wish Pericles luck (I.1.78); the statue of Pericles at Tarsus (II.0.14); the several dumb shows; Pericles' father's armor, an archetypal marker of family identity and material memory (II.1.116–130);[16] the procession of knights before the mnemonically-named King Simonides (II.2.14–57); the chest in which Thaisa is placed and set adrift (III.1.70, 3.2.49–65) and the letter and other objects enclosed with her (III.2.65–74); the monument for the supposedly dead Marina (IV.3.42–45); Marina's wish to become a bird (IV.5.104–106); and Thaisa and Marina themselves. It is not always clear to what purpose these memory objects are deployed, nor for whom. Further, there is no central mnemonic place in *Pericles* but rather a shifting array of places, typified in the sea which wrecks and washes Pericles and his family ashore on several occasions.[17]

In *Much Ado About Nothing*, memory allegory emphasizes the limits of female autonomy. When Hero is merely a mnemonic object or a memory trace, she is no longer a person. However, in the different generic environment of the late plays, the same is not quite true. Romance (important among the genres inhabited by the late plays) is a 'processional narrative',[18] and 'its events are intermittently motivated and not necessarily tied to previous action'.[19] To the degree that it participates in this genre, *Pericles* invests more in action than in character or plot, and its allegory does not have the same gendered dynamic seen in *Much Ado About Nothing*. The 'processional' form itself is an important part of the mnemonic intellectual tradition. Ordered arrangements of striking images with no connection to one another are the very definition of the memory arts. The mnemonic images in *Pericles* serve as reminders not of the causative events in the plot (of which there are few) but of themselves, of the succession of events, objects, and persons that serve aesthetic and moral purposes more than narrative purposes. Allegory invests the figures in this play with autonomy and expands their range of meaning rather than restricting it, and this lack of intention has the effect of liberating the play's persons, to a certain extent, from gender hierarchy.

To take a central example, the memory allegory suggested by Thaisa's burial at sea defies easy interpretation. Yielding to the sailors' demand that 'the ship be cleared of the dead' (III.1.48–49) to quiet the storm, Pericles addresses Thaisa's body before carrying her off to be put overboard:

> A terrible childbed hast thou had, my dear,
> No light, no fire. Th'unfriendly elements
> Forgot thee utterly, nor have I time
> To give thee hallowed to thy grave, but straight
> Must cast thee, scarcely coffined, in the ooze,
> Where, for a monument upon thy bones
> And aye-remaining lamps, the belching whale
> And humming water must o'erwhelm thy corpse,
> Lying with simple shells. O Lychorida,
> Bid Nestor bring me spices, ink and paper,
> My casket and my jewels, and bid Nicander
> Bring me the satin coffer. [*Gives her the babe.*] Lay the babe
> Upon the pillow. Hie thee, whiles I say
> A priestly farewell to her. Suddenly, woman.
>   [*Exit Lychorida.*]
> SAILOR: Sir, we have a chest beneath the hatches, caulked and bitumed ready.
>   (3.1.56–71)

Faced with the task of improvising a funeral service,[20] Pericles laments the absence of the usual reminders of the dead and offers multiple substitutes. Thaisa will have no 'monument upon her bones' nor 'aye-remaining lamps';[21] instead, she is left to the 'belching whales / And humming water'.[22] In this unstable condition, Pericles surrounds his wife with a series of boxes—coffin, casket, 'satin coffer' ('coffin' in the Quarto), and chest—which suggest the receptacles often associated with an ordered memory: *scrinium* (a box for keeping books), treasure chest, money-bag. 'Caulked and bitumed ready', the chest in which Thaisa is placed evokes Noah's ark, itself a memory image.[23] The jewels, spices, and writing materials are both practical expedients and common mnemonic cues. Next to Thaisa's body, Pericles places the baby, which Lychorida earlier calls 'this piece / Of your dead queen' (III.1.17–18). Pericles surrounds Thaisa's body with mnemonic apparatus, but he retains none of it for himself, not even his infant daughter.

The image of a body overwhelmed not just by the unpredictable motion and vast space of the sea but by noise—'belching', 'humming'—further suggests how thoroughly Thaisa's body will be 'o'erwhelm[ed]' in death.

When Thaisa's body is found by Cerimon, the mnemonic pageant resumes. Like Friar Laurence in *Romeo and Juliet*, Cerimon is a medical practitioner who knows the qualities of 'vegetives, . . . metals, stones' (III.2.36) and who keeps his medicines in 'all my boxes in my closet' (III.2.80), a mnemonic ordering which is also a common metaphor in the memory arts. Again, the mnemonic imagery seems excessive. It is unnecessary for the audience to remember Thaisa; she is found by Cerimon in the scene immediately following her burial at sea. Pericles is absent. Cerimon cannot 'remember' someone who shares no part in his past. The mnemonic imagery serves no purpose other than its central one: to invest the image with importance, to suggest the excessiveness and serendipitous working of memory itself.

Although she is temporarily silenced by her apparent death, and although she retreats to the temple of Diana after being revived by Cerimon, Thaisa's reappearance signals her function as a rememberer as well as an object to be remembered. Pericles calls her a 'nun' (V.3.15), and this along with the fact that Pericles does not recognize her suggests that she is veiled;[24] and in fact, if her face is covered like those of the nuns in *Measure for Measure* she may embody Lucina, on whom Pericles calls during Marina's birth. Although she is not recognized by Pericles, she recognizes him in spite of his covering beard and long hair: 'Voice and favour! / You are, you are, O royal Pericles!' (V.3.14) (In a sense, he is also veiled.) She emphatically 'of [her] own accord discovereth [her]self', but she is still not recognized. Upon recovering from her faint, she demands visual confirmation and claims ownership of Pericles:

> O, let me look!
> If he be none of mine, my sanctity
> Will to my sense bend no licentious ear,
> But curb it spite of seeing. O my lord,
> Are you not Pericles? Like him you spake,
> Like him you are. Did you not name a tempest,
> A birth and death?
> PERICLES: The voice of dead Thaisa!
> THAISA: That Thaisa am I, supposed dead
> And drowned.
>
> *(V.3.28–36)*

Unlike Hero, Thaisa claims continuity with her past selves: she is 'dead Thaisa', or rather, as she corrects Pericles, she is 'Thaisa . . . *supposed* dead / And drowned'. Her identity accumulates by modification, not opposition or rupture. Further, to Thaisa Pericles is 'mine'. Her ownership of Pericles entirely reverses gender hierarchy. Thaisa's wish to look is fraught with erotic significance, since it seems that rules for Diana's 'nun' are similar to those that regulate the order of Catholic nuns in *Measure for Measure*,[25] and that desire, evident from her first encounter with Pericles, is to consume and envelop: 'All viands that I eat do seem unsavoury, / Wishing him my meat' (II.3.30–31).[26] Thaisa's wish to devour Pericles, like Juliet's wish for Romeo to be scattered after her death 'in little stars' and Cleopatra's 'dream' of an Antony so huge that realms fall out of his pockets, distorts the body of the male beloved with its intensity. All of this takes place in the Temple of Diana at Ephesus, a location that might seem to be a stable, ordered alternative to the shifting environs of the sea and the brothel, but which is in fact far from stable. A temple is *the* typical mnemonic *locus*, but this temple, formerly one of the wonders of the world, had in the seventeenth century 'sunk twenty feet into the silt'.[27] In its prime associated with the cult of mother-worship,[28] the temple reverses the hierarchies that allowed both trained memory and heterosexual marriage to function. The temple works not so much to create order as to emphasize the importance of disorder, most notably the self-dissolving power of sexual desire:

> You shall do well
> That on the touching of her lips I may
> Melt and no more be seen. O, come, be buried
> A second time within these arms.
> 					(V.3.41–44)

The separation of mnemonic structures from the functioning of memory is above all evident in the figure of Marina, the daughter who cannot remember her father but who nonetheless 'by her own most clear remembrance . . . / Made known herself [his] daughter' (V.3.12–13). This miraculously 'clear' memory is simply Marina's account of herself, partly learned from Lychorida (now dead) and recited to Pericles at his prompting. Her ability to narrate her own life restores Pericles. As a grown daughter who resembles her supposedly dead mother, Marina also recalls the past in her person, as Pericles recognizes before he learns her story: 'My queen's square brows, / Her stature to an inch, as wand-like straight, / As silver-voiced, her eyes as jewel-like / And cased as richly' (V.1.99–102). However, without Marina's own memory, this resemblance might be understood by Pericles as merely coincidental; if she were only an object, Marina would do nothing. Marina is preserved not just as an object but as a remembering subject able to absorb and retell memories that are hers and those that have been told to her. Her preservation is notable due to the scattershot working of memory in the play and, of course, due to the nature of the place (another mnemonic *locus*) where she is found. The brothel is a place of stagnation and dissolution; rape and resulting venereal disease threaten to destroy, even dissolve, the body that has been miraculously preserved thus far; that this does not occur suggests the durability of the memory in spite of disorder and even because of it.

However, despite her association with 'good', orderly memory, Marina's deepest wish, while in the brothel, is one that is more easily associated with disorderly memory or oblivion. She wishes not for return, for restoration, or for rescue, but for dissolution—the very fate which the brothel threatens in any case. She wishes 'that the gods / Would set me free from this unhallowed place / Though they did change me to the meanest bird / That flies i'th' purer air!' (4.5.103–106) Her wish for escape is also a wish to be lost, a wish that suggests a loss of place and the abandonment of mnemonic ordering. The wish to be transformed into a bird associates Marina with Philomel, and through Philomel the ability to speak after this aggressive act of silencing and to escape physically the site of the assault. Further, the image of an escaping bird evokes the long association between birds and memory, articulated by Plato (among other ancient sources) to 'supplement his primary image of the [memory as] wax in order to convey what that image conspicuously misses: the sense that memories often seem alive, fluttering, and elusive'.[29] Marina's wish for freedom is a wish to escape, to become unmoored from structure, not to return to a putative stable origin—which in fact she does not have, having been born at sea.

The moving statue in *The Winter's Tale*

Of the three veiled or covered women discussed in this chapter, Hermione is one whose return speaks most directly to the difference between recollection and reconciliation. As in *Much Ado*

About Nothing and *Pericles*, mnemonic allegory informs but does not fully explain the structure of *The Winter's Tale*. From the appearance of the pregnant Hermione to the revelation of her statue, the play can be understood as a lesson in the art of remembering. However, the statue of Hermione, existing as it does in a middle state between object and person, makes even more prominent the questions about gender and personhood which were introduced in *Much Ado About Nothing*. Hermione is never merely a reminder or a mnemonic image; she also remembers, and by her own account she 'preserve[s] [her]self'.

Even more clearly than in *Much Ado About Nothing* or *Pericles*, *The Winter's Tale* aligns the figure of the unruly woman with therapeutic remembering. Leontes is afflicted with the idea of his wife's infidelity; like Claudio, he focuses on her gestures and her appearance and discounts her words. When Paulina brings the newborn Perdita to Leontes, she acts as an even more than usually aggressive memory trace:

>   I
> Do come with words as medicinal as true,
> Honest as either, to purge him of that humour
> That presses him from sleep.
> LEONTES: What noise there, ho?
> PAULINA: No noise, my lord, but needful conference
> About some gossips for your highness.
> LEONTES: How?
> Away with that audacious lady! Antigonus,
> I charged thee that she should not come about me.
> I knew she would.
> ANTIGONUS: I told her so, my lord,
> On your displeasure's peril and on mine,
> She should not visit you.
> LEONTES: What, canst not rule her?
>
> (II.3.35–45)[30]

Paulina describes her intervention as the opposite of 'noise': she provides a reasonable reminder of Leontes' social duties on the birth of his child (finding 'gossips' or godparents for the christening). By uprooting evil ideas from Leontes' brain, she will allow him to find the 'sleep'—both literal sleep and forgetfulness—that will help him return to his proper self. The baby herself is a small version of Leontes: 'Although the print be little', she is 'the whole matter / And copy of the father' (II.3.97–98). Her resemblance to him should function as a reminder, but does not. Resistant to her husband's 'rule' in the cause of justice, Paulina is an unprompted memory trace as well as a woman who exceeds the boundaries of acceptable feminine behavior. It is no mistake that Leontes orders first Paulina and then both Hermione and Perdita to be burned in the fire (II.3.93–94, 112–114, 130–140, 154–155). As well as the prescribed penalty for female traitors, fire was a traditional remedy in the art of memory for obliterating unwanted memory images.[31] Abandoning the baby is also a gesture of forgetting, but one that allows chance to work its magic and bring the play toward a felicitous conclusion.

In contrast to the resemblance between Marina and Thaisa, the resemblance between Perdita and both her father and mother is problematic rather than therapeutic. Leontes experiences the resemblance between himself and Mamillius as, among other things, emasculation:

>   Looking on the lines
> Of my boy's face, methoughts I did recoil
> Twenty-three years, and saw myself unbreeched,
> In my green velvet coat; my dagger muzzled,
> Lest it should bite its master, and so prove,
> As ornaments oft does, too dangerous.
> How like, methought, I then was to this kernel,
> This squash, this gentleman.
>   *(I.2.153–160)*

Leontes' first child is a temporal paradox who causes his father to 's[ee] [him]self unbreeched', returned to the undifferentiated state before he is old enough to assume all the markers of adult masculinity, a loss of dignity (if also a potentially regenerative new beginning[32]) emphasized by another sense of 'unbreeched', naked. Blunted and miniaturized, this Leontes meets his son as a diminished equal, unnerved by their close resemblance and by the memory of himself as a young child. 'Another / As like Hermione', Perdita is a potential replacement for her mother, not a reminder of her. Marriage-plot comedy is comedy because it promises children who will resemble their parents and grant them a measure of immortality by living on beyond their lifetimes. This form of continuity is denied to us in *The Winter's Tale*.

The problems with the second generation make Hermione's return all the more important. Hermione's statue is veiled and then uncovered, revealing a figure that, like Thaisa in *Pericles*, is not entirely the Hermione remembered by her husband. She is a survivor, as well as, or more than, the memory image she initially seems to be. The details of Hermione's reawakening are too familiar to need much rehearsal: she reappears as a sculpted image, both her appearance and her location in an enclosed space suggesting the internal drama of memory theatre. However, the image quickly begins to strain against this framework: she is more 'wrinkled' and more 'aged' than the Hermione whom Leontes remembers (V.3.28, 29); she is unfinished; she seems to 'breath[e]' and her 'veins' seem to 'bear blood' (V.3.64, 65); she moves; movingly, 'she's warm' (V.3.109); and she directs her first and final words not to her husband, for whom the spectacle is supposedly presented, but to her daughter. Leontes initially treats the statue as a reminder: 'There's magic in thy majesty', he says, 'which has / My evils conjured to remembrance' (V.3.39–40). However, Hermione's revivification requires him to do more than recall his past deeds, and Hermione's own stated motivation—that she has 'preserved / [Her]self to see the issue' (V.3.127–128)—makes her far more than a mnemonic stimulus. As someone who 'see[s]', Hermione is a witness, not just a reminder. She 'preserve[s] / [Her]self'; she is not preserved by others, either by Leontes, as a remembered image, or even by Paulina as a work of art. Indeed, as a self-preserved figure she cannot quite be said to be remembered at all. Perdita, a double for her mother and for her dead brother Mamillius—and, of course, a returning figure in her own right, lost as an infant (as her name indicates) and now found—also participates in the mnemonic drama, at a somewhat more distant remove. In both cases, a figure who might in other circumstances be an unruly memory trace takes on instead a subjectivity defined by resistance to being memory and even to being remembered. The recognition scene is complicated by the fact that the woman who has been lost is herself capable of loss and that she returns not just to be recognized, but to recognize and reclaim.

There is tragic potential in unwilled, uncontrolled remembering, as Hamlet makes clear when he wishes to stop his memory from functioning. ('Heaven and earth, must I remember?')

Interestingly, although Viola's cross-dressing plan shifts her from a memorial to an anticipatory (or future-oriented) mode, Sebastian continues to recollect the shipwreck throughout the play and to register its effect on his role in the play. Thus, in a conversation with Antonio in Act 2, he narrates his home of Messaline nostalgically:

> You much know of me then, Antonio, my name is Sebastian, which I called Roderigo; my father was that Sebastian of Messaline whom I know you have heard of. He left behind him myself and a sister, both born in an hour: if the heavens had been pleased, would we had so ended! But you, sir, altered that, for some hour before you took me from the breach of the sea was my sister drowned.
>
> *(2.1.14–22)*

Like his sister, Sebastian identifies himself through his relationship to his dead father. This lineage is not only a source of legitimacy for him, but also allows him to draw closer to Antonio with demonstrations of shared knowledge ('whom I know you have heard of'). His reference to Viola having drowned 'some hour' before his own rescue creates a sense of temporal break between the twins: although they were 'both born in an hour,' this sameness is 'altered' by Sebastian's survival, and he wishes that they had also died at the same time. The 'breach' to which he refers is not only 'the breach of the sea,' in the sense of the surf or breakers, but a breach between brother and sister, as well as between *eros* and *thanatos*. The former allows for the play's romantic denouement, and the latter constitutes an attempt to police this permeable boundary in the play. Like Viola's formulation of this divide in Act 1 – 'And what should I do in Illyria? / My brother he is in Elysium' (1.2.3–4) – Sebastian draws attention not only to actual geographic places but also to remembered spaces of the living and the dead.

Strikingly, this divide also informs the court of Olivia, characterized by mourning, a practice unsuited to the generic demands of comedy. Susan Snyder reminds us that singleness is unacceptable in comedy:

> Comic conventions, for all their diversity, do reveal common assumptions. The mode is too rich to enclose in any one formula, but the most pervasive principle is surely the rejection of singleness. The single self is seen as deficient, in more senses than one ... Shakespeare's comedies in particular stress the uneasiness of isolation, whether self-imposed or not.[12]

Although Viola comes to know Illyria by remembering Orsino the bachelor, Olivia's mode of mourning is anti-romantic in its remorseless concern with loss, division and solitude. Interestingly, in a play that is obsessively concerned with potential forms of coupling, the Captain and Viola's exchange in I.2 about Olivia's isolation figures her court as a closed space:

> *Viola.* O that I serv'd that lady,
> And might not be deliver'd to the world,
> Till I had mine own occasion mellow,
> What my estate is.
> *Captain.* That were hard to compass,
> Because she will admit no kind of suit,
> No, not the Duke's.
>
> *(I.2.42–6)*

In *The Winter's Tale*, the excesses, the escaping trails and wisps of memory grow toward comic and regenerative recovery—in part. The loss of Mamillius, as many critics remind us, cannot be repaired by remembering him or by the reappearance of any of his doubles (Hermione, Florizel, Leontes). His memory is not allegorized as return. He is simply gone, his absence unremarked, and the recovery and recuperation of the final scene is incomplete.

Conclusion

In an essay on memory in *Love's Labour's Lost* published in *Shakespeare Quarterly* in 1973, Trevor Lennam suggests that the play puts forward the claim that women are a better alternative to books:

> If they do not win the ladies, at least they find through love's labors that 'the ground of study's excellence' far from being a bookish acquisition lies in 'the beauty of a woman's face' and, as Berowne sweetly argues, that women 'are the ground, the books, the academes, / From whence doth spring the true Promethean fire' (IV.3.299–300).[33]

Figuratively equating women with knowledge is hardly unique to *Love's Labour's Lost*, and celebrations of this equivalence can be found in sources other than the late Dr. Lennam's scholarship (which, in addition to this article, consists of a minor book on the Children of Paul's). To call Berowne's statement 'swee[t]', however, is to miss half the point of the play. In *Love's Labour's Lost*, knowledge may be gained through study and patient application, but lovers cannot, even if desire is mutual. The poems and speeches composed by Berowne and his companions out of the 'true Promethean fire' of love are ridiculous, not sublime. Women are not knowledge. The equivalence does not hold.

Shakespeare's comedies explore gender hierarchy and gendered subjectivity by creating an unstable memory allegory. Hero is a mnemonic object and also to a small degree a remembering subject, and to different degrees and in different ways so are Thaisa (and Marina) and Hermione. Not merely 'alive, fluttering, and elusive', women who function as memory images have the potential to speak and remember in their own right and thus to challenge the entire structure of artificial memory—which, as commentators from Augustine to Montaigne make clear, is always unstable. The allegory is an indictment: as memory is unstable, so too are power relationships based on gender.

Acknowledgment

I would like to thank Randi Saloman for her comments on an earlier version of this chapter.

Notes

1. Augustine, *Confessions of St. Augustine*, trans. E.B. Pusey (Westminster, MD: Modern Library, 1999), p. 210.
2. Garrett A. Sullivan, Jr., *Memory and Forgetting in English Renaissance Drama* (Cambridge: Cambridge University Press, 2006), p. 39.
3. John Willis, *Mnemonica* (London, 1661), sig. K4^{r-v}.
4. Sullivan, *Memory and Forgetting*, p. 39. On masculinity and the memory arts, see also Lina Perkins Wilder, *Shakespeare's Memory Theatre: Recollection, Properties, and Character* (Cambridge: Cambridge University Press, 2010), pp. 25–32; Andrew Hiscock, *Reading Memory in Early Modern Literature* (Cambridge: Cambridge University Press, 2011), pp. 3–6, 13–15.

5 On the relationship between returning mothers and the churching ritual following childbirth, see Caroline Bicks, 'Backsliding at Ephesus: Shakespeare's Diana and the Churching of Women', in *Pericles: Critical Essays*, ed. David Skeele (New York: Garland, 200), esp. pp. 213–217.
6 My argument is somewhat at odds with Janet Adelman's argument that returning mothers are purified and desexualized. See Adelman, *Suffocating Mothers: Fantasies of Maternal Origin in Shakespeare's Plays, Hamlet to The Tempest* (New York: Routledge, 1992), p. 36.
7 Peter of Ravenna, *The Book of Memory, that Otherwyse is called the Phenix* (London, 1545), sig. A7^{r-v}; see Wilder, *The Art of Memory*, pp. 35–36.
8 Quotations from *Much Ado About Nothing* follow Claire McEachern's third-series Arden edition (London: Thomson Learning, 2006).
9 Stephen F. Dobranski, 'Children of the Mind: Miscarried Narratives in *Much Ado About Nothing*', *Studies in English Literature*, 38, no. 2 (1998), 242.
10 On reckoning, see Cynthia Lewis, '"We know what we know": Reckoning in *Love's Labour's Lost*', *Studies in Philology*, 105, no. 2 (2008 Spring), 247.
11 Hester Lees-Jeffries, *Shakespeare and Memory* (Oxford: Oxford University Press, 2013), p. 193.
12 Vincenzo Cartari, *The fountaine of ancient fiction*, trans. Richard Linche (London, 1599), sig. H1^{r-v}.
13 See Suzanne Gossett, 'Introduction' to *Pericles* (London: Thomson Learning, 2004), p. 119.
14 David Cressy, 'Thanksgiving and the Churching of Women in Post-Reformation England', *Past & Present*, 141 (November 1993), 132–140.
15 I set aside the question of memorial reconstruction. See Gossett, 'Introduction' to *Pericles*, pp. 22–30.
16 Ann Rosalind Jones and Peter Stallybrass, *Renaissance Clothing and the Materials of Memory* (Cambridge: Cambridge University Press, 2000), esp. pp. 245–268.
17 On the sea in *Pericles*, see Steve Mentz, *At the Bottom of Shakespeare's Ocean* (London: Continuum, 2009), 68–69.
18 Northrop Frye, *A Natural Perspective: The Development of Shakespearean Comedy and Romance* (New York: Columbia University Press, 1965), pp. 27–28.
19 Gossett, 'Introduction' to *Pericles*, p. 108.
20 As Gossett points out, there was no set service in the Book of Common Prayer for those buried at sea until 1662. Gossett, *Pericles*, p. 287n.
21 On the textual crux—the Quarto reads 'ayre remayning'—see Gossett, *Pericles*, p. 285n.
22 The lamps are a marker of Catholic piety outlawed during the reign of Henry VIII. Gossett, *Pericles*, p. 409n.
23 Sarah Novacich, *Ark and Archive: Narrative Enclosures in Medieval and Early Modern Texts* (unpublished dissertation); Gossett, *Pericles*, p. 287n.
24 Gossett, *Pericles*, p. 399n.
25 Ibid.
26 Ibid.
27 Bicks, 'Backsliding', p. 206.
28 See Bicks, 'Backsliding', pp. 206–207, 211–212; F. Elizabeth Hart, '"Great is Diana" of Shakespeare's Ephesus', *Studies in English Literature*, 43, no. 2 (Spring 2003): 347–374.
29 Stephen Greenblatt, *Hamlet in Purgatory* (Princeton, NJ: Princeton University Press, 2001), pp. 214–215; see also Wilder, *Shakespeare's Memory Theatre*, p. 67.
30 Quotations from *The Winter's Tale* follow John Pitcher's third-series Arden edition (London: Methuen, 2010).
31 Mary Carruthers describes a modern example in *The Book of Memory: A Study of Memory in Medieval Culture* (Cambridge: Cambridge University Press, 1990), p. 77.
32 See Lees-Jeffries, *Shakespeare and Memory*, pp. 177, 183–184.
33 Trevor Lennam, '"The ventricle of memory": Wit and Wisdom in *Love's Labour's Lost*', *Shakespeare Quarterly* 24, no. 1 (1973 Winter), 55.

18

ILLYRIA'S MEMORIALS

Space, memory, and genre in Shakespeare's *Twelfth Night*

Susan Harlan

This chapter will consider how the relationship between space and memory in Shakespeare's *Twelfth Night* (1602) informs our understanding of romantic comedy in this play. Comedy is future-oriented in its commitments to marriage and procreation, but it also often engages in forms of nostalgia, or concerns with a lost past. Originally, nostalgia had referred to homesickness, or a longing for home (*nostos*): however, this deployment of place in a broader discourse of belonging resonates closely with the displacement that characters often experience in romance. Susan Stewart has defined nostalgia as:

> a sadness without an object, a sadness which creates a longing that of necessity is inauthentic because it does not take part in lived experience. Rather, it remains behind and before that experience. Nostalgia, like any form of narrative, is always ideological: the past it seeks has never existed except as narrative, and hence, always absent, that past continually threatens to reproduce itself as a felt lack.[1]

These emphases upon self-narrativization and insufficiency clearly underpin the beginning of *Twelfth Night*, which is shaped in terms of Olivia's mourning and Viola's acute experience of alienation: emphases, as I will suggest, which also underpin the play's fragile conclusions of reunions and matchmaking. For Stewart, nostalgia negotiates that which does not exist – that which must be invented as narrative. It is about a 'felt lack.' In a similar manner, the beginnings and endings of plays are boundaries between what does and does not exist: they delineate what has been narrated and what has not – and will not be.

Spaces of memory

In direct comparison with Shakespeare's late romances, *Twelfth Night* delivers a number of its characters into a hostile, unknown, and in some ways undefined space. Elin Diamond argues that comedic landscapes are alien, for

> The comedies' devotion to magic means, of course, that landscape and human shape are subject to change without notice; more than that, magic suggests another reality, largely unseen, coexisting with the one we know. It may be comical yet frightening like Friar Bacon's devils, or beautiful like the tiny society of Titania's elves. In any case, it is other.[2]

Raphael Lyne similarly refers to 'the other-worldly atmosphere of romance,'[3] emphasizing that romantic spaces like Illyria become on stage indeterminate or ambivalent planes of reference. One way of navigating through such spaces is with the resources of memory for both character and audience.

This concern with the relations between space and memory is also evident in one of Shakespeare's later plays, *The Winter's Tale* (c. 1610–11). In both plays, memory is a key means by which affective locales are fashioned. The limitations of memorial reconstruction may often draw the audience's attention to the boundaries of the plays themselves (what narratives can and cannot be played out in these spaces), as well as addressing larger questions of a character's insider or outsider status. What Viola remembers about her home, and about the place 'Illyria' in which she finds herself, gestures toward what 'remains behind and before … experience,' to return to Stewart's phrase. From one perspective, this is a past that does not really exist – in the sense that it is not staged and thus cannot truly be verified or known by anyone other than the figure that remembers, but we are repeatedly asked to attend to its significance.

Both *Twelfth Night* and *The Winter's Tale* urge audiences to reflect at length upon the magical, the wondrous, and the threatening lands while investing in romantic tropes governed by expectations of betrothal and marriage. In general terms, David Wiles has argued that, 'The context for a history of performance space is a history of space. Classical and medieval space was finite and bounded, but the renaissance and the enlightenment introduced the new conception that space was infinitely extensible.'[4] In its embrace of voyages to unknown and fantastical lands, romance can certainly present space as 'infinitely extensible' – even as the performance venue of a play limits and circumscribes space. This concern with unknown, fantastical space in *The Winter's Tale* gives rise to perhaps Shakespeare's most famous stage direction ('Exit pursued by a bear' (III.3.58)) when Antigonus finds himself in 'The deserts of Bohemia' (III.3.2). In response to Antigonus' inquiry, the Mariner explicitly urges audiences on and offstage to attend to the relationship of alien lands to 'ill time':

> ANTIGONUS. Thou art perfect, then, our ship hath touch'd upon
>   The deserts of Bohemia?
> MARINER. Ay, my lord, and fear
>   We have landed in ill time: the skies look grimly,
>   And threaten present blusters. In my conscience,
>   The heavens with that we have in hand are angry,
>   And frown upon 's.
>   (III.3.1–7)

The 'present blusters' that the Mariner identifies situates the voyagers in the present, or the most immediate time frame, whereas their geographic displacement invokes the past of the play and gestures forward in time and narrative by invoking the familiar tropes of romance. This is a hostile landscape, and indeed the Mariner's warning that, 'this place is famous for the creatures / Of prey that keep upon 't' (III.3.12–13) soon finds expression in the demise of Antigonus. Before this occurs, however, the aging courtier offers a lengthy recollection of a dreamlike encounter with Hermione's ghost that engages with 'what may follow' (3.3.51) for the baby Perdita:

> The storm begins: poor wretch,
> That for thy mother's fault art thus expos'd
> To loss and what may follow! Weep I cannot,
> But my heart bleeds; and most accurs'd I am
> To be by oath enjoin'd to this. Farewell!
>   (III.3.49–53)

In a short space of time, Antigonus' regret is quickly replaced by the Shepherd's forward-looking comedic certainty that, "'Tis a lucky day, boy, and we'll do good deeds on't' (3.3.136–7). However, in due course in this new-found land, 'ill time' must give way to the Chorus Time, who allows for the lapse of sixteen years that renders the first three acts of the play a memory for both the characters and the audience. Time himself exhorts his audience to remember in the service of comedy: 'remember well / I mentioned a son o' the king's, which Florizel / I now name to you' (4.1.21–3). Perdita's suitor is thus introduced drawing upon the resources of future recollection.

The romantic locales of *The Winter's Tale* allow for, or indeed mandate, certain memorial modes for the characters and theatrical audience. Of course, 'romance' as a generic category post-dates the *First Folio* of 1623, but it may be unhelpful to distinguish too sharply between the dramatic undertakings of these two genres. As Lawrence Danson notes of Shakespeare's late plays,

> Although they are like the comedies (they end in reconciliations which include marriages and the repair of broken marriages, and with the promise of new beginnings through birth and dynastic succession), they are separated by several years – and several tragedies – from Shakespeare's earlier comedies ... Separating them out too rigidly risks obscuring the ways in which the last plays are examples of Shakespeare's continual experimentation, his variation, revision, and subversion of his own and his contemporaries' idea of generic practice.[5]

The shipwreck in *Twelfth Night*, for example, produces a location that gives rise to certain memories. Memories of place proliferate in the opening act of the play, particularly for Viola and Sebastian, and these memories inform their understandings of the roles that they will play in a romantic comedy. So, in one sense, memory becomes a means by which they recognize themselves, one another, and the genre in which they are embedded. In his work on maps and mortality, William Engel directs our attention to the 'jagged lines of demarcation between physical nature and significance.'[6] *Twelfth Night* negotiates several such jagged lines as it maps out what Illyria will allow regarding characters' pasts, presents, and futures.

Remembering Illyria

That *Twelfth Night* was performed at Middle Temple Hall on February 2, 1602 and not in a public outdoor amphitheatre may serve to complicate our understanding of the play's treatment of space and memory. As Frances Yates outlined in *The Art of Memory*, the design of the early modern theatre was influenced by classical and medieval understandings of how the art of memory relied on imagined architectural spaces, including memory theatres.[7] The Inns of Court were a different matter: they were established to teach the common law and to train Serjents at law, or judges. A Lord of Misrule was elected to preside over Middle Temple's Christmas celebrations, which were among the most important events in the Inn calendar, and indeed *Twelfth Night* is inextricably linked to the revelry of holiday, as C.L. Barber influentially argued.[8] John Manningham, a student at the Middle Temple, recorded in his diary that the play was performed at a feast:

> At our feast wee had a play called Twelve Night or What You Will ... a good practice in it to make the Steward believe his Lady widdowe was in Love with him by counterfeiting a letter as from his Lady in general termes, telling him what she liked best in his and prescribing his gesture in smiling, his apparaile &c. And then when he came to practice making him believe they tooke him to be madde.

That the play should be figured as an event that occurs *at* the feast – 'At our feast wee had a play called Twelve Night' – reminds us that this is not a theatrical space, but a space that is accommodating a play. In the same ways that space and time were found to jostle for position in the characters' understandings of belonging and desire, for Manningham, the play was claiming a presence in an environment given over customarily to quite different purposes.[9]

However, to return to the question of the transformation of time and space in Shakespeare's dramaturgy, *Twelfth Night* is a play which is firmly committed to the labors of constructing memory. The melancholic opening at court immediately gives way to a post-shipwreck romantic locale in which Viola and the Captain attempt to situate themselves. Viola's first question – 'What country, friends, is this?' (1.2.1) – is both a statement of ignorance and an attempt to locate herself in a place she does not recognize but will find that she remembers. Her question is addressed to the Captain and the sailors, and twenty lines later she asks the Captain directly, 'Know'st thou this country?' (1.2.21). The term 'country' can refer to the land of one's residence, or homeland, but Viola is probably using it in the sense of land, terrain, or a region. However, the repetition of the term 'perchance' three times in so many lines establishes that the narratives this location will enable are uncertain:

> VIOLA.   And what should I do in Illyria?
> My brother he is in Elysium.
> Perchance he is not drown'd: what think you, sailors?
> CAPTAIN.   It is perchance that you yourself were sav'd.
> VIOLA.   O my poor brother! and so perchance may he be.
>   *(I.2.3–6)*

Viola's sense of displacement ('And what should I do in Illyria?') establishes her as lost in the geographic sense and yet seeking a form of selfhood through kinship memory: she has no sense of her role apart from her dead brother. This disorientation links directly to her theatrical trajectory: what *will* she do in Illyria? Her first use of the term 'perchance' ('Perchance he is not drown'd') engages both the definitions of *perhaps* and *by chance*. The former sense sets up a counterfactual statement, a desire for an alternative narrative to the one in which she finds herself. The latter shifts the emphasis onto the question of luck, suggesting that this may be a space of unlikely wonders. The Captain's response – 'It is perchance that you yourself were sav'd' – draws on this meaning, reading the shipwreck as a fortunate deliverance. In her response ('O my poor brother! and so perchance may he be'), Viola brings the two layers of meaning together: he may potentially/perhaps be dead, and he may be dead by (unlucky) chance. More broadly, the role of potential in the play is underscored by its subtitle 'What You Will' – a capacious invitation to the audience to rewrite the title if they see fit. The audience's will, understood as a demand predicated on taste and desire, has its own potential: by generating its own title, the audience might write another kind of narrative. Viola herself has a will, both in her wish for her brother's survival and in her cross-dressing plan, and this will finds expression in the notion of what 'perchance' may be. Writing of Iachimo's 'competing stories' in *Cymbeline* about the supposed seduction of Imogen in *Cymbeline*, J.K. Barret notes that, 'The playwright privileges the theater's capacity to put multiple, co-present options on imaginative, rather than physical, display, and encourages the consideration and memory of multiple story lines, even when only one set of actions happens onstage.'[10] If the early modern period may be characterized in part by its concern with 'extensible' planes of space and time, both *Twelfth Night* and *The Winter's Tale* show themselves determined to investigate such propositions with remarkable tenacity by exploiting the creative resource of potential experience. The Captain in *Twelfth Night*, for example, is at some pains to present a detailed counterfactual narrative based in 'chance' to soothe Viola:

> True, madam, and to comfort you with chance,
> Assure yourself, after our ship did split,
> When you and those poor number sav'd with you
> Hung on our driving boat, I saw your brother,
> Most provident in peril, bind himself
> (Courage and hope both teaching him the practice)
> To a strong mast that liv'd upon the sea;
> Where, like Arion on the dolphin's back,
> I saw him hold acquaintance with the waves
> So long as I could see.
> (1.2.8–17)

That Sebastian's possible survival is presented a form of 'comfort' suggests that this narrative may not, in fact, be true (as does the comparison between Sebastian and Arion), but the Captain's claims to truth are far less important than the space of possibility that this narrative opens up. Indeed, Viola attaches a monetary value to this hope:

> For saying so, there's gold:
> My own escape unfoldeth to my hope,
> Whereto thy speech serves for authority,
> The like of him. Know'st thou this country?'
> (I.2.18–21)

Such a story of reassuring witness establishes an authority that she hopes will extend to geographic knowledge, and the Captain reveals himself to be both local to Illyria and privy to its gossip and rumors about Orsino. We learn that the Captain has traveled between Illyria and the unknown, off-stage location that represents the beginning of their journey (possibly Messaline): 'For but a month ago I went from hence' (I.2.31). Viola's own knowledge of the Duke has its roots in memory and, once again, in relations of kinship: 'Orsino! I have heard my father name him. He was a bachelor then' (I.2.28–9). Her 'then' turns toward the past, but also a potential environment for romantic-comedic narrative for the young, unmarried protagonist. Her reference to 'then' constructs vague temporality, like the 'Once upon a time' of fairy tales or Antonio's 'once' later in the play: 'Once in a sea-fight 'gainst the Count his galleys, / I did some service, of such note indeed, / That were I ta'en here it would scarce be answer'd' (3.3.26–8). His 'once' refers to a solitary event, the consequence of which persists into the present and the future, but it is also 'once' as an undesignated moment. Interestingly, this nebulous sense of pastness creates theatrical space for examining questions of belonging, kinship, and potentially romantic bonds that also look to the future and set up certain generic expectations for the theatrical audience. This play has a past, but it remains occluded, and it is felt chiefly in these moments of recollection.[11] Unlike Antonio's 'once,' which will ultimately alienate him from Illyria and from the play's romantic plotlines, Viola's 'then' is quickly absorbed into comedic mandates, for it allows the Captain to establish Orsino as romantically available.

Viola's question 'And what should I do in Illyria? / My brother he is in Elysium' also draws attention to the tranformations of time and space which the heroine is being called upon to enact.

Viola's wish to be 'admit[ted]' to Olivia's court is quickly replaced with her plan to serve Orsino. However, as in the first line of Sonnet 116 – 'Let me not to the marriage of true minds admit impediment' – the term 'admit' takes on both a cognitive and a spatial sense: it means *acknowledging the existence of* and *allowing into*. Like Olivia's court, Sonnet 116 is a closed space; the speaker quite literally will not admit the possibility of an alternate definition of love, in the sense of allow into, into his tightly crafted, legal-esque argument (and poetic text).[13] Olivia will not acknowledge Orsino's suit, and she will not allow others into her court. Valentine informs Orsino in I.1, 'So please my lord, I might not be admitted' (I.1.24), and this language is echoed by Sir Toby at the beginning of I.3, who asks, 'What a plague means my niece to take the death of her brother thus? I am sure care's an enemy to life' (I.3.1-3). Olivia's mourning, and her resulting isolation, constitutes a dangerous threat to the marriage-oriented generic demands of comedy at the beginning of this play. Her court and her body are off limits: no one will be admitted.[14] The Captain tells Viola that her plan 'were hard to compass,' and although the Arden editors J.M. Lothian and T.W. Craik gloss 'compass' as 'contrive,' the term also implies encircling, surrounding, or encompassing. This sense of spatial delineation establishes the court initially as apart from the romantic space into which Viola, the Captain, and the sailors are thrust.

For the expectations of comic narrative to be fulfilled, Olivia's commitment to mourning (or morbid remembering), like that of Viola and Sebastian for each other, must fall into abeyance. Premiered on the stage in the same years as *Hamlet*, *Twelfth Night* remains unusually concerned with death, memory, and *memento mori* in its progress toward comic resolution. Feste's song in II.4 goes some way to add momentum to this undertaking in its rejection of all conventional gestures of mourning, including that of weeping:

> *Not a flower, not a flower sweet,*
> *On my black coffin let there be strewn:*
> *Not a friends, not a friend greet*
> *My poor corpse, where my bones shall be thrown:*
> > *A thousand thousand sighs to save,*
> > > *Lay me, O where*
> > *Sad true lover never find my grave,*
> > > *To weep there.*

This song anticipates Feste's final song – 'For the rain it raineth everyday' – which situates itself, epilogue-like, in the liminal space between the theatrical audience and the play and suggests a return to the play's melancholy tone that the final scene of promised marriages is unable to entirely correct. That this song should echo his earlier prohibition against weeping may serve to activate audience memory, and the assertion that 'it raineth everyday' creates a stable and unchanging pattern predicated on knowing the past. Nonetheless, *Twelfth Night* comes to indicate how difficult it is to exploit knowledge of the past and places radically into question our ability to secure a comprehensive understanding of that past. As the play repeatedly underlines, Olivia seeks to preserve her brother's memory, but her mode of preservation differs markedly from Viola's. In Act 1, Valentine characterizes Olivia's tears for her dead brother as preserving this brother, or holding him in the realm of the living:

> *The element itself, till seven years' heat,*
> *Shall not behold her face at ample view;*
> *But like a cloistress she will veiled walk,*

And water once a day her chamber round
With eye-offending brine: all this to season
A brother's dead love, which she would keep fresh
And lasting, in her sad remembrance.
(I.1.26–32)

Her 'eye-offending brine' (1.1.30) prefigures the sea invoked by Viola and the Captain, and Olivia's 'chamber' becomes a garden that produces not life, but death kept 'fresh / And lasting, in her sad remembrance.' The regularity with which this death-garden is watered ('once a day') suggests not only the rituals and practices central to mourning practices, but also the labor required to keep memory alive. In Act 2, Sebastian notes of his sister that, 'She is drowned already, sir, with salt water, though I seem to drown her remembrance again with more' (II.1.29–31). Here, tears of grief are figured as both excessive ('more') and repetitive ('again'). Conversely, in the final scene, Sebastian will set up the possibility of tears that would represent recognition and repair, or a turn away from the mode of memory represented by mourning and grief: 'Were you a woman, as the rest goes even, / I should my tears let fall upon your cheek, / And say, "Thrice welcome, drowned Viola"' (V.1.237–9). Mourning and grief are found to be policed in Illyria. Olivia's 'sad remembrance' echoes Claudius' reference to remembering his own dead brother 'together with remembrance of ourselves' (I.2.7) in Act 1 of *Hamlet*. Illyria is both a remembered romantic place for the characters and the theatrical audience and a place that discourages memory that divides one from the realm of *eros*. However, as we have seen, memory can be dangerously melancholic. One of the most melancholic lines of the play – Sir Andrew Aguecheek's 'I was adored once too' (2.3.181) – also obliquely registers loss in the context of comedy and reminds that audience that he, too, will have no place in the play's couplings.

Memorials and relics

Twelfth Night's dominant masculine friendship between Antonio and Sebastian exists in a space that that is designated as apart from Illyria, or as another part of it, and this location also has implications for the play's understanding of genre. The location of II.1 and III.3 is not quite so clear as in Rowe's *dramatis personae* list, which identifies it as 'another state further along the co[a]st of the Adriatic.' Robert Weimann notes that:

> On Shakespeare's stage, the localization of dramatic action must be viewed in conjunction with the endeavor to establish a firmly controlled, closely circumscribed mode of staging the text. In a good many comic scenes but especially in an early comedy like *The Two Gentlemen of Verona*, there was no specific imaginary locale; as the text of the play reveals, the playwright simply was uninterested in whether the location, in accordance with the represented action, actually was 'Milan' or, as the Folio has it, 'Padua' (2.5.2); whether later it still was 'Milan' or perhaps 'Verona' (3.1.81); or whether the play's final scene was no longer set in 'Milan' but yet again, 'Verona' (5.4.129).[15]

In these scenes between Sebastian and Antonio, we also have no 'specific imaginary locale.' We do not seem to be in Illyria, but we are close to it – in a place outside of Orsino's duchy. The spatial vagueness here is not evidence of a lack of dramatic interest, but a means of engaging with the relationship between memory, place, and genre. Although this place remains unspecified, it has several striking qualities that underscore what characters remember about it. In III.3, when Sebastian is reunited with Antonio, he suggests that they do some sight-seeing: 'What's to do? / Shall we go see the relics of this town?' (3.3.18–19). When Antonio replies 'To-morrow, sir; best first go see your lodging' (3.2.20), Sebastian expresses both an unexpected knowledge of the city in which they find themselves and a further desire to see its attractions:

> I am not weary, and 'tis long to night.
> I pray you, let us satisfy our eyes
> With the memorials and the things of fame
> That do renown this city.
> *(3.3.21–4)*

His dual interest in 'the relics of this town' and 'memorials and the things of fame / That do renown this city' suggests that this other, nearby state has a past that it remembers. Although the play is largely interested in what particular characters remember, or in personal memories, here memory takes on a communal, cultural sense. The editors of the Arden edition gloss 'relics' as 'antiquities'; however, the term 'relic' might also resonate with a specifically lost, Catholic past for Shakespeare's audiences. Philip Schwyzer notes that relics have a 'strong association with a particular past sets them apart from daily life. They are screened from the present, as it were, under glass, and generally owe their survival (and in some cases destruction) to that separation.'[16] He directs our attention to how the relic negotiates a complex relationship between the present and the past; they are 'screened from the present' so that they may continue to dwell, and encourage their viewers to dwell, in the past. Relics mark absent subjects in partial form, as Alexandra Walsham argues:

> At the most basic level, a relic is a material object that relates to a particular individual and/or to events and places with which that individual was associated. Typically, it is the body or fragment of the body of a deceased person, but it can also be connected to living people who have acquired fame, recognition, and a popular following.[17]

Relics offer contact with an individual, and they also constitute material memories.[18] In this context, the figuration of relics is corporeal: the fragments of saints' bodies, leftovers from another religious tradition, holy things. As in the case of the Ghost in *Hamlet*, this term opens up a space for the Catholic in a place otherwise at least tangentially associated with a Protestant present. However, when Antonio mistakes Viola for Sebastian, he 'But O how vile an idol proves this god!' (III.4.374). Viola is not only the 'image' (III.4.371) of Sebastian – a term Antonio uses several lines earlier – but an 'idol,' an illegitimate and debased copy. Equally importantly, Sebastian may also be indicating a desire to see ruins of the city: relics of its own, architectural past. Indeed, Antonio notes that Sebastian will have time to 'feed [his] knowledge / With viewing of the town' (III.3.41–2).

Sebastian's invocation of 'memorials and the things of fame / That do renown this city' indicates that this location does indeed have a past. *The Oxford English Dictionary* defines 'memorial' as both an object set up to commemorate and preserve the memory of a person or event, as well as something remembered, or worthy to be remembered, that may not have a material marker. Customs and observances might be 'memorials,' as might chronicles and records. Nonetheless, the term can also designate something intended to assist the memory, or an aid.

These 'memorials' seem to be material rather than figurative – perhaps statues or monuments that echo Viola's earlier memory of herself as 'Patience on a monument, / Smiling at grief' (II.4.115–16) and Orsino's reference to Olivia as a 'marble-breasted tyrant' (V.1.122). These instances figure the human subject as a statue – both conventional in their formulations, and both feminized. These memorials imply a past, a history. 'History' is the term Orsino uses to inquire after Viola's father's daughter in 2.4, but in this instance, the term is personal: her story, her own past. Sebastian's reference to memorials suggests that this location embodies communal memories that give rise to memorials. As Michael Neill notes,

> In the medieval theatre the tomb has been a sign of spiritual triumph, the Christian victory over death; but in the new popular theatre it quickly developed an extended range of secular meanings, influenced by the classical idea of the monument, and reflecting the increasingly temporal bias of Renaissance funeral art.[19]

These objects suggest both 'memorial and *memento mori* aspects'; they are backward-looking and forward-looking, or monitory, monuments. The fact that they remain largely undefined, unknown, and unvisited is appropriate in a play that constantly invokes the past but, as a comedy, is obligated to look to the future. Because Antonio is being pursued by the law – he notes that, 'I do not without danger walk these streets' (3.3.25) – Sebastian does not in fact go to see these relics and memorials, and they disappear from the play. They are, in a sense, forgotten. However, this is not the only reason that their potential outing does not take place. Antonio is also concerned with finding lodgings for Sebastian. He mentions several times that he should go to the Elephant: 'In the south suburbs, at the Elephant, / Is best to lodge' (3.3.39–40). Antonio maps a contemporary urban geography onto this imprecise romantic locale, as well as designating a place that emblematizes his and Sebastian's intimacy, apart from the play's mandated marriages.[20] The Elephant reappears in Act 4 when Sebastian wonders:

> Where's Antonio then?
> I could not find him at the Elephant
> Yet there he was, and there I found this credit
> That he did range the town to seek me out.
> *(4.3.4–7)*

That Antonio himself should disappear from this place, only to reappear briefly in the final scene, further underscores his outsider and excluded status.

The play's comic conclusion reunites a number of characters, who in turn must recognize one another. The conclusion demonstrates a marked preoccupation with the extent to which recognition depends on whether, and what, a character recollects. As a number of critics have noted, Antonio's love of Sebastian cannot be absorbed into the drive toward heterosexual marrying which conventionally defines the undertaking of comedy.[21] In Act 5, he recollects saving Sebastian 'From the rude sea's enrag'd and foamy mouth' (5.1.76), only to be rejected. Significantly, this rejection is figured as forgetting:

> For his sake
> Did I expose myself (pure for his love)
> Into the danger of this adverse town;
> Drew to defend him, when he was beset;

> Where being apprehended, his false cunning
> (Not meaning to partake with me in danger)
> Taught him to face me out of his acquaintance,
> And grew a twenty years' removed thing
> While one would wink.
>
> *(5.1.80–8)*

That Antonio understands Viola/Cesario's lack of recognition as an indication that he has '[grown] a twenty years' removed thing' suggests that a lack of recognition constitutes a failure to recollect. The 'remove' of which he speaks is the remove of time – or the distance it enables – but the term also implies elimination: Antonio understands that he is at an emotional remove from Sebastian and, indeed, he has been removed progressively from the play's romantic narratives. By imagining this as the result of the passage of time, a romantic trope familiar to the theatrical audience, he accounts for Viola/Cesario's surprising behavior and underscores its injustice. When Olivia encounters Viola/Cesario and takes him for Sebastian, she asks, 'Hast thou forgot thyself? Is it so long? (5.1.139). Her second question – 'Is it so long?' – similarly attempts to account for Viola/Cesario's failure to perform the role of Sebastian by invoking the passage of time. If Viola/Sebastian does not remember her, Olivia can only understand this as a mode of self-forgetting: that he does not know who he is. Sullivan reminds us that, 'forgetting is a form that subjectivity – a relationship to identity that represents the shattering of identity – frequently takes on the early modern stage.'[22]

The play's resolution assures the substitution of Sebastian for Cesario, a figure who must disappear from the play's double marriages. This disappearance is marked most clearly in Orsino's nostalgic musings – 'Boy, thou hast said to me a thousand times / That thou never should'st love woman like to me' (5.1.265–6) – and his demand to 'see thee in thy woman's weeds' (5.1.271) remains beyond the boundaries of the play. That he still addresses her as 'Cesario' (5.1.384) at the very end of the play suggests that Olivia's mourning for her brother may indeed have been replaced by Orsino's mourning for his lost, loved page. In this final scene, recollecting their home becomes the means by which Viola and Sebastian's identities are reclaimed and assured. This becomes the manner in which they recognize one another. Sebastian says:

> I had a sister,
> Whom the blind waves and surges have devour'd:
> Of charity, what kin are you to me?
> What countryman? What name? What parentage?
>
> *(V.2.226–9)*

The term 'countryman' recalls Viola's questions in I.2 regarding the 'country' in which she found herself, and his attention to 'parentage' echoes also her own memory of her dead father in that scene. It is by recollecting their shared father and Messaline that these twins are able to re-establish their kinship bond.[23] Viola responds that she is 'Of Messaline: Sebastian was my father; / Such a Sebastian was my brother too' (5.1.230–1). By invoking Messaline, as she had in I.2, she establishes this off-stage place as necessary to her own and her brother's sense of belonging. They must once again lay claim to a past geography in order to enter into their respective romantic narratives. What has been lost can be remembered.

Notes

1. Susan Stewart, *On Longing* (Durham, NC, and London: Duke University Press, 1993), p. 23. Phyllis Rackin also attends to the pervasive nostalgia of Shakespeare's history plays. See in particular Chapter 3: 'Anachronism and Nostalgia', in *Stages of History: Shakespeare's English Chronicles* (Ithaca, NY: Cornell University Press, 1990), pp. 86–145.
2. Elin Diamond, *Writing Performances* (London: Routledge, 1995), p. 51.
3. Raphael Lyne, *Shakespeare's Late Work* (Oxford: Oxford University Press, 2007), p. 26.
4. David Wiles, *A Short History of Western Performance Space* (Cambridge: Cambridge University Press, 2003), p. 4.
5. Lawrence Danson, *Shakespeare's Dramatic Genres* (Oxford: Oxford University Press, 2000), 13. On 'the romantic element' in early modern English comedy, see Madeleine Doran, *Endeavors of Art: A Study of Form in Elizabethan Drama* (Madison: The University of Wisconsin Press, 1954), particularly pp. 171–85.
6. William Engel, *Mapping Mortality: The Persistence of Memory and Melancholy in Early Modern England* (Amherst: The University of Massachusetts Press, 1995), p. 131.
7. Frances Yates, *The Art of Memory* (Chicago: The University of Chicago Press, 1966). See also Mary Carruthers, *The Book of Memory: A Study of Memory in Medieval Culture* (Cambridge: Cambridge University Press, 1990).
8. See Barber, *Shakespeare's Festive Comedy: A Study of Dramatic Form and its Relation to Social Custom* (Princeton, NJ: Princeton University Press, 1959).
9. Marvin Carlson reminds us that, 'Normally when we think of theatrical performance we imagine it taking place within an architectural space designed for that purpose, although history and quite likely our own experience can provide us with examples of theatre taking place in other sorts of locations as well.' See Carlson, *Places of Performance: The Semiotics of Theatre Architecture* (Ithaca, NY, and London: Cornell University Press, 1989), p. 6.
10. J.K. Barret, 'The Crowd in Imogen's Bedroom: Allusion and Ethics in *Cymbeline*', *Shakespeare Quarterly*, 66.4 (Winter 2015): 440–62.
11. Garrett Sullivan defines recollection as 'the process by which memory traces are retrieved and brought into consciousness' – as opposed to *memoria*, or 'not only the faculty that stores images in the brain, but also the site of that storage (often metaphorized in the period as a treasury or a wax tablet, and occupying the hindmost ventricle in the brain).' Garrett A. Sullivan, *Memory and Forgetting in English Renaissance Drama* (Cambridge: Cambridge University Press, 2005), p. 7.
12. Snyder, *The Comic Matrix of Shakespeare's Tragedies: Romeo and Juliet, Hamlet, Othello, and King Lear* (Princeton, NJ: Princeton University Press, 1979), p. 51.
13. Alexander Leggatt reminds us that, 'A stage is a tightly defined space, and comedy concerns itself with the way people live in spaces, the open space of a park or wood, the closed space of a room with practicable doors.' See Leggatt, *English Stage Comedy 1490–1990: Five Centuries of a Genre* (London and New York: Routledge, 1998), p. 9.
14. As Leonard Tennenhouse notes, Olivia's court requires the figure of Malvolio to police its boundaries: 'Malvolio can only imagine the community to which he aspire as one that arbitrarily excludes him. On this basis, he takes it upon himself to enforce the principle of exclusion when acting as the overseer of Olivia's household.' See Tennenhouse, *Power on Display: The Politics of Shakespeare's Genres* (New York and London: Methuen, 1986), p. 67.
15. Robert Weimann, *Author's Pen and Actor's Voice: Playing and Writing in Shakespeare's Theatre*, ed. Helen Higbee and William West (Cambridge: Cambridge University Press, 2000), p. 183.
16. Philip Schwyzer, *Shakespeare and the Remains of Richard III* (Oxford: Oxford University Press, 2015), pp. 103 and 105. Please see the introduction to Harlan, *Memories of War in Early Modern England: Armor and Militant Nostalgia in Marlowe, Sidney, and Shakespeare* for a more detailed discussion of relics.
17. Alexandra Walsham, 'Introduction: Relics and Remains', *Past and Present*, 206.5 (2010): 9–36, 9.
18. I borrow this term from Ann Rosalind Jones and Peter Stallybrass, *Renaissance Clothing and the Materials of Memory* (Cambridge: Cambridge University Press, 2000).
19. Michael Neill, *Issues of Death: Mortality and Identity in English Renaissance Tragedy* (Oxford: Clarendon Press, 1997), p. 310.
20. See Stephen Mullaney's seminal account of the relationship between early modern theater and the geography of the city in *The Place of the Stage: License, Play, and Power in Renaissance England* (Ann Arbor: The University of Michigan Press, 1988).

21 Shakespearean comedies have notoriously fraught endings. Kiernan Ryan argues that, 'The utopian closure of Shakespearean comedy and romance is qualified by the intrusion of these harsher, unredeemed realities and disquieting intimations which it cannot repress, and which stress the fragile fictionality and incompleteness of its state of concord.' See Ryan, 'Shakespearean Comedy and Romance: The Utopian Imagination', in *Shakespeare's Romances*, ed. Alison Thorne (New York: Palgrave, 2003), pp. 27–52, 39.
22 Sullivan, p. 12.
23 Of the role of the absent father, Leggatt notes that, 'It is Viola's reunion with her twin brother Sebastian that resolves the romantic plot, and at the centre of their recognition scene is the shared memory of their father's death, the day Viola turned thirteen. (So presumably did Sebastian, but it is a sign of the centrality of the father–daughter relationship for Shakespeare that they both measure the loss by *her* birthday.) Not only does their reunion take place under his aegis; on the brink of marriage, they recall his death, suggesting that the new life they are about to begin is an answer to that death, something offered to his memory' (pp. 107–8).

19

'HAVE YOU FORGOT YOUR LOVE?'

Material memory and forgetfulness in *Love's Labour's Lost* and *Measure for Measure*

Christine Sukic

One of memory's most common metaphors is that of the book, a material association that is supposed to give tangibility to that sometimes elusive notion.[1] In Shakespearean drama, one of the famous examples of that need for concreteness and search for signs is when Hamlet asks for his 'tables' (I.5.107) in order to better remember the injunction of his father's ghost, after having decided to erase all previous encumbering facts from the 'table of [his] Memory' (I.5.98),[2] thus associating memory with the written text, in both the metaphorical and the literal sense. However, early modern practices of memory did not necessarily favour the written word, and paper memory was sometimes an object of suspicion, with or without the reference to Plato's *Phaedrus*, the most often quoted origin for this mistrust. The *topos* that the use of the written word favours laziness and hinders the capacity to reminisce is thus found throughout the early modern period, from William Fulwood who, in his translation of Guglielmo Gratarolo's treatise *The castel of memorie* (1562) recommended his readers 'Take heede leste the writinge of things doe not hurte your Memorye',[3] to Edward Reynolds, in his *Treatise of the Passions and Faculties of the Soule of Man* (1640), who pointed to the limitations of writing in the practice of reminiscence, opposing the external memory of the desks to that of the mind:

> Plato telleth us, that the use of Letters, in gathering *Advarsaria* and Collections, is a hinderance to the Memorie; because those things which wee have deposited to our Desks, wee are the more secure and carelesse to retaine in our Minds.[4]

Thus memory is placed within this contradiction of being induced by reminiscence relying on material objects such as books and letters, while the use of such objects is supposed to actually hinder the practice of memory.[5] Both *Measure for Measure* and *Love's Labour's Lost* seem to be correlated with that contradiction, in that they counterbalance the materiality of memory with many instances of oblivion — deliberate or not. In *Love's Labour's Lost*, the oath signed on paper in the first scene of the play is almost immediately broken and constitutes the starting-point of the plot. In *Measure for Measure*, Angelo urges Isabella to forswear her vow of chastity while he himself deliberately forgets about his promise of pardon, as he also chose to forget his promise to marry Mariana. Although both plays set numerous written objects before the spectators' eyes, they also point to the unreliability of the written text to prompt memory, so that they both seem to be subject to the 'razure of oblivion' seen by the Duke as one of the dangers of the 'tooth of time' in *Measure for Measure* (V.1.13–14).

That Shakespeare would be questioning the validity of paper memory is, after all, not very surprising for a playwright and actor confronted with — for himself or his fellow actors — the task of memorizing lines to be uttered in the playhouse,[6] but his mistrust of the written text as a source of memory is first and foremost of an aesthetic nature in those two comedies: rejecting the idea of a stable written word as fixed in marble, he favours mutability over fixity when it comes to the written text. His contemporary Montaigne expressed the same kind of inclination for changeability by relating reading and forgetting: 'if I be a man of some reading, yet I am a man of no remembring, I conceive no certainty'.[7] I would like to examine the question of memory and forgetfulness in *Love's Labour's Lost* and *Measure for Measure* by taking into account that early modern interrogation of the written word and its legitimacy, since the text is often envisaged in its erasable form, and therefore as a constant palimpsest, by Shakespeare, Montaigne, and many of their contemporaries. The figure of Memory itself, in emblem books, is usually represented with a pen and a book, which is sometimes identified as a palimpsest,[8] to suggest the reversibility and changeability of a text constantly threatened by oblivion. The status of the written word in the early modern period and the palimpsestic aspect of the early modern page not only testify to a culture of borrowing, imitating, and appropriating but they also, and more deeply, inform us on an aesthetics based on the notion of effacement and erasure.

Forgetting the word of the law

Frederick Kiefer has noted the importance of written materials, more especially poems, as stage-properties, in *Love's Labour's Lost*.[9] In *Measure for Measure* as well, objects that are or bear forms of writing appear, either literally as stage-properties, or metaphorically as a sort of secondary text meant to elicit the characters' memory primarily of laws and rules. For that effect, the written text is of a prescriptive nature.

In *Love's Labour's Lost*, the oath signed on paper in the first scene of the play is a prescriptive element that suggests that the signatories — the four young men — will remember its contents and therefore conform to its terms, as Navarre reminds them:

> You three, Berowne, Dumaine, and Longaville,
> Have sworn for three years' term to live with me,
> My fellow-scholars, and to keep those statutes
> That are recorded in this schedule here.
> Your oaths are passed, and now subscribe your names.
> (I.1.15–19)

The verb 'recorded' is related by its etymology (through the Latin verb *ricordari*) and one of its older meanings to a process of recollection.[10] The necessity that document be signed completes the association with memory. The signatures attest to the written nature of the law and reinforce its prescriptive nature. In his dedicatory letter to King James in *The Advancement of Learning* (1605), Francis Bacon associates inscription and prescription, especially if the text is placed within the power of a king. The royal inscription turns the text into a 'monument' of fixed memory:

> This propriety [of knowledge and learning] inherent and individuall attribute in your Majestie deserveth to be expressed, not onely in the same and admiration of the present time, nor in the Historie or tradition of the ages succeeding; but also in some solide worke, fixed memoriall, and immortall monument, bearing a Character or signature, both of the power of a king, and the difference and perfection of such a king.[11]

In *Love's Labour's Lost*, Navarre's claim of the prescriptive nature of the subscription is reinforced by his initial reference to 'fame' being 'registered upon [their] brazen tombs' (I.1.2) even though, as William C. Carroll has shown, fame is at first 'something noble here, a power which can defeat mutability' before it changes meaning in the course of the scene and turns 'from written inscription to oral rumour' when Berowne uses the word a few lines down: 'Too much to know is to know naught but fame' (I.1.92).[12] Of course, a prescriptive text such as a law can be written or unwritten, but it is related to memory.[13] Andy Wood has pointed to the importance of that relation, especially in England, where the law is often unwritten (*jus non scriptum*) and must therefore be remembered through 'textual' or 'verbal' means.[14]

The legal dimension of *Measure for Measure* has long been documented, prescription and punishment being determinant in the plot to the point that the play ends on the actual performance of a trial.[15] However, the law, when Duke Vincentio purports to leave the power of government and of the law in the hands of Angelo, seems to have gone into disrepute and is no longer prescriptive since, as Claudio tells Lucio, it is hardly ever used, like an old and neglected suit of armour, until, of course, Angelo steps in:

> but this new governor
> Awakes me all the enrolled penalties
> Which have, like unscour'd armour, hung by th'wall
> So long, that nineteen zodiacs have gone round,
> And none of them been worn; and for a name
> Now puts the drowsy and neglected act
> Freshly on me
>
> *(I.2.154–60)*

The idea that the law is dead if it is forgotten is confirmed by the Duke in the next scene, when he complains to Friar Thomas that 'decrees' are 'dead' (I.3.27–8). The wear and tear of the law is thus described as carelessness or absent-mindedness ('we have let slip', I.3.21), as if its prescriptive aspect required an active use of one's memory. While in *Love's Labour's Lost* the play starts on the active prescription of a set of rules, in *Measure for Measure* Angelo's action is prompted by what is seen by some as a neglect of the law and a passive attitude of both state and subjects.

However, in both cases, and even though the plays abound in references to acts of writing or written objects, the claim for a prescriptive use of an oath or the law is soon forgotten and rendered obsolete by mere oblivion. In *Love's Labour's Lost*, as early as act I, scene 1, this pattern is acted out on stage when Berowne reads out items from the written oath, and announces in the same breath the arrival of the Princess of France, and so the necessity of breaking the article he was reading out, which becomes, perforce, 'in vain' (I.1.137). Oblivion is concomitant with the written word, as Navarre expresses it: realizing that 'this was quite forgot' (I.1.139), he immediately decides that they 'must of force dispense with this decree' (I.1.145).

Antimnemonic objects

The instability of the written word in the text of *Love's Labour's Lost* is seen in the numerous instances of the word 'forswear' (and variants such as 'forsworn'). This emphasis on the disregard for prescriptive texts could be confronted with the many instances of, or references to, written objects in the play.[16] When Navarre first meets the Princess and announces that he has 'sworn an oath' (II.1.97), she immediately points to the danger of such an act: 'Our Lady help my lord! He'll be forsworn' (II.1.98). The oath is still present in the audience's minds, as it appears as a stage-property in I.1 as a sort of mnemonic object reminding the spectators, not of the prescriptive effect of the document, but on the contrary, of its total neglect. The same could be said about the piece of paper given to Navarre by the Princess ('resolve me in my suit', II.1.110). Most editors place a stage direction at this point indicating that the Princess gives Navarre 'a paper'. The suit is not mentioned again until V.2.733 ('my great suit so easily obtained'), when the spectators suddenly remember the reason for the Princess's visit to Navarre. Written objects are thus mnemonic stage-properties in as much as they point to the characters' or the spectators' forgetfulness. They are displayed or handled on stage as a reminder of the worthlessness of the written word. In act II.1, once it is ascertained that the king is about to forswear his oath, he himself is turned into a written object by Boyet, who remarks that, Navarre's heart being 'impressed' with the Princess's 'print' (II. 1. 235), his face now looks like the page of a book: 'His face's own margin did quote such amazes' (II.1.245). In early modern practices of note-taking, as Richard Yeo has pointed out, the page margin was often used as a place of recollection.[17] The margin could be a creative and a methodical space, as in James Cleland's *Hero-paideia, or the institution of a young noble man* (1607), in which the author recommends using the margin 'for the exercising of your owne judgment and confirming your memorie', especially if the book being read 'be a Rapsodie, without anie coherenes of the parts therof, as Criticall and lawe bookes are'.[18] The margin is a place of memory but one related to the instability of a disparate text. As Grant Williams has stressed, the term 'rhapsody' is related by writers such as Robert Burton and Thomas Browne to an 'epidemic of error': they associate the danger of forgetfulness with the proliferation of knowledge and of the printing press.[19]

In act IV, scene 3, the stage is also invaded with pieces of paper that, at once, testify to the love of the men towards the women, but are also mnemonic objects reminding spectators of the four young men's having forgotten the oath as well as their betrayal of each other. The papers thus appear as double visual signs, being reminiscent at once of a practice of love poetry based on the Petrarchan tradition, as well as of the young men's inability to stick to their previous oath. Writing about Desdemona's handkerchief, Hester Lees-Jeffries sees it as a material object becoming a palimpsest on which both texts (the erased one and the new one) can still be read: 'More allusively, it can refer to any image or text (or even an object) where another version as it were shows through'.[20] The same image of the palimpsest can be applied to the textual objects of *Love's Labour's Lost*, since they are the basis of two contradictory texts, both simultaneously readable by the spectators. Although this scene is based on the visual accumulation of written objects as stage-properties and reading materials (with the successive entrances of the four young men each holding a paper as well as Berowne's letter produced by Jaquenetta when she enters (l.185)), it constantly reminds us that the written text is imperilled by the young men's ability to erase it from their memory in order to replace the old text (the 'old decree', IV.3.213) with something new. Berowne is able to express this constant erasure by a paradox: 'we have made a vow to study, lords, / And in that vow we have forsworn our books' (IV.3.292–3). By saying so, he turns forswearing into a necessity: 'It is religion to be thus forsworn' (IV.3.337). By confronting the concreteness of the written paper with the ability of the young men to metaphorically erase their signed name on another piece of paper, Shakespeare does not only represent with a visual sign the *tabula rasa* effect of love on these four young men, he also points to an inherent textual reversibility that is part and parcel of the play's aesthetics.

Erasing memory

In *Measure for Measure* the written text as well as the signature serves as a sign of legitimacy, as when the Duke (acting as Friar Lodowick) asks the Provost to recognize his hand and seal: 'Look you, sir, here is the hand and seal of the Duke: you know the character, I doubt not, and the signet is not strange to you?' (IV.2.190–3). Again, the visual display of the letter is supposed to convince the Provost of the Friar's legitimacy because he can remember the Duke's handwriting. For the spectators, the use of this stage-prop is both a visual reminder of the Duke's authority as well as of the ambivalence of the written word, being an instrument in the hands of the Duke to manipulate his interlocutors. It is also interesting that memory is often associated with the image of the seal, with Aristotle as a common source, when he describes the imprinting of an image in memory: 'the change that occurs marks in a sort of imprint, as it were, of the sense-image, as people do who seal things with signet rings'.[21] The reference to the seal reinforces the idea of an imprint of images in memory but at the same time jeopardizes its validity since the spectators know about the Duke's double dealing.

This double reading of the written text is confirmed by the several instances of written stage-properties in the same scene, this time attributed to Angelo. Having been entrusted with executive and legislative power by the Duke, Angelo is in charge of the authority of the written word: he intends to remind the people of Vienna of the validity of the law, since it has been forgotten until then. The law must be part of a constant memorial process that is based on visibility. Angelo often claims the need to make things visible, as when he requires to see Claudio's head after his execution. As he tells Escalus, during a dialogue about Claudio's upcoming condemnation and execution, 'what we do not see, / We tread upon, and never think of it' (II.2.25–6). The 'precise Angelo' (III.1.93) is not only characterized by a strict observance of rules but also by exactness in his understanding of the law, not only in the spirit but also in the letter. In act IV, scene 2, the warrant for Claudio's death is displayed by the Provost, who stresses its prescriptive value by pointing to its presence on stage: 'Look, here's the warrant, Claudio, for thy death' (IV.2.61). For the spectators, this memorial object serves as a reminder of Angelo's puristic application of the law, even though the Duke/Friar Lodowick is adamant that the 'countermand' (IV.2.90) will turn up and annul the warrant. The prescriptive value of the warrant is substantiated by the arrival on stage of a messenger who brings a new 'note' (IV.2.100). Far from being a 'countermand', the note is meant to remind the Provost of his task: 'that you swerve not from the smallest article of it, neither in time, matter, or other circumstance' (IV.2.101–3). In other words, the note is a verbatim repetition of the warrant: memorial accuracy is of prime importance in this case. In order to make things clear, Shakespeare has the 'note' read out by the Provost. Angelo reiterates the necessity of having visual proof of the execution: 'For my better satisfaction, let me have Claudio's head sent me by five' (IV.2.120–1). In a way, his memorial activity is characterized by two ways of memorizing: verbatim memorization as well as *memoria rerum*, the memory of things.[22]

However precise Angelo is, he is also versed in the art of forgetting, being ready to do away with the word of the law. He combines an image of erasure with scatological and erotic metaphors: 'Having waste ground enough, / Shall we desire to raze the sanctuary / And pitch our evils there?' (II.2.170–2). In the early modern period, erotic pleasure was said to be a cause for amnesia, which Helkiah Crooke marvels at in *Mikrokosmographia*, in which he associates sexual ecstasy, oblivion, and moral depravity:

> For were it not that the God of Nature hath placed heerein so incredible a sting or rage of pleasure, as whereby wee are transported for a time as it were out of our selves, what man is there almost who hath anie sense of his own divine nature, that would defile himselfe in such impurities.[23]

Angelo uses images that are comparable, being ready to give way to lusty oblivion (to 'raze the sanctuary') and to forget about the letter of the law in order to deposit his 'evils' into the sanctuary of Isabella's body. By doing so, he is also requiring of her that she forgets about her future vows, since she is still 'unsworn' (I.4.9). Should she yield to his sexual advances, she would, paradoxically, be 'forsworn' before she is 'sworn'.

More than a man of memory and a stickler for the letter of the law, Angelo is rather a forgetful, absent-minded character given to amnesia. His relation to Mariana can also be read in terms of the written word as prescriptive evidence being at the same time forgotten and replaced, like a palimpsest, by another type of narrative. In fact, the plot seems to be based on the oblivion of a written text that has to be reminded to forgetful, or amnesic characters. Even the Duke's written word is subject to a form of effacement and replacement by another text: 'Every letter he hath writ hath disvouched other' (IV.4.1), Escalus tells Angelo. As for Claudio and Juliet's 'true contract' (I.2.134), it is only partly remembered by the two lovers who forget about a formal marriage. Angelo himself is Mariana's husband 'on a pre-contract' (IV.1.72) but this contract, far from representing a form of prescription, has fallen into oblivion: 'my husband / Knows not that ever he knew me' (V.1.187–8). Even though the word 'forswear' is not as frequent as in *Love's Labour's Lost*, Angelo can be described as having forsworn his words to Mariana. She reminds him of his utterance of those words, as well as of the contract, made unbreachable through their vows: 'I am affianc'd this man's wife, as strongly / As words could make up vows' (V.1.226–7). In act V, Isabella kneels before the Duke to expose and confront him as being 'forsworn' (V.1.40). Just like in *Love's Labour's Lost*, forswearing becomes one of the bases of the plot and the text of the law is submitted to the menace of reversibility. Isabella, at this point in the play, like Mariana, is the depository of memory.

Effacement of body memory

The memory of the written word is thus unreliable. Both plays seem then to accredit the idea that, more than the written word, the body can be the receptacle of memory, as well as its visual emblem on the stage. The 'true contract' of the marriage between Juliet and Claudio having been forgotten, the written text becomes the 'character' written on Juliet's body, as Claudio himself acknowledges (I.2.143–4). Mariana also points to the importance of the body in the memory of her engagement with Angelo, as she tells him: 'This is the hand which, with a vow'd contract, / Was fast belock'd in thine' (V.1.206–9). Finally, the Duke forces Angelo to remember Mariana's body by staging the substitution of Isabella by Mariana. In both plays, *Love's Labour's Lost* and *Measure for Measure*, the body becomes the textual depository of a certain type of memory.

In *Love's Labour's Lost*, when Berowne tells Rosaline: 'These lords have visited: you are not free, / For the Lord's tokens on you do I see' (V.2.422–3), he is using the word 'token' as a polysemic term, meaning both the small gifts given by the young men to the ladies, as well as the 'plague spots', the signs of the plague. This word was often used in a medical context as a synonym of 'symptom'.[24] Its double meaning is here particularly relevant, since it refers to both an object and a body part, and in both cases is a sign, either a proof of love, or evidence of death to come, but also an object of memory: the token bears at once the memory of the deathly disease, and it reminds the ladies of the young men's love. The tokens given by the young lords are, indeed, 'remembrances' – the word Ophelia uses in *Hamlet* – that is to say objects to be kept as a memorial. They are interesting as signs since, like written objects, they are supposed to elicit remembrance that they signify in their material aspect. What is more, as symptoms, they suggest that the body itself is the seat of memory, an idea that is also suggested every time a body part is compared to a written text. This objectification of the body as a seat of memory could be related to the search for a specific space within the body devoted to memory, of which there are several examples in the early modern period, as well as earlier ones.[25] That memory is related to the body is also obvious in the bodily metaphors used to define it, as for instance when Edward Reynolds quotes Saint Augustine – 'some have called the Memorie, the Belly of the Soule' – and recommends long-term digestion in order to preserve it: 'it is true in the Minde, as in the Stomach; too quick digestion doth always more distemper than nourish, and breedeth nothing but Crudities in Learning. Nor can I call so much Studie, as agitation and restlesnesse of the Minde'.[26] However, in *Love's Labour's Lost*, it is not so much the identification and localization of material memory that is at stake, but the idea that the body itself is a memento. There are several examples in the play, such as Navarre's heart being turned into an imprinted object ('His heart, like an agate with your print impressed', II.1.235), or his face into the page of a book ('His face's own margin did quote such amazes', II.1.242). The pedants also have a physical relation to the text and the way to absorb knowledge as Nathaniel suggests when saying about Dull that 'he hath never fed of the dainties that are bred in a book, / He hath not eat paper, as it were; he hath not drunk ink' (IV.2.24–5).

Far from being statufied and treated as a worthy monument, the body is subject to objectification as a memento. In *Measure for Measure* this is particularly obvious, first in the character of Juliet, whose body bears the memory of the consummation of her marriage to Claudio before the 'denunciation': 'The stealth of our most mutual entertainment / With character too gross is written on Juliet' (I.2.143–4). As Janet Adelman has rightly pointed out, Juliet's body bears the frightful memory of an original sin and as such, is the cause of Claudio's condemnation, and yet, it seems to disappear from the text of the play as well as the space of the stage:

> Juliet's pregnant body is the originating site for this play's confrontation with sin and death; it itself is the 'character too gross' (1.2.144) in which Claudio's sin is written and hence the material cause of his subjection to death. As such, it is a visible reminder of maternal origins and of the danger that is their inheritance. But the body so prominent in the beginning is curiously effaced by the action of the play, as the relationship between Juliet and Claudio is effaced; and this effacement seems to me a sign of the play's uneasy relation to sexuality and to the pregnant female body as the site of origin.[27]

The same process of effacement can be observed in Isabella, and even more so with Mariana, who is, more than a memento, an object of amnesia, Angelo having 'swallowed his vows whole, pretending in her discoveries of dishonour' (III.1.226–7). Forgetfulness is here a devouring act through which Angelo has erased Mariana's body from his memory, while she herself appears as a figure of memory, or even hypermnesia: 'This forenamed maid hath yet in her the continuance of her first affection' (III.1.239–40). The lyrics of the song sung for her at the beginning of act IV, scene 1 point to her hypermnesic state of mind – she is entirely turned towards the memory of her former lover – while, again, the vows she took having lost their legitimacy, the body seems to be subject to a process of effacement:

> Take, o take those lips away
>   that so sweetly were forsworn,
> And those eyes, the break of day
>   lights that do mislead the morn:
> But my kisses bring again,
>   bring again;
> Seals of love, but seal'd in vain,
>   seal'd in vain.
>   *(IV.1.1–6)*

The effacement of her body is further stressed when Angelo sleeps with her without realising it. The interchangeability of the two women's bodies turns them into generic women, with a loss of their identity and whatever makes a body memorable to all the senses. Mariana's body is thus the seat of Angelo's oblivion, while his memory of Isabella's body is completely wrong. The reversibility of the two bodies makes it impossible to remember them as seats of love.

That there is a commodification, not only of Isabella's body but of women's bodies in general, in *Measure for Measure* is quite obvious.[28] Angelo can be seen as one of the great consumers in that trade, but more than buying, he mainly objectifies women's bodies and uses them as palimpsests of his own desires. He manages to erase Mariana from his memory – he is, the Duke says, 'a marble to her tears' (III.1.229), as if no memory of her could ever be written again on him – at the same time erasing the desire for her body in order to better replace it with Isabella's, as Mariana states it when questioned by the Duke about her husband: 'that is Angelo, / Who thinks he knows that he ne'er knew my body, / But knows, he thinks, that he knows Isabel's' (V.1.201–3). The substitution of Isabella by Mariana, and then the revelation of the trick by the Duke in the final scene, provides shock-treatment for Angelo's amnesia, he being reminded by Mariana – using deictics – of what, and whom, he had forgotten:

> This is that face, thou cruel Angelo,
> Which once thou swor'st was worth the looking on:
> This is the hand which, with a vow'd contract,
> Was fast belock'd in thine.
>   *(V.1.206–9)*

Having been shown what is beneath Mariana's veil – her face, suddenly reappearing and revealed on stage – he finally admits to having been 'contracted' to Mariana (V.1.373–4). The commodification of bodies as erasable seats of memory is confirmed in the play by the substitution of Claudio's head with that of Ragozine. There is a first attempt at erasing all memory of Barnardine's head in order to re-create a substitute Claudio, but Barnardine refuses. Being drunk most of the time, he is remarkably devoid of any kind of memory: 'careless, reckless, and fearless of what's past, present, or to come' (IV.2.141–2). Conversely, the Duke is able to erase all of Ragozine's identity, even though the pirate is endowed with a certain notoriety (IV.3.70), but his face testifies to its palimpsestic possibilities: 'A man of Claudio's years; his beard and head / Just of his colour' (IV.3.71–2). Hence Ragozine's head simply becomes 'the head' (IV.3.91), and confirms the palimpsestic qualities of the human body in the play.

Comedy and forgetfulness

Memory is first and foremost an unstable notion in *Love's Labour's Lost* and *Measure for Measure*, if only because of Shakespeare's ability to re-write known – or unknown – source material and his selective memory, or his distortion of a source that he may have re-written from memory. More importantly, we may wonder whether oblivion and a certain aesthetic instability are pre-requisites of comedy. After all, Shakespeare's tragedies seem to be based on the memory, even the rumination of, indeed the obsession for, certain facts or objects, maybe because they are based on foundational scenes that provide the ground for the tragedy — the equivalent of the classical tragic fault. One of Whitney's emblems, *Scribit in marmore laesus* ('the wronged man writes in marble') associates memory and pain. As the words of the wronged man are inscribed in marble, their memory is therefore indelible. Whitney also stresses the erasability of happiness, as opposed to grief:

> In marble harde our harmes wee alwayes grave,
> Bicause, wee still will beare the same in minde:
> In duste wee write the benifittes wee have,
> Where they are soone defaced with the winde.[29]

While pain is part of a memorial process, oblivion or misused memory could be seen as a cause for comedy. In *Love's Labour's Lost*, the main comic situation is the immediate forswearing of the oath by the four young men, already anticipated by Berowne, who ironizes on the 'necessity' of that breach of faith: 'If I break faith, this word shall speak for me: / I am forsworn on "mere necessity"' (I.1.151–2). Paradoxically, the little 'academe' of learning is quite forgotten and from then on, the young men seem to devote themselves to short-term memory only, in particular the arrival of the French princess and her three attending ladies. Anything that goes beyond this recent event seems to be dismissed by the characters and to disappear from the plot. The Princess's suit, for instance, although it is the pretext of her visit to Navarre, is forgotten twice, being, as the king states it in I.1, 'quite forgot' (139), then described in act II, scene 1, but forgotten again: it does not reappear into the plot until the very end of the play, when, at V. 2. 733, we learn that the suit has been granted but with no further details. Other elements of the comic plot involve a loss of memory, as when Costard, who is in charge of delivering letters, cannot remember who gave him each letter, and who to deliver it to. The possibility of a blunder is announced when Berowne asks him to do something for him. Costard agrees but leaves before he knows what it is, since, as he states it himself, 'I shall know, sir, when I have done it' (III.1.154). He thus demonstrates that his memory works through experience, not language, whether written or oral: he acts, therefore he knows, but his knowledge does not seem to be containable. As a forgetful character, he is a valuable source of comedy in the play, since his knowledge of words is only partial, and based on association, rather than accumulation. For instance, the word 'enigma' reminds him of 'egma', which he seems to take for some sort of enema or clyster-pipe (III.1.69). His inability to remember the meaning of 'remuneration' (which he takes to mean 'the Latin word for three-farthings', III.1.134), is also the source of sexual puns – 'Why it is a fairer name than French crown' (III.1.137–8) – and more comedy. The 'remuneration' turns in fact into a quid pro quo: instead of a reward or recompense for a well-accomplished work, as well as the 'guerdon' used by Berowne (III.1.164), it instead leads to a substitution of letters resulting in Armado being further mocked while Berowne's love for Rosaline is exposed to his friends in act IV, scene 3.

Dull is another character whose comedic energy is based on his inability to remember the proper form of words. His malapropisms invade the text and point to its reversibility – 'reprehend' for 'apprehend'; 'farborough' for 'thirdborough' (I.1.181, 182) – and even contaminate Costard who turns 'contents' into 'contempts' (I.1.187). The same could be said of Elbow in *Measure for Measure*, who is unable to remember words properly and turns their meaning inside out, the two malefactors becoming 'two notorious benefactors' (II.1.50). Again, comedy is based on surprise effects and produced by characters whose memory of language is very selective.

Nonetheless, there are characters who represent a certain type of memory, while being clearly the subject of comedy. In *Love's Labour's Lost*, the pedants (Holofernes, Nathanael and Armado) are all three devoted to a certain knowledge of the past, seen in their use of Latin, for instance, or in their references to classical authors. Armado should be set apart, since his memory is also selective, being unable to remember figures – 'I am ill at reckoning', he says in act I, scene 2 – and whose mythological knowledge is incomplete, so much so that he has to question Moth, his page, on basic facts, asking 'Comfort me, boy, what great men have been in love?' (I.2.63). At the same time, Armado is able to remember the most complex and rarest of words, such as 'indubitate' (IV.1.66) or combine the memory of two words into one, such as his 'annothanise' (IV.1.68) or 'infamonise' (V.2.674).

The pedants Holofernes and Nathanael can be related to a specific practice of memory, since they pride themselves on their keen knowledge of rare words as well as of Latin. Holofernes in particular, illustrates the importance of memory and of learning by heart in the classroom, where the 'table-book' drawn by Nathaniel (V.1.15) was commonly used to take notes. Nathaniel is particularly interested in remembering the word 'peregrinate' just used by Holofernes – a word coined by Shakespeare – so he writes it down in order to have a little reminder with him. Holofernes' and Nathaniel's knowledge is based on their faculty for remembering the most obscure and useless elements of knowledge, which affords them the opportunity to add variety to their copious language. Holofernes himself describes the way in which his memory works:

> This is a gift I have, simple, simple – a foolish extravagant spirit, full of forms, figures, shapes, objects, ideas, apprehensions, motions, revolutions. These are begot in the ventricle of memory, nourished in the womb of *pia mater* and delivered upon the mellowing of occasion.
>
> *(IV.2.65–70)*

As William C. Carroll has observed, Holofernes' mind is not gifted with the power of imagination; it is simply full of material he can summon up when he needs a synonym in order to introduce *varietas*.[30] Variety is brought about by synonymy, which suggests that any word can be substituted by its synonym, its roughly equivalent. Holofernes, for instance, manages to use three synonyms suggesting the deer killed by the Princess was in prime condition, as well as four synonyms for the word 'sky': 'The deer was, as you know, *sanguis*, in blood, ripe as the pomewater, who now hangeth like a jewel in the ear of *caelo*, the sky, the welkin, the heaven' (IV.2.3–5). Armado, by the way, is given to the same kind of idiosyncracy.

This capacity to consider any word the equivalent of another can be related to the technique of the palimpsest, suggesting that a text can replace another after wiping out the original text. This was, by the way, common in the use of table-books: these were made up of tablets, that is to say sheets, of various materials, but erasable ones. According to Richard Yeo, words written on table-books were usually wiped away because they represented short-term information (such as shopping-lists) or 'moved into more permanent notebooks for storage, analysis, and subsequent communication'.[31] Black slate, or *palimpsestus*, was also an object used in the early modern classroom, as described in the book by the schoolmaster Charles Hoole, *An easie entrance to the Latine tongue* (London, 1649). In the part entitled 'Of a school' devoted to objects used in a classroom, Hoole illustrates the importance of writing and re-writing by including such elements as 'a black-slate, *Palimpsestus*', or 'a sponge to rub out what is written, *Spóngia delétilis*'.[32] The pedants' memory involves several superimposed texts, testifying to short-term memory, improperly digested, as Holofernes' style often suggests:

> *Fauste precor, gelida quando pecus omne sub umbra Ruminat*—
> And so forth. Ah, good old Mantuan, I may speak of thee as the traveller doth of Venice:
> *Venetia, Venetia,*
> *Chi non ti vede, non ti pretia.*
> Old Mantuan, old Mantuan, who understandeth thee not, loves thee not. [*He sings*].
> Ut, re, sol, la, mi, fa.
>
> (IV.2.91–9)

The macaronic aspect of those lines can be read as a superimposition of words of various languages as well as a juxtaposition. They evoke short-term memory as they can be forgotten, erased from one's memory as soon as they are uttered. Language, as well as situation, is thus often subject to a palimpsestic process.

More than the pattern of reminiscence that seems to be at stake in many tragedies, *Love's Labour's Lost* and *Measure for Measure* are characterized by amnesia and forgetfulness. Forgetting, as an essential part of the economy of comedy, often paves the way for surprise effects, mistakes, and misunderstandings that allow for subversive strategies, such as the mocking four young men about to forego the company of women or the revelation of hypocrisy of self-righteousness. But more than this, oblivion and absent mindedness give the text of these plays, as well as their performance on stage, an unstable quality, allowing for a palimpsestic aesthetics. Instead of a direct, straightforward access to knowledge, these two comedies display a poetics of oblivion whereby the truth of the text is not to be found in its capacity to assert and memorize, but, on the contrary, in its ability to forget, subvert, and substitute. While in *Love's Labour's Lost*, the written word is constantly escaping us, being either faulty, or unreliable, and given to complete reversal, in *Measure for Measure*, oblivion and substitution suggest the impossibility of fixing meaning. In both cases, truth is fleeting, and relative. The nature of the text for Shakespeare is always, as for Montaigne, susceptible to forgetfulness, change, and substitution. Montaigne did not hesitate to admit to being himself forgetful: 'There is not a Man living, whom it would so little become to speak of Memory as my self, for I have none at all; and do not think that the World has again another so treacherous as mine'.[33] Shakespeare displays this same contradiction as Montaigne: while steeped in a culture of borrowing, based on the memory of other works, he constantly reminds us of the reversibility of the text.

Notes

1 See Mary Carruthers, *The Book of Memory: A Study of Memory in Medieval Culture* (Cambridge University Press, 2008).
2 On this subject, see the seminal article by Peter Stallybrass, Roger Chartier, J. Franklin Mowery and Heather Wolfe, 'Hamlet's Tables and the Technologies of Writing in Renaissance England', *Shakespeare Quarterly*, 55.4 (Winter 2004), pp. 379–419.

3 Guglielmo Gratarolo, *The castel of memorie ... Englished by Willyam Fulwood*, 1562, sig. G1ᵛ.
4 Edward Reynoldes, *A treatise of the passions and faculties of the soule of man* ..., 1640, p. 17.
5 See Richard Yeo, *Notebooks, English Virtuosi, and Early Modern Science*, University of Chicago Press, 2014.
6 On the subject of actors and memory, see Lina Perkins Wilder, *Shakespeare's Memory Theatre: Recollection, Properties, and Character*, Cambridge University Press, 2010, pp. 32–35, and on the question of rehearsal in general in the early modern period, see Tiffany Stern, *Rehearsal from Shakespeare to Sheridan*, Oxford, Clarendon Press, 2000.
7 Michel de Montaigne, *Essays* ..., transl. John Florio, London, 1613 edition, Book II, chapter 10, 'Of bookes', p. 226.
8 Commenting on a figure of Memory that appears in the margin of Queen Elizabeth's Prayer Book, William E. Engel remarks: 'Memory is appropriately tagged here as being "a treasure house", and is easily recognized by her traditional attributes of a pen (or stylus) in her right hand and a book (or palimpsest) in the other' ('The Decay of memory', in Christopher Ivic and Grant Williams (eds), *Forgetting in Early Modern English Literature and Culture. Lethe's Legacies*, London and New York, Routledge, 2004, pp. 21–40, here p. 25).
9 Frederick Kiefer, 'Poems as Props in *Love's Labour's Lost* and *Much Ado About Nothing*', in *Reading and Literacy in the Middle Ages and Renaissance*, ed. Ian Frederick Moulton, Brepols Publishers, 2004, pp. 127–41.
10 The *OED* gives, as one of the obsolete meanings of the verb: 'To learn by heart, to commit to memory, to go over in one's mind; (also) to repeat or say over as a lesson or portion of memorized text, to recite'.
11 Francis Bacon, *The two bookes of Francis Bacon. Of the proficience and advancement of learning, divine and humane*, 1605, 'To the King', sig. A2ᵛ–A3ʳ.
12 William C. Carroll, *The Great Feast of Language in* Love's Labour's Lost, Princeton, NJ, Princeton University Press, [1976], 2015, pp. 22, 23.
13 On the relation between law and memory, see for instance John Goodrich, *Oedipus Lex. Psychoanalysis, History, Law*, Berkeley and Los Angeles, California, University of California Press, 1995, pp. 182–3.
14 Andy Wood, *The Memory of the People: Custom and Popular Senses of the Past in Early Modern England*, Cambridge University Press, 2013, pp. 247–86.
15 See Ervene Gulley, '"Dressed in a Little Brief Authority": Law as Theater in *Measure for Measure*', in *Law and Literature Perspectives*, Bruce L. Rockwood, ed., Peter Lang, 1996, pp. 53–80.
16 On the use of written objects in the play, see Christine Sukic, ' "I am sure I shall turn sonnet": Writing or Being Written in *Love's Labour's Lost*', *Love's Labour's Lost ou l'art de séduire*, Christian Gutleben (ed.), *Cycnos*, volume, no. 1, 2015, Paris, L'Harmattan, pp. 35–46.
17 Richard Yeo (*op. cit.*) describes for example John Evelyn's marginal note-taking (pp. 60–1) or John Locke's use of marginal Heads in his journal (pp. 205–6). Mary Carruthers, in *The Book of Memory*, writes on marginal notes or designs in medieval manuscripts as a way of 'distinguishing the book' drawn from mnemonic techniques (p. 309).
18 James Cleland, *Hero-paideia, or the institution of a young noble man* ... Oxford, 1607, p. 160.
19 Grant Williams, 'Textual Crudities in Robert Burton's *Anatomy of Melancholy* and Thomas Browne's *Pseudodoxia Epidemica*', in *Forgetting in Early Modern English Literature and Culture. Lethe's Legacies*, Christopher Ivic and Grant Williams (eds), London and New York, Routledge, 2004, pp. 67–82, p. 75.
20 Hester Lees-Jeffries, *Shakespeare and Memory*, Oxford Shakespeare Topics, Oxford University Press, 2013, p. 157.
21 Aristotle, *On Memory*, 450a 25, transl. R. Sorabji, Providence, RI, Brown University Press, 1960, quoted in Mary Carruthers, *The Book of Memory, op. cit.*, p. 19.
22 On those two memorizing techniques used in the Middle Ages, see Mary Carruthers, *The Book of Memory, op. cit*, pp. 113–18.
23 Helkiah Crooke, *Mikrokosmographia a description of the body of man* ..., 1615, p. 200, quoted by Elizabeth D. Harvey, 'Pleasure's Oblivion: Displacements of Generation in Spenser's *Faerie Queene*', in *Forgetting in the Early Modern Period, op. cit.*, pp. 53–64, p. 53.
24 On the meaning of the word 'token' in *Love's Labour's Lost*, see Christine Sukic, ' "I smell false Latin, dunghill for *unguem*": Odours and Aromas in *Love's Labour's Lost*', *Actes des congrès de la Société française Shakespeare* [online], 32, 2015, online since March 20th 2015, consulted on November 21st 2015. URL: http://shakespeare.revues.org/3289
25 In *Reading Memory in Early Modern Literature*, Andrew Hiscock gives several examples of this constant inquiry into the human body in order to locate the seat of memory (Cambridge University Press, 2011, pp. 28–31).

26 *A treatise of the passions*, p. 16.
27 Janet Adelman, *Suffocating Mothers: Fantasies of Maternal Origin in Shakespeare's Plays,* Hamlet *to* The Tempest, New York and London, Routledge, 1992, pp. 88–9.
28 See for example Marc Shell, *The End of Kinship:* Measure for Measure, *Incest, and the Ideal of the Universal Siblinghood*, Stanford, CT, Stanford University Press, 1988: '*Measure for Measure* explores the significance not only of paying money for a body but also of using a body as money, for in this play heads and maidenheads are traded as if they were commensurate' (p. 125).
29 Henry Green (ed.), *Whitney's 'Choice of Emblemes'*, A fac-simile reprint, London, Lovell Reeve & Co., 1866, p. 183.
30 '[Holofernes'] power, 'begot in the ventricle of memory,' therefore depends not on the imagination or the phantasy but on a large remembered vocabulary which may be summoned up for 'variation,' yet for nothing that we could term a genuine transformation of language' (William C. Carroll, *The Great Feast of Language, op. cit.*, p. 138.
31 Richard Yeo, *op. cit.*, p. 21.
32 *An easie entrance to the Latine tongue ... a work tending to the school-masters's eas, and the weaker scholar's encouragement in the first and most wearisome steps to learning*, London, 1649, p. 270.
33 *Essays, op. cit.*, p. 44.

PART V

Poetry

20
'SUPPOSE THOU DOST DEFEND ME FROM WHAT IS PAST'

Shakespeare's *Venus and Adonis* and *The Rape of Lucrece* and the appetite for ancient memory

Andrew Hiscock

My poetic metres will sing of you, most chaste virgin monarch, powerful Elizabeth [...] Sad Lucretia is praised with great honour [...] you have deserved greater praise. She was fortunate to be born from noble parents, but your lineage makes you semi-divine [...] The land of Rome bore her, but England, which should be held equal to Rome, gave you your milk as she bore her power. [...] O Elizabeth [...] most sacred monarch, you are welcome as you come to us [...] O goddess worthy of God.

Juno has filled you, Queen, with most abundant riches, Pallas Athena has given you a full share of serious wisdom and the other most distinguished virtues of the mind; but Venus (as she is the goddess of beauty) has given you a tall body, and has added an attractive appearance.

[...] according to Valerius Maximus, those household gods, that state, that kingdom will easily stand securely for ever, where lust for the powers of Venus, and for money, have insinuated themselves the least.[1]

The excerpts above date from the opening decade of Elizabeth I's reign when she was being welcomed ceremonially on her periodic visits to seats of learning in her realm. Fulsome panegyrics, such as these originally framed in Latin, were participating in a particularly favoured political discourse of heroic tribute circulating widely throughout the courts of early modern Europe. Recourse to classical allusion, underpinned by years of studying texts surviving from antiquity, constituted a commonplace expectation for those seeking to celebrate all forms of authority and, indeed, for their learned audiences on such occasions, whether they were Elizabeth's native-born courtiers or foreign visitors. Thus, by the close of the sixteenth century, Shakespeare's narrative poems *Venus and Adonis* (1592–3) and *The Rape of Lucrece* (1593–4) were engaging fully with the markedly recursive motion in evidence across Europe to understand its own cultural relationships of power and affect in terms of mythologies of origin and belonging nurtured by ancient Greek and Roman forebears.

The present discussion interrogates the ways in which these seemingly distant pasts were put to service in late Elizabethan poetics and the ways in which the faculty of memory might be deployed in such instances to test the normative pressures of (self-)government in sixteenth-century England. In *De Inventione* Cicero had notably identified *memoria* as a subdivision of *prudentia* and his taxonomy continued to have enormous influence in succeeding centuries, not only in the writings of Augustine (who, in the *Confessions*, argued that memory became the *venter animi* or 'the stomach of the mind'[2]), but also in those of Thomas Aquinas, for example, in his commentaries upon Aristotle's *De Memoria et Reminiscentia*:

> The role of prudence is to direct the prudent man to do what ought to be done by considering not only the present but also the past. This is why Cicero sets down as the parts of prudence not only foresight, through which future things are attended to, but also understanding, through which present things are considered, and memory, through which past things are apprehended.[3]

Early modern writers remained richly sensitive to these intellectual legacies. Indeed, in the chivalric world of Spenser's epic poem *The Faerie Queene*, for example, the urgent exhortations to remember and to remember oneself are certainly exercised vigorously in the ethical instructions dispensed to the many and various *errant* and *erring* figures in his narratives: 'Vnlucky Squire (said *Guyon*) sith thou hast / Falne vnto mischiefe through intemperaunce, / Henceforth take heede of that thou now hast past, / And guyde thy waies with warie gouernaunce' (II.iv.36).[4]

All too often, in their encounters with the visual arts, musical performance, theatrical entertainment, civic ceremonial and, indeed, the reading matter dedicated to them, early modern monarchs and members of their courtly entourages were invited into the company of the pantheon of Olympian gods and antique heroes.[5] Interestingly, when Spenser's questers enter Castle Joyeous (the house of Malecasta), they discover that 'The wals were round about appareiled / With costly clothes of *Arras* and of *Toure*, / In which with cunning hand was pourtrahed / The love of *Venus* and her Paramoure, / The fayre *Adonis*, turned to a flowre, / A worke of rare deuice and wondrous wit' (III.i.34). Elsewhere, in Marlowe's own epyllion *Hero and Leander* (pub. 1598), the very garments of the heroine ('Venus' nun', 319[6]) are wondrously decorated: 'Her wide sleeves green, and border'd with a grove, / Where Venus in her naked glory strove / To please the careless and disdainful eyes / Of proud Adonis, that before her lies' (11–14). In the 1569 painting 'Elizabeth and the Three Goddesses' attributed to Hans Eworth, the final Tudor monarch keeps company with Pallas Athena, Juno and Venus,[7] and in John Bartlet's *A booke of ayres with a triplicitie of musicke* (1606), the lovesick singer has no possible hope of winning his mistress of 'immortall beautie [...] Since Adone Venus would not woo'.[8]

Nonetheless, as the kaleidoscope of references to myth expands in early modern print and manuscript culture, it soon becomes evident that whether we revisit the supposed travails and tribulations of pagan gods or those of national heroes, the emphasis falls squarely upon the need to render the present legible and its relations of power more susceptible to scrutiny with these shared narratives from the remote past.

Shakespeare's retrospective poetics

By 1605, Richard Barnfield was waxing lyrical in praise of Shakespeare, 'Whose *Venus*, and whose *Lucrece* (sweet and chaste) / Thy name in fames immortall Booke have plac't'.[9] Indeed, it is thought that *Venus and Adonis* was the first production which Shakespeare oversaw through the presses; and if the 1623 First Folio did not *eternize* any of his poems, *Venus and Adonis* proved to be the most popular of his productions at the booksellers, enjoying edition after edition through to the end of the early Stuart period: none of the plays attributed to him could rival the four editions of *The Rape of Lucrece* and the six editions of *Venus and Adonis* printed by 1600. For all eyes, *Venus and Adonis* (1194 lines in 199 sixains) and the 'graver labour'[10] *The Rape of Lucrece* (1855 lines in 265 septets) presented a striking letter of introduction penned by a new writer for a patron, Henry Wriothesley, Earl of Southampton, and, more generally, for the broader reading public of late Elizabethan England.

In recent times, the cultural theorist Richard Terdiman has cautioned that,

> Most often we think of memory as a faculty constituting our consciousness and our self-awareness, as the means by which our coherence and our history is constructed and sustained. Such mnemonic activity is fundamental. But there is another side to memory – memory as a *problem*, as a site and source of cultural disquiet.[11]

Strikingly, such queryings of the faculty were equally prevalent in the early modern period itself. In the new reign of James VI/I, the Dean of St. Pauls, John Donne, reminded his congregation, 'in this survey of sin, thy first care must be, to take heed of returning too diligently to a remembrance of those delightful sins which are past; for that will endanger anew'.[12] The delving of Shakespeare's narrative poems into antique pasts seems similarly to have provoked queasiness and feelings of unease among at least some of his early modern readers. By the 1630s Richard Braithwait was complaining that,

> *Books* treating light subiects, are Nurseries of wantonnesse [...] *Venus and Adonis* are vnfitting Consorts for a Ladies bosom. Remoue them timely from you, if they euer had entertainment by you lest, like the *Snake* in the fable, they annoy you.[13]

With even more vigour, one R. Henderson insisted that 'carnal men [...] England and Romish Jezebels and Italian Courtesans [...] will be frying, boiling, and broiling in their luxurious desires [...] [like that] wanton Venus'.[14] Indeed, nearly two hundred years later, William Hazlitt might be discovered lamenting that,

> It has been the fashion of late to cry up our author's poems, as equal to his plays: this is the desperate cant of modern criticism [...] The two poems of Venus and Adonis and of Tarquin and Lucrece appear to us like a couple of ice-houses. They are about as hard, as glittering, and as cold.[15]

Whatever the remarkable strength and candour of the responses voiced down the centuries with regard to these poems, the labours surrounding the unpicking of ambiguities, equivocations, sometimes opaque correlations and elsewhere teasing correspondences between antique figures and those within living memory often appear to have constituted pleasure principles in the reading strategies of a large number of sophisticated Elizabethan consumers. The latter, and a goodly number of their successors, enjoyed being tempted into deciphering games when being transported to mythological and heroic (nay, seemingly Homeric) settings: 'Even as the sun with purple-coloured face / Had ta'en his last leave of the weeping morn' (*Venus and Adonis*, 1–2). With a most deliberate purpose, Spenser had written 'clowdily'[16] of his knights' adventures in Faerie Lond, and Philip Sidney cautioned in *The Apologie for Poetrie* (1595) that, 'Sometimes, vnder the prettie tales of Wolues and Sheepe, can include the whole considerations of wrong dooing and patience'.[17] However, a generation earlier, in the opening years of the reign of Elizabeth's half-sister Mary, Thomas Wilson might already be found arguing at length in *The Arte of Rhetorique* (1553) that,

> The Poetes were wise men, & wished in harte the redresse of thinges, the whiche when for feare they durst not openly rebuke, thei didde in coloures paynte theim oute, and tolde menne by shadowes what they shoulde do in good south.[18]

James VI/I was certainly most cognisant of this vigorous desire to encode and to decode in the textual cultures across the British nations and made his wrath known when he felt his 'mother deceased', Mary Queen of Scots, was being depicted in *The Faerie Queene*;[19] and later when a certain *History of the World* rolled from the presses in 1614. Ralegh's unfinished work never progressed beyond the narrative of the Second Macedonian War, but by January 5th 1615, John Chamberlain was writing to Sir Dudley Carleton, 'Sir Walter Raleighs booke is called in by the Kinges commaundment, for divers exceptions, but specially for beeing too sawcie in censuring princes'.[20]

If there is every evidence that Elizabethans derived great delight from the challenges of decoding evocations (both textual and visual) of a remote past under political, moral, spiritual terms, there was certainly an impressive number of publications available to the late sixteenth-century reader offering guidance in this pursuit. Stephen Batman's *Golden Booke of the Leaden Goddes* (1577), for example, counselled that from the image of Venus 'figured in a Garden of Flowers, naked, with a Garland of Flowers and Roses on her head: her Wagon was drawen with two white Swannes, and a payre of whyte Doues', the reader should take note that

> Her Garland of Roses doth signifie the superfluity which wantons require, and being naked, ye shamelesse care of Uirginitie: The Garden of Flowers, the variable alluremnentes of amorous Louers, her Wagon betokeneth Pleasure: the Swannes, stoutnesse of swift reuenge.[21]

Equally important in contributing to these particular pleasures of textual consumption might be the recognition of stylistic influences and textual sources which shaped encounters with the world of pagan myth. In direct comparison with Shakespeare's *Venus and Adonis*, Francis Beaumont's *Salmacis and Hermaphroditus* (1602) remained eager to roll back the centuries to the erotically charged environment of which 'sweet-lipp'd Ovid long ago did tell'.[22] Such was the explicitly *charged* nature of the poetics to be found in these epyllia that in Marlowe's *Hero and Leander*, for example, the 'yielding hearts' of the protagonists appear to generate electrifying effects in the environs – 'The air with sparks of living fire was spangl'd' (187–8); and in George Chapman's *Ovid's Banquet of Sence* (1595) when Ovid 'layde his hand vpon [Corinna's] side, / [...] [It] made her start like sparckles from a fire'.[23] It was acknowledged by at least one contemporary critic that Shakespeare maintained analogous aims of *aemulatio* in his own narrative poems: in *A comparative Discourse of our English poets with the Greeke, Latine, and Italian Poets* (1598), Francis Meres signalled, 'As the soule of *Euphorbus* was thought to liue in *Pythagoras*: so the sweete wittie soule of *Ouid* lives in mellifluous & hony-tongued *Shakespeare*, witnes his *Venus and Adonis*, his *Lucrece*, his sugred *Sonnets* among his priuate friends, &c.'.[24] Indeed, when Shakespeare's *Venus and Adonis* was published, its title-page was accompanied with an epigraph from another of Ovid's productions, the *Amores*: 'Villa miretur vulgus; mihi flavus Apollo / Pocula Castalia plena ministret aqua' (Let the common herd be amazed by worthless things; but for me let golden Apollo provide cups full of the water of the Muses).[25]

The profound legacies of Ovidian poetics in early modern England (most especially the *Metamorphoses* detailing the many and various frantic exchanges and resistances between mortals and immortals) have been widely appreciated in scholarship over recent decades.[26] The *Metamorphoses* had been strategically renewed for Tudor readers by Sir Arthur Golding's verse translation of books I–IV, and then of the complete work in 1567. It soon emerged as a key resource for students, poets and, more generally, for the literate public at large for cultural (frequently, moral) debate. As a consequence, four further editions had rolled from the presses by 1612, but even Golding himself urged his readers to take heed of the potential for disquiet which such writing might generate:

> Some naughtie persone seeing vyce shewd lyvely in his hew [might] take occasion by and by like vices too ensew [...] / That men [...] should not let their lewd affections have the head [...] / For under feyned names of Goddes it was the Poets guyse / The vice and faultes of all estates too taunt in covert wyse.[27]

The sense of strain is palpable here in Golding's prefatory text as he endeavours to train his readers' attentions upon questions of ethics rather erotics, upon *nomos* rather than *physis*.

In both the contexts of *Venus and Adonis* and *The Rape of Lucrece*, readers are offered no option but to focus hard upon the unruliness of human appetite; and perhaps, as Peter Brooks has persuasively underlined more generally in his discussion of narrative construction, such pressures are at work from the very beginning of all our textual encounters:

> Narratives both tell of desire and arouse and make use of desire as dynamic of signification [...] Desire is always there at the start of the narrative [...] the need to tell as a primary human drive that seeks to seduce and to subjugate the listener.[28]

The teasing and beguiling pleasures that are released in such encounters can only be further amplified when the poems in question appeal to the memory in a recessive vision of unbiddable desire and vain resistance. In both *Venus and Adonis* and *The Rape of Lucrece*, Shakespeare tests and creatively adapts our knowledge of earlier mythical narratives which may figure Venus's success, Adonis's virility or the Roman Republic being founded. However, the fine operations of selection, ellipsis, erasure and supplement exemplified in Ovidian verse writings (and Shakespeare's narrative poems) may be found to shadow the arresting practices of acceleration, imposition, enhancement, excision, fragmentation and disjunction to which the faculty of memory itself is subject.

Mythologising and remembering the ancients

> I can think of only one reason why no one has tried to explain these stories: no one has really understood the art of mythology. If anyone explained some of the stories, he never got beyond the outer layer, the simple exposition obvious to everyone. We still lack an acceptable expositor (at least that is my opinion) to reveal the deepest, most concealed secrets of the stories [...][29]

Such was the complaint voiced in Natale Conti's (Natalis Comes') enormously influential *Mythologiae sive Explicationis Fabularum* (1567). His investigations into pagan mythology enjoyed widespread circulation in early modern Europe, and it was a familiar handbook for such diverse writers in Britain as Spenser, Bacon, Chapman, Jonson, Ralegh and Milton. Conti's

Mythologiae found its way into Tudor classrooms, into James VI/I's library and into university collections, such as that at Christ Church, Cambridge. Indeed, it constituted one amongst a host of sixteenth-century humanist endeavours to enrich the current state of knowledge, moral and spiritual wisdom, through the excavation of the classical past. Interestingly, this aim seems to have been in evidence from some of the earliest considerations of mythical narrative. In *Concerning the Gods and the Universe* (4th century AD), for example, Sallustius had insisted that the recounting of myth should lead us to 'enquire [...] [that we might] not keep our intellects in idleness'. However, moral anxieties were already being expressed that 'Those who would learn about the gods need to have been well educated from childhood and must not be bred up among foolish ideas [...] good and intelligent by nature, in order that they may have something in common with the subject'.[30]

By the early modern period, the value of the rich treasury of myth as a means not only to bridge the centuries with antiquity, but also to access a richly nuanced vocabulary for meditating the human condition was broadly recognised – and further guidance through this complexly wrought mythological world became available as a consequence. Thus, if readers of *Venus and Adonis* were compelled to cogitate that 'worse than Tantalus' is [the goddess's] annoy' (599) or those of *The Rape of Lucrece* were being asked to scrutinise 'still-pining Tantalus' (858) or 'Philomel, that sing'st of ravishment' (1128), help might be at hand. Boccaccio's *De Genealogia Deorum* (Venice, 1472) served as a seminal text for later European productions, such as Lilio Gregorio Giraldi's *De Deis Gentium* (Basel, 1548), Vincenzo Cartari's *Le Immagini dei Dei degli Antichi* (Venice, 1556) and, as we have seen, Conti's *Mythologiae* (Venice, 1567) with its marked taste for extended symbolic exegeses. Each production built incrementally upon the wealth of knowledge offered by its predecessors.

Conti, for example, evoked the vision of 'Venus, whom the common people thought of as the goddess of every pleasure and delight, charm and grace' and, as the appetite for delving deeper into the pagan myths had persisted since antiquity, the goddess had come to be attributed with an ever growing number of identities: the earthly, hedonistic Venus (*Venus vulgaris*); the fecund Venus (*Venus genetrix*); the warrrior Venus (*Venus armata*); the cunning Venus (*Venus mechanitis*); the promiscuous Venus (*Venus meretrix*) and so on. In his *Bibliotheca* (1542) Elyot summoned up his vision of '*Venus, ueneris,* called goddesse of loue, sometyme lechery, also carnall appetite, also beautie, by whiche a man is stired to loue'; some twenty years later, Cartari submitted, 'I do say that Venus certainly seemed to be the chief deity of the prostitutes'.[31] Interestingly, the narratives contained in such collections as those of Cartari and Conti found their way into Elizabethan print culture in the many and various editions, for example, of Thomas Cooper's *Thesaurus* (1565), of (as we have seen) Stephen Batman's *Golden Booke of the Leaden Goddes* (1577) and, indeed, in the broad compendium of Abraham Fraunce's *Third part of the Countesse of Pembrokes Ivychurch* (1592) where 'to the wilde wood went too wilde and wilful *Adonis*'.[32] Cartari's collection was rendered in abbreviated form for English-speaking audiences in Robert Linche's *The Fountain of Ancient Fiction* (1599), and in the years after James VI/I's death, George Sandys published his extensive collection, *Ovid's Metamorphosis Englished, Mythologiz'd, and Represented in Figures* (1632), which brought together elements from all the productions which had circulated during the Tudor period.

In Linche's *Fountaine of Ancient Fiction* the Elizabethan reader was reminded that

> According [...] to the opinion of the Poets, Venus was taken to be the goddesse of wantonnes & amorous delights [...] the mother of loue, because that without a certaine loue & simpathie of affections, those desires are sildome accomplished. And vnto hir they ascribe the care and charge of marriages and holie wedlockes.[33]

In this way, the English-reading public was reminded of the intensely supple nature of the narrative resource of myth. Figures such as Spenser, Milton and Chapman were clearly acquainted with a number of the above collections, indicating the key handbook status which such productions from home and abroad had attained. Indeed, in his wonted satiric mode, the dramatist John Marston submitted the following:

Reach me some Poets Index that will show.
Imagines Deorum. Booke of Epithetes,
Natales Comes, thou I know recites,
And mak'st Anatomie of Poesie.[34]

Flexing memory in *Venus and Adonis*

Shakespeare's *Venus and Adonis*, dedicated to 'the world's hopeful expectation', initially appears to have a consuming interest in *most immediate* action between 'rose-cheeked Adonis'[35] and 'sick-thoughted Venus': 'Look when a painter would surpass the life'; 'Now quick desire hath caught the yielding prey' (dedication, 3, 5, 289, 547). However, it swiftly becomes apparent that there is more than one cycle of experience competing for our attention: 'His art with nature's workmanship at strife, / As if the dead the living should exceed' (291–2). The insistently dynamic present constructed by the highly stimulated narrator ('Look how he can, she cannot choose but love' 79) and played out between the resisting youth, the endlessly resourceful goddess ('where she ends she doth anew begin' 60) and the fauna of this most fertile landscape, is continually shaped by recursive movements to earlier scenes of ungovernable desire. 'More lovely than a man' (9), Adonis is discovered unripe or ill-suited[36] for Venus's advances and repeatedly confirms his own, more focused passions, preferring to hunt than to become the quarry. Subjected to the searing attentions of an immortal, he makes repeated attempts to remove himself from every manifestation of *great creating Nature*: 'Fie, no more of love! / The sun doth burn my face; I must remove' (185–6). The fleetingly exasperated Venus ('Now which way shall she turn? What shall she say?' 253) attempts to disarm her coy subject ('unapt to toy' 34) and, like Shakespeare himself, seeks to beguile by conjuring up an erotically charged account from an Olympian past: 'I have been wooed as I entreat thee now, / Even by the stern and direful god of war [...] / Over my altars hath he hung his lance, / His battered shield, his uncontrolled crest' (97–8, 103–4). Significantly, the forceful authority of one seduction myth from the past segues into another as the goddess seeks to gain purchase on resisting agents both on and beyond the page: 'Narcissus so himself himself forsook, / And died to kiss his shadow in the brook' (161–2).

More generally, this fractious drama of the appetitive female and the intractable youth ('Who blushed and pouted in a dull disdain, / With leaden appetite' 33–4) is re-enacted in a wide variety of epyllia from the early modern period, shadowing Ovid's depictions of the demure figures of Hermaphroditus and Adonis. In Marlowe's *Hero and Leander*, 'Fair Cynthia wish'd his arms might be her sphere; / Grief makes her pale, because she moves not there' (59–60), whereas as early as Thomas Peend's *Hermaphroditus and Salmacis* (1565) we discover a juvenile who 'blusht as red as blood, / He wyst not then what loue dyd meane'.[37] Equally teasingly, in Drayton's *Endimion and Phoebe* (1595) 'The shag-haird Satyrs Mountain-climing race, / Haue been made tame by gazing in his face. / For this boyes loue, the water-Nymphs haue wept', but the indomitable youth 'requests, that [Phoebe] would stand aside, / Because the fish her shadow had espide'.[38] Clearly, one of the major challenges of the poet in such instances is to identify strategies with which the (stubbornly) virginal youth may counteract the manoeuvres of his temptress. Interestingly, rather than submitting to the weight and authority of past experience, the male subjects of epyllia offer constant testimony of their ill-acquaintance with the past, of their inability to be inscribed within the remembered experience of others. Their young bodies and minds are not to be claimed in this way on account of their insistent commitments to the present and future pleasures of hunting, fishing and sports liberated from the world of coupling: 'all my mind, my thought, my busy care, / Is how to get my palfrey from the mare' (383–4). Indeed, at moments of particular pressure, Shakespeare's 'flint-hearted boy' (95) repeatedly disengages from Venus's remorseless vision of the procreating landscape ('Art thou a woman's son and canst not feel / What 'tis to love [...]?' 201–2) and emphasises his ambition to forge a definitive self in the *anticipated* pleasures of the forest: '"I know not love", quoth he, "nor will not know it, / Unless it be a boar, and then I chase it"' (409–10). If Venus attempts to trigger a transformation in her loved one by drawing him into intimate spaces ('The tender spring upon thy tempting lip / Shows thee unripe; yet mayst thou well be tasted' 127–8), Adonis fences mentally with his voluptuous assailant by insisting upon his pre-sexual state, the very newness of his entry into a goddess's world which seems congested with the erotic memory and bodily knowledge of others: 'Measure my strangeness with my unripe years. / Before I know myself seek not to know me' (524–5). Furthermore, Adonis's energetic refusals to be incorporated into Venus's record of achievement renders him impervious to any counsel from his assailant. However, we are forcefully reminded that, in death, Adonis has no agency whatsoever – he is ultimately held captive within the memorial motions of the goddess's thoughts, deeds and words: 'And now she beats her heart, whereat it groans, / That all the neighbour caves, as seeming troubled, / Make verbal repetition of her moans' (829–31).

Venus's interventions as speaker dominate almost a half of the entire poem, whereas those of 'the wayward boy' (344) amount to little more than seven per cent of its narrative. In the midst of the verbal (and physical) fireworks which she generates, the goddess not only seeks to figure forth the irresistible authority of past experience, she attempts to elide the passage of time, to close the record of experience and thus to silence the indignant youth: 'Here come and sit, where never serpent hisses, / And being set, I'll smother thee with kisses' (17–18). With great rhetorical dexterity, Venus constantly draws attention to the intensely changeful environment in which Adonis finds himself, multiplying angles of vision on the past and the landscape, redrawing the axes of time and space: 'Ten kisses short as one, one long as twenty. / A summer's day will seem an hour but short, / Being wasted in such time-beguiling sport' (22–4). The goddess seeks to scramble the youth's ethical investments in memory and conscience and, like the speaker of Shakespeare's sonnets, condemns the barren aspirations of the headstrong addressee: 'What is thy body but a swallowing grave'? (757). The undaunted Venus seeks to disorient Adonis by transporting him into a world beyond his desires for customary exercise to her own volatile environment governed by remorseless appetite: 'He saith she is immodest, blames her miss; / What follows more she murders with a kiss' (53–4). However, these desperate exchanges and perceivedly destructive urges look forward irrevocably to more deadly ones as we are asked to envisage the gladiatorial struggle with the fearful boar whose 'snout digs sepulchres where'er he goes' (622).

The vigorous, penetrative and deadly encounter of Adonis with what John Weever termed in *Faunus and Melliflora* (1600) 'the anger-froathing boare' and with what Vincenzo Cartari conceived to be 'a very good symbol of the winter',[39] is vividly rendered in Golding's translation of Ovid: 'And hyding in his codds his tuskes as farre as he could thrust / He layd him all along for dead vppon the yellow dust'. In the subsequent narrative, Golding's Ovid has Venus fashion an anemone from the youth's spilt blood – a 'remembrance' of her fallen love.[40] Prefiguring this fate, Shakespeare's goddess initially salutes 'The field's chief flower, sweet above compare, / Stain to all nymphs, more lovely than a man' (8–9), and subsequently (again, in direct comparison with the speaker of the *Sonnets*) impresses upon the subject the impermanence of his own desires: 'Fair flowers that are not gathered in their prime / Rot and consume themselves in little time' (131–2). At the close of the poem, the grieving Venus submits, 'Poor flower [...] / [...] it is as good / To wither in my breast as in his blood' (1177, 1181–2), and thus draws him into closer proximity than she had ever achieved with him in life. Ovid's *Metamorphoses* specifically urges that this narrative moment be configured in memorial terms: 'My grief, Adonis, shall have an enduring monument, and each passing year in memory of your death shall give an imitation of my grief. But your blood shall be changed to a flower'.[41] Adopting a similar mode, Abraham Fraunce in *The third part of the Countesse of Pembrokes Yuychurch* (1592) has his Venus rail against the 'Hellish Fates' and determine 'In despite of you, shall yearely remember *Adonis*, / Yearely remember mee, by remembring yearely *Adonis*'.[42] However, in the final moments of Shakespeare's poem in which the aftermath of Adonis's death is briefly evoked, we are greeted primarily with the maternal *Venus genetrix* drawing her loved ones into the intimate spaces of body and memory:

> 'Here was thy father's bed, here in my breast.
> Thou art the next of blood, and 'tis thy right.
> Lo, in this hollow cradle take thy rest,
> My throbbing heart shall rock thee day and night;
> There shall not be one minute in an hour
> Wherein I will not kiss my sweet love's flower.'
> *(1183–8)*

Future remembering and *The Rape of Lucrece*

In turning to the travails of Rome in the sixth century BC and, most particularly, to one whom Sir Thomas Elyot had described in his *Bibliotheca* as 'Lucretia, a noble woman of Rome', Shakespeare might reach for a number of widely available texts. In Ovid's *Fasti* the wayward Tarquin is transported by blind love (*et caeco raptus amore furit*) on his first meeting with Collatine's wife – indeed, the reader learns that she only increased in beauty as he continued to recall her (*recordanti plura magisque placent*).[43] Elsewhere, in his accounts of the early history of Rome, Livy is characteristically more preoccupied with the military and political life of the city state. However, if this particular narrative begins with siege warfare against Ardea (the main town of the Rutuli), the reader is nonetheless informed of the fatal supper when Tarquin took the resolution to rape Lucretia, subsequently threatening her with dishonour by placing the dead body of a slave beside her own, seemingly adulterous body, if she fails to submit to his will. Amongst his post-classical sources Shakespeare might have drawn upon Chaucer's *Legend of Good Women*, where the narrator feels himself called upon 'to preyse and drawen to memorie / The verray wife, the verray trewe Lucresse' who was overcome by the 'blynde lust' of her aggressor.[44] John Gower's *Confessio Amantis* also foregrounded the famous narrative where the violated heroine, succumbing to the same fate, turned to her Roman kin and 'Hire tale betwen schame and drede / Sche tolde, noght withoute peine'.[45] Matteo Bandello drew upon Livy for his own *Novelle* (1554, 4th Book 1573) which Shakespeare may have known in the original Italian or in French translations (Pierre Boaistuau's *Histoires Tragiques* (1559) and, later, François de Belleforest's *Histoires Tragiques* (1566–83)). In due course, Bandello, amongst a number of other sources, was transposed by William Painter into

The palace of pleasure (1566) where the Lucretia narrative appears in 'The seconde Nouell': here, the reader discovers Sextus Tarquinius 'incensed with a libidious desire, to construprate and defloure *Lucrece*'.[46]

In the prefatory 'Argument' accompanying the publication of Shakespeare's *The Rape of Lucrece* we learn of the initial wagering between the Roman nobleman in the military camp concerning the 'virtues' of their wives, and of the company's visit to Collatine's villa to see Lucretia, a woman of 'incomparable chastity'. Significantly, Shakespeare excises these sections of the intrigue from his subsequent poetic narrative and communicates them tactically through the fecund memory of the aggressor, Tarquin: 'Now thinks he that her husband's shallow tongue, / [...] In that high task hath done her beauty wrong, / Which far exceeds his barren skill to show' (78, 80–1). The nobleman's memorial prowess is then figured forth in the public domain as he, like Othello, charms his female auditor with vivid tales of past heroics: 'He stories to her ears her husband's fame, / Won in the fields of fruitful Italy' (106–7). To the sometimes profound discomfort of many readers and critics,[47] in this first half of Shakespeare's poem we are forced to keep most close company with the rapist, attending to the fine distinctions and contrary motions of his thoughts:

> Here, pale with fear, he doth premeditate
> The dangers of his loathsome enterprise,
> And in his inward mind he doth debate
> What following sorrow may on this arise.
> *(183–6)*

This expert textual manoeuvring to bring us into uneasy proximity with a destructive mind to excite our attention and scramble our faculties of sympathy and judgement will characterise Shakespeare's writing throughout the length and breadth of his career. Here, locked in a consciousness with malice aforethought, the reader attends to an unexpectedly meditative aggressor who responds most keenly to the ways in which he will be claimed by future remembering: 'Yea, though I die, the scandal will survive, / [...] my posterity, shamed with the note, / Shall curse my bones, and hold it for no sin / To wish that I their father had not been' (204, 208–10).

The Rape of Lucrece emphatically denies us the satisfaction of dismissing Tarquin as a mindless agent of monstrous violence. Instead, we are compelled in the opening phases of the narrative to take heed of a brutal, unstable figure whose sensibilities are wholly focused upon anxiety-ridden ruminations on memory and desire: 'I have debated, even in my soul / What wrong, what shame, what sorrow I shall breed' (498–9). In direct comparison with an impressive number of Shakespeare's villainous characters, Tarquin's final determination ('strive I to embrace mine infamy' 504) is inextricably linked to the exercise of (admittedly, impassioned) reasoning: 'I know repentant tears ensue the deed, / Reproach, disdain, and deadly enmity' (502–3). If, under the pressure of Venus's remorseless scrutiny, Adonis seeks to empower himself by seeking refuge in unclaimed narratives of future experience, the finely grained consciousness of Tarquin lucidly foresees his own ceaseless damnation in anticipated cycles of scornful remembering.

Thus, in the violent confrontation of minds and bodies which ensues between Tarquin and Lucrece in her chamber, it is perhaps unsurprising that he rebuffs the stinging, moral appeals made by the resisting reader of his desires. Initially, in her extension of hospitality to this man of war, Lucrece (like Adonis) meets the insistent attentions of her visitor with disarming innocence and perplexity: 'But she, that never coped with stranger eyes / Could pick no meaning from their parling looks' (99–100). However, subsequently in her chamber, the heroine is terrorised physically and mentally. Before her body is forced to succumb to Tarquin's assaults, he explains that he reserves precisely the same future for her that he has painfully envisaged for himself. Lucrece is treated to a pitiless account of the years ahead in which she will become a pariah – moreover, the doleful narrative that Tarquin unfolds is articulated under specifically gendered terms:

> Thy issue blurred with nameless bastardy;
> And thou, the author of their obloquy,
> Shalt have thy trespass cited up in rhymes
> And sung by children in succeeding times.
> *(522–5)*

Thus, sorely pressed by the prospects of both present and future trauma, Lucrece has to contemplate the very thing she abhors, her inability to secure an identity independent of his sexual violence: 'The blemish that will never be forgot' (536). In Sonnet XXV, we learn 'The painful warrior famousèd for might, / After a thousand victories, once foiled / Is from the book of honour razèd quite, / And all the rest forgot for which he toiled' (9–12). Significantly, in Tarquin's bleak vision of the future for his victim, Lucrece will not only find herself wiped from 'the book of honour', but Collatine too will become the 'scornful mark of every open eye' (520). Shrewdly, Lucrece seeks to resist Tarquin's narratives of her future identity and belonging with the analogous resources of monitory memory. 'O, be remembered', she urges in her moment of utmost need, 'no outrageous thing / From vassal actors can be wiped away' (607–8). Nonetheless, her impassioned attempts to weaken her aggressor with appeals concerning his own tainted future ('How will thy shame be seeded in thine age' 603; 'wilt thou be the school where Lust shall learn?' 617) meet inevitable defeat in Shakespeare's narrative, because the villain has already pre-empted them with his own, finely honed cogitations.

If, in *Venus and Adonis*, the goddess is fleetingly allowed to apostrophise the 'hard-favoured tyrant' Death (931), in the more desperately troubled world of ancient Rome, the abandoned Lucrece surrenders to the lure of keeping company with 'comfort-killing Night', 'vile Opportunity' and 'misshapen Time' (764, 895, 925). Aristotle had affirmed in *De Memoria et Reminiscentia* that the human ability to remember, amongst other cognitive acts, was articulated with a lexis of visual apprehension – 'Without an image thinking is impossible'.[48] And indeed, richly sensitive to the manifold temptations on offer to a sinning populace of early modern London, the Puritan lawyer and author William Prynne not only railed in *Histrio-mastix* (1633) against the activities of the playhouses located in the suspect, leisureful and seemingly labourless 'liberties' of the city ('O therefore let Stage-Players *perish, yea, for ever perish, which thus revive the cursed memory of Pagan Idols, and their infernall wickednesses*, whose remembrance should for ever be forgotten lest we perish by them'), he chose precisely to strike an Aristotelian note by reminding his audience, 'Nothing more powerfully sinkes into the memory, then that which is apprehended by the eye'.[49]

Subsequently, in ekphrastic mode ('No object but her passion's strength renews' 1103), Lucrece focuses hard down upon a 'skilful painting made for Priam's Troy' (1367) where her own painful memories are distilled in this vision taken from collective memory 'where all distress and dolour dwelled' (1446). Rather than mentally fencing with Tarquin in formulating accounts of future remembering, she now communes mentally with this scene of universal devastation. Such is the intensity of this engagement that Lucrece has her own trauma vividly commemorated in the details of the Sack of Troy: 'even as subtle Sinon here is painted, / So sober-sad, so weary, and so mild, / [...] To me came Tarquin armed' (1541–2, 1544). The Roman spouse concentrates fixedly upon the figure of 'despairing Hecuba' (1447) agonising over the butchering of her loved ones. Indeed, in the entire period subsequent to her rape, Lucrece is characterised by her memorial exertion and is stung anew by the prospect of being rendered nothing more to future minds than Tarquin's victim: 'The nurse to still her child will tell my story, / And fright her crying babe with Tarquin's name' (813–4). From the perspective of the richly imaginative *mise-en-abîme* which Lucrece constructs, it appears that generation after generation will know her only as a product of others' desires: 'Feast-finding minstrels, tuning my defame, / Will tie the hearers to attend each line, / How Tarquin wronged me, I Collatine' (817–19). Thus, in her highly stimulated mind wracked with trauma, Lucrece emerges as a shame-ridden phoenix, continually being reborn in the infamy of Tarquin's act: 'So of shame's ashes shall my fame be bred, / For in my death I murder shameful scorn; / My shame so dead, mine honour is new-born' (1188–90). This mode of complaint fuelled by the resources of memory had been renewed for late Elizabethan interest not only onstage in tragedies and history plays in the theatres, but also in a succession of poetic productions which included Samuel Daniel's *The Complaint of Rosamund* (1592), Thomas Lodge's *The Complaint of Elstred* (1593) and Richard Barnfield's *The Complaint of Chastitie* (1594). Acknowledging the popularity of the mode for the early 1590s audience, Lucrece's extended complaint is exploited as a vehicle for vividly exploring possible narratives of memory and, indeed, possible modes of self-identification as she narrates the pasts of others and her own futures.

When the company of Collatine and his comrades-at-arms return to the villa, Livy has the heroine declare before the assembled company, 'My body only has been violated. My heart is innocent, and death will be my witness'.[50] Livy and his imitators spend a significant period of time contemplating the future of the Roman Republic through the fraternal convergence of the dishonoured male kin in a common cause: after Lucretia kills herself, for example, Painter's 'Seconde Nouell' has it that '*Brutus* perswaded the *Romanes*, that thei should [...] take weapons in their handes, and shewe themselues like men'.[51] However, Shakespeare curtails significantly such an account in order to remain in a more sustained manner in the company of the heroine. Rather than construing the Roman auditors at the end of the poem as sole agents of justice, dominating the poetic narrative Lucrece pronounces and enacts her own sentence. Through a consciously purgative act of violence, she rejects Tarquin's compositional hand that 'never be forgot in mighty Rome / Th'adulterate death of Lucrece and her groom' (1644–5), and thus robs the aggressor of his claims to appropriate both the present and future. In turn, she imperiously compels upon her auditors a remorseless course of slaughter ('Be suddenly revengèd on my foe— / Thine, mine, his own. Suppose thou dost defend me / From what is past' 1683–5), affirming, 'For sparing justice feeds iniquity' (1687). If, as Lynn Enterline has argued, 'in Shakespeare's poem Lucrece explicitly uses her body as a text, turning suicide into a kind of writing',[52] the lifeless body at the close of the poem also becomes a prime site of male competition and ownership: 'The father says "She's mine." "O, mine she is", / Replies her husband' (1795–6). She is thus memorialised emphatically, absorbed within the relentless narrativisation of the Roman *civitas* ('They did conclude to bear dead Lucrece thence, / To show her bleeding body thorough Rome, / And so to publish Tarquin's foul offence' 1850–2) in which the shrewd political aspirant Brutus, 'Began to clothe his wit in state and pride, / Burying in Lucrece' wound his folly's show' (1809–10).

Concluding thoughts

In *De Natura Deorum* Cicero reflected at length upon the appetite in evidence down the centuries for figuring forth deities when seeking to enquire upon the conditions of human existence:

> [Epicurus] alone perceived, first, that the gods exist, because nature herself has imprinted a conception of them on the minds of all mankind. For what nation or what tribe of men is there but possesses untaught some "preconception" of the gods?[53]

In this way, the pantheon of the gods became a most convenient instrument for positing ontological principles. This was recognised as keenly in the early modern period as it had been in the first century BC. In his *Mythologiae* Natale Conti reasoned with disarming insight that

> If the names Venus and Cupid did not exist, or if we did not think of them as gods, but rather desires and raw passions (which is what they really are) then we would have nothing left but the repulsive and disgusting name of lust and people acting as crazy and as wild as animals.[54]

The purpose of the present discussion has been not only to explore the ways in which the compendium of mythological knowledge was being made increasingly available to sixteenth-century readers across Europe as a discourse of artistic ambition, cultural investment and philosophical reflection, but also the ways in which Shakespeare's narrative poems in particular compel us to consider the status and functions of memory in all its guises (recollection, commemoration, monitory memory, future remembering, anterior narratives of origin and selfhood, and so on). In the *Sonnets*, Shakespeare's reader is repeatedly urged to consider the anxiety-ridden prospect of human erasure ('But as the riper should by time decease, / His tender heir might bear his memory'[55]), and his narrative poems are similarly obsessed with resisting the invidious forces of (self-)forgetfulness and how these impulses become inextricably linked to trauma and (self-)violence in a reality hostile to human success. Unable to recover a past anterior to the knowledge of violent sexual assault, in different ways both Adonis and Lucrece inscribe themselves within a dynamic mode of futurity, anticipating redemption secured in yet unrealised cycles of existence.

In the context of this consideration of the two very different victims depicted in Shakespeare's poetic narratives, Jonas Barish would seem most persuasive in his more general contention that memory 'carries an inescapable moral dimension for Shakespeare'.[56] In the face of differing forms of menace, Adonis and Lucrece become variously typified by ethical promptings, wistful longings, bitter anxieties and hortative modes of expression. The faculty of memory invariably invests in that which is lost and in that which attenuates our experiences of absence. Convincingly, Richard Stamelman has argued that

> The fissures of memory cannot be repaired. The memory of presence is not itself presence, but an image, a simulacrum, a *re*-presentation. Presence, existing as it does for a mere instant, can be repeated only through remembrance: the re-suturing, the re-membering of fragments, not all of which will come together to make a seamless whole.[57]

If, as we witnessed earlier in the discussion, memory may easily constitute *a problem* for those performing its labours, it equally frequently becomes, as Aristotle had advised, a committed desire to recapture, to search out (often desperately) that which has been lost. By way of conclusion, it might be added that if readers' encounters in *Venus and Adonis* and *The Rape of Lucrece* with evocations of the past (particularly a past fractured by violence and trauma) lead effortlessly to a re-interrogation of the cultural present, these same encounters must also compel us to pluralise our consumption of the past, to re-visit its perplexing indeterminacy.

Notes

1 See respectively: Giles Fletcher the elder, epigram 5 and elegiacs in 'Verses Addressed to the Queen at Windsor by Eton Scholars, 19 September 1563'; Edward Franckline, epigram 17 in 'Verses Addressed to the Queen at Windsor by Eton Scholars, 19 September 1563'; Anon., 'To the most powerful and serene Queen Elizabeth [...] the cohort of her Etonians sends greetings' in a presentation manuscript 'Verses Addressed to the Queen at Windsor by Eton Scholars, 19 September 1563'. See John Nichols, *John Nichols's 'The Progresses and Public Processions of Queen Elizabeth I': A New Edition of Early Modern Sources*, ed. Elizabeth Goldring et al., vol. I: 1533–1571 (Oxford: Oxford University Press, 2014), pp. 318, 323, 328–9.
2 Saint Augustine, *Confessions*, bk. X, xiv (21), trans. Henry Chadwick (New York: Oxford University Press, 1991).
3 'Commentary on *On Memory and Recollection*', in St. Thomas Aquinas, *Commentaries on Aristotle's 'On Sense and What is Sensed' and 'On Memory and Recollection'*, trans. Kevin White and Edward M. Macierowski (Washington, DC: Catholic University of America Press, 2005), p. 184. For more general discussion here, see Andrew Hiscock, *Reading Memory in Early Modern Literature* (Cambridge: Cambridge University Press, 2011), p. 18ff.
4 All quotations are taken from *The Faerie Queene* are taken from Edmund Spenser, *The Faerie Queene*, ed. A.C. Hamilton et al. (Harlow: Longman, 2001).
5 In this context, see Andrew Hiscock, '"Achilles alter": the heroic lives and afterlives of Robert Devereux, 2nd Earl of Essex', in A. Connolly and L. Hopkins (eds.), *Essex: The Cultural Impact of an Elizabethan Courtier* (Manchester: Manchester University Press, 2013), pp. 101–32.
6 All references to *Hero and Leander* are taken from Sandra Clark (ed.), *Amorous Rites: Elizabethan Erotic Verse* (London / Rutland, VT: Everyman / Charles E. Tuttle, 1994).
7 The inscription accompanying this painting is 'IVNO POTENS SCEPTRIS ET MENTIS ACVMINE PALLAS / ET ROSEO VENERIS FVLGET IN ORE DECVS / ADFVIT ELIZABETH IVNO PERCVLSA REFVGIT OBSVPVIT PALLAS ERVBVITQ VENVS'. Translation: 'Pallas was keen of brain, Juno was queen of might, / The rosy face of Venus was in beauty shining bright, / Elizabeth then came, And, overwhelmed, Queen Juno took flight: / Pallas was silenced: Venus blushed for shame'. For further information, see the Royal Collection at Windsor Castle at www.royalcollection.org.uk / collection / 403446 / elizabeth-i-and-the-three-goddesses
8 John Bartlet, *A booke of ayres with a triplicitie of musicke* (1606), sig. F2ᵛ.
9 *The Shakspere Allusion-Book: A Collection of Allusions to Shakspere From 1591 to 1700*, II vols, ed. C.M. Ingleby, Lucy Toulmin Smith, Frederick James Furnivall, John James Munro (London / New York: Chatto & Windus / Duffield & Co., 1909): I.51.
10 Shakespeare's dedicatory text for *Venus and Adonis*. All references to Shakespeare's poetry are taken from William Shakespeare, *Shakespeare's Poems*, ed. Katherine Duncan-Jones and H.R. Woudhuysen (London: Arden Shakespeare, 2007). In this instance, see p. 128.
11 Richard Terdiman, *Present Past: Modernity and the Memory Crisis* (Ithaca, NY / London: Cornell University Press, 1993), p. vii.
12 John Donne, *The Sermons of John Donne in ten volumes*, ed. and intro. George R. Potter and Evelyn M. Simpson (Berkeley and Los Angeles: University of California Press, 1953–62): I.3.194.
13 Richard Braithwaite, *The English gentlewoman* (1631), p. 139.
14 Qtd. in Philip C. Kolin (ed.), *Venus and Adonis: Critical Essays* (New York, NY: Garland, 1997), p. 11.
15 William Hazlitt, *Characters of Shakespear's Plays* (London: Taylor & Hessey, 1818 – 2nd ed.), pp. 347–8.
16 Letter to Raleigh. See Spenser, *The Faerie Queene*, ed. Hamilton, p. 716.
17 Sir Philip Sidney, *An apologie for poetrie* (1595), sig. F2ᵛ.
18 Thomas Wilson, *The arte of rhetorique* (1553), sig. CC4ᵛ.
19 See Richard A. McCabe, 'The Masks of Duessa: Spenser, Mary Queen of Scots and James VI', *English Literary Renaissance* 17 (1987), 2, 224–42.

20 John Chamberlain, *The Letters of John Chamberlain*, vol. I, ed. Norman Egbert McClure (Philadelphia: American Philosophical Society, 1939), p. 568.
21 Stephen Batman, *The golden booke of the leaden goddes* (1577), sig. 6^v.
22 Francis Beaumont, 'The Author to the Reader', l.7. All references to *Salmacis and Hermaphroditus* are taken from Clark, *Amorous Rites*.
23 George Chapman, *Ovid's Banquet of Sence* (1595), sig. E3^r.
24 Francis Meres, *Palladis tamia Wits treasury being the second part of Wits common wealth* (1598), pp. 281–2.
25 Translation taken from William Shakespeare, *The Complete Sonnets and Poems*, ed. Colin Burrow (Oxford: Oxford University Press, 2002), p. 173.
26 Some notable interventions in this field of scholarship include: Jonathan Bate, *Shakespeare and Ovid* (Oxford: Clarendon Press, 1993); Lynn Enterline, *The Rhetoric of the Bod:. From Ovid to Shakespeare* (Cambridge: Cambridge University Press, 2000); Raphael Lyne, *Ovid's Changing Worlds: English Metamorphoses 1567–1632* (Oxford: Oxford University Press, 2001); Liz Oakley-Brown, *Ovid and the Cultural Politics of Translation in Early Modern England* (Farnham, UK: Ashgate, 2006); A.B. Taylor (ed.), *Shakespeare's Ovid: The 'Metamorphoses' in the Plays and Poems* (Cambridge: Cambridge University Press, 2000).
27 'To the Reader', in Ovid, *The. xv. bookes of P. Ouidius Naso, entytuled Metamorphosis, translated oute of Latin into English meeter, by Arthur Golding Gentleman* (1567), sig. A3^r.
28 Peter Brooks, 'Narrative Desire', in Brian Richardson (ed.), *Narrative Dynamic:. Essays on Time, Plot, Closure, and Frames* (Columbus, OH: Ohio State University Press, 2002), pp. 130–7 (pp. 132, 136).
29 Qtd. in John Mulryan and Steven Brown, 'Venus and the Classical Tradition in Boccaccio's *Genealogia Deorum Gentilium Libri* and Natale Conti's *Mythologiae*', *Mediaevalia*, 27 (2006), 135–56 (p. 143).
30 Sallustius, *Concerning the Gods and the Universe*, ed. and trans. Arthur Darby Nock (Cambridge: Cambridge University Press, 1926), p. 3.
31 See respectively: Sir Thomas Elyot, *Bibliotheca Eliotae Eliotis librarie* (1542), sig. MM6^v; Vincenzo Cartari, *Vincenzo Cartari's Images of the Gods of the Ancients: The First Italian Mythography*, trans. John Mulryan (Tempe, AR: Arizona Center for Medieval and Renaissance Studies, 2012), p. 420.
32 Abraham Fraunce, *The third part of the Countesse of Pembrokes Yuychurch* (1592), sig. 44^v.
33 Richard Linche, *The fountaine of ancient fiction* (1599), sigs. CC2^{r-v}.
34 John Marston, *The Works of John Marston*, ed. A.H. Bullen, III vols. (London: John C. Nimmo, 1887): III. 270.
35 'Rose-cheekt Adonis' also appears in Marlowe's *Hero and Leander* (93).
36 For further discussion here, see Richard Rambuss, 'What it feels like for a Boy: Shakespeare's *Venus and Adonis*', in Richard Dutton and Jean E. Howard (eds.), *A Companion to Shakespeare's Works*, vol. IV: The Poems, Problem Comedies, Late Plays (Oxford: Blackwell, 2003), pp. 240–58.
37 Thomas Peend, *The pleasant fable of Hermaphroditus and Salmacis* (1565), sig. A5^v.
38 Michael Drayton, *Endimion and Phoebe Ideas Latmus* (1595), sigs. B2^v, C2^r.
39 See respectively: John Weever, John, *Faunus and Melliflora or, The original of our English satyres.* (1600), sig. C4^v; Cartari, *Vincenzo Cartari's Images of the Gods of the Ancients*, trans. Mulryan, p. 425.
40 Ovid, *Metamorphosis, translated [...] by Arthur Golding* (1567), sigs. 134^v, 135^r.
41 Ovid, *Metamorphoses*, II vols., Eng. trans. Frank Justus Miller (London / New York: W. Heinemann / G.P. Putnam's Sons, 1916): II.722 (bk. X).
42 Fraunce, *The third part of the Countesse of Pembrokes Yuychurch*, sig. 45^r.
43 Translations: 'transported by blind love [Tarquin] raved'; 'In memory's life more fair and fair she grew'. Ovid *Fasti* bk. 2, ll. 762, 770. See Ovid, *Ovid's Fasti*, trans. Sir James George Frazer (London / New York: W. Heinemann / G.P. Putnam's Sons, 1931), pp. 112–13.
44 Geoffrey Chaucer, *The Legend of Good Women*, ll.1685–6, 1756. See Geoffrey Chaucer, *The Complete Poetry and Prose of Geoffrey Chaucer*, ed. Mark Allen and John H. Fisher (Boston: Wadsworth, 2012), p. 658ff.
45 John Gower, *Confessio Amantis*, ed. Russell A. Peck (Canada[?]: Medieval Academy of America, 1980), VII.5048–9 (p. 405).
46 William Painter, *The palace of pleasure* (1566), sig. 5^v.
47 Maurice Evans argues, for example, that 'Tarquin is so remarkable a study of lust that for many readers it splits the poem in half and throws the interest, if not the sympathy, on to the villain at the expense of the wronged Lucrece'. See William Shakespeare, *The Narrative Poems*, ed. Maurice Evans (Harmondsworth: Penguin, 1989), p. 25.
48 On Memory, 450a1 1. See translation by J.I. Beare, in Aristotle, *The Complete Works of Aristotle*, revised Oxford translation, ed. Jonathan Barnes, Bollingen Series LXXI 2 (Princeton, NJ: Princeton University Press, 1984), p. 714.

49 William Prynne, *Histrio-mastix The players scourge, or, actors tragaedie* (1633), pp. 93, 357.
50 Livy, *The Early History of Rome. Books I–V of 'The History of Rome from its Foundation'*, trans. Aubrey de Sélincourt (Harmondsworth: Penguin, 1971), p. 99 (I.58–9).
51 Painter, *The palace of pleasure*, sig. 6^v.
52 Enterline, *The Rhetoric of the Body*, p. 153.
53 Cicero, *De Natura Deorum, Academica*, Eng. trans. H. Rackham (London / New York: William Heinemann Ltd / G.P. Putnam's Sons, 1933), pp. 44–5 (I.xvi.43).
54 Natale Conti, *Natale Conti's 'Mythologiae' Books I–IV*, trans. John Mulryan and Steven Brown (Tempe, AR: Arizona Center for Medieval and Renaissance Studies, 2006), p. 314 (bk. iv, ch. 13 'On Venus').
55 Shakespeare, sonnet I, 11.3–4.
56 Jonas Barish, 'Remembering and Forgetting in Shakespeare', in R.B. Parker and S.P. Zitner (eds.), *Elizabethan Theater: Essays in Honor of S. Schoenbaum* (Newark / London: University of Delaware Press / Associated University Press, 1996), pp. 214–21 (p. 221).
57 Richard Stamelman, 'The "Presence" of Memory', *L'Esprit Createur*, 36.3 (1996 Fall): 65–79 (pp. 77–8).

21
MONUMENTAL MEMORY AND LITTLE REMINDERS
The fantasy of being remembered by posterity

Grant Williams

When scrutinizing Shakespeare's boast about his 'powerful rhyme' outliving 'marble', gold, and 'unswept stone', recent critics seek guidance from Horace, one of the classical sources of his boast.[1] Horace's trope of verse metalwork, *aere perennius*—'more lasting than bronze'— promotes a fantasy of perduration contingent upon a triumphant poetic materiality.[2] According to the unstated implications of this trope, a monument, whether a poem, artefact, or building, derives its wished-for immortality from an indelibly memorable mark inscribed into imperishable fabric. However, the question of what lasts in a memorial is more complicated than a narcissistic boast would have us believe, and so I want to unseat the Horatian commonplace with another Roman genealogy proper to rhetoric. During the early modern period, the idea that intellectual products could compete with physical memorials circulated widely in the expression 'monuments of wit', which, as Bacon observed, 'are more durable than the monuments of power or of the hands'.[3] The expression—a translation of *ingeniorum monumenta*—appears in Quintilian's encyclopaedic treatise on rhetoric, where he examines the challenges inherent in the topic of praising men. Because the state rarely devotes the occasion or the expense to celebrate divine honors, posthumous gratitude, and statues, Quintilian seems to distrust the staging of public memorials. Instead, 'monuments of genius', such as, plays, cities, laws, and institutions, provide a suitable topic of eulogizing, for they will have withstood the test of time: 'some, like Menander, have had a fairer deal from posterity than from their own age'.[4] This passage on the rhetoric of memorial praise introduces two key ideas in my argument. First, monumental memory's staying power depends less on the durability of materials than on securing the approval of future generations, and thus Quintilian's important insight can be extended to the rhetoric of all monuments, not just *ingeniorum monumenta*. Second, his expression 'monument of *wit*'—with my extra emphasis on wit, the mental faculty— designates my argument's destination. Despite periodically envisioning a grandiose mausoleum for himself and his beloved, Shakespeare settles for little reminders, which strive to captivate the beloved's cognition.

My discussion differs from recent readings of monumental memory that situate its fragility and failures in material conditions.[5] Centering the durability of human values on a cultural artefact—its various technologies, models, and metaphors—ignores the crucial role played by posterity. Aaron Kunin has recently pushed materialist assumptions about Shakespeare's sonnets to the extreme by considering how the poems attempt to perpetuate some trace of the beloved, turning the poet into a *de facto* university researcher engaged in an immortality project by means of exploring various technologies of preservation. If it were not for the limitations of the materials used, a storage device could overcome entropy and thereby guarantee that the defunct and his values would be remembered forever. However, Shakespeare's actual struggles with the fantasy of perduration presuppose that any cultural artefact, any material trace, lasts only insofar as its imagined posterity recognizes its worth. The permanent recognition that a monument strives to obtain emerges from the matrix of values, mores, and beliefs made possible by the monument's economy of praise. It is this immaterial and fleeting intersubjective recognition that subsists in the contingency of an inscription's cultural and historical moment and thus cannot survive the vicissitudes of the monument's passage to future generations. The sonnets lean at times towards the fantasy of securing posterity's praise, but in their sustained ruminations on ruins admit to its ultimate futility and emptiness. Nevertheless, instead of abandoning himself to the elegiac chord that readers are quick to sound when lamenting the finitude of memory, Shakespeare appeals to another posterity, one not located in an imaginary future: he reaches out to his beloved, a posterity in the present moment of monumental inscription.

When the sonnets do indulge in the fantasy of perduration consistent with his Horatian boasts, the speaker imagines future readers who will render him and his beloved the recognition that he believes they deserve. Sometimes, this imagined posterity appears to be generic mortals, who can breathe, speak, and see as in sonnets 18 and 81. Here, Shakespeare enjoys the monument's narcissistic affirmation that all of humanity will recognize who he was. Elsewhere, he does narrow his focus on a particular set of readers. 'You live in this, and dwell in lovers' eyes' (55.14), sonnet 55's final line states. Like Donne's 'Canonization', wherein pilgrim-lovers of the future pray at his verse shrines, Shakespeare appeals to tomorrow's paramours, whose appreciation of love qualifies them as proper witnesses. These few monumental sonnets presuppose a new kind of secular code or law of love, very much akin to that implied by Montague's and Capulet's promise to erect twin statues to commemorate the tragic but true love at *Romeo and Juliet*'s conclusion. Love's new natural law, trumping the canon law and the law of arms, obtains its most authoritative expression in sonnet 116.

Shakespeare's imagining of posterity here does not deviate far from that which other Elizabethan sonneteers conceive. The sonneteer's monument stands before Cupid's legislators, publicly testifying to the speaker's troth, his pledged faith. So frustrated is Samuel Daniel's speaker that he threatens to withdraw his monumental contract of praising Delia, who does not reciprocate his passion. His sonnets appeal to a posterity held in place by courtly love, whose juridical authority will requite Daniel's ill-treatment by perpetuating a punitive remembrance of Delia's cruelty. Less vindictive than Daniel's but equally monumentalizing, Sidney's sonnets laud Stella's regal grace in order to bask in a sublime honor filtered through the law of love. They create a poetic memorial so that posterity will recognize his inherent nobility, compensating for what his lineage could never yield and what Elizabeth I refused him and restoring, perhaps, the honor that he suffered when his rival Lord Rich married his intended, Penelope Devereux.[6]

However, notwithstanding his sporadic Horatian boasts, Shakespeare's many other memorials of wit have trouble reaching out to a posterity consisting of courtly love's legislators and ambassadors. The sonnets enshrine doubt concerning love's noble code over and over again to the point that they lay bare its flimsy pretence and arbitrariness. The speaker not only admits that being in love fosters self-betrayal, as in sonnet 151, but also brings to light the mutual foreswearing of the poet, the young man, and the dark lady, whose infidelities and love triangles betoken a wanton, cynical lawlessness (35, 36, 41, 42, and 152). The lovers try to pull the wool over the eyes of imagined posterity so much that the future reader starts to resemble a feeble-minded, clueless father, whom they must placate with lies or empty arguments before going about their perfunctory pleasures: in sonnet 42, the poet preserves his love for the young man and his stolen mistress by an arithmetic that enables him to turn the love triangle back into two. He can love her vicariously through the young man's lusts, and in sonnet 138, the dark lady and the poet engage in mutual self-deception as though they both needed to flatter themselves with the thought that what they have can still be recognized as love.

Heraldic recognition

The imagined posterity presupposed by Tudor sonnets finds fuller articulation in Spenser's sonnet 69, where the speaker reflects upon his economy of praise:

> What trophee then shall I most fit devize,
> In which I may record the memory
> Of my loves conquest, peerelesse beauties prise,
> Adorned with honour, love, and chastity.
> Even this verse vowd to eternity,
> Shall be thereof immortall moniment:
> And tell her prayse to all posterity,
> That may admire such worlds rare wonderment.[7]

In the monumental poetic act, the speaker praises the beloved's beauty in order to receive, in turn, two temporally separate recognitions. First, he seeks out the beloved's reciprocal recognition in that the initial act of praising is a declaration of love. Second, by exploiting a combination of the beloved's rare beauty and his elevated language, the speaker seeks out posterity's recognition for the beloved, the poet, and their amorous relationship. Spenser along with other Elizabethan sonneteers inherits his monumentalizing impulse from epideictic rhetoric as disseminated by Quintilian's *Institutes* and filtered by Petrarchanism, whose influential pun on Laura's name crystalizes what Alastair Fowler calls 'stellification'—the elevated fame secured by praise.[8]

It is in the poem's quatrain that Spenser indirectly shadows forth the specific image of posterity that holds in place his economy of praise:

> The famous warriors of the anticke world,
> Used Trophees to erect in stately wize:
> In which they would the records have enrold,
> Of theyr great deeds and valarous emprize.[9]

The trophies and records of past military deeds were studied and prized by heralds, who believed that arms commemorated the honor won by ancestral warriors on the battlefield. As John Guillim states in his heraldic treatise,

> these tokens which we call Armes ... were bestowed by Emperours, Kings, and Princes, and their Generals ... in the field upon martiall men, whose valorous merits ... required due recompence of honour answerable unto their worthy acts, the remembrance whereof could not better bee preserved and derived unto posterity.[10]

It is well documented that throughout the sixteenth century Renaissance poets adopted armorial language to memorialize the beloved,[11] and Spenser follows suit, aspiring to this economy of praise for celebrating peerless love.[12]

The Elizabethan sonnet's fantasy of monumentalization involves, at its core, a posterity in the form of heraldic recognition, whether from royalty, nobles, gentlemen, or heralds themselves. Such recognition promises to grant the sonneteer the class-inflected existential worth that, he believes, he and his beloved deserve. Tudor 'monuments'—and the word covered a range of artefacts from tombs and sepulchers to records, chronicles, histories, and any 'remembrance left to posteritie of some notable acte'[13]—invariably sought out, then, patrician remembering. Particularly germane for Shakespeare's economy of praise was the Tudor craze for elaborate funerals, which exerted an influence on how a subject should be monumentalized. Nobility initiated the vogue of tomb building—along with expensive processions and burials—on a scale never seen before to compensate for the loss of purgatory and the destruction of chantries where masses for the dead were sung and to reaffirm its solidarity during an era that saw its ranks stagnate and the monarchy become more centralized.[14] Playing instrumental roles in both interconnected vogues, heralds managed the recognition and thus remembrance of Tudor nobility, their supervision policing armorial distinctions at obsequies and during the design and construction of tombs.[15]

Unlike Spenser's, Shakespeare's sonnets subtly refuse to give the patrician monument the heraldic recognition that it assumes it deserves. As John Weever observes, the tombs and sepulchres of noble men, princes, and kings were fabricated out of precious materials, such as marble and brass,[16] both of which Shakespeare associates with deterioration in memorial contexts (55, 64, 65, 107), in effect tarnishing the funeral monument's materiality. Pejoratively qualifying 'monuments' (55.1) and 'tomb' (101.11), the modifier 'gilded' disparages the preeminent value that heraldic tinctures, the armorial color scheme, attributed to gold. As early as the procreation sonnets, tombs become shorthand for oblivion, unable to transmit heraldry's patrilineal recognition. In sonnet 3, the speaker chides the beloved's neglect of siring a child as a tomb to 'stop posterity' (3.8), while the next sonnet gives the warning that without progeny the beloved's beauty will leave no legacy, being effectively 'tombed' (4.13) within himself, an inauspicious interment paralleling his later entombment in men's eyes (81.8). Sonnet 101 expands upon this devaluation of funeral monuments, including 'sepulchres' (68.6) and 'bier' (12.8), when the speaker argues that it is within his truant Muse's power to make his beloved 'outlive a gilded tomb, / And to be praised of ages yet to be' (101.11–12).

When vaunting Horatian claims, Shakespeare strives to surpass heraldic praise, appealing to an imagined posterity of sympathetic lovers. In sonnet 106, the poet peruses the memorial records of the past so as to determine the origins of his beloved's beauty:

> When in the chronicle of wasted time
> I see descriptions of the fairest wights,
> And beauty making beautiful old rhyme
> In praise of ladies dead, and lovely knights,
> Then in the blazon of sweet beauty's best,
> Of hand, of foot, of lip, of eye, of brow,
> I see their àntique pen would have expressed
> Even such a beauty as you master now.
> *(106.1–8)*

As many commentators have pointed out, 'blazon' here does not merely signify *effictio*, the outward description of a praised person, but the verbal description praising a coat of arms either in speech or writing. Heralds busied themselves with the task of reconstructing lineages in order to authenticate, record, and publicly present the armorial bearings of English nobility. Shakespeare seems to follow suit, mobilizing the antiquarian technique of scouring records for evidence as if he were going to map out his patron's genealogical tree, whose lineal and collateral branches could reveal new affiliations and entitlements.[17]

The sestet's bold reversal, however, turns genealogy into biblical typology, through which all antique praises are but prophecies and prefigurings of the beloved's beauty. His poetic blazon negates heraldic remembering by secularizing a mode of reading scriptures that remembers 'forwards': type, the past person, impossibly recalls the anti-type—the exceptional beloved. Sonnet 59 similarly inverts the genealogical method. The speaker challenges his beloved to find his beauty in any antique book, implying that tracing lineal connections holds little relevance for gauging commemorative praise. Both sonnets teach readers how to judge the honor imparted by other blazon-poems (21, 53, 98, 99, and 130). The poet is not just creating a new language of meta-praise, but simultaneously usurping the herald's position from which his verse monument can be properly recognized.[18] Shakespeare's poetic blazons scandalously insinuate that genealogically-derived arms amount to an unfulfilled, inferior remembering.

Although it would be an overstatement to contend that the usurpation of heraldic recognition in Shakespeare's sonnets launches a veiled political attack on class structure, their competition with aristocratic monumentalization reveals a defensive posture. Funeral monuments had no place for him,[19] for they seemed out of reach at the time of composing the sonnets, and we are not sure they had a place for his beloveds either. Whether or not the Young Man was noble, the poet treats him—at the very least on account of his beauty—as his social superior, while the Dark Lady is treated as a social inferior. In sonnet 71, the speaker's desire to be forgotten by the beloved does not necessarily bespeak a self-sacrifice explained by either 'narcissistic smugness of the speaker's gesture of selflessness', in Booth's words, or, in Vendler's apt phrasing, 'a defensive construct hoping to awaken in the shallow young man the very depths of mourning that it affects to prohibit'.[20] The couplet reveals that the speaker does not want the beloved to remember his 'poor name' (71.11) lest the world will mock the beloved's grief. The impending dishonor makes clear sense when we assume that the beloved belongs to a social station higher than the poet's: the poet is too humble to warrant the mourning worthy of the beloved's gentility. The line 'when I (perhaps) compounded am with clay' (71.10) holds out the possibility that the speaker might not be buried in a common dirt grave, and yet the weak hope serves only to reinforce the disparity between their stations. The next sonnet rewords the same sentiments (72.11), while sonnet 74, fully revealing Shakespeare's cards, argues that the poet's status resides not with his 'base' person (74.12), which will return to the earth—again a common grave—but with his worthy spirit contained in the verse memorial. Sonnet 81 corroborates the speaker's ambitions, comparing his 'common grave' (81.7) with the dignified way in which the beloved will be entombed. His beloved, too, will receive an enhanced memorialization, for the poet affirms, 'Your monument shall be my gentle verse' (81.9), punning on 'gentle' as 'kind' or 'tender' but also 'well-born'. The speaker's appropriation of the beloved's heraldic commemoration subtly elevates his own status—not a preposterous tactic given that commoners who became heralds had gentlemanly status conferred on them by receiving arms at the time of their appointment.[21]

Because he occupies no place in patrician monumental culture, the speaker may very well slip into oblivion even in his beloved's mind and thus turns for consolation and symbolic refuge to his verse memorials. Appropriately enough, in sonnet 74, he splits his subjectivity into two parts, parodying the King's two bodies, or rather the nobleman's two bodies, for Nigel Llewellyn identifies twin monumental bodies, one fleshly, corruptible, and personal and the other marmoreal, so to speak, commemorative, and social.[22] The first gestures toward the corpse's physicality and putrification outside meaning, whereas the second designates the eroding place or position that the subject occupies in what Claude Lévi-Strauss and Lacan term the 'symbolic order'—the overarching customs, laws, and language that structure reality and mediate all intersubjective communication.[23] If the real of death strikes modern subjectivity, as Ariès argues, with fear and horror over the corpse's decay,[24] the pathos, if not horror, for early modern monumental culture seems to be concentrated on subjectivity undergoing utter symbolic dissolution, where being remembered by posterity is no longer possible. The articulation of this fantasy of enduring after death belonged almost exclusively to the social elite. Shakespeare's sonnets thus allow him at times to indulge in the fantasy of possessing a monumental body, albeit an alternative one to patrician memory.

The blank antiquarian gaze: ruminating on ruins

If Shakespeare's sonnets betray at times a disenchantment with heraldic recognition, they also lapse into somber reflections on the ruin—the disturbing, unrecognizable artefact that subtends the monument's fantasy. When observing that 'by Time's fell hand defaced / The rich proud cost of outworn buried age' (64.1–2), the speaker says, 'Ruin hath taught me thus to ruminate' (64.11). According to Carruthers, the ruminant image of chewing the cud was basic to understanding medieval *memoria* besides *meditatio*,[25] and so Shakespeare signals that ruins teach him to remember meditatively on his beloved's death in this sonnet and, by extension, refer to a practice continuing throughout the rest of the sequence.[26] The speaker ruminates on ruin, waste, wear, and decay plaguing the beloved's beauty, his family line, the poet's life, their love, and all sorts of worldly, mortal things.

Shakespeare's rumination on ruins invokes another important Tudor institution devoted to monuments, an institution very much complementary with heraldry. Emerging during the Elizabethan and Jacobean period, antiquarianism sought to recover remains from obscurity by collecting and describing material artefacts and finding and analyzing primary documentation.[27] As Angus Vine asserts, 'the antiquary conceived of himself as bridging the gap between past and present, affording "olden time" presence so that it might speak to or inform the current time'.[28] Vine's description also applies to heralds, who actively participated in the antiquarian movement.[29] Both antiquaries and heralds were, for instance, outspoken—yet complicit—critics of their own culture's involvement in the construction of monuments. Shakespeare's ruminations on ruins channel the suspicion of contemporary acts of memorialization by interrogating the economy of praise, which, as is well known, the speaker denigrates regularly. His verses, like gaudy tombs, are in jeopardy of material devaluation. During the post-Reformation period, there was a noted increase, Nigel Llewellyn observes, in the number of super-sized monuments.[30] The bigger, the higher, and the costlier the tomb, the more monuments were regarded as expressions of economic power and erasures of social distinction. The antiquaries John Stow and John Weever alerted readers to the middle-class intrusion into the noble domain of funeral monuments;[31] others complained too about the period's proliferation of new patents of coats of arms awarded to upstart gentlemen.[32] In Elizabethan monumental culture, the praise communicated through arms and tombs quickly lost its lustre, when the commodification of antiquarian services was seen to cheapen aristocratic value. The Elizabethan sonnet craze coincided rather fascinatingly with these fads of displaying class difference and exacerbated Shakespeare's frustration with the overuse of praise and its concomitant market devaluation. It leads him in sonnets 82 to 85 to the rhetorical tactics of identifying with plain speaking, retreating into silence, admitting the beloved's ineffable beauty, and asserting the authenticity of thoughts as opposed to writing. In sonnet 83, the poet's muteness has the virtue of not impairing the beloved's beauty, since rival poets create a moribund 'tomb' (83.12) through their verbosity. Read within the context of a heraldic market where upstarts can purchase coats of arms and build their own monuments, sonnet 130's famous rejection of the poetic blazon is not just an abstract rhetorical problem but expresses the period's jadedness with empty and exhausted monumental materiality. Such materiality, in other words, is no guarantee of communicating—let alone sustaining—recognition, since glitter and hyperbole may be socially arbitrary.

And so Shakespeare exposes the fickleness and contingency of the praiseworthy itself. Through innuendo all the way to explicit accusation, his sonnets bear witness to praise's degeneration into its epideictic opposite: a series of poems focus on the speaker's and the beloveds' shame (61, 88, 121, 140), dishonor having grave consequences on any lasting fame. For premodern societies obsessed with honor, blame and disgrace left corrosive effects on monuments, compelling the Romans to practice 'damnatio memoriae'[33] and Tudor rulers to threaten potential traitors with attainder—the forfeiture of one's estates and the right to inherit and transmit them by descent.

What Shakespeare's ruminations on ruins gravitate toward is the antiquarian fear over the monument being utterly stripped of posterity's recognition. Both antiquaries and heralds would transform a ruin into a monument by restoring the missing symbolic apparatus—the economy of praise—upon which any kind of putative remembering depends. A most noteworthy pattern in John Stow's *Survey of London*, as Andrew Gordon comments, is 'the extensive recording of church monuments within the perambulation of the wards'.[34] Noting carefully whether or not monuments were defaced, he records the dead's names and thereby hearkens back, Gordon claims, to the pre-Reformation practice of honoring the parish dead through reading the bede roll. Stow—the elder disciple of William Camden—desires to restore to his parish-ruins posterity's recognition. And yet, as Vine acknowledges, the 'resurrective impulse [of the antiquary] was frequently undercut by a sense of loss, the awareness that time could never be fully defied. Antiquaries encountered ruined buildings, dispersed libraries, and obscured genealogies, a past that was, and alas would often remain, fragmentary'.[35] Throughout the antiquary's salvaging efforts, the ruin floats precariously on symbolic speculation, being at risk of sliding back into Lethe's waters. Oblivion might result from the antiquary inserting the ruin into a symbolic apparatus alien to the monument's initial fabrication. A contemporary confidant relates how Stow omitted new monuments from his survey on the grounds that their owners had been the defacers of the monuments of others.[36] This antiquary performing a kind of hysteric heraldic role adjudicates between worthy and unworthy memorials on the basis of an economy of praise starkly different from what would have attended the monument's original erection. And oblivion might, of course, result from the antiquary failing to find any symbolic apparatus for the orphaned ruin. William Camden, perhaps the period's most respected antiquary—and herald too—confesses that Stonehenge does not prompt him to inquire into its wondrous construction but 'rather to lament with much griefe that the Authors of so notable a monument are thus buried in oblivion'.[37]

When ruminating on ruins, Shakespeare does not strive at all for any chronological specificity as though he were an antiquary incapable of restoring the monument. His mentioned ruins remain silent, unrecognizable. In sonnets 55, 107, 123, 124, and 125, the speaker suggests the monument's destruction through the calamities of accident, fashion, politics, and war, as well as ordinary deterioration. He recapitulates the philosophical tenor of his ruminations with the paradox that ruin and waste last longer than the eternity promised by monumental 'bases' (125.3).[38] Curiously enough, the aforementioned sonnets make no attempt to acknowledge the Tudor era's single most traumatic event of monumental destruction. Long into the seventeenth century, antiquaries the likes of Thomas Fuller and John Aubrey still mourned the Tudor Dissolution of the Monasteries, which despoiled and ruined architecture, statuary, and books, let alone Catholic communities.[39] Despite his Protestant antipathies toward Papist superstition, John Bale, a witness and early antiquary of the original dissolution, laments the irrevocable harm done to his nation's past: 'That in turnynge over of ye superstycyouse monasteryes, so lytle respecte was had to theyr lybraryes for the savegarde of those noble & precyouse monumentes ... (and I scarsely utter it wythout teares)'.[40] Even though the sonnets can imagine the failures of so many different memorial artefacts from books and records to tombs and pyramids, they silently pass over the greatest catastrophe visited upon Tudor monuments.

A possible exception is, of course, 'Bare ruined choirs' (73.4), an image of the architectural decay of an abbey church. The church is represented through a synecdoche in which the area around the sanctuary, the altar, and the choristers stands for the entire building. The synecdoche, a trope of fragmentation, succinctly conveys both architectural and liturgical ruin, since the choir would have been the site of numerous commemorations, including not only prestigious funeral monuments and plaques but also Requiem masses sung during pre-Reformation times. And yet the forlorn image only teases us with memory. It functions as a metaleptic figure, standing at least two removes from its tenor. 'Bare ruined choirs' symbolizes the seasonal decay of trees stripped of their leaves, and this seasonal decay, in turn, symbolizes the poet's waning life. Only the poet is being remembered by the image, which, reduced to a figure's vehicle, effectively plunges the Tudor Dissolution into oblivion. But is this not how Shakespeare treats his ruminations on ruins generally? In attributing no historical specificity to the remains, Shakespeare assumes the blank gaze of an antiquary who cannot recognize the monument's praise for the defunct. These silent ruins serve as foils for his verse's own desire for commemoration and death-prompts to spur the lovers to remember each other by.

As we saw with his denigration of the sonnet's economy of praise, Shakespeare's ruminations on ruins reflect upon his own monumentalizing activity. How could they not? He directs us to how his sonnets hover on the brink of deteriorating into inscrutable tokens of the past—even at his present moment. It is as if their passage into monumentalization is fraught with continuous peril. In sonnet 115, the poet declares, 'Those lines that I before have writ do lie' (115.1), questioning the import of one of his previous memorials and thereby echoing the fraudulence of monuments found in sonnet 123. There the speaker goes so far as to dismiss various monuments—pyramids, registers, and records—on the grounds that they change throughout time because of their hasty construction and are thus unreliable, even deceptive. He likewise argues elsewhere, 'ruined love when it is built anew / Grows fairer than at first' (119.11–12). Will not this newly built love-memorial fall prey to deterioration as well? These admissions that his verse monuments can change for the better or the worse undermine the monumentalizing fantasy, casting doubt on whether or not the decay of poetic meaning can ever be arrested. Earlier he imagines the time of his death, when his beloved will mourn him, advising him to 're-survey / These poor rude lines' (32.3–4). At that posthumous point, many rivals will have surpassed his modest craft, so he wants to be remembered for his love, not his verse's obsolete style.[41] Antiquary-like, the poet teaches the beloved how to read the failing monument, while registering its own temporal finitude.

Shakespeare's rumination on ruins dissolves the fantasy of monumentalization because it ultimately foregrounds the contingency of posterity's recognition. A monument is built facing toward an imaginary future observer inscribed within the defunct's same economy of praise. Its destiny could very well not be the recognition of a herald who would sing the praises of the defunct, but the blank stare of an antiquary, who effectively reduces it to an inscrutable artefact, meaningless remains. There is nothing transhistorical or universal in the act of recognition, for the values of different civilizations and their various economies come and go. They are, Shakespeare suggests, even contested and relativized at the originary point of monumental inscription and materialization. Thus, it is a misplaced mourning to locate the sonnets' loss in the decay of materiality given that, even if an everlasting substrate could be discovered, remembering in and of itself would not be secured. After all, an illegible ruin still possesses a brute physicality and tangibility. For the fantasy of perduration to become a permanent social reality, the symbolic order, that cultural-linguistic matrix of beliefs, mores, and values in which the defunct's subject position inheres, would have to continue untouched and unchanged for aeons.

Little monuments

Stephen Orgel articulates the underside to the sonnets' fantasy in which nothing remains but monumental failure: 'Shakespeare's volume of love poems stands as a monument to frustration and loss, anatomising the inadequacies and the radical loneliness of the self and the ultimate elusiveness of the Other'.[42] The loss observed by Orgel finds a critical currency among scholars who regard the work of the sonnets as mourning that which they cannot possess.[43] Elegizing the fragility of remembering and the inevitability of forgetting communicate an *ubi sunt* pathos for a mortal world. Contemporary memory studies encourage such pathos over loss by virtue of cultural materialist assumptions about remembrance. The fixation on the material artefact sets memory up as material perpetuation,[44] not only ignoring posterity's immaterial and contingent symbolic basis that makes possible being remembered, but also confining the monument to missed encounters between the past and the future, encounters much like those promoted by the herald and the antiquary.

In an analysis of the sonnets, Emily Vasiliauskas breaks with materialist assumptions, going so far as to argue that Shakespeare seeks refuge in 'outmodedness', an untimely space between topicality and immortality, fashion and the monument. Similarly, I see Shakespeare voicing dissatisfaction with monumental memory and converting that dissatisfaction into a positive rhetorical force. However, I do want to stress that the sonnets by no means give up on the monument, while serving their present, timely circumstances; in other words, the monument of wit need not reach out to an imaginary posterity at all, but may concentrate on the initial stage of recognition sought by the speaker's praise.[45] It is the beloved who is the sonnets' ultimate posterity. And so the speaker does not wallow in self-pity over the fragility and finitude of being remembered and, instead, adopts a *carpe diem* practice that endeavors to seize the moment in the face of death—a secular *memento mori* oblivious to the afterlife. His ruminations on ruins possess an urgency for the here and now, 'urgency' etymologically meaning to press upon the attention. 'When forty winters shall besiege thy brow' (2.1); 'When I do count the clock that tells the time' (12.1); 'When I consider every thing that grows' (15.1); 'When I have seen by Time's fell hand defaced' (64.1); and 'When in the chronicle of wasted time' (106.1), the poet implements a sort of *memento amāre*, whereby he clings to the moment of recalling his current beloved, their relationship, and his poetry. When reading the sonnets, we not only occupy future archaeological, antiquarian, and heraldic positions in studying the text as an artefactual remainder representing pastness, but also join with the poet in the present time of his desire.

Under the spell of cultural materialism, the artefact, and technology, one can easily forget that the sonnets also unfold in *real time* the lover's own 'natural memory'. I highlight this type of memory because pre-modernity did not rudely separate the artificial from the natural. Both concepts formed complex epistemological relationships throughout the period's knowledge production.[46] With respect to memory treatises, mnemotechnical devices held significance only insofar as they engaged mental faculties.[47] In Shakespeare, many examples abound of the ideational intertwining with the artefactual. Sonnet 122 argues that the beloved's gift of tables, a commonplace book, is inferior to the poet's faculty of memory, and the lover mentally encloses the beloved's image just as a treasury or a memory cabinet stores a prized possession (24, 31, 46, and 133), the poet often explicitly recalling the beloved's image or shadow, a basic component of the art of memory (27, 43, and 61).

I want to argue that the monumentalizing impulse in the sonnets, straddling the natural and the artificial, fosters a type of thinking native to lovers. In the period, the term monument could assume many guises, such as sepulchres, books, records, images, and tokens.[48] Nonetheless, the underlying principle common to all these artefacts is the mental action of remembrance. The basic etymology of *monumentum* is, after all, *monere*, to remind or put in mind of, and so a monument functions as what we would term today a 'reminder'. Yet an object cannot remind itself on its own since reminding involves a mind's interaction with the physical reminder. In this way, monuments of wit are not simply hypostatized objects from the past: they participate in the present cognition of the speaker's rhetorical and linguistic inscription. Thus, Shakespeare's speaker does not really give up on the monumentalizing impulse—only in its pretensions to outbraving time. His monuments of wit remind the beloved in the near and neighbouring present. They yield brief, yet precious moments of recognition fundamental to living lovers.

Shakespeare's monuments, no matter how temporary, serve as reminders of his beloved in a world where sensory demands and inner turmoil constantly compete for his thoughts, harassing, distracting, and hijacking his mind. Reminders refocus us on what we deem important and turn ourselves toward that with which we want to fill our minds. According to the cognitive philosopher Andy Clark, 'linguistic tools enable us to deliberately and systematically sculpt and modify our own processes of selective attention', which a subject has only so much to spare.[49] Clark's hypothesis of the *extended* mind—the view that cognition distributes itself throughout language, the environment, and its objects—also enables me to propose a corollary suggested by the sonnets.[50] Shakespeare's reminders, his little monuments, are *intended* artefacts, 'intention' meaning the action of straining and directing one's attention to something as well as the action of 'intending' the beloved, his true intended. Needless to say, 'Shakespeare encourages alertness in his reader'.[51] Attention in a way is a small interval the poet steals from time and gives to his beloved.

Recreating alertness and attention may compellingly explain the notorious complexity of a given sonnet, testified by both Booth's and Vendler's voluminous and nuanced exegeses. A sonnet requires that readers bracket off the world and concentrate on untangling a figurative, conceptual knot. A rhetoric of intense engagement induces the poet to enter into the mental state of attention during the act of writing and encourages the beloved to enter into this state during reading too: the poet transmits the cognition that he wants the beloved to appreciate and share. The beloved is invited to immerse herself or himself in the poet's cognitive environment laid out by the sonnets. Monuments, ruins, and reminders give the beloved the means to repel the competing distractions and temptations of everyday life so that his or her mind can attain the attentiveness that characterizes the deep bonds between lovers.

Even though Shakespeare's reminders, I contend, belong to what Lacan calls the imaginary order, they do not necessarily fall prey to the fantasy of monumentalization, which makes present action dependent upon the imagined horizon of future approval.[52] Shakespeare's intended artefacts do not try to enshrine an economy of praise that will outbrave time's passage. They neither seek the approval of what 'future' generations will deem honorable and praiseworthy nor attempt to outshine rival memorials with their brilliance. Their destiny is neither the blazoning herald nor the nodding antiquary. They do not fear that their words will lose their lustre and become outmoded vehicles. The intended artefact delivers its value in the moment of engagement. By clearing out a mental space of attention, reminders encourage the lovers to begin their thinking anew. Together, they prompt in the beloved a ceaseless return to the initial, the provisional, and the temporary and focus his or her mind on an attention that amounts to a real break with the symbolic order. Such attention reproduces the traumatic thrill of love at first sight or the traumatic sorrow of falling out of love—the mirror recognition in all its shock and sudden joy, whereby previous certainties and meanings are suspended.[53] At this imaginary moment, the dialectic of absence and presence, loss and possession, characteristic of the symbolic order, no longer exerts an influence. The lover loses himself in love's mindfulness, submitting himself to the urgency of the beloved's image unconstrained by obligatory memory or the lure of the future. The remarkable sonnets 29 and 30 provide cognitive scripts of the process by which reminders of the beloved can yield *jouissance* while sweeping away all the demands, calls, and interpellations of posterity, even if the hiatus is only temporary: 'But if the while I think on thee (dear friend) / All loses are restored, and sorrows end' (30.13–14). Shakespearean reminders are little monuments that do not lust for patrician memory, the distant recognition of posterity, but steal a momentary cognitive pleasure: 'For thy sweet love rememb'red such wealth brings / That then I scorn to change my state with kings' (29.13–14).

By our modern standards, the little reminders performed by Shakespeare's sonnets may seem apolitical, maybe even solipsistic. However, I do not think that this judgment could be further from the case when one considers the bigger picture of early modern memory. Carving out a space of personal remembrance, no matter how temporary, constituted a decisive political intervention on the part of Shakespeare insofar as the period's preoccupation with remembering could be said to overburden individuals. With the growing body of contemporary scholarship on memory's plurality, diversity, and ubiquity there reaches a point where one cannot avoid the aggregative impact that material culture, the mnemonic episteme, and collective memory had on the individual early modern subject.[54] Monumental culture left little room for personal or private memory not only by marginalizing, as we have seen, most of the population from the resources of commemoration but also by placing serious demands of recognition and remembering on humble subjects. If, in Žižek's analysis, postmodernity tries to conduct itself as though the Big Other—the imagined agent behind the symbolic order who runs the show—does *not* exist, early modernity suffered from a ubiquitous, importunate Big Other who would not leave subjects alone.[55] 'Remember me' was by no means a haunting call peculiar to Hamlet's father's ghost, but the Big Other's insistent mnemonic interpellation that hounded early modern subjectivity. The imperative rung throughout churches, which channelled Scripture's injunction to remember God (Deuteronomy 8.18). It echoed within school halls, where students were taught to recall Greek and Roman textual authorities through methods of thinking and composition such as commonplacing, *imitatio*, and moral exempla. It appeared in armorial bearings that spread across the surfaces of everyday life from people's bodies to furniture, from architectural interiors to exteriors, and from private estates to public places and byways;[56] and it circulated throughout the new reformed calendar, celebrations, masques, and progresses, calling upon citizens to remember their Sovereign.[57] Shakespeare, whose history plays commemorate, albeit critically at times, the formation of the Tudor nation state, added his voice to broadcasting the Big Other's frequently-heard injunction of 'Remember me'. Religious and other cultural forces sought to territorialize aggressively people's mental real estate, and any forgetting would reflexively result in disciplinary action or, at the very least, plague interiority with guilt. The famous line that Renaissance thinkers were dwarves standing on the shoulders of giants needs to be rewritten to account for the oppression of the Big Other's memory: Renaissance subjects were dwarves crushed under the weight of the past's giants.[58]

In their capacity to block out mental space for the purposes of poetic attention, Shakespeare's reminders mute the insistent mnemonic interpellation of the Big Other and thereby assert a personal and private memory site dedicated to the lovers alone. These intended artefacts assist the lovers' minds in resisting the Big Other's cognitive territorialization of subjectivity and demonstrate how one can steal moments of pleasure from authority whose imperatives to perform the duty of remembering dominate memory's monumental spaces. An extraordinary thing about the sonnets' construction of memory is that they advocate such a mundane practice: they veer away from antiquarian and heraldic monumentalization towards embracing the privacy of little reminders.

In this respect, the fleeting and private memories encoded in the sonnets deviate widely from the status and functions of public and mythological memory inscribed in Shakespeare's narrative poems, *Venus and Adonis* and *Lucrece*. Their privacy wins out both in its refusal to yield an autobiographical narrative or overarching temporal scheme[59] and in its eschewal of memorializing the Young Man's name as well as the Dark Lady's.[60] Repudiating the *longue durée* of memory, isolated, non-sequential reminders valorize the present moment and the mind's participation in that moment. As such, his little monuments, far from suggesting the uniqueness of his remembering, reveal an everyday tactic that many subjects would have employed under the crushing weight of authoritarian Memory.

A foundational distinction in Michel de Certeau's *Practice of Everyday Life* helps me to punctuate the political significance of Shakespeare's ordinary little reminders.[61] De Certeau describes the ways in which tactics, what he calls the art of the weak, operate within the strategies deployed by those in power. The state designs, establishes, and administers the architecture and spatial logic through which ordinary folk are channelled, subordinated, and interpellated. In contrast, tactics designate the opportune and temporary practices that those individuals enact as forms of creative resistance within the state's strategic architecture. De Certeau's distinction may easily be modulated to the two types of memory, long and short, big and little, that my discussion has been considering. Shakespeare's tactical reminders occur in the institutional interstices left behind by antiquarianism and heraldry as the latter remember nobility, monarchy, and state authority. His achievement attests to how other early modern subjects would have wrested from monumental culture a personal and private monumental practice, temporary yet intensely pleasurable—less material than mindful.

Notes

1 William Shakespeare, *The Sonnets: Updated Edition*, ed. G. Blakemore Evans, The New Cambridge Shakespeare (Cambridge; New York: Cambridge University Press, 2006), sonnet 55.1, 4. All references to Shakespeare's sonnets are taken from this edition, hereafter cited parenthetically by sonnet number and line number. William N. West, 'Less Well-Wrought Urns: Henry Vaughan and the Decay of the Poetic Monument', *ELH*, 75.1 (2008), 197–217 (pp. 198–199), and Aaron Kunin, 'Shakespeare's Preservation Fantasy', *PMLA* 124.1 (2009), 92–106 (pp. 93–94) both immediately turn to Horace in their discussion of the monument. West also provides an excellent survey of the early modern poetic trope of *aere perennius*.

2 *Horace: The Odes and Epodes*, trans. by Charles E. Bennett (Cambridge, Mass.; London: Harvard University Press; Heinemann, 1964), 3.30.1.

3 *The Advancement of Learning* quoted in William E. Engel, Rory Loughnane and Grant Williams, *The Memory Arts in Renaissance England: A Critical Anthology* (Cambridge: Cambridge University Press, 2016), p. 199.
4 *The Institutio Oratoria of Quintilian*, trans. by Harold E. Butler, 4 vols (Cambridge, Mass.; London: Harvard University Press; Heinemann, 1953), I, 3.7.17–18.
5 Peter Stallybrass and others, 'Hamlet's Tables and the Technologies of Writing in Renaissance England', *Shakespeare Quarterly*, 55.4 (2004), 379–419; Amanda Watson, '"Full Character'd": Competing Forms of Memory in Shakespeare's Sonnets', in *A Companion to Shakespeare's Sonnets*, ed. by Michael Schoenfeldt (Malden, Mass.: Blackwell, 2007), pp. 343–60; West, 'Less Well-Wrought Urns: Henry Vaughan and the Decay of the Poetic Monument'; Kunin, 'Shakespeare's Preservation Fantasy'; and Hester Lees-Jeffries, *Shakespeare and Memory* (Oxford: Oxford University Press, 2013).
6 Katherine Duncan-Jones, *Sir Philip Sidney: Courtier Poet* (London: Hamish Hamilton, 1991), pp. 199–200.
7 Edmund Spenser, *Edmund Spenser's Poetry*, ed. by Hugh Maclean and Anne Lake Prescott (New York: WW Norton, 1993), sonnet 69.5–12.
8 Alastair Fowler, *Time's Purpled Masquers: Stars and the Afterlife in Renaissance English Literature* (Oxford: Clarendon Press, 1996), pp. 61–86.
9 Spenser, sonnet 69.1–4.
10 John Guillim, *A Display of Heraldrie* (London, 1610), p. 4.
11 See Nancy Vickers, '"The Blazon of Sweet Beauty's Best": Shakespeare's Lucrece', in *Shakespeare and the Question of Theory*, ed. by Patricia Parker and Geoffrey Hartman (New York: Methuen, 1985), pp. 95–115, and Jonathan Sawday, *The Body Emblazoned: Dissection and the Human Body in Renaissance Culture* (London; New York: Routledge, 1995), pp. 191–212.
12 Though Spenser addresses heraldric language explicitly in sonnets 20, 69 and 70, many sonnets make use of subtler armorial motifs in their blazons.
13 See under 'Monimento', *John Florio: A Worlde of Wordes*, ed. by Hermann W. Haller (Toronto: University of Toronto Press, 2013), p. 410.
14 Michael Neill, *Issues of Death: Mortality and Identity in English Renaissance Tragedy* (Oxford: Clarendon Press, 1997), pp. 40–41; Lawrence Stone, *The Crisis of the Aristocracy, 1558–1641* (Oxford: Oxford University Press, 1965), p. 97.
15 Stone, p. 578; Nigel Llewellyn, *The Art of Death: Visual Culture in the English Death Ritual, c. 1500–c. 1800* (London: Reaktion Books, 1991), p. 72.
16 John Weever, *Ancient Funerall Monuments* (London: 1631), sig. B5.
17 New lineage connections could be the basis of land claims as well as increased prestige. The herald Robert Cooke forged documents for Henry Sidney's pedigree after Philip was insulted by the Earl of Oxford. See Duncan-Jones, *Sir Philip Sidney: Courtier Poet*, p. 165.
18 John Kerrigan, 'Introduction', in William Shakespeare, *The Sonnets and A Lover's Complaint*, ed. by John Kerrigan (Harmondsworth, Middlesex; New York: Penguin, 1999), pp. 7–63 (pp. 18–26), argues that Shakespeare ethically critiques the language of praise and false-compare as mercantile. Perhaps the most famous theoretical examination of Shakespeare's radical praise in the sonnets is Joel Fineman, *Shakespeare's Perjured Eye: The Invention of Poetic Subjectivity in the Sonnets* (Berkeley: University of California Press, 1986).
19 The fact that Holy Trinity Church, Stratford-upon-Avon, honored him with a funerary effigy had more to do with his status as a poet and not his social position as a son of a glover and an actor by trade. See Park Honan, *Shakespeare: A Life* (Oxford; New York: Oxford University Press, 1998), pp. 402–403.
20 William Shakespeare and Stephen Booth, *Shakespeare's Sonnets* (New Haven, Conn.: Yale University Press, 1977), p. 257; Helen Vendler, *The Art of Shakespeare's Sonnets* (Cambridge, Mass.: Belknap Press of Harvard University Press, 1997), p. 329.
21 All heralds must be gentlemen and, if they have no arms, they will be given them. See *A Collection of Curious Discourses Written by Eminent Antiquaries*, ed. by Thomas Hearne, 2 vols (London, 1773), I, p. 145.
22 Llewellyn, pp. 46–47. He builds on the famous notion from Ernst H. Kantorowicz, *The King's Two Bodies: A Study in Mediaeval Political Theology* (Princeton, N.J.: Princeton University Press, 1957).
23 For a sound introduction to this term, see Tony Myers, *Slavoj Žižek* (London; New York: Routledge, 2003), pp. 22–24.
24 Philippe Ariès, *The Hour of Our Death* (New York: Knopf, 1981), p. 28, distinguishes between the tame death of premodernity and the wild, dangerous death of modernity.
25 Mary J. Carruthers, *The Book of Memory: A Study of Memory in Medieval Culture* (Cambridge; New York: Cambridge University Press, 1990), p. 165.

26　For Spenser's extensive use of the art of memory in relation to ruins, see Rebeca Helfer, *Spenser's Ruins and the Art of Recollection* (Toronto; Buffalo: University of Toronto Press, 2012).
27　For a discussion of the historical activity of the first English antiquaries, see Daniel R. Woolf, 'Erudition and the Idea of History in Renaissance England', *Renaissance Quarterly*, 40.1 (1987), 11–48.
28　Angus E. Vine, *In Defiance of Time: Antiquarian Writing in Early Modern England* (Oxford; New York: Oxford University Press, 2010), pp. 5–6.
29　The Elizabethan Society of Antiquaries also included heralds besides lawyers. See Vine, p. 53.
30　Llewellyn, p. 106.
31　Weever, sig. B5^v–B6^r; John Stowe, *Survey of London*, ed. by C.L. Kingsford, 2 vols (Oxford: Clarendon Press, 1908), I, pp. 177, 253; II, p. 248.
32　Henry Peacham, *The Complete Gentleman* (London: 1620), pp. 138, 150.
33　Eric R. Varner, *Mutilation and Transformation: Damnatio Memoriae and Roman Imperial Portraiture* (Leiden; Boston: Brill, 2004).
34　Andrew Gordon, *Writing Early Modern London: Memory, Text and Community* (New York: Palgrave Macmillan, 2013), p. 116.
35　Vine, p. 7.
36　Gordon, p. 114.
37　William Camden, *Britain, or A Chorographical Description*, trans. by Philemon Holland (London: 1610), p. 253.
38　William Shakespeare, *Shakespeare's Sonnets*, ed. by Katherine Duncan-Jones (London: Arden Shakespeare, 1997), p. 362, identifies this paradox.
39　For antiquarian reactions to the Dissolution, see Margaret Aston, 'English Ruins and English History: The Dissolution and the Sense of the Past', *Journal of the Warburg and Courtauld Institutes*, 36 (1973), 231–255.
40　John Bale, *The Laborous Journey and Search for John Leland* (London, 1549), sig. Aviii^r.
41　Emily Vasiliauskas, 'The Outmodedness of Shakespeare's Sonnets', *ELH*, 82.3 (2015), 759–787.
42　Stephen Orgel, 'Introduction', in Shakespeare, *The Sonnets: Updated Edition*, p. 20. The Other is an alternative name for the Lacanian symbolic order.
43　Watson, '"Full Character'd": Competing Forms of Memory in Shakespeare's Sonnets', p. 356; Joyce Sutphen, '"A Dateless Lively Heat": Storing Loss in the Sonnet', in *Shakespeare's Sonnets: Critical Essays*, ed. by James Schiffer (New York: Routledge, 2000), pp. 199–217 (p. 214).
44　Take for example, Lees-Jeffries, *Shakespeare and Memory*, p. 138, who says, 'The sonnet will remember love when even the lover cannot. As remembrances or love tokens, sonnets have a status as material objects'.
45　I am referring to the first moment of recognition mentioned when discussing Spenser's sonnet 69. With regard to Vaughan's failed monuments, West, pp. 212–213, arrives at a conclusion resonant with my argument's: the poetic artefact, despite a message that does not endure, can be 'the basis for a community of practice' in the present.
46　For an overview of a complex relationship, see Bernadette Bensaude-Vincent and William R. Newman, *The Artificial and the Natural: An Evolving Polarity* (Cambridge, Mass.: MIT Press, 2007).
47　See, for example, Guglielmo Gratrolo, *The Castle of Memory*, and Hugh Plat, *The Jewel House of Art and Nature*, in Engel, Loughnane and Williams, pp. 54–64 and pp. 66-69.
48　See endnote 14.
49　Andy Clark, 'Word, Niche and Super-Niche', *Theoria. Revista de Teoría, Historia y Fundamentos de la Ciencia*, 20.3 (2005), 255–268 (p. 259).
50　Andy Clark and David Chalmers, 'The Extended Mind', *Analysis*, 58.1 (1998), 7–19 and Miranda Anderson, *The Renaissance Extended Mind* (Houndsmill, Basingstoke: Palgrave Macmillan, 2015).
51　Vendler, *The Art of Shakespeare's Sonnets*, p. 28.
52　For an explanation of this term, see Myers, pp. 21–22.
53　I am referring here to Lacan's mirror stage, Jacques Lacan, 'The Mirror Stage as Formative of the I Function as Revealed in Psychoanalytic Experience', in *Écrits*, trans. by Bruce Fink (New York: WW Norton, 2006), pp. 75–81.
54　For the impact of memory on early modern culture, see 'Introduction', in Engel, Loughnane and Williams, pp. 1–32.
55　Slavoj Žižek, 'The Big Other Doesn't Exist', *Journal of European Psychoanalysis* (1997) www.lacan.com/zizekother.htm [accessed 1 November 2016] (para. 8 of 26).
56　Stone, p. 25.

57 David Cressy, *Bonfires and Bells: National Memory and the Protestant Calendar in Elizabethan and Stuart England* (London: Weidenfeld & Nicolson, 1989).
58 For an example of this adage, see Robert Burton, *The Anatomy of Melancholy* (Oxford: 1624), sig. B2^r.
59 For the critical controversy over the autobiography of the sonnets, see James Schiffer, 'Reading New Life Into Shakespeare's Sonnets', in *Shakespeare's Sonnets: Critical Essays*, pp. 3–71. For example, Heather Dubrow, '"Incertainties Now Crown Themselves Assur'd": The Politics of Plotting Shakespeare's Sonnets', in *Shakespeare's Sonnets: Critical Essays*, pp. 113–133, dismantles the accepted division between the Young Man and Dark Lady sonnets on the basis that many sonnets do not address a gendered pronoun.
60 Many have noted this fact, for example, Orgel, 'Introduction', in Shakespeare, *The Sonnets: Updated Edition*, p. 16; Kerrigan, p. 21; Kunin, p. 99.
61 Michel de Certeau, *The Practice of Everyday Life*, trans. by Steven Rendall (Berkeley: University of California Press, 1984), pp. 34–39.

PART VI

Review

22
THE STATE OF THE ART OF MEMORY AND SHAKESPEARE STUDIES

Rebeca Helfer

The Routledge Handbook of Shakespeare and Memory represents the scholarly state of the art, to be sure, but to place this volume in its necessary critical and historical context, in this chapter I survey this exciting and evolving field of study from roughly the new millennium to the present day. After the introduction, 'From mnemonics to memory studies', my discussion divides into two main sections, 'Remembering and forgetting' and 'Materializing and embodying', followed by a conclusion, 'The future of memory and Shakespeare studies.' Rather than attempting to be all-inclusive (a near impossibility, given the richness and range of emerging critical conversations), instead I try to provide a big picture of where Shakespeare and memory studies intersect, and to illuminate these important points of contact. While exploring the interdisciplinary nature of memory studies, and thus such varied topics as history, materiality, cognition, embodiment, performance, and pedagogy, I emphasize English literature broadly and Shakespeare's writing specifically.

From mnemonics to memory studies

One of the most passionate and prolific proponents of early modern memory studies, William Engel, complained approximately twenty-five years ago (in 'Mnemonic Criticism and Renaissance Literature: A Manifesto') that the 'instrumental role of memory in humanist theories of knowledge and pedagogy' had been largely ignored by literary critics since the work of Paolo Rossi and Frances Yates.[1] Without a doubt, early modern memory studies was built in large part upon the groundbreaking work of Yates and Rossi on the history of artificial memory, much of which was published over half a century ago. In her enormously influential study *The Art of Memory* (1966), Frances Yates described the development of the art of memory (aka, mnemonics, mnemotechnics, locational or spatial memory, *ars reminiscendi*, and so on) from its classical origins – particularly in Roman rhetoric, in which the mnemonic method of creating mental structures (usually books and buildings) filled with vivid images allowed orators to first memorize material and then recollect it during the course of delivery, in effect by 'reading from' or 'travelling through' the orderly structure that had been created – to its radical transformation in the Renaissance as a quasi-magical and hermetic art directed toward philosophical, pedagogical, and political ends, as well as religious reform. By contrast, Paolo Rossi's *Logic and the Art of Memory: The Quest for a Universal Language* (1960) traced a more rationalist history of early modern artificial memory, charting the art of memory's advancement from magical thinking about universal knowledge, to logic and, finally, to new scientific discourses.[2]

Rossi and (to a lesser extent) Yates were influenced by Walter Ong's foundational study of early modern pedagogy and print, *Ramus, Method, and the Decay of Dialogue: From the Art of Discourse to the Art of Reason* (1958) which argued that the sixteenth-century educational reformer, Peter Ramus, radically altered the oral and rhetorical art of memory by absorbing it into a method of logic that nevertheless depended on mnemonic visual aids, resulting in a revolution made possible by the rise of print.[3] Albeit in very different ways, both Yates and Rossi defended the residual relevance of an oral art of memory in print culture. Approximately thirty years later, Mary Carruthers made the case against this shift from orality to literacy with her seminal study *The Book of Memory: A Study of Medieval Culture* (1990), asserting instead that the so-called oral art of memory was always visual and literate, bound to the book (so to speak) as a key mnemonic locus from its classical inception to the highest middle ages. Carruthers challenged the notion that the memory arts were superseded first by writing and then by print, and also clarified the crucial role of thinking broadly construed to processes of recollection, demonstrating the simultaneously creative and cognitive, sacred and secular uses of memory in medieval culture.[4] Other valuable studies of the history of memory followed, especially (for the early modern period) Lina Bolzoni's *The Gallery of Memory: Literary and Iconographic Models in the Age of the Printing Press* (1995): a magisterial work focused less on artificial memory per se than on manifold memorial practices and their representation in sixteenth-century Italian culture.

Things have changed dramatically since Engel first lamented the lack of attention to memory in early modern literature, aided in no small part by Engel's innovative work at the intersection of mnemonics and aesthetics, prose and poetics, history and theory, which has helped to shape the field as we know it today. Engel's first two studies, *Mapping Mortality: The Persistence of Memory and Melancholy in Early Modern England* (1995) and *Death and Drama in Renaissance England: Shades of Memory* (2002), both 'resume Frances Yates's argument that renewed attention to the classical Memory Arts is a prerequisite for advances in Renaissance scholarship.'[5] Drawing upon early modern visual culture, especially emblematics and allegory, Engel's studies demonstrate how and why metaphorics of memory and mortality pervade early modern literature and culture, shaping Renaissance cognitive processes and symbol systems across a wide range of authors and genres. In these works as in *Chiastic Designs in English Literature from Sidney to Shakespeare* (2009), which explores the pervasive chiastic mnemonic patterning in Renaissance literature, Engel demonstrates the memorializing mentality and methodology that underlie so much of early modern authorship, writing, and culture.

As Donald Beecher and Grant Williams so aptly observe in the introduction to their valuable essay collection, *Ars Reminiscendi: Mind and Memory in Renaissance Culture* (2009), 'Renaissance memory studies are no longer strictly mnemonic – that which pertains to the enhancement of memory – but "memorial" – taking a legitimate interest in that which the memory is culturally induced to retain, and by extension all that societies create in order to recollect themselves'.[6] Although they resist the notion that 'memory, cut loose from its moorings in mnemotechnology, should rightfully become a history of everything', the volume's impressive scope – with sections on 'Revisioning the Classical Art of Memory,' 'Manuscripts, Commonplace Books, and Personal Recollection,' 'Learning, Rhetoric, and the Humanist Challenge,' 'Nations, Historiography, and Cultural Identity,' 'Natural Memory vs. Artificial Recollection,' and a comprehensive 'Overview of Renaissance Memory' by Beecher – nevertheless speaks volumes about the expansion of early modern memory studies.[7] In what follows, I try to chart the field's growth from mnemonics-driven research to the current state of early modern memory studies, which embraces a wide range of methods and matters, and which includes the theoretical and practical concerns of contemporary memory studies.[8]

Remembering and forgetting

This expansion of memory studies owes much to the desire to remember the past and speak with the dead, and thus it owes much to history – or, more accurately, to older and newer forms of historicism. For Shakespeare studies and indeed for early modern literary studies, Stephen Greenblatt's work looms large, having influenced a generation of scholars by showing how the convulsive historical changes in early modern Europe – particularly Protestantism, print, and power, especially in relation to the rise of the nation-state – dramatically transformed early modern authorship and identity, including memory.[9] In the context of this discussion, *Hamlet in Purgatory* (2001) best exemplifies this historical, cultural poetics. Greenblatt examines the central role of memory in *Hamlet* through the figure of the ghost, which he places in the context of Reformation debates about the status of Purgatory and the issue of remembering the dead, whether through prayer or indulgences.[10] Here, as elsewhere, Greenblatt shifts the focus from psychological interpretations to historical and cultural ones: he asserts that 'Psychoanalytical readings of the play in the twentieth century [had] the odd effect of eliminating the Ghost as ghost, turning it into the prince's traumatic memory or, alternatively, into a conventional piece of dispensable stage machinery', contending instead 'that the psychological in Shakespeare's tragedy is constructed almost entirely out of the theological, and specifically out of the issue of remembrance that ... lay at the heart of the crucial early-sixteenth-century debate about Purgatory'.[11] With Purgatory's elimination in Protestant England and the memorializing religious rituals and practices therein, Greenblatt concludes that 'the space of Purgatory becomes the space of the stage' and the 'theater ... a cult of the dead'.[12]

Of course, new and revised critical methods have since emerged, exemplified by Zackariah Long's recent article, '*The Spanish Tragedy* and *Hamlet*: Infernal Memory in English Renaissance Revenge Tragedy' (2014), which returns to reading memory in *Hamlet* psychologically, albeit with a difference. Calling the figure of the revenger 'the early modern mnemonic subject *par excellence*,' Long asserts that 'revengers experience infernal memory not only as a psychological but an ecological event – an example of the imbrication of interior and exterior worlds that has become the focus of recent critical work on the early modern mind-body'.[13] Hamlet 'projects Purgatory' onto his world 'only because he first *introjected* it,' Long contends, reframing Purgatory as an external expression of Hamlet's inner world, a model for the 'theater of his mind'.[14] Drawing upon recent studies of early modern cognition and performance that I will discuss later, which view the psychological in terms of the relation between mind and matter, or embodiment and environment, Long's reading of an infernal *Hamlet* is clearly a long way from Greenblatt's *Hamlet in Purgatory*, but also clearly linked to it.

Historicist approaches remain influential in early modern studies, but with a new (or renewed) emphasis on memory itself as a subject of study, with important implications for how the past is remembered. In *Writing Early Modern London: Memory, Text and Community* (2013), Andrew Gordon explicates the complex 'textual negotiations of memory and urban community,' especially relating to the 'remembrance of the dead,' and the ways in which the 'Reformation re-coding of death that disrupted patterns of communal remembrance provoked profound reflection upon the functions of remembrance within urban society'.[15] This work combines historical and literary approaches to early modern memory, reading (for example) John Stow's *Survey of London* in legal as well as literary terms, and Isabella Whitney's poetic will and testament to London in economic and civic terms. Gordon complements this study with his and Thomas Rist's edited collection, *The Arts of Remembrance in Early Modern England: Memorial Cultures of the Post-Reformation* (2013), illustrating the ways in which 'the arts of remembrance were tangible, legible and visible everywhere in the early modern surrounds'.[16] This volume pursues the relation of the memory arts to post-Reformation theology, emphasizing transformations in modes of memorializing. Yet this focus does not limit the collection's broad exploration of memory over three parts – 'Materials of Remembrance,' 'Textual Rites,' and 'Theatres of Remembrance' – which span historicist, materialist, and literary approaches to memory, including Shakespeare's. As Gordon and Rist conclude, and as their volume bears witness, 'the contested cultural inheritance of the early modern period found no more powerful expression than in the rich flowering of the arts of remembrance'.[17]

Andrew Hiscock's far-reaching study, *Reading Memory in Early Modern Literature* (2011), at once synthesizes and significantly enlarges upon varied approaches to early modern memory, offering something of a meta-history of England. Hiscock's work considers memorializing processes from a variety of perspectives, including gender, theology, epistemology, pedagogy, politics, materiality, and, of course, history. In the service of 'exploring the very different cultural appetites and motivations that governed the cultural perception of memory in the early modern period', he reveals the complex and contested ways that England was remembered throughout the early modern period, across a wide range of authors and genres.[18] Although Hiscock discusses Shakespeare in the introduction, he avoids the usual suspects of early modern memory studies (such as Shakespeare, Spenser, Sidney, and so on), and instead explores how a variety of authors from Surrey to Mary Sidney (including the women so often forgotten within this tradition) engaged with contentious issues of memory in the process of remembering the past and memorializing themselves in the process – and, further, how readers (then as now) continue such memorializing processes. Throughout *Reading Memory*, Hiscock demonstrates the prominent and pervasive role of memory in early modern English literature, revealing how remembrance was an activity fraught with both cultural peril and possibilities, which helped to shape identity for authors and audiences alike, while always expanding reading communities.

As scholars have increasingly reimagined early modern memory studies, one of the most significant turns has been toward forgetting – or more precisely, the dynamic and dialectical relationship between remembering and forgetting. Christopher Ivic and Grant William's signal edited collection, *Forgetting in Early Modern English Literature and Culture: Lethe's Legacies* (2004), helped to inaugurate this turn by 'mov[ing] beyond the paradox inherent in the closed dialectic between the presence and absence of memory,' asserting instead that 'memory is not a totalizing field, and forgetting is neither the outside nor a lack within such an idealized field'.[19] This volume illustrates the art of forgetting over four parts (Embodiments, Signs, Narratives, and Localities) and across a range of authors (including Spenser, Donne, Burton, Brown, and, Shakespeare), showing that 'forgetting is fully dialectical with remembering' and the 'art of oblivion is integrated with the art of memory' in early modern English literature (11).

Garrett Sullivan's influential study, *Memory and Forgetting in English Renaissance Drama* (2005), further refocused scholarly interest on forgetting in early modern memory studies. Sullivan 'insists that we see forgetting as more than a mere failure of memory,' and aims to correct the bias or 'critical over-emphasis on artificial memory evident since at least the groundbreaking work of Frances Yates'.[20] As Sullivan affirms, moments of forgetfulness in Shakespeare, Marlowe, and Webster function as representations of a character's interiority, and crucial instances of identity reformation. 'Forgetting is a form that subjectivity – a relationship to identity that represents the shattering of identity ... on the early modern stage,' he contends, which can be read as expressing 'emergent notions of individuality'.[21] Sullivan also reframes memory from being a mind-based, interior process to a 'fully embodied process' that always interacts 'with the environment,' drawing on cognitive studies that I discuss below.[22]

With *Memory in Shakespeare's Histories: Stages of Forgetting* (2012), Jonathan Baldo elucidates the complex dynamic of remembering and forgetting in the context of Shakespeare's history plays, specifically the second tetralogy.[23] Baldo's study examines the ways in which 'Shakespeare's history plays ... stage vigorous explorations of the shifting and tenuous partnerships between historical memory and forgetting, changing religious practices and doctrine, social stability, the power of the English state, and nationhood'.[24] Due to such dramatic historical changes, many Elizabethans experienced a profound, even traumatic break from their recent past, a sense of historical rupture that, Baldo asserts, the history plays reflect in 'the fluidity and uncertainty of the values the history plays attach to remembering and forgetting'.[25] More than observing competing historical memories in Shakespeare's histories, Baldo reveals that 'the power to forget and to make others forget, and the related power to revise or rewrite historical memory,' in fact shapes English national identity in these plays.[26]

Isabel Karremann's *The Drama of Memory in Shakespeare's History Plays* (2015) skilfully builds upon the work of Baldo, Sullivan, and others, including Lina Perkins Wilder's *Shakespeare's Memory Theatre: Recollection, Props, and Character* (2010), discussed below. Focusing on 'theatrical practices' in Shakespeare's history plays, which create 'a dynamic interplay between remembering and forgetting through which the collective memory is formed and transformed ... [and] *performed*,' Karremann stresses that 'we ... need to take into account the specific mnemonic devices of theatrical dramaturgy as another formative condition that enables not simply *what* is remembered or forgotten on the early modern stage, but *how*': to this end, she pursues such subjects as oral and written history, ceremony, embodiment, distraction, and nostalgia.[27] As I will now elaborate, Karremann's study of Shakespeare's history plays diverges from older forms of new historicism, and instead draws upon recent trends in early modern memory studies: the turn toward mind and matter, or more broadly, embodiment and environment, especially in the context of early modern performance studies.

Materializing and embodying

Peter Holland's landmark edited collection, *Shakespeare, Memory and Performance* (2006), helped dramatically enlarge the field of Shakespeare performance studies by linking it more intimately to memory studies.[28] In his introduction, Holland opines that 'Shakespeare studies and, in particular, Shakespeare performance studies have so far ... tended to ignore the recent theorization of memory and investigation of its cultural and social practices, in spite of Shakespeare's own sustained concern with the functioning of memory'.[29] Holland vows to change this, inaugurating the study of memory in Shakespeare performance studies with this volume, and clarifying how and why memory matters to Shakespeare performance critics: 'memory is fundamental to the processes of performance, from the actors' remembering their lines, through the ways performances remember each other, to the ways in which audiences remember what they have seen – and Shakespeare performance critics are themselves members of those audiences'.[30] As such, this experimental and theoretical volume treats the three-fold subject of Shakespeare, memory, and performance expansively, with topics ranging from performances of memory within Shakespeare's plays, to reconstructions of Shakespeare performances, to the editing of Shakespeare's texts, to costumes and bodies, to collections and museums, to technology both old and new, in varied forms of media and archives.[31]

Holland's edited volume owes much to the materialist turn in early modern memory studies, exemplified by Ann Rosalind Jones and Peter Stallybrass' collaborative work, *Renaissance*

Clothing and the Materials of Memory (2000), which explores the relation between fashion and self-fashioning from historical, materialist, and Marxist perspectives.[32] Jones and Stallybrass work to reveal how clothing mattered to status, gender, sexuality, and religion in the early modern period as a 'material mnemonics ... central both to the economic and social fabrication of Renaissance Europe and to the making and unmaking of Renaissance subjects'.[33] *Hamlet* figures centrally in their contention that to 'rethink clothes as habits is to rethink ... both the materiality of social hierarchy and the materiality of memory'.[34] Stallybrass continues this work in a collaborative essay with Roger Chartier, John Mowery, and Heather Wolfe, 'Hamlet's Tables and the Technologies of Writing in Renaissance England' (2004), which considers the material role of erasable writing notebooks, especially Hamlet's 'tables,' in early modern memorial culture, both remembering and forgetting. 'If table-books played an important role in the Renaissance art of memory,' they argue, 'they also provided an antithetical model of the mind,' for just as 'remembrance can be erased from one's tables, it can be erased from one's mind,' and so 'tables materialize the opposition between memory and forgetfulness'.[35]

Early modern memory studies has increasingly turned toward examining the interaction between mind and matter, and more broadly, cognition and culture. John Sutton's contribution to Mary Floyd-Wilson's and Garrett Sullivan's edited collection, *Embodiment and Environment* (2007), 'Spongy Brains and Material Memories,' joins the work of Jones, Stallybrass, Evelyn Tribble (see below), and others, by examining the 'spongy, changeable brain' in relation to 'mechanisms and media of memory' like 'writing-tables,' and in the context of early modern drama.[36] This essay extends Sutton's own foundational work in *Philosophy and Memory Traces: Descartes to Connectionism* (1998) and especially 'Body, Mind, and Order: Local Memory and the Control of Mental Representations in Medieval and Renaissance Sciences of the Self' (2000), where he proposes a 'set of analytical devices for historical cognitive science'.[37] In 'Body, Mind, and Order,' Sutton works to develop an historical model of memory by adopting and adapting Extended Mind theory (which grew out of philosophy and which sees the workings of the mind as shaped by external as well as internal forces) as well as Distributed Cognition, an interdisciplinary field which grew out of cognitive science, but which draws upon research from philosophy (especially Extended Mind Theory), psychology, sociology, anthropology, education, artificial intelligence, and so on, and which posits that cognition is off-loaded into the environment through technology and social means.[38] Whereas in 'Mind, Body, and Order,' Sutton asserts that mnemonic systems create a mind–body divide, using 'cognitive order and discipline' to tame threats of mental and bodily disorder,[39] in 'Spongy Brains' he revises this thesis, instead observing the imbrication of natural and artificial memory, suggesting that 'embodiment and environment ... were not (always) merely external influences on feeling, thinking, and remembering, but (in certain circumstances) partly constitutive of these activities'.[40] Rather than seeing 'the arts of memory ... [as] the cognitive wing of a heavily moralized civilizing process,' Sutton concludes here that 'embodied human minds operate in and spread across a vast and uneven world of things – artifacts, technologies, and institutions which they have collectively constructed and maintained through cultural and individual history'.[41] Throughout history, in short, natural memory and artificial memory invariably intertwine.

Evelyn Tribble and Nicholas Keene's *Cognitive Ecologies and the History of Remembering: Religion, Education, and Memory in Early Modern England* (2011) considerably enlarges the work of Sutton and others on historical cognition by taking 'the English Reformation as a test case ... for an ecological approach to the question of the relationships among memory, cognition and culture'.[42] Drawing on Extended Mind/Distributed Cognition, they argue 'that the mind is both embedded in and extended into its worlds,' and 'rather than seeing "cognition" as a set of interior trans-historical mental processes, extended and distributed models hold a hybrid and integrative view, in which the realm of the mental extends into physical and social systems'; in so doing, they seek to bridge disciplinary divides and conceptual dichotomies between natural and artificial, inner and outer, social and collective, cognition and culture.[43] Tribble and Keene pursue this model in relation to profound changes wrought by the Reformation, arguing that 'the twin capacities of memory and attention underpin most of the Reforming project,' which they explore through subjects such as prayer, print, sacred space, and song.[44] They conclude by considering early modern educational systems, and 'significant shifts in the history of mnemonic practices and theory that came about in the wake of the Reformation'.[45]

Published this same year, Tribble's *Cognition in the Globe: Attention and Memory in Shakespeare's Theatre* (2011) begins by observing that 'early modern adult playing companies coped with enormous mnemonic loads, apparently performing up to six different plays a week ... while learning and mounting a new play more than once a month,' and 'seeks to answer a seemingly simple question: How did they do it?'.[46] To do so, Tribble considers how '"thinking" is not detached from embodiment, affect, and the environment' but 'embedded within and extended out into the world'.[47] Producing 'a theory of cognition and memory that is both historically and socially aware,' Tribble explores the physical environment of the stage and the cognitive materials therein; the use of an actor's voice, gesture, body, and mind; and the role of social cognition within playing companies.[48] Tribble further develops this influential model in a volume edited with Laurie Johnson and John Sutton, *Embodied Cognition and Shakespeare's Theatre: The Early Modern Body-Mind* (2014), which endeavors to 're-cognise' the old mind–body problem in light of new views on the inter-relatedness of cognition and embodiment.[49]

Drawing upon a wide range of approaches to early modern memory, from historicism and materialism to cognition and embodiment, Lina Perkins Wilder's innovative study, *Shakespeare's Memory Theatre: Recollection, Props, and Character* (2010), returns to the ancient memory arts albeit in a new way: by spotlighting their role in Shakespeare's dramaturgy, and thus 'emphasizing the practical and conceptual interaction between the memory arts and the mnemonic space that is the early modern English stage'.[50] In asserting that 'the materials of theatre are, for Shakespeare, the materials of memory,' Wilder treats the term 'materials' doubly, even paradoxically: she proposes that the physical materials of theater (stage, props, and players) are frequently represented in their absence, and as such they 'become the materials for a mnemonic dramaturgy that shapes language, character, and plot,' creating a reciprocal relationship between physical and memorial materials, such that just 'as the plays enable remembering, so remembering shapes the formal qualities of the plays'.[51] Place-based mnemonics function as a theatrical language, whereby an intangible past is made present – frequently in the form of the female body, which, Wilder clarifies, represents a clear inversion of the dominantly male-gendered memory arts.[52] Such absent-presence at once engages the audience's collective memory, while producing the illusion of a character's individual history and unique subjectivity. 'By withholding the physical presence of many of these objects,' Wilder concludes in part, Shakespeare's complex mnemonic dramaturgy has the ironic effect of challenging 'the whole notion that memory can be made tangible, that it can be given order'.[53] Shakespeare's memory theatre thus dramatizes the negative capability of memory itself.

With *Memory and Intertextuality in Renaissance Literature* (2016), Raphael Lyne demonstrates that cognitive approaches to early modern literature represent a two-way street, with benefits in both disciplinary directions: 'theories of memory can tell us things about literary intertextuality,' he contends, 'but literary intertextuality can tell us things about theories of memory'.[54] Lyne's study divides into two main sections, the first of which examines implicit and explicit memory, adapting terms from experimental psychology as a way to rethink the relationship between intentional and unintentional intertextuality in early modern literature. Here, Lyne explores the intertextual presence of Ovid and Erasmus in Shakespeare's Sonnets, suggesting how the complex remembrance of their work paradoxically serves to raise questions about the ownership or possession of an individual's memory. The second section considers how cognitive theories of schema and fragment function as models of memory with which to examine the relation between a work and its predecessor, specifically the issue of what is remembered or forgotten in intertextual representation, which Lyne pursues in the context of *Antony and Cleopatra* and the complex role of Plutarch's history therein. 'As a contribution to Memory Studies,' Lyne concludes, 'this book aims to value its primary subject matter as a source of insight in itself, even as it exposes ... Shakespeare [and others] to a set of scientifically derived criteria,' ultimately arguing for 'a form of interdisciplinarity that avoids self-denial on the part of literary criticism'.[55] Lyne's assertion of the value of reading early modern literary memory through modern cognitive studies in effect brings this chapter full circle, at once marking a return to the kind of argument that William Engel made long ago for the importance of early modern memorial culture, while also marking the enormous distance travelled since 'Mnemonic Criticism and Renaissance Literature: A Manifesto' was first published.

The future of memory and Shakespeare studies

What, then, is the future of memory and Shakespeare studies? To answer this question, and by way of a conclusion, I consider an apparent miscellany of scholarly works, which though clearly related to the topics and trends traced above, do not fit neatly within them. Rather, I am suggesting, these studies and their varied subjects – which include technology, sexuality, song, sonnets, skepticism, and time – point to emerging areas of interest in these intersecting fields.

Given that early modern mnemonics represent various techniques or technologies for storing, retrieving, and even creating memory, surprisingly little attention has been paid to its relationship to post-modern technologies of artificial memory and intelligence. Neil Rhodes and Jonathan Sawday's edited collection *The Renaissance Computer: Knowledge Technology in the First Age of Print* (2000), though more concerned with print than memory, nevertheless marks a partial exception to this rule, particularly Leah Marcus' contribution to this volume, 'The Silence of the Archive and the Noise of Cyberspace,' which links old and new forms of artificial memory by exploring 'the extent to which the computer has fulfilled the ancient dream of creating an "encyclopaedic memory"'.[56] Although Marcus considers, for example, the role of visual icons in ancient and modern memory technologies, she focuses more explicitly on how 'the computer and the noisy world of cyberspace allow us to recapture some of the sociable and auditory elements of early modern reading and memory' that have been rendered silent in the archives and library, in a sense returning to the oral and rhetorical aspects of communication.[57] Despite the relative paucity of work comparing old and new forms of memory explicitly, a host of new studies on Shakespeare and technology, comparing old and new media, point the way.[58]

Even as embodiment and bodies generally have been hot topics in memory studies and Shakespeare studies for some time, less work has been done to link memory to long established critical discourses on sexuality – hence, the timeliness of the collection, *Sexuality and Memory in Early Modern England: Literature and the Erotics of Recollection* (2015), edited by John Garrison and Kyle Pivetti. 'Seeking out the ways in which the faculties of recall inform and construct the sexual experience,' and 'search[ing] for not just *the recollection of erotics* but *the erotics of recollection*,' they contend that the conjunction of memory and sexuality has the capacity to reshape and revise both fields.[59] The volume divides into three parts: 'Legacies of Desire' explores 'how new texts revivify past desires but also how these revivified desires become models for future forms of sexual expression';[60] 'Bodies, Remember' considers the 'eroticized body' as an 'mnemonic vessel' that raises issues of personal and collective memory;[61] and 'Intimate Refusals' views 'the active refusal to remember' as a means of memorializing, and as 'generat[ing] ... the mechanisms of erotic memory'.[62] Many of the essays concern either Shakespeare or Spenser, though some also treat writers such as Marlowe and Middleton.

Although most studies generally consider the relation between memory and the visual, Erin Minear's *Reverberating Song in Shakespeare and Milton: Language, Memory, and Musical Representation* (2011) examines the 'insistently sonic aspect to Shakespeare's memory.'[63] Arguing that musical memory works very differently from a place-based visual mnemonic, Minear explains that 'Shakespeare often does not so much stage music as stage the process by which characters' language becomes musical,' revealing how 'such verbal reproduction of effects attributed to music can occur on the page as well as on the stage'.[64] In the context of *Hamlet*, for example, Minear considers the ways in which for a play thoroughly steeped in sound, 'music in *Hamlet* ... no longer serves as a symbol of divine harmony' but 'becomes instead a ghostly manifestation' of disorder across a range of registers, from the internal to the cosmic.[65] 'By repeatedly dramatizing the working of songs, melodic phrases, and rhythmic patterns in the memory,' as Minear makes clear, 'Shakespeare suggests that music and its effects on the mind serve as a model for the paradoxical way that forgetfulness and remembrance cling together and reinforce one another,' in ways that influence Milton.[66]

Amanda Watson's "Full character'd': Competing Forms of Memory in Shakespeare's Sonnets' (2007) deals insightfully with a subject that has received surprisingly little attention: the role of the memory arts in Shakespeare's lyric poetry.[67] As Watson's in-depth essay illustrates, 'the sonnet's speaker invokes a wide variety of discourses about memory ... shifting commemorative strategies [that] jar against each other,' and which lead readers to question whether 'poetry [can] live up to the claims some of the sonnets make for its power to memorialize'.[68] She surveys Shakespeare's main metaphors of commemoration related to sight, especially images associated with love; smell, observing that the power of this 'sensory recall seems oddly overlooked in the memory literature';[69] and, finally, writing and its role in establishing 'the persistence of memory,' in evident tension with 'the speaker's doubts about the permanence of memory'.[70] Watson concludes by discussing 'oblivion as a way of remembering,' suggesting that 'memory is always already a partial forgetting,' but finally that 'forgetting is also a starting point for poetry'.[71]

Anita Gilman Sherman's *Skepticism and Memory in Shakespeare and Donne* (2007) looks back to classical skepticism (and more recently to Stanley Cavell) to rethink the art of memory within a skeptical philosophical tradition, considering how 'the so-called art of memory becomes ... an art of doubt'.[72] Sherman contends that 'Shakespeare and Donne are engaged in skepticism's imaginative reshaping of memory,' which she sees 'not only in connection with mourning, but as a source of comic potential for recoveries from skepticism'.[73] Arguing for a dialectical relationship between memory and forgetting, as well as individual and collective memory, Sherman first explores Shakespeare's and Donne's responses to classical skepticism, mediated in large part through Montaigne, and then moves on to discuss key theoretical and historical concepts that inform her work: 'Framing,' 'Countermonuments,' 'Disnarration,' and 'Exemplarity.' Attempting to 'lay to rest at least one complaint lodged against skepticism – that it results in relativism,' Sherman's study powerfully demonstrates that skepticism 'inspires high art and enlightened ethics,' even (or especially) for skeptics like Shakespeare and Donne.[74]

By contrast, J.K. Barret looks to the future in 'The Crowd in Imogen's Bedroom: Allusion and Ethics in *Cymbeline*' (2015), as in *Untold Futures: Time and Literary Culture in Renaissance England* (2016), to reframe the role of memory in early modern literature in terms of multiple and competing temporalities rather than the past alone. In 'The Crowd in Imogen's Bedroom,' Barret connects literary allusion with ekphrasis, relating descriptive memories of the plastic arts to the art of memory, arguing that visual mnemonics 'make the audience *retrospectively* aware of [a] range of competing options' because they produce a tension between what *might be* in the future and a counterfactual (or imaginative) vision and version of the past, what *might have been*.[75] These alternative versions of the past 'stick to the present as unforgotten prospects,' Barret explains, creating 'uncertainty about both the past and the present' that 'compels us to make ethical judgments,' while exposing the complex implications of these interpretive choices.[76] Barret concludes that in *Cymbeline* 'art brings a broad spectrum of possibilities into view,' both good and bad, through which 'Shakespeare ... stages an active process of ethical choice that troubles any assumption that literature's power lies in its capacity to render our futures better'.[77]

As memory studies and Shakespeare studies evolve in increasingly interdisciplinary ways, an important new resource, William E. Engel, Rory Loughnane, and Grant Williams' *The Memory Arts in Renaissance England: A Critical Anthology*, offers students at all levels a way to access and appreciate the historically interdisciplinary nature of the memory arts. Spanning from 1500–1700, with sections on rhetoric and poetry, education and science, history and philosophy, religion, and literature, this anthology shows the vast scope of the memory arts, revealing both its diversity and ubiquity. Even as the editors understand the memory arts to designate a specifically Renaissance concern with the revival of Greek and Roman culture, and even as they endeavor to preserve the historical and cultural difference of pre-modernity from collapsing into the concerns of contemporary memory studies (e.g., trauma, repression, political protest, and so on), *The Memory Arts in Renaissance England* nevertheless speaks powerfully to the growth and potential of early modern memory studies, as well as Shakespeare's place within it – and to the fact that these fields have already been transformed by modern memory studies. The recent swell of scholarly works in contemporary memory studies and the practical and theoretical concerns therein increasingly finds a central place in early modern memory studies, despite the challenge of maintaining historical and disciplinary integrity. If past is indeed prologue, then the current critical state of the art would seem to predict that the conjoined future of Shakespeare and memory studies will be not only increasingly interdisciplinary and international, but also trans-historical in the best possible sense: as engaging with concerns at once old and new, which cross disciplinary and spatial as well as temporal boundaries.[78] Finally, with the superb example of *The Routledge Handbook of Shakespeare and Memory* before us as a model, we might even say that the future is now.

Notes

1 W.E. Engel, 'Mnemonic Criticism and Renaissance Literature: A Manifesto.' *Connotations*, 1.1 (1991): 12–33 (p. 12). Cf. A. Assman, *Cultural Memory and Western Civilization: Functions, Media, Archives* (Cambridge: Cambridge University Press, 2011, orig. 1999), p. 18.

2 For related works on early modern knowledge, see: W. West, *Theatres and Encyclopedias in Early Modern Europe* (Cambridge: Cambridge University Press, 2002); R. Lewis, *Language, Mind and Nature: Artificial Languages in England from Bacon to Locke* (Cambridge: Cambridge University Press, 2007).

3 On orality and literacy, see also: M.T. Clanchy, *From Memory to Written Record: England, 1066–1307* (Oxford: Blackwell, 1979); R. Lewis, *Language, Mind and Nature: Artificial Languages in England from Bacon to Locke* (Cambridge: Cambridge University Press, 2007). On memory in relation to print and pedagogy, see D. Beecher and G. Williams (eds.), *Ars Reminiscendi: Mind and Memory in Renaissance Culture*

(Toronto: CRRS, 2009); and M.T. Crane, *Framing Authority: Sayings, Self, and Society in Sixteenth-Century England* (Princeton, NJ: Princeton University Press, 1993).

4 See also: M.J. Carruthers, *The Craft of Thought: Meditation, Rhetoric, and the Making of Images, 400–1200* (Cambridge: Cambridge University Press, 1998); J. Coleman, *Ancient and Medieval Memories: Studies in the Reconstruction of the Past* (Cambridge: Cambridge University Press, 1992); J.P. Small, *Wax Tablets of the Mind: Cognitive Studies of Memory and Literacy in Classical Antiquity* (London, New York: Routledge, 1997).

5 W.E. Engel, *Death and Drama in Renaissance England: Shades of Memory* (Oxford: Oxford University Press, 2002), p. 26. See also: W.E. Engel, 'Kinetic Emblems and Memory Images in *The Winter's Tale*', *Late Shakespeare, 1608–1613*, ed. A.J. Power and R. Loughnane (Cambridge: Cambridge University Press, 2013): 71–87. My own work builds upon Yates' scholarship, both my first study (R. Helfer, *Spenser's Ruins and the Art of Recollection* (University of Toronto Press, 2012) and my current project on the role of artificial memory in early modern literary theory, 'The Art of Memory and the Art of Writing in Early Modern England'.

6 Beecher and Williams, *Ars Reminiscendi*, p. 17.

7 Beecher and Williams, *Ars Reminiscendi*, p. 18.

8 Defining works for memory studies (including many of the essays here) include: B. Anderson, *Imagined Communities: Reflections on the Origin and Spread of Nationalism* (London: Verso, 1991); M. Halbwachs, *On Collective Memory*, trans. L.A. Coser (Chicago: University of Chicago Press, 1992, orig. 1941); P. Nora, *Realms of Memory: The Construction of the French Past*, ed. L.D. Kritzman, trans. A. Goldhammer (New York: Columbia University Press, 1998, orig. 1984).

9 On early modern history and memory, see: D. Cressy, *Bonfires and Bells: National Memory and the Protestant Calendar in Elizabethan and Stuart England* (Berkeley and Los Angeles: University of California Press, 1989); B. Gordon, and P. Marshall (eds.), *The Place of the Dead: Death and Remembrance in Late Medieval and Early Modern Europe* (Cambridge: Cambridge University Press, 2000); P.H. Hutton, *History as an Art of Memory* (University Press of New England, 1993); E. Kuijpers, J. Pollmann, J. Müller and J. van der Steen (eds.), *Memory Before Modernity: Practices of Memory in Early Modern Europe* (Leiden, Boston: Brill, 2013); J. Le Goff, *History and Memory*, trans. S. Rendall and E. Claman (New York: Columbia University Press, 1992, orig. 1977); P. Ricoeur, *Memory, History, Forgetting*, trans. K. Blamey and D. Pellauer (Chicago: University of Chicago Press, 2004).

10 On *Hamlet* and memory, see also: J.J. Schiffer, 'Mnemonic Cues to Passion in *Hamlet*', *Renaissance Papers*, ed. G.W. Williams and B.J. Baines (Durham, NC: Boydell & Brewer, 1995): 65–79; A.M. Cohen, 'Hamlet as Emblem: The *Ars Memoria* and the Culture of the Play', *Journal for Early Modern Cultural Studies*, 3.1 (Spring/Summer 2003): 77–112; A. Dawson, 'Priamus is Dead: Memorial Repetition in Marlowe and Shakespeare', *Shakespeare, Memory and Performance*, ed. P. Holland (Cambridge: Cambridge University Press, 2006): 63–84; A. Dawson, 'The Arithmetic of Memory', in A. Dawson and P. Yachnin (eds.), *The Culture of Playgoing in Shakespeare's England: A Collaborative Debate* (Cambridge: Cambridge University Press, 2001).

11 S. Greenblatt, *Hamlet in Purgatory* (Princeton, NJ: Princeton University Press, 2001), p. 229.

12 Greenblatt, *Hamlet in Purgatory.*, pp. 257–8.

13 Z.C. Long, 'The Spanish Tragedy *and* Hamlet: Infernal Memory in English Renaissance Revenge Tragedy', *ELR*, 44.2 (2014): 153–92 (p. 154).

14 Long, 'The Spanish Tragedy *and* Hamlet', p. 189.

15 A. Gordon, *Writing Early Modern London: Memory, Text and Community* (New York: Palgrave, 2013), p. 5. On national memory, see: K. Pivetti, *Of Memory and Literary Form: Making the Early Modern English Nation* (Newark: University of Delaware Press, 2015); P. Schwyzer, *Literature, Nationalism, and Memory in Early Modern England and Wales* (Cambridge: Cambridge University Press, 2004); J. Summit, *Memory's Library: Medieval Books in Early Modern England* (Chicago: University of Chicago Press, 2008).

16 A. Gordon and T. Rist (eds.), *The Arts of Remembrance in Early Modern England: Memorial Cultures of the Post Reformation* (Farnham, UK: Ashgate, 2013), p. 3.

17 Gordon and Rist, *The Arts of Remembrance*, p. 15.

18 A. Hiscock, *Reading Memory in Early Modern Literature* (Cambridge: Cambridge University Press, 2011), p. 19.

19 C. Ivic and G. Williams (eds.), *Forgetting in Early Modern English Literature and Culture: Lethe's Legacies* (London, New York: Routledge, 2004), p. 1. On forgetting, see: J. Baldo, *Memory in Shakespeare's Histories: Stages of Forgetting in Early Modern England* (London, New York: Routledge, 2012); G.A. Sullivan, Jr., *Memory and Forgetting in English Renaissance Drama* (Cambridge: Cambridge University Press, 2005); H. Weinrich, *Lethe: The Art and Critique of Forgetting*, trans. S. Rendall (Ithaca, NY: Cornell University Press, 2004, orig. 1997).

20 Sullivan, *Memory and Forgetting*, p. 2.
21 Sullivan, *Memory and Forgetting*, pp. 12, 22, 24.
22 Sullivan, *Memory and Forgetting*, p. 7.
23 On memory in historical drama, see: I. Karremann, *The Drama of Memory in Shakespeare's History Plays* (Cambridge: Cambridge University Press, 2015); J. Mazzaro, 'Shakespeare's "Books of Memory": *1* and *2 Henry VI*', *Comparative Drama*, 35.3/4 (Fall/Winter 2001-02): 393–414.
24 Baldo, *Memory in Shakespeare's Histories*, p. 1.
25 Baldo, *Memory in Shakespeare's Histories*, p. 2.
26 Baldo, *Memory in Shakespeare's Histories*, p. 132.
27 Karremann, *The Drama of* Memory, pp. 32, 188.
28 P. Holland (ed.), *Shakespeare, Memory and Performance* (Cambridge: Cambridge University Press, 2006), p. 3. On memory and performance studies, see: M. Carlson, *The Haunted Stage: The Theatre as Memory Machine* (Michigan University Press, 2001); and A. Favorini, *Memory in Play: From Aeschylus to Sam Shepard* (New York: Palgrave, 2008). On Shakespeare and performance broadly, see: Hatchuel and Vienne-Guerrin, ed., *Shakespeare on Screen* series; and B. Hodgdon and W.B. Worthen (eds.), *A Companion to Shakespeare and Performance* (Malden, MA: Blackwell, 2005).
29 Holland, *Shakespeare, Memory and Performance*, p. 3.
30 Ibid.
31 On memory and editing / textual studies, see: L.E. Maguire, *Shakespearean Suspect Texts: The Bad' Quartos and their Contexts* (Cambridge: Cambridge University Press, 1996); J. Tronch Pérez, 'Playtext Reporters and *Memoriones*: Suspect Texts in Shakespeare and Spanish Golden Age Drama', *Shakespeare and the Mediterranean*, ed. T. Clayton, S. Brock and V. Forés (Newark, NJ: University of Delaware Press, 2004): 270–85; M.J. Kidnie and S. Massai (eds.), *Shakespeare and Textual Studies* (Cambridge: Cambridge University Press, 2015). On memory and performance/theatre history, see: T. Stern, *Rehearsal from Shakespeare to Sheridan* (Oxford: Clarendon Press, 2000); T. Stern and S. Palfrey, *Shakespeare in Parts* (Oxford: Oxford University Press, 2007).
32 On materiality and memory, see: W. West, 'No endless moniment: Artificial Memory and Memorial Artifact in Early Modern England', *Regimes of Memory*, ed. S. Radstone and K. Hodgkin (London, New York: Routledge, 2003): 61– 75; J.S. Peters, 'Theater and Book in the History of Memory: Materializing Mnemosyne in the Age of Print.' *Modern Philology*, 102.2 (November 2004): 179–206; R. Shankar, 'Marking Time: Memory and Market in *The Comedy of Errors*', *Shakespeare Quarterly*, 56.2 (Summer, 2005): 176–205; P. Sherlock, *Monuments and Memory in Early Modern England* (Farnham, UK: Ashgate, 2008); N. Korda and J. Gil Harris (eds.), *Staged Properties in Early Modern English Drama* (Cambridge: Cambridge University Press, 2002); C. Richardson, *Shakespeare and Material Culture* (Oxford: Oxford University Press, 2011).
33 A.R. Jones and P. Stallybrass, *Renaissance Clothing and the Materials of Memory* (Cambridge: Cambridge University Press, 2000), p. 14.
34 Jones and Stallybrass, *Renaissance Clothing*, p. 277.
35 P. Stallybrass, R. Chartier, J.F. Mowery, and H. Wolfe, 'Hamlet's Tables and the Technologies of Writing in Renaissance England', *Shakespeare Quarterly*, 55.4 (2004): 379–419 (pp. 412–14).
36 J. Sutton, 'Spongy Brains and Material Memories', *Environment and Embodiment in Early Modern England*, ed. M. Floyd-Wilson and G.A. Sullivan, Jr. (New York: Palgrave, 2007): 14, 22–3.
37 J. Sutton, 'Body, Mind, and Order: Local Memory and the Control of Mental Representations in Medieval and Renaissance Sciences of the Self', *1543 and All That: Image and Word, Change and Continuity in the Proto-Scientific Revolution*, ed. G. Freeland and A. Corones (Dordrecht, Boston, London: Kluwer, 2000), 117–50 (p. 117).
38 On Extended Mind Theory and Distributed Cognition, see: A. Clark and D.J. Chalmers, *The Extended Mind*, ed. R. Menary (Cambridge, MA: MIT Press, 2010 [org. 1998]): 27–42; E. Hutchins, *Cognition in the Wild* (Cambridge, MA: MIT Press, 1995). On literary cognitive studies, see: M. Turner, *Reading Minds: The Study of English in the Age of Cognitive Science* (Princeton, NJ: Princeton University Press, 1991); M. Turner, *The Literary Mind* (Oxford: Oxford University Press, 1996); M. Turner, *The Artful Mind: Cognitive Science and the Riddle of Human Creativity* (Oxford: Oxford University Press, 2006). On early modern cognition, see: M. Anderson, *The Renaissance Extended Mind* (New York: Palgrave, 2015); D. Beecher, *Adapted Brains and Imaginary Worlds: Cognitive Science and the Literature of the Renaissance* (Montreal: McGill-Queen's University Press, 2016); M.T. Crane, *Shakespeare's Brain: Reading with Cognitive Theory* (Princeton, NJ: Princeton University Press, 2001); R. Lyne, *Shakespeare, Rhetoric and Cognition* (Cambridge: Cambridge University Press, 2011); R. Lyne, *Memory and Intertextuality in Renaissance Literature* (Cambridge: Cambridge University Press, 2016); E. Spolsky, *Word vs Image:*

Cognitive Hunger in Shakespeare's England (New York: Palgrave, 2007); E. Spolsky, *The Contracts of Fiction: Cognition, Culture, Community* (Oxford: Oxford University Press, 2015).
39 Sutton, 'Body, Mind, and Order', pp. 117, 119.
40 Sutton, 'Spongy Brains and Material Memories', p. 14.
41 Sutton, 'Spongy Brains and Material Memories', p. 27.
42 E. Tribble and N. Keene, *Cognitive Ecologies and the History of Remembering: Religion, Education, and Memory in Early Modern England* (New York: Palgrave, 2011), p. 2.
43 Tribble and Keene, *Cognitive Ecologies and the History of Remembering*, pp. 2, 7.
44 Tribble and Keene, *Cognitive Ecologies and the History of Remembering*, p. 15.
45 Tribble and Keene, *Cognitive Ecologies and the History of Remembering.*, p. 132.
46 E. Tribble, *Cognition in the Globe: Attention and Memory in Shakespeare's Theatre* (New York: Palgrave, 2011), p. 1.
47 Tribble, *Cognition in the Globe*, pp. 2–3.
48 Tribble, *Cognition in the Globe*, p. 12.
49 On embodiment and environment, see: G.K. Paster, *The Body Embarrassed: Drama and the Disciplines of Shame in Early Modern England* (Ithaca, NY: Cornell University Press, 1993); G.K. Paster, *Humoring the Body: Emotions and the Shakespearean Stage* (Chicago: University of Chicago Press, 2004); Floyd-Wilson and Sullivan, *Environment and Embodiment in Early Modern England*; L. Gallagher and S. Raman. *Knowing Shakespeare: Senses, Embodiment and Cognition* (New York: Palgrave, 2010).
50 L.P. Wilder, *Shakespeare's Memory Theatre: Recollection, Props, and Character* (Cambridge: Cambridge University Press, 2010), p. 13.
51 Wilder, *Shakespeare's Memory Theatre*, pp. 1–2.
52 On memory and gender, see Kate Chedgzoy, *Women's Writing in the British Atlantic World: Memory, Place and History, 1550–1700* (Cambridge: Cambridge University Press, 2007); and Weber, *Memory, Print, and Gender in England*.
53 Wilder, *Shakespeare's Memory Theatre*, p. 58.
54 Lyne, *Shakespeare, Rhetoric and Cognition*, p. 2.
55 Lyne, *Shakespeare, Rhetoric and Cognition*, pp. 240–41.
56 L.S. Marcus, 'The Silence of the Archive and the Noise of Cyberspace', *The Renaissance Computer: Knowledge Technology in the First Age of Print*, ed. N. Rhodes and J. Sawday (London, New York: Routledge, 2000): 18–28 (p. 18).
57 Marcus, 'The Silence of the Archive', p. 27.
58 On memory, media, and technology, see: A. Assman, *Cultural Memory and Western Civilization: Functions, Media, Archives* (Cambridge: Cambridge University Press, 2011, orig. 1999); C. Carson and P. Kirwan (eds.), *Shakespeare and the Digital World: Redefining Scholarship and Practice* (Cambridge: Cambridge University Press, 2014); A.M. Cohen, *Shakespeare and Technology: Dramatizing Early Modern Technological Revolutions* (New York: Palgrave, 2006); D. Draaisma, *Metaphors of Memory: A History of Ideas About the Mind*, trans. P. Vincent (Cambridge: Cambridge University Press, 2000, orig. 1995); A. Galey, *The Shakespearean Archive: Experiments in New Media from the Renaissance to Postmodernity* (Cambridge: Cambridge University Press, 2014).
59 J.S. Garrison and K. Pivetti (eds.), *Sexuality and Memory in Early Modern England: Literature and the Erotics of Recollection* (London, New York: Routledge, 2015), p. 4.
60 Garrison and Pivetti, *Sexuality and Memory in Early Modern England*, p. 7.
61 Garrison and Pivetti, *Sexuality and Memory in Early Modern England*, p. 8.
62 Garrison and Pivetti, *Sexuality and Memory in Early Modern England*, p. 10.
63 E. Minear, *Reverberating Song in Shakespeare and Milton: Language, Memory, and Musical Representation* (Farnham, UK: Ashgate, 2011), p. 10. On music and memory, see also: P. Iselin, 'Myth, Memory and Music in *Richard II, Hamlet*, and *Othello*', *Reclamations of Shakespeare*, ed. A.J. Hoenselaars (Amsterdam; Atlanta, GA: Rodopi, 1994): 173–86.
64 Minear, *Reverberating Song*, p. 13.
65 Minear, *Reverberating Song*, p. 15.
66 Minear, *Reverberating Song*, p. 111.
67 See also G.A. Sullivan, Jr., 'Voicing the Young Man: Memory, Forgetting, and Subjectivity in the Procreation Sonnets', *A Companion to Shakespeare's Sonnets*, ed. M. Schoenfeldt (Malden, MA: Blackwell, 2007): 331–42.
68 A. Watson, '"Full character'd": Competing Forms of Memory in Shakespeare's Sonnets', *A Companion to Shakespeare's Sonnets*, ed. M. Schoenfeldt (Malden, MA: Blackwell, 2007): 343–60 (p. 343).
69 Watson, '"Full character'd"', p. 349.

70 Watson, '"Full character'd"', p. 354.
71 Watson, '"Full character'd"', pp. 355, 358.
72 A.G. Sherman, *Skepticism and Memory in Shakespeare and Donne* (New York: Palgrave, 2007), p. ix.
73 Sherman, *Skepticism and Memory*, pp. xiii, 40.
74 Sherman, *Skepticism and Memory*, pp. 191–2.
75 J.K. Barret, 'The Crowd in Imogen's Bedroom: Allusion and Ethics in *Cymbeline*', *Shakespeare Quarterly*, 66.4 (2015): 440–62 (p. 441).
76 Barret, 'The Crowd in Imogen's Bedroom', p. 442.
77 Barret, 'The Crowd in Imogen's Bedroom', pp. 458, 462.
78 Recent companions and collections on Shakespeare and/or memory studies, valuable resources for students and scholars alike, include: C. Calvo and C. Kahn (eds.), *Celebrating Shakespeare: Commemoration and Cultural Memory* (Cambridge: Cambridge University Press, 2015); I.R. Makaryk and M. McHugh (eds.), *Shakespeare and the Second World War: Memory, Culture, Identity* (Toronto: University of Toronto Press, 2012); H. Lees-Jeffries, *Shakespeare and Memory* (Oxford: Oxford University Press, 2013); M. Rossington and A. Whitehead (eds.), *Theories of Memory: A Reader* (Edinburgh: Edinburgh University Press, 2007); A. Whitehead, *Memory* (London, New York: Routledge, 2009); A. Arcandeli and M. Tamm (eds.), *The Cultural History of Memory in the Early Modern Age* (Bloomsbury, *Forthcoming*, 2017); A. Erll, A. Nünning and S.B. Young (eds.), *A Companion to Cultural Memory Studies* (Berlin: De Gruyter, 2010); S. Kattago (ed.), *The Ashgate Research Companion to Memory Studies* (Farnham, UK: Ashgate, 2015); S. Radstone and B. Schwarz (eds.), *Memory: Histories, Theories, Debates* (New York: Fordham University Press, 2010).

BIBLIOGRAPHY

Adams, T.R. and N. Barker, 'A New Model for the Study of the Book', in N. Barker (ed.), *A Potencie of Life: Books in Society* (London: British Library, 1993), pp. 5–43.
Adelman, J., *Suffocating Mothers: Fantasies of Maternal Origin in Shakespeare's Plays,* Hamlet *to* The Tempest (New York: Routledge, 1992).
Agamben, G., *Homo Sacer: Sovereign Power and Bare Life,* 1995, trans. D. Heller-Roazen (Stanford, CA: Stanford University Press, 1998).
Alexander, P., '*Troilus and Cressida,* 1609', *The Library,* 4th series, 9 (1928–9), 267–86.
Allan, D., *Commonplace Books and Reading in Georgian England* (New York: Cambridge University Press, 2010).
Allen, M.J.B., 'Jacques against the Seven Ages of the Proclan Man', *Modern Language Quarterly,* 42 (1981), 331–46.
Amine, K., 'Shakespeare's Tragedies in North Africa and the Arab World', in M. Neill and D. Schalkwyk (eds.), *The Oxford Handbook of Shakespearean Tragedy* (Oxford: Oxford University Press, 2016), pp. 847–63.
Anderson, M., *The Renaissance Extended Mind* (New York: Palgrave, 2015).
Anderson, R. (ed.), *A Brush with Shakespeare: The Bard in Painting 1780–1910,* exhibition catalogue (Montgomery Museum of Fine Arts, 1986).
Anon., *Garrick's Vagary; or, England run mad, with particulars of the Stratford Jubilee* (London: S. Bladon, 1769).
Aquinas, T., *Commentaries on Aristotle's 'On Sense and What is Sensed' and 'On Memory and Recollection',* trans. K. White and E.M. Macierowski (Washington, DC: Catholic University of America Press, 2005).
Arcandeli, A. and M. Tamm (eds.), *The Cultural History of Memory in the Early Modern Age* (Bloomsbury, forthcoming, 2017).
Archer, W., *Henry Irving: Actor and Manager* (London: Field and Tuer, 1883).
Archer, W., *Study and Stage* (London: Grant Richards, 1899).
Ariès, P., *The Hour of Our Death* (New York: Knopf, 1981).
Aristotle, *The Complete Works of Aristotle,* revised Oxford translation, ed. J. Barnes, Bollingen Series LXXI 2 (Princeton, NJ: Princeton University Press, 1984).
Ashcroft, B., G. Griffiths, and H. Tiffin (eds.), *The Empire Writes Back: Theory and Practice in Post-Colonial Literatures* (London: Routledge, 1989, 2002).
Assmann, A., *Cultural Memory and Western Civilization: Functions, Media, Archives* (Cambridge: Cambridge University Press, 2011).
Assmann, J., 'Collective Memory and Cultural Identity', trans. J. Czaplicka, *New German Critique,* 65 (Spring/Summer 1995), 125–33.
Assmann, J., *Religion and Cultural Memory* (Stanford, CA: Stanford University Press, 2006).
Aston, M., 'English Ruins and English History: The Dissolution and the Sense of the Past', *Journal of the Warburg and Courtauld Institutes,* 36 (1973), 231–55.
Auberlen, E., '*King Henry VIII*: Shakespeare's Break with the "Bluff King Harry" Tradition', *Anglia,* 98 (1980), 319–47.
Auerbach, N., *Ellen Terry: Player in Her Time* (London: J.M. Dent & Sons, 1987).

Bibliography

Augustine, *The Confessions of St. Augustine*, trans. R. Warner (New York: New American Library, 1963).
Augustine, *Confessions*, trans. H. Chadwick (New York: Oxford University Press, 1991).
Augustine, *Confessions of St. Augustine*, trans. E.B. Pusey (Westminster, MD: Modern Library, 1999).
Auslander, P., *Liveness: Performance in a Mediatized Culture* (London and New York: Routledge, 1999).
Austin, J.L., *How to Do Things with Words* (Cambridge, MA: Harvard University Press, 1962; 2nd edn 1975).
Bacon, F., *The two bookes of Francis Bacon. Of the proficience and advancement of learning, divine and humane* (London, 1605).
Baker, D.W., 'Jacobean Historiography and the Election of Richard III', *HLQ*, 70 (2007), 311–42.
Baker, M., *Live to Your Local Cinema: The Remarkable Rise of Livecasting* (Basingstoke: Palgrave Macmillan, 2013).
Bakhtin, M.M., *Rabelais and His World*, trans. H. Oswolsky (Bloomington: Indiana University Press, 1965).
Bakhtin, M.M., *The Dialogic Imagination* (Austin: University of Texas Press, 1981).
Baldo, J., *Memory in Shakespeare's Histories: Stages of Forgetting in Early Modern England* (New York: Routledge, 2012).
Baldwin, T.W., *William Shakspere's Smalle Latine and Lesse Greeke* 2 volumes (Urbana: University of Illinois Press, 1944).
Bale, J., *The Laborous Journey and Search for John Leland* (London, 1549).
Ball, R.H., *Shakespeare on Silent Film: A Strange Eventful History* (London: George Allen & Unwin, 1968).
Barber, C.L., 'The Saturnalian Pattern in Shakespeare's Comedy', *The Sewanee Review*, 59.4 (1951), 593–611.
Barber, C.L., *Shakespeare's Festive Comedy: A Study of Dramatic Form and Its Relation to Social Custom* (Cleveland, OH and New York: Meridian, 1959).
Barish, J., 'Remembering and Forgetting in Shakespeare', in R.B. Parker and S.P. Zitner (eds.), *Elizabethan Theater: Essays in Honor of S. Schoenbaum* (Newark and London: University of Delaware Press/Associated University Press, 1996), pp. 214–21.
Barnes, J., *Talking It Over* (London: Jonathan Cape, 1991).
Barret, J.K., 'The Crowd in Imogen's Bedroom: Allusion and Ethics in *Cymbeline*', *Shakespeare Quarterly*, 66.4 (2015), 440–62.
Barret, J.K., *Untold Futures: Time and Literary Culture in Renaissance England* (Ithaca, NY: Cornell University Press, 2016).
Barrie, R., 'Telmahs: Carnival Laughter in *Hamlet*', in M.T. Burnett and J. Manning (eds.), *New Essays on Hamlet* (New York: AMS, 1994), pp. 83–100.
Barthes, R., *Camera Lucida*, trans. R. Howard (London: Flamingo, 1984).
Bartlet, J., *A booke of ayres with a triplicitie of musicke* (1606).
Bartlett, F.C., 'Some experiments on the reproduction of folk stories', *Folk-Lore*, 31 (1920), 30–47.
Bartlová, M., '*In Memoriam Defunctorum*: Visual Arts as Devices of Memory', in L. Dolezalová (ed.), *The Making of Memory in the Middle Ages* (Leiden: Brill, 2010), pp. 473–86.
Barton, J. with P. Hall, *The Wars of the Roses* (London: BBC, 1970).
Batman, S., *The golden booke of the leaden goddes* (1577).
Beecher, D., *Adapted Brains and Imaginary Worlds: Cognitive Science and the Literature of the Renaissance* (Montreal: McGill-Queen's University Press, 2016).
Beecher, D. and G. Williams (eds.), *Ars Reminiscendi: Mind and Memory in Renaissance Culture* (Toronto: CRRS, 2009).
The Belvedere Trust, 'The Theatre: Shoreditch', http://idox.hackney.gov.uk/WAM/doc/Design%20and%20Access%20Statement377424.pdf?extension=.pdf&id=377424&location=VOLUME1&contentType=&pageCount=1
Benedict, B., 'The "Beauties" of Literature, 1750–1820: Tasteful Prose and Fine Rhyme for Private Consumption', *1650–1850: Ideas, Aesthetics, and Inquiries in the Early Modern Era*, 1 (1994), 317–46.
Bensaude-Vincent, B. and W.R. Newman, *The Artificial and the Natural: An Evolving Polarity* (Cambridge, MA: MIT Press, 2007).
Berger, H., Jr., 'Sneak's Noise or Rumor and Detextualization in *2 Henry IV*', *The Kenyon Review*, N.S. 6 (1984), 58–78.
Berger, H., Jr., *Imaginary Audition: Shakespeare on Stage and Page* (Berkeley: University of California Press, 1989).
Berger, H., Jr., *Harrying: Skills of Offence in Shakespeare's Henriad* (New York: Fordham University Press, 2015).
Bergeron, D., 'Shakespeare Makes History: *2 Henry IV*', *SEL*, 31(1991), 231–45.
Bergson, H., *Matiere et mémoire* (Paris: F. Alcan, 1900 2nd edn. 1st pub. 1896).
Bicks, C., 'Backsliding at Ephesus: Shakespeare's Diana and the Churching of Women', in D. Skeele (ed.), *'Pericles': Critical Essays* (New York: Garland, 2000), pp. 205–27.
Black, J., 'The Visual Artistry of *Romeo and Juliet*', *SEL*, 1500–1900, 15.2 (1975), 245–56.

Blinde, L.M., 'Rumored History in Shakespeare's *2 Henry IV*', *ELR*, 38:1 (2008), 35.
Blom, Ina, 'The Autobiography of Video: Outline for a Revisionist Account of Video Art', *Critical Inquiry*, 39.2 (Winter 2013), 276–95.
Bloom, H., *Falstaff* (New York: Chelsea House, 1992).
Blundeville, T., *True Order and Method of Writing and Reading Histories* (London, 1574).
Bolton, W.F., 'Ricardian Law Reports and *Richard II*', *Shakespeare Studies*, 20 (1988), 53–65.
Bolzoni, L., *The Gallery of Memory: Literary and Iconographic Models in the Age of the Printing Press*, trans. J. Parzen (Toronto: University of Toronto Press, 2001, orig., 1995).
Bolzoni, L., *The Web of Images: Vernacular Preaching from Its Origins to Saint Bernardino da Siena* (Aldershot, UK: Ashgate, 2004).
Booth, P., *Digital Fandom: New Media Studies* (New York: Peter Lang, 2010).
Borden, I., 'The Blackfriars Gladiators: Masters of Fence, Playing a Prize, and the Elizabethan and Stuart Theater', in P. Menzer (ed.), *Inside Shakespeare: Essays on the Blackfriars Stage* (Selinsgrove, PA: Susquehanna University Press, 2006).
Boris, E.Z., *Shakespeare's English Kings, the People, and the Law* (Madison, NJ: Fairleigh Dickinson University Press, 1978).
Bouchard, G., 'Unforgiving and Wasted Memory in Shakespeare's *2 Henry IV*' (unpublished paper, 2015).
Bouissac, P., *The Semiotics of Clowns and Clowning: Rituals or Transgression and the Theory of Laughter* (London: Bloomsbury, 2015).
Bowsher, J., *Shakespeare's London Theatreland: Archaeology, History and Drama* (London: MOLA, 2012).
Bowsher, J., 'Shakespearean Playhouse Development', *Theatres Magazine*, 35 (Spring 2013), 18–21.
Boydell, J., et al., *A Collection of Prints from Pictures Painted for the Purpose of Illustrating the Dramatic Works of Shakspeare*, vol. 1 (London: John and Josiah Boydell, 1803).
Bradford, A.T., 'Jaques' Distortion of the Seven-Ages Paradigm', *Shakespeare Quarterly*, 27 (1976), 171–6.
Braithwaite, R., *The English gentlewoman* (1631).
Bray, G. (ed.), *Documents of the English Reformation* (Cambridge: James Clarke and Co., 1994).
'Brexit Special', *Morning Ireland*, Radio Telefís Éireann, RTE1, 24 June 2016, 7am.
Brigden, S., *London and the Reformation* (Oxford: Clarendon Press, 1989).
Brockway, M., 'Commonplace Book, ca. 1833–1835', Brown University, John Hay Library, Hay Manuscripts, Ms. Harris Codex 1278.
Brooks, P., 'Narrative Desire', in B. Richardson (ed.), *Narrative Dynamics. Essays on Time, Plot, Closure, and Frames* (Columbus, OH: Ohio State University Press, 2002), pp. 130–7.
Brownlie, S., 'Does Memory of the Distant Past Matter? Remediating the Norman Conquest', *Memory Studies*, 5.4 (2011), 360–77.
Bruno, G., *De Umbris Idearum et Ars Memoriae*, trans. S. Gosnell (New York: Huginn, Muninn, 2013).
Bruntjen, S., *John Boydell 1719–1804: A Study of Art, Patronage and Publishing in Georgian London* (New York: Garland, 1985).
Bruyneel, K., 'The King's Body: The Martin Luther King Jr. Memorial and the Politics of Collective Memory', *History and Memory*, 26.1 (Spring/Summer 2014), 75–108.
Buchanan, J., *Shakespeare on Silent Film: An Excellent Dumb Discourse* (Cambridge: Cambridge University Press, 2009).
Bullough, G. (ed.), *Narrative and Dramatic Sources of Shakespeare*, vol. 6 (London: Routledge and Kegan Paul, 1966).
Burkhardt, S., *Shakespearean Meanings* (Princeton, NJ: Princeton University Press, 1968).
Burnett, M.T., 'Parodying with Richard', in S. Hatchuel and N. Vienne-Guerrin (eds.), *Shakespeare on Screen: Richard III* (Rouen: Presses des Universités de Rouen et du Havre, 2005), pp. 91–112.
Burnett, M.T., *Shakespeare and World Cinema* (Cambridge: Cambridge University Press, 2013).
Burnett, M.T. and J. Manning (eds.), *New Essays on Hamlet* (New York: AMS, 1994).
Burnett, M.T. and R. Wray, *Shakespeare, Film, Fin-de-Siècle* (Houndmills, Basingstoke, and London: Macmillan, 2000).
Burt, R., 'All that Remains of Shakespeare in Indian Film', in D. Kennedy and Y. Li Lan (eds.), *Shakespeare in Asia: Contemporary Performance* (Cambridge: Cambridge University Press, 2010), pp. 73–108.
Burton, J., 'Lay on, McGuffey: Excerpting Shakespeare in Nineteenth-Century Schoolbooks', in C. Kahn, H.S. Nathans, and M. Godfrey (eds.), *Shakespearean Educations: Power, Citizenship, and Performance* (Newark: University of Delaware Press, 2011), pp. 95–111.
Burton, R., *The Anatomy of Melancholy* (London, 1624).
Busse Berger, A.M., *Medieval Music and the Art of Memory* (Berkeley and Los Angeles: University of California Press, 2005).

Calbi, M., *Spectral Shakespeares: Media Adaptations in the Twenty-First Century* (Houndmills, Basingstoke and London: Macmillan, 2013).
Calderwood, J.L. 'Styles of Knowing in *All's Well*', *Modern Language Quarterly*, 25 (1964), 272–94.
Calvo, C. and C. Kahn (eds.), *Celebrating Shakespeare: Commemoration and Cultural Memory* (Cambridge: Cambridge University Press, 2015).
Camden, W., *Britain, or A Chorographical Description*, trans. P. Holland (London: 1610).
Campbell, T., *The Life of Mrs. Siddons*, 2 vols. (London: Effingham Wilson, 1834).
Carlson, K.A., 'The Impact of Humor on Memory: Is the Humor Effect about Humor?', *Humor: International Journal of Humor Research*, 24.1 (2011), 21–41.
Carlson, M., *Places of Performance: The Semiotics of Theatre Architecture* (Ithaca, NY and London: Cornell University Press, 1989).
Carlson, M., *The Haunted Stage: The Theatre as Memory Machine* (Ann Arbor: Michigan University Press, 2001).
Carr, J.F., S.L. Carr, and L.M. Schultz, *Archives of Instruction: Nineteenth-Century Rhetorics, Readers, and Composition Books in the United States* (Carbondale: Southern Illinois University Press, 2005).
Carroll, W.C., *The Great Feast of Language in Love's Labour's Lost* (Princeton, NJ: Princeton University Press, 1976).
Carroll, W.C., '"The Form of Law": Ritual and Succession in *Richard III*', in L. Woodbridge and E. Berry (eds.), *True Rites and Maimed Rites: Ritual and Anti-Ritual in Shakespeare and His Age* (Urbana, IL and Chicago: University of Illinois Press, 1992), pp. 203–19.
Carruthers, M., *The Book of Memory: A Study of Memory in Medieval Culture* (Cambridge: Cambridge University Press, 1990).
Carruthers, M., *The Craft of Thought: Meditation, Rhetoric, and the Making of Images, 400–1200* (Cambridge: Cambridge University Press, 1998).
Carruthers, M. and J.M. Ziolkowski (eds.), *The Medieval Craft of Memory: An Anthology of Texts and Paintings* (Philadelphia, PA: University of Philadelphia Press, 2002).
Carson, C. and P. Kirwan (eds.), *Shakespeare and the Digital World: Redefining Scholarship and Practice* (Cambridge: Cambridge University Press, 2014).
Cartari, V., *The fountaine of ancient fiction*, trans. R. Linche (London, 1599).
Cartari, V., *Vincenzo Cartari's Images of the Gods of the Ancients: The First Italian Mythography*, trans. J. Mulryan (Tempe, AR: Arizona Center for Medieval and Renaissance Studies, 2012).
Cavell, S., *The Claim of Reason: Wittgenstein, Skepticism, Morality, and Tragedy* (Oxford: Oxford University Press, 1979).
Chamberlain, J., *The Letters of John Chamberlain*, vol. I, ed. N. Egbert McClure (Philadelphia: American Philosophical Society, 1939).
Chapman, G., *Ovid's Banquet of Sence* (1595).
Chartier, R., 'Laborers and Voyagers: From the Text to the Reader', trans. J.A. González, *Diacritics*, 22 (1992), 49–61. http://dx.doi.org/10.2307/465279
Chaucer, G., *The Complete Poetry and Prose of Geoffrey Chaucer*, ed. M. Allen and J.H. Fisher (Boston: Wadsworth, 2012).
Chedgzoy, K., *Women's Writing in the British Atlantic World: Memory, Place and History, 1500–1700* (Cambridge: Cambridge University Press, 2007).
Christos, G., *Memory and Dreams: The Creative Human Mind* (New Brunswick, NJ: Rutgers University Press, 2003).
Cicero, *De Natura Deorum, Academica*, Eng. trans. H. Rackham (London and New York: William Heinemann and G.P. Putnam's Sons, 1933).
Clanchy, M.T., *From Memory to Written Record: England, 1066–1307* (Oxford: Blackwell, 1979, 2nd ed. 1993).
Clark, A., 'Word, Niche and Super-Niche', *Theoria. Revista de Teoría, Historia y Fundamentos de la Ciencia*, 20.3 (2005), 255–68.
Clark, A. and D.J. Chalmers, 'The Extended Mind', *Analysis*, 58.1 (1998), 7–19.
Clark, A. and D.J. Chalmers, *The Extended Mind*, ed. R. Menary (Cambridge, MA: MIT Press, 2010 [org. 1998]), pp. 27–42.
Clark, S. (ed.), *Amorous Rites: Elizabethan Erotic Verse* (London and Rutland, VT: Everyman/Charles E. Tuttle, 1994).
Cleland, J., *Hero-paideia, or the institution of a young noble man...* (Oxford, 1607).
Clubb, L.G., *Italian Drama in Shakespeare's Time* (New Haven, CT: Yale University Press, 1989).
Cohen, A.M., '*Hamlet* as Emblem: The *Ars Memoria* and the Culture of the Play', *Journal for Early Modern Cultural Studies*, 3.1 (Spring/Summer 2003), 77–112.

Bibliography

Cohen, A.M., *Shakespeare and Technology: Dramatizing Early Modern Technological Revolutions* (New York: Palgrave, 2006).

Coleman, J., *Ancient and Medieval Memories: Studies in the Reconstruction of the Past* (Cambridge: Cambridge University Press, 1992).

Colie, R., *The Resources of Kind: Genre-Theory in the Renaissance*, ed. B.K. Lewalski (Berkeley: The University of California Press, 1973).

Colie, R., *Shakespeare's Living Art* (Princeton, NJ: Princeton University Press, 1974).

Collinson, P., *The Birthpangs of Protestant England: Religion and Cultural Change in the Sixteenth and Seventeenth Centuries* (Basingstoke: Macmillan Press, 1988).

Conford, D., 'The Tarot Fool', in V.K. Janik (ed.), *Fools and Jesters in Literature, Art, and History: A Bio-Bibliographical Sourcebook* (Westport, CN: Greenwood, 1998), pp. 453–8.

Connerton, P., *How Societies Remember* (Cambridge: Cambridge University Press, 1989).

Conti, N., *Natale Conti's 'Mythologiae' Books I–IV*, trans. J. Mulryan and S. Brown (Tempe, AR: Arizona Center for Medieval and Renaissance Studies, 2006).

Cook, D., 'Authors Unformed: Reading "Beauties" in the Eighteenth Century', *Philological Quarterly*, 89 (2010), 283–309.

Corazza, Juan Carlos, Dir., *Hijos De Shakespeare*, Theatro de la Reunion (Conde Duque, Madrid), 2015.

Cordner, M. and P. Holland (eds.), *Players, Playwrights, Playhouses: Investigating Performance, 1660–1800* (Basingstoke: Palgrave Macmillan, 2007).

Cormack, B., *A Power to Do Justice: Jurisdiction, English Literature, and the Rise of Common Law, 1509–1625* (Chicago: University of Chicago Press, 2007).

Counsell, C., 'Introduction', in C. Counsell and R. Mock (eds.), *Performance, Embodiment and Cultural Memory* (Newcastle-upon-Tyne: Cambridge Scholars Publishing, 2009), pp. 1–15.

Crane, M.T., *Framing Authority: Sayings, Self, and Society in Sixteenth-Century England* (Princeton, NJ: Princeton University Press, 1993).

Crane, M.T., *Shakespeare's Brain: Reading with Cognitive Theory* (Princeton, NJ: Princeton University Press, 2001).

Crawforth, H., S. Dustagheer, and J. Young, *Shakespeare in London* (London: Arden Shakespeare, 2014).

Cressy, D., *Bonfires and Bells: National Memory and the Protestant Calendar in Elizabethan and Stuart England* (Berkeley: University of California Press, 1989).

Cressy, D., 'Thanksgiving and the Churching of Women in Post-Reformation England', *Past & Present*, 141 (November 1993), 106–46.

Crooke, H., *Mikrokosmographia a description of the body of man...* (London, 1615).

Crowl, S., *Shakespeare at the Cineplex: The Kenneth Branagh Era* (Athens: Ohio University Press, 2002).

Crowl, S., *Shakespeare and Film: A Norton Guide* (New York and London: Norton, 2008).

Cubeta, P.M., 'Falstaff and the Art of Dying', *Studies in English Literature*, 27.2 (Spring 1987), 197–211.

Cummings, B., '"Dead March": Liturgy and Mimesis in Shakespeare's Funerals', *Shakespeare*, 8 (2012), 368–85.

Daniel, S., *The Complete Works in Verse and Prose of Samuel Daniel*, ed. A.B. Grosart, 5 vols (New York: Russell & Russell, 1963), I.

Danson, L., *Shakespeare's Dramatic Genres* (Oxford: Oxford University Press, 2000).

Darnton, R., 'What is the History of Books?', in *The Kiss of Lamourette: Reflections in Cultural History* (New York: Norton, 1990), pp. 107–35.

Darnton, R., '"What is the History of Books?" Revisited', *Modern Intellectual History*, 4 (2007), 495–508. http://dx.doi.org/10.1017/S1479244307001370

D'Assigny, M., *The Art of Memory* (London, 1699).

Davidson, A., *Shakespeare in Shorthand: The Textual Mystery of King Lear* (Newark: University of Delaware Press, 2009).

Dawson, A., 'The Arithmetic of Memory', in A. Dawson and P. Yachnin (eds.), *The Culture of Playgoing in Shakespeare's England: A Collaborative Debate* (Cambridge: Cambridge University Press, 2001), pp. 161–81.

Dawson, A., 'Priamus is Dead: Memorial Repetition in Marlowe and Shakespeare', in P. Holland (ed.), *Shakespeare, Memory and Performance* (Cambridge: Cambridge University Press, 2006), pp. 63–84.

Dawson, A.B. and P. Yachnin, *The Culture of Playgoing in Shakespeare's England* (Cambridge: Cambridge University Press, 2001).

de Certeau, M., *L'Invention du quotidien, I: Arts de faire* (Paris: Union Générale d'Editions, 1980).

de Certeau, M., *The Practice of Everyday Life*, trans. S. Rendall (Berkeley: University of California Press, 1984).

de Grazia, M., 'Shakespeare in Quotation Marks', in J.I. Marsden (ed.), *The Appropriation of Shakespeare: Post-Renaissance Reconstructions of the Works and the Myth* (New York: St. Martin's Press, 1991), pp. 57–71.

Deiter, K., *The Tower of London in English Renaissance Drama: Icon of Opposition* (New York: Routledge, 2008).
Delabastita, D. and L. D'Hulst (eds.), *European Shakespeares: Translating Shakespeare in the Romantic Age* (Amsterdam and Philadelphia: John Benjamins, 1993).
Delabastita, D. and T. Hoenselaars (eds.), *Multilingualism in the Drama of Shakespeare and his Contemporaries* (Amsterdam: John Benjamins, 2015).
Dent, R.W., *Shakespeare's Proverbial Language: An Index* (Berkeley: University of California Press, 1981).
Diamond, E., *Writing Performances* (London: Routledge, 1995).
Dias, R., *Exhibiting Englishness: John Boydell's Shakespeare Gallery and the Formation of a National Aesthetic* (New Haven, CT and London: Yale University Press, 2013).
Dillon, J., 'Scenic Memory', in A. Gordon and T. Rist (eds.), *The Arts of Remembrance in Early Modern England* (Farnham, UK: Ashgate, 2013), pp. 195–209.
Dionne, C. and P. Kapadia (eds.), *Bollywood Shakespeares*, Reproducing Shakespeare: New Studies in Adaptation and Appropriation (London: Routledge, 2014).
Dobranski, S., 'Children of the Mind: Miscarried Narratives in *Much Ado About Nothing*', *Studies in English Literature*, 38.2 (1998), 233–50.
Dobson, M., *The Making of the National Poet: Shakespeare Adaptation and Authorship 1660–1769* (Oxford: Clarendon Press, 1992).
Dodd, W., *The Beauties of Shakespear: Regularly Selected from Each Play. With a General Index, Digesting Them under Proper Heads. Illustrated with Explanatory Notes, and Similar Passages from Ancient and Modern Authors* (London: Printed for T. Waller, 1752).
Dollimore, J., *Radical Tragedy* (Brighton: Harvester, 1984).
Donne, J., *The Sermons of John Donne in ten volumes*, ed. and intro. G.R. Potter and E.M. Simpson (Berkeley and Los Angeles: University of California Press, 1953–62).
Donne, J., *John Donne*, ed. J. Carey (Oxford and New York: Oxford University Press, 1990).
Doran, M., *Endeavors of Art: A Study of Form in Elizabethan Drama* (Madison: The University of Wisconsin Press, 1954).
Döring, T., *Performances of Mourning in Shakespearean Theatre and Early Modern Culture* (New York: Palgrave Macmillan, 2006).
Draaisma, D., *Metaphors of Memory: A History of Ideas About the Mind*, trans. P. Vincent (Cambridge: Cambridge University Press, 2000, orig. 1995).
Drayton, M., *Endimion and Phoebe Ideas Latmus* (1595).
Drohan, D. (Dir.), 'Show Information', *Tempest!* Project Arts Theatre, Dublin 2003. http://dev.project artscentre.ie/archive/archive-p-detail/114-tempest
Drohan, D., 'By Moonlight: In the Light of Day', *Frontline: The Irish Voice of Intellectual Disability*, 63 (12 June 2005). http://frontline-ireland.com/by-moonlight-in-the-light-of-day/
Dubrow, H., '"Incertainties Now Crown Themselves Assur'd": The Politics of Plotting Shakespeare's Sonnets', in J. Schiffer (ed.), *Shakespeare's Sonnets: Critical Essays* (New York: Routledge, 2000), pp. 113–33.
Duffy, E., *The Stripping of the Altars: Traditional Religion in England 1400–1580* (New Haven, CT: Yale University Press, 1992).
Duncan-Jones, K., *Sir Philip Sidney: Courtier Poet* (London: Hamish Hamilton, 1991).
Dunthorne, J., 'This Week in Books', *The Guardian*, 28 February 2009. www.theguardian.com/ books/2009/feb/28/shakespeare-shoreditch-roberto-bolano-smiths
Dutton, R. and J.E. Howard (eds.), *A Companion to Shakespeare's Works*: vol II, *The Histories* (Oxford: Blackwell, 2003).
Eagleton, T., *William Shakespeare* (Oxford: Blackwell, 1986).
Eagleton, T., *Literary Theory: An Introduction* (1983; Oxford: Blackwell, 2008).
Eco, U. and M. Migiel, 'An *Ars Oblivionis*? Forget It!', *PMLA*, 103 (1988), 254–61.
Edelmen, C., *Brawl Ridiculous: Swordfighting in Shakespeare's Plays* (Manchester: Manchester University Press, 1992).
Egan, G., *The Struggle for Shakespeare's Text: Twentieth-Century Editorial Theory and Practice* (Cambridge and New York: Cambridge University Press, 2010).
Eger, E. (ed.), *Bluestockings Displayed: Portraiture, Performance and Patronage, 1730–1830* (Cambridge: Cambridge University Press, 2013).
Elyot, Sir T., *Bibliotheca Eliotae Eliotis librarie* (1542).

Bibliography

Engel, W.E., 'Mnemonic Criticism and Renaissance Literature: A Manifesto', *Connotations*, 1.1 (1991), 12–33.
Engel, W.E., *Mapping Mortality: The Persistence of Memory and Melancholy in Early Modern England* (Amherst: University of Massachusetts Press, 1995).
Engel, W.E., *Death and Drama in Renaissance England: Shades of Memory* (Oxford: Oxford University Press, 2002).
Engel, W. E., 'The Decay of Memory', in C. Ivic and G. Williams (eds), *Forgetting in Early Modern English Literature and Culture: Lethe's Legacies* (London and New York: Routledge, 2004).
Engel, W.E., *Chiastic Designs in English Literature from Sidney to Shakespeare* (Farnham, UK: Ashgate, 2009).
Engel, W.E., 'Kinetic Emblems and Memory Images in *The Winter's Tale*', in A.J. Power and R. Loughnane (eds.), *Late Shakespeare, 1608–1613* (Cambridge: Cambridge University Press, 2013), pp. 71–87.
Engel, W.E., R. Loughnane, and G. Williams (eds.), *The Memory Arts in Renaissance England: A Critical Anthology* (Cambridge: Cambridge University Press, 2016).
Enterline, L., *The Rhetoric of the Body: From Ovid to Shakespeare* (Cambridge: Cambridge University Press, 2000).
Erll, A., 'Cultural Memory Studies: An Introduction', in A. Erll and A. Nünning (eds.), with S.B. Young, *Cultural Memory Studies: An International and Interdisciplinary Handbook* (Berlin: Walter de Gruyter, 2008), pp. 1–15.
Erll, A., *Memory in Culture*, trans. S.B. Young (Basingstoke: Palgrave Macmillan, 2011).
Erll, A., A. Nünning, with S.B. Young (eds.), *A Companion to Cultural Memory Studies* (Berlin: De Gruyter, 2010).
Erne, L., The First Quarto *Romeo and Juliet* (Cambridge and New York: Cambridge University Press, 2006).
Erne, L., *Shakespeare and the Book Trade* (Cambridge: Cambridge University Press, 2013).
Estill, L., *Dramatic Extracts in Seventeenth-Century English Manuscripts: Watching, Reading, Changing Plays* (Newark: University of Delaware Press, 2015).
Favorini, A., *Memory in Play: From Aeschylus to Sam Shepard* (New York: Palgrave, 2008).
Febvre, L. and H-J. Martin, *The Coming of the Book: The Impact of Printing 1450–1800*, trans. D. Gerard (London: Verso, 1976).
[Felton, S.], *Imperfect Hints Towards a New Edition of Shakespeare* (London: Logographic Press, 1787).
Fineman, J., *Shakespeare's Perjured Eye: The Invention of Poetic Subjectivity in the Sonnets* (Berkeley: University of California Press, 1986).
Finkelstein, D. and A. McCleery, *An Introduction to Book History* (New York: Routledge, 2005).
Fisher, B.D., *Falstaff* (New York: Opera Journeys, 2004).
Fisher, S. and R.L. Fisher, *Pretend the World is Funny and Forever: A Psychological Analysis of Comedians, Clowns, and Actors* (Hillsdale, NJ: Lawrence Erlbaum, 1981).
Fitzgerald, P. (ed.), *The Life, Letters and Writings of Charles Lamb*, vol. 3 (New York: Cosimo, 2008).
Florio, J., *John Florio: A Worlde of Wordes*, ed. H.W. Haller (University of Toronto Press, 2013).
Foakes, R.A. and R.T. Rickert (eds.), *Henslowe's Diary* (Cambridge: Cambridge University Press, 1961).
Ford, S.A., 'Reading Elegant Extracts in *Emma*: Very Entertaining!', *Persuasions On-Line*, 28 (2007). www.jasna.org/persuasions/on-line/vol28no1/ford.htm
Fowler, A., *Time's Purpled Masquers: Stars and the Afterlife in Renaissance English Literature* (Oxford: Clarendon Press, 1996).
Fox, A., *Oral and Literature Culture in England, 1500–1700* (Oxford: Clarendon, 2000).
Fraser, R.S., '"The king has killed his heart": The Death of Falstaff in *Henry V*', *Sederi*, 20 (2010), 145–57.
Fraunce, A., *The third part of the Countesse of Pembrokes Yuychurch* (1592).
Frenda, S.J., R.M. Nichols, and E.F. Loftus, 'Current Issues and Advances in Misinformation Research', *Current Directions in Psychological Science*, 20.1 (2011), 20–3.
Frere, W.H. and W.P.M. Kennedy (eds.), *Visitation Articles and Injunctions. Vol. 3: 1559–1575* (London: Longmans, Green and Co., 1910).
Friedman, W., *Boydell's Shakespeare Gallery* (New York: Garland, 1976).
Frizell, N., 'Pop Up Plays at Rift's Shakespeare in Shoreditch Festival', http://now-here-this.timeout.com/2014/10/08/pop-up-plays-at-rifts-shakespeare-in-shoreditch-festival/
Frye, N., *The Anatomy of Criticism* (Princeton, NJ: Princeton University Press, 1957).
Frye, N., *A Natural Perspective* (New York: Harcourt, Brace & World, 1965).
Fulwood, W., *The Castel of Memorie* (London, 1562).

Bibliography

Gadd, I., 'The Use and Misuse of *Early English Books Online*', *Literature Compass*, 6.3 (2009), 680–92.
Galey, A., *The Shakespearean Archive: Experiments in New Media from the Renaissance to Postmodernity* (Cambridge: Cambridge University Press, 2014).
Gallagher, L. and S. Raman, *Knowing Shakespeare: Senses, Embodiment and Cognition* (New York: Palgrave, 2010).
Garber, M., *Dream in Shakespeare: From Metaphor to Metamorphosis* (New Haven, NJ: Yale University Press, 1974).
Garber, M., *Shakespeare's Ghost Writers: Literature as Uncanny Causality* (New York and London: Methuen, 1987).
Gardiner, E.R., 'Commonplace Book, [189?]', Brown University, John Hay Library, Hay Manuscripts, Ms. Harris Codex 1219.
Garrison, J.S. and K. Pivetti (eds.), *Sexuality and Memory in Early Modern England: Literature and the Erotics of Recollection* (London and New York: Routledge, 2015).
Gillis, J.R., 'Memory and Identity: The History of a Relationship', *Commemorations: The Politics of National Identity*, ed. J.R. Gillis (Princeton, NJ: Princeton University Press, 1994), pp. 3–26.
Girard, R., *Violence and the Sacred*, trans. P. Gregory (Baltimore, MD: Johns Hopkins University Press, 1972). http://globalshakespeares.mit.edu/ http://globetoglobe.shakespearesglobe.com
Goddard, H.C., *The Meaning of Shakespeare*, 2 vols. (Chicago: University of Chicago Press, 1951).
Goldsmith, R.H., *Wise Fools in Shakespeare* (East Lansing: Michigan State University Press, 1955).
Goodland, K., '"Obsequious Laments": Mourning and Communal Memory in Shakespeare's *Richard III*', *Religion and the Arts*, 7 (2002), 31–64.
Goodrich, J., *Oedipus Lex: Psychoanalysis, History, Law* (Berkeley and Los Angeles: University of California Press, 1995).
google.com/trends/topcharts#vm=cat&geo=US&date=201510&cid
Gordon, A., *Writing Early Modern London: Memory, Text and Community* (New York: Palgrave, 2013).
Gordon, A. and T. Rist (eds.), *The Arts of Remembrance in Early Modern England: Memorial Cultures of the Post Reformation* (Farnham, UK: Ashgate, 2013).
Gordon, B. and P. Marshall (eds.), *The Place of the Dead: Death and Remembrance in Late Medieval and Early Modern Europe* (Cambridge: Cambridge University Press, 2000).
Gower, J., *Confessio Amantis*, ed. R.A. Peck (Canada[?]: Medieval Academy of America, 1980).
Gratarolo, G., *The castel of memorie...Englished by Willyam Fulwood* (London, 1562).
Green, H. (ed.), *Whitney's "Choice of Emblemes"*, A fac-simile reprint (London, Lovell Reeve & Co., 1866).
Greenblatt, S., *Shakespearean Negotiations* (Berkeley: University of California Press, 1988).
Greenblatt, S., *Hamlet in Purgatory* (Princeton, NJ: Princeton University Press, 2001).
Greenblatt, S., 'Afterword: Shakespeare in Tehran', in D. Callaghan and S. Gossett (eds.), *Shakespeare in Our Time: A Shakespeare Association of America Collection*, The Arden Shakespeare (London and New York: Bloomsbury, 2016), pp. 343–52.
Greene, G., 'Shakespeare's Cressida: "A kind of self"', in C.R. Swift Lenz, G. Greene, and C.T. Neely (eds.), *The Woman's Part: Feminist Criticism of Shakespeare* (Urbana: University of Illinois Press, 1980), pp. 133–49.
Greg, W.W., *The Shakespeare First Folio* (Oxford: Clarendon Press, 1955).
Grene, N., *Shakespeare's Serial History Plays* (Cambridge: Cambridge University Press, 2002).
Grimes, R.L., *Ritual Criticism* (Columbia: University of South Carolina Press, 1990).
Grimes, R.L., 'Reinventing Ritual', *Soundings*, 75 (1992), 21–41.
Grootenboer, H., *Treasuring the Gaze: Intimate Vision in Late Eighteenth-Century Eye Miniatures* (Chicago: University of Chicago Press, 2013).
Gross, R.A., 'Reading for an Extensive Republic', in R.A. Gross and M. Kelley (eds.), *An Extensive Republic: Print, Culture, and Society in the New Nation, 1790–1840*, A History of the Book in America, 2 (Chapel Hill: University of North Carolina Press, 2010), pp. 516–44.
Guéron, C., 'Forgetful Audiences in *Julius Caesar*', Actes des congrès de la Société française Shakespeare, 30 (2013): *Shakespeare et la mémoire*. https://shakespeare.revues.org/1959?lang=en
Guillim, J., *A Display of Heraldrie* (London, 1610).
Guillory, J., 'Genesis of the Media Concept', *Critical Inquiry*, 36.2 (2010), 321–62.
Gulley, E., '"Dressed in a Little Brief Authority": Law as Theater in *Measure for Measure*', in B.L. Rockwood (ed.), *Law and Literature Perspectives* (Bern: Peter Lang, 1996).
Gurr, A. and J. Orrell, 'What the Rose Can Tell Us', *Antiquity*, 63.240 (September 1989), 421–9.
Hadfield, A., *Shakespeare and Renaissance Politics* (London: Methuen, A&C Black, 2004).

Bibliography

Hagen, S.K., 'The Visual Theology of Julian of Norwich', in F. Willaert, H. Braet, T. Mertens, and T. Venckeleer (eds.), *Medieval Memory: Image and Text* (Turnhout: Brepols, 2004), pp. 145–60.

Halbwachs, M., *The Collective Memory*, trans. F.J. Ditter, Jr. and V. Yarzdi Ditter (New York: Harper & Row, 1980).

Halbwachs, M., *On Collective Memory*, ed. and trans. L. Coser (Chicago and London: University of Chicago Press, 1992).

Hamilton, D.B., 'The State of Law in *Richard II*', *Shakespeare Quarterly*, 34 (1983), 5–17.

Hampton-Reeves, S. and C. Chillington Rutter, *The Henry VI Plays* (Manchester and New York: Manchester University Press, 2006).

Harlan, S., *Memories of War in Early Modern England: Armor and Militant Nostalgia in Marlowe, Sidney, and Shakespeare* (New York: Palgrave Macmillan, 2016).

Hart, F.E., '"Great is Diana" of Shakespeare's Ephesus', *Studies in English Literature*, 43.2 (Spring 2003), 347–74.

Harvey, E.D., 'Pleasure's Oblivion: Displacements of Generation in Spenser's *Faerie Queene*', in C. Ivic and G. Williams (eds.), *Forgetting in the Early Modern Early Modern English Literature and Culture: Lethe's Legacies* (London and New York, Routledge, 2004), pp. 53–64.

Hassel, R.C. Jr., *Renaissance Drama and the English Church Year* (Lincoln: University of Nebraska Press, 1979).

Hatchuel, S., *Shakespeare: From Stage to Screen* (Cambridge: Cambridge University Press, 2004).

Hatchuel, S., *Shakespeare and the Cleopatra/Caesar Intertext: Sequel, Conflation, Remake* (Madison, NJ: Fairleigh Dickinson University Press, 2011).

Hatchuel, S., 'The Shakespearean Films of the 90s: Afterlives in Transmedia in the 21st Century', in *Shakespeare 450*, Actes de la Société Française Shakespeare, April 2015. http://shakespeare.revues.org/2945

Hatchuel, S. and N. Vienne-Guerrin, 'Remembrance of Things Past: Shakespeare's Comedies on French Television', in S. Hatchuel and N. Vienne-Guerrin (eds.), *Television Shakespeare: Essays in Honour of Michèle Willems* (Rouen: Presses des Universités de Rouen et du Havre, 2008), pp. 171–97.

Hatchuel, S. and N. Vienne-Guerrin, '"O Monstrous": Claude Barma's French 1962 TV *Othello*', in N. Vienne-Guerrin and P. Dorval (eds.), *Shakespeare on Screen in Francophonia* (2010–), Montpellier (France), University Montpellier III, Institut de Recherche sur la Renaissance, l'Âge Classique et les Lumières (IRCL), 2014. www.shakscreen.org/analysis/barma_othello

Hattaway, M., B. Sokolova, and D. Roper (eds.), *Shakespeare in the New Europe* (Sheffield: Sheffield Academic Press, 1994).

Havens, E., *Commonplace Books: A History of Manuscripts and Printed Books from Antiquity to the Twentieth Century* (New Haven, NJ: Beinecke Rare Book and Manuscript Library, 2001).

Hawkes, T., *Meaning by Shakespeare* (London and New York: Routledge, 1992).

Hazlitt, W., *Characters of Shakespear's Plays* (London: Taylor & Hessey, 1818 – 2nd ed.).

Hazlitt, W.C., *English Drama and Stage Under the Tudor and Stuart Princes: Documents and Treatises* (London: Roxburghe Library, 1869).

Hearne, T., *A Collection of Curious Discourses Written by Eminent Antiquaries*, ed. T. Hearne, 2 vols (London: 1773), I.

Hedrick, D., 'Distracting Othello: Tragedy and the Rise of Magic', *PMLA*, 129.4 (2014), 649–71.

Helfer, R., *Spenser's Ruins and the Art of Recollection* (University of Toronto Press, 2012).

Heywood, T., *The First and Second Parts of King Edward IV*, ed. R. Rowland, Revels Plays (Manchester: Manchester University Press, 2005).

Hiatt, C., *Ellen Terry and Her Impersonations* (London: George Bell and Sons, 1898).

Highet, G., *Anatomy of Satire* (Princeton, NJ: Princeton University Press, 1962).

Hills, M., *Fan Cultures* (New York: Routledge, 2002).

Hirsh, J., *Shakespeare and the History of Soliloquies* (Cranbury, NJ: Associated University Press, 2003).

Hiscock, A., *The Uses of This World: Thinking Space in Shakespeare, Marlowe, Cary and Jonson* (Cardiff: University of Wales Press, 2004).

Hiscock, A., *Reading Memory in Early Modern Literature* (Cambridge: Cambridge University Press, 2011).

Hiscock, A., '"Achilles Alter": The Heroic Lives and Afterlives of Robert Devereux, 2nd Earl of Essex', in A. Connolly and L. Hopkins (eds.), *Essex: The Cultural Impact of an Elizabethan Courtier* (Manchester: Manchester University Press, 2013), pp. 101–32.

Hodgdon, B., *Shakespeare, Performance and the Archive* (London and New York: Routledge, 2016).

Hodgdon, B. and W.B. Worthen (eds.), *A Companion to Shakespeare and Performance* (Malden, MA: Blackwell, 2005).

Bibliography

Hodgkins, C., 'Plays Out of Season: Puritanism, Antitheatricalism and Parliament's 1642 Closing of the Theatres', in D.W. Doerksen and C. Hodgkins (eds.), *'Centered on the Word': Literature, Scripture, and the Tudor-Stuart Middle Way* (Newark, DE: Delaware University Press, 2005), pp. 298–318.

Holderness, G., 'Boxing the Bard: Shakespeare and Television', in G. Holderness (ed.), *The Shakespeare Myth* (Manchester: Manchester University Press, 1991), pp. 173–89.

Holderness, G., '"Author! Author!": Shakespeare and Biography', *Shakespeare*, 5.2 (April 2009), 122–33.

Holinshed, R., *Holinshed's Chronicles*, ed. H. Ellis, 6 vols (London: J. Johnson, 1807–08).

Holland, P. (ed.), *Shakespeare, Memory and Performance* (Cambridge: Cambridge University Press, 2006).

Honan, Park, *Shakespeare: A Life* (Oxford and New York: Oxford University Press, 1998).

Hoole, C., *An easie entrance to the Latine tongue … a work tending to the school-masters's eas, and the weaker scholar's encouragement in the first and most wearisome steps to learning* (London, 1649).

Horace, *Horace: The Odes and Epodes*, trans. C.E. Bennett (Cambridge, MA and London: Harvard University Press and Heinemann, 1964).

Howell, W.S., *Logic and Rhetoric in England, 1500–1700* (Princeton, NJ: Princeton University Press, 1956).

Howsam, L., *Old Books and New Histories: An Orientation to Studies in Book and Print Culture* (Toronto: University of Toronto Press, 2006).

Huang, A. and E. Rivlin (eds.), *Shakespeare and the Ethics of Appropriation*, Reproducing Shakespeare: New Studies in Adaptation and Appropriation (New York: Palgrave Macmillan, 2014).

Hutcheon, L., *A Theory of Adaptation* (New York: Routledge, 2013).

Hutchins, E., *Cognition in the Wild* (Cambridge, MA: MIT Press, 1995).

Hutton, P.H., *History as an Art of Memory* (Lebanon, NH: University Press of New England, 1993).

Ingleby, C.M., L. Toulmin Smith, F.J. Furnivall, and J.J. Munro (eds.), *The Shakspere Allusion-Book: A Collection of Allusions to Shakspere from 1591 to 1700*, II vols (London and New York: Chatto & Windus and Duffield & Co., 1909).

Iselin, P., 'Myth, Memory and Music in *Richard II*, *Hamlet*, and *Othello*', in A.J. Hoenselaars (ed.), *Reclamations of Shakespeare* (Amsterdam and Atlanta, GA: Rodopi, 1994), pp. 173–86.

Ivic, C., 'Reassuring Fratricide in *I Henry IV*', in C. Ivic and G. Williams (eds.), *Forgetting in Early Modern English Literature and Culture: Lethe's Legacies* (London: Routledge, 2004), pp. 99–109.

Ivic, C. and G. Williams (eds.), *Forgetting in Early Modern English Literature and Culture: Lethe's Legacies* (London and New York: Routledge, 2004).

Iyengar, S., 'Moorish Dancing in *The Two Noble Kinsmen*', *Medieval and Renaissance*, 20.1 (2007), 85–107.

Jackson, R., *Theatres on Film: How the Cinema Imagines the Stage* (Manchester: Manchester University Press, 2013).

James, H., *Shakespeare's Troy: Drama, Politics, and the Translation of Empire* (Cambridge: Cambridge University Press, 1997, rep. 2013).

Jauss, H.R., *Toward an Aesthetic of Reception*, trans. T. Bahti (Minneapolis: The University of Minnesota Press, 1982).

Jenkins, A., '1000 Plays', www.annies1000plays.com

Jenkins, A., *Annie's 1000 Plays: Volume One* (London: Shakespeare in Shoreditch, 2015).

Jenkins, H., *Textual Poachers: Television Fans & Participatory Culture* (New York: Routledge, 1992). jmediagroup.net/top-10-most-searched-authors-of-2015/

Johnson, L., J. Sutton, and E. Tribble (eds.), *Embodied Cognition and Shakespeare's Theatre: The Early Modern Mind-Problem* (London and New York: Routledge, 2014).

Jones, A.R. and P. Stallybrass, *Renaissance Clothing and the Materials of Memory* (Cambridge: Cambridge University Press, 2000).

Jonson, B., *The Alchemist*, in D. Bevington, M. Butler and I. Donaldson (eds.), *The Cambridge Edition of the Works of Ben Jonson*, vol. 3, 7 vols (Cambridge: Cambridge University Press, 2012), pp. 541–710.

Jung, C.G., *Man and His Symbols* (Garden City, NJ: Doubleday, 1964).

Kansteiner, W., 'Finding Meaning in Memory: A Methodological Critique of Memory Studies', *History and Theory*, 41 (2002), 179–97.

Kantorowicz, E.H., *The King's Two Bodies: A Study in Mediaeval Political Theology* (Princeton, NJ: Princeton University Press, 1957).

Karremann, I., 'Rites of Oblivion in Shakespeare's History Plays', *Shakespeare Survey*, 63 (2010), 24–36.

Karremann, I., *The Drama of Memory in Shakespeare's History Plays* (Cambridge: Cambridge University Press, 2015).

Kastan, D.S., *'All's Well That Ends Well* and the Limits of Comedy', *ELH*, 52 (1985), 575–89.

Kastan, D.S., *Shakespeare and the Book* (Cambridge and New York: Cambridge University Press, 2001).

Kattago, S. (ed.), *The Ashgate Research Companion to Memory Studies* (Farnham, UK: Ashgate, 2015).

Kelly, C.E., *In the New England Fashion: Reshaping Women's Lives in the Nineteenth Century* (Ithaca, NY: Cornell University Press, 1999).

Kernan, A., '*The Henriad*: Shakespeare's Major History Plays', in A.B. Kernan (ed.), *Modern Shakespeare Criticism: Essays on Style, Dramaturgy, and the Major Plays* (New York: Harcourt Brace Jovanovich, 1970), pp. 245–75.

Kerrigan, J., *Revenge Tragedy: Aeschylus to Armageddon* (Oxford: Clarendon Press, 1996).

Kewes, P., 'The Elizabethan History Play: A True Genre?', in R. Dutton et al. (eds.), *A Companion to Shakespeare's Works: The Histories* (London: Blackwell, 2003), pp. 170–93.

Kichuk, D., 'Metamorphosis: Remediation in *Early English Books Online (EEBO)*', *Literary and Linguistic Computing*, 22.3 (2007), 291–303.

Kidnie, M.J. and S. Massai (eds.), *Shakespeare and Textual Studies* (Cambridge: Cambridge University Press, 2015).

Kiefer, F., 'Rumor Fame and Slander in *2 Henry IV*', *Allegorica*, 20 (1999), 3–44.

Kiefer, F., 'Poems as Props in *Love's Labour's Lost* and *Much Ado About Nothing*', in I.F. Moulton (ed.), *Reading and Literacy in the Middle Ages and Renaissance* (Turnhout: Brepols, 2004).

Kirkman, F., *The Wits, or sport upon sport* (London, 1662) [with permission, Folger Shakespeare Library].

Kitch, A., 'Bastards and Broadsides in "The Winter's Tale"', *Renaissance Drama*, 30 (1999), 43–71.

Knowles, K., *Shakespeare's Boys: A Cultural History* (New York: Palgrave MacMillan, 2014).

Kolin, P.C. (ed.), *Venus and Adonis: Critical Essays* (New York: Garland, 1997).

Korda, N. and J. Gil Harris (eds.), *Staged Properties in Early Modern English Drama* (Cambridge: Cambridge University Press, 2002).

Kott, J., *Shakespeare Our Contemporary*, trans. B. Taborski; preface by P. Brook (London: Methuen, 1967, sd. ed.).

Kuijpers, E., J. Pollmann, J. Müller, and J. van der Steen (eds.), *Memory Before Modernity: Practices of Memory in Early Modern Europe* (Leiden and Boston: Brill, 2013).

Kunin, A., 'Shakespeare's Preservation Fantasy', *PMLA*, 124.1 (2009), 92–106.

Lacan, J., 'The Mirror Stage as Formative of the I Function as Revealed in Psychoanalytic Experience', in *Écrits*, trans. B. Fink (New York: W.W. Norton, 2006), pp. 75–81.

Lafont, A., 'Mythological Reconfigurations on the Contemporary Stage: Giving a New Voice to Philomela in *Titus Andronicus*', *Early Modern Literary Studies* (2013). https://extra.shu.ac.uk/emls/si-21/11-Lafont_MythologicalReconfigurations.htm

Lanham, R., *The Motives of Eloquence: Literary Rhetoric in the Renaissance* (New Haven, CT: Yale University Press, 1976).

Lanier, D., 'Michael Almereyda's *Cymbeline*: The End of Teen Shakespeare', in S. Hatchuel and N. Vienne-Guerrin (eds.), *Shakespeare on Screen: The Romances* (Cambridge: Cambridge University Press), forthcoming in 2017.

La Primaudaye, P. de, *The Second Part of the French Academie* (London, 1594).

Larcom, L., *A New England Girlhood, Outlined from Memory* (Boston: Houghton, Mifflin, 1889).

Lees-Jeffries, H., *Shakespeare and Memory* (Oxford: Oxford University Press, 2013).

Leggatt, A., *Shakespeare's Political Drama: The History Plays and The Roman Plays* (New York: Routledge, 1988; repr. 1989).

Leggatt, A., *English Stage Comedy 1490–1990: Five Centuries of a Genre* (London and New York: Routledge, 1998).

Le Goff, J., *History and Memory*, trans. S. Rendall and E. Claman (New York: Columbia University Press, 1992, orig. 1977).

Lennam, T., '"The Ventricle of Memory": Wit and Wisdom in *Love's Labour's Lost*', *Shakespeare Quarterly*, 24.1 (Winter 1973), 54–60.

Lerer, S., 'Epilogue: Falling Asleep Over the History of the Book', *PMLA*, 121 (2006), 229–34.

Lesser, Z. and P. Stallybrass, 'The First Literary Hamlet and the Commonplacing of Professional Plays', *Shakespeare Quarterly*, 59 (2008), 371–420.

Levenson, J., *Romeo and Juliet: Shakespeare in Performance* (Manchester: Manchester University Press, 1987).

Levin, H., 'Sitting Upon the Ground (*Richard II*, iv.i)', in J. Mucciolo (ed.), *Shakespeare's Universe: Renaissance Ideas and Conventions: Essays in Honor of W.R. Elton* (Aldershot, UK: Scholar Press, 1996), pp. 3–20.

Levin, R., 'Women in the Renaissance Theatre Audience', *Shakespeare Quarterly*, 40.2 (Summer 1989), 165–74.

Levine, L.W., *Highbrow/Lowbrow: The Emergence of Cultural Hierarchy in America* (Cambridge, MA: Harvard University Press, 1988).

Lewis, C., '"We Know What we Know": Reckoning in *Love's Labour's Lost*', *Studies in Philology*, 105.2 (Spring 2008), 245–64.

Lewis, R., *Language, Mind and Nature: Artificial Languages in England from Bacon to Locke* (Cambridge: Cambridge University Press, 2007).

Lewis, W.S. (ed.), *Horace Walpole's Correspondence*, vol. 33 (Oxford: Oxford University Press, 1983).

Liebler, N.C., 'The Mockery King of Snow: *Richard II* and the Sacrifice of Ritual', in L. Woodbridge and E. Berry (eds.), *True Rites and Maimed Rites: Ritual and Anti-Ritual in Shakespeare and His Age* (Urbana, IL and Chicago: University of Illinois Press, 1992), pp. 220–9.

The Life of Sir John Oldcastle (1600), Malone Society Reprint (Chiswick: Charles Whittington at the Chiswick Press, 1908).

Linche, R., *The fountaine of ancient fiction* (1599) (see also V. Cartari).

Lippitt, J., 'Commonplace Books, April 26, 1814', 1814, Brown University, John Hay Library, Hay Manuscripts, Ms.12.31, folder 1 of 3. www.litencyc.com

Litvin, M. (guest ed.), *Critical Survey*, 19.3, Special issue: 'Arab Shakespeares' (December 2007).

Livy, *The Early History of Rome. Books I–V of 'The History of Rome from Its Foundation'*, trans. A. de Sélincourt (Harmondsworth: Penguin, 1971).

Llewellyn, N., *The Art of Death: Visual Culture in the English Death Ritual, c. 1500–c. 1800* (London: Reaktion Books, 1991).

Lodge, T., *Rosalynde* (London, 1590).

Loftus, E.F., 'Planting Misinformation in the Human Mind: A 30-Year Investigation of the Malleability of Memory', *Learning and Memory*, 12.4 (2005), 361–6.

London Word Festival, 'Shakespeare in Shoreditch', The Londonist, http://londonist.com/2009/03/london_word_festival_shakespeare_in.php?showpage=5#gallery-1

London Word Festival, 'Shakespeare in Shoreditch', Vimeo, https://vimeo.com/8116764

Long, Z., '"Unless you could teach me to forget": Spectatorship, Self-Forgetting, and Subversion in Antitheatrical Literature and *As You Like It*', in C. Ivic and G. Williams (eds.), *Forgetting in Early Modern English Literature and Culture: Lethe's Legacies* (London: Routledge, 2004), pp. 151–64.

Long, Z.C., 'The Spanish Tragedy and Hamlet: Infernal Memory in English Renaissance Revenge Tragedy', *ELR*, 44.2 (2014), 153–92.

Lorenz, P., *The Tears of Sovereignty: Perspectives of Power in Renaissance Drama* (New York: Fordham University Press, 2013).

Luis-Martinez, Z., 'Shakespeare's Historical Drama as *Trauerspiel*: *Richard II* – and After', *ELH*, 75 (2008), 673–705.

Lyne, R., *Shakespeare's Late Work* (Oxford: Oxford University Press, 2007).

Lyne, R., *Shakespeare, Rhetoric and Cognition* (Cambridge: Cambridge University Press, 2011).

Lyne, R., *Memory and Intertextuality in Renaissance Literature* (Cambridge: Cambridge University Press, 2016).

Lyons, T.L., 'Serials, Spinoffs, and Histories: Selling "Shakespeare" in Collection before the Folio', *Philological Quarterly*, 91.2 (2012), 1–37.

Mack, B., 'Archaeology of a Digitization', *Journal of the Association for Information Science and Technology*, 65.8 (2014), 1515–26.

Mack, P., *Elizabethan Rhetoric: Theory and Practice* (Cambridge: Cambridge University Press, 1996).

Macknik, S.L., S. Martinez-Conde, and S. Blakeslee, *Sleights of Mind: What the Neuroscience of Magic Reveals about our Everyday Deceptions* (Macmillan, 2010).

Maguire, L.E., *Shakespearean Suspect Texts: The 'Bad' Quartos and their Contexts* (Cambridge: Cambridge University Press, 1996).

Makaryk, I.R. and M. McHugh (eds.), *Shakespeare and the Second World War: Memory, Culture, Identity* (Toronto: University of Toronto Press, 2012). The Malachites, www.themalachites.co.uk/#!shakespeares-shoreditch/c1nsx

Maley, W., 'Recent Issues in Shakespeare Studies: From Margins to Centre', in A. Hiscock and S. Longstaffe (eds.), *The Shakespeare Handbook* (London: Continuum, 2009), pp. 190–205.

Marche, S., "Mocking Dead Bones: Historical Memory and the Theater of the Dead in *Richard III*', *Comparative Drama*, 37 (2003), 37–57.

Marcus, L.S., 'The Silence of the Archive and the Noise of Cyberspace', in N. Rhodes and J. Sawday (eds.), *The Renaissance Computer: Knowledge Technology in the First Age of Print* (London and New York: Routledge, 2000), pp. 18–28.

Bibliography

Mariner, D.D., 'Gems of Poetry', 1837, Brown University, John Hay Library, Hay Manuscripts, Ms. Harris Codex 1188.

Marlowe, C., *Doctor Faustus and Other Plays*, ed. D. Bevington and E. Rasmussen (Oxford: Oxford World's Classics, 1995).

Marshall, P., *Beliefs and the Dead in Reformation England* (Oxford: Oxford University Press, 2002).

Marston, J., *The Works of John Marston*, ed. A.H. Bullen, III vols. (London: John C. Nimmo, 1887).

Marston, J., *The Malcontent*, ed. B. Harris (London: Ernest Benn, 1967).

Maus, K.E., '[Introduction to] *Titus Andronicus*', in S. Greenblatt, W. Cohen, S. Gossett, J.E. Howard, K.E. Maus, and G. McMullan (eds.), *The Norton Shakespeare: Third Edition* (New York: W.W. Norton, 2015), pp. 491–8.

Mayer, J.-C., 'The "Parliament Sceane" in Shakespeare's *King Richard II*', *XVII–XVIII, Bulletin de la société d'etudes anglo-americaines des XVIIe et XVIIIe siècles*, 59 (2004), 27–42.

Mazer, C.M., 'Sense/Memory/Sense-Memory: Reading Narratives of Shakespearian Rehearsals', *Shakespeare Survey*, 62 (2009), 328–48.

Mazzaro, J., 'Madness and Memory: Shakespeare's *Hamlet* and *King Lear*', *Comparative Drama*, 19.2 (Summer 1985), 97–116.

Mazzaro, J., 'Shakespeare's "Books of Memory": *1* and *2 Henry VI*', *Comparative Drama*, 35.3/4 (Fall/Winter 2001–02), 393–414.

McCabe, R.A., 'The Masks of Duessa: Spenser, Mary Queen of Scots and James VI', *English Literary Renaissance*, 17.2 (1987), 224–42.

McDonald, R., *The Bedford Companion to Shakespeare: An Introduction with Documents* (New York: St. Martin's Press, 1996).

McKenzie, D.F., *Bibliography and the Sociology of Texts* (Cambridge and New York: Cambridge University Press, 1999).

McMullan, G. and J. Hope (eds.), *The Politics of Tragicomedy: Shakespeare and After* (London: Routledge, 1992).

Melchiori, G., *Shakespeare: Genesi e struttura delle opere* (Roma: Editori Laterza, 2003).

Mentz, S., *At the Bottom of Shakespeare's Ocean* (London: Continuum, 2009).

Menzer, P., *Anecdotal Shakespeare: A New Performance History* (London: Bloomsbury, 2015).

Meres, F., *Palladis tamia Wits treasury being the second part of Wits common wealth* (1598).

Merlo, G., 'Shoreditch Was Always Where It's At', *Cultural Wars*, 18 March 2009. www.culturewars.org.uk/index.php/site/article/shoreditch_was_always_where_its_at/

Michaelian, K., 'The Information Effect: Constructive Memory, Testimony, and Epistemic Luck', *Synthese*, 190.12 (2013), 2429–56.

Milner, M., *The Senses and the English Reformation* (Aldershot, UK: Ashgate, 2013).

Minear, E., *Reverberating Song in Shakespeare and Milton: Language, Memory, and Musical Representation* (Farnham, UK: Ashgate, 2011).

Miola, R., *Shakespeare's Rome* (Cambridge: Cambridge University Press, 1983).

Mirandola, P. della, 'The Dignity of Man', in J.B. Ross and M.M. McLaughlin (eds.), *The Portable Renaissance Reader* (New York: Viking Press, 1953), pp. 476–9.

Montagu, E., *An Essay on the Writings and Genius of Shakespeare, compared with Greek and French dramatic poets, with some remarks on the misrepresentations of Mons de Voltaire* (London: J. Dodsley, 1769).

Montaigne, M. de, *Essays...*, trans. John Florio (London, 1613).

Montrose, Louis, '"The Place of a Brother" in *As You Like It*: Social Process and Comic Form', *Shakespeare Quarterly*, 32 (1981), 28–54.

Moore, S.F. and B.G. Myerhoff (eds.), *Secular Ritual* (Assen: Van Gorcum, 1977).

More, H., *Florio, a Tale, for Fine Gentlemen and Fine Ladies: And The Bas Bleu, Or, Conversation: Two Poems* (London: T. Cadell, 1786).

More, T., *Complete Works*, 15 vols II: *The History of Richard III*, ed. R.S. Sylvester (New Haven, NJ: Yale University Press, 1963).

Moss, A., *Printed Commonplace-Books and the Structuring of Renaissance Thought* (Oxford: Clarendon, 1996).

Mucciolo, J. (ed.), *Shakespeare's Universe: Renaissance Ideas and Conventions; Essays in Honor of W.R. Elton* (Aldershot, UK: Scholar Press, 1996).

Mueller, M., 'The EEBO-TCP Phase I Public Release', *Spenser Review*, 44.2.36 (Fall 2014).

Mullaney, S., *The Place of the Stage: License, Play, and Power in Renaissance England* (Ann Arbor: The University of Michigan Press, 1988).

Mulryan, J. and S. Brown, 'Venus and the Classical Tradition in Boccaccio's *Genealogia Deorum Gentilium Libri* and Natale Conti's *Mythologiae*', *Mediaevalia*, 27 (2006), 135–56.

Murphy, A., *Shakespeare in Print: A History and Chronology of Shakespeare Publishing* (Cambridge: Cambridge University Press, 2003).
Murphy, A., *Shakespeare for the People: Working-Class Readers, 1800–1900* (Cambridge and New York: Cambridge University Press, 2008).
Mustashrik, *Manga Julius Caesar* (London: Self-Made Hero, 2008).
Myers, T., *Slavoj Žižek* (London and New York: Routledge, 2003).
Neely, C.T., *Distracted Subjects: Madness and Gender in Shakespeare and Early Modern Culture* (Ithaca, NY: Cornell University Press, 2004).
Neill, M., *Issues of Death: Mortality and Identity in English Renaissance Tragedy* (Oxford: Clarendon Press, 1997).
Neill, M., 'English Revenge Tragedy', in R. Bushnell (ed.), *A Companion to Tragedy* (Oxford: Blackwell, 2005).
Newman, K., '"And wash the Ethiop white": Femininity and the Monstrous in *Othello*', in J.E. Howard and M.F. O'Connor (eds.), *Shakespeare Reproduced: The Text in History and Ideology* (London and New York: Routledge Press, 1987).
Nichols, J., *John Nichols's 'The Progresses and Public Processions of Queen Elizabeth I': A New Edition of Early Modern Sources*, ed. E. Goldring et al., vol. I: *1533–1571* (Oxford: Oxford University Press, 2014).
Nims, J.F. (ed.), *Ovid's 'Metamorphoses': The Arthur Golding Translation 1567* (Philadelphia: Pau Dry Books, 2000).
Nora, P., *Les lieux de mémoire* (Paris: Gallimard, 1984–92).
Nora, P., 'Between Memory and History: Les Lieux de Mémoire', *Representations*, 26 (Spring 1989), 7–25.
Nora, P., *Realms of Memory: Rethinking the French Past*, volume 1, ed. L. Kritzman, trans. A. Goldhammer (New York: Columbia University Press, 1996).
Nora, P., *Realms of Memory: The Construction of the French Past*, volume 3, ed. L.D. Kritzman, trans. A. Goldhammer (New York: Columbia University Press, 1996–8).
Nora, P., *Rethinking France*, trans. M. Trouille (Chicago: University of Chicago Press, 2001–06).
Norbrook, D., '"A Liberal Tongue": Language and Rebellion in *Richard II*', in J. Mucciolo, J. (ed.), *Shakespeare's Universe: Renaissance Ideas and Conventions; Essays in Honor of W.R. Elton* (Aldershot, UK: Scholar Press, 1996), pp. 37–51.
Norgaard, H., 'Never wrong but with just cause', *English Studies*, 45 (1964), 137–41.
North, M.L., 'The Sonnets and Book History', in M.C. Schoenfeldt (ed.), *A Companion to Shakespeare's Sonnets* (Malden, MA: Blackwell, 2007), pp. 204–21.
Novacich, S., *Ark and Archive: Narrative Enclosures in Medieval and Early Modern Texts* (unpublished dissertation).
Old Comedian, *The Life and Death of David Garrick, Esq, the Celebrated English Roscius* (London: J. Pridden, et. al., 1779).
Olson, E.T., 'Personal Identity', in E.N. Zalta (ed.), *The Stanford Encyclopedia of Philosophy* (Spring 2016 Edition), http://plato.stanford.edu/archives/spr2016/entries/identity-personal/
O'Neill, S., *Shakespeare and YouTube: New Media Forms of the Bard* (London: Bloomsbury Arden, 2014).
Ong, W.J., *Ramus, Method, and the Decay of Dialogue: From the Art of Discourse to the Art of Reason* (Chicago: University of Chicago Press, 1958).
Ong, W.J., *Orality and Literacy: The Technologizing of the Word* (Methuen, 1982).
Orgel, S., 'Introduction', in G. Blakemore Evans (ed.), *The Sonnets: Updated Edition*, The New Cambridge Shakespeare (Cambridge and New York: Cambridge University Press, 2006), pp. 1–22.
Orgel, S., 'Shakespeare and the Art of Forgetting', in M. Marrapodi (ed.), *Shakespeare and Renaissance Literary Theories: Anglo-Italian Transactions* (Farnham, UK: Ashgate, 2011), pp. 25–35.
Oritz, J.M., 'By the Book: Blazoning the Subject in Shakespeare's History Plays', in D. Uman and S. Morrison (eds.), *Staging the Blazon in Early Modern English Theatre* (Burlington, NJ: Ashgate, 2013), pp. 125–36.
Orwell, G., *Nineteen Eighty-Four* (London: Penguin Books, 1990).
Osborne, B.S., 'Landscape, Memory, Monuments and Commemoration: Putting Identity in Its Place', *Canadian Ethnic Studies*, 33.3 (2001), 39–77. http://search.proquest.com/docview/215637580?accountid=14777
Otto, B.K., *Fools are Everywhere: The Court Jester Around the World* (Chicago: University of Chicago Press, 2001).
Ovid, *The. xv. bookes of P. Ouidius Naso, entytuled Metamorphosis, translated oute of Latin into English meeter, by Arthur Golding Gentleman* (1567).

Bibliography

Ovid, *Metamorphoses*, II vols., Eng. trans. F.J. Miller (London and New York: W. Heinemann and G.P. Putnam's Sons, 1916).
Ovid, *Ovid's Fasti*, trans. Sir J.G. Frazer (London and New York: W. Heinemann and G.P. Putnam's Sons, 1931).
Painter, W., *The palace of pleasure* (1566).
Palfrey, S.H., 'Commonplace Book, Boston, ca. 1841–1876', Brown University, John Hay Library, Hay Manuscripts, Ms. Harris Codex 1029.
Pape, W., and F. Burwick (eds.), *The Boydell Shakespeare Gallery* (Bottrop: Peter Pomp, 1996).
Paster, G.K., *The Body Embarrassed: Drama and the Disciplines of Shame in Early Modern England* (Ithaca, NY: Cornell University Press, 1993).
Paster, G.K., *Humoring the Body: Emotions and the Shakespearean Stage* (Chicago: University of Chicago Press, 2004).
Pater, W., *Walter Pater: Three Major Texts*, ed. W.E. Buckler (New York: New York University Press, 1986).
Patterson, A., *Reading Holinshed's Chronicles* (Chicago: University of Chicago Press, 1994).
Peacham, H., *The Complete Gentleman* (London, 1620).
Peend, T., *The pleasant fable of Hermaphroditus and Salmacis* (1565).
Pendleton, T.A. (ed.), *Henry VI: Critical Essays* (New York and London: Routledge, 2001).
Pérez, J. Tronch, 'Playtext Reporters and *Memoriones*: Suspect Texts in Shakespeare and Spanish Golden Age Drama', in T. Clayton, S. Brock, and V. Forés (eds.), *Shakespeare and the Mediterranean* (Newark, NJ: University of Delaware Press, 2004), pp. 270–85.
Peter of Ravenna, *The Book of Memory, that Otherwyse is called the Phenix* (London, 1545).
Peters, J.S., *Theatre of the Book 1480–1880: Print, Text, and Performance in Europe* (Oxford: Oxford University Press, 2001).
Peters, J.S., 'Theater and Book in the History of Memory: Materializing Mnemosyne in the Age of Print', *Modern Philology*, 102.2 (November 2004), 179–206.
Phelan, P., *Unmarked: The Politics of Performance* (London: Routledge, 1993).
Phelan, P., 'Playing Dead in Stone, or When is a Rose Not a Rose?', in E. Diamond (ed.), *Performance and Cultural Politics* (London and New York: Routledge, 1996), pp. 65–88.
Pivetti, K., *Of Memory and Literary Form: Making the Early Modern English Nation* (Newark: University of Delaware Press, 2015).
Plett, H.F., *Rhetoric and Renaissance Culture* (Berlin: Walter de Gruyter, 2004).
Plutarch, *Lives*, vol. 7. *Demosthenes and Cicero, Alexander and Caesar*, trans. B. Perrin, Loeb Classical Library 99 (Cambridge, MA: Harvard University Press, 1919).
Pratt, A.T., 'Stab-Stitching and the Status of Early English Playbooks as Literature', *The Library*, 16 (2015), 304–28. http://dx.doi.org/10.1093/library/16.3.304
Price, L., *The Anthology and the Rise of the Novel from Richardson to George Eliot* (Cambridge and New York: Cambridge University Press, 2000).
Pringle, Brandon, Perkins and Will, 'The Stage: Shoreditch Development', http://uk.perkinswill.com/news/the-stage-shoreditch-development-planning-permission.html
Prynn, J., '800million Development will Kill the Soul of Shoreditch', *Evening Standard*, 23 January 2015, www.standard.co.uk/news/london/800m-development-will-kill-the-soul-of-shoreditch-9998504.html
Prynne, W., *Histrio-mastix The players scourge, or, actors tragaedie* (1633).
Purcell, S., 'The Impact of New Forms of Public Performance', in C. Carson and P. Kirwan (eds.), *Shakespeare and the Digital World* (Cambridge: Cambridge University Press, 2014), pp. 212–25.
Puttenham, G., *The Arte of English Poesie* (London, 1589).
Puttenham, G., *The Art of English Poesy*, ed. F. Whigham and W. Rebhorn. (Ithaca, NY: Cornell University Press, 2007).
Quarles, F., *Divine Fancies* (London, 1632).
Quinn, G. (Dir.), 'Programme notes', *MAC-BETH 7*, Project Arts Theatre, Dublin, 2004. http://dev.projectartscentre.ie/archive/archive-p-detail/1005-macbeth-7
Quintilian, *The Institutio Oratoria of Quintilian*, ed. H.E. Butler, 4 vols (Cambridge, MA and London: Harvard University Press and Heinemann, 1953), I.
Rackin, P., *Stages of History: Shakespeare's English Chronicles* (Ithaca, NY: Cornell University Press, 1990).
Radstone, S. and B. Schwarz, *Memory: Histories, Theories, Debates* (New York: Fordham University Press, 2010).

Raleigh, W., Sir, *The History of the World* (London, 1614).
Rambuss, R., 'What It Feels Like for a Boy: Shakespeare's *Venus and Adonis*', in R. Dutton and J.E. Howard (eds.), *A Companion to Shakespeare's Works*, vol. IV: *The Poems, Problem Comedies, Late Plays* (Oxford: Blackwell, 2003), pp. 240–58.
Relihan, C.C., 'Liminal Geography: *Pericles* and the Politics of Place', in A. Thorne (ed.), *Shakespeare's Romances* (New York: Palgrave, 2003).
Renan, E., 'What is a Nation?', trans. M. Thom, in H. Bhaba (ed.), *Nation and Narration* (London: Routledge, 1990).
Repton, H., *The Bee, or a Companion to the Shakespeare Gallery* (London: T. Cadell, [1789]).
Reynoldes, E., *A treatise of the passions and faculties of the soule of man...* (London, 1640).
Ribner, I., *The English History Play in the Age of Shakespeare* (Princeton, NJ: Princeton University Press, 1965).
Richard II, in *The Wars of the Roses* (1990), dir. M. Bogdanov with M. Pennington.
Richards, B., 'Hamlet and the Theatre of Memory', *Notes and Queries*, 223 (1988), p. 53.
Richardson, C., *Shakespeare and Material Culture* (Oxford: Oxford University Press, 2011).
Ricoeur, P., *Memory, History, Forgetting*, trans. K. Blamey and D. Pellauer (Chicago: University of Chicago Press, 2004).
Roach, J., *Cities of the Dead: Circum-Atlantic Performance* (New York: Columbia University Press, 1996).
Robertson, W.G., *Time Was* (London: Hamish Hamilton, 1931).
Robson, C., *Heart Beats: Everyday Life and the Memorized Poem* (Princeton, NJ: Princeton University Press, 2012).
Rose, J., 'Rereading the English Common Reader: A Preface to a History of Audiences', *Journal of the History of Ideas*, 53 (1992), 47–70. http://dx.doi.org/10.2307/2709910
Rose, J., *The Intellectual Life of the British Working Classes* (New Haven, CT: Yale University Press, 2001).
Rose Lipman Building, www.themillcoproject.co.uk/spaces/the-rose-lipman-building/
Rossi, P., *Logic and the Art of Memory: The Quest for a Universal Language*, trans. S. Clucas (University of Chicago Press, 2000, orig., 1960).
Rossington, M. and A. Whitehead (eds.), *Theories of Memory: A Reader* (Edinburgh: Edinburgh University Press, 2007).
Rothwell, K.S., *A History of Shakespeare on Screen: A Century of Film and Television*, 2nd edition (Cambridge: Cambridge University Press, 2004 [1999]).
Rowe, K., 'Dismembering and Forgetting in *Titus Andronicus*', *Shakespeare Quarterly*, 45 (1994), 279–303.
Rowe, K., '"Remember me": Technologies of Memory in Michael Almereyda's *Hamlet*', in R. Burt and L.E. Boose (eds.), *Shakespeare The Movie II, Popularizing the Plays on Film, TV, Video, and DVD* (London: Routledge, 2003), pp. 37–55.
Rubin, J., *Songs of Ourselves: The Uses of Poetry in America* (Cambridge, MA: Belknap Press, 2007).
Rumbold, K., 'Shakespeare Anthologized', in M.T. Burnett, A. Streete, and R. Wray (eds.), *The Edinburgh Companion to Shakespeare and the Arts* (Edinburgh: Edinburgh University Press, 2011), pp. 88–105.
Ryan, K., 'Shakespearean Comedy and Romance: The Utopian Imagination', in A. Thorne (ed.), *Shakespeare's Romances* (New York: Palgrave, 2003).
Salingar, L., 'Memory in Shakespeare', *Cahiers Élisabéthains*, 45 (1994), 59–64.
Sallustius, *Concerning the Gods and the Universe*, ed. and trans. A.D. Nock (Cambridge: Cambridge University Press, 1926).
Samuel, R., *Theatres of Memory*, vol. 1: *Past and Present in Contemporary Culture* (London: Verso, 1994).
Sanderlin, G., 'The Repute of Shakespeare's Sonnets in the Early Nineteenth Century', *Modern Language Notes*, 54 (1939), 462–66. http://dx.doi.org/10.2307/2910858
Sanders, J., 'Mixed Messages: The Aesthetics of *The Two Noble Kinsmen*', in A. Dutton and J.E. Howard (eds.), *A Companion to Shakespeare's Works*, Vol. 4: *Poems, Problem Comedies, Late Plays* (Oxford: Blackwell, 2003), pp. 445–61.
Sanders, J., *Adaptation and Appropriation*. The New Critical Idiom (London: Routledge, 2006).
Saul, N., *Richard II* (New Haven, CT: Yale University Press, 1997).
Sawday, J., *The Body Emblazoned: Dissection and the Human Body in Renaissance Culture* (London; New York: Routledge, 1995).
Schachter, D., *Searching for Memory* (New York, Basic Books, 1995).
Schachter, D. and J.T. Coyle, *Memory Distortion: How Minds, Brains, and Societies Reconstruct the Past* (Cambridge, MA: Harvard University Press, 1997).
Scheil, K.W., *She Hath Been Reading: Women and Shakespeare Clubs in America* (Ithaca, NY: Cornell University Press, 2012).

Bibliography

Schiffer, J.J., 'Mnemonic Cues to Passion in *Hamlet*', in G.W. Williams and B.J. Baines (eds.), *Renaissance Papers* (Durham, NC: Boydell & Brewer, 1995), pp. 65–79.

Schiffer, J., 'Reading New Life into Shakespeare's Sonnets', in J. Schiffer (ed.), *Shakespeare's Sonnets: Critical Essays* (New York: Routledge, 2000), pp. 3–71.

Schmitt, C., *Political Theology*, 1922, trans. G. Schwag (Chicago: University of Chicago Press, 2005).

Schuler, R.M., 'Magic Mirrors in *Richard II*', *Comparative Drama*, 38 (2004), 151–81.

Schwyzer, P., *Literature, Nationalism, and Memory in Early Modern England and Wales* (Cambridge: Cambridge University Press, 2004).

Schwyzer, P., 'Lees and Moonshine: Remembering Richard III, 1485–1635', *Renaissance Quarterly*, 63.3 (2010), 850–83.

Schwyzer, P., *Shakespeare and the Remains of Richard III* (Oxford: Oxford University Press, 2015).

Scott, W.O., 'Landholding, Leasing, and Inheritance in *Richard II*', *SEL*, 42 (2002), 275–92. https://shakespeareinireland.wordpress.com

Shakespeare, W., *The Works of Shakespear: In Which the Beauties Observed by Pope, Warburton, and Dodd, Are Pointed out: Together with the Author's Life, a Glossary, Copious Indexes, And, a List of the Various Readings.*, ed. Hugh Blair, 8 vols (Edinburgh: Printed by Sands, Murray, and Cochran, for W. Sands [and 6 others], 1753).

Shakespeare, W., *Troilus and Cressida*, New Variorum, ed. H.N. Hillebrand and T.W. Baldwin (Philadelphia: J.B. Lippincott, 1953).

Shakespeare, W., *All's Well That Ends Well*, ed. G.K. Hunter, The Arden Shakespeare Second Series (London: Methuen; Cambridge, MA: Harvard University Press, 1966).

Shakespeare, W., *William Shakespeare: The Complete Works*, ed. S. Wells, G. Taylor, J. Jowett, and W. Montgomery (Oxford: Clarendon Press, 1986).

Shakespeare, W., *The Narrative Poems*, ed. M. Evans (Harmondsworth: Penguin, 1989).

Shakespeare, W., *The Plantagenets* (London: Faber, 1989).

Shakespeare, W., *Titus Andronicus*, The Arden Shakespeare, ed. J. Bate (London: Routledge, 1995).

Shakespeare, W., *The Norton Shakespeare*, ed. S. Greenblatt, W. Cohen, J.E. Howard, and K.E. Maus (London and New York: W.W. Norton & Co., 1997).

Shakespeare, W., *Shakespeare's Sonnets*, ed. K. Duncan-Jones (London: Arden Shakespeare, 1997).

Shakespeare, W., *Troilus and Cressida*, The Arden Shakespeare, ed. D. Bevington (Walton-on-Thames, UK: Thomas Nelson, 1997).

Shakespeare, W., *Julius Caesar*, Arden Third Series, ed. D. Daniell (Walton-on-Thames, UK: Thomas Nelson, 1998).

Shakespeare, W., *King Henry VI, Part II*, Arden Third Series, ed. R. Knowles (Walton-on-Thames, UK: Thomas Nelson, 1999).

Shakespeare, W., *The Sonnets and A Lover's Complaint*, ed. J. Kerrigan (Harmondsworth and New York: Penguin, 1999).

Shakespeare, W., *King Henry VI, Part I*, Arden Shakespeare, Third Series, ed. E. Burns (London: Thomson Learning, 2000).

Shakespeare, W., *King Henry VI, Part III*, Arden Shakespeare, Third Series, ed. J.D. Cox and E. Rasmussen (London: Arden Shakespeare, 2001).

Shakespeare, W., *The Arden Shakespeare Complete Works*, ed. R. Proudfoot, A. Thompson, and D.S. Kastan (London: Arden Shakespeare, 2002).

Shakespeare, W., *The Complete Sonnets and Poems*, ed. C. Burrow (Oxford: Oxford University Press, 2002).

Shakespeare, W., *King Richard II*, ed. C.R. Forker (London: Arden Shakespeare, 2002).

Shakespeare, W., *Romeo and Juliet*, The New Cambridge Shakespeare, ed. G. Blakemore Evans (Cambridge; New York: Cambridge University Press, 2003).

Shakespeare, W., *Troilus and Cressida*, The New Cambridge Shakespeare, ed. A. Dawson (Cambridge: Cambridge University Press, 2003).

Shakespeare, W., *As You Like It*, Arden Shakespeare, Third Series, ed. J. Dusinberre (London: Thomson Learning, 2006).

Shakespeare, W., *Hamlet*, Arden Shakespeare, Third Series, ed. A. Thompson and N. Taylor (London: Thomson Learing, 2006).

Shakespeare, W. *Much Ado About Nothing*, ed. C. McEachern (London: Thomson Learning, 2006).

Shakespeare, W., *The Sonnets: Updated Edition*, The New Cambridge Shakespeare, ed. G. Blakemore Evans (Cambridge and New York: Cambridge University Press, 2006).

Shakespeare, W., *Shakespeare's Poems*, ed. K. Duncan-Jones and H.R. Woudhuysen (London: Arden Shakespeare, 2007).

Bibliography

Shakespeare, W., *Othello*, ed. M. Neil (Oxford: Oxford University Press, 2008).
Shakespeare, W., *Richard III*, Arden Third Series, ed. J.R. Siemon (London: Bloomsbury Arden Shakespeare, 2009).
Shakespeare, W., *The Winter's Tale*, ed. J. Pitcher (London: Methuen, 2010).
Shakespeare, W., *The Arden Shakespeare Complete Works*, ed. R. Proudfoot, A. Thompson, and D.S. Kastan (London: Methuen Drama; Bloomsbury, 2011).
Shakespeare, W., *The Two Noble Kinsmen*, The Arden Shakespeare, ed. Lois Potter (London and New York: Bloomsbury, 2014).
Shakespeare, W. and S. Booth, *Shakespeare's Sonnets* (New Haven, CT: Yale University Press, 1977).
Shakespeare, W. and G. Wilkins, *Pericles*, ed. S. Gossett (London: Arden Shakespeare, 2004).
Shakespeare in Shoreditch Festival, www.shakespeareinshoreditch.in/
Shakespeare in Shoreditch Festival: Brad Birch, *Pit of Clay*, www.youtube.com/watch?v=jWu1IH1CfYc&list=UUz0RHBDoE4n3EVRr6gdfE5Q&index=54
Shakespeare in Shoreditch Festival: Sabrina Mahfouz, *Disnatured*, www.youtube.com/watch?v=1d9GB029GXc&index=52&list=UUz0RHBDoE4n3EVRr6gdfE5Q
Shakespeare in Shoreditch Festival: Thomas McMullan, *Three Loose Teeth*, www.youtube.com/watch?v=wlbVh5zzjZA
Shankar, R., 'Marking Time: Memory and Market in *The Comedy of Errors*', *Shakespeare Quarterly*, 56.2 (Summer 2005), 176–205.
Shapiro, I.A., 'Robert Fludd's Stage-Illustration', *Shakespeare Studies*, 2 (1966), 192–209.
Shaughnessy, R., 'The Shakespeare Revolution Will Not be Televised: Staging the Media Apparatus', in P. Holland (ed.), *Shakespeare, Memory and Performance* (Cambridge: Cambridge University Press, 2006), pp. 305–28.
Shaughnessy, R., 'One Piece at a Time', in S. Werner (ed.), *New Directions in Renaissance Drama and Performance Studies* (Houndmills, Basingstoke: Palgrave Macmillan, 2010), pp. 15–29.
Shell, M., *The End of Kinship*: Measure for Measure, *Incest, and the Ideal of the Universal Siblinghood* (Stanford, CA: Stanford University Press, 1988).
Sherlock, P., *Monuments and Memory in Early Modern England* (Farnham, UK: Ashgate, 2008).
Sherman, A.G., *Skepticism and Memory in Shakespeare and Donne* (New York: Palgrave, 2007).
Sherman, D., '"What more remains?": Messianic Performance in *Richard II*', *Shakespeare Quarterly*, 65.1 (2014), 22–48.
Sidney, Sir P., *An apologie for poetrie* (1595).
Sidney, Sir P., *The Poems of Sir Philip Sidney*, ed. W.A. Ringler (Oxford: Clarendon Press, 1962).
Sillars, S., *Painting Shakespeare: The Artist as Critic 1720–1820* (Cambridge: Cambridge University Press, 2006).
Silver, G., *Paradoxes of Defence* (London, 1599).
Singh, J.G., 'The Bard in Calcutta, India, 1835–2014', in D. Callaghan and S. Gossett (eds.), *Shakespeare in Our Time: A Shakespeare Association of America Collection* (London and New York: Bloomsbury, 2016), pp. 171–5.
Small, J.P., *Wax Tablets of the Mind: Cognitive Studies of Memory and Literacy in Classical Antiquity* (London and New York: Routledge, 1997).
Smith, B.R. and K. Rowe (eds.), *The Cambridge Guide to the Worlds of Shakespeare*, 2 vols (Cambridge: Cambridge University Press, 2015).
Smith, L., *Victorian Photography, Painting and Poetry: The Enigma of Visibility in Ruskin, Morris and the Pre-Raphaelites* (Cambridge: Cambridge University Press, 1995).
Smith, N., *The Royal Image and the English People* (Aldershot, UK: Ashgate, 2001).
Snyder, S., *The Comic Matrix of Shakespeare's Tragedies:* Romeo and Juliet, Hamlet, Othello, *and* King Lear (Princeton, NJ: Princeton University Press, 1979).
Snyder, S., '*All's Well That Ends Well* and Shakespeare's Helens: Text and Subtext, Subject and Object', *ELR*, 18 (1988), 66–77.
Snyder, S., 'The Genres of Shakespeare's Plays', in M. de Grazia and S. Wells (eds.), *The Cambridge Companion to Shakespeare* (Cambridge: Cambridge University Press, 2001).
Sohmer, S., *Shakespeare's Mystery Play: The Opening of the Globe Theatre 1599* (Manchester and New York: Manchester University Press, 1999).
Spenser, E., *Edmund Spenser's Poetry*, ed. H. Maclean and A. Lake Prescott (New York: W.W. Norton, 1993).
Spenser, E., *The Faerie Queene*, ed. A.C. Hamilton et al. (Harlow: Longman, 2001).

Spolsky, E., *Word vs Image: Cognitive Hunger in Shakespeare's England* (New York: Palgrave, 2007).
Spolsky, E., *The Contracts of Fiction: Cognition, Culture, Community* (Oxford: Oxford University Press, 2015).
Squire, L.R., *Memory and Brain* (Oxford: Oxford University Press, 1987).
Stallybrass, P., R. Chartier, J.F. Mowery, and H. Wolfe, 'Hamlet's Tables and the Technologies of Writing in Renaissance England', *Shakespeare Quarterly*, 55.4 (2004), 379–419.
Stalpaert, C. (ed.), *Peter Greenaway's* Prospero's Books*: Critical Essays* (Ghent: Academia Press, 2000).
Stamelman, R., 'The Presence of Memory', *L'Esprit Createur*, 36.3 (Fall 1996), 65–79 (pp. 77–8).
Stanton, K., '*Hamlet*'s Whores', in M.T. Burnett and J. Manning (eds.), *New Essays on* Hamlet (New York: AMS, 1994), pp. 167–88.
Starks, L.S., '"Remember me": Psychoanalysis, Cinema, and the Crisis of Modernity', *Shakespeare Quarterly*, 53 (2002), 181–200.
St Clair, W., *The Reading Nation in the Romantic Period* (Cambridge and New York: Cambridge University Press, 2004).
Stern, T., *Rehearsal from Shakespeare to Sheridan* (Oxford: Clarendon Press, 2000).
Stern, T., *Making Shakespeare: From Stage to Page* (London and New York: Routledge, 2004).
Stern, T., 'This Wide and Universal Theatre: The Theatre as Prop in Shakespeare's Metadrama', *Shakespeare's Theatres and the Effects of Performance*, ed. F. Karim-Cooper and T. Stern (London: Bloomsbury, 2013).
Stern, T. and S. Palfrey, *Shakespeare in Parts* (Oxford: Oxford University Press, 2007).
Stewart, A., *Shakespeare's Letters* (Oxford: Oxford University Press, 2008).
Stewart, S., *On Longing* (Durham, NC and London: Duke University Press, 1993).
Stockton, A., '"Annis Stockton, 1819" (cover Title), Bound Volume', 1819, Princeton University Library, Stockton Family Papers, Manuscripts Division, Department of Rare Books and Special Collections.
Stone, L., *The Crisis of the Aristocracy, 1558–1641* (Oxford: Oxford University Press, 1965).
Stowe, J., *Survey of London*, ed. C.L. Kingsford, 2 vols (Oxford: Clarendon Press, 1908).
Sukic, C., '"I am sure I shall turn sonnet": Writing or Being Written in *Love's Labour's Lost*', *Love's Labour's Lost ou l'art de séduire*', in C. Gutleben (ed.), *Cycnos*, volume no. 1 (Paris: L'Harmattan, 2015).
Sukic, C., '"I smell false Latin, dunghill for *unguem*": Odours and Aromas in *Love's Labour's Lost*', *Actes des congrès de la Société française Shakespeare* [online], 32, 2015.
Sullivan, G.A., Jr., *Memory and Forgetting in English Renaissance Drama* (Cambridge: Cambridge University Press, 2005).
Sullivan, G.A., Jr., 'Voicing the Young Man: Memory, Forgetting, and Subjectivity in the Procreation Sonnets', in M. Schoenfeldt (ed.), *A Companion to Shakespeare's Sonnets* (Malden, MA: Blackwell, 2007), pp. 331–42.
Sullivan, G.A., Jr., *Sleep, Romance and Human Embodiment: Vitality from Spenser to Milton* (Cambridge: Cambridge University Press, 2012).
Summit, J., *Memory's Library: Medieval Books in Early Modern England* (Chicago: University of Chicago Press, 2008).
Sutphen, J., '"A Dateless Lively Heat": Storing Loss in the Sonnet', in J. Schiffer (ed.), *Shakespeare's Sonnets: Critical Essays* (New York: Routledge, 2000), pp. 199–217.
Sutton, J., *Philosophy and Memory Traces: Descartes to Connectionism* (Cambridge: Cambridge University Press, 1998).
Sutton, J., 'Body, Mind, and Order: Local Memory and the Control of Mental Representations in Medieval and Renaissance Sciences of the Self', in G. Freeland and A. Corones (eds.), *1543 and All That: Image and Word, Change and Continuity in the Proto-Scientific Revolution* (Dordrecht, Boston, and London: Kluwer, 2000), pp. 117–50.
Sutton, J., 'Spongy Brains and Material Memories', in M. Floyd-Wilson and G.A. Sullivan, Jr. (eds.), *Environment and Embodiment in Early Modern England* (New York: Palgrave, 2007), pp. 14–34.
Sutton, J., C.B. Harris, P.G. Keil, and A.J. Barnier, 'The Psychology of Memory, Extended Cognition, and Socially Distributed Remembering', *Phenomenology and the Cognitive Sciences*, 9.4 (2010), 521–60.
Sweet, A.L., 'Commonplace Book, Providence, R.I., ca. 1837–1843', Brown University, John Hay Library, Hay Manuscripts, Ms. Harris Codex 1150.
Sypher, W., 'Magical Mystery Tour', *New York Review of Books*, 29 January 1970, 23–5.
Taylor, D., *The Archive and the Repertoire: Performing Cultural Memory in the Americas* (Durham, NC: Duke University Press, 2003).
Taylor, G. and R. Loughnane, 'The Canon and Chronology of Shakespeare's Works', in G. Taylor and G. Egan (eds.), *Shakespearean Authorship: A Companion to the New Oxford Shakespeare* (Oxford: Oxford University Press, forthcoming 2017).

Bibliography

Tennenhouse, L., *Power on Display: The Politics of Shakespeare's Genres* (New York and London: Methuen, 1986).
Terdiman, R., *Present Past: Modernity and the Memory Crisis* (Ithaca, NY and London: Cornell University Press, 1993).
Terry, E., *Four Lectures on Shakespeare*, ed. C. St. John (London: Martin Hopkinson, 1932).
T.F., *News from the North* (London, 1579).
The London Chronicle.
The Public Advertiser.
Thompson, A. and N. Taylor (eds.), *Hamlet*, Arden (London: Thomson Learning, 2006).
Tribble, E., *Cognition in the Globe: Attention and Memory in Shakespeare's Theatre* (New York: Palgrave, 2011).
Tribble, E. and N. Keene, *Cognitive Ecologies and the History of Remembering: Religion, Education, and Memory in Early Modern England* (New York: Palgrave, 2011).
Turner, F., *Shakespeare and the Nature of Time* (Oxford: Clarendon Press, 1971).
Turner, M., *Reading Minds: The Study of English in the Age of Cognitive Science* (Princeton, NJ: Princeton University Press, 1991).
Turner, M., *The Literary Mind* (Oxford: Oxford University Press, 1996).
Turner, M., *The Artful Mind: Cognitive Science and the Riddle of Human Creativity* (Oxford: Oxford University Press, 2006).
Tylee, C., 'The Text of Cressida and Every Ticklish Reader: *Troilus and Cressida*, the Greek Camp Scene', *Shakespeare Survey*, 41 (1989), 63–76.
Uphaus, R.W., 'Vicesimus Knox and the Canon of Eighteenth-Century Literature', *The Age of Johnson: A Scholarly Annual*, 4 (1991), 345–61.
Utterback, R., 'The Death of Mercutio', *Shakespeare Quarterly*, 24.2 (1973), 105–16.
Varner, E.R., *Mutilation and Transformation: Damnatio Memoriae and Roman Imperial Portraiture* (Leiden and Boston: Brill, 2004).
Vasiliauskas, E., 'The Outmodedness of Shakespeare's Sonnets', *ELH*, 82.3 (2015), 759–87.
Vendler, H., *The Art of Shakespeare's Sonnets* (Cambridge, MA: Belknap Press of Harvard University Press, 1997).
Verney, L., 'The Office of Recorder of the City of London', *Transactions of the Guildhall Historical Association*, 8.9 (2000), 1–7. www.guildhallhistoricalassociation.org.uk/docs/The%20Office%20of%20 Recorder%20of%20the%20City%20of%20London.pdf
Vickers, N., '"The blazon of sweet beauty's best": Shakespeare's Lucrece', in P. Parker and G. Hartman (eds.), *Shakespeare and the Question of Theory* (New York: Methuen, 1985), pp. 95–115.
Vine, A.E., *In Defiance of Time: Antiquarian Writing in Early Modern England* (Oxford and New York: Oxford University Press, 2010).
Voloshinov, V.N., *Marxism and the Philosophy of Language* (Cambridge, MA: Harvard University Press, 1986).
Walker, E., 'Julie Taymor's *Titus* (1999), Ten Years On', in S. Hatchuel and N. Vienne-Guerrin (eds.), *Shakespeare on Screen: The Roman Plays* (Presses des Universités de Rouen et du Havre, 2009), pp. 23–65.
Walsh, B., *Shakespeare, the Queen's Men, and the Elizabethan Performance of History* (Cambridge: Cambridge University Press, 2009).
Walsham, A., *Church Papists: Catholicism, Conformity and Confessional Polemic in Early Modern England* (Woodbridge, UK: The Boydell Press, 1999).
Walsham, A., 'Introduction: Relics and Remains', *Past and Present*, 206.5 (2010), 9–36.
Walsham, A., 'History, Memory, and the English Reformation', *The Historical Journal*, 55 (2012), 899–938.
Warnock, M., *Memory* (London: Faber & Faber, 1982).
Watson, A., '"Full character'd": Competing Forms of Memory in Shakespeare's Sonnets', in M. Schoenfeldt (ed.), *A Companion to Shakespeare's Sonnets* (Malden, MA: Blackwell, 2007), pp. 343–60.
Watson, A., 'Shared Reading at a Distance: The Commonplace Books of the Stockton Family, 1812–40', *Book History*, 18 (2015), 103–33. http://dx.doi.org/10.1353/bh.2015.0006
Weber, H., *Memory, Print, and Gender in England, 1653–1759* (New York: Palgrave, 2008).
Weever, J., *Faunus and Melliflora or, The original of our English satyres* (1600).
Weever, J., *Ancient Funerall Monuments* (London: 1631).
Weimann, R., *Shakespeare and the Popular Tradition in the Theater*, ed. R. Schwartz (Baltimore, MD: Johns Hopkins University Press, 1978).

Bibliography

Weimann, R., *Author's Pen and Actor's Voice: Playing and Writing in Shakespeare's Theatre,* ed. H. Higbee and W. West (Cambridge: Cambridge University Press, 2000).

Weinrich, H., *Lethe: The Art and Critique of Forgetting,* trans. S. Rendall (Ithaca, NY: Cornell University Press, 2004, orig. 1997).

Wells, S., 'The Canon in the Can', *Times Literary Supplement,* 10 May 1985, p. 522.

Wells, S., *Shakespeare: A Life in Drama* (New York: W.W. Norton, 1997).

Welsford, E., *The Fool: His Social and Literary History* (Garden City, NY: Anchor, 1961).

West, S., *The Image of the Actor: Verbal and Visual Representation in the Age of Garrick and Kemble* (London: Pinter, 1991).

West, W., *Theatres and Encyclopedias in Early Modern Europe* (Cambridge: Cambridge University Press, 2002).

West, W., 'No Endless Moniment: Artificial Memory and Memorial Artifact in Early Modern England', in S. Radstone and K. Hodgkin (eds.), *Regimes of Memory* (London and New York: Routledge, 2003), pp. 61–75.

West, W.N., 'Less Well-Wrought Urns: Henry Vaughan and the Decay of the Poetic Monument', *ELH,* 75.1 (2008), 197–217.

West, W.N., 'Replaying Early Modern Performances', in S. Werner (ed.), *New Directions in Renaissance Drama and Performance Studies* (Houndmills, Basingstoke: Palgrave Macmillan, 2010), pp. 30–50.

Wheeler, R., *Shakespeare's Development and the Problem Comedies* (Berkeley: University of California Press, 1981).

White, H., *The Content of the Form: Narrative Discourse and Historical Representation* (Baltimore, MD: Johns Hopkins University Press, 1990).

White, W.C., *Orlando: Or Parental Persecution, a Tragedy* (Boston, 1797).

Whitehead, A., *Memory* (London and New York: Routledge, 2009).

Whiting, R., 'Abominable Idols: Images and Image-Breaking under Henry VIII', *Journal of Ecclesiastical History,* 33 (1982), 30–47.

Wickham, G., H. Berry, and W. Ingram (eds.), *English Professional Theatre, 1530–1660* (Cambridge: Cambridge University Press, 2000).

Wiggins, M., in association with C. Richardson, *British Drama: A Catalogue,* Vol. VI: *1609–1616* (Oxford: Oxford University Press, 2015).

Wilder, L.P., *Shakespeare's Memory Theatre: Reflections, Properties and Character* (Cambridge: Cambridge University Press, 2010).

Wilder, L.P., 'Playing Sodomites: Gender and Protean Character in *As You Like It*', in M.W. Shurgot and Y.J. Ko (eds.), *Shakespeare's Sense of Character: On the Page and From the Stage* (Farnham, UK: Ashgate, 2012), pp. 189–207.

Wilder, L.P., '"My Exion is Entered": Anatomy, Costume, and Theatrical Knowledge in *2 Henry IV*', *Renaissance Drama,* 41.1–2 (2013), 57–84.

Wiles, D., *A Short History of Western Performance Space* (Cambridge: Cambridge University Press, 2003).

Willeford, W., *The Fool and His Scepter: A Study of Clowns and Jesters and Their Audience* (Evanston, IL: Northwestern University Press, 1969).

Willems, M., 'Verbal-Visual, Verbal-Pictorial or Textual-Televisual? Reflections on the BBC Shakespeare Series', in A. Davies and S. Wells (eds.), *Shakespeare and the Moving Image: The Plays on Film and Television* (Cambridge: Cambridge University Press, 1994), pp. 69–85.

Williams, Jr., F.B., 'Commendatory Verses: The Rise of the Art of Puffing', *Studies in Bibliography,* 19 (1966), 1–14.

Williams, G., 'Textual Crudities in Robert Burton's *Anatomy of Melancholy* and Thomas Browne's *Pseudodoxia Epidemica*', in C. Ivic and G. Williams (eds.), *Forgetting in Early Modern English Literature and Culture: Lethe's Legacies* (London and New York: Routledge, 2004).

Williams, G., 'Early Modern Blazons and the Rhetoric of Wonder: Turning Towards an Ethics of Sexual Difference', in T. Krier and E.D. Harvey (eds.), *Irigaray and Premodern Culture* (London: Routledge, 2005), pp. 126–37.

Williams, G., 'Double Exposure: Gazing at Male Fantasy in Shakespearean Comedy', in D. Uman and S. Morrison (eds.), *Staging the Blazon in Early Modern English Theatre* (Burlington, NJ: Ashgate, 2013), pp. 13–24.

Willis, J., *Mnemonica* (London, 1661).

Willis, S., *The BBC Shakespeare Plays: Making the Televised Canon* (Chapel Hill, NC and London: The University of North Carolina Press, 1991).

Wilson, J.D., *The Fortunes of Falstaff* (Cambridge: Cambridge University Press, 1943; repr. 1979).

Wilson, T., *The arte of rhetorique* (1553).
Winter, J., *Sites of Memory, Sites of Mourning: The Great War in European Cultural History* (Cambridge: Cambridge University Press, 1998).
Wolfson, S.J., 'Shakespeare and the Romantic Girl Reader', *Nineteenth-Century Contexts*, 21 (1999), 191–234.
Wood, A., *The Memory of the People: Custom and Popular Senses of the Past in Early Modern England* (Cambridge: Cambridge University Press, 2013).
Woodbridge, L. and E. Berry (eds.), *True Rites and Maimed Rites: Ritual and Anti-Ritual in Shakespeare and His Age* (Urbana, IL and Chicago: University of Illinois Press, 1992).
Woolf, D.R., 'Erudition and the Idea of History in Renaissance England', *Renaissance Quarterly*, 40.1 (1987), 11–48.
Worthen, W.B., 'Fond Records: Remembering Theatre in the Digital Age', in P. Holland (ed.), *Shakespeare, Memory and Performance* (Cambridge: Cambridge University Press, 2006), pp. 281–304.
Wotton, Sir H., *Life and Letters of Sir Henry Wotton*, ed. L.P. Smith, vol. II (Oxford: Clarendon Press, 1907).
Wright, T., *The Passions of the Minde in Generall by Thomas Wright, a reprint based on the 1604 edition* (Urbana: University of Illinois Press, 1971).
Yates, F.A., *Giordano Bruno and the Hermetic Tradition* (Chicago: University of Chicago Press, 1964).
Yates, F.A., *The Art of Memory* (Chicago: University of Chicago Press, 1966).
Yates. F.A., 'The Stage in Robert Fludd's Memory System', *Shakespeare Studies*, 3 (1967), 138–66.
Yates, F.A., *Theatre of the World* (Chicago: University of Chicago Press, 1969).
Yates, F.A., *Astraea: The Imperial Theme in the Sixteenth Century* (London: Routledge & Kegan Paul, 1975).
Yeo, R., *Notebooks, English Virtuosi, and Early Modern Science* (Chicago: University of Chicago Press, 2014).
Yoshino, K., 'The Choice of the Four Fathers: Henry IV, Falstaff, the Lord Chief Justice, and the King of France in the *Henriad*', *Yale Journal of Law and the Humanities*, 22.2 (2013), 417–39.
Žižek, S., 'The Big Other Doesn't Exist', *Journal of European Psychoanalysis* (1997), www.lacan.com/zizekother.htm

INDEX

Ackroyd, Peter, 95
acting *see* player and playing
actor *see* player and playing
Adams, Thomas R., 24
Adelman, Janet, 272
aemulatio see emulation
aesthetics, 11–12, 29, 65, 68, 150, 161, 219, 246, 267, 270, 274, 276, 316
Albott, Robert, 84
al-Haddad, Najib, 39
Allan, David, 27, 28
allegory, 167, 173, 233, 240, 245–246, 248–249, 251, 316
Alleyn, Edward, 217
Alleyn, Giles, 93
Almereyda, Michael, 68
American readership, 24, 25, 27–31
Amine, Khalid, 39
Amleth, 19, 65
amnesia *see* forgetting
anachronism, 156, 199–200
anagnorisis see recognition (*anagnorisis*)
analogy, historical, 283–284
Anderson, John William, 52
Andrewe, Laurence, 78–80, 82, 84
anthologies, 25–31
antiquarianism, 301–305, 308, 317–318
Anton, Robert, 84
aphorisms, 29
Aquinas, St. Thomas, 282
'Arab Spring', 38, 39
Arab world, 38–44
Archer, William, 56, 58
archetype, 143–146, 227
archive, 98–99, 209–211, 215–216, 322
Arden Shakespeare Series, 43
Aristotle, 282, 291, 293–4

Arne, Thomas, 48
ars memorativa see memory, arts of; memory images; memory places
ars moriendi, 172, 175
ars vivendi, 172
Arthur, King, 174
articles (*Richard III*) *see* memory, stage properties and
Asbury, Kelly, 69
Assmann, Aleida, 47, 94, 95
Assmann, Jan, 47, 94, 209, 218
Aubrey, John, 304
audience, 17, 105, 149, 151–153, 159, 165–166, 170, 180–189, 191–205, 208–220, 227, 236, 259
Augustine, St., 231, 239, 241, 251, 272, 282
Austen, Jane, 26
Austin, John, 211, 216
Avignon Theatre Festival, 63

Bacon, Francis, 81, 85, 267–8, 285, 297
Bakhtin, Mikhail, 192, 209
Baldo, Jonathan, 5, 6, 135–136, 168, 169, 170, 199, 319
Bale, John, 304
Ball, Robert Hamilton, 63
Bandello, Matteo, 289
Banks, Thomas, 52
Bara, Theda, 63
Barber, C. L., 168, 255
Bardolatry, 39, 49
Barish, Jonas, 83, 293
Barker, Nicolas, 24
Barma, Claude, 65
Barnfield, Richard, 282, 292
Barret, J. K., 256, 324
Barrett (Browning), Elizabeth, 29
Barthes, Roland, 47, 58, 59
Bartlet, John, 282

Index

Bartlett, Frederick, 112
Barton, John, 186
Bate, Jonathan, 118
Batman, Stephen, 284, 286
Bayly, Lewis, 84
BBC, 66
Beaumont, Francis, 284
Beckett, Samuel, 36
Bedford Shakespeare, 75
    Beecher, Donald, 316
Beerbohm, Max, 58
Bell, John, 51, 53
Belleforest, François de, 289
Berger Jr., Harry, 210
Bergson, Henri, 47
Berkeley, William, 79
Berlin Wall, 38
Bernard of Clairvaux, 152
Best, Michael, 75
Billingsley, Henry, 77
biography, of Shakespeare, 94–97, 99
Birnie, William, 87
Black, James, 110
Blackfriars Theatre, 77, 79
Blair, Hugh, 26
blazon, 173
Blinde, Loren, 194
Bloom, Harold, 167
Blyth, Ben, 92, 93, 97, 98
Boaistuau, Pierre, 289
Boas, F. C., 112
Boccaccio, Giovanni, 286
body, discipline of, 17, 167–168
body, monumental, 302
body, opposed to soul or mind, 13, 145, 225, 271–273, 292, 318–323
body language, 211, 216, 218
Bollywood, 39
Bolzoni, Lina, 316
books, 16, 18, 67–68, 77–79, 121, 124, 151–152, 191, 213, 217, 231, 240, 246, 251, 266–267, 269, 272, 282–284, 291, 301, 304, 306, 315; *see also*, memory, stage properties and; memory, book history and; memory, print and
Booth, Stephen, 306
Bose, Siddhartha, 92, 96, 97
Bouchard, Gary, 175
Bouissac, Paul, 172
Bowdler, Henrietta, 25–6
Bowdler, Thomas, 25–6
Boyd, Michael, 183
Boydell, John, 51, 52
Boydell Shakespeare Gallery, 46, 51–52, 53, 56
Boyle, Robert, 81
Braithwait, Richard, 283
Branagh, Kenneth, 62, 66–67, 68, 69
Brando, Marlon, 65

Brexit *see* European Union
Brinsley, John, 81, 84
British Museum, 38, 39
Brockway, Maria, 29
bronze, compared to poetry, 297, 300
Brookes, Nathaniel, 79
Browne, Thomas, 269, 318
Brownlie, Siobhan, 95
Brownlow, Frank, 77
Bruno, Giordano, 82, 83, 88, 170
Bruyneel, Kevin, 97
Bryson, Bill, 95
Buchanan, Judith, 62
Burbage, James, 77, 93
Burbage, Richard, 217
Burckhardt, Sigurd, 150–151
burial, 67, 117, 119, 123, 130–132, 155, 240, 246–247, 292, 300
Burnett, Mark Thornton, 63, 64, 67
Burns, Edward, 180
Burt, Richard, 62–3, 65
Burton, Jonathan, 28
Burton, Richard, 65
Burton, Robert, 81, 269, 318
Byron, Lord (George Gordon), 28

cabbalism, 18
Cagney, James, 64
Cairncross, Andrew, 180
Calbi, Maurizio, 68
Cambridge Guide to the Worlds of Shakespeare, 43
Cambridge University, 38
Camden, William, 303
Camillo, Giulio, 4, 11–15, 16, 18, 19–20, 82
Campbell, Thomas, 56
Carleton, Dudley, 284
carnivalesque, 167–168, 172, 209
carnivals, 92, 167
carpe diem trope, 305
Carpenter, John, 87
Carroll, William C., 214–215, 268, 275
Carruthers, Mary, 149, 153, 302, 316
Cartari, Vincenzo, 244–245, 286, 288
Carter, Elizabeth, 30
Carter, George, 49, 50–51
Catalogue of English Literary Manuscripts, 76
Cavell, Stanley, 215, 323
Caxton, William, 79
celebrity, 49
Chamberlain, John, 284
Chapman, George, 123, 284, 285, 287
character, 11, 13, 19–20, 48, 50, 53, 56–57, 69, 93, 96, 105, 107–114, 117, 122–124, 135, 137, 139, 141–142, 145, 149–150, 165–178, 183–186, 189, 193–194, 197, 199–200, 206, 210, 225–237, 246
characterization *see* character

352

Index

Charles II, 80
Chartier, Roger, 25, 320
Chaucer, Geoffrey, 34, 289
Cheere, John, 49
childbirth, 244–245
children, 1–2, 25–27, 37, 42, 67, 118, 120, 122–123, 127, 135–138, 140–141, 226, 230, 234–235, 244–251, 286, 291–292, 300
Chivers, Tom, 92, 94, 97, 99
Christos, George, 136–138, 145
Cibber, Colley, 185
Cicero, 77, 85, 282, 293
cinema and Shakespeare *see* Shakespeare, William, film productions
city comedy, 199
class, social, 38, 301–302
Cleland, James, 269
Clubb, Louise George, 209
cognition, distributed, 137–138
Coles, Elisha, 86
Colie, Rosalie, 167
Colman, Ronald, 64
Comes, Natalis *see* Conti, Natale
commonplace books, 27–31
complaint (literary mode), 122, 133, 292
Connerton, Paul, 94
Conti, Natale, 285, 286
Cooper, Thomas, 286
Copland, Robert, 80, 81, 83
Corazza, Juan Carlos, 42
Cotton, Charles, 81
Counsell, Colin, 94
Craig, Alexander, 84
Craik, T. W., 259
Cressy, David, 151
Crooke, Helkiah, 271
Crowl, Samuel, 67
crown *see* memory, stage properties and
cud, chewing the *see* rumination
Cukor, George, 64
Cummings, Brian, 208, 219
Curtain, The (early modern playhouse), 92, 93, 97
Czech Republic, 38

Dallington, Robert, 84
da Messina, Antonello, 67
Daniel, Samuel, 292, 298
Daniell, David, 151
Danson, Lawrence, 255
Darnton, Robert, 24
D'Assigny, Marius, 79, 81
databases: *British History Online*, 75; *Bymewilliamshakespeare.org*, 75; *Catalogue of English Literary Manuscripts*, 76; *Early English Books Online*, 73–76, 78–88; *Internet Shakespeare Editions*, 75; *Literature Online* (LION), 73–76, 87; *Lost Plays Database*, 75; *Oxford Scholarly Editions Online*, 75; *Scriptorium*, 76; Shakespearedocumented.org, 75; *Shakespeare in Quarto*, 75; *Shakespeare Quartos Online*, 75; *Six Degrees of Francis Bacon*, 75
d'Avity, Pierre, 84
Day, Richard, 87
de Certeau, Michel, 68, 308
Dee, John, 77
de Havilland, Olivia, 64
Deiter, Kristen, 218
Delabatista, Dirk, 41, 43
Denison, John, 84
design, Vitruvian, 77
Dessingué, Alexandre, 55
Devereux, Robert (Earl of Essex), 76
Diamond, Elin, 253
Diana, temple of, 247–248
Diana, tripartite *see* Lucina
Dicsone (Dickson), Alexander, 76, 83, 88
Dieterle, William, 64
digitisation, 74
Dillon, Janette, 209
disability, 40–41
Dobson, Michael, 48
Dodd, William, 26, 27, 28, 30
Donaldson, Peter S., 43
Donne, John, 81, 283, 298, 318, 323
Drayton, Michael, 183, 287
Droeshout, Martin, 47
Drohan, Declan, 40
Dromgoole, Dominic, 41
Dryden, John, 81
Duffy, Eamon, 153
Duncan, Francesca, 92, 93
Duncan-Jones, Katherine, 95
Dunne, Derek, 44
Dunthorne, Joe, 92, 94–95, 96
d'Urfé, Honoré, 79
Dustagheer, Sarah, 4

Eagleton, Terry, 167–8
Early English Books Online (EEBO) *see* databases
Edelstein, Jean Hannah, 92
editors of Shakespeare, 24
education, 2, 77, 275, 318, 323; *see also* rhetoric
Edward VI, 152, 153
Edwards, J. Gordon, 63
Edzard, Christine, 67
Eire *see* Ireland, Republic of
ekphrasis, 175, 291–292, 324
elegiac, 29, 48, 86, 298, 305
Elizabeth I, Queen, 151–153, 165, 281, 282, 284, 298
Elyot, Thomas, 289
emblems, 18, 125, 131n28, 146, 155, 170, 173–175, 183, 215–217, 227, 267, 271, 274, 316
empire, 34–44, 161
emulation, of the ancients, 284–285

Engel, William E., 5, 234, 315, 316, 322
Enterline, Lynn, 292
epideictic *see* memory, fame and
Erasmus, Desiderius, 322
Erll, Astrid, 94
Essex, Earl of *see* Devereux
Euclid, 77
European Shakespeares, 38
European Union, 34, 37, 38
Eworth, Hans, 282
eyewitness testimony, 111

Facal, Darío, 35
Fairbanks, Douglas, 64
Febvre, Lucien, 24
Felton, Samuel, 51
Fenton, Geoffrey, 83
fighting *see* stage combat
First Folio (Shakespeare), 25, 283
Fisher, Rhoda L., 142–143
Fisher, Seymour, 142–143
Fletcher, John, 79, 84, 87, 192, 201
Floyd-Wilson, Mary, 320
Fludd, Robert, 11, 12, 76, 77
Fonda, Henry, 69
Ford, John, 69
foreshadowing, 170, 185–186, 196–197
forgetting, 3, 39, 62, 92–94, 99, 114, 117–121, 123–129, 145–146, 149–150, 153–155, 157, 159–161, 165–166, 168, 194, 212–213, 225, 228, 231, 235–236, 240, 245, 248–249, 262–263, 266–276, 293, 303–304, 317–319, 323; *see also* memory, displacement and; memory, distraction and; memory, order and
forgiveness, 169, 177, 244
Forker, Charles R., 216
Foster, Donald, 75
Fowler, Alistair, 299
France, 39, 52, 63–64, 68
Fraunce, Abraham, 84, 286, 289
Frye, Northrop, 226
Fuente, Oscar de la, 35–36
Fuller, Thomas, 304
Fulwood, William, 80, 81, 83, 266
Fuseli, Henry, 52, 53
future, 24–25, 67, 85, 97, 127, 129, 137, 142, 145–146, 154–155, 158–159, 181, 184–186, 214, 226, 253, 255, 257–258, 262, 271, 282, 288, 324; *see also* remembering, future

Gainsborough, Thomas, 58
Garber, Marjorie, 146
Gardner, Edna Rose, 29
Garrick, David, 48, 49, 50, 51, 64
Garrison, John, 322
Gavira, Emilio, 35
Gielgud, John, 67

Gieskes, Ed, 5
Gillis, John R., 116
Giraldi, Lilio Gregorio, 286
Girardot, Annie, 64
Globalisation, 39
Globe Theatre, 12, 15, 17, 77, 91, 92, 93
Globe Theatre (20th-century reconstruction), 41, 43, 98
glove *see* memory, stage properties and
Goddard, Harold C., 140–141
Godden, Selena, 92
Godskall, James, 84
Godwin, Simon, 42
Golding, Arthur, 285, 288
Goldsmith, Robert, 142
Gordon, Andrew, 303, 317–318
Gossuin of Metz, 79
Gower, John, 289
Grammaticus, Saxo, 65
Gratarolo, Guglielmo, 80, 81, 84, 88, 266
Grazia, Margreta de, 27
Greenaway, Peter, 67
Greenblatt, Stephen, 38, 39, 43, 95, 208, 317
Greene, Robert, 93, 198
Greenham, Richard, 84
Grene, Nicholas, 5
Grimes, Ronald, 209, 216, 218, 219
Guillim, John, 299
guilt, 186–187

Halbwachs, Maurice, 47, 55, 94, 209
Hall, Edward, 184, 212
Hall, Joseph, 84
Hall, Peter, 65, 186
Hamilton, William, 53
Hampton-Reeves, Stuart, 183
hand, severed *see* memory, stage properties and
handkerchief *see* memory, stage properties and
Hanson, John, 87
Harlan, Susan, 6
Harry, King, bluff, 202
Hart, A. C., 180
Hatchuel, Sarah, 4, 154
Hathway, Thomas, 183
Hawes, Stephen, 82, 84
Hawkes, Terence, 95
Hawkins, Sam, 92
Hazlitt, William, 283
heads, severed *see* memory, stage properties and
Hedrick, Donald, 107
Hegel, Georg Wilhelm Friedrich, 47, 59
Helfer, Rebeca, 3, 6–7
Henderson, R., 283
Henry VIII, King, 152, 202, 205
Henslowe, Philip, 180
heraldry, 173, 299–303, 305, 307–308
Herdson, Henry, 81

Index

hermeticism, 18
Herrick, Robert, 81
Heywood, Thomas, 183
Hiatt, Charles, 58
Hirsh, James, 139
Hiscock, Andrew, 6, 116, 141, 171, 318
historicism, 317–319
Hoenselaars, Ton, 41, 43
Hoffman, Michael, 67
Hogarth, William, 53, 55
Holderness, Graham, 66, 95, 96
Holinshed, Raphael, 81, 84, 218
Holland, Peter, 319
Homer, 123–124
Hong Kong, 37
honour, 118–119, 122–124, 159, 168, 177, 187
Hoole, Charles, 276
Horace, 297, 298, 300
Hoskins, John, 84
Howard, Leslie, 64
Howell, William, 81
Huang, Alexa, 43
Hugh of Lincoln, 151–152, 153
humours, 198–199
Humphries, A. R., 194
Hungary, 38
hypermnesia, 62, 273

identity, 94–97, 99, 116, 119–120, 124, 126–127, 149–150, 159–161, 225–237, 239–251, 263, 291, 301–302, 307, 318–319
imagination, 12–13, 47, 51, 53, 55, 58, 67, 97, 116–117, 128, 140, 158, 165, 167, 174–175, 177, 194–195, 203, 205, 220, 227, 231, 235–236, 256, 306–308
imagines see memory images
imitation, 52, 289, 307
immortality, 49, 64, 250, 268, 282, 285, 287, 297–299, 305
improvisation, 91, 141, 209–211, 213–214, 216–217, 246
indictment (*Richard III*) *see* memory, stage properties and
information effect *see* memory, false
interiority, 3, 18, 189, 225, 245, 308, 317–321
internet searches, 74
inwardness *see* interiority
Iran, 38, 39, 43
Ireland, Northern, 37
Ireland, Republic of, 35–39, 40, 43–44, 157
Irish, language *see* Ireland
Irving, Henry, 46, 56
Ivic, Christopher, 318

James, Heather, 117
James VI/I, King, 15, 151, 204, 267, 283, 284, 286
Japan, 37, 39–40, 66

Jenkins, Anne, 96
Jenkins, Henry, 68
Jerome, Stephen, 87
Jolly, Thomas, 63
Jones, Ann Rosalind, 319–320
Jones, Inigo, 77
Jones, Osheen, 68
Jonson, Ben, 73, 84, 93, 105–106, 199, 285
Jung, Carl, 143, 145

Kansteiner, Wulf, 47
Kar, Ajoy, 65
Karremann, Isabel, 117, 172, 319
Kastan, David Scott, 25, 226
Kattago, Siobhan, 46
Keene, Nicholas, 320–321
Kemble, John Philip, 53
Kiefer, Frederick, 267
King James Bible, 152
King Jnr., Martin Luther, 96
King's Men, The, 34
Kirkman, Francis, 168
Klein, Katia, 36
knowledge, 12–14, 203, 209, 227–231, 234–237, 245, 251, 268, 274–275, 285–287, 318, 322
Knowles, Katie, 43
Knowles, Ronald, 180, 181
Knox, Vicesimus, 26, 27, 30
Kott, Jan, 66
Kozintsev, Grigori, 66
Kristeva, Julia, 35
Kunin, Aaron, 297
Kurosawa, Akira, 39, 66
Kurzel, Justin, 62
Kyd, Thomas, 197
Kyle, Barry, 36, 40

Lacan, Jacques, 302, 306
Lamb, Charles, 55
Langley, Thomas, 84
Larcom, Lucy, 27
Lees-Jeffries, Hester, 117, 244
le Goff, Jacques, 46
Lemnius, Levinus, 84
Lennam, Trevor, 251
Lerer, Seth, 30
Lesser, Zachary, 27
letters *see* memory, stage properties and
Levenson, Jill, 110
Levin, Harry, 216
Lévi-Strauss, Claude, 302
lieux de mémoire, 46, 48, 50–51, 63, 94, 209, 215
Linche, Robert, 286
Lindsay, David, 87
Linn, John Blair, 30
Lippitt, Julia, 28
literacy *see* orality, opposed to literacy

Index

Literature Online (LION) *see* databases
livecast *see* Shakespeare, William, stage productions, on film
Livy, 122, 289, 292
Llewellyn, Nigel, 302
Lloyd, Lodowick, 83, 85
Lull, Ramon, 82
loci see memory places
Lodge, Thomas, 229–230, 231, 292
Loncraine, Richard, 67
London Chronicle, 48
London Word Festival, 92–99
Long, Zachariah, 3–4, 225, 317
Longfellow, Henry Wadsworth, 29
looking-glass (*Richard III*) *see* memory, stage properties and
Lost Plays Database see databases
Lothian, J. M., 259
Loughnane, Rory, 4, 44, 324
Lucina, 244–245, 247
Luhrmann, Baz, 67, 69
Lyne, Raphael, 254, 321–322

Maastricht Treaty, 38
Macknik, Stephen, 106–107
Madden, John, 69
magic, 106–107
Malachites, The, 92, 93, 96, 97, 98
malapropism, 275
Mankiewicz, Joseph, 65
mantle *see* memory, stage properties and
Manton, Thomas, 81
marble, as building material, 161, 262, 297, 300
marble, as writing surface, 262, 267, 273–274
Marcus, Leah, 322
Mariner, David, 30
Markham, Gervase, 84
Marlowe, Christopher, 93, 189, 193, 197, 198, 217–218, 219, 282, 284, 287, 318, 323
marriage, 2–3, 19, 139, 174, 181–182, 187, 214, 226, 240, 242, 244–245, 248, 250, 253–255, 259, 262–263, 271–272, 286
Marston, John, 77, 78, 287
Martin, H.-J., 24
Martinez-Conde, Susan, 106–107
Massinger, Philip, 79, 81
Mature, Victor, 69
Mayer, Jean-Christophe, 218
'McDonald[s], Ronald', 39
McGuffey Readers, 28
McKenzie, D. F., 24
McMullan, Gordon, 203, 204
McMullan, Thomas, 93, 96
McPartlin, Marie, 92
Medieval drama, 217
Melchiori, Giorgio, 198

Melton, John, 81
memento mori, 85–87, 172, 175, 177, 262, 305
memorials *see* monuments
memoria rerum see memory of things
memorization, of lines, 267
memorization, verbatim, 270
memory: action and, 209; alienation and, 19, 225–237; ambiguity and, 175; book history and, 4, 23–31, 67, 316, *see also* memory, print and; burial and, 123, 139, 192, 240, 288, 300–302; calendar and, 149–152; Catholicism and, 150–154, 260–261, 317–318, 324; classical world and, 116–129, 149–161, 281–294, 322–324; clothing and *see* memory, costume and; clown and *see* memory, fool and, *see also* memory, humor and; cognitive science and, 106–107, 136–140, 145–146, 306, 320–322; comedy and, 1–3, 6, 114, 168–169, 223–278; constructedness of, 25, 30, 47, 52, 58, 67, 69, 92, 94–97, 105–107, 116; conventionality and, 112; costume and, 50, 63, 98, 144, 216, 230, 319–320; Creation and *see* memory, Genesis, book of, and; displacement and, 136, 144–145, 235, 256, *see also* forgetting; distortion and, 3, 25, 106, 138, 200, 236, 247, 274, 285, *see also* forgetting; memory, false; distraction and, 16–21, 149–161, 319, *see also* forgetting; *divisio* and, 16, 18; ethics and, 149, 156, 172, 244, 282, 285–286, 288, 293–294, 323, *see also* memory, morality and; empathy and, 232–234, 237; exemplarity and, 183, 323; experience and, 2–3, 47, 53, 68, 106–107, 113, 119, 123, 140, 143, 226–237, 253–254, 274, 288, 290, 293; faculty psychology and *see* memory, physiology of; fame and, 116, 118, 124, 176, 268, 299–308; fiction and, 19–20, 191–205; fidelity, sexual, and, 112–113, 126–127, 232; film and, 4, 62–70; fool and, 135–137, 141–146, 165, *see also* memory, humor and; Genesis, book of, and, 13–14, 78; gender and, 239–251, 318, 321; genre and, 3, 114, 135, 158, 165, 226, 240, 246, 253–263, 323; ghosts and, 154, 156–157, 317; hearing and, 25, 78, 105, 107, 192, 194, 199–200, 203–204, 323; history and, 3, 5, 127, 160–161, 163–222, *see also* memory, historical; humor and, 136–137, 174, 201, *see also* memory, fool and; images (religious) and, 149, 152–154; impression and, 230, 235–236; language and, 2, 28, 34–42, 94–95, 98, 111, 154, 158, 160, 167–168, 193–200, 203; law and, 208–220; lineage and, 116; love and, 125–128, 227–231, 235–237, 241–242, 248, 273, 298–299, 305–306; manipulation and *see* memory, false; material culture and, 25, 266–276, 297, 303, 305–306, 318–322; matter and, 16, 297–298; misogyny and, 112; morality and, 283–285,

356

see also memory, ethics and; new media and, 4, 73–88, 322; order and, 12, 239–240, 245–248, 321; ownership of, 2, 35, 70, 247, 292, 303, 322; passions and, 17, 241; performance and, 4, 34–44, 91–99, 180–189, 291, 319–321; physiology of, 230, 241, 272, 320–321; playbooks and see memory, scripts of plays and; poetry and, 191–192, 279–312; post-colonial adaptation and, 4, 34–44, 65; print and, 23, 25, 31, 56, 74, 78–88, 316, see also memory, book history and; programmes and, 38, 62; prompt books and, 62, 98; Protestantism and, 150–154, 261, 317–318, 321, 324; *prudentia* and, 3, 85, 282; quotation and, 25–31; Reformation and see memory, Protestantism and; memory, Catholicism and; report and see memory, storytelling and; reputation and see memory, fame and; retailing and see memory, storytelling and; ritual and, 47, 49, 92, 98, 117–118, 121–122, 130, 175, 208–220; Rome and see memory, classical world and; scripts of plays and, 27, 67, 98; seal and, 270, see also memory, impression and; self and see memory, identity and; sea and, 240, 245–247, 256–258, 260; Shakespeare's plays and see *individual titles*; Shakespeare's poems and see *individual titles*; skepticism and, 213, 323; sight and, 2, 12, 46–47, 153, 156, 194, 241, 291, 316, 323; sound and see hearing and; space and, 141, 253–263; stage properties and, 98, 112–113, 117, 120, 128, 155–156, 211–213, 215–218, 267–271, 321; storytelling and, 107–114, 191–197, 205, 285; stress and, 140; theatres and, 4, 11–21, 53–59, 62, 76–77, 91–92, 255–256, 291, 321, see also memory places, memory images, memory, arts of; tragedy and, 3, 4–5, 103–162; Troy and see memory, classical world and; truth and, 19–20, 47, 53, 92, 96, 191–205, 245; virtue and, 149–161; visual culture and see visual arts, sight and memory; water and see sea and; writing and, 23, see also works by title; see also remembering
memory, arts of, 19, 73–74; 76–85, 87–88, 136, 165–178, 218, 239–240, 246–249, 251, 255, 306, 315–318, 320, 323–324; see also memory places, memory images; memory, theatre and
memory, collective, 47–48, 55–56, 94, 116, 135, 160, 209, 321
memory, communicative see memory, collective
memory, cultural, 94, 97–98, 209, 260–261, 316
memory, episodic, 106
memory, excessive see hypermnesia
memory, false, 105–107, 138–139, 144–145
memory, flashbulb see memory, stress and
memory, historical, 191–205, 319
memory image, body as, 122, 167–168, 172–175, 177, 245–248, 261, 271–273, 292

memory images, 2, 13, 15–16, 19–21, 73, 78, 81–82, 166–167, 170, 173, 175, 177, 239–251, 306; see also memory, arts of; memory, images (religious) and
memory, long-term, 136–137
memory, natural, 80–81, 138, 306, 316, 320–321
memory, obligatory, 118, 120, 128, 155, 158, 307–308
memory of things, 270
memory places, 11–21, 73, 78, 81–82, 170, 218–219, 246–248; see also memory, arts of
memory places, body as, 271–273, 289, 292
memory, public see memory, collective
memory, scenic, 209
memory, short-term, 274, 276
memory, social see memory, false; see also memory, storytelling and
memory technology, 2, 12, 74–76, 316, 319–320, 322
memory, therapeutic, 41, 240–243, 249
Mendelssohn, Felix, 64
Meres, Francis, 83, 284
Merlo, Giulia, 95
metempsychosis, 225
Meyerhoff, Barbara, 214
Michaelian, Kourken, 106
Middleton, Thomas, 323
milieux de mémoire see *lieux de mémoire*
Milner, Matthew, 152–153
Milton, John, 30, 285, 287
Minear, Erin, 1, 6, 239, 323
Mirandola, Pico della, 14
misinformation effect see memory, false; see also memory, storytelling and
MIT Global Shakespeare see databases
mnemonics see memory, arts of; memory images; memory places
Molière, 39
monarchy, 208–220
monasteries, 73, 304
Montaigne, Michel de, 251, 266, 276, 323
monuments, 49, 110, 117, 149, 158, 161, 234, 260–262, 268, 297–308, 317–318, 323
Moore, Sally, 214
Moore, Thomas, 28
More, Hannah, 26
More, John, 87
More, Thomas, 210, 212, 213–214
mortality, 14, 85, 229, 255, 285, 302, 316; see also immortality
Mortimer, Felix, 92, 93, 94, 95, 97–98
Mosse, Miles, 84
mourning, 50, 87, 118, 188, 219, 220n7, 241, 244, 253, 258–260, 263, 301, 304–305
Mowbray, Alan, 69
Mowery, John, 320
multi-media, 68–69
Munday, Antony, 183

Napoleon (Buonaparte), 39
Nashe, Thomas, 73, 84, 87, 204
nation, 34–35, 38–39, 157, 170
nationalism, 46, 48, 51, 53, 66, 168
nationality, 38
National Theatre (London), 63, 97
Nawras, Joshua, 92, 93
Neely, Carol Thomas, 149–50
Neill, Michael, 112, 113, 155, 262
neoplatonism, 13, 18
New Cambridge Shakespeare series, 43
New Oxford Shakespeare series, 75
Nicholl, Charles, 95
Noble, Adrian, 67, 186
Noh Theatre (of Japan), 40
Nora, Pierre, 46, 50, 63, 94, 209, 215
Norbrook, David, 217
Northcote, James, 52, 53, 54
Norton Shakespeare, 75
nostalgia, 46, 123, 126, 128, 132, 150, 160, 169, 174, 204, 253, 258, 263, 319
note-taking, 269–270, 276, 277n17
noting (mnemonic), 158, 242, 284, 290, 303
Nunn, Trevor, 67

oaths (language), 172, 230; *see also* vows
oblivion *see* forgetting
O'Brien, Emily, 44
obsolescence, 268, 304–305, 307
Olivier, Laurence, 62, 65, 66, 185
Ong, Walter, 316
orality, opposed to literacy, 74, 209–211, 268, 274, 316, 319, 322
Orgel, Stephen, 305
Orwell, George, 155
Otto, Beatrice, 137
outmodedness *see* obsolescence
Ovid, 117, 119, 121–122, 217, 284–285, 288–289, 322
Oxford Dictionary of National Biography, 75
Oxford Handbook of Shakespearean Tragedy, 43
Oxford Scholarly Editions Online see databases

Pacino, Al, 68
Painter, William, 289–290, 292
Palfrey, Sarah Hammond, 29
palimpsest, 136, 150–154, 214, 267, 269, 271, 273, 275–276
panegyric, 281
papers *see* memory, stage properties and
Parker, Oliver, 67
Partridge, Bernard, 56
Pasquier, Etienne, 84
Pater, Walter, 216
Patiño, Javier L., 35

Patterson, Annabel, 201, 218
Pecke, Thomas, 84
Peele, George, 198
Peend, Thomas, 287
Pendleton, Thomas, 181
Pennington, Michael, 217
peripeteia see reversal
Perkins, William, 88
Persia *see* Iran
Peter Pan Theatre Company, 37
Peters, Julie Stone, 12
Petrarchanism *see* Petrarch, Francesco
Petrarch, Francesco, 83, 174, 269, 299
Phaedrus, 23, 266
Phelan, Peggy, 92, 99
Pickford, Mary, 64
Pierpoint, John, 27
pillow (*Richard II*), putative *see* memory, stage properties and
Pivetti, Kyle, 322
Plaix, Cesar de, 84
Plat, Hugh, 79, 82, 83, 85
Plato, 23, 248, 266
player and playing (early modern), 20
Playfere, Thomas, 84
Plutarch, 152, 322
Poland, 38
Polanski, Roman, 66
politics, 24, 34, 37–39, 42, 68, 92, 94, 96–99, 116–117, 119, 121–122, 150–151, 160, 168, 172, 182, 187, 194, 204, 208–220, 281–282, 318, 324
Polsted, Ezekiel, 79
posterity, 66, 191–192, 290, 297–308
Potter, Lois, 36
power, 1, 35, 41, 47, 70, 99, 140–144, 150, 152–161, 171, 187, 208–221, 240, 251, 267–268, 270, 281–282, 302, 308, 317, 319
Power, Andrew J., 4
praise *see* memory, fame and
Price, Leah, 29
Price, Sampson, 81, 84
print culture *see* books; memory, book history and; memory, print and
privacy, 82, 117–118, 122–123, 154, 156, 170–171, 242, 245, 307–308
property development, 96–98
proverbs *see* aphorisms
Prynne, William, 291
psychoanalysis, 317, 324
purgatory, 19
Puritanism, 157, 291
Puttenham, George, 83, 191–192

Quick Bright Things (theatre company), 40–41
Quinn, Gavin, 37, 38, 40
Quintilian, 77, 297, 299

Raleigh (Ralegh), Walter, 230–231, 284, 285
Ramus, Peter, 316
Rankins, William, 87
rape, 119, 121, 248, 271, 281–294
Ravenna, Peter of, 80, 81, 84, 88
recognition (*anagnorisis*), 23, 35, 39–41, 49–50, 112–113, 133, 143, 145–146, 152, 167, 172, 176, 199, 214, 232–233, 245, 247–248, 262–263, 299, 305
recollection *see* remembering
Reformation, 150, 152, 153, 157, 302–304, 317, 318, 320, 321
Reinhardt, Max, 64
relics, 49, 153, 235, 260–262
religion *see* memory, Catholicism and; memory, Protestantism and; memory, ritual and; Puritanism; Reformation
remembering, 49, 117, 185–189, 191–205, 225–237, 244, 257, 262–263, 317–319; *see also* memory
remembering, future, 120, 126–127, 129, 161, 290–291, 297–308, 323; *see also* future
Renan, Ernest, 150
repertoire (Diana Taylor), 209–220
res see memory images
revenge, 117–122, 128
reversal, 209, 216, 244, 276, 301
Reynolds, Edward, 266, 272
Reynolds, Joshua, 58
rhetoric, 2, 73, 77, 79, 83–84, 88, 166, 316, 324; *see also* education
Rhetorica ad C. Herennium, 77
Rhodes, Neil, 322
Ribner, Irving, 201
Rich, Penelope, 298
Richard, Bernard, 11
Richard III, King, exhumation of, 192
Richardson, Tony, 66
Rist, Thomas, 318
Roach, Joseph, 92, 94
Robertson, Graham, 57
romance (genre), 40, 63, 68, 171–172, 174, 192, 201, 246, 253–263
Rooney, Mickey, 64
Rose, Jonathan, 30
Rose Theatre, The, 92, 93
Rossi, Paolo, 315–316
Rothwell, Kenneth S., 64, 67, 69
Roubiliac, Louis-François, 49, 52
Rourke, Lee, 92
Rowe, Katherine, 43, 62
Rowe, Nicholas, 51
Rowlands, Samuel, 87
Royal Academy of Arts, 48, 51
Royal Shakespeare Company, 36, 40, 42, 63, 183, 186
ruins, 21, 26, 62, 117, 129, 261, 298, 302–306

rumination, 302
Russia, 38
Rutter, Carol Chillington, 183
Rymer, Thomas, 113
Rysbrack, John Michael, 49

Said, Edward, 36
Sallustius, 286
Sanders, Julie, 35, 36
Sandys, George, 286
Sargent, John Singer, 57–58
satire, 123–128
Saunders (Sanders), Richard, 79, 80
Sawday, Jonathan, 322
sayings *see* aphorisms
scenario (Diana Taylor), 209–210
sceptre (*Richard III*) *see* memory, stage properties and
Scheemakers, Thomas, 49, 52
schoolbooks *see* anthologies; education; *McGuffey Readers*
Schuler, Robert M., 216
Schwyzer, Philip, 261
Scotland, 34, 36, 37, 39, 65
Scriptorium, 76
sea, 121, 150, 160, 188, 240, 245–248, 257–258, 260
search engine optimization (SEO), 73
secularization, 208, 219–220
Semple, Edel, 44
Seneca, 121
Senecan tragedy, 19, 121
sexuality, 36–37, 68, 127, 174, 240, 245, 248, 259, 262, 271–272, 274, 283–294, 322–323
Shakespeare in Quarto see databases
Shakespeare in Shoreditch Festival, 92–93, 94, 96, 97, 98
Shakespeare Quartos Archive see databases
Shakespeare, William, adaptations, 34–41, *see also* Shakespeare, William, film productions; Shakespeare, William, stage productions; *The Best Pies in London*, 93; *By Moonlight*, Quick Bright Things, 40; *Falstaff*, Giuseppe Verdi, 169; *Heir to the Throne*, 93; *Hijos de Shakespeare*, 42; *Indian Tempest*, Footsbarn, 43; language and, 35, 38–41; *MAC-BETH*, Pan-Pan Theatre, 37–38; *Macbeth 7*, Quinn's, 40; *Othello*, Siddhartha Bose, 96–97; otherness and, 34–35; *Plantagenets, The*, dir. Adrian Noble (1988), 186; Shakespeare in Shoreditch, London Word Festival (2009), 92; *Tempest!*, Quick Bright Things, 41; *Three Loose Teeth*, 93; *War of the Roses, The*, dir. Michael Bogdanov (1990), 216
Shakespeare, William, film productions: *Anarchy (Cymbeline)*, dir. Michael Almereyda (2014), 68; *Antony and Cleopatra*, dir. J. Gordon Evans (1917), 63; *As You Like It*, dir. Christine

Index

Edzard (1992), 67; *As You Like It*, dir. Kenneth Branagh (2006), 66–67; BBC Shakespeare Series (1978–1985), 66; *In the Bleak Midwinter*, dir. Kenneth Branagh (1995), 69; *The Children's Midsummer Night's Dream*, dir. Christine Edzard (2001), 67; *Chimes at Midnight*, dir. Orson Welles (1965), 65; *My Darling Clementine*, dir. John Ford (1946), 69–70; digitisation and, 62–64; *A Double Life*, dir. George Cukor (1947), 65; *Gnomeo & Juliet* (2011), 69; *Hamlet*, dir. Grigori Kozintsev (1964), 66; *Hamlet*, dir. Franco Zeffirelli (1990), 65–66; *Hamlet*, dir. Kenneth Branagh (1996), 66–67; *Henry V*, dir. Laurence Olivier (1944), 65; *Henry V*, dir. Kenneth Branagh (1989), 66–67; *Julius Caesar*, dir. Joseph Mankiewicz (1953), 65; *King Lear*, dir. Peter Brooks (1971), 66; *King Lear*, dir. Grigori Kozintsev (1971), 66; *Looking for Richard*, dir. Al Pacino (1996), 68; *Love's Labour's Lost*, dir. Kenneth Branagh (2000), 66–67; *Macbeth*, dir. Orson Welles (1948), 65; *Macbeth*, dir. Roman Polanski (1971), 66; *Macbeth*, dir. Justin Kurzel (2015), 62; *A Midsummer Night's Dream*, dir. Max Reinhardt (1935), 64; *A Midsummer Night's Dream*, dir. Peter Hall (1968), 66; *A Midsummer Night's Dream*, dir. Michael Hoffman (1999), 67; *A Midsummer Night's Dream*, dir. Adrian Noble (1996), 67; *Much Ado About Nothing*, dir. Kenneth Branagh (1993), 66–67; *Othello*, dir. Orson Welles (1952), 65; *Othello*, dir. Oliver Parker (1995), 67; preservation and, 62–64; *Prospero's Books*, dir. Peter Greenaway (1991), 67; *Ran*, dir. Akira Kurosawa (1985), 39–40, 66; rehearsal in, 69; *Richard III*, dir. Richard Loncraine (1995), 67; *Romeo and Juliet*, dir. George Cukor (1936), 65; *Romeo + Juliet*, dir. Baz Luhrmann (1996), 67; *Saptapadi*, dir. Ajoy Kar (1961), 65; scholarship on, 64; *Shakespeare in Love*, dir. John Madden (1999), 69; *ShakespeaRe-Told* (2005), 66; *The Taming of the Shrew* (1929), 64; *The Taming of the Shrew*, dir. Franco Zeffirelli (1968), 65; *Throne of Blood*, 39–40, 66; *Titus*, dir. Julie Taymor (1999), 67–68; *Twelfth Night* (1957), 64; *Twelfth Night* (1962), 64; *Twelfth Night*, dir. Trevor Nunn (1996), 67; world cinema and, 63–64

Shakespeare, William, stage productions: *A Midsummer Night's Dream*, The Malachites, 93; digital resources on, 43–44; Globe to Globe *Hamlet*, 41–42; *Hamlet* (2000), RSC, 42; *Henry IV, Part 2*, Shakespeare Theatre (2004), 193; *Henry VI*, dir. Thomas Jolly, 63; *Henry VI*, dir. Michael Boyd (2000), RSC, 183–184; histories cycle, dir. Michael Boyd (2006), RSC, 183–184; history plays, performed as a sequence, 180–189; *King Lear*, The Malachites, 93; *Macbeth*, The Malachites, 93; on film, 63, 98–99; scholarship on, 43; *see also* Shakespeare, William, adaptations

Shakespeare, William, works: *All Is True (Henry VIII)*, with John Fletcher, 5, 28, 191, 201–205, 208; *All's Well That Ends Well*, 6, 225, 234–237; *Antony and Cleopatra*, 5, 149–150, 154, 157–161, 322; *As You Like It*, 6, 28, 225–234; comedies, sources of, 229–231, 274; *Hamlet*, 5, 11–12, 14–21, 28, 29, 41–42, 77, 135–146, 172; *Henry IV*, Part 1, 5, 85, 166–178; *Henry IV*, Part 2, 5, 167–178, 191–201; *Henry V*, 5, 93, 165–166, 168, 171, 173–178; *Henry VI*, Part 1, 5, 77, 180–189; *Henry VI*, Part 2, 5, 180–189; *Henry VI*, Part 3, 5, 180–189; *Henry VIII see All Is True*; histories, compared to works by other playwrights, 183, 219; histories, sources of, 184, 201, 205, 210–214, 216, 218–219; *Julius Caesar*, 5, 28, 149–157, 184; *King John*, 28; *King Lear*, 5, 39–40, 135, 142–146, 184; *Love's Labour's Lost*, 6, 251, 266–276; *Macbeth*, 39–40; *Measure for Measure*, 6, 28, 266–268, 270–276; *A Midsummer Night's Dream*, 1–3, 29, 34–37, 40–41; *The Merchant of Venice*, 28, 30; *The Merry Wives of Windsor*, 5, 168–169; *Much Ado About Nothing*, 6, 240–245, 251; *Othello*, 5, 28, 29, 107, 110–114; *Pericles*, 6, 240, 245–248, 251; poetry, sources of, 288–290; *The Rape of Lucrece*, 6, 281–287, 289–294, 308; *Richard II*, 5, 166, 208–210, 215–220; *Richard III*, 5, 180–189, 191, 208–215, 218–220; *Romeo and Juliet*, 5, 93, 107–110, 113–114; Shoreditch and, 19, 93; sonnets, 6, 30, 297–308, 322–323; *The Tempest*, 41, 171, 240; *Timon of Athens*, 28; *Titus Andronicus*, 5, 116; *Troilus and Cressida*, 5, 116; *Twelfth Night*, 6, 142, 253–263; *Two Gentlemen of Verona*, 28, 77, 260; *The Two Noble Kinsmen*, 34–37, 40; *Venus and Adonis*, 6, 281–289, 293–294, 308; *The Winter's Tale*, 6, 23, 240, 248–251, 254–255

Shapiro, I. A., 77
Shapiro, James, 95
Shearer, Norma, 64
Sherman, Anita Gilman, 5, 323
Sherry, Richard, 84
Shoreditch, London, 19, 91–99
Siddons, Sarah, 53, 56, 58
Sidney, Mary, 318
Sidney, Philip, 85, 283–284, 298
Sillars, Stuart, 53
Singh, Jyotsna G., 39
Six Degrees of Francis Bacon see databases
Slater, Anna Pasternak, 113
sleeve and *see* memory, stage properties and
Slovakia, 38
Smith, Bruce R., 43

Smith, Lindsay, 58
social media, 68–69, 75
Southampton, Earl of *see* Wriothesley, Henry
Southey, Robert, 30
Spain, 35, 41–42
speech-acts, 211, 216–217
Spenser, Edmund, 282, 283, 284, 285, 287, 299, 300, 318, 323
Spenser, Gabriel, 93
Squire, Larry L., 136, 140
stage combat, 107–111, 113, 125
Stallybrass, Peter, 27, 319–320
Stamelman, Richard, 293
Stanton, Kay, 5, 6
Starks, Lisa S., 64
statue of Pompey *see* memory, stage properties and; visual arts, sculpture
St Clair, William, 25
Stewart, Alan, 113
Stewart, Susan, 253
Stocker, Thomas, 83
Stockton, Annis, 28
Stow, John, 78, 218, 302, 303, 317
Strafford, Thomas Wentworth, 86
Stratford Shakespeare Jubilee (1769), 46, 48, 49, 50, 51, 52
subjectivity *see* identity
suicide, 292–293
Sukic, Christine, 6
Sullivan, Garrett A., 83, 171, 225, 318–319, 320
Sutton, John, 106, 320
Sweet, Anna L., 29
Sylvester, Josuah, 86
synecdoche, 304

table-books, 235, 266, 275–276, 306, 320
tables *see* table-books
Tarlton, Richard, 93
tarot, 143
Taviani, Paolo, 69
Taviani, Vittorio, 69
Taylor, Diana, 92, 94, 98, 209, 219
Taylor, Elizabeth, 65
Taylor, Gary, 180
Taylor, John, 81
Taylor, Sam, 64
Taymor, Julie, 68
technology, 62–64, 74–76, 87, 297–298, 306
technology, mnemonic *see* memory technology
Terdiman, Richard, 283
Terry, Ellen, 46, 56–57, 58, 59
Text Creation Partnership (TCP) *see* databases
Theatre, The (early modern playhouse), 91, 92, 93, 94, 97
theatregrams, 209
theatre of the world, 12, 18

theatrum mundi see theatre of the world
theatrum orbis terrarum see theatre of the world
Theobald, Lewis, 151
Thomson, James, 30
Tonson, Jacob, 51
Tower of London, 218–219; *see also* memory places
transmigration of souls *see* metempsychosis
trauma, 38, 46, 62, 119, 138–139, 291–293, 304, 317, 324
Tribble, Evelyn, 5, 320–321
Tronch, Jesús, 5
Truck, Ridley, 92

Vasiliauskas, Emily, 305
Vendler, Helen, 306
Verdi, Giuseppe, 169
Vienne-Guerrin, Nathalie, 4
Vine, Angus, 302
Viret, Pierre, 83
Virgil, 117, 202
visual arts, 4, 46–59; lithography, 56; painting, 49–58, 217; photography, 56–59; sculpture, 49, 149, 152–156, 217, 248–251, 297
Vitruvian man *see* design, Vitruvian
Voloshinov, Valentin, 193
Voltaire, 52
vows, 15–18, 119–121, 127, 135, 140–141, 158, 168, 172, 186–187, 217, 254, 266–269, 271–274

Wagner, Richard, 180, 189
Walker, Elsie, 68
Walkington, Thomas, 87
Walpole, Horace, 54
Walsham, Alexandra, 153, 261
Ware, Henry, 29
Warnock, Mary, 46–7
Watson, Amanda, 4, 323
Watson, Caroline, 49
Wayland, John, 82
Webbe, William, 84
websites *see* databases
Webster, John, 73, 77, 78, 84, 318
Weever, John, 288, 300, 302
Weimann, Robert, 210, 260
Weir, Peter, 69
Welles, Orson, 62, 65
Wells, Stanley, 95, 123, 180
Welsford, Enid, 141
Wesley, John, 29
West, Shearer, 4
Westall, Richard, 52, 53
Westminster Hall, 218–219; *see also* memory places
White, Hayden, 193
White, William Charles, 28
Whitney, Geoffrey, 273

Whitney, Isabella, 317
Wickham, Glynne, 77
Wiggins, Martin, 75
Wilde, Oscar, 37, 38
Wilder, Lina Perkins, 6, 15, 18, 107, 136, 140, 146, 321
Wiles, David, 254
Willeford, William, 142, 143, 144
Willems, Michèle, 66
Williams, Grant, 6, 173, 174, 269, 316, 318, 324
Willis, John, 12, 15, 81, 239
Willis, Susan, 66
Willsford, Thomas, 82–83
Wilson, J. Dover, 167, 181, 194
Wilson, Robert, 183
Wilson, Thomas, 84, 284
witness memory *see* eyewitness testimony
Wolfe, Heather, 320
women, in history plays, 203–204
women, in theatre audiences, 203–204
Wood, Michael, 95
Wordsworth, William, 47
World Shakespeare Festival (2012), 42
World's Shakespeare 1660–Present, The, 43
Wotton, Henry, 205, 208
Wray, Ramona, 67
Wright, Joseph (of Derby), 53
Wriothesley, Henry (Earl of Southampton), 283

Yates, Frances A., 11, 76, 77, 81, 82, 83, 87, 88, 255, 315, 316, 318
Yeo, Richard, 269, 275–276
Young, Edward, 30

Zakarian, Abi, 93
Zeffirelli, Franco, 65
Žižek, Slavoj, 307–308